Translating Empire

TRANSLATING EMPIRE

Emulation and the
Origins of Political Economy

SOPHUS A. REINERT

HARVARD UNIVERSITY PRESS
Cambridge, Massachusetts, and London, England
2011

Library of Congress Cataloging-in-Publication Data

Reinert, Sophus A.
Translating empire : emulation and the origins of political economy / Sophus A. Reinert.
p. cm.
Includes bibliographical references and index.
ISBN 978-0-674-06151-4 (alk. paper)
1. Economics—Europe—History—18th century. 2. Philosophy, European—18th century. 3. Europe—Intellectual life—18th century. 4. Enlightenment—Europe. I. Title.
HB83.R45 2011
330.1094—dc23   2011017919

Til Francesca

In all the pursuits of active and speculative life, the emulation of states and individuals is the most powerful spring of the efforts and improvements of mankind.

—EDWARD GIBBON, *The History of the Decline and
Fall of the Roman Empire* (1788)

I have sometimes thought, that if these Kingdoms lay not under the confusion and unintelligibleness of Understanding in Trade, as the Builders of Babel did in Languages, we might without the Sin of those arrogant Architects, erect such Towers in Trade as might overtop the Universe in that Mystery.

—FRANCIS BREWSTER, *Essays on Trade and Navigation* (1695)

Contents

Figures

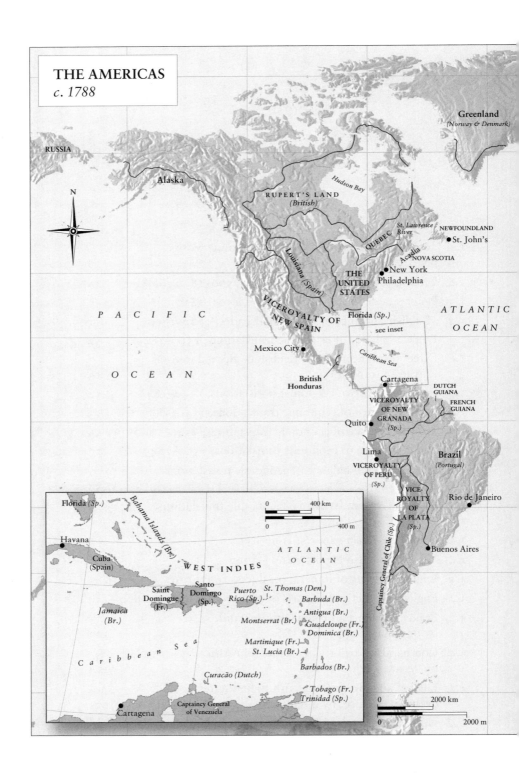

THE AMERICAS
c. 1788

RUSSIA

Greenland
(Norway & Denmark)

Alaska

Hudson Bay

RUPERT'S LAND
(British)

NEWFOUNDLAND
St. Lawrence River
●St. John's

QUEBEC

Acadia
NOVA SCOTIA

THE
UNITED
STATES

●New York
Philadelphia

Louisiana
(Spain)

P A C I F I C

VICEROYALTY OF
NEW SPAIN

Florida *(Sp.)*

A T L A N T I C

O C E A N

see inset

O C E A N

Caribbean Sea

Mexico City ●

British
Honduras

●Cartagena

DUTCH
GUIANA

FRENCH
GUIANA

VICEROYALTY
OF NEW
GRANADA

Quito●

(Sp.)

Lima ●
VICEROYALTY
OF PERU
(Sp.)

Brazil
(Portugal)

VICE-
ROYALTY
OF
LA PLATA
(Sp.)

●Rio de Janeiro

Captaincy General of Chile *(Sp.)*

●Buenos Aires

Florida *(Sp.)*

Bahama Islands *(Br.)*

0   400 km

●Havana

Cuba
(Spain)

W E S T   I N D I E S

A T L A N T I C
O C E A N

0   400 m

Jamaica
(Br.)

Saint
Domingue
(Fr.)

Santo
Domingo
(Sp.)

Puerto
Rico *(Sp.)*

St. Thomas (Den.)

Barbuda (Br.)

Antigua (Br.)

Montserrat (Br.)
Guadeloupe (Fr.)
Dominica (Br.)

Martinique (Fr.)
St. Lucia (Br.)

Barbados (Br.)

C a r i b b e a n   S e a

Curaçao (Dutch)

Tobago (Fr.)
Trinidad (Sp.)

●Cartagena

Captaincy General
of Venezuela

0   2000 km

0   2000 m

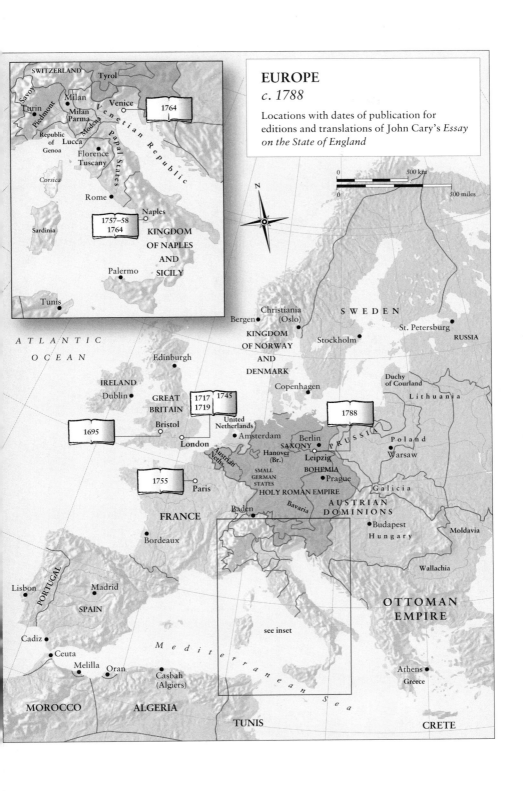

SWITZERLAND
Tyrol
Savoy
Turin
Piedmont
Milan
Milan
Parma
Venice
1764
Venetian Republic
Modena
Republic of Genoa
Lucca
Florence
Tuscany
Papal States
Corsica
Rome
Naples
1757–58
1764
KINGDOM
OF NAPLES
AND
SICILY
Sardinia
Palermo
Tunis

EUROPE
c. 1788

Locations with dates of publication for
editions and translations of John Cary's *Essay
on the State of England*

0   500 km
0   500 miles

N

ATLANTIC
OCEAN

Bergen
Christiania
(Oslo)
SWEDEN
St. Petersburg
KINGDOM
OF NORWAY
AND
DENMARK
Stockholm
RUSSIA

Edinburgh

IRELAND
Dublin
GREAT
BRITAIN
1717
1719
1745
Bristol
1695
London
United
Netherlands
Amsterdam
Copenhagen
Duchy
of Courland
Lithuania
Berlin
SAXONY
Hanover
(Br.)
Leipzig
PRUSSIA
Poland
Warsaw
1788
Austrian
Neths.
SMALL
GERMAN
STATES
BOHEMIA
Prague
Galicia
1755
Paris
HOLY ROMAN EMPIRE
AUSTRIAN
DOMINIONS
FRANCE
Baden
Bavaria
Budapest
Hungary
Moldavia
Bordeaux
Wallachia

Lisbon
PORTUGAL
Madrid
SPAIN
Cadiz
Ceuta
Melilla
Oran
Casbah
(Algiers)
Mediterranean Sea
see inset
OTTOMAN
EMPIRE
Athens
Greece

MOROCCO
ALGERIA
TUNIS
CRETE

Introduction

The English statesman and philosopher Francis Bacon famously asserted that "knowledge is power," but some forms of knowledge are more conducive to power than others. Among them is the study of *imperium*, of power itself.[1] The dark science of achieving greatness and dominion over others has taken many names and forms: it constituted the backbone of Plato's *Republic,* where the doctrine of the "noble lie" taught elites to deceive and control the masses; it was codified in later epochs as Tacitus's *arcana imperii,* the "state secrets" of Roman rule; it thrilled and frightened readers in the form of Niccolò Machiavelli's "reason of state." Yet gradually thinkers and statesmen discovered that political tools no longer sufficed to secure empire, since power depended to an ever greater extent on economic factors. Between people and polities, comparative wealth became a measure of relative might. The study of power came to embrace knowledge of how to become and remain rich in competitive contexts, a field of learning that emerged with time under the heading of political economy: "wealth," as Adam Smith paraphrased Thomas Hobbes, "is power."[2] This book argues that we have misunderstood the history of this discipline.

Economic historians have been right to emphasize how the proliferation of "useful" texts and practices contributed to the rise of the West in early modernity, but those with real and lasting influence are seldom eulogized in the historiography of political economy.[3] In effect, a vast discrepancy exists today between the economic ideas that historically were most influential on the one hand and those most rigorously studied by academics (and quoted by pundits) on the other. And our traditional canon of economics is equally impossible to reconcile with the actual economic strategies pursued by Europe as it first took off comparatively to the rest of the world. It is difficult, for example, to find a definition of "The Enlightenment" anywhere which does not include among its central tenets faith in peaceful progress through "free trade," and it is often explicitly argued that Britain and then Europe only forged ahead internationally once they had overcome the phase of "mercantilism" and embraced variations of *laissez-faire* during the same period.[4] Building on more recent work by leading economic historians of the early modern period, however, it is becoming increasingly evident that if history teaches us anything regarding the mechanisms of economic development, it is that while production, entrepreneurship, and technological change are keys to growth, they are not necessarily automatic outcomes of market mechanisms. The economy is intrinsically political, in that it is woven together in the process by which individuals and communities administer their material lives and engage with those of others, and the traditionally understood origins of economics and of economic development need to be rethought in light of the historical evidence.[5]

The present study contributes to this project by revealing the conflicted roots of political economy in the long eighteenth century and the seminal roles played in its institutionalization by the translations of texts and practices; by the pressures of international competition; and by what contemporaries knew as "emulation," a noble alternative to "envy" broadly signifying the desire to imitate and improve on superiors without harming them in the process. This, in turn, sheds light on the extent to which the broadly conceived West consciously rose to global predominance also through ruthless and widespread government interventions aimed at competitively encouraging and emulating "industrial" activities, and how the historical mainstream of political economy theorized this process. The early modern period witnessed the codification in European vernaculars of variations of the word "industry" as signifying not only a personal quality but also sectors of the economy and a specific form of economic activity related to manufacturing, and a principal point of international emulation came to revolve around the competitive politics of this change, the means by which political communities could both encourage "industrious" workers and proper "industrial" establishments, related to but distinct from older traditions of so-called "proto-industry."[6]

By accepting historical standards of influence for past works of political economy and by adopting an international perspective, the history of economic analysis, the history of economic policy, and economic history align in ways which can tell us a great deal about the historical development of capitalism in the world. England, and Europe generally, industrialized while adhering to theories and pursuing policies which have little to do with the historiography of political economy invented retroactively in Britain in the second half of the nineteenth century. By then their empire had matured and their needs had changed, but to understand the foundations of that empire we must deprovincialize our discourse and aim for a far more rigorous reconstruction of international political economy in historical perspective.

"The Enlightenment," a heuristically useful if much maligned periodization, was an age of globalization much like ours, but to only think about it in one or two languages is to do it grave injustice. Monoglot globalization is a form of imperialism, and at the time there were many competing imperialisms, conversing with and emulating each other. To keep up with one's competitors was an existential imperative for most political communities, but this truth is often lost in isolated case studies. This book contests this historiographical tendency by considering Enlightenment debates about political economy as an interconnected whole, whose centrifugal force was mediated by the centripetal pull of competing local contexts. Simultaneously comparative and diachronic, it draws inspiration from recent calls to unite the traditions of "entangled" and "comparative" historiography, aiming to analyze Enlightenment political economy in comparative terms while simultaneously telling a coherent story.[7]

Following the opening, conceptual chapter on the roles of emulation and translation in the codification of early modern political economy, this study latches on to an extraordinary series of cumulative translations of a single book, by the Bristol merchant John Cary, to structure its analysis. Though not a riveting read, the 1806–1807 edition of Johann Georg Meusel's *Literature on Statistics* describes the book in question well:

> Essay on the State of England's Trade, *in London (in Paris)* 1755. 2 vols. in 12.—A free translation by a conscientious Du Mout [*sic*] of an English work by JOHN CARY, who lived as a merchant in Bristol at the end of the 17th century. *Anton Genovesi*, former Professor of the Science of Trade and National Economy at the University of Naples, translated it into Italian (*Naples* 1757. 3 vols. In 8.) and added a Commentary to it. M. *Christian August Wichmann* translated this, alongside the original, into German, Leipz. 1788. 8.[8]

Virtually unknown today, the work catalogued by Meusel is yet unique in the annals of book history. Composed in one volume in late seventeenth-century Bristol, Cary's book grew to two volumes in French translation and three volumes in the subsequent Italian translation, only to revert to one volume in its final rendition in German, nearly a century after it first was published. All the while, no translator merely returned to Cary's original. Every new translation was made from a previous one, changes in each instance sedimenting neatly for excavation by later historians. A textual equivalent of the Burgess Shale popularized by Stephen Jay Gould, the book's translations are a rich fossil bed whose layers contain isolated yet evolutionarily interconnected microcosms.[9] One could mine the archaeological site represented by Cary's *Essay* in translation for many things. This study uses it to explicate how European political communities competed between the "Glorious Revolution" and the French Revolution, how some grew wealthy while others became poor, and how they struggled to be free in a world where industry to an ever greater extent secured liberty and greatness through violent economic rivalries.[10] More specifically, this book examines how "political economy" emerged as a "science" for succeeding in such competition.

Its title plays on the theme of *translatio imperii*. Just as Constantine transferred the *imperium* from Rome to Byzantium in 330, so, declared Otto of Freising in his 1143–46 *Chronicle or History of the Two Cities,* the acclamation of Charlemagne as Holy Roman Emperor by Pope Leo III on 25 December 800 represented a *translatio imperii* back west.[11] A transitional enterprise, the *translatio* referred to the succession of an imperial identity. As Aachen, the old capital of the Holy Roman Empire, simultaneously was Aix-la-Chapelle and Aquisgrana, among many other names in linguistic translation, so, in terms of cultural, spiritual, and political translation, it was also Constantinople and therefore Rome itself, embodying a millennial dream of Western civilization. *Translatio imperii* narrowly understood reflected the geographical movement of empire, just as the parallel tradition of *translatio studii* represented the spatial shift in the center of learning from Greece to Rome to France and, eventually, to England and the New World.[12] In terms of international competition, a more broadly conceived process of *translatio imperii* drove the early modern world economy: a contested and competitive process by which different states, at different times and with varying degrees of constancy, have managed to claim hegemony. Empire was translated in early modern Europe, and translations were an important but neglected vehicle of its movements. There was, in short, a relationship between *translatio studii* and *translatio imperii,* knowledge and power.

As testified to by its first appearance in a book's title, and though its variations later were legion, the term "political economy" was born in a context of intense international competition and explicitly institutionalized as a vehicle of emulation.[13] The dramaturge Antoine de Montchrétien, a fugitive from the law following an illegal duel in Paris, sought refuge in

England in the opening years of the seventeenth century. On returning to France, he presented the king with a recipe for economic development in the form of his 1615 *Treatise on Political Economy*. While principally reflecting the theoretical insights of Plato, the French jurist Jean Bodin, and the Piedmontese renegade Jesuit Giovanni Botero on the matter, not to mention Montchrétien's own experiences in the fast developing English economy, this work also showed unmistakable kinship both with its author's previous occupation and the cause of his exile: commerce, it argued, was ceaseless conflict, often with tragic consequences, and there was "nothing but necessity which should force people to get elsewhere what they have not." This was less a call for autarky than a plea that France should follow England and Holland's lead out of national dependency by competitively nurturing certain economic activities above others, and principally by encouraging domestic manufactures. Their economies, he argued, provided as clear an example to emulate in 1615 as the "Republics of Genoa and Venice" had for their "ancestors"; "Our life," he maintained, "is almost entirely conducted by example." Although Montchrétien was subsequently shot, quartered, and incinerated during a Huguenot uprising, fortunately in that order, his work survived to coin the term for one of *the* defining concerns of the Enlightenment, "political economy," and delineated some of its basic tenets: liberty, as independence of other powers; industry, both as a personal quality and as an economic activity related to manufacturing; emulation, as noble competition.[14]

From Giovanni Botero's codification of foreign economic policies in his 1589 *Reason of State* to the 1607 establishment of "Flemish fashion" tapestry manufactures in Paris, through Veit Ludwig von Seckendorff, who inaugurated the science of Cameralism in the 1665 *Additions* to his *German Princely State* following a formative sojourn in Holland, to Alexander Hamilton, describing the glory of industry in his 1791 *Report on the Manufactures* in Philadelphia after surveying the factory systems of the Old World, Montchrétien's bellicose conceptions of liberty and emulation were representative of economic practice from "the Renaissance" through "the Enlightenment," chronologically as well as geographically.[15] But because many lacked the resources of these luminaries, one of the principal mediums of emulation became textual translation: if one was unable to convey the sights and impressions of other countries firsthand or through extensive research, one could nonetheless render understandable the words of those who were. Some canonical economic works, in that and in later periods, were in fact far more influential in new contexts abroad than they ever were in the place and time of their writing, from Richard Cantillon's *Essay on the Nature of Commerce* to Karl Marx's *Capital*.[16]

In one of his most celebrated essays, the Turinese novelist Italo Calvino defined "the classics" as those "books that come down to us bearing the traces of readings previous to ours, and bringing in their wake the traces they have left on the culture or cultures they have passed through."[17] Like Calvino's classics, Cary's *Essay* gained notoriety through readings across different contexts, through which it concomitantly influenced and was influenced by the ideas, manners, and institutions it encountered. Our ancestors' classics are not always our classics, and as classics sometimes go, this one went: out of Europe's literary imagination, out of its subject's spectrum of economic correctness, and out of the canon so perceived.[18] Yet the distinctive process of cumulative translation that the *Essay* represents uniquely illuminates the emulative interaction of political and economic cultures in eighteenth-century Europe and the ways overarching problematics reached local resolutions. So though the *Essay* itself repeatedly became influential, this study of how and why English political economy was codified and emulated is a preamble to explore larger issues at work: how terms so currently crucial as free trade originally were conceived; how similar economic aims were achieved through different policies in diverse contexts; how certain technologies of power and security were diffused and the role they played in countervailing empires and religions; the tenuous relation between civil and economic liberties, social and natural sciences; and how ancient virtue and erudition readjusted to a world increasingly dominated by economic concerns. Finally, the translations of the *Essay* tell of how great power, or *imperium,* has been contested historically, and how it eventually changes hands. But in reconstructing the lives, times, and theories of Cary and his translators, this book also contributes to contemporary debates.

Most important among them is the dispute over the historical role of economic policy, the legislative application of theory, understood both in terms of individual acts and of overarching political commitments. To what extent can political communities fruitfully influence the course of their economic lives, to what extent was the so-called rise of the West a corollary of conscious strategies, and which theories were most often and most successfully translated into practice? While it is generally agreed that England, then Britain, rose to greatness through laissez-faire and that this was why it was emulated abroad, this book shows how England was among the most interventionist states of its age, and how the harrowing success of these policies made England's economy and the ideas on which it was based worthy of guarded emulation. The common retort to such arguments is that one confuses correlation with causation. Assuming that laissez-faire is good and interventions are bad, one can argue that England became wealthy in spite of its economic policies, not because of them. "The best case to be made for mercantile policy," it was recently argued, is that it "did not impede Britain's transformation into the first modern industrial economy."[19] This book maintains that the historical evidence now is so heavily in favor of industrial and military policies successfully encouraging long-term economic development in England, admittedly through far more complex means than simply setting tariffs to encourage domestic manufactures, that the burden of proof falls on neoclassical economics, not on the historical record. This is of course not to say that economic interventions *always* pay off, only that they historically have done so in some contexts and that their *absence* in no way can be conceived of as a precondition for economic development.

This problem also touches on the ongoing controversy over the purportedly peaceful nature and interaction of commercial societies. Does trade always promote peace? Does it promote liberty, however defined? What is the political fallout of economic inequality, not only between individuals but between regions, states, and empires? The doctrinaire stance that commercial relations always bring peace, liberty, and public happiness enjoys considerable credit along the entire spectrum of modern politics, from world leaders to Nobel laureates and the mainstream media.[20] Although they always considered such a dichotomy problematic, the conceptual opposition between ancient conquest and modern commerce was originally elucidated in the works of John Locke, François Melon, and Montesquieu. Later, their tentative schemes were institutionalized as an amazingly abiding Whig narrative whereby primitive war was overcome by the "sweet," "gentle," and "civilizing" consequences of trade.

This interpretative hypothesis, known as the *"doux-commerce* thesis," has proven rewarding in recent years and become nothing less than a mantra of modernity, but was far from the only way of conceptualizing international trade in the early modern world.[21] The global economy of the eighteenth century was also characterized by what contemporary writers knew as "jealousy of trade."[22] The problem, as Alexander Hamilton among others pointed out, was that jealousy of trade, while arguably immoral, had historically been extremely effective.[23] A trade-off existed between ethics and power in international relations. From the city-states of Italy through Holland to England, the center of the European economy had consistently shifted as new nations mastered the synergy of war and wealth better than their predecessors.[24] This was the dominant logic of early modern political economy as it was practiced, and this was the spirit in which Cary wrote and was translated. Commerce, like war, could be a means of coercion and a path to empire.

The ideas Cary promulgated in Europe were at odds with those of many of his now canonical contemporaries, but the fact that the refined (and usually more elite) thinkers currently favored by historians were often ignored for centuries might say more about our own conceits than we care to admit. One must, for example, have a remarkably narrow conception of civil society to argue that Ciceronian ambivalences toward wealth as a source of moral corruption were "widely held in the Renaissance and early modern period."[25] Not only have leading archival historians demonstrated that, even in the "upper class" of Republican Florence during the Renaissance, "wealth was associated with *virtù* and honor, poverty with dishonor" but, at the risk of being maudlin: most people in history have worried about feeding their families.[26] The neatest and now most fashionable theories were not necessarily the most influential, and those works that emerge as particularly important historically seldom correspond to the canon of economics established in the late nineteenth and twentieth centuries.[27] Historiographical "precursorism" has profoundly skewed our understanding of the history of political economy, and if one's interest is in ideas, their origins, and their repercussions in historical context, a study of the history of economic texts in translation suggests that a fundamental revision of the established canon is not only possible but absolutely necessary.[28]

The modalities of this process, however, are seldom as simple as unit ideas spreading through the aether.[29] The very cultural distinctiveness that drives political communities to compete for survival also inflects the ways they conceptualize each others' political economies. In 1898, for example, the Japanese commissioner Tentearo Makato was instructed to travel east, to the West, in search of how "economics" increased standards of living. While he succinctly stated the need for emulation in international trade and the indisputable importance of economic concerns for political life, his report also underlines the pitfalls of translating such debates. For the field Makato studied reminded him only of "splendid Japanese vases,— imposing without, but within nothing but cobwebs and dust," and certain economic principles were simply too alien for his intellectual ecology to assimilate. Thus, he defined the term "NIHILISM (confined to Russia, I think)" as "the overthrow of despotic government and the setting up of representative."[30] Makato's statement seems at best bizarre if one does not consider that critics of Russian autocracy like Ivan Turgenev and Fyodor Dostoyevsky sometimes conceived of themselves, and were attacked by tzarist loyalists, as "nihilistic."[31] One must actively engage with such intellectual friction to appreciate how international emulation has influenced past political economy and how translated books acquire and tender meaning.

Emma Rothschild has poignantly defined this as "the Grandville problem," after the nineteenth-century French artist Jean-Jacques Grandville's meditations on the theme of figures changing forms across arcs of association.[32] Thoughts change as they travel through time and space, and an international history of ideas demands careful sequential contextualizations considering not only the linguistic but also the material and symbolic dimensions of transmission. Readers, and thus translators, are not passive recipients but active agents in the creation of knowledge.[33] And if what follows is an intellectual history, it unapologetically considers the wider material and cultural world, studying not only theory but also practice, not only proposal but also policy.[34]

Though prone to genetic drift and random mutations, books adapt to changing habitats like species, but ideas, like components of biological organisms tailored to specific ecologies, don't all travel equally well. To be concrete, Cary's comments about "*Popish* cut-throats" were as likely to survive in Catholic Europe as a panda in a volcano. In the spirit of Grandville's image, a widely diffused children's game can serve as a useful metaphor for the translations of Cary's *Essay*. In Norwegian it is called *hviskeleken*, in German *stille Post*, and in many countries some variation of "broken telephone." The first participant whispers a phrase to the person sitting next to him or her, who whispers the phrase to the next and so on until the phrase reaches the final participant, at which point the initial phrase is compared to the end result and laughter ensues. The politically incorrect British term for this game, however, reveals a deeper meaning. "Chinese Whispers" namely leads the explanation for the failure of communication away from technical issues like broken telephones, silent mail, and slurred speech toward a more fundamental problem of language.[35]

After Babel, it does not matter how well telephones work or how loudly one shouts if one does not share the language of one's intended audience. The difference between this game and the study of cumulative translations is that though every stage of the communication would have seemed like "Chinese" to the previous and subsequent actors in the chain, it was eminently meaningful to the given interpreter. The translations of Cary's *Essay* are thus more like the Hans Christian Andersen fable that tells of a story that was recounted and cumulatively embellished by various barnyard animals until "a feather became five hens." As in Andersen's story, the difference was not only quantitative, in that the translations of the *Essay* were simply longer than the original, but also qualitative, in terms of the information they conveyed. While every interlocutor's story in the fable deviated from the one before it, for whatever reasons they all thought it the right story to tell.

John Dunn has noted that the fate of a text usually stands "in a somewhat ironical relation to its author's original intentions," and similar insights have fueled book history in recent decades.[36] Reading, it has been argued, is "on the order of the ephemeral."[37] Yet the fleeting experience of reading can find its material anchorage in the act of translation, as inflections that otherwise would have been lost are emphasized and given prevalence over original intentions, in that and subsequent contexts. As Jorge Luis Borges echoed Bertrand Russell, translations are the "partial and precious documentation of the vicissitudes" a text incurs in encountering the spectrum of its "possible impressions."[38] By providing corroborative points of view, the cumulative and comparative study of such "impressions" clarifies not only the original text and the context in which it was meant to exist but also its bastard progeny and the worlds into which they were brought. But if the chosen subject matter seems erudite and antiquarian, the mosaic uncovered by painstaking intellectual archaeology of forgotten texts in translation cannot but concern our modern sensibilities deeply. For the image it depicts of what Europeans thought and did as modern economic growth first took shape suggests we should reconsider the very origins of political economy.

CHAPTER 1 ENGAGES WITH early modern European theories of economic competition and political liberty, focusing on how both commerce and conquest could be conceived of as means of coercion in international relations. Both were means of "giving laws" to others and thus subjecting them to one's empire. Liberty, in short, was a competitive endeavor just as trade was. Not only did the necessity of succeeding in international rivalries require that radical constitutional changes at times be engineered from within, but the capacity of wealthy nations to project their power by economic means meant such changes could also be forced on the poor and the latecoming from without. The chapter concludes by discussing early modern debates about language, empire, and translation in this context, analyzing a data-set of early modern economic translations originally collected by Kenneth E. Carpenter. Graphing the dynamic flux of economic translations between European languages in the period 1500–1848, the chapter demonstrates how they served as vehicles of emulation and represent a barometer of comparative economic success in Europe and discusses how they problematize the current canon of economics.

Chapter 2 presents Cary and his works in the context of international trade, moral reformism, and anti-Catholicism in Williamite England. The *Essay,* though intended as a strategic intervention in a very specific debate over the structure and future of England's empire, proposed generalized measures to promote economic competitiveness through the development of domestic manufactures in the spirit of the Navigation Acts. John Locke praised it as the "best discourse" he had read on the subject, and it soon triggered a violent debate over the right of Ireland to industrialize at the cost of metropolitan economic interests. Cary's ensuing legal polemic with the Irishman William Molyneux over the imperial relevance of Locke's theories led to the radical formalization of Cary's theses. For the first time in the English language, trade became a "science" in late editions of Cary's *Essay*.

Chapter 3 examines the 1755 French translation of the *Essay* by Georges-Marie Butel-Dumont, who played a cardinal role in the official program of Vincent de Gournay, the intendant of trade, of translating key works of political economy as a means of promulgating this "science of trade" and thereby emulating and countervailing Britain's industrial and military successes. In a Catholic, ostensibly absolutist France plagued by religious dissonance, chronic fiscal shortfalls and subsistence anxieties, and a looming war, Butel-Dumont's rendition of the *Essay* aligned itself with the liberal local culture of translation and grew, in response to its new contextual concerns, by a factor of six. Indeed, it became one of the most programmatic economic translations of its age, a historical catalogue of English interventions and aggressions, a theoretical work on the mechanisms of international trade and the nature of commercial society, and an urgent call to action on the eve of the Seven Years' War.

Chapter 4 shifts the focus to Italy, where Antonio Genovesi translated the French translation of the *Essay* in 1757–58 to use as textbook at his new chair of political economy at the University of Naples, the first of its kind in Italy. An abbot and an institutional academic, Genovesi updated Cary's work through a series of annotations and supplementary texts rather than translational license. This refined the analysis of the original in light of Renaissance reason of state literature, and importantly of Italy's long histories of rises and falls. Drawing on the cyclicality of economic emulation and the economic inequalities of eighteenth-century Europe, Genovesi codified what amounted to a political economy of decline, refining a theory of liberty and power in international relations based on the differential capacities of economic activities to create wealth.

Chapter 5 analyzes Christian August Wichmann's translation of Genovesi's rendition of the *Essay* into German in 1788. By this time Cary had become a posthumous celebrity in his own right, his policy proposals long implemented. The chapter contextualizes this transition, and Wichmann's revolt against it, in relation to the practical tradition of Cameralism, which stretched from Tuscany to the Scandinavian Arctic, and reconstructs the process through which Cary's *Essay* was discovered by Wichmann's Danish patron Peter Christian Schumacher on a "grand tour" to study European political economy, and particularly the school now known as Physiocracy, and the consequences of Enlightenment economic policy on the continent.

The epilogue retreats from the study of the *Essay*'s individual editions to consider the wider, global history of how Cary was read in the context of eighteenth-century political economy and international competition. Venturing briefly across the Atlantic, this book adumbrates the most recent *translatio* of empire, from the Old World to the New, demonstrating how the history explicated in the earlier chapters sheds new and significant light on the political economies of independence in North and South America, from Alexander Hamilton to Manuel Belgrano, father of Argentine independence. Both cases present striking examples of the larger processes of economic *translatio imperii,* as former colonies translated and employed metropolitan technologies of wealth and power for their own purposes, to safeguard their liberty and their development from the hostile policies of their former masters.[39] This, in turn, suggests a fundamental reconception of what "Enlightenment" political economy ultimately represented.

The need to study the early modern transmission and translation of economic ideas and practices—and the changing economic fortunes that drove them—is testified to by the fact that the very issues with which they were concerned are currently at the forefront of our political consciousness. As Istvan Hont has argued, there is little "conceptual novelty" in the way we discuss issues of globalization and economic development today, not to mention the nexus between international trade, labor, and welfare.[40] Wealthy countries with high wages still fear that poor countries might undersell them, just as Venice feared England would in the seventeenth century. And we are still vexed by the advantages and disadvantages of free trade and of formal and informal empires, by the shifting relationships between industry and finance, states and cultures, the local and the global. Alessandro Verri's statement in the pages of the Milanese Enlightenment periodical *Il Caffè* that "no nation has become excellent on its own" and that the progress of civilization depended on "enlightened imitation" rings as true today as it did in 1765.[41] Yet now, as then, this can be a harrowing process. Though history may not supply immediate answers to our most pertinent questions, the study of how competitively developing states, cultures, and economies have emulated each other and reflected on their strategies and their situations can certainly inform our thoughts and policies—as well as sharpen our awareness of just what is at stake.

CHAPTER ONE

Emulation and Translation

Liberty and the Balance of Trade

As the dust began to settle in the wake of the global Seven Years' War of 1756–63, the cosmopolitan libertines Giacomo Casanova and Ange Goudar penned the legendary *Chinese Spy*, a widely translated best seller constructed around a series of fictitious dispatches by exotic observers in the spirit of Montesquieu's *Persian Letters*.[1] The six-volume work chiefly recounted the experiences and misadventures of the mandarin envoy Champi-pi, "commissioned to examine into the present state of Europe." The spy deftly engaged with every major power and controversy of his age, but his insights into political economy were particularly poignant. On the deck of his ship, as the English coast emerged through the morning mists, Champi-pi pondered, "So this is . . . that famous potent state, which claims the dominion of the sea, *and at present gives law to several great nations!*"[2] The expression he employed to relate Britain's supremacy, "give laws," was a commonplace variation on the fearsome classicizing idiom *dare legem victis*, "to impose law on the conquered," but it was capacious enough, as used even by canonical authorities on natural law, to include both de facto and de jure forms of dominion.[3] England, the imaginary mandarin knew well, ruled not only the sea but ostensibly independent nations. *The Chinese Spy* was appropriately composed in various London coffeehouses, for that was where the English "genius for public oeconomy" was located, and from whence the English "settle the affairs of Europe." Casanova and Goudar had no doubts about the close connection between this specific "genius" and England's ability to "settle the affairs of Europe." Indeed, they argued, "the figure it makes among the other powers in Europe, is entirely owing to money." Through wealth, in short, England achieved empire over the world, and by means of this coercion it in turn grew even wealthier: "It was a good thought of this nation for enriching itself, to intermeddle with the continent," the Mandarin observed, "as otherwise it would be the poorest in Europe."[4]

But how had England embarked on this virtuous circle of commerce and conquest, this path that had made it so much more than simply a foggy, windswept archipelago off the northwestern periphery of the Eurafrasian landmass? There was, as Adam Smith observed in the concluding passage of his *Wealth of Nations,* a striking discrepancy between England's imperial project and the "real mediocrity of her circumstances."[5] Summoning a trope of the eighteenth century, Casanova and Goudar explained that the English were better at "imitation" than "invention." As a London acquaintance of the mandarin said, "Most nations outdo us in invention, but we exceed them in imitation. We beat all Europe for polishing, but cannot do without models." England had simply beaten its competitors at their own game.[6] "One single oeconomical maxim sometimes *gives a government the superiority over others," The Chinese Spy* explained, and by encouraging its agriculture and manufactures the English thalassocracy, its empire of the sea, had placed other nations in a state of *"dependence,"* rendering them *"easy to be conquered."* What the mandarin could not understand, though, given that England had imitated its way to greatness, was why legislators on the continent had not simply followed suit, why they had not themselves resorted to emulation to catch up. Sovereigns and statesmen alike worried about the balance of power and the means of safeguarding national liberties from the rise of an irresistible empire, yet they neglected the most important measures of a state's power in the modern world: agriculture, manufactures, and trade. England proved that economic factors requiring "encouragements" had become paramount in political life. Casanova and Goudar repeatedly emphasized the relationship between wealth, war, navies, and power, and the mandarin could not help but wonder why most states took "a road quite opposite" England's, since this perpetuated a situation in which the island, again, "gives law to Europe." It had found the key to empire in aggressive policies imitating its old superiors, but competing nations failed to emulate its naval and commercial superiority in turn.[7]

This was hardly the first time England was perceived to dominate others in such terms. Writing to the Venetian Senate in 1671, for example, Pietro Mocenigo had noted how England, by "serving as a counterpoise for balancing the crowns [of Europe]," both gave "peace to the Christian world" *and* had *"laid down the law* to their friends and enemies."[8] England did this by ensuring that other powers could not exert influence as it had. The great theoretician of natural law Emmerich de Vattel harnessed the same political vocabulary nearly a century later, in his 1758 *Law of Nations,* to confront these mechanisms of international relations by proposing that the "famous scheme of the political equilibrium or balance of power" should be "understood" as "a disposition of things" whereby "no power is able absolutely to predominate, or to *prescribe laws to others."*[9] But a political balance of power could not easily be maintained at the time without a concomitant balance of trade, which Mocenigo had left out of his analysis. More specifically, Casanova and Goudar now intuited that the real "balance of Europe," the concept that above all others was supposed to safeguard the liberties of independent political communities, had come ultimately to depend more on economic "encouragements" and emulation than on troop movements and dynastic politics; and that commerce too could be a form of conquest. But if their discussion of the phenomenon was particularly trenchant, *The Chinese Spy* was not alone in understanding the dynamics of power in precisely these terms.

In his celebrated 1764 work *On Crimes and Punishments,* the great Milanese statesman Cesare Beccaria noted that "the philosophical truths rendered common by the printing press have animated commerce, and a tacit war of industry has been sparked between nations."[10] Some thought of this "tacit war of industry" as an alternative to military conquest. This was the vein in which Jacques Accarias de Sérionne, a French publicist and political economist in exile, proclaimed, "it is more certain and more humane to attend to the Equilibrium [of power] through Commerce than through War. . . . If the spirit of Commerce were to spread everywhere, wars would be less frequent in Europe. The rivalry between Nations will no longer excite anything but a general emulation: one will attack with industry instead of [military] power."[11] If commerce was still fundamentally conceptualized through military analogies, it nonetheless represented a more humane way of pursuing and resolving international rivalries. If competition could not be neutralized in the modern world, commercial interests might at least mitigate its most sanguinary manifestations.

Many, however, such as Beccaria's colleague Sebastiano Franci, thought even such measured praise excessive. Instead, he saw "the war of industry," or "bloodless war," as a preamble to slaughter, a dangerous new stage in conflicts by which the great powers could justify and propagate violent action. Conquest and commerce went hand in hand in allowing some the power to "give law" to others.[12] This was the scenario that their Lombard homeland had all too often experienced in the early modern period, as it vacillated between Spanish, French, and Austrian spheres of influence, and one of the most concise statements of this equation between commerce and conquest in the balance of powers was made by Pietro Verri, Beccaria and Franci's intellectual godfather as head of the Milanese Academy of Punches: "In the last century, the enlightenment [*i lumi*] spread across Europe has given birth to a new science of finance. The nations have shaken off their lethargy; the Nations feel that the tacit war of commerce always progresses and always acts, even in peacetime, and that the balance of commerce in Europe becomes that of power."[13] If the balances of power and trade were the same, international relations could know no peace. Far from pacifying it, commerce had rendered conflict endemic in the modern world. What follows elucidates the eighteenth-century idiom "giving laws" as it was harnessed in the context of international economic rivalry, focusing especially on the role that "emulation" and "translation" played in securing national autonomy, literally, in the original Greek, the state of "having one's own laws," of being free.[14]

Jealousy of Trade

For Hobbes, political communities, driven by "jealousies," famously confronted each other "in the state and posture of Gladiators," and a recurrent dream of subsequent political theory has been to pacify international relations by substituting goods for *gladii*, commerce for conquest.[15] Historical experience nonetheless continued to stymie these hopes, primarily because eighteenth-century England, like Venice three centuries earlier, proved ambidextrous enough to gut her neighbors with one hand and sell them cheap funeral shrouds with the other. Even after the proverbial swords were beaten into ploughshares, the seminal importance of economic power in the modern world led many to think even liberty was for sale. Hence, freedom was threatened by economic rivalries whether communities faced each other in the posture of gladiators or of merchants. Yet there is still a tendency to consider commerce a peaceful influence in the eighteenth century, to the point that recent historiography takes the venerable dichotomy between the "conquest" of the ancients and the "commerce" of the moderns for granted. Montesquieu is often invoked as the architect of a paradigm that declared trade to be "gentle" and "sweet," antithetical to violence, a cure for "Machiavellianism" and "destructive prejudices" alike. In one of the most influential works in this tradition, Albert Hirschman readily accepted that Montesquieu's vision had been "proven wrong" by the historical record, but his main contention remained that the origins of capitalism could be located in an intellectual attempt to neutralize violence with commerce. There is no need to challenge Hirschman's insight that there were such "political arguments for capitalism before its triumph," or that many of these arguments indeed presented the spirit of commerce as antithetical to that of conquest.[16] Even Jean-Jacques Rousseau argued in his revision of Charles-Irénée Castel, the *abbé* de Saint-Pierre's famous *Plan for Perpetual Peace* that "commerce, which daily tends to preserve itself in equilibrium, taking from certain powers the exclusive advantages which they have derived from it, *at the same time deprives them of the great means which they had of giving laws to others.*"[17] Commerce was justified, then, by one of its staunchest critics, as an antidote to great power politics. What must be established, however, is the existence of a competing and equally, if not more widespread, way of addressing the role of commerce in early modern international relations, a way of thinking about the politics of economic interactions that was less sanguine about the future of commercial societies than the tradition Hirschman so memorably documented.[18]

The foundational insight driving this tradition was that civic survival had come to depend on success in international economic competition. Thomas Mun, that most famous of all "mercantilists," who made his fortune in the flourishing Tuscan port of Leghorn around the turn of the sixteenth century, spoke the cause of the East India Company and had honed an acute understanding of the politics of international commerce. "The Trade of Merchandize," he knew well, was "the verie Touchstone of a kingdomes prosperitie."[19] That a political community had an obligation to take care of this "touchstone" was obvious, and the story that will unfold in the chapters that follow is also an exploration of the fallout of this exigency of competitive political survival in the early modern world. "Commerce is the source of finance," the Controller-General of Finances under Louis XIV, Jean-Baptiste Colbert, put it emblematically, "and finance is the sinew of war." It was nothing less than "a perpetual and peaceful war of mind and industry among all nations."[20] Liberty, understood as independence from arbitrary superiors, depended on relative economic power. And Colbert's extensive program to ensure French superiority in Europe through economic policies had its natural outcome, observers soon noting that France's "opulence" gave "jealousy to all of Europe."[21]

The idea, institutionalized by the likes of Colbert, that true economic development depended on competitive value-added exports was tremendously influential across Europe at the time. The problem was that not everyone could import raw materials and export manufactured goods at the same time. In the historical context of early modern Europe, there were simply not enough trades subject to technological change and increasing demand (like textiles)—to go around.[22] Though the increasing complexity and differentiation of international trade certainly ameliorated the situation between the late sixteenth and late eighteenth centuries, the fact remains that few economic activities could compete with textiles as engines of economic development before the advent of coal-driven industrialization (some would say even today).[23] Given that some trades qualitatively were understood to be better than others, jealousy of trade was organically embedded in the European system of political communities competing over resources, goods, and markets. For as the celebrated French *philosophe* Guillaume Thomas François Raynal clarified, "one knows that jealousy of trade is nothing but jealousy of power."[24] Given the inherent bellicosity of the international system, there was simply no reason for a statesman *not* to fear and envy wealthier, more industrious and powerful neighbors.

An anonymous 1744 *memoire* on trade stated almost axiomatically that expanding the export of French manufactures, particularly textiles, would lead to a "prodigious turnover that would enrich the people" of France and "diminish those of the Dutch and the English," France's endemic enemies. Economic superiority was understood to be a positional good, particularly in markets for manufactures, and hierarchies of development could become hierarchies of power.[25] "Commerce," an Italian journal argued in 1766, had come to "decide" the "superiority of one Nation over another."[26] Today, we are more prone to think like Jean de Dieu-Raymond de Boisgelin de Cucé, archbishop of Aix, who wrote in a 1785 commentary on Montesquieu: "Commerce seems to have a propensity to create one single empire of all empires, one single people of all peoples, to found one single, immortal nation that has no other name but that of mankind."[27] Yet as late as 1799, the Irish political economist Thomas Brooke Clarke could summarize the lessons of history quite differently: "she who commands the Commerce, commands the Wealth; and she who commands the Wealth of the World, must command the World itself."[28] International competition over wealth, and the corrupting means of its acquisition, were understood by many to be conducive rather to hegemony than to harmony in the early modern period. And since wealth was of existential importance to political communities, the conquest of their markets was no less debilitating than that of their territories.

On 28 May 1673, for example, "The Weavers' Company of London" petitioned the king and Privy Council to prohibit the importation of foreign textiles competing with English manufactures.[29] Charles II soon issued a proclamation forbidding the wearing of silk at court and ordering foreign manufactures to be seized at customs, news of which soon reached Florence, at the time still a capital of the world's silk industry. As a Venetian spy in the city reported, the edict hit Florence like "a bombshell," costing them their "principal market" and threatening them with "poverty": it brought a "tacit and unexpected war."[30] The fates of nations were decided in the conflation of conquest and commerce. And England was not known as a lone champion of free and peaceful trade but as the most predatory of the pack. Already Queen Elizabeth I, European ambassadors observed, was "very jealous of the prosperity of the French."[31] And if she wanted "to secure a free commerce" for her subjects on the continent so that they could "increase their capital," her means of achieving this, and the violent lengths to which Englishmen would go to "foster English and restrict foreign commerce," left the rest of Europe dumbfounded. They were the "disturbers of the whole world," whose "rapacity and cruelty" had made them "odious to all nations," yet they took "glory" in becoming "formidable" this way, in achieving greatness through economic and military aggression.[32]

This impression of Englishmen as characteristically rapacious and jealous of other countries' prosperity became widespread in the eighteenth century, when England was thought, in the words of one representative observer, to uphold "large parts of its commerce" only through "violent conduct" and "wild wars," but remained common throughout the nineteenth-century era of nationalism and into that of the World Wars.[33] There are few more fitting expressions than the contemporary idiom "jealousy of trade" for describing the challenges posed by this way of conceptualizing commerce and its frightful efficiency.[34] Though David Hume's formulation might be the most famous, that offered by the nearly contemporary Sephardic political economist Isaac de Pinto defines the phenomenon succinctly: "Jealousy of commerce, and competition for power, create enmity between nations as well as between individuals. They run the same career, *and aspiring at the same object, are enemies because they are rivals.*"[35] All states sought liberty and material welfare, but since international economic competition increasingly made these positional goods, the means of autonomy were a decidedly limited resource.

Conquest, Commerce, Liberty

The difference between the ancient "spirit of conquest" and the modern "spirit of commerce" was perhaps most successfully theorized by the French political economist Jean-François Melon in his often-translated *Political Essay on Commerce* (1734).[36] His model of international trade charted the variable success of nations by focusing on different economic activities, delineating an imaginary archipelago in which the individual islands each specialized in distinct goods, such as grain, textiles, or beer. Developing the "natural and primitive" interaction of developed commercial systems, his model showed that certain structures of trade "insensibly" could make an island "less plentiful, less peopled, and at length" even "subdued, by another island, which formerly had fewer inhabitants." As these dynamics took shape, it was only a matter of time before one island broke the "Balance of Equality," attaining "a Superiority of Power" and the ability to *"give Laws to the other Islands."* By adopting "new political Maxims," the dominant island would "support the Trade of those Islands from which she fears nothing; and destroy the Trade of the Islands whose Competition might alarm her."[37]

Commerce, Melon argued, was a far more stable instrument of hegemony than conquest. Though he here reproposed John Locke's dichotomy between the destructive *esprit militaire* of the ancients and the modern *esprit de commerce,* these two spirits were often intertwined in Melon's analysis. The "Spirit of Conquest" might be inimical to the "Spirit of Preservation," but this was not the case with the "Spirit of Commerce," which was "always accompanied by the Wisdom necessary for Preservation." Rome had only succeeded in conquering Carthage "by Means of particular Circumstances." Had the Carthaginians only nurtured war as they nurtured wealth, modernity would have been the legacy of Africa, not Europe. The synergy of wealth and war secured a polity's stability and power to give others laws. The civilizations of antiquity had manifested one or the other, paradigmatically in the confrontation between military Rome and commercial Carthage, but now France should learn from them both.[38]

Melon was not alone, and the near ubiquity of similar juxtapositions of conquest and commerce in eighteenth-century Europe testifies to the longevity of the Renaissance political tradition of reason of state, and the extent to which Hobbes's gladiator had learned to peddle his wares. "Has England thus unlearned the art of war?" Saint-Pierre asked in those tumultuous decades after Britain first emerged as a great economic power, "Rome and Carthage are no longer here, and there is no longer a military people which subjects a mercantile people . . . [now] one always finds the superiority of troops where there is a superiority of money."[39] Or, as John Dryden more poetically had put it, "The lab'ring Bee, when his sharp Sting is gone / Forgets his Golden Work, and turns a Drone."[40] If industry and commerce were helpless without power to support them in international trade, then imperial expansion could be justified by defensive necessity.

Inspired by the very same changes in the relation between politics, war, and economics, Montesquieu also elaborated on the dangers of economic empires in a section of the *Spirit of the Laws* that he might have composed in discussion with Melon, and that Voltaire rightly described in a marginal note as a "portrait of England."[41] His passage about England's gorgonization of the Irish woolen industries at the end of the seventeenth century, to which I soon will return, clearly explicates the limitations of his celebrated dichotomy between conquest and commerce, and blurs the thin line separating Anglomania from Anglophobia at the time. England had *"given"* Ireland *"its own laws,"* "enslaved" it and forced it into a state of "great dependence" by economic means, but as a result it possessed "a great commerce," and its "navy" became "superior to that of all other powers."[42] It was an act of ruthless reason of state that Montesquieu could not help but simultaneously condemn and commend. That England would be able to treat other powers similarly was a universal preoccupation in eighteenth-century Europe, and increasingly so with its growing power around the time of the Seven Years' War.[43] In effect, the testimony of Jan Pieterszoon Coen, an officer of the Dutch East India Company and twice governor-general of the East Indies, retained its cogency as an indicator of just how winners in international trade explained their success: "one cannot do commerce without war, nor war without commerce."[44]

Far from representing an Indian summer for reason of state, Pieterszoon defined the disposition with which political economy would be institutionalized across Europe in the mid-eighteenth century, when continental authors and statesmen first seriously turned to translating English economic texts and emulating English economic policies. It is clear from studying the patterns of emulation in early modern Europe that England's gradually more positive balance of trade—exemplified in its transition from being an exporter of raw wool to one of manufactured textiles—and the military might this ensured was followed by a positive balance of translations, and, ultimately, a positive linguistic and cultural balance first seriously evident in the 1750s.[45] For "England," as the historian of economics Giuseppe Pecchio would note in 1829, "is for the moderns what Crete was to the ancient philosophers."[46] As a polity it was the linchpin of modernity par excellence, the "object," as one observer put it during the French Revolution, "of universal envy" throughout "this century."[47] Yet England crossed the line between conquest and commerce with abandon, with powerful repercussions for European life and legislation.[48]

France was forced on all levels to face up to England's military and economic challenge. Just as the transfer of technology across the Channel at the time was spearheaded by state-sponsored acts of espionage, so political economy emerged as a discipline in France under the tutelage of *intendant du commerce* Vincent de Gournay, who administered an impressive program of translation and emulation through his administrative network of patronage in the 1750s.[49] Annotating his translation of the 1694 edition of Josiah Child's *Discourse of Trade,* Gournay delineated the basic tenets of the new "science of commerce" and the spirit of his whole endeavor: *"one cannot repeat it often enough, the destiny of commerce and of the arts depending on it will always be like that of war."*[50] Even symbolically, in terms of its metaphorical linkages, political economy was a bellicose science. As a contemporary review of Gournay's translation warned: "England has never had a conqueror the sword of which has served them as well as Child's pen."[51]

The very same idea was promulgated also in Italy, the geographical region that, through its relative decline in the seventeenth century, had most severely felt the political and cultural consequences of failure to keep up in international competition.[52] And again, England's example would set the agenda, from one end of the peninsula to the other. The reformer Giovanni Battista Zanobetti, for example, annotating in 1751 a Leghorn edition of the bestselling *Of Commerce,* by the papal banker Girolamo Belloni, noted how "It seems indeed that the genius of commerce and that of conquest are contradictory within the same nation. . . . Today, though, one sees these two geniuses united in some Kingdoms, and the happy peoples who have this fate are superior to the Romans because uniting commerce and conquest allows them to keep what they have acquired, binding the conquerors and the conquered and all the parts of the empire with mutual benefits."[53] Commerce, he argued, could bring "mutual benefits," but not through a prism of peaceful laissez-faire. The focus of Zanobetti's discussion was, of course, England, which also was the subject of Francesco Algarotti, the Venetian nobleman and translator of Isaac Newton, in his 1764 *Treatise on Commerce:* "The English, who by land and by sea make use of their own arms, demonstrate well that one can graft military valor onto the mercantile profession; and *if they pursue commerce with Carthaginian subtlety, they do not lack Roman virtù in war."*[54]

Niccolò Machiavelli had influentially argued that the Swiss harbored Roman *virtù* because they relied on their own arms rather than on mercenaries, and while this preoccupation remained in Algarotti, he was among the many who, by the time Britannia was ruling the waves, had abandoned the Florentine secretary's mistrust of commerce.[55] England had successfully fused wealth—through international trade rather than landed property—and civic virtue, a conflation of conceptual categories that challenges the basic assumptions of the republican paradigm with regard to the supposedly irrevocable dichotomy between wealth and virtue in the eighteenth-century imagination.[56] As some saw it, liberty and *virtù* had become ineffective in the modern world without the wealth to back them up, and it was accordingly "a mistake to believe," as the Neapolitan political economist and jurist Michele De Jorio put it, "that riches, which are the daughters of commerce," as opposed to agriculture, were "incompatible with valour," adding that "one should not search for the model of civic *virtù* in a poor and military Nation, [for] a State cannot really be happy, and formidable, if it is not opulent."[57]

The Neapolitan reformer and diplomat Ferdinando Galiani reiterated this message about war and wealth in his *Dialogues on the Grain Trade* (1770), noting that "England" was "simultaneously agricultural, industrial, warlike, commercial," and elsewhere stated quite unequivocally that "advantageous commercial treaties are solely the effect of victories and of conquests."[58] This was Franci's above-mentioned "bloodless war," or "war of industry," a phraseology for making sense of modern commercial relations that was also picked up by Italy's third professor of political economy, the poet Agostino Paradisi of Modena. Lecturing to his students on how Holland's merchants were like "Conquerors," Paradisi underlined how Holland owed "the prosperity of its Commerce to the malignity with which it exercised it."[59] Moreover, as an anonymous, late eighteenth-century Piedmontese manuscript on economic reform reveals, the ideal of modern commerce freeing itself from the logic of conquest could go hand in hand with the painful realization that it had failed to do so:

> The importance of commerce has, with prosperous success, already occupied all the governments of Europe for two centuries. [But] extremely advantageous cures degenerated to maintain animosities between peoples, and produced disagreements, and wars. The heavens would have wanted that they, driven by laudable emulation, had only competed through the superiority of their industry, and had not taken to violence, and to slaughter, which have transformed the sacred knot with which providence has wanted to tie men together into the most painful scourge of humanity![60]

Yet the conceptual conflation of conquest and commerce among many eighteenth-century political philosophers meant that even commerce on its own became a threat to the autonomy of political communities. It was gradually understood that one could "give law" and conquer peoples and markets solely through structures of international trade. This was explicitly argued across the European world, and memorably so already by William Paterson, architect of the abortive Darien venture to establish a Scottish colony on the Isthmus of Panama in 1698–1700. Were Scotsmen to dominate cross-peninsular trade between the Caribbean and the Pacific, he argued, they would be able *"to give laws to both oceans and become arbitrators of the commercial world, without being liable to the fatigues, expanses and dangers of contracting the guilt and blood of Alexander and Caesar."*[61] Commerce could be a means of achieving *imperium* without "guilt and blood," of having one's proverbial cake and eating it too. By being physically and emotionally detached from their conquests, their subjects, and their victims, Paterson hoped that economic imperialists might escape the corrupting and destabilizing effects that had toppled past empires in the historical record and thus achieve a durable dominion over others. A consumer in Edinburgh would never need to see any slaves, any plantations, any factories; he could pleasantly and virtuously enjoy the spoils of Scotland's economic empire. As Paterson would soon learn, though, commerce remained soundly anchored to the imperatives of reason of state, and the great powers of the time deemed his venture no less dangerous to the established order than they would have deemed a full-scale Scottish invasion of Central America, and quickly put an end to it by military means.[62]

A frequently translated mid-eighteenth-century essay on Genoa's commerce calls into question the obsessive dogmatism of modern historiography with regard to conquest, commerce, and liberty in precisely these terms:

> In this particular there is no difference between a warlike and a trading republic: on the contrary both ought to be considered from the same point of view. . . . An incontestable proof of this assertion is the jealousy and disquiet that appears when another power extends its trade, and penetrates into the places where she has established her commerce: disquiets as violent and attended with the same effects as those of a military state, who sees one of its neighbours receive a considerable increase in dominion.[63]

In material as well as symbolic terms, conquest and commerce had salient similarities in early modern Europe, and some would go so far as to call these similarities synergies.

Not surprisingly, this way of thinking about economic relations reached one of its highest degrees of theoretical sophistication in the Kingdom of Naples, which for centuries had endured asymmetrical patterns of trade and subjection to foreign masters, exporting its raw materials in exchange for manufactured goods.[64] Antonio Genovesi, Italy's first professor of political economy, warned that Naples and other nations producing raw materials would be forever "dependent on foreigners" and become *"in certain ways tributaries,"* "instruments of their wealth and power."[65] National independence was as meaningless as it was fleeting without the economic power, and more specifically the industrial and thus military power, to guard it from foreign interests. Political economy was not merely the science of reforming institutions and making the kingdom wealthy, it rendered nations viable as political entities in the midst of international rivalries, and to do this it had to open people's eyes to the congruence of conquest and commerce. Similarly, Genovesi's student De Jorio wrote extensively on the legal and political consequences of commerce in historical perspective, and could only acknowledge that "the history of the most warlike nations is that of their commerce no less than of their conquests."[66] Why? Because it is really "a state enriched by Commerce . . . that makes others fear the loss of their liberty." Though the sources of wealth had differed greatly between Spain, Holland, Sweden, and England, all had sought to "give laws" to Europe. The question was how states employed their resources to dominate competitors, and, historically, De Jorio saw some technologies of imperialism work better than others. While England reigned triumphant, Spain had disappeared from the world's scene, and Germany was still "rule[d] by the empire of foreign industry," for "dependence on necessities" was tantamount to "slavery."[67]

Contrary, then, to an influential argument in modern historiography, the possibility that an empire might be established through economic as well as military means was clearly articulated in the eighteenth century. Conquest was not always a corruption of trade's intrinsic telos; it could be its most natural consequence. Similarly, republicanism and commercial society were never simply an antidote—or a subsequent paradigm—to universal monarchy.[68] They could also be its midwives, and from this perspective, De Jorio wrote, "England seems to have hit the bull's eye." Indeed, commerce had bestowed on England "dominion" even where it sent no troops, and aspiring to "Universal Monarchy" through "industry," it had established *"a different kind of Empire."*[69] Though ostensibly friendly and reciprocal, free trade could, for De Jorio and the science of legislation on which he drew, establish "empires" and enable political communities to "give laws" to one another. An autonomous state could lose its "liberty" without a single shot being fired or a single gladius hitting home. In this sense, liberty was not simply the monopoly of specific political constellations like "republics," for real liberty—whether understood in individual or collective terms, as personal autonomy or national sovereignty—in the end depended on laws and on the agency of legislation, ultimately dictated by international relations of power no less than internal organizations of political life.[70]

Giving and Receiving Laws

Surveying the varied landscapes of political economy, one indeed finds that the idioms of "giving" and "receiving laws" were then as universally employed as they are now neglected. The expression *dare* or *dicere leges victis,* "to give" or "to dictate the law to the conquered," was a variation on the equation in classical antiquity of power with the ability to "give laws," a condition often explored by Thucydides, and derived from the idea that liberty demanded subjection only to one's own legislation. The alternative was to be unfree, to be *alieni iuris,* subject to the *juris-diction* of another, as later stipulated in Roman law.[71] This idea, harnessed by Moses the Law-giver and by Livy, by Roman jurists and by prostrate Carthaginians forced to "receive the law" at the feet of Scipio Africanus at the end of the Second Punic War, was nearly ubiquitous in early modern Europe, even tendering abstract meanings. A "public granary," one Basque merchant put it, could "give the law to commerce."[72] Yet most often the phrase was explicitly political. The undisputed right to "give laws to subjects," like that of "war and peace," belonged to sovereigns, indeed it was the essence of sovereignty according to the celebrated French jurist Jean Bodin, and Giovanni Botero, a founding author of the reason of state tradition, used the phraseology of giving and receiving laws repeatedly to signify both concrete conquests and de facto empires.[73] The expression's proliferation was intimately linked to solidifying theories of sovereignty in Europe—for, as Locke would put it, "what can give Laws to another, must needs be superiour to him"—and to the gradual shift from dynastic to national rivalries on the continent, sometimes identified with the idea that individuals in a stable political community could be empowered by the collective demonstration of force over "foreigners" in international competition.[74] So widespread did the idiom eventually become that it even was institutionalized in late eighteenth-century dictionaries. "To give the law to one," a Spanish-English dictionary explained in 1797, should be translated "Dar la ley á alguno."[75]

After all, political units were largely conceived of in the tradition of the body politic in early modern Europe, by which, as suggested in Emperor Justinian's *Digest* of Roman law, free men and free states alike had to be "in their own power" and not "under the power of someone else" in order to enjoy their *libertas.*[76] Machiavelli's platitude that "rulers should do their best to avoid being at the discretion of others" might well have derived from Alcibiades' timeless admonition to the Athenians, on the eve of the Sicilian expedition, that "there is a danger that we ourselves may fall under the power of others unless others are in our power," and both maxims facilitated expansionist politics.[77] Their realist intuitions were rendered more formally in the eighteenth century. Denis Diderot was one of many to argue that "political liberty is the situation of a people who have not alienated their sovereignty, and who either make their own laws or are associated to some degree in their legislation."[78] To "dictate the laws," De Jorio wrote in this vein, was "the most important role of Government."[79] Given this assumption that liberty was to live in a state of laws rather than arbitrariness, then precisely who set those laws was of cardinal importance.

Yet there were more ways for a state to be "enslaved" than those most often considered by modern historiography. In the "republican" or "neoroman theory of free states" explored by Quentin Skinner, for example, a state could be enslaved in "two distinct ways": through "colonisation or conquest" or by virtue of its "internal constitution."[80] Yet the idiom of "giving" and "receiving" laws was employed to convey dominions not only of physical conquest but also of commerce, and many Europeans feared that a state could be enslaved by purely economic means. In particular, England's triumph in the contest to "give" rather than "receive" laws through trade became the sun around which many founding fathers of political economy revolved, from the architects of the Williamite Settlement after the 1688-9 Revolutions and the Gournay circle in Paris to Genovesi's school in Naples and Alexander Hamilton in Washington.[81] As the London pamphleteer Charles Davenant transposed Machiavelli's doctrines to the question of international economic relations, "No Wise State, if it has the Means of preventing the Mischief, will leave its Ruin in the Power of another Country"; and with this he justified armed interventions abroad to "interrupt the too sudden growth of any neighbour nation."[82]

If differences in economic power could impose hierarchical relations between political communities, the politics of international trade acquired heightened importance. Jurisdiction could of course be more or less formal, and the concept of "giving laws" also expressed such greyscale relations. The Irish political economist Bernardo Ward, writing in the service of Ferdinand VI of Spain, argued that Spain, at the height of its powers, had managed to "conquer a new world, and give the law to the greater and principal part of the old." In a world of competing commercial societies, liberty depended not only on military but also on economic power to resist that conflux of conquest and commerce known, and feared, as *imperium*.[83] Throughout the European world, economic policies, conscious acts to administer the material world and regulate economic relations, became all-important as the means through which sovereigns—kings, city councils, parliaments—could influence the welfare and political destinies of their polities.[84] Success in trade, the ability to give laws, and commercial jealousy were impossible to extricate as the modern world economy took shape, and would resonate as such into the nineteenth century.[85] Where a state was located in the architecture of the global economy—what it produced and traded and how—remained of literally existential importance.

As Genovesi's greatest heir, Gaetano Filangieri, observed in his magisterial and hugely influential *Science of Legislation,* "commerce" had become "essential to the organization and to the existence of political bodies." For "in the midst of opulence your name will be feared, your alliance will be desired, your rights respected, your pretensions supported well, [and] you will give the law to your neighbors, but they will give it to you if you are poorer than they are."[86] Ancient ideals had come to depend on forces much larger than those addressed by the canonical philosophers; wealth had become a cause rather than a simple consequence of greatness and what a vibrant tradition of eighteenth-century political philosophy still referred to as the "common good," derived from late medieval Christian notions of the "ben comune" as a higher good than that capable of being aimed for and experienced by individuals. Machiavelli's dictum that it was "not the particular good but the common good that makes cities great" had a long afterlife in the age of political economy.[87]

Though the phrase "universal monarchy" is currently equated with the historical goals of either Spain or France, the growing fear in eighteenth-century Europe, at least after its troops thundered across the fields of Blenheim in 1704, was that England would enslave the world by giving it laws.[88] It was a latecomer to power politics; its forceful rise to prominence in the early modern period met with awe and wonder, fear and jealousy. These sentiments were clearly expressed in a 1704 Danish manuscript marveling at the island's recent history. From a humbling past in which the Hansa had "prescribed the laws to the English," England had turned the tables entirely.[89] The Navarrese political economist Gerónimo de Uztáriz echoed this idea in 1724. Because of the immense wealth secured for Holland through its empire in the East Indies, it was able to "impose laws" on the English in 1662, "after a bloody and expensive war, moved by jealousy and commercial competition," but their places had irrevocably changed.[90] The question that even Englishmen asked around the turn of the seventeenth century, however, was whether England had not gone too far, no longer seeking simply freedom from others but power over them as well. A self-critical British dystopia of 1712, for example, argued that "O-Brazilians" (Englishmen in the allegorical architecture of the account) look "upon it as their undoubted Birth-Right to Revile, Slander, and Insult all the World; *nay to give Laws to all other Nations.*"[91]

This suggests that historiography has long overlooked one of the principal vectors of political liberty in early modern Europe—a vector that not only sidelined but in effect trumped debates about civic virtue and self-representation.[92] No virtuous citizen militia could compete with the artillery of the Royal Navy. A state could no longer safeguard its liberty by closing itself off from international trade, for no closed commercial state—at least in Europe—could long resist the aggressive power of the great trading nations.[93] As even Davenant admitted in 1699, amid fears of virtue's decline in the modern world, though "trade" was "in its nature a pernicious thing," it was "a necessary evil" given the "posture and condition of other countries." Commerce might have been a negative influence on human existence, but it was also a necessity for the survival of an independent polis in the face of hostile foreign powers. Virtue alone could no longer hold the fort, but there can be no doubt that this was a compromise for Davenant: "if trade cannot be made subservient to the nation's safety, it ought to be no more encouraged here than it was in Sparta."[94]

So if the "doux commerce" model of political communities envisaged that states could secure their freedom under the aegis of peaceful commercial relations, the alternative tradition of economic rivalry made liberty itself competitive. Since the economic sphere too followed certain laws, with some economic activities being more conducive to agonistic autonomy than others, the competitive management of the material world became a cardinal aspect of statecraft. "Trade," Hume aptly argued, had become "an affair of state."[95] And he, like Goudar and Casanova, saw only one way of securing liberty and independence in the modern world: an endless process of mutual emulation in order to countervail international inequalities of economic power and "forced dependencies." Only in this way could political "independency" be safeguarded.[96]

The Virtue of Emulation

The European Renaissance had been an "Age of Emulation" in two ways. It was a moment when architects, artists, humanists, and sovereigns drew extraordinary energies from contemplating the past glory of Rome and from emulating its greatness, but also when northern states in the European periphery first began to seriously imitate and surpass the Italian core.[97] What follows will focus less on the aesthetic contemplation of Rome than on practices of economic emulation, without suggesting that the former did not inform the latter. Like the idea of "giving" and "receiving" laws, emulation was a venerable concept in early modern Europe, having been established as the constructive alternative to the passion of "Envy" already in Aristotle's *Rhetoric*. As Hobbes defined it in his influential translation of that work, "*Envy* is grief, for the prosperity of such as our selves, arising not from any hurt that we, but from the good that they receive." Envy was a negative jealousy of other people's prosperity, even when the envious party itself was unaffected. "Emulation," on the other hand, was "grief arising from that our Equals possess such goods as are had in honour, and thereof we are capable, but have them not; not because they have them, but because not we also." It was a noble, positive passion manifested by "Young and Magnanimous Men."[98]

Similar definitions appeared often in the dictionaries of the period: Elisha Coles's *English Dictionary* defined "Emulation" as "a striving to excel others," and so did Nathan Bayley in his *Orthographic Dictionary*. "To Emulate," he explained, was "to strive to exceed one."[99] Ephraim Chambers's great *Cyclopædia* defined it "a noble jealousy."[100] As the eighteenth century progressed, however, the word's historical aporias were discussed more openly. One Latin dictionary noted that esteemed classical authors had differed in their use of the term. *Aemulatio* to Cicero had meant "Emulation either in a good or bad sense," whereas for Quintilian it signified "Imitation with a desire to excel," and to the bleaker Livy it was "hatred, and contention, the usual effects, where one of the parties cannot obtain his desire." An *Aemulator*, however, was a "rival, an imitator," as Cicero (and Hobbes) had argued, and was the meaning "more frequently used."[101] An important French dictionary came to consider it generally as a "noble and generous passion which, admiring merit, beautiful things and the actions of others, attempts to imitate them, or even to surpass them, striving to this end courageously and with honourable and virtuous principles."[102] Emulation was no longer a static passion seeking to equalize fortunes but rather the principle of competitiveness itself, possibly—but not necessarily— encouraging a cycle of virtuous economic one-upmanship.[103] But if emulation often was praised for its virtues, the word retained darker connotations. An English-Italian dictionary from the middle of the century defined "Emulation" as "a striving to excel or go beyond another in any thing," which could be translated both as "Emulazione" and as "Gara," in other words "race" or "competition," valid also for the words "strife, contention, jarring, emulation."[104]

Emulation, as such, enjoyed a wide array of meanings in a variety of contexts, from a noble virtue helping everyone progress to an elegant euphemism for cutthroat competition. The sphere of activity in which it enjoyed the most powerful resonance was probably art.[105] In dictionaries of love the concept could take on its darker and less rigorous signification, describing the vying interests of rival suitors, while pedagogically it was the driving principle behind biographical collections published in early modern England to foster a "Spirit of Emulation," an endeavor in turn emulating a Sallustian trope often rehearsed in European humanist circles.[106] In the "very ancient town" of Oswestry, a geographical dictionary explained in 1759–60, there was similarly a "charity-school" in which "a laudable emulation" was "excited" by "little premiums."[107] The step from pedagogy to politics was short; in the cultural lexicon of the day, emulation could be fostered by judicious encouragement, a meaning that would become exceedingly relevant in the context of governmental interventions in the economy.[108] Yet such manipulation went both ways, and just as emulation could be cultivated, so it could be extinguished. True excellence depended on the impermanence of its individual loci, glaring concentrations of greatness smothering all competition and thus emulation, inviting decadence and decline.[109] Monopolies of power, whether in markets, at court, in love, or in intellectual debate, were equivalent to stagnation, an insight that would influence elite sociability in France throughout the eighteenth and nineteenth centuries.[110] Worldly melioration was intrinsically intertwined with individual initiative, but the latter in turn depended on careful calibration by higher powers to bloom.[111] Emulation, a Roman economic journal explained in the 1770s, could be "directed."[112]

There thus existed a politics of administering the tension between jealousy and emulation to ensure not only that competition existed, but that it aligned with the "common good." And to complicate matters further, this problem was understood to transcend the interactions of individuals to act on goods and nations as well, a process galvanized across Europe in the eighteenth century by myriads of official regulations as well as private societies encouraging national emulation.[113] Harrowingly, international emulation was even more prone to counteract the concept's ostensibly noble origins than individual emulation. For as success in the international theatre of emulation was a great source of national pride, so failure could trigger the most desperate gambits to overcome adversity. As Jean-Paul Rabaut de Saint-Etienne prophetically proclaimed in 1789, France was "made, not to follow examples, but to give them."[114] The necessity of harnessing emulation and of keeping it true to its noble ideals was evident, for in Europe's history, as many noted, genocidal imperialism was the most natural outcome of "emulation" between people and polities.[115]

And these two kinds of emulation, individual and national, were profoundly related. Their synergy in terms of success in international competition was analyzed explicitly by the great London political economist Malachy Postlethwayte. "Emulation," he wrote, was synonymous with

"Rivalship" and as such "the most active Principle of useful Commerce." He envisaged emulation as taking place on two levels, national and international, and that the latter depended on the former. "Emulation in Work between the Subjects" of a nation "alone contributes more than any other Means to procure a Nation that foreign Rivalship by which she grows rich and powerful." Emulous citizens made for an emulous body politic. "Emulation among their Artists and Workmen within their own Country," Postlethwayte repeated in an analysis of France, "is the best Preparatory to enable them to vye with Foreigners."[116] Integration in international markets could successfully encourage domestic "emulation," rendering a nation more flourishing, argued a Tuscan woolworker in the 1770s, but only if the government helped its manufacturers "compete with foreigners."[117] A person's emulation depended on the capacity of its community to do so, and vice versa.

Raynal thought "commerce, which prevailed after the discovery of the New World," had "increased" the "powers" of nations by "exciting universal emulation";[118] and Hume, who frequently invoked the term *emulation* in his work, thought it was "the greatest Encourager of the noble Arts," indeed "the source of every excellence." Not only did it "naturally arise" among states "connected together by commerce and policy," but it was so important that "domestic commerce itself would languish for want of emulation, example, and instruction." Although Hume forcefully argued that "emulation among rival nations" served to "keep industry alive in all of them," later commentators have exaggerated his penchant for laissez-faire. In the cultural terminology of the day, emulation could be generated through encouragement, and Hume's argument for the English economy was in principle no different from that of the Oswestry schoolmasters: a "tax" to encourage "home manufactures," like the "little premiums" of the charity school, was never "prejudicial."[119] Hume's friend Adam Ferguson followed suit in his 1767 *History of Civil Society,* noting with woe that extinguishing "the emulation which is excited from abroad" would "break or weaken the bands of society at home" and "close the busiest scenes of national occupations and virtues."[120]

Yet, like the young Hobbes himself, these two Scottish philosophers doubted the practical possibility of differentiating between emulation and jealousy in the context of competing commercial societies. Hume often referred to a hybrid "jealous emulation," while Ferguson argued that "emulation" was "rarely unmixed with envy and jealousy," and, importantly, that in fact "the emulous are enemies of each other."[121] And though that even more celebrated Scotsman Adam Smith often would praise the virtue of emulation, and essentially thought that it resulted from "unrestrained competition," he also warned that "mutual emulation and the desire of greater gain" could lead men to "hurt their health by excessive labour."[122] The sculptor Jean-Baptiste Boudard's famous *Iconology* had pictured this blurred distinction well some years earlier. The image of "Jalousie" includes a cock, since "the cock, a jealous and vigilant animal, is its symbol," while that of "Emulation" depicts two, for "its attributes are two cocks ready to fight."[123] This ambivalence had linguistic origins as well: Aristotle's original term for emulation was *zelos,* the root of the word jealousy in many European languages.[124]

To appreciate the ambiguity of emulation it is useful to keep in mind the scheme later elaborated by the conservative politician and philosopher Edmund Burke. While he abandoned the term emulation itself, he found in its component passions of "sympathy," "imitation," and "ambition" the engine of all civilization.[125] As the early modern world made abundantly clear, however, sympathy was the decidedly weakest link of the triad, without which emulation became merely ambitious imitation. As such, emulation was often the noble veneer for jealous attempts at attracting the envy of others. If catching up economically was philosophically justifiable by recourse to emulation, few successful nations would not subsequently revert to jealously guarding their position. Greatness, again, was an eminently positional good.[126] Emulation could ideally spell a way out of mankind's wars and miseries by leading the way to constructive competition, but given actual conditions of economic development and rivalry, it was seldom more than a rhetorical ploy.[127] A Venetian pamphlet described the state of the world anno 1770 in precisely these terms. "Commerce," it argued, "can be compared to fire, which, depending on whether it is used well or poorly, benefits us, or hurts us." The problem was that "emulation degenerates into jealousies, into discords, into hatreds, into rabid wars; the effects of which rarely compensate the damage they do to Commerce and to the National Economy, and the jealous emulation, root of the discord, remains ever alive."[128] Emulation and jealousy were two sides of the same coin. Like fire and trade, emulation could both burn and illuminate, and it took craft to harness safely.

The Curse of Babel

However difficult it was to practice virtuously, emulation was further hampered in early modern Europe by the same cultural and linguistic factors impeding contemporary Grand Tourists: faced with the linguistic plurality of the continent, emulation was inflected by the tortured practices of transmission and translation. The latter had been a cause of technical and theological contention since time immemorial. Though the world's cultures share surprisingly similar explanations for the original loss of a common language, the Western tradition rests on the rubble of the Tower of Babel and the linguistic fragmentation resulting from its fall.[129] Genesis 11:1–9 tells the story of a God, incensed by the overconfidence of men, sundering their towering achievement along with the instrument of their greatness: the universal language that bound them together; the uncorrupted communication that enabled their seamless cooperation. The incident of the tower also introduced substantial theological concerns about translation itself, for was it not blasphemy to circumvent God's will, to assume what he had denied? Or was the curse of Babel, like the expulsion from Eden, an invitation to achieve grace and perfection in this world, to redeem humanity for its insolence and hubris through human agency?

As the seemingly infinite variety of plants discovered during the age of exploration invited botanists to reconstruct Eden, so could perhaps the world's variety of languages reveal a singularity in the multiplicity, the *clavis universalis* that, through mortal ingenuity, could undo the vice that brought down Babel.[130] Centuries of medieval and early modern European scholarship therefore sought to weld the pieces of the biblical tower together again; the thirteenth-century Majorcan philosopher Ramon Llull sought the key to universal understanding in the "white magic" of Christian cabbala, while the Jesuit Athenasius Kircher looked to Egyptian hieroglyphics three hundred years later.[131] Individual translations might not recover the architectural blueprint of Babel Llull and Kircher searched for but nonetheless contributed to its reconstruction, word by word, much as dictionaries could be justified as means of transmitting synthetic knowledge in a context of linguistic diversity.[132] Redemptive vocabularies were similarly applied to worldlier translations of political economy, as is evident from a 1767 review of Giovanni Francesco Scottoni's Venetian translation of the French edition of Cantillon's manuscript *Essay on the Nature of Commerce in General* that asserted that the work was "enlightening" and apt for "Holy Religious men."[133]

Such hyperbole was not universally convincing; legions of authors continued to bewail the futility of translation. Chambers even went so far, when faced with the contemporary tendency to use "Definitions promiscuously" and the "Uncertainty" this had "introduc'd into Language," as to argue that "all the confusion of Babel is brought upon us hereby; and people of the same country, nay the same profession, no longer understand one another."[134] Babel had come to stand for the problems of communication itself. Yet while some feared the very possibility of society in a world of miscommunications, society and communication themselves went ahead rather unperturbed.[135]

More technically, Dante had influentially declared the impossibility of translating anything "touched by the muses." But the poet's distinction is significant.[136] For better and worse, early modern economic administrators and merchant pamphleteers were rarely poetic or primarily concerned with invoking emotions, although their tales of plight and hunger certainly *could*. Rather, such men concerned themselves with the communication of ideas and experiences, theories and practices. As the Florentine book censor Giuseppe Pelli Bencivenni pondered after deciding to translate a Latin dissertation that had appeared in a Swiss journal:

> I find it difficult because it is in a German Latin, which very poorly can be transported to Italian with any exactness. Therefore it is necessary that I conserve the sense without being attached to the words. In works that are not of eloquence, or of poetry, this method of translation seems to me the best, because at the end, in books on science, it is important only to know the sentiments of the authors, and not the way in which they expressed them, unless they are those greatest luminaries of knowledge of whom even the small things are venerated.[137]

Some years later, Pelli again returned to the difficulty of translation, practically equating it with that of original composition, but also to the difference between translating historical and scientific works and translating philosophical and poetical works. There was something indefinably different about translating principles, recipes, and discoveries as compared to poetry, and it is precisely in this space of purpose-driven communication that political economy would lodge in the long eighteenth century.[138] Economic translators tended to be clear in their intentions and transparent in their political sensibilities, often formulating them both in terms of national emulation in the pursuit of power.

As a result of the very specific political constellation of the European states-system after the War of Spanish Succession, what J. G. A. Pocock has called the "Utrecht Enlightenment," the myth of Babel was inflected to the point where the separation of languages came to be evaluated positively. The Peace of Utrecht of 1713 brought the confessional anarchy and the subsequent Wars of Religion that had dominated politics on the continent since the Reformation to a momentary close, inaugurating a period when the European order of states, linked by the mutual emulation of commerce and manners, subsumed religious practices to civil society, thus freeing it from Edward Gibbon's millennial yoke of "Barbarism and Religion."[139] In 1751, the abbé Noël-Antoine Pluche delineated the positive consequences of the fall of Babel in light of this new world order. Civilization and the advances of the nation-state were made possible only by the forced subdivision of men occasioned by the episode of the tower, by the concentration and internal development enforced by the isolation of linguistic communities.[140] Translation was more important than quixotically questing for a universal language, for it was the competitive interaction of nations that begat civilization, and only through translation could one hope to emulate the achievements of others. The art of translation, like the European system of states itself, sought to escape its submission to religion, and what mattered to the reformers of the Utrecht Enlightenment was how translation could facilitate communication and emulation between states, not whether this was reconcilable with scripture. Religion came to coexist with other sources of authority but continued to influence and justify economic translation and emulation: "Look that thou make them after the pattern," Ustáriz's English translator selectively quoted Exodus 25:40, "which was shewn thee."[141]

Admittedly, the languages of Europe were affected differently by the curse of Babel, and much as Latin for centuries had been able to unify the learned across the continent, so French took on an unrivaled role as the vehicle of linguistic mediation in the early modern period. The Florentine Cosimo Alessandro Collini, for example, wrote his 1761 *Discourse on the History of Germany* directly in French, "a language which has become that of merchants, of peace treaties, that of nearly all the Courts of Europe and the majority of men of letters."[142] Why would someone not versed in French care about the book in the first place? It made perfect sense for a Tuscan to write a German history in French. Pelli argued the same regarding a forthcoming Siennese translation of Raynal: "whoever is capable of appreciating this marvelous book must know French, and whoever does not know it is too ignorant to know its merit."[143] French was the language of high diplomacy but also of high international exchange, and was recognized as such by the literati of Europe. Yet translations of economic works influenced deeper social strata as well. Peter Burke's work on the popularity of ancient historians in early modern Europe is enlightening in this regard. Not only did the most frequently republished works of ancient history (say Valerius and Curtius) not correspond to those emphasized by modern historians (say Thucydides and Polybius) but the most popular works in the wider vernacular markets (Plutarch, Curtius) were not those most popular in the more restricted learned readership engaging with texts in Greek and Latin (Sallust, Suetonius).[144] Books catered to different audiences, and to appreciate the history of political economy one must be far more attuned to actual market conditions for works in different languages, and particularly so in terms of their appearances in elite languages, first Latin, then French, and the wider world of less universal vernaculars. The point of the revolution in the publication and translation of economic works was not to render books available to scholars and diplomats, who already were able to engage with the originals (and serious readers often preferred original editions, unless they were rare, or valuable additions had been made in translation).[145] The point was rather to introduce such works to entirely new segments of society and empower them to think critically about the most pressing issues of modernity: emulation, liberty, and public happiness, not to mention more practical matters such as new agricultural techniques. The Spanish translation of Galiani's *Dialogues* encapsulated this attitude well: "Though there are many in our day who can read the original, since the French language is so common, there are also many who do not understand it, principally in the interior parts of the Provinces, which is where the doctrine it contains perhaps can be most important."[146]

Though such schemes are overly tidy, it has been argued that the European linguistic imagination changed from "vertical" to "horizontal" around the time of Petrarch. From a hegemonic hierarchy in which Latin, sanctified, presided over the vernaculars of Europe, the Renaissance began to see its dethronement in favor of a dynamic field of languages engaged in the mutual exchange of words and ideas.[147] It was in this secular context that questions of temporal power, measured also according to perceived economic performances, began to influence the relationships between languages without reference to their proximity to scripture. Centuries later, the Salernitan natural scientist Giuseppa Eleonora Barbapiccola stated not only that she intended to "share" her translation of René Descartes *Principles of Philosophy* "with many others, particularly women" but also that operational differences between vernaculars meant that some languages, in practical and emulative terms, inherently were more communicative than others: "our language," she wrote, "can render a version of this work that conforms even more closely to the Latin text" than others. Most important, however, she noted the secularization of languages and the process of *translatio studii* through a historical rendition of translation patterns, with the core of European culture shifting from Greek to Latin to Italian to French, and, in the period here under analysis, to English.[148]

As *The Chinese Spy* pointed out, this process was complicated by the interrelationship between the trajectories of linguistic and temporal power, *translatio studii* and *translatio imperii*: "The Italians, who in every thing have set the example in this part of the world, were the first in polishing language; the other nations indeed have followed so good a pattern."[149] In

his elegant last book, Richard Helgerson demonstrated how the "new poetry" of sixteenth-century Europe was deeply preoccupied with scaffolding
contemporary empires with eloquent vernaculars, with ensuring that a
country's culture did not lag behind its power. Spain, England, and France
did not merely compete economically and militarily for the throne of
Rome. They also competed culturally, and the literary efforts of poets such
as Joachim du Bellay and Edmund Spenser were precisely aimed at supplying their native languages with poetry as capable of sophisticated articula-
tion as the Latin of Cicero and Virgil or the Italian of Petrarch. Only by
fusing worldly and cultural power could the elusive *translatio* of Rome
materialize. This required a careful balancing of imitation, innovation, and
tradition. It required emulation. The paradigm was embodied by the
warrior-poet Garcilaso de la Vega, uniquely playing both Scipio and Virgil
to Charles V's Caesar during his 1535 North African campaign, but a
similar preoccupation with language and empire would structure poetry
from Augustan Britain to the United States of Ralph Waldo Emerson and
Walt Whitman.[150] *Translatio imperii* was anchored in *translatio studii,* in
the emulation of language, power, and their union.

Cycles of Emulation and Translation

From their origins in rediscovered texts of ancient moral philosophy, these
ideals of emulation were eventually expressed across a variety of literary
genres, from party pamphlets and technical briefs to novels. An anonymous
early eighteenth-century poem on *Fishery* in fact formulated the role of
emulation in the rise of England's empire as well as any learned treatise:

> The Ancients fancy'd half the *Globe* conceal'd,
> But where, or how it lay, was not reveal'd;
> At length *Columbus* drew the *Western* Scene,
> Disclosing all those Wond'rous Views within.
> From his Success, our Emulation came,
> We ventur'd out, and we atchiev'd the same.[151]

As the poem continues, England not only caught up with Spain but superseded it. And soon it was the English empire that showed "merit" worthy
of emulation, with some of its writers on matters of political economy
becoming deeply alarmed by what damage their well-intended works
might do in the wrong hands—by how, in other words, they could inadvertently inspire and instruct foreigners through this passion or virtue of emulation they themselves had harnessed.[152]

For in the microcosm of man and in the macrocosm of the body politic alike, success was a desperately evanescent phenomenon. The "falling behind" of the Italian city-states at the end of the Renaissance, the second decline, had robbed Rome of its historical monopoly on the theme.[153] Though its history would remain a canon with which other declines could be compared, contrasted, and conflated, Rome was by the eighteenth century joined by a legion of unsuccessful states and empires, a despondent roster that included the Spanish, the Portuguese, and the Dutch, not to mention a veritable hecatomb of ancient civilizations observable, in their Ozymandian transience, only through the scattered fragments uncovered by antiquarians.[154] There was an inherent cyclicality to greatness and emulation. The Spanish and, more directly, the Dutch had after all been vanquished by English emulation in recent memory. It was the "Spirit of Envy or Emulation" the Dutch empire had inspired that had rendered it ephemeral, an Englishman argued in 1750, and the Dutch themselves, as the famous French statesman and political economist Véron de Forbonnais noted shortly afterward, had only "imitated" the Italian city-states on a "more solid foundation."[155] Just as the consequences of international competition in many ways remained unaltered, so greatness based on commerce was no more permanent than that based on conquest. All empires would in time be overtaken by their competitors, and many considered emulation the means by which the wheel of the world turned, the engine, so to speak, of *translatio imperii*.[156]

Adrian Johns has recently emphasized the piratical element of "the Enlightenment" and the ways metaphors of piracy trailed the transmission of ideas in the long eighteenth century.[157] Translations were part and parcel of this "Piratical Enlightenment." A late eighteenth-century translator of François Fénelon, for example, wished to "give away" copies of his book so that "perhaps some person will dare to pirate the translation, and thus the public will obtain it at last." Only by surrendering the rights to his own work could he ensure its promulgation.[158] Yet in few areas was the tension between creative and commercial exigencies more pronounced than in the field of political economy, in which competition divided peoples, not people. Josiah Child, a governor of the East India Company whose works were widely circulated in his time, knew the double-edged power of economic emulation all too well. The first edition of his *Discourse on Trade*, a work explaining the virtues of lowering the interest rate on money, repeatedly argued that England should look toward the economic successes of the continent for inspiration, in terms of not only interest, but also industry: "*If we intend to have the Trade of the World,*" he maintained, "*we must imitate the Dutch, who make the worst as well as the best of all*

Manufactures, that we may be in a capacity of serving all Markets, and all Humors." England should indulge in economic nationalism by judiciously emulating Dutch industrial practices.[159] But emulation went both ways, and Child included a very telling caveat in the fourth edition of his *Discourse*:

> I think it necessary, for caution to my Countrymen, to let them know what effects these discourses have had on others. When I wrote my first treatise, interest was in the Island of Barbados at 15 *per cent*. where it is since by an Act of the Country brought down to 10 *per cent*. a great fall at once, and our weekly Gazettes some months past informed us, that the Swedes by a law had brought down their interest to 6 *per cent*. neither of which can have any good effects upon us, but certainly the contrary, *except by way of emulation they quicken us to provide in time for our own good and prosperity.*[160]

Observing the international implementation of his ideas, Child found succor in the "good and prosperity" resulting from perpetual emulation. By creating a permanent state of precarious competition, Child and his contemporaries across Europe came to consider economic emulation through translations a constructive, if nerve-wracking phenomenon that ultimately would make everyone better off, fuelling a virtuous circle of one-upmanship. This, incidentally, was the precise mechanism by which eighteenth-century Europeans believed their continent had embarked on a path of progressive development, associated with what we now would call "capitalism," rather than, as that of the contemporary Chinese, of stability. Child formulated in emulative economic terms what Pluche had formulated in terms of translations.[161]

As in Hobbes's translation of Aristotle, emulation was ideally a constructive phenomenon that, by perpetuating a state of precarious competition, ultimately made everyone better off. But it was not always peaceful. A review of the French translation of Child, undertaken by the same group subsequently responsible for that of Cary, explained not only how he had proposed to "transform" England's "envy into emulation" but also how he had "divined" the "mystery" of commerce, which the Dutch had been "hiding," becoming, in a symbolically pregnant phrase, "the legislator of all of Europe." Political economy codified successful practice, but once secretive reason of state acquired written form, emulation could ensure universal Enlightenment—an ambivalent prospect in light of international competition. For though the instruments of empire were circulated freely, their bellicose purpose remained unaltered. The review's conclusion is telling with regard to the nature of political economy as it first was institutionalized across Europe. Child was the "Newton" of commerce, and *"We will never beat the English in commerce if not with the weapons which Child forged for them.*"[162] And as a French translator justified his endeavor in the 1750s, "nothing contributes advantage in sustaining our emulation" more than "contemplating the acts of our enemies."[163]

The importance of economic translations as vehicles of cyclical jealous-emulation was expressed with striking clarity also by Malachy Postle-thwayte in a 1749 essay on his translation of Jacques Savary's epic *Dictionary of Commerce*.[164] Hoping his rendition would produce the same "happy effects in *Great Britain*" as the original had in France, Postlethwayte noted that if "they have improved upon us, we may, perhaps, in our turn go still further, and improve upon them." Postlethwayte delineated a virtuous process of continual cyclical emulation between competing nations, presenting translation as the means of its achievement. Equally remarkably, he addressed the anxiety experienced by statesmen as the secretive paradigm of reason of state gave way to the early modern public sphere. Just as Child pondered the explosive encounter of valued knowledge and portable print culture, Postlethwayte could not help but praise the rival French for being such "generous and communicative people." Why? Because "there never was so much knowledge of trade ever exhibited to the world before" the publication of Savary's *Dictionary*. Everyone could now harness centuries of accumulated administrative and commercial know-how in an expensive but manageable set of volumes, translate them, and disseminate their insights. Yet Postlethwayte's moral compass remained soundly anchored to the coordinates of reason of state. His hopes were namely that the translation would "universalize" economic knowledge not to serve mankind, but to "prove instrumental in raising such an emulous spirit of trade and merchandizing in Great Britain, as may prevent our Britons from being outdone in the practical part thereof, by any rival country whatsoever."[165] Though England had emulated the supremacies of Holland and France, they in turn had emulated those of the Italian city-states, and so on, he may have shared the perennial hubris of all imperialists: that their own empire should be the last.

As the soon-to-be Marquis de Pombal expressed in Portugal, emulation was an endlessly dynamic endeavor: "All European nations have improved themselves through reciprocal imitation; each one carefully keeps watch over the actions taken by the others."[166] As such, emulation is a crucial analytical category for understanding the competing and competitive technologies of greatness in the history of the European world. The perpetual process of one-upmanship that emulation fueled ensured what some would call "progress," and Daniel Defoe rejoiced at seeing how, after centuries of emulation, competing states "ambitious of imitating us in the same Manner, and to rival our Manufactures, are obliged to hire Instructors from hence, and to learn of those who were but Learners before."[167] Raynal's description of Britain's economic conquest of Portugal in his celebrated *History* is in this sense indicative of the political-economic imagination of the eighteenth century:

> As soon as Great Britain had condemned it to a state of inaction, it is fallen into such barbarism as is scarce credible. The light which had shone all over Europe did not extend itself to the frontiers of Portugal. *That kingdom was even observed to degenerate, and to attract the contempt of those whose emulation and jealousy it had before excited.*[168]

To stop emulating, or to lose the capacity to do so, was to wither away. But though many agreed that emulation through translation was a double-edged sword, there was less consensus regarding its practical consequences. Raynal provided one of the most cogent refutations of the dangers of emulation: "The fertility of invention will ever be beforehand with the quickness of imitation."[169] Progress, civil as well as economic, depended on a constant stream of innovation and betterment, a stressful current that could secure nations from the efforts of others to surpass them. As England had demonstrated to reformers like Alessandro Verri, however, progress depended on "enlightened" rather than "slavish imitation."[170] The nature of emulation and the oscillating degrees of censorship it encountered in Europe meant translation was a preeminent vehicle of such "enlightened" emulation.[171] Though political and religious arguments often were overturned in translation, this facilitated the exchange of economic ideas and policies between radically different social and political structures. Perhaps the technical development of economic analysis was even furthered by the deconstruction of political economy into its constitutive parts, politics and economic analysis.

But translation and emulation were difficult for the science of legislation to administer. A widely recognized problem was, for reasons of both political stability and cultural coherence, that not all information was equally worthy of translation. As one Spanish censor wrote in 1758, to "translate" books that "damage custom" or "understanding" would be like importing "pestilential merchandise," like loading "exotic birds [*Guacamayos*], and monkeys, instead of gold and silver, and raw materials for factories."[172] Translations could have revolutionary consequences.[173] Furthermore, by the very act of claiming supremacy in trade, a state changed the rules of the game for those coming after it: hence the difference between imitation and emulation.[174] One could not simply apply economic theories and policies formulated in the world's most powerful economies in less developed contexts.[175] Added to this was an even more insidious problem contemporaries identified as resulting from the explicit politics of emulation and the problems inherent in trying to resist the cyclicality of international competition.[176] There were strategies, in other words, for counteracting attempts by latecomers to catch up with leading nations.

However reasonable it seemed to imitate English policies, England's counter-emulation, an admittedly incongruous concept, could derail their competitors' attempts. At the height of the French Revolution, Gaetano Sotira, a Neapolitan scholar in Parisian exile, explicitly warned against the "errors," the propaganda and the disinformation, promulgated by certain "political writers" with regard to the causes of "England's greatness." Rather than locating it in centuries of imperial policies and interventions to "encourage manufactures," said writers explained it simply by recourse to the "form of its Government," English "national character," or even it "being an island." The "English themselves," he argued, "have accredited such errors, which *serve greatly to render their emulation by other Peoples more difficult.*"[177] Similar fears that "theorists" might falsify the historical record were voiced on both sides of the Atlantic in the second half of the eighteenth century and paved the way for the great German-American economist Friedrich List's later statement that

> It is a commonplace rule that when someone has attained the summit of greatness, he throws away the ladder by which he has climbed up, in order to deprive others of the means of climbing up after him. Herein lies the secret of Adam Smith's cosmopolitical teachings, the cosmopolitical tendencies of his great contemporary William Pitt, and of all their heirs in the British government administration.[178]

Having achieved greatness through emulation, England, now Great Britain, sought to resist its cyclicality by sabotaging the emulation of others. What was the alternative? As political economy was institutionalized and the science of the legislator actively opened its eyes to international trade, a common way to resist such legerdemain was to let emulation be informed by the actual histories of more successful nations rather than simply by theoretical speculation. At times, legislators even emulated each other directly, bypassing theory entirely.[179] The same pattern of emulating the successful economic policies of rival nations rather than their most fashionable theories occurred across the European world in the second half of the eighteenth century and is easily chartable through existing publication data.[180]

Genovesi's statement is emblematic of how the science of the legislator adapted to economic rivalry through translation and enlightened emulation: "If one wants to plant the science of commerce in a nation, and be certain that it grows, nothing is more useful than to give it the history of the commerce of those nations that most exercise it and best understand it."[181] Only by translating histories of economic policy could legislators empower their citizens to defend their liberty against all comers in the agon of trade, a sentiment reiterated throughout the continent. Returning to Stockholm after several years in London, for example, the Swedish statesman and political economist Anders Nordencrantz promoted the idea that only "imitation" of England's "artificial improvements" could secure Sweden's "happiness." For this to take place, however, a statesman had to heed Clio's lessons; delineating both the sweet shores of England's success and the bitter shoals of Spain's failure, history was a map no legislator could do without.[182] Yet the great Galiani might have defined the mainstream of Enlightenment political economy best. Ridiculing theoretical dogmatism, he argued that political economy was a science mediating between simple general theories and complex local contexts, a historical form of knowledge without which the translation and emulation of foreign theories could become downright dangerous.[183]

Emulation through Translation

In spite of Raynal's assurances, countries *could* supersede each other through emulation, a process about which changing patterns of economic translations can convey powerful insights. Daniel Milo once proposed that translations represented a "cultural barometer"; using UNESCO's *Index translationum* to chart the "global stock market of translation" in the twentieth century, he showed how the most valuable authors, in terms of volume of translations, shifted from Tolstoy, Dickens, and Balzac to Agatha Christie, Walt Disney, and Jules Verne in the decades after World War II.[184] Besides the change in translation patterns shown by Milo, it is worth noting that the most translated authors in the period remained strictly limited to the realm of fiction, and that the changes he documented in the end measured cultural and literary rather than political and economic desirability. The relations between cultural preferences and economic forces remain elusive, but what follows elucidates the means by which economic texts and practices were codified, evaluated, and transmitted with greater clarity by focusing on translations of broadly defined "economic" works. Though this exercise claims no cliometric rigor, a quantitative study of such translations might then serve as a barometer of economic success in early modern Europe, measuring the fluctuating values assigned to national economies by their competitors. The quantitative study of translations here undertaken aims to inform a qualitative discussion about the origins of political economy, not to lay down rigid theorems. But if power is *imperium*, that axiomatic Machiavellian liberty that expands at the expense of others', and *imperium* is vied for through an economic competition shaped and informed by emulation, then the study of changing patterns of economic translation indeed sheds light on the nature of freedom, the evanescence of power, and the history of *translatio imperii*.

Applying Milo's method to the economic rather than the literary sphere and throwing the net back centuries, however, poses the problem of providing data for a period centuries before that covered by UNESCO. To complete a perfect data-set of early modern "economic" translations between all European languages is in fact impossible, no different from the utopian visions of universal libraries proposed by past bibliophiles.[185] Sometimes, even canonical texts were translated but never published.[186] Similarly, the very term "economic" is itself open to different interpretations, and it is surprisingly hard even to draw the line where gardening ends and agriculture begins. Yet Kenneth E. Carpenter came close to this Borgesian ideal during his long tenure as curator of the Kress Collection at Harvard Business School's Baker Library, where he amassed a vast catalogue of European economic translations before 1849, the end-date of the collection. Since the development of this data-set over the past years, it is now possible to analyze a set of around 2,500 "economic" translations, a critical mass housed in the world's greatest libraries and specialized collections of economics. It cannot be emphasized enough that the set is not complete and that the criteria for its composition remain arguable. That said, the criteria for selection have been rather stringent. The data-set does not include merchants' handbooks just because they mention money and exchange-rates, but does include those merchants' handbooks which theorize about double entry bookkeeping for government. It does not include works of eighteenth-century travel literature just because they mention the presence of merchants in Hamburg, but does include those that explicitly theorize about international trade.

Given these caveats, the data at hand hold precious heuristic value for understanding the dynamic interconnection of power, translation, and emulation from 1500 to 1849, between Ludovico Sforza's final march on Milan and Britain's annexation of the Punjab. This range of dates might be fortuitous, but it is surprisingly fitting. Though it remained eerily similar in many ways, the globalization of the nineteenth century proceeded at a different pace than that of the long eighteenth century. As the Italian revolutionary Giuseppe Mazzini observed in 1847,

Europe is now so closely united that it is not possible for a new idea to emerge in one country, without thousands of translators seeking to make it popular everywhere else; it is so closely united at the level of commercial interests that no rise or fall of exchange rates can take place in London or Paris without the shock being felt in Vienna, Genoa, Amsterdam, and Hamburg.[187]

Mazzini described a world very much like our own; the data-set originally put together by Carpenter elucidates how it got that way.

As shown in Figure 1.1, economic translations are few and far between in the sixteenth and seventeenth centuries. There is a modest increase in the second half of the seventeenth century that grows further in the opening years of the eighteenth. A very sudden break occurs in the mid-eighteenth century, when the number rises to 134, and again in the 1760s, when it peaks at 339, before declining to 166 in the 1770s. With the exception of a trough during the Napoleonic Wars in the 1810s, economic translations then remained at a permanently high plateau. If an English translator could declare in 1654 "We are fallen into an Age of *Translations*," the age of economic translations had to await the 1750s, around the same time as English technologies seriously began to be transferred to the continent through emulation and conscious acts of industrial espionage.[188] Conspicuously, the translations of Cary's *Essay* all coincided with peaking periods. These changing patterns of translation could conceivably reflect a general trend of publishing; more economic works being translated in certain decades simply as corollaries of an expanding book trade. Yet aggregate data

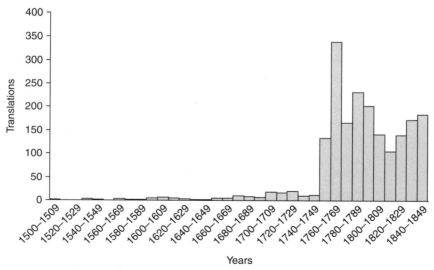

FIGURE 1.1. Total European translations of economic works per decade, 1500–1849

of European publishing between 1454 and 1794 show no massive percentage increases taking place in the 1750s and 1760s. The Swedish book trade was exploding in those years, and an upward trend is observable throughout the century, but no spikes can be identified in the decades in question looking at the continent as a whole. Such deviations from a state of steady increase are, however, readily observable around the time of the English civil war, with the decline of Italian publishing toward the late seventeenth century, and with the advent of the French Revolution.[189] The sudden peak in the number of translations of political economy evident in the 1750s and 1760s, then, reflects an increase with respect to the overall output of books, as such works came to occupy a larger share of the eighteenth-century book trade and market for knowledge.

An important qualification must be made before exploring the data-set more thoroughly, and that regards the role of censorship laws in shaping the development of European political economy. I will touch on the comparative liberty of presses as it treats specific cases, but it lies beyond this study's scope to make rigorous arguments about censorship and political economy more generally. Censorship laws and, more important, their enforcement, varied widely across national and even regional boundaries, but they were of cardinal importance. The case of Denmark-Norway is characteristically idiosyncratic. As a result of Johan Friederich Struensee's relentless work, relative press freedom was instituted by royal decree on 27 December 1770 to "enlighten" the kingdom.[190] Government had begun to actively encourage economic debate as part of their more widespread program to encourage national industry in the mid-1750s, and by the 1760s the country printed an average of four hundred books a year. The year 1771 saw nearly eight hundred books published in Denmark-Norway, and 1772 nearly 850. Among these, books in the category of "state sciences," stretching across the realms of political writing from the highly abstract to the patently ad hominem, enjoyed a tremendous upsurge. After about six such books were published in 1770, nearly thirty-five were published the following year.[191] This outpouring of critical works shocked authorities, and censorship was reintroduced after Struensee met a grisly fate on the scaffold; yearly political publications soon returned to hover around five.[192] Most of the nations of Europe had similarly distinctive experiences with press freedom. Generally, however, the existence of censorship laws can only lead us to emphasize the human element in the transmission of ideas, the ways individual decisions to approve of specific books influenced intellectual history on a grand scale.

Looking beyond censorship and total numbers of published translations, it is similarly evident that different countries had different cultures of translation, and that different national discourses of political economy were evaluated very differently on the international stock market of translations suggested by Milo. It has been impossible, for the sake of comparative macro studies of economic performance, to really differentiate between, say, Naples and Venice or London and Bristol. For bibliophiles and local historians this is an unthinkable omission, and future studies will highlight this data-set's power at the regional rather than linguistic level. Furthermore, to appreciate the shock that jolted the market of economic translations in the 1750s, one must momentarily leave the empirical study of translations behind. Anatole France once claimed that "the only exact knowledge" was the publication date and format of books, but if one dares to venture beyond the safety of material artifacts into the realm of conjecture, a millennial perspective on the world economy published by the Organization for Economic Co-Operation and Development (OECD) sheds important light on the dynamics of early modern economic translations.[193]

As shown in Figures 1.2 and 1.3, in the year 1500, when the gaze of the world still rested safely on Renaissance Italy, the gross domestic product of the Atlantic archipelago now called the United Kingdom was nearly $3 billion (or $714 per capita). By comparison the Italian peninsula was a staggering $11.5 billion ($1,100). By the year 1700, however, the gross domestic product of the United Kingdom had reached $10.7 billion while

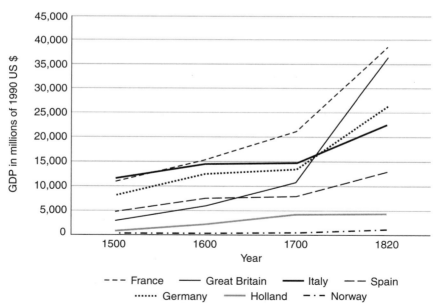

FIGURE 1.2. Economic development in Europe, 1500–1820 (based on Maddison 2006, 244–247, 263–265)

Italy had experienced only a moderate increase to $14.6 billion. In terms of per capita distribution during the same period, that of the United Kingdom had reached $1,250 while that of Italy tellingly had remained stagnant at $1,100. In other words, the economy of Great Britain had increased by 256 percent between 1500 and 1700 while that of Italy had increased only by a mere 27 percent. The mean rate of economic growth in the period was nearly ten times higher in the United Kingdom than in Italy. This takeoff continued into the eighteenth century, for by 1820 the economy of the United Kingdom had grown by a staggering 1287 percent since the year 1500, while that of Italy only had grown by 195 percent. Whereas the United Kingdom's percentage share of world GDP had risen from 1.1 to 5.2, that of Italy had sunk from 4.7 to 3.2.[194]

A very similar story emerges from existing demographic data. Of the population of Italy, 22 percent were urban in 1500, and 16 percent were rural nonagricultural. Three centuries later, these percentages were 22 and 20. In England, on the other hand, which only enjoyed a meager 7 percent urbanization in 1500, with 18 percent employed in nonagricultural rural activities, these percentages had risen to 29 and 36, respectively, by 1800. Whereas England had been the most agricultural nation in Europe west of

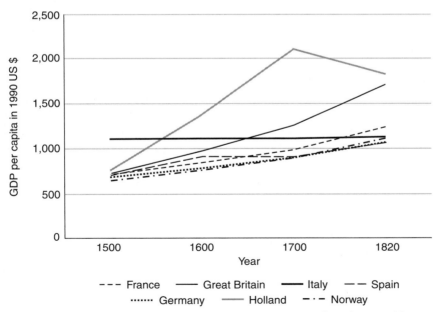

FIGURE 1.3. Per capita development in Europe, 1500–1820 (based on Maddison 2006, 244–247, 263–265)

the Rhine in 1500, by 1800 it was the least so by a wide margin.[195] Already in the late seventeenth century, English wages were taking off compared to most of continental Europe, and a more rigorous history of political economy can help us better understand the policies and strategies behind this great transformation.[196]

The data for GDP are conjectural, but it is evident that the most radical changes in the European economic theatre were the relative declines of Italy, Spain, and Holland and the dramatic rise of the United Kingdom, at the time known interchangeably as "England" and "Britain." While France enjoyed the highest GDP in Europe because of its enormous population, England was wealthier per capita, and a variety of well-known factors contributed to its eventually acknowledged dominance in world affairs. From being a peripheral exporter of raw wool in the sixteenth century, England had come to conquer its surrounding Celtic crescent and had, through reason of state, an agricultural revolution, and aggressive protectionist measures become a proverbial workshop of the world. English economic interests successfully warded off Irish attempts to industrialize in the late seventeenth century, and it shocked the world through a series of unforeseeable military victories, first during the Nine Years' War following the Williamite settlement and then during the War of Spanish Succession. The War of Austrian Succession culminating in the 1748 peace of Aix-la-Chapelle might technically have ended in a stalemate, but it returned European territorial possessions overseas to the Anglo-friendly antebellum status quo established by the 1713 Treaty of Utrecht. And as England asserted itself as a great power, the status of its language rose hand in hand with the balance of its trade. Just as England went from being an exporter of raw materials to one of manufactured goods in the early modern period, the English language came from being an importer of foreign vocabulary in the sixteenth century to being a net exporter in the eighteenth.[197] A concomitant change would soon be evident in its balance of economic translations, for as the humanist Antonio de Nebrija had explained to Queen Isabella of Spain already in 1492, language was not only itself a "tool of conquest" but "has always been the consort of empire, and forever shall remain its mate."[198]

The rampant successes of England's credit-based war financing had invalidated the venerable trope of political philosophy, maintained by the likes of Machiavelli, that virtuous men rather than money were the "sinews of war," and all over Europe statesmen were forced to reconsider many of their most basic assumptions. Frederick the Great was right, "the face of Europe is entirely different from what it was in the age of Machiavelli," and it was acutely evident that the mechanisms of commerce now posed both clear limits and provided pertinent possibilities for national as well as international politics.[199] Whether one lived in Stockholm, Leipzig, or Milan, there was a pressing need to understand the intertwined phenomena of wealth, war, and public happiness, and it was also increasingly obvious that lessons of political economy were best learned by observing and emulating more successful economies.[200] The radical increase in the total number of translations observable in the wake of the War of Austrian Succession is therefore not surprising, given the European political and economic context of the period. Observing Paris, Galiani wrote that this passion for economic thought was "an enthusiasm, a fashion, a Crusade," an observation valid of the continent generally.[201] And as the balance of economic translations between English and the continental languages in Figure 1.5 shows, the boom can in large part be explained by the wish to emulate the successes of Great Britain, which had succeeded Italy and the Low Countries as the principal target of emulation in Europe. Considering the large number of English economic works arriving in various European countries through intermediary French translations, the role of Great Britain appears even more domineering. The important role played by translations in bringing the Renaissance to England has often been emphasized, but why, how, and what did economic translations bring back during the Enlightenment?[202]

It seems from a conjoined reading of the charts (Figures 1.1–3) with regard to England that its positive economic transition—from being an exporter of raw wool to one of manufactured goods—and the military might this ensured was followed by a positive balance of economic translations and, ultimately, a positive linguistic and cultural balance first seriously evident in the 1750s. One can go one step further and present what Cary would have known as the "English" balance of trade. Figure 1.4 is simply

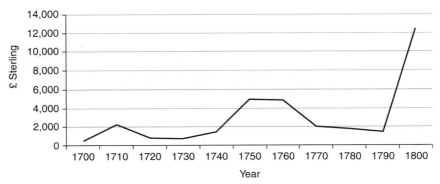

FIGURE 1.4. "English" balance of trade, by decades, 1700–1800 (based on Schumpeter 1960, 15–16)

made from subtracting official import data from official export data for all major goods, and though economic flows are far more complex than that and the data do not differentiate between types of products exchanged, the result is not devoid of heuristic value. By comparing the graphs on English success in international trade during the eighteenth century with a graph showing the English "balance of economic translations" at the time (Figure 1.5), the correlation becomes suggestive. As English trade "took off" internationally in the 1740s and 1750s, so translations of English economic works on the continent skyrocketed.

Though English broke even consistently only from the 1740s onward, the net balance of translations for the entire period 1550–1849 was an unparalleled 615 exports to 144 imports. The picture becomes even more striking in light of contemporary demography. Of all European translations in the 1750s, for example, 37 percent were direct translations from English, not counting translations of English works going through intermediary languages. Comparably, England had a population of approximately 5.74 million in 1750, or 3.5 percent of Europe's estimated 163 million souls.[203] Of Europe's population, then, 3.5 percent produced economic works that, in the Western market for translations on the subject, represented 37 percent of all direct translations (Figure 1.6). And while French, as a lingua franca of the eighteenth century, in total exported the same number of economic works (well within a hypothetical margin of error), it also imported more,

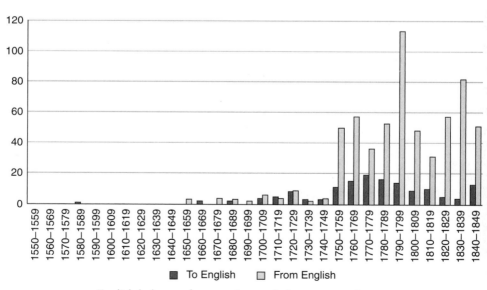

FIGURE 1.5. English balance of economic translations, 1500–1849

enjoying a ratio of 615 exports to 464 imports (Figure 1.7). English was the clear winner in the contemporary balance of translations. Although it is not surprising that the insularity of English is reflected also in its willingness to import foreign works, it is almost unimaginable that English equaled French in the total number of exported economic translations, and likewise striking that Great Britain remained a net importer of economic works as late as the 1730s. The dramatic increase thus did not reflect changes in the long-term comparative economic development of Europe, or the gradual growth of the European book trade, but the impact, on the historical level of the "event" theorized by Fernand Braudel, of Britain's increasing military presence in the world in the first half of the eighteenth century and its following arms race for trade and empire with France leading up to the Seven Years' War.[204]

Inexorably intertwined with the rise of England, the second important piece of information revealed by the OECD statistics is the relative decline of Italy and of the Spanish dominions, areas all too aware of their changing fortunes. While the former was thought to have botched the transition from city-state to nation-state in the late Renaissance and stagnated economically since, no country in Europe had suffered the dark side of early modern political economy more than Spain, whose enormous influx of gold and silver from the New World was thought to have paid for mercenary armies and foreign manufactures.[205] Their empire, once almost universal in scale and scope, had seemingly failed to adapt to the exigencies of economic

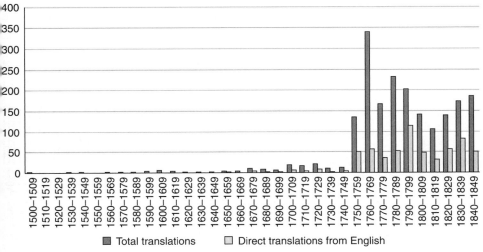

FIGURE 1.6. Direct translations from English compared to total European translations, 1500–1849

competition. The different attitude British economic writers had to the political economic discourses of other countries in the mid-eighteenth century are clearly evident from a simple comparison of translators' introductions to French and Spanish works. Where France posed a tangible threat nurturing anger and anxiety, Spain no longer did.[206] Trade with Spain was lucrative because it still consisted largely in the exportation of British manufactures in exchange for Iberian and Latin American raw materials, and a translation was justified as a way of monitoring the situation and ensuring necessary measures could be taken to maintain its profitability. In the end, the question was one of knowing what one's enemy was up to in order to counteract the tools of its empire or, alternatively, its emulation of one's own.[207]

Genovesi presented the complementary analysis to that offered by Defoe and the aforementioned translators when, in the 1750s, he set out to render a series of English works on political economy in Italian to use as textbooks at his newly established chair of political economy at the University of Naples, emphasizing the cyclicality of emulation explicitly. Ironically, Italians now had to emulate England as the English once had emulated Italy.[208] As Figure 1.8 demonstrates, Italy remained a net exporter of economic works throughout the sixteenth and seventeenth centuries, a trend that becomes even more pronounced if one considers the number of Italian translations

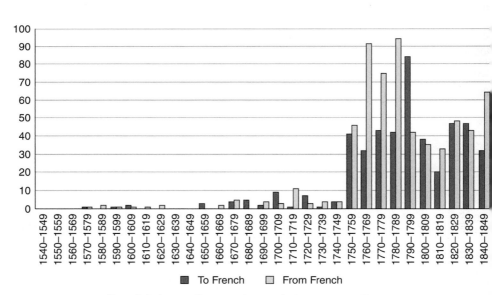

FIGURE 1.7. French balance of economic translations, 1540–1849

of classical authors and works by Italians originally written in Latin. From the 1730s onward, however, and dramatically so from the 1750s, Italy would suffer from a vertiginous translation imbalance with the rest of Europe, and mainly with England and France.

A similar endeavor of emulative translation was launched in Spain by Juan Enrique de Graef, author of the *Mercurial Discourses* published in the period 1752–56, when he sought to encourage a renewal of the empire by translating and "compiling what foreigners write on the principal matters of commerce, cultivation and exercise of the arts."[209] Generally speaking, the 1540–1849 Spanish balance of economic translations matches the barometer of economic success at the time (see Figure 1.9). One of the few exporters of economic works in the sixteenth century, Spanish became a clear net importer during most of the seventeenth and eighteenth centuries. The only exceptions were in the 1740s and 1750s, when multiple editions and translations of Géronimo de Uztàriz's work on how to mitigate decline by investing in national productive capacities appeared throughout Europe. As a Spanish economic translator emblematically wrote in a 1771 rendition of a work on Anglo-French economic competition, "it seems to me that our language, arts, and Muses will extend their empire, and take the tribute of

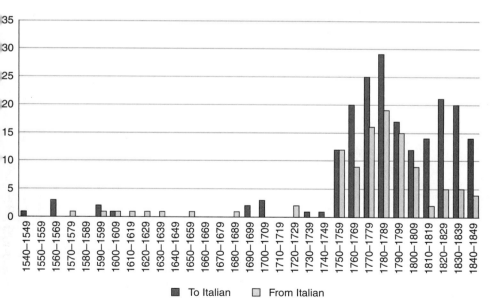

FIGURE 1.8. Italian balance of economic translations, 1540–1849

commendation from the emulating nations, which until this point they scornfully have denied us." This was why he hoped "the translation of a book" could demonstrate the "commerce undertaken by two rival nations, and the way in which they have arrived at the opulence they have acquired."[210] The careful emulation of foreign political economy was a widespread practice and warranted response to the problems of relative decline among Spanish statesmen and scholars of the eighteenth century.[211]

Though the Dutch too for some time held a nearly hegemonic position in the European economy, however, this failed to translate into a prominent role for translations of Dutch economic works in the European book market. Between 1500 and 1849, the Dutch imported 190 works while exporting only 45 (see Figure 1.10), a good percentage of which were editions of the one Dutch economic best seller: Pieter de la Court's 1662 *Interest of Holland*.[212] But the history of Dutch translations is otherwise indicative of the changes occurring in Europe. The first Dutch translation of an English economic work was in the 1660s, while the first in general seems to have been of a Latin work by an Italian through an intermediary French translation in the 1580s.

The general response observable in declining powers was shared in the Scandinavian countries as well, which, though they never had reached the peaks of Italy, Holland, or Spain, saw the same principle of emulation guide attempts to stymie the growing dominance of the English and French.

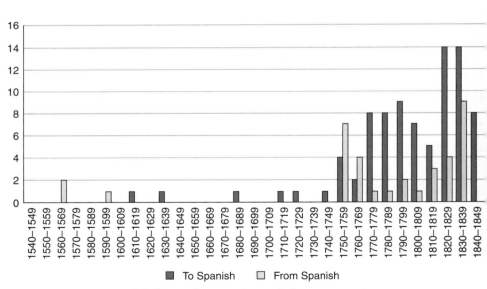

FIGURE 1.9. Spanish balance of economic translations, 1540–1849

Erik Pontoppidan, the bishop of Bergen, for example, founded one of the first economic journals in Denmark-Norway to emulate wider European trends, noting how Danes and Norwegians, "in this seemingly oeconomic century," finally were following the "example" of southern countries by turning to political economy. And numerous academies across Sweden and Denmark-Norway were at the time preoccupied with the problems and possibilities of emulation in an international system in which they were decidedly junior members.[213]

Although the fact that France exported about as many works as England in the period suggests that the French empire proved a model to emulate for most European countries (see Figure 1.11), and although the question whether control of the seas and of the New World would fall on France or on Great Britain remained unanswered at midcentury, French political economy was also thought to have emerged as a discipline in the 1750s largely through the mediation of English works. As the January 1756 issue of the *Journal Oeconomique* emblematically asserted, *"the ardour, with which the English apply themselves to all that can make commerce flourish, should no doubt excite our emulation."*[214] Yet translations never made up a very large percentage of the total number of all broadsides, pamphlets, brochures, and works on economic subjects broadly conceived.[215] Perhaps the solution to this conundrum is simply the extraordinarily coherent program undertaken by the group of philosophes, statesmen, and

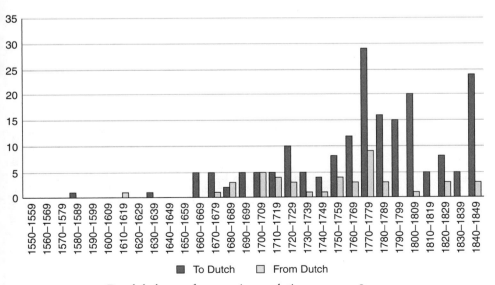

FIGURE 1.10. Dutch balance of economic translations, 1540–1849

former merchants gathered around Gournay in the 1750s. What mattered was not merely the *quantity* of works on political economy; some of the output of Gournay's circle proved to be *qualitatively* extremely influential in jump-starting debates. Their adopted program of translation included not only the greatest English works on political economy but, tellingly, also those of Spain, a fact that poses difficulties for the hypothesis that translations can be studied as measures of relative economic success. The contrasting economic experiences of the two empires taught complementary lessons, but whereas British works were translated as guides to how to conduct an imperial economy, Spanish works could be translated as guides to how *not to*.[216]

This furor of translation went so far in France that even homegrown French economic works were presented as foreign imports. In 1755, a journal quipped that "all work on the commercial enterprises of the English" duplicitously were published "under the title *'translated from English.'* "[217] In effect, when Gournay's friend Plumard de Dangeul had sought to publicize his economic ideas in 1754, he pretended to translate a work by the imaginary English merchant Sir John Nickolls, in the process translating large parts of a real tract by the Bristol divine Joshua Tucker. Al-

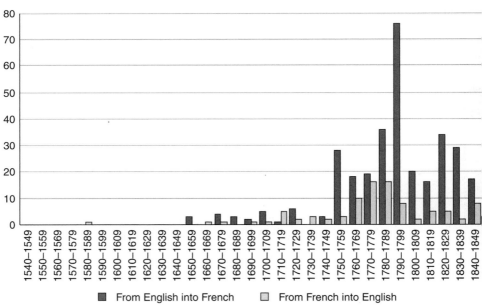

FIGURE 1.11. English-French balance of economic translations, 1540–1849

though Dangeul had little confidence in the French public's faith in homegrown political economy, his work caused a sensation in France and was quickly translated into English (1754), Swedish (1754), Danish (1756), German (1757), Italian (1758), and Spanish (1755 and 1771) in a dialogue of emulation that at least problematizes the assertion of Lucien Febvre and Henri-Jean Martin that the decline of Latin as a "universal language" established "permanent divisions" between European cultures.[218] Dangeul's English translator was bemused by the circularity of producing a real English translation of a French translation of a "pretended" English original, and while their two countries were the principal protagonists of the debate, the assertion of Dangeul's Danish translator succinctly summarized the virtue of emulation for laggard countries: "it is and remains undeniable that the exact knowledge of other countries is useful for the citizens of any country," particularly as manifest in the realm of "state-administration and government." That the book in question was Anglo-French dialogue of political economy was in effect only an advantage, because "the two great countries" *both* served "as Example and Pattern to all of Europe."[219] As the Duke of Almodóvar soon would put it, one had to look to both France and England because they were the only ones able to "give the law to Europe."[220] The French, however, turned to England more often than the English returned the favor.

The French illness that contemporaries dubbed Anglomania, which manifested itself through the imitation of English gardens, institutions, and apparel, was one of the principal reasons for the dramatic change in translation patterns observable in the second half of the eighteenth century.[221] As Edward Gibbon noted in the wake of the Seven Years' War, at a time when the Atlantic archipelago had become the greatest imperial power in history, "The name of Englishman inspires as great an idea at Paris, as that of Roman could at Carthage, after the defeat of Hannibal."[222] Although the numbers for the early centuries are too small to risk generalizations, English and French vied for a positive balance of translations until the 1740s, when a century of Anglomanie set in that would peak with the Revolution. France was nonetheless Great Britain's main rival, and charting the balance of economic translations between English and other continental languages shows a more marked discrepancy. Compared to 173 direct German translations of English economic works, only 15 German works had made their way to Great Britain by 1849. And the 1750s were again a turning point, the decade in which English books for the first time began to vie with French imports at the Easter book fair in Leipzig.[223] Overall, German was the clear loser in the European balance of translations (see Figure 1.12), importing

776 works but only exporting 197, but though the argument could be made that it simply had nothing to offer in terms of political economy, the first chairs devoted to the subject in the world were established in early eighteenth-century Germany, a century before anything similar appeared in England.[224] Moreover, the now dated *Bibliography of Cameralism,* the quintessentially German tradition of state administration at the time, covers several thousand entries for the period in question.[225] As one Cameralist observed, his discipline could "fill entire libraries."[226]

Different national or regional cultures of political economy were characterized by different degrees of openness to foreign ideas and practices, and, though a continuous circulation of economic translations existed in Europe, the English language taught far more than England was willing or needed to learn about the subject. Translations of economic works were so symptomatic of these larger changes in European economic and linguistic relations because they represented an ideal case of emulation. They were both themselves emulative acts *and* the foundation for further emulation. An English-German dictionary exemplified this toward the end of the century: "As the English Nation is taking the Lead in almost every Art and Science, so it is become necessary to Foreigners aiming at Perfection in any Branch of Business the English chiefly excel in, to gain a proper Knowledge of the English Tongue."[227] As emulation affected people and empires, however, so it affected translated texts about them.

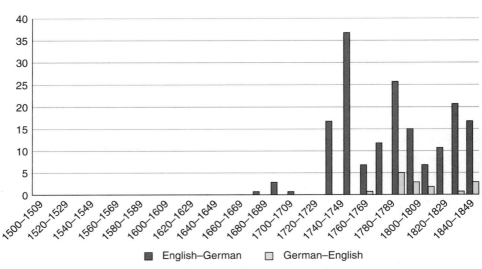

FIGURE 1.12. English-German balance of economic translations, 1540–1849

Emulative Cultures of Translation

Early modern European political economists showed a clear awareness of the interrelationship between traffic and translation, between trade, ideas, and languages.[228] The bishop and savant Pierre Daniel Huet, for one, acutely described the redemptive relationship between commerce and communication: "the Confusion of Languages followed the Flood, as did also the Dispersion of the People. Trade then became more difficult, but much more necessary."[229] Like the Pentecostal charism of glossolalia, trade could reconcile men after the fall of Babel.[230] A similar insight was soon echoed by the Neapolitan scholar Giambattista Vico, and it was not without reason that Jean le Rond d'Alembert spoke of the "mutual *commerce* of ideas" in the *Encyclopédie,* and Hume thought the related but distinct terms "*industry, knowledge,* and *humanity*" were "linked together by an indissoluble chain."[231] Huet would remain tremendously influential in early modern political economy and translation theory alike, and Cary's translator Genovesi was one of many to take his teachings to heart.[232] But although authoritative and erudite, Huet fell back on one of the oldest maxims of translation. Working on his fourth-century rendition of the gospels in the Latin vulgate, St. Jerome—appropriately the patron saint of translators—echoed Horace's *Art of Poetry* and his own master Evgarius of Antioch in arguing that one should translate "sense for sense and not word for word" unless handling the biblical mysteries.[233]

Their examples of rendering "sense for sense" rather than "word for word" became the baseline for the Western theory and practice of translation.[234] At times, however, the protean definition of "sense" opened the way for rather creative, not to mention voluminously expansive, translations. Added to this was the issue of emulation, a variance of which manifested itself also in the realm of philology. This emulative tension between imitation and innovation was present as early as Quintilian's first-century *Institutes of Oratory,* where he argued "It is dishonourable . . . to rest satisfied with simply equaling what we imitate."[235] This was the passage Huet translated, in his seminal 1680 *On the Best Kind of Translating,* when he stated "I do not want translation to be a paraphrase, but rather a struggle with and emulation of the original which renders the same sense," an attitude he had also found in Pliny the Younger.[236] Their aim, in short, was to improve and adapt the texts they translated for the sake of their own contexts. This agenda was explicitly resurrected in the late Renaissance and would profoundly shape the cultures of early modern translation. Translators were "merchants," peddling goods that they refined in worth and value.[237]

This culture of philological emulation problematized the art of translation; hostilities invariably arose between different approaches often believed to be institutionalized along national lines, alternatively leaning toward faithful or liberal renditions. Like syphilis, bad cultures of translation could be thought of as a plague originating in whatever country one disliked the most; one Italian went so far as to project one of the most elegant and untranslatable expressions of his language on the English: it is "an English proverb, and almost a truth of every language, that translators are traitors [*i Traduttori sono traditori*]."[238] But as many contemporaries remarked, the originally Roman license to "improve" on the original text to assimilate it to local customs went furthest in eighteenth-century France, where linguistic nationalism and the ruthless domestication of translated texts went hand in hand. Rather than appreciating the richness of foreign cultures, French translators were notorious for rewriting texts entirely to make them fit contemporary canons of "sense" and propriety.[239] The dangers of such polishing often became glaring: Émilie du Châtelet's 1734 manuscript translation of Mandeville's *Fable of the Bees* conveniently censored its indigestible paradoxes regarding the beneficial consequences of selfishness by substituting them with the "golden rule"; from the original's provocative equation "private vices—public benefits" to the platitudinous "private virtues—public benefits."[240]

Yet for all its literary licentiousness French culture thirsted for foreign knowledge, and Diderot's entry on "Encyclopédie" in the fifth volume of the *Encyclopédie,* one of the strongest Enlightenment defenses of translation, would also play an important role in promulgating political economy. Although he retained mystic longings for a "common language" that could "establish a correspondence between all parts of the human species" and void all distances in "time" and "space," Diderot maintained, in the meantime, that only translations could sustain humanity's progress beyond the lives of individuals and nations.[241] He made translations the vehicle to disseminate man's achievements and advance civilization and, similarly, defined "The Enlightenment" by urging "let us make haste to render philosophy popular."[242] Translation was the eminent vehicle for popularizing philosophies of all kinds, encouraging emulation and setting up a *perpetuum mobile* of progress in the spirit of the Utrecht settlement. As a late edition of the Chambers *Cyclopædia* would observe, *"the emulation of improvement has spread through most of the nations of Europe."*[243]

But the problem of language remained. Enlightened cosmopolitanism aside, Diderot and Voltaire betrayed their cultural preferences by ultimately abandoning the spiritual pursuit of semantic universality in simple favor of French. Only the French syntax, the two argued, corresponded to the linear argument of reasoning itself, making it the ideal nexus of all languages. French, as the "Republic of Letters" had accepted at least since the time of Pierre Bayle, was the perfect language of the encyclopedic project and indeed of the age.[244] It is therefore fitting that the most indicative example of this emulative and contributive practice of translation is Diderot and d'Alembert's *Encyclopédie.* Rousseau reminisced that this work "was at first to be merely a sort of translation of Chambers," and the 1782–1832 expanded sixty-six-volume edition of the *Encylopédie* indeed contained the Jeromian "sense" of the "translated" two-volume 1728 *Cyclopædia.*[245] Of course, it also contained a whole lot more, and the relationships between early modern encyclopedias clarify the interactions of different cultures of translation.

The first Italian translation of Chambers, published in Naples (1747–54), approached the issue very differently. Its editor assured his ideal readers that they would "not be defrauded throughout the entire work, not even by a single word," even when culturally abhorrent.[246] The divergence from the method adopted by contemporary Frenchmen is striking, but the Neapolitan rendition of Chambers nonetheless contained numerous additions, a license the editors of the contemporary Venetian translation of the *Cyclopedia* (1748–53) did not fail to criticize and capitalize on in marketing their product. The competition between the two contemporaneous editions revolved around providing the most faithful translation, but if the Venetian edition sought to be "exact and complete," there were both political and theological reasons for resorting to some degree of self-censorship even there, as when Chambers turned his sometimes malefic glance on Venice and in treating religious dogmas, Church censors having little patience for literal translations. As the abbé Pietro Ercole Gherardi wrote to the Modenese antiquarian Lodovico Antonio Muratori regarding Chambers's often "heretical sentiments" and the dangers of translation: "I expect to hear some good ones from the Englishmen, when they see one of their highly esteemed authors appear so castrated and, above all, transformed from a Calvinist into a Catholic."[247]

Like the German, Italian, and often Spanish, the English and later British culture of translation in the eighteenth century demonstrated a sometimes dolorous fidelity.[248] In clear contrast to the endeavors of the French to assimilate foreign works to their norms, the English translator of Beccaria's work *On Crimes and Punishments,* working with a prior French translation at hand, could not resist chastising his predecessor's adulteration. He himself had "preserved the order of the original" except "in a paragraph or two," but "the French translator hath gone much farther," having "transposed . . . every paragraph in the whole book." By doing so, "he hath assumed a right which belongs not to any translator, and which cannot be justified," for while the new version "may appear more systematical" than the original, to improve it that way was to "pervert" its "meaning."[249] The republican politician Walter Moyle similarly noted his limitations translating Xenophon's *Poroi,* one of the earliest works on political economy in the Western canon, writing, "I have rather chosen to render the sense and meaning of the author, than his words or his manner." But since "the purity, politeness, and the unaffected simplicity of his stile, are graces not to be copied by the barrenness and barbarity of our modern languages," he hoped his translation anyway was "faithful and exact."[250] Toward the end of the century, the anonymous Irish translator of Augustin Barruel thought his "duty" had been "fulfilled" simply through a "most literal exactness." Another anonymous translator said that his translation of Cardinal Alberoni's *Scheme for Reducing the Turkish Empire to the Obedience of Christian Princes* was done with "utmost fidelity" because, reflecting the continued biblical sway over the issue of translation, it would have been "almost unpardonable to have committed Errors, in a Scheme, calculated for promoting Christianity and the Good of Mankind."[251]

Fidelity in translation, however, did not preclude the possibility of emulation. The English translation of Louis-Antoine de Bougainville's account of his voyage is a good example. Although its many maps and charts were "reduced to a sixteenth part of the surface of the originals," they were nonetheless "infinitely superior to them in point of neatness, convenience, and accuracy," and where Bougainville was "misled by false reports" or "prejudiced in favour of his nation," the translator had corrected him only "in some additional notes." A translator was always allowed to add a superior scholarly apparatus, in the form of maps, appendixes, and annotations. And although even this judicious translator had succumbed to the temptation to omit a "discourse on the nature of the language of Tahiti," which he considered a "very trifling performance," the fact that he apologized publicly is a case in point.[252] Though such "tastes" changed over time, the general ideal, in England as in Italy, was fidelity in translation, irrespective, unlike in the French case, of the different manners and customs of nations.[253] Even Alessandro Verri, whose translation of Homer's *Iliad* systematically adapted the Greek original to the rhythm of the Italian language, found "great pleasure" in the "strangeness" of Homeric "customs" and therefore did not attempt, like contemporary Frenchmen, to polish Achilles before introducing him to the salons.[254]

This general ideal, however, was often shackled by political and religious considerations, as well as in cases where the translator's task took him outside Europe, by the often inscrutable nature of the exotic. Much as

Europe's common classical heritage unified certain conceptions of the past in the continent's historical traditions, the very tradition of emulation and translation in which works like Cary's *Essay* participated served both as means and medium for the international exchange of economic theory and practice. In spite of the frequent warfare between changing constellations of early modern European polities, a conceived cultural compatibility resulting from the continent's millennial historical heritage facilitated international interactions. The commerce of customs and ideas that philosophers praised had very tangible consequences for the interaction of European cultures. While continental translations of Adam Smith, for example, often were done selectively or politically, there was no need to invent an entirely new vocabulary, of political economy or of cultural practice, within which to locate the translated terminology. The same was not true for Leo Africanus's attempt to describe the Muslim world to Renaissance Europe, with the first Chinese translation of *The Wealth of Nations,* or the translation of Western liberal political philosophy during the period of *Bunmei-Kaika,* a slogan translatable as "Civilization and Enlightenment," during which Meiji Japan consciously sougth to emulate Western practices. In all these cases, relatively straightforward textual translation necessitated a far deeper translation of cultural and symbolic parameters.[255] Translators lost the security of compatibility when they turned to extra-European languages and traditions. This posed less of a difficulty to cultures of translation like the French, accustomed to imposing norms on received texts, than to an ideally faithful one like the English. The British Indianist Francis Gladwin's infelicitous excuses for his failure to be "strictly literal" in his celebrated 1783-6 translation of Emperor Akbar's sixteenth-century Persian *Institutes* is a representative example of the anxieties that resulted when a rigorous culture of translation encountered the varying degrees of otherness characterizing the wider world.[256]

Translational fidelity was further problematized by the inevitable divergences of purpose between author and translator.[257] As Jacob Soll has elucidated, translations could justify the most radical overthrow of political intentions, transforming, in the case of Machiavelli and Amelot de la Houssaye, a work often understood to represent tyrannical absolutism into one of political resistance.[258] By default, the illocutionary force of a translated text differs from that of the original. Though Barbapiccola's 1722 translation of Descartes was professionally done, the apparatus she added rendered it "a manifesto of women's right to learn."[259] Much can be said about Descartes's *Principles of Philosophy,* but few would primarily have read them as such on their first Latin publication. However literal the Bristol merchant John Frampton's seventeenth-century translations of

Spanish botanical, economic, and navigational lore were, they were also a way of getting back at the Spanish Inquisition for torturing him. By rendering important information regarding the Spanish empire and its technologies available for an English-speaking audience, Frampton was, like so many other translators, marshaling knowledge in a war of trade and empire.[260]

Similarly, among the many publications to see the light of day during the great English recoinage crisis of 1695–96 one finds Bernardo Davanzati's *Discourse upon Coins*. Originally presented to a Florentine audience in 1588, the treatise was literally translated by Locke's friend John Toland and nimbly inserted into the debate in support of his arguments. Davanzati's original call to return to the "old way of *casting Money*" had only meant that the coinage should be recast so that its bullion value equaled its nominal value: coins being returned to their original status. A century later in London, the same words by default contradicted William Lowndes's proposed debasement and gave Locke's side of the argument the added weight of historical authority.[261] Even without purposefully changing words, Barbapiccola, Frampton, and Toland radically inflected their respective arguments by situating them in new cultural contexts, giving them new coordinates of time, space, and debate.[262]

The Empire of Emulation

"Political oeconomy" was indeed, as the *Wealth of Nations* put it, "a branch of the science of a statesman or legislator," but, though many shared Smith's vision of a future in which interdependent commercial societies peacefully competed through trade and culture, most thinkers and legislators emphasized the discipline's actively political element more than he did.[263] Historical cases like that of Portugal's conceived economic enslavement by English merchants and policy through the 1703 Methuen Treaty, an aggressive military treatise, part of the War of Spanish Succession, which famously stipulated a customs-free exchange of Portuguese wine for English textiles, informed a widespread conception of the politics of trade in eighteenth-century Europe which was far removed from Smith's more eldritch passages on the benevolence of the natural order and the virtues of laissez-faire.[264] For if conflict might never be exorcised completely from the modern states system, policies and politics could at least alleviate the tension, realizing, however fleetingly, a golden mean between succumbing to the pressures of international competition and overpowering others economically; a moment, in Hobbes's political phantasmagoria, in which equally matched gladiators could exchange superfluities to their advantage. "It is one thing for a country *to be in a posture not to receive the law from others,*" Alexander Hamilton wrote, "and a very different thing for her *to be in a situation which obliges others to receive the law from her.*"[265] As another American commentator put it in the wake of the War of Independence, "political salvation" demanded an active science of legislation informed by the emulation of manifestly successful political economies rather than by the conjectural histories of moral philosophers. And, most important, it required competitive, emulative manufacturing.[266]

The Neapolitan De Jorio went even further, arguing that the very dynamism of the modern world economy, of competition, and of Hume's "jealous emulation" meant that autarky ultimately was as elusive as universal monarchy. Today, he wrote, "one cannot form an economic system in a Government, which does not have influence over other [states]." Autonomy was a chimera, and to serve public happiness legislators had to master the competitive administration of material and human resources, be constantly informed about competing states, and be endlessly nimble in continuously adapting tariffs and other interventions to calibrate international trade and secure peace and political fulfillment. Nonetheless, a state in which the citizenry had achieved "the greatest possible happiness" was the "Philosopher's Stone" of politics, no different from a mathematician's quest to "square the circle" or a physicist's search for "the true general system of the Universe."[267] Liberty and happiness could never be more than liminal states in the crucible of emulation. And if the acquisition of relative economic power uniformly had become a cardinal task of the science of legislation, for which common recipes continuously were translated, circulated, and emulated, the means and ends of deploying said power in international relations remained political and moral questions of incessant polyvalence.

In hindsight, we know that there indeed were pertinent synergies between conquest and commerce in the early modern period, that trade rivalries led to war, and that the viability of political communities depended on success in economic competition.[268] Far from outsiders to the world of eighteenth-century political economy, Casanova and Goudar were deeply attuned to the theoretical currents of their time. Venerable conceptions of liberty, whether understood as individual autonomy or the direct participation in a sovereign community, had become inexorably intertwined with economic concerns, with radical consequences for the nature of political philosophy. Though states of more or less peaceful competition between political communities—the *ideal* scenario for theorists of economic emulation—were within the realms of the possible, this was by no means a fall-back position in human interactions; it was not something that could be achieved easily, nor would it necessarily last once realized. Even if competitive policies appeared to fail in the short run—even if independent kingdoms like Naples continued to suffer under the debilitating yoke of asymmetrical trade after the Seven Years' War—the very dynamism of trade meant no hegemonies could be perennial.[269] Success in international trade was increasingly attributed to the fickle favors of "Lady Commerce" in the eighteenth century, and her wantonness might naturally have appealed to Casanova and Goudar.[270] Yet the two libertines discerned a silver lining in the dark clouds of foreign "laws" brooding over dependent nations: "Liberty is productive of a certain uneasiness to the mind, from which slavery exempts it. A nation under slavery has something to think of, which is to break its chains. A free nation has nothing. Now, when the imagination is left to itself, uneasiness will be working it." Uncontested power fostered ennui. "There are some English families," the imaginary mandarin Cham-pi-pi claimed, "who have not been known to laugh for ten generations," not to mention that "the greater part of Britons, unable to get the better of their vexations, hang or drown themselves."[271]

Greatness, a venerable trope had it, undermined itself. So though the English seemingly had achieved everlasting *grandezza* in the 1760s, to the extent that nothing remained for them to do but die, reality soon caught up. Their "secret poison," to borrow a phrase from Edward Gibbon, was emulation itself, for in harnessing it so successfully, they had irrevocably inspired it in others.[272] And as emulation spread and the War of American Independence changed the face of European politics, the English got something to worry about again. Then, echoing the moral of Thucydides' Melian dialogue, an Englishman warned his countrymen that "the *world* will be united against us, we shall be beat to a jelly, and *obliged to receive the law from those powers to whom in the hour of prosperity and insolence we unwisely assumed the right to give it.*"[273] In the garden of history, empire was a delicate rose, not an everlasting amaranth.[274] And even for reasons of expediency, those fleetingly imbued with power could not afford turning a blind eye to ethics.

The early modern discourse of economic emulation was essentially about power and liberty. Translations were intrinsic to this in more ways than through the idioms of *translatio studii* and *translatio imperii*, which is why the luminaries of the age so often encouraged the free circulation of books. As John Florio had put it in his translation of Montaigne's *Essayes*: "What doe the best then, but gleane after others harvest? borrow their colours, inherit their possessions? What doe they but translate?"[275] Economic translations were themselves vehicles of emulation and thus of independence, informing an "Enlightened" science of legislation that, by virtue of its embeddedness in international networks of trade and competition, was intrinsically responsive to the exigencies of real economic conditions.[276]

Traditionally, economic policies had been safely confined to the secret sphere of early modern statecraft, the realms of reason of state and Tacitus's *arcana imperii*.[277] The Florentine humanist Leonardo Bruni had joined a growing chorus when, in the opening years of the fifteenth century, he noted "it is sometimes difficult to know the policies of neighboring states; how much more difficult is it to know what distant peoples are planning."[278] The political paradigm now known as reason of state would revel in the paradox that, while it increasingly took published form, it nevertheless continued to extol the dangers of publication. As Francis Bacon justified dissimulation, "where a man's intentions are published, it is an alarum to call up all that are against them."[279] It was in this tradition that Girolamo Alberti reported to the Venetian doge from London in 1672 that "it has always been difficult to understand commerce thoroughly and at the present time especially it has become a secret, for everyone applies himself to it devotedly, and the powers take an interest in the matter because of the immense advantage to be derived for their territories and subjects."[280] As the importance of commerce grew in the world, so did the imperative to safeguard its secrets and harness its benefits. And even as late as 1750, Dutch diplomats feared that Prussia might learn "the most hidden secrets of commerce" and that way beat them at their own game.[281]

Gradually, however, a continental discourse of political economy wrested itself loose from the structural and censorial restrictions of the Old Regime, incrementally and, on occasions, in leaps and bounds. Despite the idiosyncrasies of early modern European censorship, the trend was clear. Pietro Verri noted in the early 1760s that "now" one could "find the true interest of States, and their real and physical force, in bookshops." Mysteries of state were a thing of the past: "governing a nation is no longer a magical art, but rather a published science subject to the laws of reason."[282] And emulation, his group knew, was both a problem of and a solution to modern politics.[283]

Furthermore, this transition from secretive to public cultures of learning in Europe was problematized by contemporary notions of the impermanence of knowledge, of intellectual copyright, and of the economic reasons for guarding certain kinds of information. Early dictionaries encountered the problem of codifying the oral and practical knowledge of artisans who, adhering to traditional notions of guild arcana as a means of conserving the professional skills on which their competitive advantages and material welfare depended, tended to be weary of publishing their know-how, not to mention that they resisted attempts to strip the artisanal classes of their culture and relative autonomy. Later encyclopedias ran into the similar problem of expropriating and publicizing fields of knowledge relevant to international power politics, whether in terms of finance or national defense.[284] The emergence of political economy added related tensions to the development of the Republic of Letters in Enlightenment Europe.[285] For as theories and practices that could keep political communities ahead in international economic rivalries were codified, published, and translated, they undermined their own efficiency by ensuring a level playing field of knowledge. There were ways political economy failed as a practice precisely when it thrived the most as a science, a paradox that could be resolved only by continuous recourse to the restless virtue of emulation. Economic knowledge had to be made public, but political economy, as a tradition of statecraft, was seldom less conflictual than reason of state had been.[286] It was often competition, not concord, that united subjects of this empire of emulation, a quixotic community unified by the sovereign power of economic expediency and justified by the promise of perpetual civil war.

Emulation, Translation, and Historiography

The historiography of economics generally relegates the dawn of economics as a "science" to William Petty's *Political Arithmetick,* its cockcrow to François Quesnay's *Economic Table,* and its glorious daybreak to Adam Smith's *Wealth of Nations.* An analysis of the discipline's development from the perspective of translations unveils a different picture. Economic works were qualitatively diverse carriers of influence in translation, but those that emerge as particularly important in a European context seldom correspond to the canon of economics established in the nineteenth and twentieth centuries. Where historiography long has lionized Physiocracy, for example, it was the Anti-Physiocrats who won the day as the system erected by Quesnay's men degenerated into dearth and famine.[287] Similarly, the most studied "British" economic writers of the late seventeenth century—pamphleteers, usually of a "free trade" inclination, like Nicholas Barbon, Dudley North, and the early Henry Martyn—were amazingly uninfluential in terms of editions and translations. Although the current fame of some authors like Thomas Mun does reflect a wide readership in early modern Europe, this is a proverbial exception that proves the rule. Digital databases indicate that contemporaries hardly ever referred to North and Barbon, who seem to have *never* been republished after their lifetimes, *never* translated, and practically *never* read before John Ramsay Mc-Culloch rediscovered them in the 1850s, by which point the strategies they unsuccessfully expounded in their lifetimes had gained new currency.

Yet the policies pursued by Britain in the wake of the Repeal of the Corn Laws cannot be thought characteristic also of proceeding centuries, and increased attention to the translation history of political economy sheds important light not only on the intellectual history of economics but also on the parallel history of economic policy. For continental statesmen and translators in the long eighteenth century had looked to authors and pamphleteers that were deemed more in line with actual British strategies at the time of its economic takeoff: now-neglected "mercantilists" like Cary, the authors of the *British Merchant,* and Joshua Gee. These were men of practice rather than philosophers who momentarily turned their gaze to worldlier concerns, and the economic policies they spearheaded—in short, pursuing profits through armed coercion, freeing internal trade, and encouraging domestic industry with bounties and high tariffs on the exportation of raw materials and the importation of manufactured goods—are a far cry from those proposed today by economists, those historically thought to have been influential, or, for that matter, considered representative of "Enlightenment economics."

It is thus impossible to ignore that a certain bias toward "precursorism," toward charting the genealogy of current ideas and ideologies rather than studying ideas in their own contexts, has profoundly skewed our understanding of the history of political economy in Europe. Our currently misconstrued idea of what Enlightenment political economy was about is more than simply historically problematic, reflecting neither the ideas nor the policies dominant in the European world. By virtue of how the supposed apotheosis of peaceful laissez-faire in the eighteenth century daily justifies choices and informs pundits, scholars, and world leaders alike, it has concrete consequences for practical matters today.

The only satisfying alternative is to explore it empirically from the proverbial bottom up, to redraw the complex picture of *what* happened to the early modern European economies; *what* people wrote about these changes; *how* these texts were read and translated; and *how* they changed history through immediate reforms and longer-term cultural changes.[288] And a study of the history of economic texts in translation suggests that a fundamental revision of the established canon is in order. J. G. A. Pocock long ago called for a more thorough history of translations, arguing that "we must consider what happened when Grotius was read in London or Hobbes in Leiden, Locke in Naples or Montesquieu in Philadelphia." He concludes that the Dutch reading of Hobbes meant "no more than that *Leviathan* has many histories, and figures in the creation and diffusion of languages through many kinds of contexts," but one must push beyond this to get at the core of the problem.[289] For if one respects contexts, the question cannot simply be how the inhabitants of Casalpusterlengo read Locke's economic works or how those of Skippagurra appropriated Quesnay, a method that reproduces all of the prejudices and none of the pleasures of teleology. By almost exclusively devoting themselves to the study of a small handful of canonical texts, historians and their audiences in other disciplines run the risk of convincing themselves that these texts are somehow representative of their times. Indeed, many have conflated canonical ideas (handpicked for a host of reasons over the intervening centuries) with historical practices (still largely unknown or marginalized). This is to put the cart before the horse. We must study the canon historically, not history canonically.

The insights discussed in this chapter contributed to the creation of a widespread market in Europe for translations of works on political economy and histories of economic policy, a vast and varied market that historians too long have ignored. Occasionally before and systematically after 1750, translations became a principal catalyst of the process by which political communities resisted conquering economies, supplying them with the measures to emulate instruments of imperialism. Whether the context was the explosive rivalry between giants like France and Great Britain or the more anxious attempts by new nations like Naples to find a place under the already crowded sun, translation was, as Goethe would write to Thomas Carlyle in July 1827, "one of the most important and valuable concerns in the whole world of affairs."[290]

CHAPTER TWO

Cary's *Essay on the State of England*

The Merchant of Bristol

England, people said at the turn of the seventeenth century, was the new Venice, the millennial commercial empire translated, across the crucible of emulation, from the Canal Grande to the Thames. Today, we cherish James Harrington's Anglo-Venetian political paradigm, the spread of Italian institutional innovations like insurance and double-entry bookkeeping, and Canaletto's vistas of London in galleries around the world. Less known, but more striking, is William Marlow's extraordinary *Capriccio,* which literally placed St. Paul's on a Venetian canal. For the viewer, the bustling canal—and what it represented in terms of industry, commerce, and dominion over the seas—becomes a path straight to the heart of the British Empire. Yet the lighting is different in Venice and London, demarcating the threshold of *translatio imperii.* The visual effect underlines Marlow's point. Bound by intellectual and institutional continuity, Venice and London were nonetheless different. Sharing the viewers' field of vision, a figure in the painting's lower right corner overlooks the canal and the distant Anglican skyline. He could be one of so many early modern Venetians in the twilight of their empire, gazing on a future they knew would be England's.[1] Distracted by the extravagant and the canonical, however, our attention seldom descends to the lowlier people and policies ultimately responsible for this epochal shift in the geography of power. People like John Cary, who, although reaching the peaks of political economy in eighteenth-century Europe, has since largely been delegated to oblivion by historians, economists, and political scientists alike.[2]

Shunning prolonged engagements, scholars of the infelicitous term "mercantilism" have singled him out as a pioneer in regarding the economy as a separate field of "scientific" inquiry; historians of political thought have similarly argued he precociously conceived of England's empire as a colonial system; and he has been mentioned by economic historians as an early proponent of technological change as an engine of development.[3] The interwar Chicago economist Jacob Viner presented him as a forerunner of the "favourable balance of trade" theory and one of the few dissenters to the doctrine "that low wages were desirable."[4] The ever-encyclopedic Joseph A. Schumpeter concluded that in terms of "carrying analysis beyond the obvious" all Cary's attempts ended in "failure," whereas J. Keith Horsefield unflatteringly summed him up with the statement that he "wrote a good deal, not very intelligently, about trade and credit."[5] Neither is this relative historiographical neglect placated by consensus among the few exceptions to the rule. Cary has been called "shrewd, narrowly nationalistic, and naïvely brutal" but also "a man of quite exceptional public spirit, an inflexible enemy of uncontrolled private interest and a widely respected figure"; he was both "a prominent and respectable theorist of free trade" and "one of the ablest exponents of mercantilism."[6]

Cary himself was born in Bristol in 1649, the eldest son of a merchant family stretching back to the fourteenth century, at a time when the city was fully joining the Atlantic economy as an important center of manufacture and a favorite port of call on England's western seaboard. His father Shershaw traded sugar on the Iberian Peninsula and in the West Indies, and was for a while master of the local Society of Merchant Venturers before passing away in Lisbon, and his sixteenth-century ancestor and namesake John Cary was also a daring merchant and warden of the Merchant Venturers who traded in contraband spices, and had his goods confiscated in Portugal in 1569 to his "greate losse," but managed to marry the mayor's daughter.[7] Second only to London in terms of commercial significance, Bristol was a place where the country's rapid economic growth was particularly evident.[8] Similarly echoing recent political developments, the cathedral city was also characterized by an extremely wide electoral culture, a stable Whig hegemony established in 1693 that kept Tory sentiments in check until 1710, and a profound religious influence on political life, often manifesting itself in the form of Quakerism.[9] Coming of age at the time when the politics of trade was in everyone's mouth, and when

English officials first began formulating a coherent economic policy for the colonies, Cary would draw on all these features of his native soil.[10]

Records indicate that, as was customary for members of Bristol's merchant class, he entered an apprenticeship—with a linen draper—before becoming a merchant and freeman of the city in 1672.[11] He captained ships around the Atlantic, the Caribbean, and the Mediterranean, trading in raw materials and manufactured goods, on one occasion barely evading legal repercussions for failing to load the agreed-on tonnage of sugar at Barbados. Cary became intimately involved with the politics of economic and social reform, signing petitions for everything from reducing the duties on imported sugar and herring to opening the slave trade to Bristolians.[12] Fathering numerous children, he was an active Anglican, serving terms as churchwarden for Bristol parishes. This religious persuasion involved him in pastoral movements, but more specifically the Bible presented him with a repository of moral and economic knowledge, particularly in terms of sanctifying labor. Cary's social success is testified to by his numerous apprentices and his early election into the Society of Merchant Venturers in 1677, the first step toward a lengthy career in corporate and civic affairs that would see him become warden in 1683 and, portentously, appointed to the common council of Bristol in 1688, the year of the "Glorious Revolution" he would defend so spiritedly.[13] England's political revolution, and the concomitant revolution in its financial system, profoundly informed his political vision of self-government through broad representation.[14] But it also inflected his belief in the capacity of commercial society to lift even its lowest members into wealth and virtue, and his jealous, belligerent attitude toward foreign countries. He dedicated his career to the economic aggrandizement of England's empire through conquest and commerce but, contrary to historiographical tropes, also emphasized the importance of "introducing a Habit of Virtue amongst us," a loaded phrase in which he conflated pagan civic and Christian religious ideals of moral excellence. Virtue, for Cary, was self-sacrificing patriotism as well as Christian charity, both of which he thought were empowered rather than threatened by commercial society.[15] Just as Cary enthusiastically embraced the Williamite settlement, so he enthusiastically embraced central tenets of English national identity in the period: Protestantism, parliamentarism, militarism, commerce.[16]

He also took part in the emerging English culture of toleration by stressing the importance of a "*Liberty of* Conscience." An octosyllabic poem he seems to have composed before 1696 nonetheless conveys the essence of his beliefs and the pertinent limits of his tolerance. After describing the successful overcoming of the Roman Catholic monarchs Charles II and James II at length, he concluded, illustrating what these "intestine Jarrs" and "bloody Wars" of the body politic would bring about,

> The Pope shall have a fatall fall,
> And never visit more Whitehall;
> Then shall the Nation be in peace,
> And Wealth & Honour shall increase,
> And discord in Religion cease.[17]

His aversion to Catholicism was the religious manifestation of a general dislike of "Arbitrary Power," which he associated with the Catholic James II in an early note. The opening paragraph of his *Essay* stressed the importance of a prosperous trade for defending the security of "Religion, Liberty, and Property," and his last major work was a singular attack against all absolutist abuses of power, in this case against him personally: "Arbitrary Power," he would write from jail after encountering financial problems, "knows no Bounds."[18] Incidentally, this moment also culminated Cary's lifelong fascination with the works of John Locke—"I think the Nation obliged by the service you have done" he wrote him in a letter of 11 January 1696[19]—by arguing for the importance of securing "the Liberties and Properties of the People, from all Encroachments endeavoured to be made on them."[20]

Cary took many of the basic tenets of classical republicanism to heart—the importance of civic virtue and representative government, the equation of dependency with slavery, the moral and political paradigm of the common good; ignored others—faith in a citizen militia, distrust of commerce; and empowered the result with a clear belief in the possibility of worldly melioration through economic development. Yet he saw nothing automatic in this process, and as he often emphasized his active striving for the "publick good," so he feared that private interests might thwart the common weal. These preoccupations led him to become a founding member of the Whig-oriented Society for the Reformation of Manners of Bristol, one of a number of such associations dedicated to moral reform that emerged across England in the aftermath of the 1688–89 revolutions, and to become the guiding force of its associated Corporation for the Poor, dedicated to employing vagrant and unemployed young women, and later men, in the city.[21] "Self Interest," he argued forcefully, was "the overthrow of all publicque affairs," a sentiment that poignantly expresses his anthropological assumptions and the sociological foundations of his approach to regulation and his conception of political economy.[22]

Yet sometimes the two would meet. Only after his ship *Samuell and George* was "taken by the French" on its way to Antigua in 1694 did Cary write his *Essay,* subsequently tackling all the major issues facing pamphleteers in the Williamite economy.[23] Principal among these was the fundamental question of how to structure the imperial economy, which ever since the time of Richard Hakluyt had been based on the synergistic interrelationship between a core committed to manufacturing and its colonial producers of raw materials.[24] Then came, in broad terms, the issue of how to organize and encourage trade, particularly as related to the role of a central council of trade, of joint stocks, monopolies, special privileges, and the insistence of the East India Company on importing manufactured calicoes; the problem of poverty, vagrancy, and how England's productive apparatus could best mobilize the idle elements of its workforce; the questions of recoinage and the moral, military, and political viability of the new public debt.[25]

Cary followed up the initial success of the *Essay* with several pamphlets on particular problems raised in it, and several parts of it were reprinted as stand-alone contributions to specific debates like that over the profitability of the African slave trade. His influence among the Merchant Venturers of Bristol only increased with these publications, to the point where he was elected member of a "committee to consult matters in relation to the benefit of trade" in Bristol in 1696 and subsequently sent by the Merchant Venturers to "our Representatives in Parliament as our commissioner" in London.[26] Given his surviving correspondence, it seems the Merchant Venturers of Bristol felt the need for a local presence due to their dissatisfaction with their MPs, and Cary had indeed been in regular correspondence with the latter for some time, soliciting interventions on behalf of the former.[27] The 1696 appointment of members to the Royal Council of Trade and Plantations, the "Board of Trade," a body practically identical to the council he had proposed in his *Essay,* was of particular interest to Cary, and the subject of many heated letters.[28] He hoped to pursue his political and economic agenda from a seat in the House of Commons, but his ambitions were thwarted by a political alliance, and he received the least votes of all the candidates in his district when he ran for office in 1698.[29]

Around this time, the *Essay*'s arguments for safeguarding the imperial economy against Irish manufactures were invoked as inspiration for a renewed, intensified debate over the island's sovereignty. Cary's confrontation with the Irish scientist and parliamentarian William Molyneux over the right of the Irish to manufacture their own wool made such an impression that he thereafter was invited by the English Parliament to be an overseer of the Williamite confiscations in Ireland and, as the detrimental consequences of England's measures there became impossible to ignore, to formulate palliative policies for the Irish economy. An almost stereotypical representative of the revolution in England's economic, political, and scientific culture, Cary was given a coat of arms for his efforts, becoming apostle, architect, and agent of empire.[30] His traces disappear in Ireland until he begins republishing his works in the late 1710s, systematizing them by introducing a rigorous legal and scientific vocabulary that he had first been forced to adopt in his reply to Molyneux's erudite arguments for the Irish right to industrialize. Cary's private papers reveal that uncovering and codifying basic principles and mechanisms to produce practical and systematic knowledge were a constant preoccupation for him, and include, alongside poetry of an uneven quality, a sketch of the "great Blazing Starre" of 1680, descriptions of various comets, a self-composed treatise on chymical geology, and a short venture into veterinary medicine. "Use and Experience," he claimed generally, "make us at last Masters of every thing."[31] By 1717, he had come to believe that his commercial experience could be codified as a robust "science" with a distinct set of principles to be studied and applied. Cary's fortunes then changed, and in his last known publication he bewailed the loss of habeas corpus from jail shortly before passing away around 1720. Yet, while his life's work might have come to an end then, his work's life had barely begun.

The *Essay*

The immediate context for Cary's writing was the Nine Years' War (1688–97). Though Charles II and James II both had shown insouciance with regard to French expansionism in the second half of the seventeenth century and had actively resisted ministerial efforts to foster Francophobic popular sentiment, the Protestant reign of William and Mary made aggressive patriotism a central tenet of English national identity, now distinguished as being free from absolutist hierarchies of power whether politically despotic or ecclesiastically Catholic.[32] England joined the war against Versailles also to stymie French support for the Jacobite cause of rethroning James II. The originally continental war supposedly waged to contain the expansionism of Louis XIV, and settle the European balance of power, quickly became global when England broke its neutrality following the coronation of William III, stretching across secular and spiritual domains from the Indian subcontinent across Europe into the Americas.[33]

By the summer campaigns of 1695, all parties were financially exhausted by a costly war of maneuvering, and the loss of English industry to foreign competition was no "chymerical fancy," one observer put it, but a clear and present danger.[34] Many feared that the measures necessary to fund a prolonged resistance, especially public debt, would deplete the country's finances, underlying economic structures, and future capacity to collect revenue and wage war.[35] Because the "Art of War" had been "reduced to Money," the Tory political economist Davenant warned, hostilities would neither end for lack of "Hatred" nor "Men," only "Money."[36] Having himself lost a ship to the French, Cary counted among those who had not only observed but experienced directly how war strained the "*Nerves* and *Sinews*" of England's "Treasure," and he presented his *Essay* as a guide to overcoming these obstacles without undermining the "Foundations of Wealth."[37]

For more was at risk than simple profit margins: losing dominion over the world's textile market would jeopardize the legacy of the "Glorious Revolution." These high stakes were all too clear also to Cary, who concomitantly argued not only England but "the *Protestant* Interest in *Europe*" depended on its outcome—liberty and salvation alike required that England resist what contemporaries referred to as Louis XIV's "designs of Universal Monarchy."[38] In the end, the weavers of Wolverhampton were the last line of defense against what Cary called "Popish cut-throats" from the continent, bulwarks against hostile religions, political paradigms, and manufactured goods alike.[39] "If Trade were well secured," he assured his readers, "the War would scarce be felt."[40] In the final instance, the *Essay* was "an Anatomy of the Trade of England, dissected and laid open so as to discover its Vitals," thus uncovering "the principles of all our trade."[41] It described not only how trade had changed England and the possibilities it offered but also the measures needed to encourage, defend, and, ultimately, calibrate it to maintain cultural coherence, a "true *English* Spirit," in the face of the fluctuations of commercial society.

Cary's correspondence with Locke shows he felt a duty to codify his experiences for the "publick good."[42] While more famous pamphleteers of the period often drew on a venerable tradition of European thought, sometimes only for rhetorical reasons, Cary's practical intellectual formation meant that he never approached wealth, war, and empire by recourse to the classical canon of political philosophy; where more learned contemporaries rallied against Louis XIV with the lexis of "universal monarchy," Cary warned only against kings "aiming at unlimited power."[43] There are no traces of Cicero, Tacitus, Machiavelli, or Grotius in any of his writings, nor are such influences easily traceable in his vocabulary.[44] Apart from allusions to the popular fables of Æsop, one of the only references to the world of erudition in Cary's entire corpus is a—seemingly—secondhand invocation of Livy, serving as a preamble to a biblical reference, the likes of which abound in his writings.[45] The specific passage in question, Genesis

3:19, was frequently invoked in the period and defined labor as Adam's punishment after the Fall: with the gates of Eden forever barred to man, only hard work would ever bring him sustenance.[46] If Locke, whose ideas so often were close to Cary's, repeatedly paraphrased this divine decree in his *Second Discourse,* their initial correspondence is nonetheless indicative of their different backgrounds: Cary's first letter to Locke pointed out Locke's errors in calculating exchange rates; Locke gently retaliated by noting Cary's poor Latin grammar.[47]

Lack of erudition is not lack of structure, however, and the *Essay* unfolds methodically, exploring a number of taxonomies often partitioned into descriptions and prescriptions.[48] It consists of three main sections of greatly decreasing size, dealing with trade, the poor, and taxes, respectively. Each is subject to further subdivisions. The first pages present "Trade" as consisting of "Inland *and* Outland Trade," in which "*the* Inland" was comprised of "*three parts,* viz. Buying *and* Selling, Husbandry, *and* Manufactures"; "Husbandry" is further "*divided into* Pasture *and* Tillage." These, however, provided only a "very small Summ" compared to that "*raised by* Manufactures, Trade, *and* Labour,

> the first of which . . . is the most profitable part of our *Inland Trade,* being That whereby our Product is advanced in its value, and made fit both for our own use, and also for Foreign Markets; from whence are again imported hither sundry other Materials, the Foundations of *Manufactures* different in their Natures from our own.[49]

"Trade" connoted several things for Cary and likeminded contemporaries: a vocation, for which "industry" was a qualifier and of which it represented a distinct subfield related to manufacturing; the act and process of international exchange; and, as his use of the term "Inland Trade" suggests, something like our modern term "economy."

From the outset, Cary thus distances himself from contemporary writings on trade which, drawing on a classical trope, justifyied it on the basis of some providential distribution of commodities: the Heavens had assured that different lands produced different goods, so that the necessity of exchanges could bring peace and, in the word's original significance of exchange and communication, "commerce."[50] The *Essay* is, instead, an encomium to labor, industry, and manufactures in alignment with the Whig political economy of the 1688–89 revolutions.[51] The "Profits" of the country arose "Originally from its Products and Manufactures at home," "from "Fisheries," and from "Husbandry," all "Raised by the Industry of [England's] *Inhabitants.*"[52] It mattered little what resources naturally occurred in one's lands. What mattered, "experience" taught him, was the competitive export of ever more sophisticated work, an economic world-view conducive to international competition rather than cooperation, hegemony rather than harmony.

Cary's approach was not unprecedented, but marked a radical shift in the nature of economic discourse compared to its more famous phase in the early seventeenth century. In line with Francis Bacon's insistence on "observation and experience" as the means of increasing factual knowledge, merchant-pamphleteers now openly flaunted their familiarity with commerce as an exploitable source of authority in economic affairs.[53] Steve Pincus has argued that this was a predominantly Whig methodology, as opposed to the Tory argument of Child that only a merchant who had joined the landed gentry carried authority on the subject, around the 1688 revolution.[54] The aristocrat merchant and writer Sir Dudley North was praised for his "Knowledge and Experience of Trade," which "could not be attained, unless he were a Trader himself." His work was marketed as representative of the "new Philosophy" emanating from "*Des Carte's* excellent dissertation *de Methodo*," and his introduction concluded that "Knowledge" was becoming "Mechanical," meaning "built upon clear and evident Truths," but lamented that the approach had been monopolized by the "studious and learned" rather than by the "Common-Seaman," who "with all his Ignorance, proves a better Mechanick, for actual Service, than the Professor himself, with all his Learning." If trade was to become a Cartesian, mechanical knowledge, it had to be derived from the empirical observations of practicing merchants.[55]

But since a relative liberty of press allowed Englishmen to comment on controversial issues of policy, contemporaries soon realized that merchants drew widely differing conclusions from their experiences in often widely different trades.[56] Cary's aim of presenting a total analysis of England's trade can only be understood in light of his fear of being dismissed as a mere propagandist for some specific trade or written off as a "Projector," a fear his esteemed correspondents quickly banished but that later would return to haunt him.[57]

A Conjectural History of Commercial Society

For the same reason, Cary's *Essay* quickly drew back from immediate concerns to present a conjectural history of the concomitant origins of commerce and civilization. Surveying the economic principles guiding history, he systematically explored the various elements of the wealth of nations as they emerged.

> The first Original of Trade both Domestick and Foreign was Barter. . . . As People increased so did Comerce, this caused many to go off from *Husbandry* to *Manufactures* and other ways of living, for Convenience whereof they began Communities which being found necessary for *Trade,* their *Inhabitants* were increased by expectation of Profit; this introduced *Forreign Trade,* or *Traffick* with Neighbouring Nations.

Sociable communities and then "Nations" were collaterals of economic interaction. While Cary drew extensively on Locke in his writings, comparing this passage to the *Second Treatise* nonetheless illuminates striking divergences between their historical narratives. "Every Compact," Locke argued, did not "put an end to the State of Nature between men," only that of "agreeing together mutually to enter into one Community" did so. The political contract marking the birth of society was of an entirely different order from that of commercial contracts:

> The Promises and Bargains for Truck, *&c.* between the two Men in the Desert Island, mentioned by *Garcilasso De la vega,* in his History of *Peru,* or between a *Swiss* and an *Indian,* in the Woods of *America,* are binding to them, though they are perfectly in a State of Nature, in reference to one another. For Truth and keeping of Trust belongs to Men, as Men, and not as Members of Society.[58]

The work Locke had in mind, Inca Garcilaso de la Vega's 1609 *Royal Commentaries of the Incas,* opened with a description of the misadventures of Pedro Serrano, shipwrecked with a fellow European on a desolate island off Peru.[59] His story of how the two men met, divided their labor, quarreled, and finally reunited showed the power of Christianity to bond strangers even at ends of the earth, but Locke, undoubtedly assisted by a liberal French translation, interpreted it very differently. The inflections sustained by Garcilaso's text in translation, and their consequences for political theory, are a precious omen of the chapters to come.

Garcilaso rendered the two Christian castaways' association in mercantile terms, recounting how "ellos mismos, cayendo en su disparate, se pidieron perdón y se hicieron amigos y volvieron a su compañía."[60] Garcilaso's French translator rendered their interaction less institutionally: "en fin la necessité les r'appella, & les mit bien ensemble."[61] The subsequent English translator, however, working directly from the Spanish original, presented a far more political account: "for *the better government in their way of living,*" the two men came together, and though they briefly fell out of friendship, they were reconciled by the "comfort which mutual society procures."[62] Locke's odd reference to this account is consistent with a note he made in his diary on 8 February 1687: *"Pedro Serrano that lived three years in a desolate island alone and after that time another shipwrecked man came to him and being but two they could not agree. Garcilasso de la*

Vega, Histoire des Incas, I.I.c.8." Locke's citation of this work in French corresponds with the language of the copy in his library.[63] By ignoring everything subsequent to the altercation in Garcilaso's account, Locke argued that the disagreement testified to the fragility of human interactions—no matter the necessities they satisfied—in the absence of an original social contract. The question regarded whether political, economic, or religious interests first lifted man out of the state of nature. Where Locke argued that mere economic necessity could not break the state of nature in the absence of politics, Cary located the origin of civil society squarely in commerce rather than compact.

Even at its most scholarly, then, the *Essay* and its conjectural history never left the world of merchant practicality behind. As such, it envisioned societies to rest on a demographic synergy between country and community, agriculture and manufactures. As trade expanded, so did the specialization of merchants to conciliate the mutual needs of husbandmen and manufacturers, from which a legal system eventually emerged to smooth interactions: "And as Trade increased so *Courts* of *Justice* were Appointed in several great *Towns* and *Cities,* which being of different Natures, Multitudes of People gave Attendance, expecting to get livelihoods by them" to the point where riches gave birth to luxury, sickness, and, as a result, the need for medical practitioners. Once society had reached this level of complexity, it bloomed into civic maturity. "Ripe Parts were fitted for the Service of the Church, other of the State," and supportive social, legal, religious, and political structures became sound enough to allow for the real proliferation of mutually supportive economic activities.[64] Thus, Cary argued later on, "one is serviceable to another without invading each others Province," and "the Country supplies the City with Provisions, and that the Country with Manufactures."[65]

The moral of Cary's conjectural history was simple. Civilization resulted from an ever intensifying division of labor. Comparing this account with those of contemporaries is revealing in two ways. On the one hand, it is more sophisticated than many appeals to historical authority. It was an abstract analysis of how the division of labor was a result and further cause of societal development, not merely an attempt to place England in a chronological sequence of commercial societies—usually Tyre, Athens, Rome, Venice, and the Low Countries, in that order—or a token mention of King Solomon. As will be clear later, Cary saved himself immense headaches by *not* placing England in a historical trajectory and thus by imagining that England's primacy too, like Tyre's, some day would wane; *translatio imperii* was not a coordinate of his historical imagination. On the other hand, Cary was uninterested in the politico-philosophical dimensions of his narrative, never returning to the origins of society to locate man in his state of nature or draw conclusions regarding the nature of "Power and Jurisdiction" as Locke did, or of inequality, as Rousseau famously would.[66] And it was precisely because of its economic reductionism that Cary's passage would emerge as one of the *Essay*'s most contested in translation.

Balances of Trade and Work

Following this conjectural history, the bulk of the *Essay* consists of a painstaking description of England's trades. But more than simply measuring their contributions to the wealth of the nation in terms of a balance of trade, Cary worried about the underlying balance of work.[67] His touchstone of trade and moral melioration alike was whether something encouraged England's manufactures or not. What mattered was not trade itself but *what* was traded. The *Essay* shows little evidence of the so-called Midas fallacy of chrysohedonism, the supposed "mercantilist" vice of confusing gold with wealth. Inflows of bullion were merely symptomatic of a nation's healthy productive capacity, Cary argued, real wealth being based on accumulated labor and technological developments.[68] As Steve Pincus has suggested, manufacturing industry was a veritable Whig obsession at the time, in opposition to the generally land-based political economy of James II and the Tories.[69] Locke had written that "labour makes the far greatest part of the value of things," and Cary followed suit, presenting labor as an "Addition" to the "value" of goods "by the Labour of the People."[70] Not only did labor present a far more powerful source of wealth when imbued in manufactures than in agriculture, it also helped win wars, encouraged navigation, and, most important, offered a possibility for material and social melioration, increasing workers' wages and moral rectitude while allowing them to remain competitive in foreign markets.

Aware of courting iconoclasm on this point, Cary at length addressed the question "whither the labour of our Poor in *England* being so high does not hinder the Improvement of our Product and Manufactures?" Whether, in short, high wages made industries uncompetitive, one of the fundamental preoccupations of political economy. Cary's answer, which he admitted "may seem a Paradox at first," was a resounding no, for English manufactures were made competitive by "the Ingenuity of the Manufacturer, and the Improvements he makes in his ways of working" rather than "by falling the price of poor Peoples Labour." Legions of pamphleteers had argued that low wages opened foreign markets, but Cary observed that technical and technological developments in the process of production could reduce costs while maintaining, or even raising, workers' wages.

Silk-Stockings are wove instead of knit; Tobacco is cut by Engines instead of Knives; Books are printed instead of written. . . . Lead is smelted by Wind-Furnaces, instead of blowing with Bellows . . . all which save the labour of many Hands, so the Wages of those imployed need not be lessened.[71]

Sovereignty over international trade did not depend on the suppression of domestic wages but on experience and technological progress: costs of production would fall once "Cunning crept into Trades" and "Inventions" flourished. "Mens knowledge increases by Observation," he maintained, "and this is the reason why one Age exceeds another in any sort of *Mistery,* because they improve the Notions of their Predecessors."[72] This was particularly evident in an industry with which the Carys of Bristol had been familiar for generations: technical improvements in the Caribbean sugar industry had reached a point where "the Refiner of Sugars goes through that operation in a month, which our Forefathers required four months to effect."[73] Not only was it unnecessary to suppress wages but, harnessing the same synergy he had identified in his analysis of the division of labor and the development of commercial society, Cary now showed how higher wages structurally could *increase* the wealth of the nation, as higher incomes from innovations and technological change spread, like ripples across water, through the economy in the form of higher wages and higher demand, in turn stimulating the supply of new "fashions" adding "Wings to Mens Inventions" in a continuous virtuous circle.[74]

In an age when "fashions" often were deemed sybaritic vices, Cary's faith in inventions and resulting systemic developments helped him overcome contemporary anxieties regarding (domestically manufactured) luxuries. The very whimsicality of fashion, often marking it as effeminate corruption, provided a unique impetus to widen habits of consumption that, in turn, encouraged the process of technical and material melioration, ensuring an ever-changing demand for the different textiles of which England was becoming the world's supplier. No manufactures were more central to the country's commercial identity in the period than woolens, and Cary imbued their trade with an almost mythical aura. The "Golden Fleece" of England's ruminant riches, he reminded his readers with a commonplace reference to Jason and his Argonauts, was "the *Primum* of our Wollen Manufactures" and "thereby Imploy[s] Multitudes of our People." Foreign luxuries and manufactured goods that usurped work from England's needy, on the other hand, merely encouraged vice, causing unemployment and social upheavals without any salubrious consequences.[75] This explained "why the Kingdom of *Spain* still continues poor notwithstanding its *Indies,* because all that the Inhabitants buy is purchased for its full Value in *Treasure* or *Product,* their Labour adding nothing to its Wealth, for want of *Manufactures.*"[76]

Summarizing his argument in a manuscript, Cary thought "the Interest of England" was "to improve its woollen manufactures."[77] Emphasizing the importance of wool for the English economy was itself an ancient trope dating back to Virgil's assessment that England was *terra de lana,* a "land," as Melon would present it in his economic model more than seventeen centuries later, "of wool," and Cary was obviously attuned both to the traditional sale and production of woolen manufactures and to the related phraseology of political economy.[78] But how important was wool for the English economy? Historical trade statistics is an impressionistic science. As Henry Martyn warned in his assessment of England's balance of trade in 1717–18, existing data were not perfect, yet were good enough "to know the increase or decrease of such particular trades as are beneficial or detrimental, in order to the giving encouragement to the former, or to our discouraging the latter."[79] Though historical statistics do not give us the full picture, they are not devoid of heuristic value. And considering the first decade for which official data on the value of English exports exist, it is striking, given the ban on the export of raw wool, to note the dominance of woolen manufactures. In 1698 they accounted for no less than 80 percent of known English exports (see Figure 2.1). Considering the seventy years from 1697 to 1767, woolen manufactures remained *the* key industry for English exports long after more traditional industrial goods like iron began their ascent in colonial and foreign markets (see Figure 2.2).

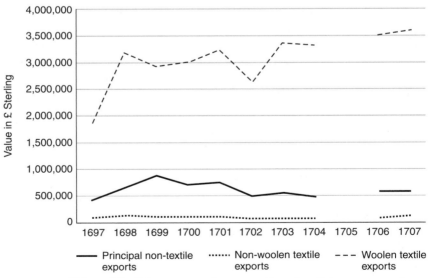

FIGURE 2.1. Value of English exports, 1697–1707 (based on Schumpeter 1960, 19, 29, 35)

But what role did international trade have in economic development, in the relation between European overseas empires, and in the advent of the so-called Industrial Revolution? Though Cary undoubtedly exaggerated the importance of international trade, downplaying the role of domestic production, consumption, and investments in economic growth, coerced overseas dominions nonetheless supplied valuable raw materials and protected markets, invigorating technological and financial developments and providing a structure for the melioration of economic practices.[80] Few doubted that England's empire and the foreign trade secured by its Navigation Acts helped make it a great power, allowing it to harness economies of scale and violence to monopolize markets for its manufactures, largely textiles.

Many economists disagree with this today, and some even go as far as arguing that if England had been bereft of its imperial supplies of cotton and dominated export markets, the "Industrial Revolution" would have occurred anyway; they would seamlessly have substituted cotton-based industrialization with "building more houses in Cheshire," a simple "shift of attention."[81] These arguments, which one must assume in one way or another are derived from what James Buchanan calls "the equality assumption" of neoclassical economics, postulating "constant returns to scale of production over all ranges of output," de facto ignores the differential capacity of economic activities to produce wealth.[82] Not all work is the same, as Cary knew well, and a "shift of attention" from subsistence agriculture to industrial mass production has tremendous consequences. Spinning cotton is not building houses. Technological development occurs unevenly across different sectors at different times and contributes unevenly to economic growth.[83]

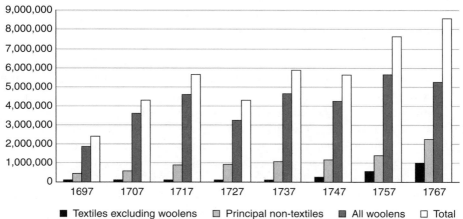

FIGURE 2.2. Value of English exports, 1697–1767 (based on Schumpeter 1960, 19–22, 25–28)

The mechanisms of economic development were similarly more complex in early modern Europe. In 1656, after yearly woolen manufactures in Venice had fallen to around eleven thousand from a high point of nearly thirty thousand pieces of cloth in 1600, only seven hundred pieces of cloth were produced for the domestic market. Even after dramatic industrial decline, Venice exported more than 93 percent of its output.[84] According to many economists, Venetians would simply have turned to other economic activities when their foreign markets for textiles were taken over by the Dutch and the British, activities that, somehow, offered the same potential for economic development. Barred from exporting advanced manufactures by their high production costs and the aggressive protectionism of foreign powers, Venice should have maintained its vast Mediterranean empire by constructing palazzi in the lagoon. Yet this is not what happened. The Serene Republic may represent a model of graceful decline, but decline it did; its empire disappeared, its population diminished, and it went from being a nexus of global trade to being a regional harbor with grandiose architecture. As a civilization, Venice, devoid of natural resources beyond fish and salt and what it drew from conquered territories on the mainland, depended on imported raw materials and the export of refined goods to faraway markets. No domestic trades could substitute for its exports; no local activities could serve as full surrogates for the export of manufactured goods to extensive markets dominated militarily and diplomatically.

Eighteenth-century England and the Industrial Revolution are a mirror image of Venice's decline. Colonial possessions absorbed up to 40 percent of incremental English industrial output between 1700 and 1775.[85] It has been estimated that increasing exports were responsible for 21 percent of England's growth of GDP and for 50 percent of its "additional industrial output" between 1780 and 1801.[86] Where England exported one-fifth of its total industrial output in 1700, by 1800 it was exporting no less than a third. More important, key sectors depended largely on foreign markets. Between 1760 and 1801, the proportion of England's total industrial output of cotton manufactures exported rose from 50 percent to 62 percent. More than three out of every five pieces of cotton manufacture—a benchmark industry of the Industrial Revolution impossible to divorce from slave labor and coerced consumers—were destined for foreign markets by the turn of the eighteenth century.[87] The changing nature of Britain's imports during its period of intensifying industrial policies is equally striking. Britain went from importing 34.7 percent raw materials and 31.7 percent manufactured goods in the period 1699–1702 to importing 62.3 percent raw materials and a mere 4.3 percent manufactured goods in the 1840s.[88] From an English perspective, the great structural transformation from an agricultural to an industrial economy occured during a period of intense economic policies to ensure precisely such a transition, *not* "after" the decline of so-called "mercantilism."[89] And Cary was an architect of this process.

Yet his *Essay* was far from insensible to the possible dark side of the manufacturing revolution, of fashions and wasteful conspicuous consumption. Commercial society had inaugurated a period of unprecedented social mobility, but just as there was a difference between working one's way to wealth and looting mines for gold, there was a fine line between working one's way up the social ladder and pretending to have already done so. "Emulation" *could* give "Opportunities of advancing [people's] Fortunes" if only encouraged properly. Similarly, where "Ale-houses" and other loci of urban sociability were supposed to "support and refresh" men in "their Labour," the contemporary vogue for hot drinks led people to loiter in "Coffee-Houses" that kept "lusty Servants," which Cary held would "breed [workers] up to nothing whereby they may be profitable to the Kingdom."[90]

The question was how to control these new institutions of commercial society to ensure economic development *and* moral rectitude.[91] Yet again, labor emerged as the nucleus of Cary's thought, for if "England" only "delighted more in improving its Manufactures," all social pathologies would be cured.[92] "Work-houses" whereby the poor could "be rather Assistants to the Manufacturers than such themselves" could whip the idle into shape, the drones of society put to work in the very luxurious industries that had corrupted them in the first place.[93] "And when once the Poor shall come by use to be in Love with Labour," Cary continued optimistically, they would be prepared for future apprenticeships requiring more skill and training.[94] Not only would such a scheme and others like it encourage "a habit of virtue amongst us," they also encouraged "Youth in an early Delight of Living by Industry, which would keep up a true *English* Spirit in them, and create a Desire to secure a Property in what they have."[95] The Welsh poet, painter, and clergyman John Dyer's 1757 epic *The Fleece,* an extraordinary commercial rendition of Virgil's *Georgics,* would put Cary's project more poetically: "Nor less they gain / Virtue than wealth, while, on their useful works / From day to day intent, in their full minds / Evil no place can find."[96]

The Role of Government in Empire and Development

Cary's analysis of the wealth of nations led him to put great faith in the organizing abilities of government, of "the State" as he put it.[97] By arguing for a stronger mercantile presence in Parliament, and for its more active role in organizing the national economy to emulate and conquer foreign competitors, he followed on a bipartisan path walked by Henry Parker, celebrated "Observator" during the Civil War, Benjamin Worsley, the supposed composer of the Navigation Acts, and even Thomas Hobbes. Parker had concluded his 1648 *Free Trade* by arguing that one should take Plato's *Republic* as inspiration and make a government not of philosophers but of merchants, and Worsley reached a similar conclusion in his semiofficial justification for the Navigation Acts, momentous documents in England's transition to a more centralized imperial venture, by recourse to emulation.[98] The "Dutch" had grown wealthy and powerful because they had made "Care and Protection of Trade abroad in all places their Interest of State." They had "prohibited English textiles" and understood the importance of an industrial policy, as was evident from the "Constant Reward and Incouragement" they gave "Inventions" and "new Discoveries," which "hath ever been" a "very great spur to Industrie." Worsley, and thus official English policy, succinctly defined the interconnection of war, wealth, and power: "it is by a Knowledge of Trade and Commerce, and the Cours of it, that one Nation or State knows perfectly how to straighten and pinch another, and *to compel a Compliance from them.*"[99] Knowledge of trade was knowledge of empire and how to achieve it: a tool, like conquest, of coercion.

Cary conceived of commerce in precisely such terms, and he too believed "it would be the great Wisdom of our Government to regulate all Foreign *Trades* by such Methods as may best make them useful in the promoting of our Manufactures."[100] Although he defined his own country as "free" in opposition to arbitrary powers on the continent, he never doubted that primarily government, and only secondarily enlightened private initiatives, could provide the necessary measures to harness the possibilities of commercial society without succumbing to its licentious and degenerative aspects, morally or economically. Cary similarly fused political, military, and economic interests when, echoing emerging canons of expertise, he proclaimed that

> TRADE REQUIRES AS MUCH POLICY AS MATTERS OF STATE, and can never be kept in regular motion by accident; when the frame of our trade is out of order, we know not where to begin to mend it, for want of a set of experienced builders, ready to receive applications, and able to judge where the defect lies.[101]

No one would build a house without consulting builders, just as no one should run a successful national economy without listening to *him*. In presenting its advice, the *Essay* followed the structural precedent established by writers like Child by proposing fourteen specific ways government could encourage the manufactures of the nation.[102] These were both direct measures—in the sense of "providing Work-houses for the Poor" (1), removing tariffs on imported raw materials and exported manufactured goods (2, 4), burdening the export of raw materials and the import of manufactured goods with heavy tariffs or prohibitions (3, 5, 11), defending English trades with vigilant warships (6)—and indirect ones, such as "lowering the interest" (7), prohibiting "privileged places" (12), and facilitating transactions (8, 9, 10, 12, 13). Finally, government was to assure, through "Treaties of Peace and other Negotiations," that foreign princes followed the opposite practices by exporting raw materials and importing manufactured goods (14).[103]

Cary's call for governmental intervention and a closer collaboration between policy and practice, however, did not entail a liking for monopolies or special privileges; "Trade" should be "laid open" and be "free."[104] By this he meant a freedom from monopolies and privileges, of vocation or "trade" in seventeenth-century parlance, not freedom of international exchange in the absence of tariffs.[105] And although he often favored tariffs, their goal was explicitly long-term industrial development rather than immediate fiscal relief.[106] His aversion to state interventions that did not encourage domestic manufactures is particularly evident in his critiques of the East India trade, the renewed polemic against which in the 1690s was an immediate context of his efforts.[107]

He had signed petitions against the Company years before, presented his grievances to Parliament, and now further denounced both its privileged nature and the detrimental consequences of its cheaply imported manufactures.[108] The East India Company was the very negation of the *Essay*'s political economy, a privileged entity with special interests, within the body politic, dedicated to importing cheap foreign luxuries that directly competed with domestic industry. Not only this, but it rested on its laurels, refusing to push English trade as far into the dark continents of the world as individual initiative would have. Had the company found new markets for English manufactures things would have been different, but at present they incarnated Æsop's fable "A Dog in a Manger," wanting neither to "supply those Plantations themselves, nor suffer others to do it."[109] The monopoly of the East India Company, like that of the African Company, embodied jealousy of trade, ironically the very same jealousy the *Essay* itself represented on a national level.

The problem was crystallized in the debate over slavery, the only nonmanufactured good Cary fought for the freedom to export being "Negroes," England's "best traffick." To sustain the African Company's monopoly on this trade was equivalent to advising "the People of *Egypt* to raise high Banks to confine the River *Nilus* from overflowing, lest it should thereby Fertilize the Lands, or the King of *Spain* to shut up his mines, lest he should fill his Kingdom too full of Silver," an oddly bullionist example in a work which otherwise tended to consider work rather than money as wealth. This "Trade," he affirmed, "is our Silver Mines," the English Potosí.[110] Why should one work the "Golden Mine" of slavery only one day a week, when its wealth could be exploited all week long? The only way Cary considered slaves to be different from other goods was that they facilitated the acquisition and elaboration of other raw materials like cotton, tobacco, and sugar, which again could be refined into more valuable manufactured goods. He not only published the relevant passages on slavery from his *Essay* as a separate pamphlet, but also petitioned Parliament on behalf of the Bristol merchant community to break the monopoly on slavery. This was achieved shortly afterward, and Bristol rose to become one of the empire's centers of slave trade.[111]

To monitor properly these and other government decisions, though, some sort of expert consulting body was necessary. Cary considered a "Council of Trade" "so necessary" that he sent the elected Bristol MPs page references to his *Essay*'s discussion of such institutions and how they best could implement his suggested policies.[112] The Bristol merchants, however, aired their worry that London would dominate the kingdom's economy further with the assistance of a partisan council; that the national interest represented by the *Essay* would be trumped by the local interests of the capital.[113] The MPs, in return, noted: "there is no doubt but the Londoners will endeavour their own interest; and the other ports of the Kingdome must bee as carefull of theirs."[114] The members ultimately appointed fulfilled all their fears, and Cary was clearly vexed by the council's composition, all too aware of the "difficulty of reducing [such plans] into practice." Although an Anglican churchwarden, he here voiced an even more sensitive concern. Cary was averse to economic privileges among Englishmen, whether manifest as an excessive clemency toward paupers or as trade monopolies on the model of the East India Company. Similarly, he dreaded that a trade council might be corrupted by ecclesiastical interests, "whither these Seminarys for Trade may not at last turn to Seminarys for Religion, & so instead of being Hives for Industrious Bees, become Nests for [i]dle . . . Drones. . . . For let religion be good or bad . . . nothing will be the product thereof but Idleness & Laziness."[115]

A War for Wealth

By not only setting the stage for production and exchange to take place but also actively encouraging manufactures and inventions with prizes and pensions, defending them against foreign wares with prohibitive tariffs and a powerful navy, Cary believed Parliament could realize his grandiose vision of an English empire resting as much on economic as on military might. The essence of the fourteen points around which he based his *Essay,* the main principles of what he later would call the "science" of commerce, in the end revolved around artificially establishing and maintaining an unequal trade with the world.[116] By importing raw materials and exporting manufactured goods, England could generate the wealth to keep economic, political, and religious pretenders at bay.[117] The looming threat was that overseas subjects would begin to emulate their subjugators, that colonial dependencies would realize the economic benefits of the manufacturing revolution and sabotage England's high-wage strategy. Sharing the same climate and resources, Ireland particularly came to play a cardinal role in Cary's political economy precisely because its woolen manufactures, like India's calicoes, could "undersell those of England." As he put it in a manuscript, Ireland produced "Plenty of good combing Wooll," and because "Manufacturers can live cheaper there then in England," it "should be the great endeavour of the Kingdome of England to discourage the working up this Wooll there, and to encourage its being brought over hither."[118] He therefore relentlessly repeated that Ireland had to be "reduced to the state of a colony" and prohibited to develop local manufactures, a point to which he soon would return with a vengeance.[119]

External threats too, chiefly France and Italy, jeopardized England's commerce along with her political and religious liberties. The former, Cary noted wearily, had already begun to protect their manufactures as England did, with possibly disastrous results. France was "like a Tavern" where Englishmen exchanged valuable raw wool for useless luxuries.[120] History, however, taught the appropriate countermeasures. The only way to respond to the consequences of Colbert's challenge in France was to imitate the old policies of Edward III, who by "keeping our Wool at home, put a stop to [Flemish] manufacture." Without English raw materials, French manufactures would fail as their Flemish predecessors had. Were this policy only possible, Cary was "apt to think their Manufactures will come to little," and the French threat thus averted.[121] He similarly explained how "prudent a Thing it is to stop an Evil in the Beginning" when praising England's success in outcompeting the Portuguese textile industry and undermining their navy with the Navigation Acts, further emphasizing the synergy between the two: "the portugueze, as they are now become bad Navigators, so they are not great Manufacturers."[122] Italy, whose manufactures once had supplied Europe and whose industry was thus hardly "in the beginning," was a tougher nut to crack. In spite of England's best efforts, the peninsula retained woolen manufactures for export, forcing Cary to suggest more ruthless remedies. Since Europe produced only so much wool every year, all of it "manufactured somewhere," it was preferable to corner the world's market for raw wool and "burn" the "Overplus" at "the Charge of the Public (as the *Dutch* do their Spices)" than to let it be fabricated elsewhere. This would elevate the value of English manufactures and cut off Italian workers from their raw materials.[123] The threat of foreign industry was so grave that in cases where merchants shipped raw wool abroad, justice should stop just short of "punishing the Exporter with Death."[124] Cary's belligerent political economy might have been particularly blunt, but it rested safely on a venerable, bipartisan tradition in England of protecting national industries at the expense of those of other nations.[125]

While the Navigation Acts might be the most notorious such laws, they were far from the first. English shipping had been nationalized already in 1381, and an act forbidding "any merchaunt straunger, by himself or by any other persone, in any yere to come bye any Wolles" was passed in 1498.[126] By 1603, Venetian officials noted with fear and awe that "The English are becoming absolute masters of these [Mediterranean] waters; for apart from rapine and robbery perpetrated daily on all sorts of vessels . . . they are utterly supplanting your subjects in the carrying trade, weakening your customs and ruining the merchant service" by ignoring and circumventing customs and thus "defrauding" *La Serenissima*.[127] The same outrage at England's militarization of trade was voiced that year by French representatives, who complained about "the pillage of French shipping and of violence committed by the English." This because the "English race in all matters of marine, not only does not esteem but actually despises every other nation in the world."[128] English economic interests were systematically protected from foreign wares by sympathetic legislation just as their workshops and citizens were defended from invasions by a vigilant navy. Their merchants and manufacturers could safely turn their hungry eyes on foreign markets, often conceived of as spaces of relentless conflict and power politics.[129] Individual merchants and importers of manufactures sometimes suffered under this regime, and so did those dependent on increasingly militarized seaways, but war offered its own opportunities for profit.[130]

The Cromwellian colonel Richard Lawrence claimed in 1682 that "a principal Piece of State-policy" for statesmen was "to know how to encrease their own and lessen their neighbours Trade," and Davenant candidly admitted, during the debates over the Board of Trade, that "for the well-governing and protection of trade many things must perhaps be done that may thwart the interest of other nations."[131] Or, as he put with regard to continuing sabotage of French economic interests, "if this Interruption of their Commerce be yet more strictly pursued, it will bring a Ruin upon them, not to be avoided by all their Oeconomy, Courage and Policy."[132] At the time, the major writers on the subject rejoiced along Cary's lines that "almost the whole World is supplied by our labour."[133] Even Barbon, whose name is so often invoked as a champion of laissez-faire, thought "all Trading Countries Study their Advantage by *Trade*, and Know the difference of the Profit by the Exchange of wrought Goods, for unwrought," and suggested laying "great Duties" on competing foreign manufactures, by which "*Trade* will continue Open, and Free."[134] By force of arms where necessary, England was to achieve a monopoly on the world's manufactures, acquiring primacy in international trade by differentiating tariffs to encourage the importation of raw materials and the exportation of finished goods. This was the essential message, formulated and executed long before the "Glorious Revolution," of which Cary's *Essay* was one of the most trenchant carriers.

Financial and Moral Reform

Primarily interested in questions of production and exchange, the *Essay* had but briefly touched on coinage and credit.[135] With the advent of the Nine Years' War, however, financial structures became so complex that a singular attention to imports and exports sufficed to explain neither economic development nor military and economic interactions between nations. For centuries, English monarchs had looked abroad for sources of sovereign lending, often with catastrophic results for all parties involved, and only with the war of 1688–97 did a proper public debt emerge in England on the Dutch model, itself an emulation of earlier Italian institutional innovations. The subsequent financial revolution could not be ignored by Cary and his contemporaries.[136] At least nineteen separate acts of Parliament passed between 1690 and 1697 regarded "granting an aid to their majesties," sometimes in the form of millions of pounds through direct taxes and, more often, through the issuing of bonds "towards carrying on a vigorous war against France."[137] The first loan issued to William III was an unprecedented £1.2 million, which London's financiers were able to subscribe at an average rate of £100.000 *a day*.[138] By the end of the Nine Years' War, the public debt reached £16.7 million, a staggering sum at a time when concentrations of capital in private business seldom exceeded £10,000.[139]

The greatest part of the public debt went to finance ongoing hostilities, particularly for expenditures relating to the Royal Navy. This inaugurated an important trend in the economic history of the British Empire, a trend that would make the English population one of the most heavily taxed in Europe.[140] The stability of the debt was of pressing strategic importance for the survival of England's liberties, and the debate that ensued among contemporary political economists betrays the way this rapidly changing framework for thinking about wealth and war increased the attractiveness of politically conservative positions. The traditionalist reaction against credit-based war financing, and its sibling vice of a standing army oppressing civil liberties, is often associated with the "Country party" and the so-called neo-Harringtonian tradition of political philosophy in the period, drawing emotional energy from the works of Machiavelli and Harrington's Anglo-Venetian utopia *Oceana*. Again, however, Cary's lack of learning saved him from the anxieties of more erudite contemporaries. Embracing the ongoing cultural revolution first sparked by the invention of gunpowder, he had no qualms about de facto arguing against the Machiavellian position. "Money," Cary wrote without pause, "we know to be the Sinews of War."[141]

Similarly, he remained unfazed by the parallel issue of the standing army, by the crisis of the ancient and Renaissance idea that a free state depended on the defensive capabilities of its armed citizenry. The logic of the division of labor at the core of Cary's conception of commercial society dictated a submission to the skill and expediency of professional armed forces. Unencumbered by canonical writings on the subject, and analytically unable or unwilling to problematize the institution of political representation, he saw no harm in entrusting the warring forces of the state to one arm of the body politic and its mercantile to another. As far as both answered to Parliament and thus the people, such a division could not infringe on their liberties or virtue. Rather, he embraced the emerging topos of the "citizen-investor" whose contribution to the security of the *patria* was greater than any soldier's.[142] As with the Navigation Acts of 1651, war and wealth went hand in hand to protect and expand the state and its citizens in ways that seriously challenged older institutions and their modern historiography.[143]

These changes in the country's financial and military structures did, however, have other repercussions to which Cary reacted more readily. By far the predominant currency at the time was the silver coin, amounting to roughly 60 percent of all money in circulation.[144] Payment imbalances during the Nine Years' War drastically reduced the output of new coins from the Tower Mint while simultaneously increasing the rate of numismatic adulterations like clipping and counterfeiting. Existing coins in circulation therefore steadily deteriorated, and the value of the silver contained in them sank compared to its nominal value. As it became cheaper to pay off foreign debts in bullion than through bills of exchange, the supply of coin contracted to the point where the problem of coinage could no longer be ignored or simply left to an increasingly draconian legal system that, considering corrupting of coinage "treason," sent a steady stream of clippers and counterfeiters to the gallows under Isaac Newton's merciless supervision.[145] Countries, Cary wrote, "guarded" their coins "with Laws, equally Sanguinary with those which secured their Crowns."[146]

A flurry of pamphlets erupted in the mid-1690s, in an episode known as the "recoinage crisis," with a general division between those arguing for a full recoinage at the original value and those arguing such a measure should be accompanied by an increase in the value of the coin reissued—a de facto devaluation in terms of foreign exchange. Lowndes, the treasury secretary, argued that the recoinage should be followed by a 25 percent increase in the value of silver coins above what their bullion content would otherwise indicate to avoid immediate resmelting by acquisitive miscreants. Locke, his most famous opponent, argued that such an increase would be meaningless, as the constancy of silver content ensured by the recoinage would stabilize prices and put a stop to social anxiety regarding the corruption of currency.[147] Locke received Cary's *Essay* in the middle of this crisis and recognized a kindred soul in the Bristol merchant. Cary's first letter to Locke was not only a passionate endorsement of his argument against debasement, it also succinctly summarized his own reasoning on the matter, indeed the very essence of his *Essay:* to find the cause of money leaving for the continent, one had to look in the realms of production, not finance.[148]

Locke's response was enthusiastic. He informed Cary not only that his *Essay* was *"the best discourse I ever read on that subject"* but also that it finally might "awaken and informe" the "country Gent" of the importance of "a right ordering of Trade."[149] In a recent monetary pamphlet, Locke had noted that "though the Country Gentleman" was "not very forward to think so," it was "an undoubted truth" that "he is more concern'd in Trade, and ought to take a greater care, that it be well manag'd, and preserv'd, than even the Merchant himself."[150] Locke recognized that he shared a program of political economy with Cary, a project of moral and economic melioration that depended on mobilizing all available resources to succeed in international competition. Cary's *Essay*, he thought, could instruct the conservative "country Gent," customarily identified with the neo-Harringtonian political persuasion, that the advent of commercial society imposed new exigencies while offering new possibilities. Soon afterward, Cary sent Locke his pamphlets related to recoinage and public finance.[151] Whereas contemporary authors like Barbon argued for separating the nominal from the intrinsic value of currency to open the way for circulating paper tenders, Cary remained close to Locke's more conservative attitude toward bullion. Coins, he maintained, "receive their values from their Weights, not from their Names, though some unthinking People have supposed otherwise."[152]

Cary was no chrysohedonist—he later proposed a form of paper currency secured in Parliament—but he insisted on this point because of the facility with which metallic currencies could be traded abroad even in wartime. In addition to his experiences in international trade, Cary had earlier ventured into alchemy and the nature of metals in an unpublished manuscript. Characteristically concluding with a comparative study of foreign coins and their values, it theorized that the international market for gold and silver expediting international trade at the time lacked a paper counterpart.[153] "The Kingdom of *England* may Trade till it becomes Bankrupt," he echoed a widespread supposition, but it was foreign, not domestic trade that made a nation rich and independent. The ontological assumptions of Cary's political economy required expanding commercial horizons, an imperialist impetus prone to acquire violent form in the context of England's widespread culture of national exceptionalism. The state's call for recoinage was an urgent affair, lest people got used to and came to accept counterfeiting and adulterations detrimental to foreign trade.[154] Cary reiterated Locke's argument that "Fear"—a central if underanalyzed coordinate in the sociology of commercial society—was the reason for currency disturbances, believing it would settle correctly once the recoinage calmed popular anxieties about market uncertainties.[155] At this point, however, Cary's theories ventured well beyond those of Locke.

Locke's writings on coinage originally stemmed from a 1668 memorandum he wrote for the Earl of Shaftesbury against Child's proposal to lower the interest on money by law and were only moderately revised to fit the economic and political climate of the 1690s.[156] Locke had certainly emphasized that the important issue of money was the "quickness of its Circulation," not its volume, but the financial structures he assumed were no longer current, leading him to underestimate "credit" as only "an Assurance of Money in some short time."[157] Locke's critique of Child, in 1668 as in the 1690s, was driven by the political aim of hamstringing the large monopolistic companies, which would have benefited more than the merchant community at large by a lowering of the interest, and he found justification for this aim in a never fully articulated faith in the existence of natural laws shaping the economic sphere. Following the ideas of Hugo Grotius and Samuel von Pufendorf, one could possibly delineate the existence of a natural rate for interest.[158] While Cary agreed with Locke's political aims as well as his proposals for policy, he arrived at them from an analysis of the emerging credit economy of commercial society rather than from the principles of natural law.

Given that labor and manufactures were the core of political economy, manipulating financial variables like interest rates and the denomination of bullion was putting the cart before the horse. Nothing good would come of raising the money, and energy should instead be invested in establishing an alternate source of national credit to the Bank of England, of which his brother Richard Cary was a director, through which existing money would travel further, animating the fortunes of widows and the elderly by putting them to the use where they were needed, among merchants and manufacturers.[159] He defined "Credit" as "That, which makes a smaller Sum of *Money* pass as far as a greater," in other words as the engine of economic circulation. But whereas the Bank of England had been dominated by the interests of London, Cary again looked for institutional structures able to encourage commerce and manufactures throughout the country, capitalizing the entire kingdom.[160] "Credit" was "as necessary to a Trading Nation, as Spirits are to the Circulation of the Blood in the Body natural," and to restrict it was to invite economic gangrene.[161]

If "secured" by government, a low-interest national bank could contribute greatly to England's wealth and make it an international financial center, a haven for foreigners seeking safe and profitable investments. "It must be a *Credit* setled on an unquestionable Foundation," the "Parliament" of England, for only that would secure "Circulation."[162] Through the financial-parliamentary nexus, citizens were both lenders and borrowers, political investors in their own futures. Once the "wheels" of trade were in "Circular Motion," profits from such credit could, "imitat[ing] our Wise Neighbours," be invested in "Rewards" for those "whose honest Heads have grown Gray in the Service of the Publick." But profits could facilitate even grander projects, peaceful as well as warlike, from irrigation to road-building, public employment, the encouragement of "inventions," and the Royal Navy to "out do our industrious Neighbours the *Dutch*, even in their own way"; England was to emulate Dutch financial institutions, if not its entrepôt trade. Just as in the *Essay*, Cary envisioned a cardinal role to be played by the state in economic affairs, and he found funding for such governmental interventions in the profits from national banking. English war expenditure was vast, but a small part could be invested in peaceful domestic activities. Yet, again, there was no point in merely manipulating financial variables when the key to wealth was production, which would be better invigorated by the establishment of a national credit than by "raising the coin." Characteristically, Cary concluded his treatise by arguing for the military necessity of a proper public credit.[163]

His second pamphlet on the subject picked up where the first one left off, with Locke's opinions on recoinage vindicated and his own call for a secure national credit established. Unlike other countries, England was uniquely endowed to establish the "Great Superstructure" of a national credit, for its foundations would be "the Peoples Liberties." As long as Englishmen enjoyed *"their own Laws,"* all would be well.[164] "The *French*" could not "Erect a Bank on any sort of Security, because the Will of that Prince being his Law, alters according to his present Occasions." No other country but England was "capable of Erecting a Bank which may draw the Eyes of *Europe*." Only the "Power with whom we intrust our Lives, Liberties, and Estates," only the sovereign citizenry, could "destroy" Cary's ambitions plans. Such Lockean rights were uniquely conducive to commercial success, but they were in turn entirely dependent on England's ever-increasing comparative wealth; liberty bred power and commerce, and vice versa. The arbitrary power of absolutist hierarchies on the other hand, which could lessen the "security" of liberty and estates, was poison to credit, to commerce, and to England itself.[165]

In the context of these debates over financial reform, it is striking that Cary, like Locke, largely ignored the vexing problems of public debt redemption.[166] Only in 1719, at the very end of his life, would he turn to the problem that nearly paralyzed Hume's sturdy economic sensibilities in the 1750s.[167] The only change Cary suggested to his earlier proposals was tying people's money to the public debt directly through the institution of a reformed national bank. While still envisioning that the bank's profits could go toward improving infrastructure and undertaking large public works, he now argued that the principal "Profits of this Bank shall wholly rebound to the Benefit of the Publick, whereby the Debts of the Nation will be sunk by degrees." Cary envisioned that the increasing public debt could be redeemed quickly and efficiently by capitalizing on the differences in percentage points at which funds were mediated through the existing public debt and the new national bank.[168] The new bank could "Lend to the Government at Five *per Cent*, what they Borrow at Four," and the "Overplus of One *per Cent*."

would alleviate the public debt and pay for public works. Experience told Cary that the difference of one percentage point, "the Foundation whereon the whole Structure is built," was consistent with reigning practice, for the national bank, with branches all over Great Britain, would be "Supported by an Universal Consent."[169] It is hard to imagine a clearer statement of the perceived interconnection between democracy and public finance, of the nexus through which people can be empowered by investing directly in their political community. There were no limits to Cary's optimism at the prospects of a commercial society based on parliamentary principles, and just as he avoided anxiety over standing armies, so his political vision saw no coming deluge in the public debt.

Theory and Practice

An internal threat Cary *did* identify regarded the organization of domestic labor, and strategic and religious motivations were irrevocably intertwined when, around the time of his *Essay*'s publication, he found himself in a position to test the practicality of his theories. The hope in cultural circles such as his own, successful enough to heed biblical concerns for those less fortunate, was that the legacy of the "Glorious Revolution" could open the way for social amelioration, whereby ever larger groups were "civilized" as the country grew wealthier.[170] The practical manifestation of this hope was the Society for Reformation of Manners.[171] The Bristol chapter of this movement was driven by the city's Merchant Venturers, their interests converging in the essential issue of establishing a proper work ethic, of shaping England's economic culture. Fueled by an Anglican emphasis on the economic importance and divine dignity of labor, this was particularly evident in Cary's conflux of theological and mercantile interests.[172]

The Society for Reformation of Manners sought not merely to turn the unemployed poor into productive members of society, but also to educate them and to empower them to partake in their own polity. With time, it was hoped that they would graduate from the workhouse to become apprentices to local merchants and manufacturers, just as Cary had been. This meant making them citizens, an undertaking that would spark a host of imitations across the British Isles at a time when now canonical republicans like Andrew Fletcher of Saltoun actively proposed a return to slavery as the best means of resolving the problem of poverty.[173] Cary's fear had always been that exporting raw materials and importing manufactured goods would create jobs abroad while unemployment ran rampant at home, and his project was also aimed at satisfying the kingdom's labor needs domestically.[174] As a contemporary remarked before encouraging putting the poor to work, "Art and Labour are the only Philosophers Stone that turns the Product of the Earth into Gold."[175]

Cary had probably encountered proposals for workhouses in Child's famous treatise, in the numerous pamphlets of Richard Haines, whom he seems to have paraphrased, and in the actual schemes realized in those years by Thomas Firmin.[176] Likewise, Locke had written a note on "Labour" sometime in 1693, castigating "the governments of the world" for their "carelessness and negligence" regarding the labors of their subjects, an issue on which he would elaborate a few years after the Bristol workhouse was successfully established. In September 1697, Locke had Cary invited to present his project to the Board of Trade, an event at which the two met in person, and it was only after this encounter that Locke composed his famous memorandum now known as *An Essay on the Poor Law*, which essentially reiterated Cary's scheme.[177] Setting the poor to work would bring about a twofold benefit: labor would "civilize" the poor and allow them to provide for their own material needs, alleviating precarious state finances strained by the costs of the Nine Years' War.[178]

The records of the Bristol Corporation of the Poor, established to organize the endeavor, confirm Cary's own description of what came to be known only as the "workhouse," at first set up on behalf of Bristol's seventeen parishes to provide work for poor girls, and later boys and "our ancient people" as well. Cary and his fellow investors in the venture provided room, board, hourly wages, and, exceptionally, free education for poor women by employing them in the preliminary treatment of raw materials for local manufactures. It was a remarkable enterprise, by "which means," he beamed, "we won them into Civility, and a love to their Labour."[179]

He had successfully proven what he had promised in his *Essay*. Street urchins could be fed, civilized, and taught to become productive members of society if only given the opportunity through employment in domestic manufactures.[180] Yet he also valued "nothing that cannot be reduced to a certainty in practice."[181] The question of the project's financial feasibility remained. "Whether," he wrote, "their Labours at the Rates we were paid, would answer the Charge of their Maintenance; and if not, our great doubt was how we might advance it, without prejudicing the Manufactures." England's place in the European hierarchy of power was precarious, and not even such a noble endeavor could be allowed to undermine England's hard-won liberties. As Cary had predicted, though, experience and technical changes in the process of production *could* increase the wages of the laboring poor, as was done within the first year of operation; "Idle drones" were made "industrious bees" while simultaneously strengthening England's position in international competition.[182] Bringing the general population into enlightenment and industry was an issue not simply of Christian charity for the sake of the next world but of immediate strategic importance in this one, and he was consequently quick to formulate the national relevance of his workhouse scheme.[183]

Countervailing Empires

Much as Cary successfully implemented the *Essay*'s plans for an industrializing enlightenment, he helped realize its imperial dimension. Securing trade with the American and Caribbean colonies against French aggression and commercial competition was a pressing concern for Bristol merchants in the 1690s. Alongside Barbados, Newfoundland had played a pivotal role in Bristol's colonial imagination since the Genoese explorer Giovanni Caboto, better known as John Cabot, had first sailed from there with a local crew to claim parts of the New World for England in 1497. Old World fishermen had reaped the rich fisheries of the area for centuries, but English interests now sought to monopolize that trade.[184] The principal area of contention was the region known as l'Acadie, permanently settled by the French in 1606, fourteen years before the *Mayflower* dropped anchor off Cape Cod. In Acadia, French settlers had forged alliances of trade and kinship with the Míkmaq Indians, developing a unique hybrid culture in the liminal land where the French and English empires intersected. They habitually proclaimed neutrality in conflicts but were, because of their special relations with the natives, consistently blamed for Indian attacks on New England. The Massachusetts General Court went as far as offering a record bounty of £50 for Indian scalps in the region, and retaliatory forces burned Acadian farms, slaughtered their cattle, and threatened to scalp them too.[185] English skirmishes with the French over fishing rights—the trade of which principally still went through Cary's Bristol—in Acadia intensified in the late seventeenth century to the point where the French invaded Newfoundland in 1696.

Noël Danican, the great "merchant-privateer" of St. Malo, had contracted with Louis XIV to conquer English Newfoundland toward the end of the Nine Years' War, one of many examples at the time of privatized state warfare, or rather of piracy acquiring a national dimension, sometimes in spite of official interests. Merchants and privateers waged war on each other, enemy interests, and shifting alliances of Indians from the Spanish Main to Hudson Bay, becoming, as James Pritchard has demonstrated, "surrogates of their respective states." The result, particularly for the

French war interest, was a debilitating lack of coordination between forces and an inadequate vision of long-term imperial development. Louis XIV, it has been argued, was still too preoccupied with dynastic affairs to conceive seriously of France's empire as an organic system of core and colonies.[186] Comparatively, Cary belonged to a new breed, writing his *Essay* to supply English policy-makers with an imperial political economy, and his involvement in the Newfoundland affair was precisely to secure the correct application of this vision.

It was reported in November 1696 that France had reinvaded Newfoundland with "eleven ships and several hundred men," taking "twenty-nine ships" and causing a "general devastation."[187] As one observer reported in an attempt to divert English ships and troops there, French forces "committed bloody and tragical hostilities" in Newfoundland ("all in Bonavista were put to the sword," another source said), requiring a "squadron of good cruising ships" to carry out "revenge." Not only were valuable fishing banks jeopardized but, "as it is America," it was conceived that there could be "silver veins in that part of the country as in Peru and Mexico" that now were lost to the enemy.[188] Similar calls for military intervention occurred frequently over the following months, but only when the West Country merchants, represented principally by Cary, demanded an expeditionary force to convoy their merchantmen to Newfoundland did the Admiralty act.[189] "We beg that two fourth-rate frigates may be sent there with all imaginable speed," he and two fellow merchants urged the authorities, along "with one hundred soldiers, ten cannon and an engineer."[190] The use of military force to win and secure foreign fisheries was entirely in line with the spirit of his *Essay*, but this time the sinews of England's empire were being strained beyond their capacity.

The Admiralty heeded these demands and more, sending three fourth-rate frigates to Newfoundland to convoy the merchantmen with which Cary was affiliated. The flotilla was joined shortly after arrival by Commodore John Norris's fleet of ten warships, by which time the English contingent to Newfoundland numbered fifteen hundred troops under the command of Colonel John Gibsone.[191] That traders like Cary could sway the allocation of scarce military resources in wartime is remarkable, but evident in the Admiralty's inquiry whether its "instructions" for deployment would "answer the service to the satisfaction of the merchants."[192] But it was equally telling of how wealth, war, and empire were conflated by contemporary statesmen. In a 1698 Admiralty report to the House of Commons, the Royal Navy totaled 266 ships, from the first-rate, one-hundred-gun ship of the line *Britannia* to the yacht *Squirrel*. At the time, *all* first- and second-rate frigates were either "In Repair" or in "Want of great Repair," only five ships composed the West-India Squadron, four the East-India Squadron, and five were set to "Attend the Plantations." Of 266 ships, only 88 were seaworthy. In the context of the final months of conflict, and in comparison with the naval presences later allotted to more famous colonial possessions, Cary had arranged a considerable investment of force.[193]

News arrived in the New World of the "expedition to Newfoundland" on 26 May 1697, but "nothing but destruction" resulting from the "barbarous fury" of the Frenchmen met Gibsone's ships when they landed at St. John's on 7 June.[194] The English had lost all but two of their settlements in the area, with losses totaling "200 killed, 700 prisoners, and 200,000 quintals of cod."[195] Taking the 1699 price of Newfoundland merchantable cod as an approximation, this amounted to a booty of £135,000, enough to pay for four first-rate warships or 8877 man-years of labor in Durham.[196] The French themselves had left, their reinforcements proving warweary.[197] Proof of the true exhaustion of the warring countries in the spring of 1697, however, came from a surprising quarter, when Baron Bernard Desjean de Pointis's storm-tossed joint-stock armada of buccaneers unexpectedly arrived laden with treasure—after sacking Cartagena and braving all that Mother Nature and Anglo-Dutch forces could muster—in Newfoundland on its way back to Brest. Seeing the freshly equipped English squadron, the baron, by now the world's most wanted man, flamboyantly decided to "offer them battle," but the English commanders declined his challenge.[198]

And, his mission effortlessly successful, Gibsone took the opportunity neither to take war to the French nor look for the fabled subarctic Potosí. Instead, going out of his way to avoid confrontations, he wrote in a reverie to the Council of Trade, describing Newfoundland's Edenic flora and fauna.[199] His rambling report was perhaps symptomatic of England's financial and military exhaustion as the most dramatic consequences of the "Glorious Revolution" came to an end. As one English colonist put it less oneirically, "we are greatly oppressed and impoverished by a tedious wasting war."[200] This exhaustion also demarcated the limits of Cary's political and economic vision. However ingenious a theory of expansion, it inevitably ran into the exigencies of practical implementation; however successful countries were at emulating the wealthier and more powerful, they would inevitably themselves be the victims of emulation. The Newfoundland affair became a festering wound in France's colonial pride, profoundly inflecting the first translation of the *Essay* fifty years later. But meanwhile, the time had come to consolidate Britannia's empire.[201]

The Case of Ireland

In his very first letter to the Bristol MPs Thomas Day and Robert Yate, Cary concluded by discussing "the affairs of Ireland, whose Trade will in a short time eat up ours, except some stop be put to it, and this doth not more affect any place as much as this City."[202] A preliminary solution appears in a subsequent letter, in which the Merchant Venturers, as represented by Cary himself, argue Ireland should be reduced "to the terms of a Colony, equall with our other settlements abroad," and that their "woollen manufactures" should be destroyed and raw wool prohibited from being sold abroad. Otherwise, England risked being undersold in foreign markets.[203] The MPs replied that these suggestions amounted to "many good thoughts," which they hoped would have their "due consideration amongst the gentlemen of England."[204] Following his success as representative of the Merchant Venturers and in the organization of the workhouse, Cary set his eyes on a seat in Parliament at the 1698 elections. The platform of his electoral campaign harnessed the only source of authority he had, both in accordance with established practice and with the more erudite "new Philosophy" of Bacon and Descartes: constituents would vote for him on the basis of his experience in, and insight into, trade and the wealth of nations, a general field of argument that he channeled into a coherent attack on the role Ireland wished to play in England's greater imperial system.[205] Having been a leitmotif of his writings, it would form the backbone of his electoral campaign.[206]

While Cary's attention to the case of Ireland might have been exceptional, he was hardly the first English political economist to turn his gaze on the neighboring island. Questions of Irish sovereignty were a constant preoccupation at least from the sixteenth century onward, from which point the island generally was assimilated with other overseas possessions in colonial debates.[207] Ireland, however, was simultaneously a colony and a kingdom, an anomalous duality fueling a rich debate around the turn of the seventeenth century.[208] Various solutions were proposed to ensure that the island remained unable to interfere with English economic interests. William Temple, onetime ambassador to Holland, had warned that Irish interests might interfere with the "Trade of *England*" in 1673, and soon afterward the merchant-pamphleteer Edward Yarranton suggested a renewal of the bill "prohibiting of *Irish*-Wools Transportation," in a dialogue that saw characters react to the rumors of wool from that island reaching Holland with exclamations like "we Clothiers may go hang our selves" and, for the sake of completeness, "I will even burn my Loom and Beam too, for I see all the World are mad."[209] William Petty proposed a more effervescent solution in his "Treatise of Ireland" a decade later: the problem could be resolved by reducing Ireland to a cattle-herding dependency of about three hundred thousand people (the Cattle Acts of 1663 and 1667 prohibiting cattle exports from Ireland were still in effect), there being no need of a "Parliament in Ireland to make Laws among the Cow-Herds and Dairy-Women."[210] Again, manufacturing activities were considered a foundational element of true political communities.

Still, nothing compared to the outflow of publications in the wake of the "Glorious Revolution," and Cary's writings were explicit contributions to the renewed debate about liberty and empire ushered in by the publication of Locke's *Two Treatises.* After a phase defying the "bloodless" moniker often assigned the revolution by historians, William III proclaimed to the Protestants gathered in Dublin in 1690 that he had come to "deliver" them from "tyranny" and "restore" their "liberties and properties."[211] Lord Sydney, inaugurating the Parliament at Dublin in 1692, similarly assured that "Their Majesties" wished that Ireland would become "as Rich and Flourishing as most of it's Neighbours." This only required "the hand of God" and the "wise, sober, and calm Determinations of your own Counsels."[212] In the absence of the former factor, however, it soon became obvious that collisions between the economic interests of England and Ireland would continue to pose a threat to Irish political sovereignty. And not surprisingly, the question of Irish wool topped the agenda when Parliament reconvened after the Nine Years' War.[213]

With the anonymous publication of the infamous *Letter from a Gentleman in the Country,* this debate over the structure of the empire turned from the economic to the explicitly political.[214] Polemically, it presented the Irish as the "most dangerous" of England's "Rivals" and a "Nursery" of "Popery and Slavery." The solution it proposed was to solidify England's imperium, ensure Ireland was "Governed by the Parliament Laws of *England.*" An argument, the anonymous author acknowledged in his concluding remarks, inspired by Cary's *Essay:* "I will trouble you no longer than to pray your Reading of Mr. *Cary of Bristols* Book, who hath writ with great Judgment and Affection to his Country on this Subject."[215] Three years after Cary first published his plans for Ireland he was explicitly invoked as foremost representative of the English imperialist side in a debate whose focus gradually evolved from Irish woolens to the political configuration of England's empire itself, over the tenuous relationship between subjects and sovereignty in that so unevenly structured political community. What exactly were the repercussions of the Williamite succession for the colonies and kingdoms united under England's Crown? What were the boundaries of their much vaunted liberties, not only in political terms of parliamentary representation but also with regard to the freedom to administer their material lives and pursue different economic activities? Until this point, Cary had only considered imperialism a question of power. Now he was forced to consider its theoretical implications as the intensified polemic came to rest on the legal and philosophical justification for reducing Ireland to the state of a colony. Could empire be legitimized, could it be just to give laws?

The *Letter* sparked a flurry of publications, some noting their indebtedness to Cary's earlier arguments.[216] The debate's high point occurred when the Irish scientist and parliamentarian William Molyneux published *The Case of Ireland, Stated,* an audacious reply to the *Letter,* defending the Anglo-Irish right to govern themselves and establish local manufactures.[217] Molyneux was a close friend and, like his nemesis Cary, an interlocutor of Locke.[218] In private correspondence he informed Locke that he had written *The Case of Ireland* with "caution and submission," but it was seldom received that way.[219] Simon Clement, one of Molyneux's more acerbic readers and seemingly an acquaintance of Cary, thought it "one of the weakest and most mistaken Books that ever was written with such a flourish of Language, and shew of Learning and Integrity," and Cary himself found Molyneux to be so "inconsistent" that he "could almost be angry."[220] The House of Commons decreed *The Case of Ireland* "of dangerous consequence to the crown and people of England," even "fatal" if "drawn into example."[221] English and Irish alike generally recoiled with horror at Molyneux's publication, many Irish fearing it only could make matters worse.[222]

Drawing on the same language of political economy as Cary, as well as a rich amalgamation of ancient constitutional precedents and natural law ("Civilians, Grotius, Puffendorf, Locke's Treat. Government, etc."),[223] Molyneux sought to make the case for Irish economic and political sovereignty on the basis of "Reason" and "Record."[224] His chosen avenues of argumentation are illuminating in the context of late seventeenth-century English legal thought. The predominant tradition of Whig jurisprudence had centered on common law as an "immemorial" custom. This argument had been undermined by the divine rights absolutist Sir Robert Filmer, whose *Patriarcha* harnessed the same vocabulary of historical precedents to show, through recourse to biblical chronology beginning with Adam, that all laws had originated in some sovereign's inalienable command, depriving proparliamentarians of their claim to political primacy. In response, building on a rich continental tradition of natural law, Locke attempted to reestablish the legal debate over parliamentary predominance on an explicitly ahistorical foundation. It was irrelevant if the House of Commons was of an "immemorial" character, for the English people anyway had a right to liberty derived from natural law.[225]

It was through the interplay of these two legal languages, through historical record and rights derived from reason, that Molyneux would make his *Case*. Returning to the earliest established English claim to Ireland, the 1171–72 conquest of Henry II, Molyneux overturned the common argument for subjection by arguing that it had been a voluntary submission, leading to an "Original Compact" between Ireland and England.[226] He relied on intellectually and emotionally loaded terms such as "original compact," "covenant," and "conquest" to make his case that "*Liberty* seems the Inherent Right of all Mankind" whether English or Irish, and thus that William III should remain faithful to his earlier promises.[227] Molyneux's argument was intricate. Henry II had only acquired power over Irishmen, not English settlers. Since the "Ancient Irish" were a minuscule percentage of the modern population, Anglo-Irish descendants of England's conquerors were Ireland's dominant inhabitants. True, England had suppressed several Irish rebellions in recent years, and these counted as "conquests" by natural law. Yet the rebels had been Catholic. Meanwhile Irish political and economic sovereignty belonged to Protestant descendants of Henry II's medieval marauders, the Anglo-Irish, who neither rebelled nor were conquered.[228] Molyneux harbored no illusions as to the efficacy of this reasoning, and wrote to Locke that "England most certainly will never let us thrive by the Wollen trade, This is their Darling Mistris, and they are jealous of any Rival."[229] He did not seek independence from England, rather regarding it as an elder sibling of a common father, the stronger equal in a composite monarchy, and a partner in empire, and hoped his argument could usher in a new era of enlightened union between the two kingdoms. He was mistaken.[230]

As one early eighteenth-century commentator noted, "several Dablers in *English* Laws and Politicks look'd upon themselves as called to *Arms*" by Molyneux's book. At least four responses were published within a year, and Cary was considered among the "prime Champions" of England's cause.[231] His long *Vindication of the Parliament of England in Answer to a Book Written by William Molyneux* was an adaptation of the general principles explored in the *Essay* to a specific problem of political economy.[232] Cary had already investigated Ireland's burgeoning wool industry in his *Essay*, concluding that it would never have arisen were it not for the Cattle Acts. Ireland, "of all the Plantations settled by the *English*," had proven the "most injurious" to their trade; "since we refuse to take the Flesh" of their animals, Cary dryly noted, "they chose to keep the Fleece."[233] It was "very convenient" for England to remain on good terms with Ireland, however, so compromise was in order.[234] Like Petty, he thought this could be accomplished if the Irish returned to their pastoral roots: "The true Interest then of *Ireland* being Husbandry, Trade and Manufactures stand diametrically opposite thereto."[235] If manufactures were absolutely necessary for Ireland, it should be limited to the less mechanizable linen trade, England being left to work the combined wool of the empire.[236] In terms of the *Essay*'s political economy, it was obvious that Ireland was relegated to poverty and dependence. Indeed, Ireland was relegated to primitivization, to a lower scale of civilization in his conjectural history of commercial societies.

Cary's earlier arguments for England's subjugation of Ireland had been based on an explicitly mercantile terminology, and they were now being contended by the arguments of an erudite scholar employing rigorous terms such as "proof," "*testimonium,*" and "evidence" to make his case.[237] "I confess my own weakness to handle a Controversie of this nature," Cary remarked, further underlining his philological inadequacy: "I shall not examine [Molyneux's] Quotations, whether they agree with the Originals or no, my Profession being not the Law, I am not furnish'd with those Books."[238] We do not know how he prepared, or whether he was helped in composing his reply to Molyneux, but he ultimately crossed the chasm that separated self-made merchants from elite legal and political theorists. Cary's earlier *Essay,* Bishop Nicholson noted in 1724, "Prepared him for a ready Encounter with Mr. *Molyneux,* whom he pursues (Paragraph by Paragraph) with a good Appearance of Skill in the Laws of both Kingdoms, and a notable Strength of Reasoning thereupon. In Short; the Merchant argues and pleads like a Counsellor at Law."[239]

But Cary nonetheless betrayed his practical intellectual formation. In his *Essay,* he had argued that "it lies in our Power to give Rules to [the Irish]," in other words to give them laws and establish empire over them in the contemporary idiom.[240] Now, he mused that it was not "very material for me to consider" on what foundations the English "*pretend* to this Power." It sufficed to "assert and prove, that the Parliaments of *England* did exercise this Power."[241] Might continued to make right, for as one Irish commentator later summarized Cary's "grand position," all privileges granted Ireland in the past could be ignored by virtue of England's "supreme dominion over all parts of the empire."[242]

Beyond the disputed legal record, however, perhaps the most surprising aspect of this polemic was the prominent part played by Locke's *Two Treatises* in setting the framework of the discourse. Was this an instance of legitimate resistance, similar to the one England herself had acted on in recent revolutions, or were the Irish merely capricious? While it is often held that Locke's authorship of the work remained unknown in the period, Molyneux's treatise explicitly named Locke as their author in print, and his critics gladly followed suit without demonstrating the least surprise. As part of his argument for the natural right of the Irish to self-government, Molyneux had referred to "an Incomparable *Treatise* . . . said to be written by my Excellent Friend, John Locke, Esq . . . [that] the Greatest Genius in *Christendom* need not disown." Privately, he confronted Locke directly over the politics of the 1699 "wool bill," stating: "How justly they can bind us without our *Consent* and *Representatives,* I leave the *Author* of the *Two Treatises of Government* to Consider." Locke himself was "mightily surprised" by Molyneux's publication.[243] The episode testifies to the wide chasm separating theory from practice. Locke, whose *Two Treatises* have been used ever since by people justifying participation in their own government, proved unwilling to abandon the tenets of reason of state and the expansive politics of power and necessity. Political principles and natural law be what they may, he reverted to his earlier more conservative persona at the very moment when his ideas could be implemented.[244] While Molyneux relied on Locke's theoretical writings to argue for Ireland's liberty to organize its economy, Locke himself, as a member of the Council of Trade and Plantations, was an influential colonial administrator translating theories into policies, and his doctrines could anyway be remarkably polyvalent.[245]

Although Locke's 1669–70 *Fundamental Constitution of Carolina* established the first European landed hereditary nobility in the New World and invested the ruling palatine with almost absolute power, it also delineated a strikingly tolerant society, and what brief passages it contained on economic issues diverged remarkably from the ideas informing the regulation of the English imperial economy at the time. In fact, the list of concerns in the comptrollers' care hardly reflects a colonial context at all, including "foreign and domestic trade, manufactures, public buildings and workhouses." Manufactures were as integral a part of civil society in the colonies as in the metropolis. Just as England's "ancient constitution" was to be exported, so was its rich economic structure.[246] This insight, so alien to Cary's scheme, emerged again when Locke was prompted to suggest ways of alleviating Virginia's grievances in 1697. He suggested not only the use of "Privileges and Immunities" to encourage trade there but also the introduction of varied manufactures and, echoing his caveats on property in the *Second Treatise,* a reform to redistribute private lands exceeding their owners' capacity to work.[247]

Locke's colonial imagination had, however, at times shown a more authoritarian vein. In his pseudo-utopian scribbles on *Atlantis* in the 1670s, he had envisioned a colonial society in which the exigencies of the common good dictated the most minute aspects of individual life.[248] Perhaps for religious reasons—toleration notoriously not extending to Catholics and atheists—Locke's approach to Irish industrialization seems inspired by his Atlantean musings rather than by his writings on Carolina and Virginia, and he spearheaded the Board of Trade's work to prohibit the exportation of Irish woolen manufactures for the common good of the English empire. Following Cary, he instead suggested the Irish could turn to linens, tempering their poverty with less lucrative manufactures that did not compete with England's staple industry.[249]

Curiously, Molyneux's critics shared the ambiguity of Locke's colonial vision, agreeing on the principles expounded by the *Two Treatises* but disagreeing on their implementation. Clement thought that "Liberty, the right of all Mankind" was "a Glorious Topick" yet claimed that the "Arguments for the Liberty and Right of all Mankind; that Conquest cann't bind Posterity, &c. are wholly misapply'd in this Case," concluding that Molyneux "abuses Mr. *Lock.*" This because the Irish "willfully" had become part of the "English Empire," abandoning the "state of Nature," and thus—Clement repeatedly invoked the widespread imperialist idiom of *dare legem* to argue—subjected themselves to its sovereignty by consenting to "receive" the "English laws."[250] Charles Leslie too sought to undermine Molyneux's appropriation of Locke's arguments: "Now, if a People can give up their own Rights (which according to Mr. Lock, & c. (from whom Mr. *Molyneux* takes it) upon Trust) is the *Original* and *Foundation* of all Government; what more *Authentick* Method can be taken, than to have them *Surrendred* by the *Cession* and *Submission* of the *Representatives* of the *People* in *Parliament.*" This was why "the *English,* as well as the *Irish,* in *Ireland,* are in the Condition of *Slaves;* and to be disposed of, both as to their *Lives* and *Fortunes,* without any *Consent* of their own."[251] William Atwood was similarly incensed by Molyneux's use of Locke: "This Gentleman," Atwood wrote, "thinks he has silenced all the *Patriots of Liberty and Property,* by his warm Appeals to them."[252] Like the other critics, Cary approved of Molyneux's argument *"That the Right of being subject only to such Laws to which Men give their own Consent, is so inherent to all Mankind, and founded on such immutable Laws of Nature and Reason, that 'tis not to be alienated, or given up, by any Body of Men whatsoever."*[253] Also like them, however, Cary's *Vindication* rejected the conclusions Molyneux drew from his reading of Locke:

> You are very much beholding to the ingenious Mr. Lock, for the fineness of your Argument, about the State of Conquest, &c. in the former part of your Book, which I do not at all blame you for, because I think no Man can handle a Subject smoothly, whereon he hath treated, that doth not follow his Copy; but I blame you for not applying those excellent Arguments more fitly.[254]

What did Cary mean by "fitly"? He had repeatedly summoned the paradigm of the body politic, concluding that "I take *England* and all its Plantations to be one great Body, those being so many Limbs or Counties belonging to it." The English empire was a person with rights to liberty. The "first Design" of its subsidiary colonies was that the "People of *England* might better maintain a Commerce and Trade among themselves, the chief Profit whereof was to rebound to the Center."[255] England had the privilege of being the "head," and, "standing like the Sun in the midst of its Plantations," it would "not only refresh them, but also draw Profits from them."[256] Cary wrote in private correspondence that letting Ireland interfere with English economic interests was nothing less than "opening a vein in man's body, and letting him bleed to death."[257] Everyone was better off with the colonial system than without it, because only imperial power and plenty could secure the liberty of all its inhabitants.[258] The alternative was dissolution and dependence on foreign powers. If Ireland kept pursuing its own good rather than that of the empire, England would "neither [be] able to support its self, nor the Plantations that depend upon it, & then consequently they must crumble into many distinct independent Governments & whereby becoming weak will be a Prey to any stronger power which shall attacque them."[259]

Though there existed pertinent feedback mechanisms between them, the political was entirely subordinated to the economic in Cary's vision. The liberty of all, procured through economic and military means, could prevail only through the submission of some. The imperial body politic was more important than its individual members, its liberty a precondition for all others': "The health of the commonwealth is to be preferred before that of any part, when it sets up a distinct interest alone, as the security of a government before that of a private person when he endeavours to overthrow it."[260] The common good supposedly trumped individual interests in Cary's social and political imagination, but his common good was better and more common in England than in its colonies.

The quid pro quo was protection. Cary offered Protestants in Ireland "Security of Religion, Liberty, and Property" as well as defense against "Foreign Powers and *Popish* Cut-throats" in exchange for submission to England's Parliament.[261] The fact that the Irish decided to call their "colonial assembly" a "Parliament" was only a matter of appearances ("you Build too much on the Name," Cary chastised Molyneux), and they still had to return to England if they wished to be "represented" politically.[262] The political zone of Cary's empire was sharply distinguished from its areas of influence and interest. The "head" was limited to the "original" geographical expanse of England, while its political subjection and economic participation had become global in reach. As such, the "empire" was primarily an economic phenomenon for Cary, a system of dominated areas providing raw materials and markets for English manufactures. It could never be properly political, though he was careful to distinguish between different degrees of subjection to England. Curiously, given his commercial interests, Cary considered himself "no Friend to Slavery," wishing to subject Ireland rather than enslave it.[263] Many may have considered the difference rhetorical, but Cary's experiences with the Bristol slave trade might have instilled in him a more nuanced appreciation of the cruel varieties of dependence.

Incommensurable epistemes clashed over Irish woolens—philosophical idealism on the one hand, realist reason of state on the other. Years later, Sir Richard Cox, originally a partisan of Irish woolens, mused on the problems of that time. "It never entered into my Thoughts, to argue about the Natural Right," he wrote, "because it was my Business to undertake that, which was most practicable." And Cox harbored no doubts as to what the result of such a confrontation was in terms of political economy:

> Indeed he seems to be simply employed, who will spend his Time, to persuade a Nation of superior Power, by his fine-spun Argument of Natural Right. . . . Speculative Men may entertain themselves with the airy Fancy of Natural Right; but Men of Practice and Discretion will submit as early as possible to Power, which they cannot conquer.[264]

Enemies of the *Essay*

While many shared Cary's opinions, numerous other voices also arose to directly and indirectly challenge them. The very metaphor of the body politic was turned against his position by one pamphleteer who argued that punishing constituent parts of the empire was a recipe for political and economic gangrene.[265] Another writer astutely disagreed with what he considered the "Tartar's Conceit" of England's outlook, "that if they kill any man, they shall immediately enjoy his Wisdom and Beauty," that England would automatically gain whatever wealth was lost to Ireland.[266] More philosophically, the moderate Tory Edmund Bohun, onetime chief justice of Carolina, wrote Cary to tell him, as Locke did, that his *Essay* was "by far the best I have ever read," but also to say "your partiality for England has misled you." With time, Bohun argued, the "trade of the world" could allow all countries to "enlarge their trades *prope ad infinitum,* without any damage to each other if the monopolizing humour, envy, and an insatiable avarice supported by fraude and violence, did not mislead them." By thinking it a duty only to increase the wealth of England, Cary contradicted "the great designe of God almighty," which Bohun said, charting it through a "rise and progress of trade" from its origins in Tyre and Sidon, was "to civilize the whole race of mankind, to spread trade, commerce, arts, manufactures, and then Christianity from pole to pole round the whole globe of the earth."[267] England's imperial mission was one of worldly melioration in the same spirit as the "Enlightenment narratives" of the eighteenth century.[268]

But whereas these narratives would show Europe's rise from barbarism *and* religion through commerce and the refinement of the arts, Bohun's narrative projected commerce, the engine of systemic change, as a way to bring barbarians *into* religion. National monopolies of trade and manufacture could only be justified by "narrow thoughts that spring up in narrow souls." Studying the history of the progress of trade, one would realize "what naked, barbarous people" inhabited the world "till they were civilized and taught manufactures, the art of war, navigation and commerce." For all his philanthropy and civic commitment, the "narrow" parameters of Cary's plan for melioration had led him astray, and supposing that "any one nation" ever could dominate "the trade of the world" was, Bohun remarked unapologetically, "a very great piece of ignorance."[269]

This was the vital difference in their visions of global commerce and one of the great tensions of early modern political economy. Both men realized that trade was not an abstract phenomenon but a term signifying countless, complex activities with very different wealth-creating potentials, and they therefore agreed that what a country imported and exported was of paramount importance for its cultural and political viability.[270] But where Bohun wanted to spread the civilizing and enriching powers of manufactures from "pole to pole," globalizing the progressive mechanisms he had uncovered studying the Mediterranean's millennial economic heritage, Cary jealously sought to guard its benefits for England, to the extent that he argued for ruining the economies it had emulated in the first place. Both required commerce to be brought to the world, but they disagreed over its architecture, over whether all should share in the power of industry or some be forced to supply England with labor and raw materials. Bohun showed no temerity when explaining what was at stake: "I am sure God will blast all those designes that are contrary to his, and ruine those nations and companys that would ingross his blessings and joine with the devil to prevent or at least retard the civilizing the rest."[271] Cary, content in the devil's company, thought Bohun's "opinion against monopoly extraordinary" but resolutely advised him "not [to] meddle with the affairs of Ireland or Scotland."[272] As subsequent chapters will demonstrate, it would be up to Cary's translators to exorcise his *Essay* of its jealousy, unknowingly turning it into the very history he himself had suggested to Bohun six decades earlier.

Unlike Bohun, however, it is striking that some of the visions most distant from Cary's in the spectrum of Williamite political economy turned around to his position as optimism regarding free global commerce encountered the stringent demands of economic reality. A year after the first reactions to Molyneux's pamphlet, Davenant engaged with the debate as a whole with tools borrowed not from Locke but from another canonical political philosopher. Closely tied to the East India Company, Davenant had earlier sought to justify their imports of Eastern manufactures by applying Machiavellian concepts to the logic of laissez-faire, arguing for the necessity of *virtù*—the manly capacity to resist the whims of fortune—to ride the international market.[273] England should abandon those of its industries that could not compete with low-wage countries in favor of producing high-quality goods. Ireland's capacity to undersell English goods, however, demonstrated the practical limitations of this vision, and Davenant suddenly found it "undoubtedly advisable" to "intercept" the Irish when "their manufactures interfere with ours." As an eighteenth-century reader noted in his marginal annotations at this point in the 1771 edition of Davenant's works, *"The jealousy Tow.ds Scotland + Ireland shown by this author is wonderful."* Davenant also followed Cary in arguing that prohibiting Irish woolens, and even linens, was "best and most expedient for the whole [of the empire]" and that England would offer its colonies "protection" in exchange for a monopoly on manufactures. All this was only "reasonable *jealousy of state*," conceptually the opposite of noble emulation.[274]

Following in the same vein, Davenant concluded his notes on Molyneux with a striking negation of his earlier arguments. Through judicious tariff policies, the international market for *all goods*, cheap as well as expensive, was to be dominated through the very "encouragement from the state" he had railed against while writing for the East India Company.[275] He maintained this new position in a later essay, where, in a passage also highlighted with a marginal annotation by the aforementioned anonymous reader, he stated, "Machiavel lays it down for a rule seldom or never subject to exception; that in matters of empire, 'Whoever is the cause of another's advancement, is the cause of his own diminution.' One nation cannot increase in power without apparent danger to its neighbours." And Davenant's reader was so taken by this passage that he copied the quotation down on the last page of the book: " 'Whoever is the cause of another's advancement is the cause of his own diminution.' *Machiavel.*"[276] Machiavelli, in short, could also be taken to justify jealousy of trade. England had no choice but to opt for ruthless reason of state in international commerce and pursue its empire by any means, precisely as Cary had less eruditely argued.

A related, less known and more personal critique of the *Essay* had, however, appeared earlier. Cary presented his case to Parliament at the height of the 1696 debates regarding the East India Company, and his position was quickly attacked by representatives of the linen drapers, forced to contend with their former colleague to protect their professional interests.[277] Their pamphlet attacked Cary's "mistaken Maxims" to demonstrate the importance of allowing Indian imports. If England prohibited "the Commodities of other Nations," they argued, said nations would retaliate.[278] Recasting Williamite Britain as heir of Themistoclean Athens, they instead stated: "Our Ships are our Walls, our Trade our Riches," so England should become a "Free Port." They agreed that manufactures should be encouraged but differed "about the method." And as Cary had drawn on his own experience and on the common-sense tropes of fables to make his argument against the East India Company, so did the drapers in their defense of it. In aiming for all, Cary's interventionist proposals risked, like another dog in another fable, losing England what it had. But what was the alternative? Agreeing with Cary that "home consumption" did not create wealth, they argued, like the early Davenant, that Englishmen should move upmarket by consuming cheap Indian manufactures at home and exporting their more expensive woolen textiles abroad.[279]

This is not to say their vision of international trade was peaceful, for they too relied on England's colonial edge over the Dutch and on the idea that others could be forced to pay for their more expensive goods. But, refusing to accept the argument that economic activities differed in anything but costs (calicoes and "Irish Cattel" were the same for them), they believed that limitless "Free Trade" would bring down the costs of "Commodities" and thus wages, which "encourages a Foreign Trade."[280] Where Cary promoted manufactures to raise wages competitively as a result of their unique productivity gains, the linen drapers sought to lower them by supplying cheaper foreign imports. The key point, for the linen drapers as for many of the Company's other supporters in the period, was thus that "Trade . . . ought to be free, sheltered against all Prohibitions; That this hath been the Practice of Holland, whose Example we should follow in taking off all Restraints from Commerce."[281] In this they echoed the cosmopolitical stance of Dudley North and his ilk: "A Nation in the World, as to Trade, is in all respects like a City in a Kingdom, or Family in a City."[282]

Cary immediately published a pamphlet in his defense, clarifying a vital point in his *Essay:* "it is not wisdom for us to prohibit the use of the Commodities of other Nations who take off ours in their stead." The exchange of domestic for foreign manufactures was a "good trade," just like exchanging manufactures for raw materials.[283] But this, he argued, was hardly the case with Indian textiles paid for in bullion. He similarly agreed that "the Profits of a Nation do not arise from its Home Consumption" but rebuffed the linen drapers' attempt to thereby justify the "use of Forreign Manufactures instead of our own." One could not straightforwardly compare the prices of English and Indian manufactures because the cost of English textiles largely consisted of domestic wages, and therefore "is all profit to the Nation." The final goods might be more expensive if produced domestically than imported from abroad, but since the higher expenses anyway rebounded within the same national market for wages, the economy could only be strengthened by it. Unlike North, whose proposals depended entirely on the abstraction that boundaries did not matter, Cary refused to ignore the political framework of economic life.

It was clear to Cary that English consumers, bound to English producers in a closed synergy of economic activities at a deeper level than the country's international relations, undermined their own purchasing power and ultimately their own country by importing manufactured goods in exchange for anything but other manufactured goods. What mattered was not only what one produced but also with whom one shared a labor market. This was why he emphasized at length that "free trade" only could mean freedom of vocation, of choosing one's trade, not freedom from regulations in international trade. After all, such an abstract freedom went against every aspect of England's political economy, the rise of its manufactures, and the very history of its economic development, from Edward III through the Navigation Acts to the Williamite settlement.[284] It is in this regard worthwhile noting that a Venetian envoy reported in 1672 that England had grown rich through "a multitude of regulations," of which "the most important" was that they realized "the disadvantage of free trade in distant countries."[285] Spain had the world's richest mines, but Cary had seen its empire crumble and its wealth usurped by England, whose prosperous empire instead rested safely on the labor of its citizens. No country could ever become rich from exporting raw materials, he ultimately argued, even if said raw materials were gold and silver.[286]

Yet competition had to be taken into consideration, and changing conditions sometimes required drastically different policies. Context mattered for political economy.[287] The drapers' argument that England should follow the Dutch in becoming wealthy through free international trade failed on this very point. "Their Modus of Trade is adopted [*sic*] to their Constitution," he maintained, "which will not at all agree with ours"; in fact the "same Trade by which the *Dutch* grow rich, would soon ruine *England*." This was because Holland, a small and urbanized commercial republic, had "but one single Interest," which was "buying and selling." Having "no Product of their own," by which one must assume he intended domestic raw materials, they specialized in traffic and shipping to the point where they had "become a Magazine of Trade or Commerce." England, on the other hand, was a territorial power with "Lands to improve." This meant that it had to provide for "two interests," those of "the Freeholder" and those of "the Trader," which were "themselves of different Natures." Only legislation could render them "serviceable to each other," and if harnessed properly their agonistic tension could form the backbone of England's success.[288] The only way the East India trade ever could become "profitable" for England was if "the Traders thither" began to "import Materials instead of Manufactures."[289] Cary's endeavor remained as much a theoretical exercise in uncovering the mechanisms of economic development as a political agenda.

Cutting through this complex debate, the 1699 bill passed both Houses and rendered restrictions on Irish wool permanent, causing anger and consternation in Ireland for centuries to come.[290] Even foreign ambassadors reported on the baneful measures by which England secured its economic ascendancy.[291] Molyneux passed away soon afterward; Cary continued on his set course. The importation of printed calicoes was prohibited in 1700, yet another of Cary's proposals to be made policy, and many more would follow in the coming years.[292] His political economy, like his workhouse, had made a name for him, and he was brought ever closer to national policy-making; he was elected trustee of the 1700 Act of Resumption and sent to Ireland to organize the Williamite confiscations alongside nobles and other notables.[293] In 1704, surprisedly noting that the bill for which he had fought so pugnaciously "hath very much lessened the Balance of [Ireland's] Foreign Trade," Cary was further commissioned by Parliament to write a plan for the establishment of linen manufactures there.[294] The mechanisms of economic development he identified remained the same, and the importance of introducing civilizing manufactures in Ireland in a way that did not hamper England continued to drive his efforts.

Seemingly oblivious as to his role in the matter, Cary noted that Ireland's situation was bleak and getting worse. The establishment of an Irish linen industry was the only solution he could imagine, "being a Manufacture no way interfering with our own." The Irish could specialize in supplying cheap ingredients, in this case linen yarn, for England's more advanced manufactures. Establishing a joint stock company for this purpose would enable the poor of Ireland to "encourage Industry, and promote Improvements, both in Product and Manufactures, which are the two things that encrease the Wealth of a Nation." In such an event England would be better off, not only because Irish uprisings would be quelled but also because their increased incomes meant they would consume "more of our Manufactures there."[295] With time, these proposals would indeed reinvigorate the Irish economy, and greatly so. Whereas linen cloth exports from Ireland in 1701 were valued at £14,000, by the 1750s they averaged £750,000.[296]

Curiously, Cary here touched on the very argument with which Bohun had criticized his *Essay,* and the surface of which he himself had grazed in replying to the linen drapers: in a peaceful world ruled by emulation rather than jealousy, everybody would be richer by buying each other's ever-improving manufactures. While he never came to fully embrace this stance, he was nonetheless forced to counter yet another argument of his *Essay.* Irish landlords, he realized, would have to "leave off the way of Husbandry they are now upon, and to turn their Lands to Hemp and Flax." This would set off a virtuous chain of events, by which the "circulation" of "ready Mony" would "encourage both the Farmer and the Manufacturer," perhaps attract a few French workers, and, with any luck, "give a fatal Blow to the Kingdom of *France* in that Manufacture." Concluding, practically as always, Cary noted the "benefits" that would arise for England "during this continuance of this War."[297] No matter the attempts to disentangle them, wealth and war remained inexorably intertwined.

A Science of Trade

Following his successful work in and on Ireland, Cary's traces seem lost until he republished his books in the late 1710s, a tumultuous period that saw the War of Spanish Succession, the Union with Scotland, and the Peace of Utrecht.[298] The 1717 edition of his *Essay* not only incorporated the arguments he had explored in other writings but was often published alongside his later pamphlets, thus presenting his internationally iron-fisted and domestically philanthropic imperial political economy in its entirety. The third and fourth editions incorporated these pamphlets as formal appendixes, distilling his life's experiences into one manageable volume. Cary's final new composition, his 1718 *Vindication of the Rights of Parliament,* written from jail, where he seems to have served time for a financial misdemeanor, was his least economic and most political. Locke's influence is even more pronounced in Cary's parliamentarianism, exasperated by the direness of the situation, and it is remarkable to what extent he was able to reapply the legal vocabulary he first internalized in his polemic against Molyneux.[299]

This, though, was only symptomatic of a larger evolution in his argumentative lexicon. Having confronted Molyneux and found himself wanting (later admitting he was "not Bred to the Law"), Cary was now well versed in the writings of the jurist and parliamentarian Lord Edward Coke and began employing legal terms such as "proof" and "evidence" in his writings.[300] Cary, who had ignored legalistic phraseologies before 1698, came to confront a supposed juridical injustice against his own person in the same way he had challenged Molyneux. Although Cary was better prepared this time, we do not know the final outcome. He emphasized the "Right every Man had to defend himself" but noted, very much mirroring his Hobbesian stance on the English empire, how once these were "given up to the Society," the "whole Body became Security for the Rights of particular Persons."[301] It was of cardinal importance that rights were not violated by the sovereignty empowered to protect them. And in a curious paradox, while lamenting the injustice of tyranny wielded against him, Cary lucidly touched on the barely veiled fault lines of his Whig ideology: "But tho' all Men are Enemies to an Arbitrary Power, when Exercised over themselves, yet, the desire of Rule is so Natural, that they are very prone to Exercise it over others, when they have Opportunities."[302]

But more than Cary's political imagination was modulated by his ventures into legal theory. If his arguments were adamant, their formulations changed markedly. Just as terms such as "proof" and "evidence" emerged in his political pamphlets, so did they concomitantly appear in the new editions of his economic works. Where Cary's 1695 *Essay* had argued that textiles should be standardized, later editions suggested that "Seals and other Marks" could offer "certain Evidences to the truth of what they certifie." Similarly, where the first edition proposed the establishment of mercantile courts to facilitate trade and questions of insurance, the later editions emphasized the importance of "Proofs" in "issues at Law."[303] And again, while he had always argued against personal and corporate monopolies, Cary's reading of Coke had finally given him a precise definition.[304] This increased linguistic—rather than truly conceptual or theoretical—rigor contributed to his most revolutionary innovation.

Whereas he had once written in the crabbed style of a merchant-pamphleteer with an above-average education (though the actual degree to which he was tutored or an autodidact remains unknown), often presenting arguments haphazardly, Cary's encounter with Molyneux's legal language precipitated a change in both the style and substance of his work: to the best of his ability, Cary came to adopt some of the vocabulary and well-ordered logic of legal discourse; moreover, he merged this legalism and its contemporary insistence on "facts" and "evidence" with his own mercantile background to present a provocative new formulation: "Trade," the 1717 edition of his *Essay* proclaimed, "hath its principles as other Sciences have."[305] Locke had written about the "principles of sciences," and Child had discussed "the Art or Science of Merchandizing," meaning the individual craft of the merchant, about which an enormous literature of merchant handbooks known as the *ars mercatoria* existed.[306] Cary himself had proclaimed his intent to explore the "principles of trade," understood as a political activity of international economic competition, already in the 1695 edition of his *Essay*. Only now, however, did he connect the dots and present the "principles of trade" as a coherent "science" of wealth, a unified set of observable first principles regarding economic development from which guidelines for practice could be derived.

Trade and learning had gone hand in hand since tariffs and patents first were invented as allied institutions in Renaissance Venice, and had profoundly shaped debates about inventions and intellectual property at the foundation of the Royal Society in 1660.[307] This connection between knowledge and economic concerns was formalized when the "haberdasher" John Graunt was invited to join the Royal Society on the basis of his ingenious "Shop-Arithmetique," an elaboration of earlier Italian developments in commercial arithmetic known as the "Rule of Three," by which three knowns could solve for a fourth unknown in a ratio relationship. He entered the Royal Society as the first representative of anything like the social sciences, leading Charles II to levy a blanket call to issue memberships to any "such Tradesmen" found worthy.[308] Petty, although hailing from far more illustrious circles, had similarly been among the original chartered members of the Royal Society and founded the art of "political arithmetick," a rigorous discipline set to analyze economies "in terms of number, weight, or measure."[309] Yet, while Cary's dual interests might have been shared by certain contemporaries, nobody in his context had ever perceived of the national organization of commerce and manufactures—of political economy so to speak—as a *science* in itself, as an autonomous field of knowledge.

The idea of a "Scientific Revolution" occurring between the ages of Copernicus and Newton has been contested frequently in recent decades. It is argued that the habitual construction of the history of science, with its complementary canon of authorities, is anachronistic and teleological, tracing the development of current concepts rather than problematizing ideas and practices in their own historical contexts.[310] A powerful trend in the historiography of the subject has instead approached early modern science through the image of the Roman god Janus, whose two faces represent the mathematical, positivist approach of modern science on the one hand and the earlier works on alchemy and natural philosophy out of which this grew on the other, the latter being intricately intertwined with hermetic and magic currents in early modern learned culture.[311] Polymathic as always, Cary had already engaged, albeit never at the level of immersion and expertise evident in his analyses of manufacturing processes or the politics of international shipping, with both these faces of "science" before making his statement about the study of trade. His papers contain not only astronomical sketches of his experiences with "great blazing starres" but also an alchemical manuscript dedicated to the "Originall production of Gold & Silver."[312]

In the end, however, he lacked the education and instruments necessary to fathom the technical dimensions of the "new Philosophy," and in his vocabulary "Egypt" did not represent the cradle of Hermetic wisdom but rather a lucrative branch of the "African Trade," good for the export of ivory, spices, and slaves, not of hieroglyph-riddled obelisks and exotic paraphernalia for the *Wunderkammern* of Europe.[313] His case is telling of how outsiders to learned circles came to appropriate the term "science" at the time, stretching it far beyond the generous parameters of natural knowledge. For while both the technical and the mystical dimensions of science were beyond him, Cary learned to appreciate the argumentative value of evidence and experience in related terms of coercive rhetoric and factual logic. Observing that the requirements for convincing his contemporaries had come to rest on positive assertions based on accurate knowledge, he argued that "trade" was a "science" because his accumulated experiences as observer of—and participant in—the early modern economy added up to an experimental conviction regarding the mechanisms of international trade. A character in a 1706 London edition of Æsop asked "in what Science" another character "had skill."[314] Cary thought his skill was in the politics of national development and economic competition, in political economy.

Though bereft of their common spatial trappings, Cary still laid claim to many of the methodological topoi of seventeenth-century sciences: he began to define a miscalculated tariff level as "a fatal Experiment"; inventions and "good Projections" should be "Rewarded some other way" than with patents to encourage wider "Experiments"; and even commercial voyages of trade and discovery were now deemed "Experiments" in his revised terminology. His meticulous account of various trades at various times, as well as their results for national welfare, now served as a roster of experimental consistency—a sort of substitute for the experimental record-keeping of the emerging natural sciences.[315]

Peter Dear has shown that artisanal groups came to "represent sources of experience" in early modern Europe through which one could access tacit expertise, and Cary deftly called on his own experiences as well as those of his social group to construct general claims about what was common and definite in commercial affairs.[316] While it was commonplace by the 1690s to consider merchants authorities on commercial issues, Cary seems unique in drawing on a variety of repositories of experience, widely shared socially and culturally, to codify his thoughts as a "science" of imperial political economy, an aspect of what Dear has defined as Western science's striving for "control of the world."[317] Cary's project drew both on the secular tradition of *ars mercatoria* and, in an almost Baconian vein, on the contemporary vogue among experimental philosophers for "experience," an element of his work that explicitly gave it currency among later readers.[318]

The 1719 third edition of the *Essay,* the last to be published in Cary's lifetime, was given a new introduction, summarizing the six most important "propositions" of his "science," an apparatus also adopted by the 1745 posthumous edition (renamed *A Discourse on Trade*) published by the London bookseller Thomas Osborne, one of the most successful booksellers of his age. The only addition was an "advertisement" that presented Cary as a "Gentleman" and "very considerable Merchant at *Bristol.*" Having met a "deserved success" when first published, the onset of the War of Austrian Succession gave Cary's work renewed cogency; trade needed "Encouragement" again, and "no Book on the Subject" could serve the purpose better than Cary's *Essay.*[319] Osborne's terminology is telling. In correspondence with Locke, Cary had expressed hopes of living up to the standards of an "English Gentleman" and had been granted arms in recognition of his success in 1700. Yet he only adopted the title of "Esquire" sometime between the 1717 second and 1719 third edition of his *Essay,* at which point he entered the five or so most powerful percent of the population.[320] In light of Steven Shapin's documentation of the connection between gentility and scientific trustworthiness in seventeenth-century England—the ways someone's social status lent credence to scientific tuth-claims—one can see how Cary's newly coined science was imbued with legitimacy by his elevation to a "gentlemanly" station, a gentlemanly status acquired by virtue of the very work to which it later lent authority.[321]

While the "mercantilist" tradition to which Cary is said to belong often has been described as a "static" system that ignores the possibility of "progress" (and classical republicanism often went hand in hand with reactionary tendencies), his science showed a clear awareness of the possibility for "improvement" and becomes incomprehensible when divorced from a broad agenda of social reformism.[322] Cary was also well aware of the historical dynamic behind his proposals, and he pointed, through the nexus of emulation, to the example of France, allegedly a haven of "popish" plots against English interests, for validation of his arguments.[323] Quite contrary to what some had argued, the French embodied a military power born from a commercial society based on professional armies and the development of national manufactures. And "opponents" of the French king, Cary mused, had quickly learned that "Monsieur *Colbert's* Head did them more Mischief than any Army in the Field."[324] The threat that foreign aggressors like France might wish to impose popish hierarchical ideologies incompatible with the political outcome of the Revolutions of 1688–89 was, in many ways, what broke the ranks of Whigs such as Locke, Molyneux, and Cary. The "Liberty" they all sought was not merely personal but also national, and the English empire's need for independence came to invade the independence of its weaker constituencies. Cary's science, in the end, formalized a tension between *imperium* and *libertas* that had haunted Europe since the Roman Eagle first spread its wings across the Mediterranean.[325] England's liberty demanded the subjection of others.

Beyond Cary

The *Essay*'s scientific formulation of economic imperialism, however haphazard, was remarkably influential. Editions were printed in octavo with laconic paratexts, encouraging accessibility both as material objects and with their straightforward prose, and were engaged with across the British Empire, by merchants, artisans, Members of Parliament, colonial expatriates, and by leading political and legal theorists.[326] The 1695 *Essay* appeared in catalogues, themselves something of an institutional innovation of the late seventeenth century, across England, with a price vacillating between a low of 6 pence through a Birmingham bookseller in 1793 and a high of 2 shillings through Carter's in London in 1768. Usually, it sold for 1 shilling or for 1 shilling and 6 pence, though no clear pattern emerges for its price during the eighteenth century.[327] Later editions made similar appearances in private libraries and bookseller's catalogues.[328] Perhaps not surprisingly, Osborne handled all of Cary's major works; his 1745 edition of the *Essay* became a mainstay of British catalogues in the second half of the eighteenth century. Its going rate in London seems to have been 2 shillings, with lower prices in regional markets.[329] By comparison, the cost of getting "dead drunk" in early eighteenth-century London was 2 pence; the cost of a chicken was 1 shilling and 6 pence. For the same price, a Londoner could either buy Cary's *Discourse* or, roughly, eat a chicken and get dead drunk. By 1785 Cary's book cost less than a chicken.[330] This was not always the case with books on similar subjects, and was less a matter of supply and demand than of costs and market segmentation.

The same London bookseller who in 1754 sold Cary's *Discourse* at the high price of 2 shillings and 6 pence, for example, sold the three-volume *British Merchant* on "royal paper" for no less than 14 shillings. This paled in comparison to a 1740 edition of Locke's works for 2 pounds and 15 shillings, or twenty-two times as much as Cary's shorter "works" collected in the *Discourse*.[331] The well-stocked 1793 catalogue of the Oxford bookseller Joshua Cooke tells much about the culture of political economy at the time and the importance of considering audiences and markets in charting historical influences. Compared to Cary's *Discourse,* which he sold for 1 shilling and 6 pence, Nugent's translation of Montesquieu's *Spirit of the Laws* priced at 10 shillings and 6 pence belongs to a different world, one that shared many of the same preoccupations but reached very different audiences. In this sense, Cooke's catalogue is striking, for it includes few of the economic works celebrated by modern historiography. There is no Barbon, no Davenant, no North, no Martyn. There is Cary, of course, and Child, who at 1 shilling belonged to the same market segment. Comparably, *The Wealth of Nations,* which Cooke presented in a 1789 edition for 1 pound and 1 shilling, cost twenty-one times more, but even Smith was cheap next to the 1792 edition of Hume's *History of England* with Tobias Smollet's continuation in 13 volumes, which sold for precisely forty-five times the cost of Cary's *Discourse,* the cost of getting drunk on gin every night for more than three years.[332] Yet the market for books did not stop there. Osborne's catalogues even offered a 1513 Aldine Plato for a princely 21 pounds.[333] Though anecdotal, this evidence adumbrates the cultural history of political economy and helps explain why Cary enjoyed such an extraordinary fortune. And, as will be clear later on, these catalogues would themselves influence the *Essay*'s reception on the continent.

In effect, between its first publication in 1695 and the last contemporary edition of 1745, England's economic policy had, apart from a brief Tory intermezzo, aligned itself ever more closely to the jealous tenets of the *Essay*.[334] Cary's ideas were consistently reflected, in practice as well as in theoretical works, in England's emphasis on protecting domestic manufactures and in terms of the violent means by which England aspired to foreign markets. His political economy was in the end one manifestation—or rather an influential codification—of a larger ideology of British imperialism centered on the mutually reinforcing relationship between naval power, manufacturing capitalism, and an exceptionalist Protestant nationalism. The founding document of this ideology was not the Magna Charta but the Navigation Act, and it was, to borrow the structuralist phraseology of Claude Lévi-Strauss for the occasion, articulated in a variety of disparate media.[335] Visually, it found elegant expression in James Thornhill's painted ceilings at Greenwich Hospital (1707–27); musically, it echoes in the fifth verse of James Thomson's powerful "Rule, Britannia":

> To thee belongs the rural reign;
> Thy cities shall with commerce shine:
> All thine shall be the subject main,
> And every shore it circles thine.
> "Rule, Britannia! rule the waves:
> "Britons never will be slaves."[336]

Or, more strikingly expressed through moral reform and commercial jealousy, in his "Patriotism":

> For oh it much imports you, 'tis your all,
> To keep your trade entire, entire the force
> And honour of your fleets; o'er that to watch,
> Even with a hand severe, and jealous eye.
> In intercourse be gentle, generous, just,
> By wisdom polished, and manners fair;
> But on the sea be terrible, untamed,
> Unconquerable still: let none escape,
> Who shall but aim to touch your glory there.[337]

And of the economic strategies debated in the wake of the "Glorious Revolution," few, if any, would embody reigning ideology better, and correspond closer to actual policies, than the *Essay*'s.

The way Cary's ideas were spread also sheds light on the historiography of economics. For it was Cary's very lack of learning that enabled him to bridge two often dichotomized economic epistemologies: secretive reason of state and "Enlightenment" political economy.[338] While his science of trade closely followed the jealous, mercilessly effective maxims of reason of state, it entirely abandoned the guarded elements of the Tacitean *arcana imperii* so dear to Machiavelli scholarship. In light of recent studies on the emergence of a "public sphere" in early modern Europe, Cary's popular conceptions of politics and political economy thus acquire new meanings.[339] When he put pressure on Bristol's MPs to secure printing privileges for W. Bonny in Bristol to establish the city's first printing press, he was not merely *partaking* in this public sphere but actively contributing to its creation.[340] Cary himself assured the means for making his thoughts public. The science proposed by the *Essay* was an exercise in economic Machiavellianism that, by virtue of England's political culture, could only achieve actual influence by appealing to Parliament and the public. Because of the nature of Williamite political discourse, and his own participatory ideology, Cary's science had to forcibly break with the arcane nature of its precursory practices. At the same time, he knew well that such public avenues of influence made well-meaning proposals exceedingly vulnerable to countervailing emulation among England's rivals—the very reason for his predecessors' secrecy.

Probably writing from jail at the end of his life, Cary's verdict on his own influence was bittersweet.[341] His ideas on public credit were still not thoroughly applied in England, yet he distressedly "Observed, that the Famous Mr. Laws" had "drawn a Scheme from it, for the Service of France." Luckily it would not be "Lasting," its "Foundation being laid on Sand," and the "Incredible Stock-Job" the Scotsman John Law had created "to Pay off the Debts of that Nation" would "in all Probability, End in Confusion and Discontent."[342] Not only did Cary realize the dangers posed by the transmissibility of the printed word but also he predicted the first great financial crisis in modern history (his patriotic sentiments blinding him to the possibility that something similar, like the South Sea Bubble, might happen on his side of the Channel). While his ideas could be transmitted, he seemed to say, the institutions and "Steady Government" on which they depended could not. Cary's greatest fame would indeed come abroad, first in France, England's "Tavern," and then in Italy, the very fountainhead of "*popish* cut-throats," before ending its journey across eighteenth-century Europe in Germany. The science he had proposed was essentially a prolonged meditation on the consequences and possibilities of manufacturing and enlightenment, seen in terms of widespread education and social empowerment. Needless to say, it would evolve considerably during this voyage, as continental thinkers, undeterred by what Cary considered the sandy foundations of their absolutist governments, sought to understand the economic pressures on modern politics and appropriate the key to English exceptionalism.

CHAPTER THREE

Butel-Dumont's *Essai sur l'État du Commerce d'Angleterre*

The Grand Tour Begins

Voltaire observed that crossing the English Channel was like crossing into another world, where "Philosophy, like every Thing else," was "very much chang'd."[1] Safely poised off mainland Europe, the archipelagic kingdom of Great Britain harbored an oceanic way of life that contemporaries were certain engendered the scientific and commercial acumen fueling its imperial ambitions.[2] France, on the other hand, was the largest territorial power west of Russia, yet an "empire rather of taste and arts" according to the Marquis d'Argenson.[3] Whereas England was the unmistakable *nouveau riche* of Europe, France had been dictating the fate of the continent for centuries. But there had been no "Glorious Revolution" there to align political and mercantile cultures with the exigencies of commercial society, and a resulting precariousness in the face of new paradigms of sociability and increasing pressures of international competition galvanized attempts by philosophes to understand the enormous changes the world was undergoing, just as the rise of industry challenged foundational institutions of the Old Regime.[4] Both countries sowed seeds of emulation in each other and across Europe, but this reciprocal transmission of ideas and practices was deeply inflected by differences in the architectures of their political economies. To understand why Cary's "science" was called on in the 1750s, and how translation came to change it, one must therefore adumbrate the French polity's blueprint and backtrack to explore England's rise to power from the perspective of its primary continental rival.

From the viewpoint of the present study, three in particular deserve emphasis among the national idiosyncrasies affecting the emulation of English political economy in France: the nation's unique subsistence imagination; the ways existing structures—often classified as remnants of a "feudal" complex—struggled to incorporate institutional innovations like the public debt and the stock market; and, on the basis of this, how the advent of commercial society in France gave birth to a struggle between competing visions of the future. In his time and place, Cary represented a very specific interest debating other pamphleteers united by a nearly uniform disregard for philosophical questions. Where he did touch on deeper issues like the relationship between wealth and virtue, the dangers of a standing army, or the moral consequences of a credit economy, he largely ignored the opposition's arguments, and even the case of Ireland boiled down to a logic of power. In France, the *Essay* was drawn into a more complex discourse that usefully can be delineated through two of its most representative figures: the quietist bishop François Fénelon and the Epicurean political economist Jean-François Melon, discussed in Chapter I, respectively representing morally conservative and radical visions of political economy and of Europe's future. Only by reconstructing this new context can one discern the nuances of emulation, the thin line separating Anglomanie from Anglophobie, and how Cary was seen to transgress that threshold with abandon.[5]

Panem et Circenses

Whereas the Estates General in Catholic France had not been called since 1614, d'Argenson believed the Protestant English were "Idolaters of Liberty," well on their way to becoming "a true democracy."[6] But platitudinous statements of religious intolerance and political bigotry aside, one of the most striking differences between the early modern English and French economic imaginations revolved around the issue of subsistence. " 'Tis in the country[side] you perceive most," a central observer wrote, "the difference there is between France and England," for in England even peasants enjoyed the luxuries of a teatime snack.[7] Though Anglophone pamphleteers of the late seventeenth century often lingered on the importance of agriculture and husbandry for economic development and the safety of their political system, they seldom raised issues of hunger and food shortage.

England was understood to primarily have based its greatness on international trade, agricultural efficiency, and the unique wealth-creating potential of manufactures, which had invigorated agriculture by encouraging the introduction of new techniques and technologies. As an anonymous pamphleteer put this "paradox" at the end of the seventeenth century, "*Mechanicks* prevent *Famin* in a nation," since "no places are more frequently afflicted with *Famin*, than those Countries which are employed in *Tillage*."[8] The record spoke clearly. Famines were the scourge of agricultural economies, not of Venice, Holland, and England, where even farmhands ate beef.[9] So conspicuous was the absence of dearth from economic debates in England that Barbon wondered in 1690 why "no great Famines" had been noticed "by Historians, in these Last Three Hundred Years?"[10] Urban poor, Cary had argued, were to be fed and clothed in workhouses for reasons of Christian rectitude, of economic efficiency, and indirectly of national security by keeping foreign manufactures at bay, but their subsistence never posed a threat to political stability per se. Concern was for idleness and uncompetitiveness, not wrathful hunger. In all his works and political activities, Cary never feared famine; it was as if the third outrider of apocalypse had been banished from the land.

In the "agricultural nation" of France, however, provisioning was a centennial and sacrosanct political obligation and a source, as d'Argenson put it, of "mortal anxiety" for the king, the country's proverbial baker of last resort.[11] "Bread," the iconoclastic philosophe Simon-Nicholas Henri Linguet emblematically wrote, "is the basis of everything in this world," and even the Anglomaniac Voltaire listed "the Art of making Bread" second in importance only to the Promethean "Discovery of Fire."[12] Bread enjoyed a "symbolic hegemony" in eighteenth century France, and the extent to which the popular subsistence anxiety was translated into elite angst is particularly evident in d'Argenson's memoirs in the 1750s, in which marauding "lower classes," "gnawed by hunger," permeated the soundscapes of Enlightenment with resonant chants of "Give us bread."[13] Officers of the monarchy fought unrest through the incessant policing of provisions, from the time seeds were sown to the moment fresh bread was brought to market. For hunger was enemy not only of political stability but of civilization, making provinces "more barbarous," laying waste to "emulation" and "civility" itself. "Hunger," d'Argenson paraphrased the classical trope *necessitas legem non habet*, "knows no law."[14]

This context offers an important avenue of explanation for the comparative radicalization of political economy in eighteenth-century France. Though trauma is notoriously difficult to confront within traditional analytical boundaries, it cannot be ignored as an explanatory device for extreme transmutations of political discourse.[15] The Parisian salons where philosophical elites debated political and economic theories might have been bastions of abundance, but their wider context was emphatically not. And the willingness of philosophes and statesmen to not only theorize but also employ experimental remedies more audacious than those simultaneously toyed with across the Channel, or for that matter elsewhere in Europe, cannot be divorced from their pressing anxieties regarding the material viability of the Old Regime and the oscillating threats of financial collapse and subsistence trauma. The opening years of the 1750s were particularly marred by dearth and disruptions of flour supplies to Paris, creating an atmosphere in which subsistence anxieties fostered famine plots—often revolving around invented, though in some sense plausible, royal conspiracies to speculate in the price of grain against the public good—that relentlessly chipped away at the foundations of authority.[16] The continuous threat that the country would be left "without bread," a threat that the Marquis d'Argenson saw manifest itself, in real and imaginary ways, with alarming frequency throughout his lifetime, created a "combustible" political climate where, he feared portentously, "a riot" could "turn into a revolt, and a revolt into a total revolution."[17]

Trust in the power of the monarchy to safeguard its subject's lifeblood had similarly been broken during John Law's scheme of financial reform and the interrelated Mississippi Bubble of the early 1720s, when a variant of the famine plot—a finance plot so to speak—undermined faith not only in authority but in the nature of commercial society itself. Given Cary's fear of being considered a "projector," it is ironic that his last claim to fame was having inspired Law, the greatest projector of them all. A visionary Scottish adventurer who, like Montchrétien before him, had been forced into exile after killing his opponent in a duel, Law would become the most talked-about and, though he enjoyed significant admirers, including Melon and Voltaire, subsequently most hated man in all of France and large parts of Europe.[18] The experiences of these two duelists on opposite sides of the Channel both sparked intense periods of reciprocal emulation, but if one inaugurated the theory of political economy, the other authored its most flamboyant practical failure so far. Cary's own reception and translation in France would be heavily conditioned by the activities of Law and his acolytes, as well as by the wide-ranging consequences Cary correctly predicted the scheme would have.

The origins of the brouhaha can be traced back to the financial innovations launched across Europe at the end of the seventeenth century. The general adoption of Italian and then Dutch institutions of public debt following the Williamite succession had changed the structures of European international relations, allowing for war financing capabilities of unprecedented efficiency. But if the English country-party had felt jeopardized by the cultural consequences of the public debt during the Nine Years' War, the War of Spanish Succession was a manifest nightmare, as the public debt on both sides of the Channel rose hand in hand with the crescendo of hostilities. By 1715, the French state was practically bankrupt, and the ingenuous Law was received as something of a messiah by a pressed regent when he proposed a "system" to revitalize France after the humiliating Peace of Utrecht.[19] Given free rein, he rapidly established a national bank, introduced paper currency, centralized all the trading companies as well as the tax system under his newly established Mississippi Company, and converted the entire public debt into its equity, becoming Controller General of Finances in the process.[20] So impressive were these measures that the English, in a case of successful but ultimately catastrophic emulation, adopted many of his policies in reforming the South Sea Company, triggering the legendary South Sea Bubble.[21] Although Cary had implied the possibility of such financial crises, the dynamics of bubbles had to be incorporated into the *Essay* by its translators.

Maxims of Modernity

Financial vicissitudes on the scale unleashed by Law had concomitant cultural consequences, some as debilitating for the Old Regime as the economic instabilities themselves. The fact that commercial society affected traditional mores and institutions had been observed before Law set to work, and in opposition to the Augustinian praise of poverty and the sumptuary laws of the preceding centuries, some English merchant-pamphleteers—Cary among them—had come to praise the positive material corollaries of changing fashions already in the late seventeenth century.[22] These observations soon met their theoretical justification in the works of the Dutch émigré doctor and political economist Bernard Mandeville, whose infamous *Fable of the Bees* ruthlessly bared the paradoxes of modernity. A society embodying accepted virtues would, he argued, collapse under the weight of its own hypocrisy, for public virtue and welfare depended on individuals pursuing activities traditionally considered sinful; the sum of private vices paradoxically ensured public benefits, as passions were countervailed and siphoned into constructive manifestations by "dextrous politicians." Commercial society was the outcome of commonly conceptualized vicious behavior, and depended entirely on its continuation. Mandeville's insight derived from the encounter of Christianized Epicureanism, derived largely from Lucretius's first-century BCE poem *The Nature of Things,* and the Augustinian rigor of philosophers orbiting the Port Royal monastery in Paris, probably reaching him through the intermediation of the philosopher Pierre Bayle.[23]

Adam Smith, reacting heavily to Mandeville, would later recapitulate these subversive elements of commercial society. The emulation of the rich by lower classes, Smith noted, was driven by the principle that "We make parade of our riches" and "conceal our poverty." Examining the "oeconomy" of the poor, one realized their expenses were largely in "superfluities" to emulate gilded ways of life. Smith was quick to lament this conduct, for the poor person subsequently assumed "the equipage and splendid way of living of his superiors" without considering the consequences. The "order of society" depended on the "disposition of mankind" to "go along with all the passions of the rich and powerful," and financial vicissitudes facilitating emulation were therefore a threat to social and political stability.[24] The poor should know their place; social emulation should only go so far.

This was precisely how some Parisian aristocrats felt amid the euphoria of the Mississippi Bubble, forced to mingle at the opera with their former servants, newly bejeweled from stock speculation.[25] The dynamism of commercial society meant traditional privileges and prejudices no longer sufficed to delineate social stratifications and, consequently, the boundaries of political and cultural authority.[26] Central to this dilemma was the issue of luxury, seen not only as corrupting but also, through its ability to blur social divisions, as deeply subversive. Though Cary had founded his political economy on manufactures and popular empowerment, he had shown reserve with regard to luxury and vice. Bereft of the analytical tools of moral philosophy, he never charted the implications of his suggestions in this regard, nor realized the inherent tension in his analysis. This tension nearly exploded in France in the decade of the *Essay*'s first translation, and many of the most celebrated authors of the period, from Diderot to Rousseau, would make their names in explicit polemics over the role of luxury and self-interest in the modern world.[27]

Although d'Argenson's "total revolution" waited four decades to erupt, subsistence fears and financial upheavals, added to England's running streak of wartime victories and the escalating cost of conflict, made the French Enlightenment a rather more anxious enterprise than is often admitted. It was in this confused and contested context that political economy emerged as a remedy for the ills of the French polity, a means of regenerating the authority of the Crown, the viability of the state, and the health of the body politic. This fervor for political economy was not only remarked on by contemporaries but is easily quantifiable in hindsight. The number of published economic works skyrocketed, doubling every five years between 1745 and 1760.[28] By the 1760s, new economic works were outpacing new novels.[29] Unlike England, where discourses freely were led by individual merchants and pamphleteers, in France political economy was often codified by relatively elite figures occupying places of power in the state apparatus and with the contacts necessary to evade censorship. That said, even the Marquis de Mirabeau, a powerful noble and partisan of the radical school of political economy known as Physiocracy, was briefly arrested for his writings.[30]

The practice of economic reform itself, however, had venerable roots both in French soil and in the universal and enduring practice of reason of state. As early as the late sixteenth century, Barthélémy de Laffemas, controller general of commerce under Henry IV, published a series of pamphlets fusing the insights of late Renaissance authors like Bodin and Botero to encourage the development of domestic industries. This, he made clear, was the only way of escaping subjection to foreign powers. Montchrétien and Colbert both followed in his footsteps, noting that although rich in natural resources, France was poor and dependent on foreign manufactures.[31] A strong industrial base supported by domestic freedom of trade and external tariffs would augment agriculture and alleviate the ever-worrying subsistence situation.[32] Wealth won wars, and, as Cary realized, any fears Europeans entertained regarding France's ambitions of universal monarchy rested on Colbert's laurels.

Yet his vision of modernity did not cater to all tastes. In the best-selling work of eighteenth-century fiction the 1699 *Adventures of Telemachus, Son of Ulysses,* Fénelon presented the Duke of Burgundy with an opposite lesson in statecraft that, unintentionally, would become public and reverberate throughout the eighteenth century.[33] A mythical tale building on the Homeric epics, the *Telemachus* was really an incisive critique of contemporary political economy and a stalwart defense of the traditional nobility. "By degrees," nations had come "to look upon superfluities as necessary to life" to the point that they could not "dispense with what was counted superfluous thirty years before," with the ensuing luxury confounding "all ranks" and degrading morals. Only by abandoning the dangerous legacy of Louis XIV, which Fénelon identified with warmongering, corruption, and the encouragement of manufactures at the expense of agriculture, could France emerge as the virtuous arbiter of human affairs, a largely agricultural, heavily armed world police in alignment with God's laws and wishes.[34]

Ironically, a key to understanding the dramatic difference between the Christian agrarians like Fénelon and authors in the tradition of Cary lies in their conflicting interpretations of scripture. Curiously, Fénelon's proposals were based on an overturning of the timeless law of diminishing returns in agriculture proclaimed already in Genesis 13:6, which explained how the Abrahamites dispersed because "the land was not able to bear them." Fénelon made the diametrically opposite argument: "the earth is inexhaustible, she increases her fecundity in proportion to the number of inhabitants who take the trouble to cultivate."[35] Colbert had supposedly glorified manufacturing industry at the expense of agriculture, the true foundation of a kingdom's wealth, which needed to be encouraged by high grain prices and free international trade, ensuring a steady supply of virtuous landed gentlemen to defend France. In the contemporary spectrum of political economy, this was as far from Cary's *Essay* as one could get, but Fénelon's works resonated in a deep and widely felt cultural ambivalence toward what the world was becoming. As one of Fénelon's critics warned, the "Politicks" of the *Telemachus* entailed the "Reverse of the Government."[36]

In an idealized panorama of political economy, two traditions were emerging that will recur in the following pages. On the one hand was a tradition based on industry, urban creativity, and financial capitalism growing out of Williamite pamphleteers like Cary, through Melon to Diderot and the Gournay circle. These were the champions of what Ed Hundert has called the "Enlightenment Maxims of Modernity."[37] On the other hand a deeply conservative current existed, obsessed with agriculture as *the* source of material and moral betterment, that stretched from Fénelon to the school known as Physiocracy and well beyond.[38] More than mere clusters of technical arguments, these stances represented different ways of conceiving the good life, and a key to the continuing eudaemonic appeal of political paternalism and Christian agrarianism in France can perhaps best be sought in the deep material structures of quotidian life. The waves of grain breaking against landlocked Paris shaped social and intellectual life very differently from the Atlantic currents to which Bristol was an ever-widening gateway in early modern Europe, and it is not altogether secondary that Melon, like later Anglomanes, hailed from maritime regions like Bordeaux and spent extensive periods abroad in international commercial centers such as London and Cadiz.[39] Emulation reveled in these contrasts, nurturing new anxieties as it placated others.

Envy, Emulation, and Anglomanie

Although Rousseau emphatically declared he was "not afraid to be alone in my century to fight [Melon's] odious maxims which only tend to destroy and debase virtue," a term he imbued with a variety of connotations both pagan and Christian, others too, reading the *Telemachus,* noted that the political and social certainties of Europe were being overturned in the opening decades of the eighteenth century.[40] Among them was d'Argenson, whose memoirs convey the widespread apprehension at unraveling social structures felt in the early 1750s. Apart from the fluctuating scarcity of bread, however, no force was more perturbing for the French statesman than England itself, which, apart from ceaselessly contesting French territories in the New World, also undermined royal authority by blowing "a philosophical wind of free and anti-monarchical government" across the Channel. The boreal breeze itself was no bother, for the Marquis was the first to deplore the despotism of Louis XV. The problem was rather the violent means by which England expanded its freedom and liberties and the conceivably dramatic resultant of all these pressures on French society.

He once reported a discussion with an enlightened Englishman who envisioned a world without "jealousy," where "each could work with emulation for its own commerce, its own navigation, and the order of its internal affairs," and the Marquis clearly shared this vision. "At bottom," he wrote, "we desire the good of England," so "let us convince ourselves that we shall be more prosperous when our neighbours are most so."[41] Yet England's agenda remained resolutely envious in its bid for "universal commerce": the "English people" desired war "out of jealousy for commerce." Having "seized possession of the entire commerce of America," England now sought to do the same with the French. Not only did they prohibit the importation of French manufactures, they also encouraged the proliferation of societies like the "Anti-Gallicans," which sought the downfall of France and an "emulation in the taste for manufacturing French fashions in England." The virtue of emulation here took a dark turn, revealing itself in a competition to destroy rivals. "England," d'Argenson foresaw, "is going to annihilate us in the three parts of the world where we have colonies."[42]

But though England was perceived as "notre superbe rival" in the French geopolitical imagination, this was both tempered and aggravated by a deep fascination with its undeniable accomplishments.[43] At least since the 1704 Battle of Blenheim, England presented both a threat of oscillating intensity and a constant source of inspiration.[44] It has been theorized that wars serve as a "heuristic shortcut for states when making decisions about best practices," and in this light Blenheim marked the point when Europeans realized England had hit on something worthy of emulation.[45] It was then "fashionable," the abbé Jean-Bernard Le Blanc noted, to take the English as "models," and scholars have since often explored what contemporaries derogatorily dubbed Anglomanie, the widespread emulation of English ideas, institutions, and practices in eighteenth-century France.[46] One of the founding texts of this tradition was Voltaire's *Letters on the English Nation.* Although the *Letters* predated Voltaire's estrangement from Frederick the Great and his definite break with biographical approaches to the historical record, they nevertheless betray an intense preoccupation with the various mannerisms of the nation: not only did they introduce Bacon, Locke, Newton, and Alexander Pope to a French audience but also they explored the cultural, economic, and political aspects of England's rise to greatness. Voltaire's hope was to "give faithful Accounts of all the useful things and of the extraordinary Persons, whom to know, and to imitate." A "Traveller who writes in that Spirit," he praised himself, "is a Merchant of a noble Kind, who imports into his native Country the Arts and Virtues of other Nations."[47] As it were, Voltaire wrote back to France from London suggesting useful books for translation already in 1727.[48]

Sojourning in England, he observed that "The Members of the *English* Parliament are fond of comparing themselves to the old *Romans.*" But Englishmen had superseded their Roman predecessors, finally arriving at a political structure where "the Prince is all powerful to do good, and at the same time is restrain'd from committing evil," a consequence of its unique political constellation, "THAT mixture in the *English* government, that harmony between King, Lords and Commons."[49] This represented a fertile base not only for liberty but also for commerce, forces that he, like Cary, saw cumulatively conspire to render England ever more glorious: "AS Trade enrich'd the Citizens in *England,* so it contributed to their Freedom, and this Freedom on the other Side extended their Commerce, whence arose the Grandeur of the State." England surpassed Rome in terms of liberty and of wealth, but not, as Fénelonians argued, at the cost of its virtue. The role of private financiers in the war effort "raises a just Pride in an *English* Merchant, and makes him presume (not without some Reason) to compare himself to a *Roman* Citizen."[50] Again, and contrary to modern historiographical tropes, wealth and virtue could go hand in hand.

Voltaire's letters would prove immensely influential, coinciding with official French interest in English parliamentary proceedings, and, indirectly, paving the way for translations of English works like Cary's *Essay.*[51] Though discussing poetry at the time, Voltaire's statement that "The *English* have reap'd very great Benefit from the Writers of our Nation, and therefore we ought, (since they have not scrupled to be in our Debt,) to borrow from them" would prove equally valid for political economy. Beyond his analysis of the division of powers, many of Voltaire's observations in England became commonplaces in the subsequent French discourse of emulation: England was a "jealous" nation (not only of its "own Liberty, but even of that of other nations"), but its tax system laudably ignored aristocratic and ecclesiastical calls for exemption, it was the home of practically implemented experimental science and philosophy, and its nobles shed traditional prejudices to honorably embark on commercial pursuits.[52] By dissecting the main elements of England's success, the *Letters* propagated a model for emulation with which all subsequent writers of the period had to engage.[53] It would profoundly inspire and shape the project of translation and dissemination of political economy launched by Gournay's circle two decades later, but was further refined and tempered in one of the most influential publications of the eighteenth century, Montesquieu's *Spirit of the Laws,* a work whose importance it is difficult to underestimate for the development of European economic discourse in general and the continental reception of Cary's *Essay* in particular.

A baroque masterpiece, the *Spirit of the Laws* voyaged through the varied landscapes of human knowledge in search of the "principles" driving the "histories of all nations." Its basic outline is famous. "Many things govern men," Montesquieu maintained, "climate, religion, laws, the maxims of the government, examples of past things, mores, and manners," and from these "a general spirit" was "formed as a result." Laws and regulations were of cardinal importance because they were the means by which legislators could influence this "general spirit" and the course of commercial civilization. Fruitful reforms required keen insights into the contextual specificities of a nation, and commercial society itself had emerged from a slow struggle against nature.[54] This civilizing "revolution" in commerce had broken the back of barbarism, counteracting "destructive prejudices" by encouraging "gentle mores." Commercial society was a cure for "Machiavellianism," putting men "in a situation such that, though their passions inspire in them the thought of being wicked, they nevertheless have an interest in not being so." Economic self-interest paradoxically counterbalanced the passions, forging a commercial society of intersecting private interests, a society whose "natural effect" was to bring "peace" through reciprocal dependency; "all unions" being "founded on mutual need."[55] But is this the full story?[56]

Whereas the analytical core of the *Spirit of the Laws* may have sought to reconcile the northern, Teutonic *thèse nobiliaire* with the southern, Roman *thèse royale* regarding the nature of the French political constitution, Montesquieu's remarkable interest in economic affairs had a different orientation, and the most striking country in his economic imagination was England.[57] "Other nations," he noted, "have made commercial interests give way to political interests," but "England has always made its political interests give way to the interests of its commerce." As a result, the country was "sovereignly jealous" of its own and other people's trade. And while Montesquieu's eulogy of peaceful trade and emulation brought him to mistrust "exclusions" and commercial prohibitions, the evident success of economic policies forced him to acknowledge the very possible benefits of governmental interventions. "Liberty of commerce," he explained, "is not a faculty granted to traders to do what they want; this would instead be the servitude of commerce." In effect, the most interventionist country in Europe, England, was also the freest one and that with the most flourishing commerce. It "hampers the trader, but it does so in favor of commerce."[58]

Montesquieu returned to the case of England's economic empire during a lengthy discussion of mores and manners later in the *Spirit of the Laws*, the previously mentioned passage annotated by Voltaire as a "portrait de l'Angleterre."[59] The individual liberty embedded in England's political structure imbued its financial system with tremendous trust and credit, citizens investing in a polity in which they were active participants. And Montesquieu could only hope, with Melon, that the peaceful ideal of commerce would keep England from channeling this "immense fictional wealth" into military misadventures by becoming a "conquering nation."[60] But while Montesquieu wished it would establish colonies "to extend its commerce more than its domination," he could not ignore England's commercial bellicosity and "natural pride." "Jealous," it had "conquered" and "enslaved" Ireland, "given that nation its own laws," and as a consequence ruled the seas. Quoting Xenophon, "But if the Athenians lived on an island and had also empire on the sea, they would have the power to harm others and no one would be able to harm them, so long as they remained masters of the sea," Montesquieu added, "You might say that Xenophon intended to speak of England."[61]

England had known to benefit from colonialism, whose purpose was to "engage in commerce under better conditions than one has with neighbouring peoples with whom all advantages are reciprocal," and to justify such unequal relations of trade Montesquieu resorted to the topos of protection, just as Cary had done: "the disadvantages to the colonies, which lose the liberty of commerce, is visibly compensated by the protection of the mother country, which defends them by her arms or maintains them by her laws."[62] Even if England's reduction of Irish industry could be justified by the protection it offered, Montesquieu's caveats regarding the dark side of commercial relations were succinct. For even without direct coercion, free international trade could create not only liberal relations of interdependence but also of dependence *tout court*, of empire:

The avarice of nations disputes the movables of the whole universe. There may be a state so unhappy that it will be deprived of the movable effects of other countries and also even of almost all its own; the owners of its land will be but the colonists of the foreigners. This state will lack everything and will be able to acquire nothing; it would be far better for it to have commerce with no nation in the world; in these circumstances commerce has led to poverty. A country which always sends out fewer commodities or less produce than it receives puts itself in equilibrium by impoverishing itself; it will receive less, until, in extreme poverty, it receives nothing.[63]

The Spirit of the Laws was exceedingly clear. Unless guided by politics, commerce could lead to conquests. This caveat aligns poorly with reigning historiography, which rather emphasizes Montesquieu's penchant for peace and liberty through free trade and construes policies, as manifestations of commercial jealousies, as perversions of "normal" trade.[64] Yet, historically, it made eminent sense; as an anonymous Italian later annotated Montesquieu's writings at this point, "this passage says something that everyone knows."[65] Though Montesquieu clung to the idea that economic mechanisms could equalize the fortunes of nations once one nation became so wealthy that increasing wages pushed its costs of production beyond the internationally competitive, banishing the possibility of a "universal monarchy," England had demonstrated how astute policies could circumvent this situation by coercing weaker nations and colonies—by sword, law, or diplomacy—into submitting to an international division of labor greatly favoring its own ends.[66] The only solution Montesquieu proposed to this perennial tragedy of global trade was autarky: "It is not the peoples who have enough among themselves but those who have nothing at home who find it advantageous to trade with no one."[67]

The English model was a Janus-faced phenomenon that haunted the economic imagination of eighteenth-century Europe. Trade could unite humanity with bonds of culture and commerce, but it could also cause the enslavement and desolation of entire countries. Montesquieu therefore argued that one had to calibrate it carefully and draw on it more selectively than Voltaire had seemed to suggest. Notably, he warned against letting the nobility engage in commerce, arguing that it was against the "spirit" of the French monarchy.[68] By allowing careless emulation of foreign practices, France risked following England into a treacherous situation where no intermediary body of interests, constitutional strictures aside, could mediate the authority of the Crown.[69]

A "moderate government" required a very different political structure, one that called to mind the methods by which statesmen had to police commercial society, for "one must combine powers, regulate them, temper them, make them act; one must give one power a ballast, so to speak, to put it in a position to resist another; this is a masterpiece of legislation."[70] The seeming volatility of English liberty, caused by its failure to separate powers, and Montesquieu's deep respect for contextual differences, curbed his enthusiasm for emulation.[71] Different social worlds adapted differently to the exigencies of commercial society and the limits it posed on traditional norms and values. This was why the English model played such an ambiguous role in Montesquieu's works and why international trade never could be left to fate.[72] A manuscript note he wrote in the spirit of d'Argenson suggests what peaceful federation of states Montesquieu envisioned once jealousy of trade was overcome and states were free to harmoniously develop their own and each other's economies.[73] This federation of cooperatively competitive states, however, remained a distant dream in an age when England sought global hegemony, not as Rome through conquest, nor through Carthaginian commerce, but as the fabled heir of both forewarned by Melon; an invincible empire based on conquest *and* commerce, just as Cary had wanted.

Gournay, Diderot, and Industrial Enlightenment

One of Montesquieu's sources for writing the *Spirit of the Laws* had been a philosophical epistolary with the abbé Le Blanc, common friend of Melon, future translator of Hume, and colleague of Cary's translator Butel-Dumont. Le Blanc had resided in England in the late 1730s and 1740s, and his 1745 *Letters of a Frenchman* became one of the period's most astute analyses of economic life and cross-Channel "jealousy."[74] His basic analysis of English economic behavior drew on Voltairean tropes; in other words, Englishmen were "jealous" not only of the "glory of their nation" and their "pretended liberties," a poignant reminder of the varieties of liberty in eighteenth-century Europe, but also of their "manufactures" ("because they know their importance"), but Le Blanc's analysis of the advent of commercial society in Europe in many ways served as a link between the generation of Montesquieu and that of the *Essay*'s subsequent translator.[75]

Though Le Blanc too admitted that climate was of paramount importance in the development of national character and that there was "some sort of contradiction between morality and policy" on the issue of luxury, he nonetheless thought "industry" mattered more than "nature" and embraced superfluity as the "father of labour and industry." Not only did luxury "promote commerce," but, as the "English" knew from "experience"—the basis of all economic and other knowledge for Le Blanc as it had been for Cary—it made flourish "arts and manufactures," which were "more abundant sources of riches than mines of gold." Indeed, so much more powerful was industry than gold that even those who possessed abudant mines of the latter were "obliged to submit to those countries, which produce only iron-mines." This was the fate of Spain, which by neglecting "manufactures" remained "poor, amid all the gold of the Indies."[76] Though England today seldom is thought of as benefiting from mineral wealth before the early nineteenth century, it had structurally become a coal fuel economy by 1700, and French government officials argued that France should imitate England in this as early as 1738.[77] A look at eighteenth-century mineral exports from England demonstrates their importance at the time, and the reasons why continental powers sought to emulate it (see Figure 3.1).[78]

Focusing only on comparative exports and imports of iron products, kept alive by the importation of raw Swedish ore, England's rise to become what Le Blanc called a nation of "iron-mines" able to dominate those who only had "mines of gold" becomes evident (see Figure 3.2).[79] Though a very clear net importer of iron when Cary originally composed his *Essay*, English policy and English capitalists had focused intensively on that sector to make the country a clear net exporter by the time of Le Blanc's writings. In effect, whereas Britain had been a "technological debtor" until the late seventeenth century, J. R. Harris demonstrated, English innovations allowing for the coke smelting of iron inaugurated its ascendancy to a position of global technological leadership.[80]

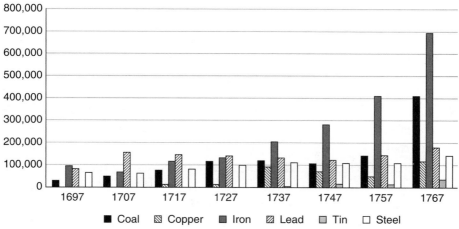

FIGURE 3.1. English exports of mineral products, 1697–1767 (based on Schumpeter 1960, 19–22)

Again, urban sociability founded on industry emerged, in this idealized depiction, as the prerequisite of modern civilization, encouraging "emulation" and Mandevillian situations where "the vices of some, turn to the advantage of others." This, in turn, encouraged culture, sciences, mechanical arts, and finally military might. Praising both the English political system and Colbert's role in making France a great power, Le Blanc drew inspiration from Melon's idea that economic power was a safer way than mere military conquest to *"give laws"* to other nations, but was more explicit in emphasizing the "mutual connexion" between "Commerce, arms and learning," to the extent that he envisioned "commerce" ensuring "the conquests of a state."[81] Far from opposing poles representing ancients and moderns in the political imagination of the time, conquest and commerce were as intertwined for Le Blanc as they were for Cary, and while he lamented destructive commercial jealousies and national animosities, it seemed uncomfortably clear that the only way to safeguard a country's independence was to threaten that of others.

Incidentally, one of his sources for this dismal insight in turn provides yet another bridge between the worlds of Cary, Montesquieu, and Butel-Dumont. Given England's relative importance as a source of economic and political lessons for the *Spirit of the Laws,* it is notable that Montesquieu only had a single English work of political economy in his library at La Brède apart from those of his friend Henry St. John, 1st Viscount Bolingbroke. This happens to be the only one quoted by Le Blanc in his letters:

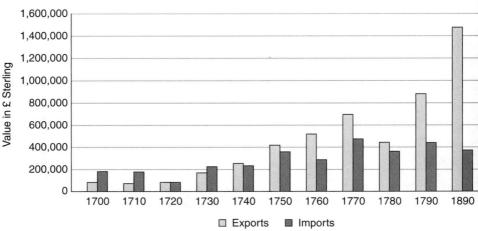

FIGURE 3.2. English exports and imports of iron products, 1700–1800 (based on Schumpeter 1960, 19–22, 25–28)

Joshua Gee's 1729 *Trade and Navigation of Great-Britain Considered*.[82] Only a year after the publication of the *Spirit of the Laws*, it was translated into French by none other than Montesquieu's own son, Jean-Baptiste Secondat, as the first really influential French rendition of an English economic treatise since Thomas Mun's *England's Treasure by Forraigne Trade* had crossed the Channel in 1674.[83]

Little is known regarding Gee and his life, but he was a wealthy merchant, industrialist, and advisor to the Board of Trade who is surmised to have been a Whig contributor to the *English Merchant* and enemy of the East India Company.[84] It was a symbolic book to translate in light of the cyclical virtue of emulation, for Gee had originally written with hopes that the "Example of the *French*" would inspire Englishmen to entrust trade to "the Care and Protection of the Government."[85] Unlike that disseminated by Cary's *Essay*, Gee's jealousy of France was modulated by a respect that muted its most vitriolic expressions, and he similarly attacked the commonplace assertion that "Trade can never thrive under an absolute monarchical Government."[86] Far from an aficionado of political liberties, trade was an unprincipled mistress whose favor went to those who embraced her with "the greatest Cheerfulness" and "the most Encouragement," and was veritably blooming across the Channel.[87] While this stance facilitated the transmission of Gee's ideas into France, it also conveyed a deeper concern with French economic hegemony; for if trade would not flee the country in repugnance of absolutism, it would have to be expunged by force. A military confrontation with France over the future control of global commerce was a tacit inevitability for this paradigmatic representative of English political economy.[88]

Yet the practical policies suggested by Gee differed little from those of Cary, and there are numerous indications that he was familiar with the *Essay*.[89] The "Head and Seat" of the empire was to ensure that colonial dependencies did not undermine its core manufactures, conceived of as the very pillar of the imperial enterprise. And the policy debacle by which Parliament had been forced to encourage linens in Ireland in exchange for a ban on its wool had taught Gee a valuable lesson: colonial manufactures should be smothered in the cradle by all means necessary.[90] By strengthening the Navigation Acts and prohibiting the construction of machinery and establishment of manufactures overseas, England could ensure that its colonies specialized in agriculture and the production of raw materials. Without industry, colonials would never attempt to "cast off the *English* Government." And he particularly praised French policies; as France had once emulated England, so it was now England's turn to emulate France.[91]

Gee's most symbolic contribution to the French debates of the 1750s, however, might have been an offhand remark. To make knowledge of "Trade, Manufactures and Colonies" public, he mused, it first had to "be espoused by great Men who have Power and Influence to put others on the Work," and a "Nation" would be "greatly obliged" to such a "noble Lord."[92] Not only should the nobility be commercial, but it should actively be involved in the promulgation of a given political economy. As it were, the French would emulate not only Gee's suggested policies but also his proposed means for their realization.[93] The model of a powerful figure galvanizing others to promote economic knowledge was exactly what occurred in Paris in the early 1750s, when England's wartime success made it painfully obvious that new remedies were needed to resist its jealous quest for universal commerce, and that it no longer was convincing to argue, in the fashion of Machiavelli, that empire in the modern world ultimately depended on anything but pecuniary power.[94]

The person to embody this notion in France was Jacques-Claude-Marie Vincent de Gournay, a merchant and government agent who, following his marriage into nobility, became a well-regarded *intendant du commerce* in the decade leading up to the Seven Years' War. Although Gournay's importance as mentor for a generation of economic thinkers has long been acknowledged, his inability to publish his most succinct thoughts on the matter, and his followers' later attempts to politicize his legacy, have obfuscated his exact role in the discourse of the 1750s.[95] In spite of his efforts to translate and publish a number of decidedly "mercantilist" tracts, the historiography of political economy has traditionally lionized Gournay as progenitor of that most apocryphal of economic statements, "Laissez faire, laissez passer," and he has been indiscriminately lumped together with the "Harbingers of Liberalism" and even "libertarians." More specifically, he is considered François Quesnay's soul mate and "cohort" and, in a tradition dating back to the eighteenth century, a "co-founder of the Physiocratic system," a "physiocrat."[96] This interpretation has long been contested, however, and some today agree with Takumi Tsuda that Gournay was "betrayed" by his descendants and appropriated by a tradition with which he had little in common.[97] Gournay's circle has been situated as an incubator of Anglomania, though its members were profoundly Anglophobic in other respects, and their politics have been found to be representative of what Simone Meyssonnier has dubbed "liberal egalitarianism."[98] The network established by Gournay is today most studied as a mediator between international currents of political economy and local French traditions and as an exponent of a new "public sphere" in France.[99]

Like so many political economists before him, Gournay's vision of political economy was forged not in the salons of Paris but through extensive practical experience with economic matters abroad and throughout France, including fifteen years as a merchant in Cadiz, Spain's gateway to the New World, and prolonged sojourns in England, Holland, and Germany.[100] It was during these journeys that foreign authors first inspired him to fuse the practice of economic policy with the study of its laws and maxims, in other words to codify a "science" of political economy reconciling, just as Cary had done, the empirical knowledge of merchants and the statesman's need to harness it politically.[101] Gournay embarked on industrial espionage for the naval minister Jean-Frédéric Phélypeaux, Count of Maurepas, in London in the 1740s, the same decade in which the French Bureau of Commerce actively turned from a program of simple economic regulation to one of competitive "amelioration," asking further permission to do the same in Germany and Hungary.

Following his purchase of the post of *intendant,* Gournay in turn established a wide network of economic agents and informants across France that kept him updated on the state of the kingdom and pursued his projects by proxy.[102] His 1758 letter of resignation eloquently summarized his emulative endeavors: "If I have proposed any principles that have seemed strange," he explained, "they have not been new. I have taken them from the writings and practices of the nations that surround us, and that have taken commerce as the principal object of their preoccupations and their politics." Why? Because "twenty-five years of study and experience in this matter have persuaded me that these principles are the right ones for extending commerce." And his writings orbited the problem of English economic policy obsessively. "Les Anglais," he knew, "view with great jealousy the progress that commerce has made in France," and his political economy supplied instruments not only for national development but also for national defense against Britannia's bid for global hegemony.[103]

Gournay deduced that if production was taken care of, consumption would follow, and that likewise a healthy real economy would secure the financial needs of the kingdom even in the face of wars and public debts. This was manifest in a neo-Colbertian emphasis on importing raw materials and exporting manufactured goods and on the need to encourage national emulation on three levels: of foreign discourses of political economy; of English economic policy; and of English commercial culture.[104] Emulation, his circle knew, was a naturally cyclical phenomenon, but it was now France's turn to imitate the successes of others.[105] Yet all reforms would be for naught unless the mercantile vocations could be instilled with the same sense of nobility and respect Voltaire had observed across the Channel, unless the existing social structures of the Old Regime could be made compatible with the demands of international economic competition.[106] Although their intellectual debt to Montesquieu would remain predominant, they decisively parted ways on the capacity of French culture to absorb foreign institutions.[107] It was therefore Gournay's way of disseminating economic knowledge that was the most revolutionary in the intellectually regulated France of his day. For whereas works on economic matters had long circulated freely in England, this had, with notable exceptions, not been the case in France until Gournay stepped up to the task. Translations of English works had been growing in importance at least since the time of Voltaire, but these had not been predominantly economic or political in nature.[108] By the 1750s, however, economic competition came to influence the culture of French learning on a large scale.

Gournay's chosen vehicle for changing the French economic imagination was, like Cary's in England, to harness the printing revolution and encourage public debate over trade, war, and the nature of commercial society. But Le Blanc had warned earlier that "it is better to translate good books than to make new ones, in which there seldom is any new instruction," and Gournay took this lesson to heart.[109] More particularly, he imagined economic thought and policy to be quintessentially emulative, investing greatly in the translation of foreign debates on these issues to bring the French public on par with other great powers. The nature of his enterprise, however, precluded taking it on single-handedly. For his goal was nothing less than to create a critical mass of economic literature able to inspire a new way of conceiving of the French economy as something malleable, something dynamic around which thoughts and policies could be formulated in open communication with the intellectual capital of the nation. It was about overturning the most fundamental prejudices of French society against mercantile occupations, about banishing Fénelon's ghost, though Gournay's goal was neither morally subversive nor politically revolutionary in any deeper sense. The country's social and political architecture was to be made hospitable to trade, but it was not to be consumed by it. As Gee had suggested, Gournay sought to inspire and encourage a circle of friends and acquaintances of varying degrees of intimacy to join his program of institutional reform. His personal history rendered him uniquely positioned to embark on such a project, as the network he carefully had nurtured first as a merchant, then as a spy, economic administrator, and finally as a noted political figure uniquely intersected what were often divided and ossified strata of French society.

Gournay himself, like Cary before him, embodied the ideal of social mobility at the heart of commercial society, and it was only by drawing on friendships and experiences at each stage of his ascent that he was able to project his vision on the French publishing world. The differences between a practical man like Gournay and a hereditarily privileged scholar such as Montesquieu lay precisely in that. No other association would subsequently do more to promote the ideals of commercial nobility at the time— most famously argued for by the abbé Gabriel François Coyer but evident in all their work—something to which Montesquieu had remained stalwartly opposed.[110] Like a Renaissance merchant prince, Gournay delegated publications and translations across the field of his influence in exchange for favors, friendship, and positions in the French administrative apparatus. Though the affairs of state giving birth to the project suggest that the nature of his patronage network was an example of *clientelismo* on the ancient Roman model of political corruption, it might be more appropriate to consider it an example of *mecenatismo,* of artistic and cultural sponsorship. For if the goal of Gournay's enterprise was political and economic like the first archetype of patronage, the means of its achievement followed the rules and practices of the second, where favors were exchanged for participation in and contribution to a larger cultural project rather than simple political allegiance in the strictest sense.[111]

Among the members of Gournay's network, which for some brief years became a stable and coherent "community of interpretation," were Le Blanc, Claude Carlier, Simon Cliquot-Blervache, Coyer, Henri-Louis Duhamel du Monceau, Plumard de Dangeul, Forbonnais, André Morellet, Anne-Robert-Jacques Turgot, Montesquieu's son Jean-Baptiste Secondat, and of course Butel-Dumont.[112] Membership was structured on a series of concentric circles, whose inner core authors like Forbonnais, Dangeul, and Butel-Dumont can be seen to have occupied, rather than as a more homogenous "group" or, as the Milanese Academy of Punches shortly would call themselves, "coterie."[113] Nor were all the members direct contributors to Gournay's project. One of the community's most important affiliates was Chrétien-Guillaume de Lamoignon de Malesherbes, then practically in control of the French organ of book censorship. The economy had, for the longest time, been an affair of state, and a revolution in the public understanding of it depended entirely on a revolution in the state's censorial opinion on the subject made possible by Gournay's personal relationship with Malesherbes and, as will become clear, with Butel-Dumont.[114]

The French edition of Gee by Montesquieu's son was perhaps the first of many similar translations of foreign economic works that, by affiliation or circumstance, can be traced to this circle, and this translation may, through the mediation of Montesquieu the elder, in fact have contributed greatly to this circle's emergence. From 1753 to Gournay's death in 1759, his wider

circle was responsible for more than forty publications on economic issues.[115] While the majority of their translations were of English originals,
the group also published important French editions of Spanish works of
political economy. Though influential, these works in many ways corrobo-
rated the English model, demonstrating, through the bleak history of Spain
and the New World, that not even mountains of gold and silver could save
an empire lacking in thriving manufacturing industries and the social and
cultural institutions to harness them. As Gournay himself argued, "wealth
does not lie in gold and in money but rather in what land and industry
produce."[116] His project for achieving such wealth through emulation
found its most explicit formulation in Forbonnais's translation of Uztáriz:
"Knowledge of the practices employed by strangers, is the shortest & safest way to get there, because it presents reason with experiences & objects
of comparison."[117]

A similar but more famous attempt to reform knowledge was launched
in the same years in the form of the *Encyclopédie* of Diderot and
d'Alembert, and Gournay's project was closer to their economic sensitivities than often thought. Their political-economic goal, like Cary's, was
educating society, disseminating useful knowledge, and teaching people to
care about their economic conditions and supplying them with the tools to
critically engage with the structures of the state, of the domestic economy,
and of international competition. And just as Cary believed that forcibly
putting the supposedly corrupt and the destitute to work in manufacturing
would better them as moral and political beings, so Diderot entertained a
vision of mechanical industries as instruments of what Daniel Roche calls
"moral improvement." Yet, mirroring Cary's refusal to let moral melioration get in the way of international manufacturing competitiveness, Diderot's project was explicitly aimed at securing "better products" from
lower-class workers. For all their "enlightenment" and rhetoric of artisanal empowerment, a fundamentally expropriating impetus nonetheless
guided these industrializing ideologies.[118] But in actively relating empiricism and experimentalism to a moral rehabilitation of the arts and crafts
and a vivid description of the productivity gains inherent in the division
of labor, Diderot's seminal article "Art," in the very first volume of the
Encylopédie, laid down nothing less than a manifesto of industrial enlightenment, of human melioration through industry and the technological
ability to domesticate nature.[119]

The proliferation of technical know-how acquired through experience
was so important that Diderot argued that keeping "useful knowledge secret" was tantamount to "theft from society." This was an obvious segue to
the *Encyclopédie*'s "Preliminary Discourse," but whereas it had argued for

the necessity of translations in terms of universal human betterment, the realities of international competition clearly inflected Diderot's ideas about the spread of technical knowledge. "Let the artisan contribute his manual skill," Diderot went on, "the academician his knowledge and advice, the rich man the cost of materials, time and trouble; and soon our arts and manufactures will possess all the supremacy we could wish over those of other peoples."[120] France's future depended on wealth secured through competitive international trade, and this in turn depended on the comparative quality and cost of its manufactures. The means of achieving that was to foster a more organic relationship between classes and fields of knowledge, between artisans, academics, and what can only be called capitalists.

But why did industry, both as a personal quality and as a type of economic activity, contribute so disproportionally to human melioration? The key lay in the unique characteristics of manufacturing that Diderot exemplified through contemporary pin factories, decades before Adam Smith followed suit:

> The swiftness of the labour and the perfection of the product depend entirely on the number of assembled workers. When a workshop is large, every operation is performed by a different man. Each worker undertakes and throughout his whole life will do only one particular thing; everyone does something different; from which it follows that every task is performed well and swiftly, and that the best manufactured product is the one made at least cost.[121]

Industry differed from agriculture because of its capacity to absorb the productive gains of an increasing division of labor. Diderot theorized this with greater sophistication than Cary had, but they promoted and partook in a very similar culture of political economy.

England's role in eighteenth-century France as a source of inspiration, emulation, and trepidation ensured that the *Encyclopédie* was forced to qualify the cosmopolitanism of its epistemology already from the outset. Whereas it was "theft" for an artisan to secrete information, the aim of publicizing technical knowledge and establishing domestic manufactures—to undersell foreign competitors—in effect put clear limits on its ideal geographical distribution.[122] Like Gournay, Diderot wanted French manufactures to excel over those of others; knowledge was no less political for the encyclopedic "public sphere" than it had been for the earlier paradigm of reason of state. Knowledge was itself competitive, and if ideas had no passports in Diderot's world, the people who put them to use did.

The *Encyclopédie*'s own definition of "cosmopolitanism" simplified a Montesquieuian dictum thus: "I put my family above myself, my country above my family, and the human race above my country."[123] A cosmopolitan's emotional commitments were universally distributed, a viewpoint influentially adopted by Immanuel Kant and many others.[124] Material concerns were a preeminent litmus test of such loyalties, shaping, nurturing, and reflecting economic identities. In few cases is the chasm separating rhetoric from reality wider than in the case of Diderot's *Encyclopédie*. Economic differences decided international relations of power and thus political and cultural hierarchies in the eighteenth century, a context in which trade could hardly be a universal solvent of patriotic commitments. Scholars have often emphasized that the *Encyclopédie* served as a vehicle for the publication of Quesnay's first articles on Physiocracy, an ideology to which I will soon return. Yet there can be no doubt that Diderot's political economy was better reflected by the article "Commerce" he commissioned for the 1753 third volume of the *Encyclopédie* from one of the most active members of Gournay's circle, Forbonnais, today remembered as Quesnay's "most virulent analytical critic."[125] Cary's French translation was, as such, part and parcel of the French industrial enlightenment.

Acadia Redux

Whatever Cary's influence on Law and later authors, the first mention of the *Essay* in translation appears in Joseph d'Hémery's *Journal de la Librairie*. Inspector of the book trade from 1748 to 1769, d'Hémery kept a catalogue of books he received, read, and evaluated every week. Although the *Essai sur l'État du Commerce d'Angleterre,* literally the *Essay on the State of England's Commerce,* was published anonymously, d'Hémery's trustworthy journal identifies Georges-Marie Butel-Dumont as the author in a note of 13 March 1755.[126] Only two days later, the same work, "drawn from a fairly short document published toward the end of the last century by John Cary" and authored by "M. Dumont," is reviewed in the *Correspondance litteraire.*[127] The book was sold by a Lausanne book dealer in 1772 for 3 livres and 10 sous, or nearly nine times the "normal" prerevolutionary cost of a four-pound loaf of bread in Paris at a time when per-capita bread consumption averaged a pound a day. Calorically, this was more than Cary's *Essay* cost relative to English poultry, but the book still occupied a different literary world compared to a first folio of the *Encyclopédie*, which cost no less than 2,450 such loaves.[128]

Though probably born to a Paris merchant in 1725, little is known of Butel-Dumont except that he graduated in law to become an accredited lawyer and royal censor for belles-lettres and history, doubtlessly an important post for Gournay to have influence over. "Mercantilistically inclined," he had by this time already assisted Gournay in translating Child and written a work on the New World of his own, *History and Commerce of the English Colonies in North America,* which due to delays in publication also appeared in 1755.[129] "Some eminent men," he wrote in private correspondence around this time, "have turned my studies to commercial things," and it seems these works can be traced back to his early incorporation into Gournay's fledgling circle, who from the outset were alarmed by England's aggressive expansionism in North America. Butel-Dumont's efforts were not for naught, and he later wrote that his "ouvrages" landed him a job as secretary to the very commission established at the signing of the Treaty of Aix-la-Chapelle to sort out the Acadian border disputes.[130]

In fact, it is obvious that Butel-Dumont was emerging, in 1755, as the foremost Americanist of the group, if not of the entire country. Given the remarkable topical and theoretical kinship between the *Essay* and Butel-Dumont's prior work, he must therefore have been the ideal member of Gournay's circle to undertake its translation.[131] And interestingly, his censorial work too was affected by the crisis unfolding across the Atlantic. One of Butel-Dumont's censorial reports approved Mathieu-François Pidansat de Mairobert's *Letter . . . on the true limits of English and French possessions in America* for publication, and Butel-Dumont returned to the question of Acadia's boundaries in his remarks.[132] But though many works were published on the subject, Butel-Dumont cited few besides those of Montesquieu and Gee. In effect, he encountered the problem of Newfoundland before he encountered the problem of Cary, a meeting that merits further scrutiny to make sense of the *Essay*'s first translation.

The tense international relations shadowing French writings on England through the 1730s and 1740s were aggravated in the years leading up to the Seven Years' War, often through disagreements over the exact meaning of certain articles of the 1713 Treaty of Utrecht, which had ended the War of Spanish Succession. Although much turmoil had assailed the European states-system in the intervening years, venerable specters returned to haunt international relations as the 1748 Treaty of Aix-la-Chapelle reestablished the status quo antebellum as settled at Utrecht thirty-five years earlier. Considered favorable toward England's interests, the epistolaries of its main architects are revealing of what England's "most essentiall Pretensions" had been: "France should recognize . . . the Protestant Succession, oblige the Pretender to retire out of the French Dominions, recall the Duke of Anjou & deliver up the Entire Monarchy of Spain, restore Newfondland & Hudson Bay, & Demolish the Fortifications & ruin the Port of Dunkirk." Though the war ostensibly had been over the Spanish Succession, this item was tertiary to the cessation of French support for James Stuart, and one step above the Newfoundland fisheries. This and surrounding letters again underline the dangers of overemphasizing the practical implementation of canonical texts and their arguments. Given the historiography of political philosophy, one might assume that the exchanges between the dukes of Marlborough, Townshend, and Savoy delineating the Utrecht Settlement would be replete with references to universal monarchies, *virtù*, liberty, and the common good, perhaps with some Tacitus and "perpetual peace" thrown in. One finds instead talk of cod and cannonballs.[133]

Among the central points of the resulting treaty, it was stipulated that France should cede Hudson Bay, Acadia "with its ancient Boundaries," and Newfoundland to the English while retaining certain fishing rights along with all the islands "in the Mouth of the River of St. *Laurence*, and in the Gulph of the same Name."[134] This proved to be an excruciatingly vague framework for colonial policy, and the crux of a long debate between hired geographers came to be the delineation of Acadia's original extent and ascertaining whether it enveloped the entirety of Nova Scotia south of the St. Lawrence River, the smaller peninsula south of the Bay of Fundy, or just a small slice of the latter; whether New France would forever be sandwiched between the nebulous contours of the Hudson Bay area and the St. Lawrence River or be able to forge its own territorial empire in North America, claiming vital riverways linking Quebec to the Atlantic in the winter months when the St. Lawrence iced.[135]

Not only were the Newfoundland fisheries by far the most lucrative element of France's colonial commerce on the continent, comparable to its sugar islands, they were also a crucial "nursery" for the navy, training as many as a quarter of its sailors. The European balance of power was seen to depend largely on France's ability to stand firm against the British navy. This in turn demanded a strong French presence in the Newfoundland theatre—a presence the English were equally insistent on demolishing.[136] As Gournay wrote to Maurepas already in 1747, "Canada and Mississippi are presently the objects of their jealousy."[137] Skirmishes and acts of British aggression were constant along the Anglo-French frontiers of North America during the buildup to the Seven Years' War, causing no little consternation in France, and British ruthlessness—ably capitalized on by official French propaganda measures—was largely responsible for a tangible shift from Anglomanie to Anglophobie in dominant strata of the French collective imagination.[138] How was one to react to a nation that accepted no international law or rules of engagement, acting as an outlaw state not bound by universal codes of right and honor?[139]

This conflict was aggravated by the English royal geographer Thomas Jefferys, whose 1754 pamphlet *The Conduct of the French, With Regard to Nova Scotia* argued for a definite English right to North America.[140] Not only had the French no rights south of the St. Lawrence River—the very name Nova Scotia being proof that it was a Scottish, thus British, and ultimately English dominion—they had no right to any presence in North America at all. The *"English,"* he insisted, "by right of discovery of the Cabots, in 1497, claim all North America, from 34 to 66 or 67 degrees of north latitude," from the top of Florida to the Arctic Circle. Not content with the Treaty of Utrecht, Jefferys went on the offensive in response to French interests in Acadia. For since the French supposedly "lay pretensions to the whole *British* empire in *America*," the *"English"* had no choice but to "revive their antient claim to *Canada*."[141] Jefferys's pamphlet, as d'Argenson noted, "made a great noise," and "all England" was "seduced" by this vigorous instigation to imperial war over the riches of the New World.[142] Later that year, in fact, Jefferys's patron William Pitt received parliamentary approval for rolling back the borders of New France in a series of military actions from the Ohio River to Newfoundland.[143]

Newfoundland, in particular, had long been a thorn in the side of Whitehall because of its continuing French cultural presence. Nominally British, large parts of Nova Scotia's population remained French-speaking Acadian, a disconcerting fact that eventually drove the government to break this population's cultural coherence, culminating in their murder and mass deportation. Driven by imperial jealousy, this project was a case of conscious ethnic cleansing, mobilizing a wide range of resources for the express purpose of not only transposing French-speaking British subjects but of annihilating them entirely. Acadians were hounded, terrorized, and finally fragmented throughout the British Empire at the cost of thousands of lives, their records and cultural integrity destroyed. Though causing outrage in Europe at the time, such genocides, justified biblically, were frequent in the English-speaking world of the eighteenth and nineteenth centuries, from the Scottish clearances to the Trail of Tears.[144] As Hume and Robertson had hinted at, imperial emulation all too often devolved into jealousy, and jealousy in turn into slaughter. It was "envy," Raynal later wrote, that ultimately had "depopulated" Acadia.[145] Understandably, Jefferys's pamphlet galvanized French apprehensions over England's imperial aggression, and it was soon translated by Butel-Dumont, who almost simultaneously published his translation of Cary's *Essay*.[146] The research he had undertaken to write his *History* had prepared him well for the work of these two imperialists.

His *History and Commerce of the English Colonies in North America* had been a systematic analysis of England's North American colonies, which, three years later, was followed by one on its colonies in the Caribbean, the *History and Commerce of the English Antilles*.[147] Much in line with the Gournay circle's program, Butel-Dumont wrote it explicitly to fill a lacuna in French publishing, since all that was available on the subject was Savary's *Dictionary*, whose information was either "incomplete, or confused, or false," and "translations" of "ancient" English works, presumably the likes of Mun.[148] The motivation was nothing but facilitating emulation, for now

> All of Europe fixes their eyes on [England], to learn, through the examination of their conduct, by what resources a Kingdom of such a small extent as England has arrived at a power equal the vastest states. . . . I will observe in the course of the work the secret ways of the English in all of North America; the jealousy with which it regards the vicinity of the French, & the measures through which it tends to render themselves sole masters of these immense countries.[149]

The woolen island of Melon's model had, as fearfully predicted, arrived at "giving laws" to distant countries. And a reviewer did not fail to identify the principle guiding Butel-Dumont's work: "Knowledge of these Colonies can enlighten our emulation."[150] But one wonders, in such instances, whether the real question was not that of facilitating revenge.

Although the Gournay circle's main preoccupation was the Old World, Butel-Dumont followed Melon and Montesquieu in considering the European balance in light of a planetary commercial theatre.[151] And he similarly followed Montesquieu in abandoning the Machiavellian mantra, reiterated by the likes of Hobbes and Spinoza, that laws could not change the constitution of man but had to align with man's fundamental proclivities. The key to understanding global commerce and economic inequality, Butel-Dumont argued, was legal, "Because it is the Laws of a State that shape the men as they are; industrious or without genius, entrepreneurial or timid, active or parasitical." Yet, with the exception of Montesquieu, scholars had "strongly neglected the science of making Laws," that "great Art of legislation." Butel-Dumont's institutional account of England's empire was an attempt to remedy this, the only means of understanding why the American colonies were the key to England's power, "the principal source of their force & of their opulence," contributing "infinitely to entertaining a rapid movement in the course of internal commerce in the Kingdom." And the differentiated nature of colonial constitutions enabled Butel-Dumont to make some reserved verdicts regarding the relationship between laws, politics, and economic life in an imperial system. While the "northern colonies," for example, generally represented a "powerful" positive influence on England's "balance of external commerce," this relationship did not always benefit the colonies in turn.[152]

Breaking somewhat with the tradition established in Voltaire's *Letters,* the *History* acknowledged that France too was a victim of national economic envy and was "jealous" of its "emulators" in the New World. Not only that, Butel-Dumont acknowledged that "The French established themselves on the Isle of Newfoundland much later than the English." This had not implied immediate hostilities, and "whatever the case" was regarding who came there first, "the one & the other went peacefully around their establishments" until the English, first after the Williamite Settlement, then during the War of Spanish Succession, demanded monopoly rights to the Newfoundland fisheries. His initial caveats aside, Butel-Dumont reflected a widely shared belief that France had been wronged at Utrecht and that warmongering was a largely English occupation.[153] He heatedly wrote that the English were "jealous," wanting ever larger chunks of the world's commerce, and that their "evil conduct" had almost botched their imperial endeavors in the New World. While later colonies had been more successful, this in turn made England "jealous" even of the "riches" and "power" of its own dependencies. Carolina, whose "constitutions fondamentales" he knew were "elaborated by the famous Locke," left "little liberty to the people," making the "Palatin" a "Monarque absolu." If Butel-Dumont was consistent in his terminology, this was tantamount to "Machiavellism." Again, demonstrating the Gournay circle's torn indebtedness to Montesquieu, he showed a clear adhesion to the Teutonic *thèse nobiliaire* by approving of local assemblies in states like Connecticut, Rhode Island, and Massachusetts as a means of counteracting these conditions by imbuing inhabitants with "all of the authority." Compared to the flourishing states of these colonies, Georgia was languishing because "constraint" had been "substituted for the liberty necessary to the formation of colonies."[154]

The English in North America had benefited from their employment of African slaves in the plantation trade and thus "understood their commerce," but due to the strictures of the Navigation Acts, there was practically no manufacturing on the North American continent. A "sort of poverty" therefore resulted from the exchange of raw materials for European manufactures, and colonists were further divided by great distances that by "slowing down the interior circulation influenced the exterior commerce." The balance between supply and demand even in addictive raw materials was so fragile that the English twice decreed that surplus tobacco be burned following the "Dutch example" of burning spices, much as Cary suggested one should do with raw wool, to inflate prices.[155] This was not to say Butel-Dumont was against imperial economic policies per se, but it does emphasize the importance Gournay's circle—like that formed around

Diderot—allotted to manufacturing industries in the development of civilization. Where Cary's *Essay* had denied political agency to colonial subjects, Butel-Dumont in the end hoped colonies could be empowered with a political capacity without this undermining the empire's economic viability. Local assemblies, however, could never become more than palliative political measures in light of England's much vaunted Navigation Acts, a theme to which he would return in his translation of the *Essay*.

Butel-Dumont's New World was an immense source of wealth for England, a mosaic of more and less functional political communities of different eudemonic potentials, and an area of necessary and immediate military contention. Well aware of the developing crisis of international relations over Acadia and England's claims to the entirety of North America, he also surveyed the history of European interactions with the continent to document that "it was known long before Columbus & that even if the French were not the first to establish themselves in the New World the Basques went there, like they also did to the coasts of Acadia, to exercise fishing before the other peoples of Europe had heard of these lands."[156] Just as Jefferys had argued that Nova Scotia, by virtue of being Scottish, belonged to the British Empire and thus to England, so perhaps Butel-Dumont thought tracing the act of original discovery to the Basques, through their current subjection to French rule, likewise authorized a French presence there. The immemoriality of the first sighting of North America, however, ultimately undermined justifications of current conquests by recourse to claims of original discovery.

Given this earlier work on English interests in North America, it is not surprising that Butel-Dumont translated Jefferys's *Conduct*. It embodied the worst excesses of English imperialism, and though far more literal than Butel-Dumont's translation of Cary's *Essay*, notes and additions nonetheless expanded Jefferys's pamphlet from 77 to 295 pages. Englishmen, Butel-Dumont emphasized, were "jealous of the establishments of other peoples in the New World," and "with no other title but cupidity, they want to make England sole master of the commerce of all America." If the reach of this conflict was conceived to be global, it emanated from a European balance of power where France was the "sole Power" that could present an "obstacle to the execution of this project." Butel-Dumont's principal response appeared in the fourth annotation to his translation, which stretched for eighteen pages and to which he referred repeatedly. "England" sought to "blind Europe to the consequences of [its] excessive pretensions & to remove the apprehensions these should give birth to for the general liberty of commerce" by projecting its vices onto France. While the English defamed France for its protectionist quest for universal monarchy, they were realizing their own. "All English writers" were in unison issuing "declamations against the legitimacy of French possessions in North America"; "mercenary pens" and their "false disclosures" culminated in the current debate over Acadia. Claiming possession of all North America, the English ignored that "the French have frequented the seas that soak the coast of New France since time immemorial."[157] Butel-Dumont's solution was, again, to deny England's right by priority of discovery itself. With such arbitrary rights, claims, and natural law put aside, diplomacy and war were the only (de)structuring forces left in the legal limbo of international relations: an anarchic sphere into which all countries, rich and poor, sought to extend order in their own image. And again, Cary's strategies were harnessed for this endeavor.

St. Jerome and the *Essai*

The *Essai*'s principles of political economy reflected, for the simple reason of Cary's influence on the English debates and proposals that French authors had begun to emulate, those observable in many of the previous publications of Gournay's circle, but of all the translations published by the Gournayïtes, the *Essai* came across as by far the most programmatic in scale and scope. As late as the nineteenth century, Cary was still used as shorthand in France for British economic culture.[158] Even contemporary reviewers thought the work differed from other translations appearing in the period.[159] The goal of the publication, Butel-Dumont said, mirroring the mood of contemporary debates, was to shed light on the "general maxims" of political economy "applicable in whatever state one wants." Although he recognized, as a close reader of Montesquieu, that national differences separated continental France from its island neighbor, even the most idiosyncratic economic policies tailored to the English situation could inspire "very useful ideas," either by reversing or reworking them.[160] General principles would be difficult to comprehend if not explained properly, however, because a simple and direct translation

> would not entirely satisfy what the title promised a French reader. Cary wrote for a nation already familiar with the arguments he treated and therefore he limited himself to indicate the object [of his work] and did not focus on details unless he proposed original ideas. An Englishman familiar with the foundations on which Cary's ideas rested can appreciate its success and merit, but how to judge them if one does not master the notions his ideas presuppose?[161]

The problem, Butel-Dumont made clear, was one of understanding Cary's *context*. Rather than merely translating the two hundred or so pages of the 1745 reprint, Butel-Dumont therefore chose to update the work to include the progress of English commerce in the six decades since the *Essay* first was published.[162] Cary and his posthumous English editors had, after all, done similarly several times between 1695 and 1745, and there was thus no immediate tension between Butel-Dumont's wish to contextualize Cary and his decision to abandon the literal integrity of the *Essay*. Others in the history of the book had done the same, and utilizing the three previous English editions of 1695, 1719, and 1745, the original text(s) really became "only the canvas of the French *Essay*."[163] His colleague Le Blanc had already written that "every translation is a copy: but to copy well, a man should know how to paint," and given his experience as scholar and administrator, Butel-Dumont confidently set out to paint his panoramas, taking care to translate as French "manners prescribe."[164] "It is important to observe," he wrote, "that in this first volume, what we have taken from the English author does not amount to more than forty-three pages of his book, and that Cary's *Essay* is in fact only the outline of the French *Essai*. The second volume owes even less to Cary. We have borrowed only its general plan and themes."[165] In the utilitarian logic motivating early modern economic translations, the crux of the matter was in the end furthering the public's understanding of the English economy rather than faithfully uncovering past interpretations of the same. Beyond the demands to "polish" foreign texts characterizing French translation culture, the very endeavor of Gournay's circle required an even broader conception of translation as the idea of the *Essay*—as a book and a manifesto—emerged as the principal object of attention, overshadowing Cary, his editors, and even Butel-Dumont himself.

In the end, the French *Essai* did what the earlier English editions had done, treating the historical development of English commerce and its "state" at the year of publication, in this case anno 1755. St. Jerome's dictum that one had to translate "sense for sense" rather than "word for word" demanded such treatment. The Jeromian categories were in clear and insuperable opposition in the *Essai*'s case, for it would have been utterly senseless, if literally correct, to render the *Essay* rigorously in 1755. It would have made of the *Essay* its diametrical opposite, a work of antiquarian erudition rather than practicable policy. The cost of respecting the spirit of the *Essay* was high, though, as the translation ballooned to more than a thousand pages, in turn entailing a separation of the original *Essay* into two volumes that contemporary reviewers felt corresponded to the internal and external trades of England. Yet this did little to change the

Essay/Essai's paratext, and as a material object, it retained the same straightforward accessibility in French as in English. And it is noteworthy that the final review in the *Journal des sçavans* stated that the journal would review any future volumes to appear in what was obviously understood to be a series on the trade of England, much like the translation of Hume's essays would become.[166]

Yet, while the work grew prodigiously in volume, political and cultural requirements modulated aspects of Cary's work dramatically, shifting the focus, if not the nature, of the economic theories and reforms suggested by the *Essay*. This is evident from a crucial passage in which Butel-Dumont delineated his method of translation. "We permitted ourselves," he explained, "to eliminate the passages from the original that absolutely could regard only England and the times in which the author was writing, as well as those in which he let himself be carried away by animosity toward France, which is very common also among his compatriots."[167] This sentence encapsulates the *Essay*'s cultural contamination. The mechanisms of economic development codified by Cary survived unscathed, but their purpose would never again be the same. In practice, the passage meant that Butel-Dumont censored references to the moral and political virtues of the English republic, to matters of religion generally, to the importance of deindustrializing continental Europe, and to the ever-present threat of "popish cutthroats" and French aggression.

In extrapolating Cary's "principles," Butel-Dumont discarded the entire political and religious framework for his economic thought. Although in a less heavy-handed manner, he similarly subverted one of Cary's most pressing preoccupations: the case of Ireland became just one of a legion of similar industrial dependencies surveyed all over the world in the French translation. Ireland might, in Davenant's words, have been "the general subject of men's discourses" when the *Essay* was first published, but in Butel-Dumont's mid-eighteenth-century French agenda it largely blended into the background noise of translation, interesting largely for the recent growth of its linnen industry and its general usefulness for England's empire.[168] The ways in which French conceptions of Irish political economy at the time differed from those of Davenant's generation in England, however, simultaneously reflected the *Essay*'s historical success, for whereas Cary repeatedly had called for the "reduction" of Ireland to the state of a "colony," Butel-Dumont could ascertain five decades later that Ireland in fact *had* been "reduced" to "the same footing as the colonies in the West Indies." And not only that, but Ireland's economic dependence on wool had successfully been transformed, also because of Cary's influence, into a an imperially more organic dependence on linnen which in turn was worthy of emulation in the context of peripheral development.[169] Only the recognition of Cary's Jeromian "sense" could align past and present, proposal and policy.

Economic History and the Science of Commerce

The end result of this process was a marked reduction in the *Essay*'s belligerence. The most idiosyncratically republican elements of Cary's political economy were likewise censored in absolutist France, the very point of the translation being to identify and emulate the "universal maxims" applicable to "any" government. Finally, Cary's fear of "arbitrary" Catholic hierarchies, at least officially the raison d'être for his colonial scheme of political economy, disappeared entirely. What remained was a much longer, more learned history of English economic development built around a remarkable catalogue of sovereign interventions and parliamentary acts intended to benefit English agriculture, commerce, and manufactures. Although it would remain for Cary's second translator, Antonio Genovesi, to rename the *"State"* of England a history, a *"Storia,"* Butel-Dumont had made it a history in all but its title; a history that not only fostered an empirical approach to "scientific" political economy but also provided the raw data on which said approach depended. His colleague Le Blanc had put it well: "Let us view history on the side of her true object, as the most sure school of policy and morality."[170]

The inventory of Butel-Dumont's estate, drawn up on his death in 1789, includes a vast library. Among the few works mentioned by name, the majority are, not surprisingly given his interests, related to travel and history, including major works by Hume, Pufendorf, Voltaire, and William Robertson.[171] His historical affinity was the logical continuation of Cary's methodology; as the science of political economy derived from experience, it had no better sources than the historical record. The *Essai* in fact became *the* definite economic history of England in the period; a history that, in accordance with the canons established by Voltaire, was not simply a coronation chronology or a list of great men and their actions but a philosophical history of institutions and their development, from the perspective not of religion or civil society but of commerce.[172] To achieve this, he relied on a credible apparatus of marginal references to countless royal statutes, parliamentary proceedings, works of political economy, and statistics he presumably derived from the vast network of informants available to Gournay's handpicked circle and Butel-Dumont's own resources in the administration. Ecclesiastical matters of course played their part, but emphasis naturally fell on institutions like tariffs, the Royal Navy, and the public debt rather than on conspiracies and confessional concerns. Not only did Butel-Dumont unveil the history of the British navy, of hospitals and poorhouses, of the East India Company and of the South Sea Bubble, but he explained how and by what laws and regulations England had emerged from its peripheral position to conquer much of the planet, establish commercial hegemonies, and become the greatest power since Rome. And if far more detailed than Montesquieu in his exploration of English commerce, Butel-Dumont retained his master's mixed feelings regarding its nature and future.

Though the dimensions of the enterprise had changed dramatically, the *Essai* began much like the *Essay*, and the forty-six pages of the original that made it through the translation somewhat literally were not selected haphazardly: "To understand if the commerce, that a Nation undertakes, broadly corresponds to its interests," one had to "research the principles, on which it is founded"; this was because "commerce, like all other sciences, also has its rules," explaining how a political body could grow strong through the regulation of individual initiative and ensure the right structures of international trade.[173] Though its analysis was more refined, the *Essai* likewise retained much of the overall architecture of the *Essay*. Butel-Dumont maintained Cary's theory regarding the sources of England's wealth as being "the produce of the country" and the "colonies," the "work of its manufactures," and its "fisheries." And strikingly in the wake of Montesquieu, he translated Cary's exquisitely economic conjectural history almost literally. As "a nation becomes numerous, commerce extends equally," with a "large number of people" deciding to leave agriculture in favor of "the mechanical arts" because they are "more lucrative," thus ensuring a "mutual succor" making "society tighter." This was the origin of cities, born from the "sweetness of profit." Little commerce could be pursued in the "countryside," and so it was extended to "neighboring countries." As urban societies developed, "controversies" emerged, creating a demand for "wise men" knowledgeable of the "laws" and invested with "public authority." The establishment of such "judges" required "procurators," "solicitors," and other "officials" who understood the "intelligence of the laws." Butel-Dumont also translated the concomitant emergence of "maladies," born from the "taste for pleasure" in commercial society, giving birth to "medicine" and the study of the "human body." Finally, ever-new professions were created to supply the new needs of civilization: priests, gastronomists, entertainers, all "necessary dependents of commerce."[174] Civilization was a corollary of economic development.

Many of the topoi of English economic culture also survived the translation; Butel-Dumont wrote of the "prodigious number of sheep" across the Channel, their "famous grazing-grounds," and how English monarchs developed textile manufactures by prohibiting the exportation of raw wool, conquering the international market for such goods from the Dutch. The English state had attracted foreign artisans and experts with privileges to imitate foreign industries and had, in the true spirit of "emulation," overcome their competitors. English wool was now "the best in the entire world," and never did its artisans "lack invention," their "ability" being "such that there is nothing that they do not imitate and similarly improve."[175] If subsistence anxiety was the most uniquely pressing concern for contemporary French political economy, this did not blind them to the equivalent English cultural idiosyncrasy: the myth of the Golden Fleece and their "astonishing quantity of sheep."[176]

Drawing on a historiographical commonplace, the *Essai* located the "prosperous increase" of English woolens and other industries in Edward III's prohibition of foreign manufactures. The consequences of English policies had been so beneficial because they had targeted specific trades with particular wealth-creating potential. One is "indebted" to manufactures, the *Essai* echoed the *Essay,* "for the increase in value that natural products receive, and for the accommodation of these same to diverse uses." Selling them to "foreigners, who pay not only for the labor, and for their intrinsic value, but sometimes much more, depending on the circumstances," manufactures embodied the urbanizing, civilizing engine of the *Essay/Essai*'s conjectural history. England's insistence on importing raw materials and exporting manufactured goods was "the most copious origin of the riches of the kingdom," employing an "infinite" number of people and driving exploration overseas in search of new materials for domestic industry. It was "emulation," between artisans and between nations, that had turned the forlorn fields of medieval England into an interconnected system of manufacturing centers. "Protected" and, in the language of the French bureaucracy, "policed" with "very minute" regulations, domestic manufacturers were shielded from foreign imports with prohibitive tariffs and given freedom to export unhindered, in every possible way encouraged by the government to retain "the benefit" of manufacturing for England. "The government does not omit anything to promote manufactures whatever sort they are," Butel-Dumont concluded, "but those of wool form the principal object of its cares."[177]

The reason *why* manufactures were so important for English policymakers depended partially on the assumption that only foreign trade could make a nation wealthy, but also on the very historical success of the English economy, which had reduced its possible venues for favorable trade. Since "rents on the land" now were so much higher in England than elsewhere, they could only compete internationally by adding value to goods through skilled labor. Regulations had therefore been employed to turn "inert" and "indolent" Englishmen into "active" caretakers of their "raw materials." The only secure trade England in the end had was with its "colonies," which remained dependent on whatever it sent them. In fact, the purpose of such legislation, beyond enriching England, was to render it independent of foreign powers. Yet the independence of the British Empire entailed a total dependency of its constituent colonies on England itself, which led to peripheral discontentment and core jealousy at any attempt to spread the benefits of manufacturing and trade beyond where the Crown and Parliament thought safe. Among the examples of England's ruthless program of imperial political economy mentioned by Butel-Dumont were the abortion of Ireland's woolen industry and of the Scottish colony at Darien.[178]

This emphasis on refined manufactures naturally led into the quagmire that was the eighteenth-century luxury debate, a polemic Butel-Dumont did not yet seem keen to confront. Like Melon, Le Blanc's 1754 translation of Hume's *Essays* had already argued: "Luxury is a word of an uncertain signification, and may be taken in a good as well as a bad sense."[179] This may help explain why, although the term "luxury" played such an integral part in Cary's vision of economic development, the word *luxe* hardly makes an appearance in the vastly expanded French edition.[180] In its place, Butel-Dumont substituted words like *mode* much more frequently than Cary used the word "fashion," though still perhaps in accordance with Jerome's dictum: luxury, fashions, and "refined manufactures" were a cause of "emulation" both individual and national that gave birth to new arts, industries, and ultimately new opportunities for employment. Although never discussed as a "problem of luxuries," as Genovesi would in his subsequent Italian translation of the *Essai*, few contemporaries would have failed to appreciate what Butel-Dumont was doing.[181] Similarly, he avoided the word "virtue" in his translation, a fact that did not escape the perceptive reviewers of the *Correspondance littéraire*. Although they considered the *Essai* a culminating contribution of Gournay's circle, they wearily and at length discussed why "it is now unfashionable to speak of virtue."[182]

Idiosyncrasies of Political Economy

Just as there were issues that only interested Englishmen, however, there were issues that only interested Frenchmen, and unfailingly, the *Essai* incorporated the unique preoccupations of its French context. Though Cary had only given passing attention to agricultural concerns, Butel-Dumont praised England's incalculable quantity of grain at length and took the occasion to remind readers that it was the "best informed" country with regards to "cultivation and the other parts of the rustic economy," derived from the "most sublime sciences." Other countries had more productive lands than England, but they were "subjects" to "revolutions of bad years." England's "regularity," Butel-Dumont echoes earlier publications of the Gournay circle, resulted from the "perfection of agriculture," which had rescued the island from its former "penuries." He further elaborated on the very different subsistence-situation across the Channel by affirming that though the English "eat very little bread," what they ate, he lyricized at length, was simply "beautiful." Appropriately, Butel-Dumont inserted a table to support his inserted chapter on the quality and quantity of English flour before going on to explain the policies and laws established by English monarchs to "perfect" agriculture. Essentially, this entailed bounties for grain exports alongside the careful protection of the domestic supply with dynamic tariffs.[183]

Moreover, this was not the only time foodstuffs topped Butel-Dumont's translational agenda. The Newfoundland fisheries, like those off the coasts of New England, were "unexhausted mines" whose "prodigious" catches every year bettered England's commerce. Fisheries had "attracted the attention of the government of England" since the time of Edward III, but only with William III had official policy begun to encourage individual "emulation" rather than "particular companies" as the best way of harvesting the seas of the New World. Numerous rules and regulations had been devised to encourage such activities too, also because fisheries were the navy's natural nursery. Butel-Dumont's rendition of Cary was so gastronomically inclined, dealing with everything from horsemeat to malted beverages and symbolic flour derivatives, that he deplored that he could not embark on mouthwatering discussions of the "excellent shrimp of Chichester," the "oysters from the county of Kent," or the "freshwater fish" of "Cambridge, York, and Cumberland etc."[184] Political economy was about more than merely securing the population appropriate subsistence. It was about making the nation great in an internationally competitive context, something that had clear fallouts for the country's political structure and victual consciousness alike.

Not only did the regularity of provisions in a great nation free its inhabitants from the clutches of subsistence anxiety, but widespread wealth also increased their well-being by making better food available to more people, something Butel-Dumont himself pointed out by noting the relative absence of bread in English diets. The quality of one's bread was a clear indicator of social standing in Old Regime France, but in the context of contemporary discourses on grain prices and starving poor, his vivid smorgasbord of white bread, sausages, shrimp, and oysters for the people seemed either utopian or insensitive.[185] Yet his message was nothing like the later joke about Marie Antoinette and the brioche. Contemporary accounts such as Voltaire's letters from his 1750 journey to the court of Frederick II clearly envisioned a stage-like coevolution of bread, wealth, and culture. Westphalia, Voltaire wrote dismissingly, was inhabited by "animals that are called humans" living in "big huts that are called houses" eating bread reminiscent of "a certain hard, black and glutinous stone."[186] Though driven by opposing ideological interests, one of the essayist Jean La Bruyère's most impassioned reproaches to Colbert had concluded the same thing. Bad policies forced peasants to live in "dens" eating "bread made of black grain" or, to remind his readers of the bottom rungs on the subsistence ladder, "roots and boiled grass mixed with flour from barley and oats with some salt."[187] Even black bread, after all, was still bread, Eucharistically invested with ritual powers of redemption and transcendence.[188]

The object of a culture's subsistence anxiety was imbued with tremendous explanatory power regarding its political and economic imaginations, and good bread—even more powerfully the shift from bread to more expensive forms of nourishment—was a shorthand symptom of great social and economic melioration, of progress so to speak. Not only did Englishmen on average consume significantly more calories than Frenchmen in the early eighteenth century, they also consumed better calories which translated into considerably more energy allowing for longer working hours.[189] As civil servants, the Gournay circle sought ways to meet the king's sacrosanct obligation to feed his people. His authority and political stability alike depended on the quantity and quality of food available throughout his reign, and they chose to promote political economy, based on the policies suggested by earlier authors like Cary and Melon, as the best means to achieve this end. In light of the circle's wish to heighten people's awareness of the limits and possibilities of commercial society, there was no better way to get the attention of a broad public than hitting the rawest nerve of them all: the issues of food and subsistence keeping people hostage.[190]

The revolutionary nature of inserting such a loaded discussion of alternative paths of subsistence to the breadways of the Old Regime cannot be overstated. Through this ventriloquized attack on the victual foundations of French society, nimbly inserted in his translation of Cary's *Essay*, Butel-Dumont harnessed the Anglomania of his time to propose reforms of a far more existential nature than any tax reform or new tariff could ever represent. The panorama he painted on Cary's canvas was, in its subversive relation to contemporary rituals and institutions of subsistence, not unlike the wild attack launched against the Physiocrats by the muckraker and philosophe Simon Linguet in the late 1770s, when he declared France's pathological dependence on bread was tantamount to "slavery."[191] As George Orwell would put it, "changes of diet are more important than changes of dynasty or even of religion."[192]

There was no doubt in Butel-Dumont's mind that governmental "encouragements" had brought about the "emulation" necessary to procure such bounties for the English, and he also tellingly continued to employ the word "police," so vital in French provision politics, for English industrial policies.[193] Where such measures had not sufficed to beat foreign competitors, as the case was with Greenland whaling, regents resorted to more heavy-handed prohibitions and, more recently, the 1750 act naturalizing all Protestant foreigners who served on a whaling vessel. This practice was well established in English textile industries as well, where Indian manufactures were imitated under the protection of prohibitions, giving "incredible encouragement" to local manufactures.[194] In their political conceptions of industry and subsistence, Gournay and Butel-Dumont both remained thoroughly embedded in a paternal matrix of control that stipulated the necessity of robust state action to guide national development. And in their insistence on such interventions facilitating individual initiatives, the group remained remarkably close to Cary's original conception of "free trade" as freedom of vocation and freedom from internal tariffs.

The English model problematized other French idiosyncrasies as well, and prime among them was the debate over commercial nobility and the extent to which French political culture could absorb the comparatively more egalitarian dynamic of English commercial society. Montesquieu, for one, had replied negatively to the question of whether the French nobility should follow England's in embracing trade, but Butel-Dumont echoed the opinions of Voltaire and the Gournay's circle generally. "Charles II," he deftly inserted in his translation of Cary's *Essay*, "who more than all the other Kings knew the English, used to say that there was no nobility in England, except among the merchants. In fact a large part of the best families . . . draw their origins from tradesmen"; the "majority of these families" were "of very recent origin," among them the famous "Josia Child."[195] It was a powerful argument for commercial nobility, given that some of the principal English authors translated by Gournay's circle—Child and Cary—had become ennobled through commercial pursuits. Not only were their books vehicles of political economy, but they themselves embodied the social structures Gournay's circle sought to emulate. The absence of Montesquieu's consideration regarding the dangers of eliminating the noble counterweight to royal authority from Butel-Dumont's rendition of Cary is striking, but, as his earlier *History* made clear, there were other ways—like local assemblies—through which the principal demands of the *thèse nobiliaire* could be accommodated without resorting to a plutophobic aristocracy. Other forms of intermediary bodies could countervail "Machiavellism" and political absolutism.[196]

Recent scholarship has explored this debate in light of changing conceptions of patriotism and the ideological conflict between the tenets of commercial society and the feudal remnants of the ancient Gothic order.[197] Though certainly imbued with a dynamic internal to French frames of cultural reference, there can be no doubt that Gournay's circle conceived of the necessary reconceptualization of the nobility in light of international emulation and commercial rivalry. They were not driven by a choice between old-fashioned warfare and peaceful commerce, between wealth and virtue in the often-repeated ideological dichotomy, but by the painful realization that France's continued survival in the face of English aggression depended entirely on its ability to muster the economic resources necessary to wage and win—or at least draw—a global war for domination. This is no less evident from the language the group employed to convey their message. "Commerce," Coyer wrote, had "its own services, its own dangers" and of course "its own combats"; trade too was a way of "conquest." Or, as Gournay put it, commerce was a form of economic "besieging."[198] They agreed with Montesquieu that virtue was righteous service of the *patrie* but manifested their patriotism differently. The real cure for the deepest of France's ailments was a guarded emulation of the English model of modernity, which entailed a careful movement away from traditional mores, prejudices, and institutions, both in the realms of subsistence and, as in the debate over the commercial nobility, in the conceptualization of the social orders themselves. Political economy became the scientific oriflamme around which these different yet interconnected forces gathered, but its quotidian deployment would engage with far more practical matters.

Freedom, Protection, and Jealousy of Trade

In spite of all their praise of liberty, "prohibitions," Butel-Dumont noted, were a keystone of English economic policy. This was, for example, true in the increasingly important mining sector. He referred to these mines—remarkably both in light of Le Blanc's *Letters* and the Gournay circle's translation of Spanish authors—as the "Potosi Gallois," or "Welsh Potosì," but they were only one example of England's mineral wealth alongside numerous "fossil materials meriting to be figured in a tract of natural history."[199] England was, as economic historians have shown, "remarkably provided with industrial raw materials" in the eighteenth century.[200] Butel-Dumont traced the establishment of flourishing "iron mills" to William III, and the *Essai* quoted Gee on the subsequent development of "furnaces" in England. The same William III, Queen Anne, and George II had similarly studied how to multiply the exports of refined sugar from Great Britain. They had also resorted to "exclusive privileges," but it seemed to Butel-Dumont, sticking to Cary's own definition of "free trade," more "useful for the public to recompense similar endeavors differently, that is it would be better to leave the field free to whoever, who would like to work." This, he was certain, would "perfect manufactures." While the "multitude of artisans" keeping England independent of foreign goods and enabling it to export overseas were maintained by acts prohibiting them from establishing shops abroad, there were ways a government could interfere positively in the economic life of a nation without resorting to such monopolies.[201] As in his implicit argument for commercial nobility, Butel-Dumont again looked for ways to achieve certain goals by other means than those generally considered. Local assemblies could perform functions of a feudal in the same way that industrialization could occur through premiums rather than prohibitions.

Tariffs and prizes therefore remained the most useful governmental interventions for Butel-Dumont and, as in Cary's original *Essay,* his chapter on distilling presented the most insights into how a state could further technological change and economic growth. These were, in fact, among the only pages translated nearly literally. "The exorbitant taxes with which French aquavit is burdened in England," Butel Dumont noted, "have given English distillers the occasion to extend their commerce." Not only did this protectionism extend commerce, it enabled English workers to qualitatively improve their labor. "Experience" thus enabled workers to "add some new ideas to those, which our ancients have transmitted, with which we seek to perfect their inventions," and this again increased the value of manufactures. "The goods that give the greatest lucre" and the greatest "benefit to a nation," Butel-Dumont paraphrased Cary, "are always those, in which one buys nothing but the [raw] material." Again, the paradigmatic example was "clocks," whose value depended entirely on "labor and industry." To harness this process, government needed to rely on the wisdom of merchants, the judicious deliberations of a committee for commerce, and the establishment of workhouses for the poor. All of England could in fact be considered a "great manufacture," and he took inspiration from the *Essay*'s fourteen points to demonstrate this. Translating their sense, he expanded on their exact content.[202]

In Cary's context, for example, there was no need to fear that manufactures would cannibalize agriculture. This was for cultural reasons not the case in France, where Fénelonian fears of this were influential, and Butel-Dumont went out of his way in the conclusion to the first volume of his translation to emphasize that subsistence would be made rather more than less secure were France to move away from its agricultural focus. It was "an error," he wrote, "to believe, that manufactures hurt agriculture, like some politicians think," for the two "amicably conspire[d] to the advantage of the nation."[203] This, however, did not mean he easily endorsed all Cary's proposals or all England's policies.

Above all, Butel-Dumont was appalled by the self-love manifested on the island. He realized that "zeal for the common good" was "the source of this people's power," driving them to "improve manufactures," "establish colonies," and "cultivate the lands." Englishmen were—calling on Voltaire's image of the citizen-investor—like "an economist all applied to increase the price of his holdings, since every Englishman reputes himself a co-proprietor of Great Britain."[204] Yet, their patriotic self-admiration harbored darker consequences, not least in terms of the ruthlessness with which they pursued wealth for their nation: "The precautions one finds necessary to take in England, only to recover certain taxes [*impostations*], to assure the execution of numerous ordinances, are so bothersome, even so tyrannical, as to have the right to be surprising in a country of liberty. One needs to be very certain that the common good requires similar policies before enacting them."[205]

If Butel-Dumont only grudgingly approved of such harsh policies for furthering economic power, he was even less favorably inclined toward England's jealous economic nationalism. As documented by the long statutory quotations he listed, England had usurped the Venetian glass and crystal industry by illegally fetching artisans from Murano, had "removed" the "commerce of sugars from the Portuguese," and had stolen the manufacture of "paper" from the French during the reign of William III.[206] All the wealth of the English depended on the government's role in developing domestic manufacture at the cost of others', and this vampiric industrialization was the very quintessence of the English model publicized by Gournay's circle. Yet England itself, or "The British Empire," as writers "lately" had begun to call it, did everything in its power to hinder other countries from following suit, through endless statutes, acts, and bills: *"The emulation, which has spread throughout all Europe and by which all nations force themselves every day to work by themselves the products of their countries, causes some disquiet to the English."*[207]

Even without considering English actions in foreign parts, a comparative study of English exports and imports to France shows a marked discrepancy throughout the eighteenth century, with England, in absolute alignment with Cary's proposals, consistently exporting far more than it imported. England's endemically positive balance of trade with France during the eighteenth century and France's concomitantly negative result highlight and help explain the tension felt in French legislative circles around the time of Cary's translation (see Figure 3.3). The first half of the 1750s, when the Gournay circle formulated their political economy in the wake of the Treaty of Aix-la-Chapelle, indeed emerges as a particularly critical period.

Generally, after studying the records of English economic policy since the Middle Ages, Butel-Dumont could only conclude that "the principal interest" of England was "to interrupt the sales of other nations in foreign markets."[208] Such were the policies "presented to Parliament when the Essay *on the State of England* was published for the first time," and they had, perhaps because of Cary's influence, been adopted "with regards to the exportation of woolen cloth and the importation of drugs proper for dyeing." The Navigation Acts were extremely well thought out and a "manifest wrong" toward the colonials, but Butel-Dumont could not accept that they were simply aimed at "small" targets like blowing the Dutch out of the water. Though admittedly making goods more expensive at home, they were nothing less than the "source" of England's greatness.[209] The Navigation Acts were emblematic of English political economy precisely because

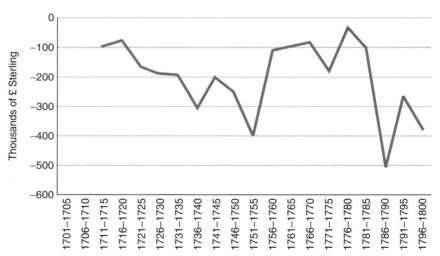

FIGURE 3.3. France's balance of trade with England, by quinquennials, 1701–1800 (based on Schumpeter 1960, 17–18)

they so effectively structured commerce as a weapon through which to further national interests at the expense of others'.[210]

Furthermore, patriotic hatred of foreigners rendered Englishmen pathologically narcissistic. For while "the excellence of English wool is certainly incontestable," it was not so "universally acknowledged" that their "manufacture of cloth" was of a "quality exclusive to all other." The "Nation too confidently praises itself" by thinking "no other people could produce fine cloths." Even worse was their purported exceptionalism:

> The impeccable love, which Englishmen have for their homeland, has made them believe, that Great Britain has been favored by nature in all ways, more than the rest of the Universe. If other places enjoy some advantage, which lacks in their country, they denigrate it, and speak with great emphasis of their equivalent. If such an advantage partakes in those, from which they enjoy, they immediately affirm, that it originates with them.

This "blind prejudice" was observable, among "numerous" other places, in England's "jealousy of seeing the discovery of the New World" and the way many Englishmen pretended Columbus in actuality was a "countryman" who had "lived in Genoa," or that a medieval Welsh prince had discovered America. "Without shame," Butel-Dumont observed, "they even affirm, in all seriousness, that the English corporeally considered are the most perfect men in the world; that they are the most vigorous, and agile."[211]

While England's treatment of Europe was bad enough, it paled in comparison to English actions overseas. Noting the "bad state of the blacks," Butel-Dumont observed that the "prosperity" of the "British Empire" depended on the "exploitation" of African slaves and that its rich colonial produce was "owed [to] their sweat."[212] A comparison of French and English slave trades at the time is illuminating in this regard (see Figure 3.4). In the decade 1751–60, France exported 70,000 slaves from Africa compared to England's 225,000. Yet the total slave population in the French West Indies was rapidly catching up with that in the British Caribbean. The reason for this discrepancy was that British slave traders supplied both powers with their Cimmerian merchandise, again demonstrating their superior technology of empire.[213]

Butel-Dumont's cosmopolitan criticism of English jealousy of trade culminated in an attack reminiscent of those that emanated from the circles of Diderot and Raynal twenty years later.[214] But this was not a mere question of race, for "to conserve for the European English the benefit of manufacture," England had prohibited everyone "the liberty of having certain manufactures in the American colonies." Normatively evaluating commerce, Butel-Dumont accepted that Europeans were guilty of an amoral and unequal trade with non-Europeans, including colonials, and that the "exploiting" institution of slavery was regretful in spite of the attenuating strictures of the Code Noir. Europeans were "arrogant" and confused "esteem" with demonstrations of military might, when all they needed was to biblically treat others as they themselves wanted to be treated.[215] The real question was whether the world's different political economies could be united by bonds of commerce—communication and trade—for the benefit of all. Cary himself had hinted at an answer in his reply to the linen drapers by noting that it was "good trade" for everyone to mutually exchange manufactures, but, as evident in his endorsement of slavery and the deindustrialization of other countries, he never cared much for humanity as such. Butel-Dumont developed this argument in the *Essai,* leaving the Jeromian "sense" of his source squarely behind. The book indeed became the negation of almost everything Cary stood for, in terms not merely of politics and confessional preferences, but of the nature of trade itself. Only mutual industrial emulation could achieve the goal of generalized economic betterment, Butel-Dumont argued, but for this to take place it was necessary to keep the economy political, to make complex moral choices, and to nurture industries with tariffs and prizes, the only security against national enslavement.

The English model of political economy was an ambiguous beast, and emulators had to be selective in their appropriations. Curiously, though,

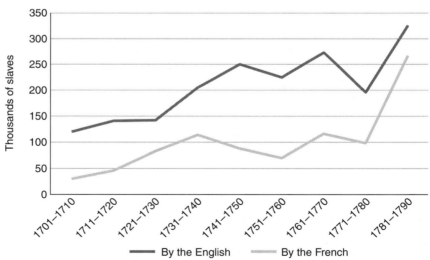

FIGURE 3.4. Comparative exports of slaves from Africa, by decades, 1701–1790 (based on Crouzet 2008, 298)

Butel-Dumont did not quote Montesquieu's caveat against Anglomania but rather Law's: "The example of another Nation, says M. Law, must not determine us to follow the same maxims, without examining if one finds oneself in the same system, and if its and our positions don't differ; so that what benefits it doesn't turn out to be damaging for us." This because "a collection of laws made by different foreign nations, cannot make do for the people, which receives them." This "point" was itself well understood in England, and implicitly more important for "Legislators" to emulate than any individual laws and regulations.[217] The Navigation Acts were a key example of the importance of context for successful emulation. For though there could be no question that France needed to emulate this example, it would have to be judiciously adapted to its new context.[217] Only this could ensure that situations like the 1720s remained a thing of the past, when emulation had gone wrong and a "spirit of madness" had gripped both sides of the Channel. Listing hundreds of phony companies that Englishmen called "*Bluettes* or *Duperies*," Butel-Dumont elucidated the downsides of emulation and commercial society in their most flamboyant folly. Simultaneously, he presented a pertinent case of how emulation should be tempered by wise and experienced political economists. For "by means of these cognitions," he concluded, legislators could generally "know, which branch to sustain, and which needs prohibiting."[218]

After more than a thousand pages of "translation," Butel-Dumont's proposals returned to simple points set out by Cary sixty years earlier: import raw materials, export manufactured goods, secure key resources for supporting home employment and the navy, assure a steady supply of seamen, and make knowledge about these matters public.[219] He disagreed less with the *Essay*'s principles than with their appropriate moral parameters: Bohun had once chastised Cary for being misled by his "partiality," and in emulating the *Essay*, Butel-Dumont began to redress the author's excessive economic natonalism. A political economy *could* create welfare without fostering violent delusions of national grandeur, and the *Essai* was indeed received by contemporary reviewers as a guide to the creation of a functioning political community, one unified by commercial bonds giving it "continual movement" and "animated circulation" ensuring that "the provinces depend one on the others."[220] Overcoming the power politics of the future depended precisely on the establishment of such synergies between economic actors, activities, and even countries.

So although the political and religious elements of Cary's *Essay* fell on deaf ears in France, the historical and economic analyses it suggested were formalized further. Butel-Dumont had sought "maxims" in Cary's science and woven them into a rich legacy of French economic thought and practice, from Colbert to Montesquieu. Yet Butel-Dumont had also taken to heart the cosmopolitan message offered by Fénelon and other critics of Louis XIV. European colonial abuses were blameworthy, but "Machiavellian" misadventures overseas were not the only possible outcome of a political economy of industrial Enlightenment. The tradition he represented was one of many at the time now lost to the dustbins of history, its place usurped by a movement that, though meaning well, created only havoc and human misery. The movement was called Physiocracy, and it erupted in the salons of Paris a mere year after Butel-Dumont translated Cary's *Essay*.[221]

Physiocracy and Anti-Physiocracy

Although Physiocracy, or the "sect" of the *économistes,* as their contemporaries called them, certainly evolved from its incipience in the mid-1750s to its fall from grace in the late 1760s, its fundamental "maxims of economic policy" remained largely unchanged.[222] Quesnay was a physician, a favorite of Louis XV's chief mistress the Madame de Pompadour, and a large landholder. Like Le Blanc and other colleagues of Gournay, he drew heavily on England's recent economic history, and particularly on the techniques—mechanization, selective breeding, four-field crop rotations—behind what we now refer to as its early eighteenth-century "agricultural revolution."[223] But where members of Gournay's circle often emphasized the importance of encouraging agriculture, even experimenting with agronomy on their lands, they did not think it sufficed to ensure a country's welfare.[224] They were, in an important sense, technologists, much like Duhamel du Monceau, perhaps the most influential transmitter of English agrarian techniques to France, who also wrote a striking description of the division of labor in pin-making.[225] The application of useful knowledge to human industry could create wealth, power, and abundance. Gournay's project was to demonstrate how England's achievement of all this resulted from a complex synergy between industrial policies, agricultural reforms, imperialist politics, and institutional structures favoring social mobility. Physiocracy proposed a far simpler, if theoretically more intricate program of political economy emphasizing agriculture and the continuing centrality of the old nobility as large landowners in a capitalist economy.[226]

As such, Physiocracy, literally "the rule of nature," presented an extraordinary all-encompassing vision of a future in which civilization could align with a presumed "natural order," but it was also in many ways an ambitiously reactionary ideology championing the reestablishment of the French monarchy on a rural foundation.[227] And though Physiocrats criticized "feudalism," their project was soon understood by many to revitalize, as far as possible within the parameters of political absolutism and commercialized labor, a "feudal," some said "retrograde" ethos favoring the rural owners of large landed estates over the emerging urban professionals.[228] Whether Quesnay's early work on the circulation of blood had echoes in his later works on the circulation of the economy, whether Benjamin Franklin's "fluid fire" inspired the Physiocrats' faith in the teleology of the natural economy, or whether an eighteenth-century clockwork presented the blueprint for their famous zig-zag by which the yearly circulation of a national economy was depicted, Quesnay's emulation of England could hardly have produced conclusions diverging further from those elaborated by Gournay's circle.[229] To buttress his claims, Quesnay, and soon his converts the Marquis the Mirabeau and Gournay's former protégé Turgot, relied on a cluster of theoretical assumptions regarding the laws of the natural economy and its concomitant political structure of "legal despotism."

Though Physiocracy often is discussed in terms of its adherents' idea of an organic, self-regulating economy, which every year produced a "net product" to be invested again, and their proposal for a "single tax" on land, their foundational theoretical assumption was that all economic activities except agriculture were "sterile"; manufactures and trade did not contribute to increasing national wealth because they could add no value to raw materials beyond what was consumed by the costs of production and the profits of the merchant.[230] On this basis, Quesnay formulated a series of "maxims," the first and foremost of which was that "industrial activities do not multiply wealth." Later, he specified that France "should facilitate an active external trade in raw produce, by means of a passive external trade in manufactured commodities that it can profitably buy from abroad," in other words export foodstuffs and raw materials in exchange for manufactured goods. This, he argued, was "the whole secret of trade: do not be afraid that by incurring this cost you will *become a tributary of other nations.*"[231]

Quesnay's explicit rejection of the contemporary equation of manufacturing superiority with power and independence in international relations only makes sense in the context of a perceived need to engage with an alternate but often ignored tradition of political economy in mid-eighteenth-century France, a tradition spearheaded by the likes of Cary, Melon, and the Gournay circle. And whereas this tradition, deeply indebted to the prudential maxims of reason of state, had been supremely aware of the dangers of emulation and the need to contextualize reforms, Quesnay preached "economic Laws that would be applicable to all Constitutions and that would make the happiness of men anywhere they were followed no matter what the Constitution might be."[232] No similarly radical set of assumptions and proposals had seriously been presented in Europe, but Physiocracy became remarkably influential in a France hungry for remedies and for bread, both of which the sect assured were the long-term consequences of its doctrine. They were instrumental in the overnight liberation of the French grain trade in the 1760s, the disorganizing consequences of which, intertwined with a series of bad harvests, created a human and political crisis in which subsistence anxiety at long last plunged into the depths of subsistence trauma.[233]

Gournay's former acolyte Turgot was one of those who, intrigued by Physiocracy, came to argue that "foreign commerce" should be free of all customs and that it was "incontestable" that "there is no other revenue possible in a state but the annual production of the earth."[234] Though Turgot fused the historiographical legacies of Physiocracy and the Gournay circle, doubtlessly also for reasons of political expediency, it must be noted that their relationship was far more ambiguous, and that some of their basic principles of political economy could not have differed more. Yet there were similarities between the approaches suggested by Butel-Dumont and by the late Turgot, and their ambitions might in the end meet at a higher level of abstraction than specific policy-proposals. When introducing his creed to Hume in a letter of 1766, Turgot presented Physiocracy as a cure for "the prejudices that you have called *Jealousy of Trade*," sadly "quite removed" from English political economy because it was "too difficult to reconcile" with "the ambition to monopolise the commerce of the world." Nonetheless, he hoped that "all those who lead nations" one day would learn to "think like Quesnay on all points."[235] The problem represented a juncture of political economy; if many agreed that jealousy of trade had to be overcome, they often disagreed on the means of doing so. This underlying preoccupation with the future of international trade might explain Butel-Dumont's decision, in the wake of Gournay's death in 1759, to approach the Physiocrats with the hopes, conceivably, of joining a network of patronage similar to that which was dissolving around him.[236]

Following his overture to Mirabeau, however, Butel-Dumont sent him, against Physiocratic protocol but understandably, given his formation under Gournay, a critique of Quesnay's *Economic Table*.[237] The problem with Physiocracy, as Butel-Dumont and so many others noted, was less their legal and political theories (though their concept of "legal despotism" was notoriously hard to swallow) than their foundational assumption regarding the causes of the wealth of nations, and most specifically their theory that all activities but agriculture were sterile. After all, the Italian, Dutch, and English economic models had, against what the Physiocrats argued, revolved around the economic power of manufactures for centuries. As Quesnay's response to Mirabeau testifies to, this was the issue at stake when the name of Cary's translator again appears in their correspondence. Though the exact argument is difficult to make out from surviving letters, it is obvious that Butel-Dumont had questioned the relationship between sterile and productive classes in the Physiocratic system

> M. Dumont has therefore pressed and detained you in reverence of the sterile class [involved in manufactures][,] which derives all of its income from the productive class [involved in agriculture][,] but he does not see that the productive class, in the case in question[,] purchases more than it sells or it gains, and that with this good management, it ruins itself, and, in ruining itself, it has progressively less to sell every year, that the sterile class cannot purchase from it if not what it must purchase from foreigners. Thus, the productive class can never find recompense.[238]

Many letters are obviously missing from Butel-Dumont's epistolary with the two Physiocrats. Yet a final mention of him in a fragment demonstrates just how important assumptions regarding basic economic dynamics were, as well as the importance of human factors in intellectual debates:

> Your letter to Mr Dumont is admirable and far beyond the reach of this tiny *monsieur*, who claims the decisive tone of a master in a science where the most instructed do not walk if not with great circumspection. Mr. Mesaigues has witnessed a scene that I had to endure with this little rebel to the point of making me know his ineptitude and his dominant character. From now on, he will have the satisfaction of always being right with me, because I do not want to throw myself against a bar of iron.[239]

We do not know how Butel-Dumont himself reacted to the exchange, but he was eventually known as an outspoken enemy of the "congrégation des Quesnayïtes."[240]

His stance was hardly atypical. Nowhere is the problem of precursorism in the history of economics more acute than with the Physiocrats, who lost every battle yet won the war of historiography. Were one to believe textbooks of economics, one would think that Physiocrats dominated the Enlightenment, and it is even argued that we should "learn" their "lesson" today.[241] Physiocrats admittedly relied on a vocabulary of "facts" and "evidence," but this rhetorical ploy merely obfuscated what many contemporaries criticized as their underlying ignorance about economic matters.[242] Quesnay's acolyte Pierre Samuel du Pont de Nemours, for example, readily admitted in his autobiography that "to control my theory, while verifying its consequences and applying them to the facts," he relied on chatter with "a few carters who worked beside the road" and "the only person whom I knew who had any rural notions, *my Father's Cook!*"²⁴³

The vehemence of Hume's own reaction to the Physiocratic solution to jealousy of trade was, in light of someone who on his deathbed considered himself "a man of mild dispositions" and "little susceptible to enmity," telling of how much was at stake in the formulation of practical policies to achieve their common aim.²⁴⁴ After a lengthy epistolary discussion of political economy with Turgot he wrote a letter to Morellet, hoping that he would take arms against the Physiocrats and "thunder them, and crush them, and pound them, and reduce them to dust and ashes! They are, indeed, the set of men the most chimerical and most arrogant that now exist. . . . I wonder what could engage our friend, M. Turgot, to herd among them."²⁴⁵ And though the Physiocrats have led a historiographically pampered existence, Butel-Dumont and Hume were far from alone in recoiling at the tangibly disastrous results of their policies. Adam Smith may have been only mildly repudiative, even considering dedicating his *Wealth of Nations* to Quesnay, but Rousseau, hardly renowned for the practicality of his political philosophy, wrote to Mirabeau that while his "system" was "very good for the people of Utopia," it was "worthless for the children of Adam," and Louis-Sébastien Mercier—incidentally Butel-Dumont's cousin and one of the best-selling authors of the age—hoped that "equitable history" would "punish" the Physiocrats.²⁴⁶ By 1770, the party of the *économistes* was nearly universally despised in France, assailed by Diderot and Voltaire alike.²⁴⁷

So though Physiocracy would seem hegemonic in the period following Butel-Dumont's translation of Cary, and to a considerable extent was implemented in the 1760s and in the 1770s under Turgot's ministry, with a lingering presence even under Charles Alexander de Calonne in the 1780s, it never eclipsed, and was in effect outlived by, an older, realist and historical tradition of industrial political economy that stretched from Colbert to Cary, whose Colbertist stamp was explicit, to his neo-Colbertist French mediator and the reaction to Physiocracy led by figures such as Jacques Necker. Physiocracy was extraordinarily successful, and might have been the first coherent doctrine of economic thought to be fully implemented by a government, but it was in no way the be-all and end-all of Enlightenment political economy. Neither was this a tension between theoretical sophistication and practical exigencies. Some of the most vehement anti-Physiocrats, from Jean-Joseph-Louis Graslin to Galiani, were also the most sophisticated theorists of the age.²⁴⁸ As one summarized his critique in 1790, the Physiocrats had presented a fallacious theory believing they would benefit large landowners, while "that of the English," understood to be not merely about flourishing agriculture but about a structural transformation of the economy away from its rural foundations, would have been a "better method."[249] The Papal political economist Paolo Vergani put it similarly in Rome on the eve of Napoleon's invasion. There was no doubt that England was the polity to emulate, but the vehicle for such emulation had to be "Giovanni Carii," not Physiocracy. For had Physiocracy "been generally adopted it would again have submerged Europe in the barbarism of the feudal centuries," into nothing less than "feudal anarchy."[250]

Anglomanie, Anglophobie, and Enlightenment

As these debates began, a very different storm was brewing in the real world that would galvanize the meaning of emulation and challenge some of the most hallowed ideals of the eighteenth century. Butel-Dumont's vision of relatively peaceful industrial emulation was one of many such hopeful schemes that were unable to wrest themselves loose from Anglo-French rivalry, and the Seven Years' War would soon painfully demonstrate that even the most tempered politics could be swept away into global war, particularly when instigated by a nation as powerful as Great Britain. The French knew well that they were not fit for a war against England, and a telling manuscript, *Memorial on the Means of Preventing the War and Arriving at a Conciliation with England,* dated February 1755, went as far as suggesting giving England large parts of Newfoundland, Quebec, and the Caribbean Islands in an attempt at appeasement.[251] The number of unprovoked British attacks only escalated that year, however, and the European intelligentsia quickly came to agree with the message of the Gournay circle and of Montesquieu's darkest moments.

England was not simply a model to imitate. It was also a model to fear. The *Observateur hollandaise,* a propaganda outlet of the French government on the eve of the Seven Years' War, noted on 1 October 1755 that England acted contrary to the "law of peoples," and Goudar observed that it ran "a completely tyrannical system" tending toward "universal monarchy." England was becoming the same bugbear that, in the guises of Colbert and Louis XIV, had justified Cary's imperialism in the first place. England's actions triggered nothing less than a crisis of values among European philosophes, demonstrating the thin line separating Anglomanie from Anglophobie and the fragile balance between nationalism and cosmopolitanism, localized and universal good. In his 1757 *Prophylactic against Anglomania,* the great cosmopolitan traveler Fougeret de Monbron succinctly described the ideological revolution at hand: "This people who have always been considered the proudest, the most jealous of their neighbor's success, the most interested, the most ungrateful and the most ferocious in the world, are, according to M. de Voltaire, the most generous, the most magnanimous, the most faithful to their commitments."[252] A reckoning was at hand.

England had given the world the *Spectator,* Locke, and Newton; it had refined earlier Dutch and Italian institutions and rendered them operational in the form of the Bank of England and the public debt; it enjoyed an effective fiscal system free from corrupting privileges; it had revolutionized agriculture; it had perfected the differentiation of tariffs to encourage domestic manufactures; and it had powerfully demonstrated the gains to be had from unleashing the passions of the bourgeois. In very few words, England stood testimony to the immense creative forces of commercial society. Yet all this had come at a cost. The "British Empire" was a blackguard empire, perfidious and terrifying, more like a buccaneer than a gentleman. As Galiani wrote in wake of the Seven Years' War, England was "a powerful and glorious nation" that considered itself "highly cultured" yet had "loudly declared to all the nations of Europe" that it did not "recognize the law of peoples, nor have room for it," instead "adopting that reason which is only apt for barbarians."[253] English patriotism, though planetary in ambition, was deeply antithetical to the cosmopolitan ideals of the age and as such impossible to reconcile with the ideal virtue of emulation.

In 1760, Butel-Dumont translated the document that was most representative of the calamities befalling Europe but ironically also contained the secret to greatness in the modern world: the English Navigation Acts.[254] By that time, even the Anglomaniac Voltaire had declared war on England.[255] And, in 1761, as the Duc de Choiseul scrambled to safeguard French interests in the New World at the closing of the Seven Years' War, he called on Butel-Dumont, deemed "one of his most capable propagandists," to publish a stinging indictment of English political economy in the form of a *Point of View on the Consequences which must Follow from the Rupture by the English of the Negotiations between France and England, from March 26 to September 20 1761.*[256] England, he observed, was realizing his worst fears. Victorious in Canada, they would harness the resources of North America, and the seamen they could train off Newfoundland, to challenge the fragile Iberian grip on the southern continent and decidedly shatter the balance of power in Europe to achieve universal empire. As in the earlier work of the Gournay circle, globalization—for that is what was at stake—was mainly a spatial expansion of the European theatre of war and wealth, not a qualifier of the nature of commercial relations. Yet, however fleetingly, the thought of what might come afterward struck Butel-Dumont. Now that North American colonists no longer required English protection from enemies in the Western Hemisphere, they would declare independence and harness the great resources of the continent for themselves. There would be yet another *translatio imperii,* across the Atlantic, and this time Europe would be left squarely behind.[257]

France nonetheless remained one of the world's great powers even after its defeat in the Seven Years' War. As Goudar and Casanova put it at the time, "Exclusive of the three great powers, France, England, and the House of Austria, the others may be looked on as intermediate, subordinate, and dependent states." Unlike England, though, the two libertines argued, France had failed to keep up with the "total change" undergone by "the European system." So though "this monarchy spreads its wings over the [Atlantic] Ocean and the Mediterranean . . . instead of being mistress of those two seas, she is insulted on her coasts." The consequence of this failure to adapt was clear, and harrowing in relation to contemporary tropes of liberty and economic competition: *"the maritime power* [England] *has given law to the continental one* [France]."[258] Needless to say, the latter continued to emulate British theories, policies, and technologies ever more intensively during the second half of the eighteenth century. Through espionage, the naturalization of foreign experts, and contraband trade in prohibited machinery, France and other powers followed on the heels of industrial Britain.

But if England's knowledge economy could be codified, translated, and transferred, the same was not true for the material world that had borne it. Butel-Dumont had praised the "Potosi Gallois," England's immense mineral resources, and no amount of guile could emulate it. Not only was France poorly endowed with coal resources, but iron, the main raw material of the industrial revolution, cost 100 percent more there than in England. However ingenious emulation was, and however refined political economy could become, one would, at times, hit the immutable reality of the commodity lottery. Hence, as Britain's industrial edge continued to sharpen into the early decades of the nineteenth century, official inquiries there decided both that it made little sense to hinder workers from taking their skills abroad and that it made a whole lot of sense to prohibit the exportation of machinery. Britain's "technological leadership" would simply not buckle as long as continental competitors lacked the actual raw materials of industrial civilization, intrinsically dependent not only on its domestic coalfields but also on its imperial supplies of organic raw materials.[259]

Butel-Dumont continued to work as a censor during the years following his *Essai*'s publication. He was elected honorary member of the Académie Royale des Sciences, des Belles-Lettres et des Arts d'Amiens in 1756, and in 1757 he was appointed first secretary to Paul-François Galucci, Marquis de L'Hospital and French ambassador to St. Petersburg, a post he was forced to resign before even starting after nearly succumbing to pneumonia in Warsaw on his way to Russia.[260] His celebrated 1771 *Theory of Luxury,* in which he finally confronted the problem of luxuries head on, systematized, under his own pen, the Gournay circle's ideas on the issues of luxury, political economy, and economic development. It was, as he would write to Benjamin Franklin, a work on the "effects of luxury considered from the point of view which might interest a statesman."[261] Accepting the need for a "security of property" emphasized by Cary, he now embraced luxury wholeheartedly because of its power to stimulate "emulation," and thus consumption, production, and ultimately material and moral welfare: nothing could drive men to better their condition more than luxuries, and nothing could "bind" their needs closer together. Without "luxury" men were "solitary like wolves." All this as long—he held on here to the *Essay*'s insights—as the object of men's desire was produced *domestically,* with all the useful consequences of employment and refinement of the arts safely secured for the kingdom.[262] Butel-Dumont's last major works were an imaginary account of an indecent philosophical voyage through Mongolia, a history of the early French kings, and an erudite history of Roman lands and taxes, the last two of which won him prizes offered by the Académie des Inscriptions et Belles-Lettres.[263] In 1779 he became secretary of the Société libre d'émulation, and in 1786 he was made *trésorier de France* by Louis XVI, a post that conferred on him the privilege of hereditary nobility.

Like Cary, Butel-Dumont thus realized the transition from merchant's son to nobility, embodying the ideal of a commercial nobility, habitually associated with Coyer, that he had argued for under Gournay decades earlier. As the poet Gérard de Nerval recounts, Butel-Dumont eventually established a "salon" bridging the gap, an "intermediary society where one encountered the *haute* bourgeoisie, *la robe,* and a bit of nobility." Frequented by the likes of the Venetian playwright Carlo Goldoni, it was "avid with readings, philosophies, paradoxes, *bons mots* and spicy anecdotes," and it was in this context that he came to be associated with libertine circles through his patronage of, and carnal competition with, the polymathic utopian pornographer Réstif de la Bretonne.[264] Their relationship was conflictual, his memoirs describing the elderly Butel-Dumont as extraordinarily "wealthy" and "très-bourgeois" with a "crapulous air." His "mouth always smelled of fried intestines" and his "mania of taking tobacco" was "repulsive." Not only did he eulogize luxury, but he practiced it as well. And so his "morals" were "relaxed," like those of "all our little *philosophistes,* who think all pleasure is permitted." He was a "character equally vile and sad" to the extent that it canceled out the "pleasures of his baseness and madness," but he was also "a great loon" and seemingly anonymous coauthor of some of Réstif's most flamboyant works.[265]

Apart from this late-life penchant for applied Epicureanism, Butel-Dumont sought to unify historical insights with the exigencies of practicable reforms, uniting his failed attempts at membership in the Académie des Inscriptions with a successful associate membership of the Société Royale d'Agriculture in 1787. His last published work, the *Historical Studies on the Agriculture of the Romans,* in effect took up the overarching argument where his *Theory of Luxury* left off. Not only did the modern world order require an overthrow of antiquated moralities, but it entailed a concomitant overthrow of nostalgia for the ancient world itself. Rome had been but a brutish vampire state that no agrarian virtue could redeem, no matter what the Fénelonians argued. Romans had preyed on the industry of others, and one could only pray to "heaven" that such a nation never appeared again on the "face of the earth."[266] Though commerce could still take on remarkably bellicose guises, the "moderns" had overcome the "ancients" in every regard. This made it all the more important for Butel-Dumont to make the academy socially and politically useful, to unite the entrepreneurial customs of the mercantile classes with the privileged profundity of elite scholarship and court culture.[267] By the time of his death on the eve of the French Revolution, all his major works had aimed at forging a functioning commercial society in a world in thrall to ruthless competition. A similar effort had been made in Naples, a kingdom even further behind in the European race for power and plenty, while Gournay was still alive. And, again, architects of the new political economy called on Cary's *Essay.*

CHAPTER FOUR

Genovesi's *Storia del commercio della Gran Brettagna*

Fortune Evanescent

The heuristic value of François Melon's model had not been exhausted with the simple identification of industrial England as the "island of wool" and agricultural France as an "island of grain" in his idealized representation of the world economy. The Italian peninsula had once been both, and found its analytical equivalent in Melon's description of a once powerful island that with time had lost the good graces of Lady Commerce. It was a motley constellation of independent republics, principalities, and subject states, a political microcosm of Europe, that twice had been the dominant force in Western civilization—during Roman times and during the Renaissance.[1] But if "Italy" was not politically united, it had been thought of as a cultural unit at least since the time of Petrarch.[2] And the relation of this cultural unit as a whole to the rest of Europe deeply influenced local life on the peninsula, particularly in terms of the contemporary understanding of the vicissitudes of time, trade, and power. For the British Grand Tourist Charles Thompson was only one of many in the eighteenth century to note that though "Italy" "once gave Laws to the World," this was no longer the case. Or, as Goudar and Casanova saw it: "Italy, which formerly gave law to the universe, is now weak and impotent, without any thing worthy the name of a power in it."[3] *Translatio imperii* had left Italy behind, and the story of Cary's Italian translation is a story of how some sought to catch up with it again.

Generally speaking, the Italian city-states had proved unable to cope with the enormous structural changes incurred by the world economy in the age of exploration. As the Atlantic and Baltic seaways increasingly usurped the importance of the Mediterranean and the larger territorial states of northern Europe took care of their own economic needs to an ever greater extent, the small Italian states found themselves unable to compete with the lower wages, larger internal markets, and ruthless economic nationalism of the great powers.[4] These dynamics force us to revisit the vexing question of the role played by international trade in economic development. As discussed earlier, the tendency of neoclassical economic historians to argue that development depends on domestic rather than foreign trade sometimes aligns poorly with the historical record. The causes of Italian decline in the seventeenth century identified by the great Italian economic historian Carlo Cipolla are interesting in this regard: "the economic prosperity of Italy was fundamentally dependent on massive exports of manufactured articles" and "on a huge volume of invisible exports such as banking and shipping services." By prohibiting the exports of its own raw wool and actively promoting that of its woolen manufactures, the very foundations of its economic miracle, England both cut off Italy's main source of raw materials *and* usurped its international markets for finished goods.[5] The result was systemic economic decline across the peninsula.

Native thinkers were all too aware of these changes, and if bellicose, papaphobic nationalism and virulent subsistence anxieties could respectively characterize the English and French debates over political economy, along, of course, with their shared hopes of global domination, then the looming awareness of decline conditioned not only national debates but likewise the reception of foreign ideas on the matter in Italy. Political and economic thought there was, for far longer than in other European contexts, simply impossible to divorce from the thanatology of nations, from the study of how cultures and political communities decline and die. As a dejected Machiavelli could not help but report home from his diplomatic missions for Florence, that city-state's relative weakness in international relations was evident already from the turn of the fifteenth century onward, and the ghastly 1527 sack of Rome by Spanish troops signaled to all the end of an era; as one eighteenth-century historian described the event, "thus Italy, that once gave laws to the world, now saw the troops of Germany and Spain, by turns, enter into her territories."[6]

Though the Venetian economy, among others, remained a Mediterranean power for some time, the season of foreign influence on the peninsula would bring about great economic consequences in the coming century. Almost a century later, after Venice's supremacy had peaked, Paolo Sarpi, a statesman, historian, and political observer of extraordinary acuity, wrote to the English ambassador Sir Dudley Carleton that "Italia" had become a gateway to the "monarchia di Europa," the battleground, not unlike the German states of the Thirty Years' War, where foreign powers could play out their ambitions with abandon. It had, as Goudar and Casanova remarked in their *Chinese Spy,* "ever been an object of emulation among the European potentates" and was a "theatre of European revolutions."[7] The only possible remedy, Sarpi had thought, was for disparate provinces of the peninsula to realize that their "common good" depended on "walking" in "common concert."[8] The particular interests of the Holy See, however, ensured that Italy—"Oh! Miserable and scrambled Italy!" as the antiquarian Scipione Maffei exclaimed—remained divided and therefore conquered; economically, culturally, and intellectually.[9] Nor did foreign observers, from George Berkeley and Montesquieu in their travel diaries to Adam Smith in his 1756 *Letter to the Edinburgh Review,* shy away from noting Italy's fall from grace.[10] The first Italian translation of Cary's *Essay* would appear a year later, as part of an increasing tide of foreign fashions and ideas, just as the troubled peninsula was seething with news of the Seven Years' War.[11]

The decline of Italy and the rise of the North indeed became one of the most powerful tropes in eighteenth-century European literature and the continent's economic imagination alike, and Italian thinkers were quick to realize that the most pertinent lessons for reform and development were now to be learned across the Alps, in the ways the great empires administered their states and their economic affairs.[12] A 1751 Savoy manuscript on the imitation of successful economic policy by the Sardinian ambassador to Britain Count Carlo Francesco Baldassare Perrone di San Martino is representative of the furor of emulation at the time as well as its particular sources of inspiration. Not only did the Count include a full translation of a pamphlet on the encouragement of manufactures by Richard Cox, lord chancellor of Ireland and opponent of Cary in the debates over Irish woolens, but also actively encouraged the imitation of foreign ideas and policies, including a chapter "containing twenty-six general maxims drawn from Davenant, Child, Gee, the British *Marchant,* Locke, Uztariz and du Tot." Its manchette, in particular, could hardly have put the phenomenon of emulation through translation more clearly: "Look aster [*sic*] good paterns [*sic*] and fallow [*sic*] them / Cherchez de bon modèles, et imitezles."[13] Though Cary was not on the list, his fame in Italy would soon supersede that of all Perron's sources combined.

Appropriately, his *Essay* would first arrive in the Kingdom of Naples, the Italian state that had cultivated the most refined historical sensitivity to decline and submission. The kingdom's idiosyncratic character was generated by two timeless facts: its proud millennial heritage, harking back to remote antiquity, and its long succession of foreign rulers. Saturating all aspects of domestic life, both were active forces shaping Naples socially, culturally, and economically: it was a cosmopolitan city, at the crossroads of Mediterranean trade and communication since Homeric times, yet often under the dominion of absentee masters.[14] Geographically one of the most extensive of the peninsula, it was endowed with copious natural resources, a gentle climate, and a magnificent natural harbor that would spellbind visitors for centuries to come. All this, though, local writers noted, had been a cause of great grief rather than joy, for whereas the barren lands of the Dutch and the Venetians drove them to better their condition, gifted people like the Neapolitans still suffered from initial complacency in the face of natural abundance.[15] Naples had, as its astute observer Galiani wrote, "not breathed the air of liberty" for two millennia and had "changed dominion more often than any other city on earth"; it was a depressed, sprawling metropolis-kingdom, plagued by dearth, poverty, and inequality under a long succession of foreign masters, and it was precisely this material and institutional backwardness that laid the foundations for the increasingly negative image of southern Italian life in Europe.[16]

The great Swiss historian Jacob Burckhardt argued that the southern Italian and Sicilian kingdom of Frederick II between 1220 and 1250 was the first "state" to be fashioned "as a work of art," but historiography has long since reassessed such laudatory treatments of his reign. What historians *do* agree on is that Frederick II's Naples was soon overtaken by northern states in terms of European economic and political development, and that few, in the intervening seven centuries, found reasons to emulate it.[17] Rather, Neapolitan civic life under the yoke of foreign rulers became a symbol of misrule in early modern Europe. Admittedly, the fifteenth-century chronicler Loise de Rosa could praise the kingdom's many foreign sovereigns—itself nothing exceptional in an era of dynastic states—for having contributed to the gradual enrichment of its soil, because "they brought with them from their countries the best," so that Naples now offered "the best fruits of the world."[18] But such panegyrics were rare. In spite of its flourishing cultural and intellectual life, Naples remained among the most economically backward regions of Europe throughout the early modern period, something akin to a periphery within the core.[19]

And in spite of the literary topos exalting southern fertility, to the extent that it was known as the "Garden of Italy" even in the eighteenth century, the largely agricultural kingdom was repeatedly plagued by dearth and famines.[20] The loose organizational system now known as "feudalism" had been instituted in southern Italy by its Norman conquerors, who, broadly speaking, exchanged fiefs for support and military service.[21] Feudal institutions were only strengthened over the subsequent centuries, as waves of foreign rulers came to depend on the local baronage for support, awarding them extraordinary concessions, including royal jurisdiction within their fiefs. By the time Goudar and Casanova turned their incisive gaze to Naples, few would have agreed with de Rosa's assessment of the outcome of the kingdom's unique history. For as the two libertines noted, foreign conquerors could bring not only "fruits" but also "vices." The reason "Neapolitans" were "the wickedest people on the whole earth" was that "the several governments" to which Naples had "been subject, have infected it with all the vices of the several climates in Europe."[22] The city, not surprisingly, came to be known as "a paradise inhabited by devils."[23]

When Charles of Bourbon routed the Habsburg rulers of Naples in 1734 to establish an ostensibly independent realm, the kingdom therefore rejoiced at the prospects of general renewal, when a much-needed economic and cultural rejuvenation could follow on the heels of political independence.[24] Economic mismanagement, however, previously at the hands of distant sovereigns continued in the wake of liberation; the new kingdom was forced to accept debilitating compromises with a legion of counteracting forces and corporations of varying degrees of coherence, from the ecclesiastics to the feudal aristocracy and the *togati,* the powerful judiciary nobility of the robe, all reducing the space in which the government could act.[25] As the possibility of significant reforms was curtailed by special interests and the monarchy's fiscal burden increasingly fell on already marginalized social groups, civil society itself seemed at stake, and the reappearance of brigandage during the 1750s—often with the support of the feudal barons—only further highlighted the waning viability of the state as such.

This dramatic situation found some if its most trenchant descriptions in the writings of foreign visitors like Charles de Brosses, a Sallust scholar and parliamentary president from Burgundy. In what would amount to the most famous French travel narrative of Enlightenment Italy, he wrote that for all its professed independence, Naples would forever remain "prey" to anyone interested in conquering it. Not only could it militarily offer "no serious resistance," but it was terminally weakened by an "incurable" internal malady: the "spirit" of its populace, which—reiterating a common trope—was "absolutely perverse, evil, superstitious, treacherous, inclined to sedition, and always ready to pillage under the guidance of the first Masaniello" that appeared, a reference to the famous democratic uprising in seventeenth-century Italy. Neapolitan, de Brosses continued, was "perhaps the most horrible and barbarous" dialect since "the tower of Babel," and aspects of the city induced "vomit." The few positive aspects of his journey to Naples, apart from the view of Capri and the marvels of the recently uncovered ruins of Herculaneum (overpowering evidence of decline), were intellectual in nature, and primary among them the discussion of "physics" and "geometry" with "abbé Entieri."[26]

The Tuscan mathematician Bartolomeo Intieri was a polymathic custodian of the Medici Grand Dukes' estates in Naples. A man of intellectual as well as practical interests, he was a sworn "enemy of sterile and abstract speculations" and deeply taken by the emerging logic of Newtonian mechanics and its possible applications in other disciplines. He was a renowned inventor, among other things of a method for conserving grain that was plagiarized by Duhamel du Monceau, and though a foreigner, he had no difficulty in seeing that Naples historically had been stuck between the imperial ambitions of the Spanish monarchy and those of the Holy See.[27] Reacting to this situation, Intieri in many ways became Gournay's Neapolitan alter ego, an administrator of knowledge fertilizing the soil of Neapolitan reformism, and it was not without reason that Franco Venturi reckoned him the source of the "Neapolitan Enlightenment" itself.[28] It was under his sway that Antonio Genovesi—the first son of a poverty-stricken farmer, born in the vicinity of Salerno in 1713—came as a young theology student in Naples.

There, the young abbé had attended the lectures of the elderly philosopher Giambattista Vico, but soon left the latter's Platonic philosophical heritage in favor of the Newtonian *novatores* of the newly established Accademia delle scienze founded by Intieri and Celestino Galiani, uncle of the better known diplomat and political economist Ferdinando Galiani.[29] Genovesi's career in the 1740s had been marked by a prolonged polemic over his theological heterodoxy and purported atheism, resulting, his eulogist wrote, from the inability of contemporaries to differentiate between "reason" and "irreligion."[30] It was during these persecutions that Genovesi was taken under Intieri's wing, and no doubt, this helped him undertake his transition from "metafisico" to "mercatante," from theologian and moral philosopher to economic reformer preoccupied principally with worldly rather than spiritual concerns.[31] In spite of these powerful influences, Genovesi believed himself above simple classification in his autobiography: "In the questions that regard God and faith, I am an orthodox believer; in the others, which enter the dominion of philosophy, I profess myself neither Aristotelian, nor Platonic, nor Epicurean, nor Stoic; I am not Greek, nor Latin; and neither Cartesian nor Newtonian, Malebranchian nor Leibnizian. Whose am I then? My own. I am rational."[32] As it turns out, however, his answer on the issue of "God and faith" had a greater impact on his wider interests than he may have liked to admit.

Political Economy, "Enlightenment," and the Public Sphere

The grand goal of Intieri's group was not institutional and economic reform per se. The previous generation of Neapolitan legal reformers had respected traditional social hierarchies and, consequently, largely failed in their efforts.[33] Having learned from this, the "enlightenment" of which Genovesi spoke and for which he fought until his death was concerned also, if not principally, with reforming people, recasting the three estates of society, and empowering hitherto marginalized groups. As Intieri had cultivated him, so Genovesi could sow the fields of the Mezzogiorno. Writing to a friend after visiting the Neapolitan countryside in 1753, he could "only hope that the inhabitants of those blessed hills understood their advantages better, and added to nature a bit of what industry and art can give." There was urgency to his vision, for people just outside the walls of Naples—one of the "greatest" cities of Europe—were more reminiscent of "Hottentots" than Europeans.[34] Yet his historical studies had taught him that Europeans had been "Huttentotti e Lapponi," the peoples now known as Khoikhoi and Saami, when the cultures of Asia and North Africa bloomed, so he knew peoples, nations, and empires were in constant flux; the Neapolitan crisis could certainly be overcome, the question was only how.[35] By joining the practical Neapolitan intellectuals attracted to the person of Intieri in the early 1750s, Genovesi, in other words, took sides in the larger reevaluation of the arts and sciences that shook the contemporary republic of letters.

Optimistically denouncing Rousseau's accusations against modern commercial society, he argued forcibly for its practical genesis, for its valuable social, economic, and even moral consequences, and for the perpetual need to refine civilization ever further.[36] "Reason," Genovesi would write in his widely influential 1753 *Discourse About the True Ends of the Arts and Sciences,* "is not useful, unless it has become practice and reality."[37] "Reason" was "the universal art," the key to uniting Genovesi's disparate interests, theory and practice, moral philosophy and political economy.[38] Although he was involved in serious theological disputes in the 1740s, he framed his reformism in generally secular terms, he abandoned the scholastic notion of a "just price" reflecting something beyond the nexus of supply and demand, and he remained true to his spiritual formation by defining "reason" as a derivative of "religion and experience."[39] The practice of reason could bring knowledge, wealth, *virtú*, and public happiness, but this would never occur unless, as Cary too had practiced in Bristol, it was brought to the common people through radical educational reform.[40] The venerable call for *libertas philosophandi* therefore found deep resonance in Genovesi's reformist spirit in this period.[41] Reason, and thus science, were the result of experience, and education was nothing but experience by proxy. "Reading, writing, and a bit of abacus" would become "almost common" in Naples if free public schools were established, and the teaching of the *Catechism* even to adults would help foster what he, echoing Cary, called the "the *virtú* of a merchant," safely based on institutions like religion and a fair system of justice.[42]

But though Genovesi was at the forefront of the major intellectual debates of the eighteenth century, irreligion never became an option for him, nor did he fully embrace the fashionable Epicurean thesis, most famously propagated by Mandeville, that the common good could result from private vices. Instead, he injected metaphors drawn from Newtonian physics— vindicated by the notion of Anthony Ashley-Cooper, the Third Earl of Shaftesbury, of virtue as a balance between private and public forces—into a basically Aristotelian moral cosmology, concluding that "*virtù* is the arithmetic middle between vices." The art of maintaining this "equilibrium in the physical laws of collision" between passions, however, the "art of living happily," required reason and insight. Consequently, most people were doomed to a life of misery.[43]

This application of a Newtonian scientific vocabulary to the moral sphere was precisely what Intieri had encouraged, but it by no means entailed that Genovesi drew the most radical conclusions of contemporary materialist moral philosophy. Against "Newton" and "Locke," he held that the "soul" was impervious to "penetration" by "ideas" through the faculties of the "senses." The bottom line was that sensual materialism was irreconcilable with theology and that no amount of theorizing could disprove his belief in the existence of an eternal soul, Lucretian atomism be damned. An existential apriorism, this baseline religiosity safeguarded Genovesi's vision from the most subversive elements of modern philosophy. Man might be hedonistic, but Genovesi's Christian beliefs by default blocked the following step of assuming him to be antagonistic; though man was "naturally *jealous* of his own good," he was "not *envious of others*."[44] Hobbesian states of nature only emerged if the equilibrium of colliding passions went unmitigated by reason, and so it was obvious, also in light of Naples's history of failed reforms, that popular enlightenment through education was the only meaningful way to achieve worldly melioration. But education in what?[45]

Genovesi's letters and autobiography bear clear witness to the Intieri group's profound interest in matters of political economy, and their discussions would often revolve around Melon, Montesquieu, the "legislator of all nations," and later the rich output of Gournay's circle: Dangeul and Forbonnais, as well as their respective translations of Ulloa and Uztáriz, Le Blanc's translation of Hume's *Essays,* and of course Cary.[46] Intieri's passion for Montesquieu was so contagious that Genovesi himself would begin an Italian translation of the *Spirit of the Laws* in earnest toward the end of his life.[47] Equally important, however, the group relied heavily on a local Neapolitan heritage of political economy after Intieri uncovered Antonio Serra's legendary 1613 *Short Treatise,* the importance of which I will emphasize below.[48] In the group's great architecture of "Enlightenment," political economy again emerged as the sturdiest keystone on which to build a better future, the chosen channel for enlightening the kingdom's lower classes, and the vehicle of reform, not only of formal institutions but of people's patterns of thought and behavior.

Naples was rich in natural resources, but these needed to be harnessed to ensure power and independence in the modern world. And though, as an agricultural kingdom, it had much to learn from the French example, Neapolitan reformers knew well that England's manufactures had ensured its subsistence safety, and that their city's former dominator Spain still suffered from having favored raw materials like gold over domestic industries. "Naples," Galiani concluded, was "a copy of Spain," hence his wish to read "the works of Uztáriz and Ulloa" "at any cost," "in original or translation."[49] The economic dynamics of Europe meant that four principal economic discourses presented themselves for emulation in Naples: its own historical one, stretching back at least as far as to the work of Serra; the French for its agricultural context, for the achievements of Colbert, and for Gournay's emphasis on the importance of translations; the Spanish for how to escape decline caused by dependence on foreign industries; and the English for how to achieve greatness through manufacturing and for having spearheaded a vision of polished commercial society. The focal point of this Neapolitan movement to emulate European currents of political economy was the establishment of a chair of "Commerce and Mechanics" at the University of Naples in 1754, the first of its kind in Italy.[50]

But though supportive of Intieri's endeavor, Galiani betrayed his usual cynicism about it in private correspondence:

> Bartolomeo Intieri has founded a chair of Commerce and Mechanics to be taught in Italian, and Genovesi will teach it. It is a general rule, that men turn to take care of things when they are coming to an end, not when they are blooming. At the time of Michelagnolo [*sic*] there was no academy of drawing in Rome, and when your Republic [Florence] was richer than Holland is today, nobody thought of founding academies of agriculture, nor of translating Locke.[51]

The establishment of academies, university studies, and, strikingly, translations of political economy were measures considered necessary to counteract Italy's relative decline in Europe. The disagreement between Galiani and Genovesi was over whether they could work; whether fate, operating through the cyclical mechanisms of history, could be fought. The chair, endowed by Intieri with a stipend of 300 ducats per annum and the donation of his considerable personal library, marked Genovesi's transition from theology to political economy, but an emerging historiographical consensus asserts the underlying unity of the two parts of his career, identifying a common thread uniting two ways of manifesting the same spirit of reform.[52] He certainly retained his penchant for intellectual cosmopolitanism throughout his life, arguing that it was not enough to encourage the language and sciences of the kingdom if one did not also look to the rest of the world, "which," Genovesi insisted only few days after his inaugural lecture, "is man's greatest school, or rather the first teacher, and always talking."[53]

Parochialism was a luxury Neapolitans could ill afford, and translation became the only means of disclosing enlightenment. Genovesi's original plan had been for his first lectures on political economy to coincide with the publication of an "introduction to the theory of commerce, destined to make these studies appreciated by the current studious youth."[54] And when his inaugural lecture was "met with applause, and immediately spread throughout the entire city," and his lecture halls turned out to always be filled with people of various "orders," he turned his mind to composing a "General discourse on commerce."[55] This would, three years later, become his *Reasoning on Commerce in General,* published as an introduction to his most considerable contribution to the program of enlightenment formulated by Intieri's group, a translation of a work that, at first sight, may seem a strange choice: Butel-Dumont's translation of John Cary's *Essay on the State of England.*[56] There is no indication of when Genovesi first encountered the French edition of Cary's *Essay,* and his unfinished autobiography unfortunately stops a year short of its publication.[57] Nonetheless, one can make educated conjectures regarding the origins of his enterprise.

The Babelian problem that plagued the great minds of Europe had been addressed by friends and acquaintances of Genovesi for years before he translated Cary.[58] Intieri himself mobilized to "publish the Italian translation of the *Spirit of the Laws*" already in 1750, Galiani cut his teeth on economic issues by translating Locke's essays on money, and a young colleague at the University of Naples, Bartolomeo de Felice, warned that Italians risked missing out on "great enlightenment [*lumi*]" if useful works remained encrypted in foreign languages. Since even Germans had begun looking toward England for inspiration, it was about time Italians did too, and de Felice did his part in counteracting the curse of the tower by publishing an anthology of largely English scientific texts for the use of Neapolitan students.[59] Genovesi similarly wrote very favorably of the Neapolitan mathematician Nicola de Martino in his autobiography, considering him "one of the great geniuses" for "showing us all the best that the English and French had produced on this subject." And in his personal correspondence around the time of Cary's first Italian edition, Genovesi wrote: "if those who know how to manage the subject and the language well would give us some translations . . . of works of natural history and experimental physics from the English and the French, all of Italy, and particularly our youth, would be in their great debt."[60] Not surprisingly, translations would take on a role of cardinal importance as vehicles for emulating political economy and economic conditions in Genovesi's personal correspondence, and he became official censor of both de Felice's anthology *and* the Neapolitan translation of Chambers's *Cyclopaedia*. With only a few amendments to make, he found the *Cyclopaedia* full of "infinite things extremely useful for the diffusion of human knowledge, proper to promote the arts, and the cognition of those things, which make the real utility and happiness of peoples."[61]

Facing up to his own challenge, Genovesi too descended into the trenches of translation, insisting not only on writing but even on teaching in the vernacular to reinforce the legitimacy of a national scientific language, something for which authorities at the university greatly criticized him and which, as he put it in private correspondence, resulted in nothing less than a "civil war."[62] "I will philosophize with the human species," he held fast, "not with the few," and translation emerged as a primary medium through which to engage with "the public."[63] These were local expressions of a common argument for the diffusion of knowledge through translations made all over Europe in that tumultuous third quarter of the eighteenth century. Ideas were no longer circulated only to get an educated elite interested in worldly melioration, and the primary focus of reformism gradually changed from formal institutions such as the legal system ("Enlightenment" from above) to informal institutions and the perceived cultural constraints on society's capacity for positive action ("Enlightenment" from below). The cosmopolitan republic of letters was by now a venerable institution fluently communicative in both French and Latin. The new imperative was providing a wider populace, in Genovesi's case stretching to include indentured farmers in the most rural parts of the kingdom, with tools for understanding the world, their possible place in it, and how they could make it better for themselves and for the common good.

This, in turn, required the careful selection of key texts to translate and the active diffusion of knowledge through explicitly nonelite channels, languages, and publications unencumbered by expensive bindings and complex paratexts. The abyss of accessibility separating Savary's prohibitively expensive *Dictionnaire* in folio from books like Cary's *Essay* in many ways reflected the very abyss between rich and poor, erudite and ignorant that Genovesi sought to bridge. He had learned an important lesson—the Enlightenment could not be published in folio, in the large and costly tomes that filled scholarly libraries, books that could be consulted but not digested; rather it required publication in octavo, to be carried, read, lived. As Voltaire would write a few years later, "Twenty folio volumes will never make a revolution: it's the small, portable books at thirty sous that are dangerous. If the Gospel had cost 1,200 sesterces, the Christian religion would never have been established."[64]

Even contemporaries noticed the similarities between Genovesi's work in Naples and Diderot's contemporary program of enlightenment; Galiani responded to a surprising inquiry by the Neapolitan minister Bernardo Tanucci as to what the *Encyclopédie* was by comparing its editor Diderot to "our Genovesi."[65] A striking kinship was their common conception of translation as an engine of enlightenment. It is noteworthy in this regard that Genovesi's early lectures demonstrate familiarity with the first six volumes of the *Encyclopédie,* and thus Diderot's self-defining article on encyclopedias and the eulogy of translations contained therein.[66] Like "many sciences," Genovesi would remark in his introduction to Cary, "that of economic philosophy" had existed in practice since the "ancients," but, through jealousy and misunderstandings, had hardly been passed down to posterity. Finally, certain "able and courageous countries" had codified it, and now all other countries could share their learning.[67] The same importance of teaching and translating foreign sciences, though, had been emphasized a few years earlier by Ludovico Muratori, a pillar of the early Italian Enlightenment and frequent correspondent of Genovesi.[68]

A librarian and antiquarian, now best known for his histories of Italy and for his paradigmatic *Public Happiness,* the erudite Modenese had insisted on the practical importance of teaching not only foreign sciences but foreign *histories.* "History," he wrote, "is a teacher of practice, showing us through human actions what theory teaches." All histories deserved "esteem," "because knowledge of the World's past serves not a little in regulating the World's present."[69] "History," Genovesi consonantly concluded in a 1759 letter discussing the very same Muratori, "is the safest and most beautiful source of the science of man."[70] More important, as he put it in his introduction to Cary, history was the emulative foundation of economic science, by which the political economy that he sought to formalize at the Intierian chair could build on the successes, and learn from the failures, of competing nations:

> If one wants to plant the science of commerce in a nation, and be certain that it grows, nothing is more useful than to give it the history of the commerce of those nations that most exercise it and best understand it. The French have therefore begun to translate into their language all the books on commerce that wise nations have written, and most of all those demonstrating the origins, the progress, and the perfection of the arts, the economy, and commerce.[71]

Genovesi was explicitly emulating the French emulation of English political economy through their very same medium: translation. It was in many ways the perfect emulation at the time, for while he continued to look to Paris as the cultural and linguistic epicenter of the civilized world, there was no getting around England's gritty primacy in matters of wealth and war.[72] Just as English Baconianism had been the model for Genovesi's call for *libertas philosophandi* in the 1740s, the history of English economic policy emerged as the model for his reformism in the 1750s, and though he would come to realize the former through the medium of the latter, this happened in light of his own unique contextual concern: an acute awareness of the cyclicality of civilization and the evanescence of power. Political economy could certainly suggest theories and practices of worldly betterment, but only history—one's own and others'—could validate its findings and lend it the authority of reason and experience.

So though he preferred to cite foreign authors, Genovesi was far from ignorant of the Italian canon on the subjects he treated. For however impotent scholars and statesmen in Italy had been in the face of decline, the vicissitudes of power they experienced proved to be an extraordinary vantage point from which to analyze the political and economic affairs of states. As the city-states that flourished after the fall of Rome gave way to the principalities, unified nation-states, and empires of the early modern period, Italians enjoyed front seats at their own apocalypse, drawing unique insights into the causes of the wealth of nations. Botero and the Neapolitan hermetic magus Tommaso Campanella, extremely influential writers of the late Renaissance, both surveyed the changing nations of the world (and in Campanella's case those of the next one) to conclude, in a manner that would echo throughout later periods, that the "real mines" in the modern world were "manufactures" and human "industry," through which Italy briefly had achieved greatness. No "mine of silver or gold in New Spain" could compare with "the power of industry," Botero argued, for the "duties from the merchandise of Milan are worth more to the Catholic King than the mines of Potosí and Jalisco."[73] Although neither Botero nor Campanella sought to explain why this was so, the Neapolitan lawyer Antonio Serra did.

Indeed, the full title of Serra's 1613 treatise, *A Short Treatise on the Causes that make Kingdoms Abound in Gold and Silver even in the Absence of Mines, with Particular Reference to the Kingdom of Naples,* indicates a direct response to their earlier inquiries. Serra essentially proposed that different economic activities operated according to different economic laws. Whereas agriculture after a certain point produced less wealth for each individual involved,

> the products of manufacturing industry can be multiplied, and this is a source of profit. Agricultural produce, on the other hand, cannot be multiplied. If a given piece of land is only large enough for the sowing of a hundred *tomoli* of wheat, it is impossible to sow a hundred and fifty there. *This is not the case with manufacturing industry; its products can be multiplied not just twofold but a hundredfold, and at a proportionately lower cost.*[74]

There were increasing returns to scale in manufacturers, which signified decreasing unit costs with increasing productivity and made them uniquely able to support ever-increasing populations without resorting to territorial conquest. The poverty, famine, and dearth of currency paralyzing Naples at the time of his writing could thus not be remedied merely through financial regulations. It was rather an illness born of the underlying structure of the economy itself, and that could only be cured through investments in productive power. And the precocious economic analysis of Botero and Serra was not without political consequences: a community was suddenly understood to be able to achieve *grandezza* through both military *and* economic means. Although Serra's treatise never had an impact during his lifetime, it was rediscovered by Intieri, who shared its insights with Galiani and Genovesi with extraordinary results. For Serra's work provided a theoretical explanation for economic development that Cary and Butel-Dumont had only adumbrated.[75]

Cary's Grand Tour Continues

Although Genovesi believed he had a "Laconic style of writing," wrote of the "annotator's duty," and claimed to have added only "very few annotations" to the French translation, the more than 1,000 pages of Butel-Dumont's two-volume edition nonetheless grew to three volumes totaling over 1,500 pages in Genovesi's hands, nearly ten times those of John Cary's original *Essay*.[76] Butel-Dumont had weeded out Cary's most rapacious and Francophobic tendencies while greatly expanding on his survey of English commerce and policy by recourse to later English writers; the end result very much invoked the type of institutional historiography lionized by Voltaire in those same years.[77] Genovesi's copious annotations self-consciously refined the *Essay*'s theoretical and "scientific" elements, but it was its historical vision that underwent the greatest conceptual changes. Italy's historical trajectory, its great series of rises and falls, now came to inform an analysis of economic change whose complexity far superseded Cary and Butel-Dumont's understanding of progress and their successive goal of material melioration.

But not all of Genovesi's additions were annotations; he also reinforced Cary's French edition with a series of supplementary texts and translations. Apart from an entirely new introduction to the work, the now retitled *History of the Commerce of Great Britain*, the volume also included Genovesi's long-gestated *Reasoning on Commerce in General* and his new works *Philosophical Reasoning on the Strengths and Consequences of Great Riches* and *Reasoning on Public Faith*, as well as an exceedingly liberal translation of Thomas Mun's *England's Treasure by Forraign Trade*, a work he would have seen praised as the origin of English economic thought in Le Blanc's 1755 appendix to the French translation of Hume's *Essays*.[78] Axiomatically, Genovesi concluded the supporting apparatus for his translation of Cary's work with a translation of the English Navigation Acts, not only the emblematic early modern English economic policy but also the most successful application of reason of state to economic concerns in Western history—three years before Butel-Dumont translated it in Paris.[79]

Genovesi knew no more of Cary than his French predecessors and thus presented Cary only as a "mercatante di Bristol," recalling the description he came to employ for his own new position at the university. It was clear, however, from Genovesi's understanding of European history and from his close reading of the text, that Cary had been tremendously influential in England and that, driven by his "love of the common good," he had contributed to that "grandezza" which "has overshadowed all of Europe."[80] The *History* itself was to be divided into three volumes: the first included his *Reasoning on Commerce in General* and charted the history of England's internal commerce; the second exposed "the most appropriate and vigorous means of promoting manufactures" and contained both his *Philosophical Reasoning* and translation of Mun; and the third treated England's external commerce, to which he appended both his translation of the Navigation Acts and his *Reasoning on Public Faith,* with which he capped the entire endeavor. Altogether, Genovesi's *History* became by far the most programmatic work of Italian political economy in the long eighteenth century. Fusing historical, theoretical, and ethical elements into a coherent whole, it produced a voluminous manifesto of enlightened economic science.

The actual process of writing and editing the billowing work was tortuous, however, as is evident from its recurring stylistic and grammatical problems. The translation of Butel-Dumont's edition was initially entrusted to Genovesi's brother Pietro, but illness slowed down his work and ultimately took his life, around the same time as Intieri's death, before he could contribute much even to the first volume.[81] Genovesi thus continued alone, sending pages to the typesetter one by one.[82] The result, translated "word for word" rather than "sense for sense" in a way about which St. Jerome would have had much to say, is undeniably staccato. Even Genovesi's eulogist observed that it was "written with some haste and negligence."[83] For all his translational license, Butel-Dumont conscientiously indicated his sources while amplifying Cary's *Essay.* Genovesi's translation partly obfuscated this. Though he makes frequent reference to other works, the particular influences of writers like Child and Davenant on the body of the text are sometimes identifiable only by recourse to the foregoing French translation.[84] Yet, in his rush, he never fundamentally changed the French rendition of Cary, preferring to emulate the original by recourse to annotations and appendixes. But though his translation of Butel-Dumont's translation of Cary was strictly verbatim, this was, curiously, not the case with the supplementary material, as is evident from his introduction to Mun's treatise. There he admits that he has not "followed the text of his author too scrupulously, as most do, like one who, being somewhat philosophical, couldn't completely take up the merchant's way of thinking, or better still, who thought he could improve his author's many thoughts and even organize them better, because they were not; and thought that the English, especially in that century, were all bad writers."[85] There is no indication whether the Italian translation of Mun was done through an intermediary French edition, since *England's Treasure by Forraign Trade* was one of the true economic best sellers of early modern Europe. The difficulty Genovesi experienced translating it could be related to the fact that its editions all had appeared in antiquated seventeenth-century vernaculars with which he was less familiar than with Butel-Dumont's polished rendering of Cary's *Essay*.[86]

Genovesi's annotations to the *History* nonetheless followed the same principle by ordering, systematizing, and refining the original arguments. The introduction set the tone for the entire work: "one might perhaps think" that the "*grandezza* and wealth of English commerce" was "the work of chance," or perhaps "of the site" or "of climate," but this would be a "total error." England's *grandezza* was the result of exceedingly conscious policy; the only reason its manufactures had risen to conquer the world's markets was the "singular art and diligence" by which they had been "promoted." As for Montesquieu, and Serra long before him, economic policy was a way of remedying deficiencies of nature. The first object of Genovesi's translation was to show the means by which England had achieved its *grandezza,* but the second and most important object was to demonstrate that "any other nation" could achieve the same, mitigating for its context, by following England's lead. This, he said, echoing Muratori, was "the principal fruit to draw from reading historians and books on politics and economics."[87] Since men were "real and not chimerical," surrounded by "things and not words," the world could only be improved on, he reiterated his earlier writings and his formation in Intieri's group, if people turned to study actual conditions.

Given the methodology of the group's political economy, it was natural to turn to the peoples and things across the Alps for inspiration. "I will not," Genovesi made clear "distance myself from the principles of the best English authors: because of all the nations of Europe, none has thought more, nor better about the economics of the state, and of commerce both external and internal, than they have. We must therefore not be reproached if in this art, of which they are such great masters, we take them as models."[88] For though Uztáriz and Ulloa, both recently translated by Gournay's circle and praised by Galiani for their relevance for Neapolitan concerns, had produced genuinely historical works that profoundly influenced Genovesi, they described the decline and fall of a wealthy country rather than a poor one's rise to greatness, and could thus ultimately teach only a negative lesson of development.[89] Their acute and tragic analysis of the "Spanish disease" had explained how a country that had imported hundreds of thousands of tons of raw wealth nonetheless remained poor and dependent on foreign manufactures for their most basic needs, and their suggestions, like Cary's, focused on encouraging national productive capacity by diversifying the manufacturing sector. But unlike Cary's, theirs were tinged with melancholy. Of all the works of political economy brought to light by Gournay's circle, only the *Essay* provided a positive, comprehensive history of the actual economic policies that a country had pursued to escape its dependence on foreign powers. Only Cary could show the full range of "springs and levers," as Genovesi put it, that England "had operated to lift itself, in all parts of its economy, to greatness."[90] It was not an abstract work about virtue, commercial ideals, and the good life, but a gritty and abrasive guide to the wealth of nations. Butel-Dumont had turned the *Essay* into a history of English economic policy, the raw material from which Genovesi distilled his academic discipline of political economy, based, in the spirit of Muratori and Intieri, on induction through accumulated historical experience rather than deduction from a priori theoretical claims. Similarly, Butel-Dumont had censored Cary's political and religious creed, cleaning the "canvas" of the *Essay* for Genovesi to paint his vision of enlightened Catholic absolutism. The manuscripts from Genovesi's first lectures in political economy indeed show that the resulting opus represented both the lectures of his first years of his teaching and, with all probability, the first textbook of economics in Italy.[91] From being a primer of economic imperialism, Cary's *Essay* came to be a general guidebook for escaping de facto colonial dependencies.

Arts, Sciences, and Political Economy

"Commerce," Genovesi never tired of repeating, "is an art, which, like all others, has an end, rules, and principles," echoing Cary's own statement following his debate with Molyneux, but which in its Neapolitan context by default gained a Galilean and Newtonian rather than legalistic air.[92] This "science of commerce," "economic philosophy," or "civil economics" was to be a "harmonious connection" of "recipes" based on accumulated "experience."[93] It was neither a doctrine for the distribution and allocation of scarce resources nor applied natural law. Essentially, it was a science of national economic development in the tradition not only of the *Essay* but also of the revolutionary conception of greatness explored by Botero and Serra, a greatness born not from territorial gains but from the power of industry. As a review in the Venetian *Giornale d'Italia* summarized the political economy of Genovesi's *History,* it was a science allowing statesmen to "increase the greatness, power, and wealth of the Nation, without at the same time aiming to enlarge the borders of what one possesses."[94] By drawing on an earlier Italian tradition of thinking politically about economic conditions and achieving independence under international pressure, Genovesi's political economy envisaged an ideal path by which to achieve greatness through commerce *without* conquest, something that, bereft of Serra's insights, neither Cary nor Butel-Dumont had ever seriously considered. That the two categories of conquest and commerce retained a tendency to conflate throughout the eighteenth century did not detract from his hope. Cary had first stated that "Trade hath its Principles, as other Sciences have," which Butel-Dumont translated as "Le commerce a ses régles ainsi que toute autre science." Though Genovesi's rendition is almost literal, the meaning of his words had in effect changed dramatically: "Ha il Commercio, siccome ogni altra Scienza, le sue regole anche egli."[95]

And whereas Genovesi thought a similar science in England would have focused on how to fight off usurpers to the economic throne of Europe, the question on the Neapolitan agenda was quite the opposite.[96] Though the English Navigation Acts were wildly successful, the path-dependent evolution of the world economy meant that straightforward attempts to copy their success by poor countries were bound to fail. Conceptually, it was a question of finding the right balance between innovation and imitation, but how, in practical terms, could a latecomer in Europe's commercial arena carve out its niche? The problem, one can theorize on the back of Benedict Anderson, was that the very presence of the emulated country fundamentally upset the rules of the game for the emulator, to a large extent voiding the structures that had allowed the former to make itself worthy of imitation in the first place.[97] How, Genovesi asked, could the countries "that come after," the ones that "come once mass has already been said," catch up?[98] In a letter written nearly ten years after his translation of Cary, he expounded his mature thoughts on the matter in terms echoing Serra's almost verbatim:

> my feeling is that one wants to know what the other nations wise in economics and politics have figured out, but their rules should be employed like doctors' prescriptions, that is, taking into account the climate, the location, the robustness of the states, and the nature and power of their inhabitants' mentalities. Some systems will be suitable for England, but wouldn't help France, and some right for Tuscany, which could harm the state of Milan. Therefore, it is good for one to read everything, but he must sift through them in order to choose.[99]

Genovesi was conscious that when emulation triggered the translation of a work of political economy from one context to another, the terms of its application changed irrevocably. History emerged as the necessary cipher to unveil not only the mechanisms of social progress but also the way to employ this knowledge, once codified, in other historical realities. Yet, as Genovesi would formalize his thoughts in later correspondence, political economy had to provide the necessary theory through which Clio's raw data could be made intelligible.[100] "Science" was the product of a long period of codifying experience and observations, and again, history was experience by proxy.[101] Between the preface and the first part of his translation of Cary, Genovesi thus inserted his *Reasoning on Commerce in General,* the introduction to political economy he had begun discussing with interlocutors already in the early 1750s. Whereas England was the ultimate "model" in economic matters, the French were the first to emulate their science and policies through the medium of translations, and in important ways his was a case of double emulation, not only of the subject matter but of the way of harnessing it.[102] Yet of the countless books available on economic affairs, Genovesi held none in higher regard than Cary's *Essay.* Unlike Huet or Savary, Cary had gone beyond chronicle and chronology to explain the "true causes" of England's *grandezza*. Cary, or rather Butel-Dumont—a fact that remained largely hidden to Genovesi by the peculiarities of the French culture of translation—had developed a historical theory that clarified the confusion of commercial society and identified key elements to be nurtured and promoted. Though the word "science" only appeared once in late editions of Cary's *Essay,* the word's importance grew in its French translation to fully bloom in Italian, where Genovesi included an entire methodological chapter devoted to the "Science of Commerce" in his *Reasoning.*

There was a difference, he said, following Cary and Forbonnais, between the "practice of merchandizing" and the "political science of commerce." The former regarded "private interest," the other that of the "entire nation." The "science of commerce" thus offered solutions to the great problems of individual nations, which were "having [*I*] the maximum possible population. *II.* having the maximum number of goods. *III.* The maximum possible wealth: *IV.* And the maximum possible power." In doing so the "science" proceeded with the "order of truth," drawing on "the universal reason of man," "history," and "experience." Though some had suggested that political economy should be limited to making the citizenry affluent, he did not think it possible to partition the aforesaid four factors, for population, wealth, and power were inexorably intertwined. His "science" was the result not of "abstract reasoning" but of the study of the "history of nations," always guided by the need for "public happiness." For this was, as for Botero and Serra, the origins of sovereign wealth and happiness as well. Agriculture was certainly the "first source" of wealth, providing food and "materials for manufactures." Its flourishing was stymied in Naples, however, by the kingdom's anachronistic social and economic structures, characterized by such banes to productivity as inequality of property and of rights, exaggerated luxury, poor circulation of money, the absence of agricultural academies, and institutions undermining "emulation." Idle vagrants became—as they had for Cary—a symbol of all that was wrong with the economy he observed, and like his English predecessor he thought "promot[ing] industry" was the only way of resolving the problem they posed. This, Genovesi assured by recourse to the same biblical authority, could only come about through education, so that "everyone is persuaded, that there is no way on earth leading to comforts besides labor alone." Symptomatically, the Gournay circle's insistence on the importance of imbuing vocations with an air of "honor," of fame and dignity, found great resonance in Intieri's group.[103]

Labor was not commerce, however, and not all commerce was good commerce. As Montesquieu, the authors of Gournay's circle, and the Spanish case so clearly had demonstrated, history proved the existence of "harmful" and "ruinous" forms of trade.[104] The difference between these trades and "useful" ones was, as for the entire tradition emanating from the *Essay,* how much work went into the goods traded and, more important, what kind of work was involved. Genovesi's reading of Ulloa and Uztáriz matured in him the same conviction regarding the nature of economic power that was manifest in Cary's response to the linen drapers. No amount of raw materials, even if said raw materials were gold and silver, could stand up to the power of industry, which fertilized agriculture, the arts, and society itself. This benefit was understood in terms not only of the wealth of a nation but of its liberty. Without manufactures, Genovesi said, invoking Melon, nations would remain "dependent on foreigners" and become "in certain ways tributaries" of foreign powers, "instruments of their wealth and power, and thus always poor."[105] National independence was as meaningless as it was fleeting without the economic power, and more specifically the industrial power, to guard it from foreign interests. Political economy was not merely the science of reforming institutions and making the kingdom wealthy, it was the science of rendering political communities viable in a world increasingly shaped by economic competition.

Observing that the line separating sovereign nations from "servants" in Europe coincided neatly with that separating exporters from importers of manufactured goods, Genovesi declared that the future of Naples in the final instance "depends on the perfection, and the increase of manufactures." The goal of political economy was thus to "make sure that the country depends as little as possible on others" for its manufacturing needs, for "the less its dependence, the greater its freedom, its wealth, and its power." Genovesi in fact went as far as declaring the independence (the "liberty") of a nation directly proportional to the refinement of its industry, conceiving of liberty as a four-tiered hierarchy in which one progressed through levels corresponding to a nation's capacity to produce ever more complex manufactures. There was no way around it, an agricultural nation could never be free. Only when "good and copious manufactures of all kinds" were added to such a foundation would a country be "near entirely free from being servant of others." The only way to render a political economy viable was thus to encourage the development of national manufactures and, significantly, luxuries. And of all the nations of Europe, none had achieved this state of "greatest liberty" more durably than England, a nation that had chosen a developmental path "opposite" that of Spain. Manufactures were in the end a question of power, for just as the economic power of an individual could be translated into political power over others in a society of people, so a state's economic power could be translated into political power over others in a society of nations.[106] Freedom could only prosper in the modern world when countries came to trade manufactures with each other, thus avoiding the relations of dominion and dependence that necessarily arose from exchanges between polities specializing in activities with differential returns to scale.

Industry and Free Trade

But why were manufactures so important for a nation's political economy? In formalizing his answer to this question, Genovesi's theoretical endeavor was facilitated by insights Intieri's coterie drew from the local reason of state tradition. His colleague Galiani would be the first author to ever laud Serra in print, ranking him above Locke and Melon.[107] He sought to republish Serra's treatise in the early 1750s, modeled practically all the theoretical and policy insights of his tremendously influential 1770 *Dialogues on the Grain Trade* on those of Serra, and finally paraphrased his insight about increasing returns in manufactures in his culminating attack on the Physiocrats' insistence on the sterility of manufactures: "And voilà the great difference between manufactures and agriculture. Manufactures increase with the number of arms you put in, while agriculture decreases." Only manufactures could be "multiplied" into "infinity," and whereas manufactures made agriculture more effective, the opposite could never be the case. So important were manufactures that Galiani envisaged a state of political perfection in which a political community was forced to import food from abroad to feed its ever-growing industrious population, "for the masterpiece of the art [of government] is to force nature and make her work a miracle such as having, on limited land, more men than its forces and means could possibly feed."[108] Political economy was the means of achieving this masterpiece, and if England had come closest to it in the eighteenth century, it had taken a Neapolitan to explain how.

Genovesi drew the same groundbreaking conclusion from the group's reading of the *Short Treatise*, utilizing an identical vocabulary of "manufactures" and "multiplication" in his translation of Cary's *Essay*. The reason manufactures had produced such great wealth in England and the policies meticulously charted by Butel-Dumont had worked so well was their multiplying effect and their ability to galvanize the larger economy. Disproportionably more people could live in a nation with developed manufactures than in one without because they made agriculture more effective, and wealthy city-states could even flourish in the absence of bountiful hinterlands, only on the revenues from exporting manufactures. English economic policy, born from the belief that it was right to "multiply" the value of goods before exporting them, had been based on "good" laws "rigorously prohibiting" the export of raw materials. Genovesi thus concluded, paraphrasing Serra, that "it is always a wise law to prohibit the extraction of raw materials, which can be worked in the nation; because the nation working them earns the manufacture, which can render 6, 10, and even 100 times as much."[109]

"Manipulating money," he also agreed with both Serra and Cary, would never help Naples, for the only way to the future lay in the development of domestic productive capacity.[110] In fact, the greater the labor and expertise needed to manufacture products, the greater the wealth they could produce. Encouraging the production of increasingly labor- and expertise-intensive goods was the key to sustained growth. Cary himself had noted, in the wake of Petty, that luxury items such as watches were the apex items of national production because the cost of labor far exceeded the cost of raw materials necessary in their making, but it took Genovesi's Neapolitan theoretical heritage to explain why this was the case. The key to material betterment was not labor itself, as Locke had so powerfully proclaimed, but what was labored on and how. Time spent laboring in subsistence agriculture simply did not have the same capacity to produce wealth as the same time spent laboring in textiles; and the reason for this was, as Serra had explained, that absolutely crucial difference between increasing and diminishing returns to scale. Political economy was partly a science of manipulating differential returns to scale in international relations.

Once the desirability of manufactures was settled "scientifically," and a clear hierarchy of economic activities established, the difficult issue of organizing the nation's economy played directly into the equally thorny problems of "free trade" and the meaning of "freedom" and "liberty" in commercial societies—questions that, paraphrasing Hobbes and Melon, Genovesi thought had "caused no lesser disputes among politicians, than among theologians."[111] In his annotations to Butel-Dumont's interpretation of England's aggressive policies to control the world's manufactures, Genovesi therefore often digressed toward the larger issues of economic liberty. "One may venture to think," he noted, "that all these regulations poorly adapt to the nature of trade, as everybody knows trade wants liberty." Was it not common knowledge that "privileges," a loaded word in terms of the contemporary social structures Genovesi wished to reform, destroyed "emulation"?[112] Yet history showed that it was necessary to dismantle certain recurring misappropriations of the term. "Liberty" was certainly the "soul of trade," but misunderstanding the psychology of commerce, the ways human passions shaped commercial society, might give men a "license that destroys all trade." Assessing the right degree of liberty, and which forms of privilege were to be defended, was a complex issue dependent on the needs of the moment, for one could "sin in this kind of government either by doing too much or by doing too little." Society needed certain rules, for just as "unpunished crimes make owners less secure in their lives and their goods," the same "insecurity" in anarchic trade would make commerce stagnant. But what were they?[113]

One of the greatest confusions regarding the meaning and benefits of "free trade," Genovesi wrote, was the persistence of some authors in the belief that only republics could have a "great commerce." These authors "confounded civil liberty with commercial liberty" and furthermore failed to understand the meaning of "civil liberty" itself, confusing the degree of concentration of executive power with the nature of its implementation.[114] For all his insistence on the importance of empowering the Neapolitan public, his faith in the positive consequences of enlightened absolutism never wavered, even in private correspondence. Unyielding conceptions of liberty, he continued, were both quixotic and harmful:

> There are those, who by liberty of trade mean two things: an absolute license for manufacturers to work without regulations of measurements, of weights, of forms, of colors, etc., and one no less absolute for merchants to circulate, export, and import everything which they like, without any restrictions, without excises, without tariffs, without customs duties. But this liberty, except among adventurous people on the Moon, does not exist in any country on Earth: on the contrary you will find it nowhere less than in those nations that best understand trade.[115]

Similarly, in his translation of Mun, he had Mun write:

> And even though one wants commerce between all nations to be free, nonetheless I think, that this liberty can and should be restrained by certain limits, because in helping others, it could hurt us, as all countries should accommodate it to its interests, without others having the right to lament: because everyone is master of his house, to whose lordship the liberty of commerce cannot contest".[116]

People who maintained this absolute definition of "free trade" would have to conclude that there existed no great commerce anywhere in the world, while the greatest works of political economy taught "that no places have more rigorous rules to preserve the bounty, and with that the esteem of manufactures, of other trades, and trust in traffic, than the three countries that now share Europe's great trade," in other words England, Holland, and France.[117] Not only had the political economies furthest away from such a radical conception of free trade bloomed the most economically, but they had also achieved the most enlightened and subsistence-secured publics, the most robust civil societies, and ultimately the most viable political existences. Given Genovesi's analysis of the different sectors of the economy, and here his close readings of Montesquieu and Melon must be taken into consideration, it was evident that the wrong kind of "free trade" could quickly lead to a country's deindustrialization and subsequent dependence on foreign powers: the very cultural and political suicide from which political economy was supposed to shield nations. Specializing in supplying the great powers with their raw materials, however freely, would only "cause the ruin of the state," and he therefore suggested the active emulation of their successful tariffs to encourage the import of raw materials and the export of manufactured goods.[118]

The problem with this scheme, as Cary's enemies had noted half a century earlier, was that since techniques and technologies in a developing country hardly could match those of a nation long established in its production, the price of imported goods often was far less than the cost of producing said goods domestically. Many, Genovesi assumed, would argue for free international traffic on these grounds. Yet he believed the terms of the argument were false, for what really mattered was with whom you shared your labor market. Paying slightly higher prices for local goods not only encouraged industrialization and greater divisions of labor within one's political community, but since trades were interconnected, this allowed for higher real wages in all trades from agriculture upward, ensuring social cohesion.[119] The reason it was better for nations to engage in manufacturing even though it would be costlier than importing goods from abroad—a question Cary had grappled with in his reply to the linen drapers six decades earlier—was that this was the only way to link the wages of the consumers to those of the producers; this was, in the end, the only way to establish the positive interdependence of trades visible in England, the cumulative causation of development that Serra had identified as underlying all thriving commercial societies. The educated public Genovesi wished to nurture could not exist in a purely agricultural economy, and the whims of fortune, he wrote with the same aversion to Stoic and Epicurean moral philosophy that his former professor Vico demonstrated, could not be entrusted with the safekeeping of civilization.

In this, as always, England remained the model to emulate, and particularly the selective burdens it imposed on commerce to further the common good: "Nowhere in Europe are these burdens in fact greater than in England, and at the same time no nation has a greater and freer trade. And the reason is, that they are situated intelligently, which is to say they all work towards a single end, which is the augmentation of the nation's agriculture and manufactures."[120] That a wealthy nation like England sought to hinder developing nations from emulating their methods and catching up was as unjust to Genovesi as it had been to Butel-Dumont:

> The law of peoples gives all nations the right to employ whatever Economy they deem appropriate to their Commerce. For if the English have prohibited foreign goods, or overburdened them with duties, they cannot reasonably lament themselves that other nations use their same laws against them. I praise the care with which they treat their Commerce; but could I criticize the other States, who treat them as they treat others?[121]

Melon, and the Colbertist legacy he represented, had been right to emphasize "liberty and protection."[122] The only sensible meaning of free trade in the end remained Cary's freedom of vocation and "that circulation of merchantable goods, which is safe, and ready, and directed not only at our private utility but good also for the nation in general, of which we are part."[123]

Luxury and Civil Thanatology

Genovesi's specific analysis of the wealth-creating potential of manufactures and the ways by which their trade should be encouraged also served as the groundwork for his original take on the troublesome problem of luxury. One of the great polemics of the Enlightenment, it was also the cause of ferocious debates across the Italian peninsula. As in France, the first notable salvo against the moralizing Augustinian doctrines on luxury in Italy came from Melon's 1734 *Essay*, followed by the first French edition of Mandeville's *Fable* in 1740.[124] Most of Genovesi's forerunners and contemporaries, however, had resisted Melon's arguments. The rather prolific Neapolitan political economists Paolo Mattia Doria and Carlo Antonio Broggia had both been remarkably outspoken in denouncing attempts to exculpate luxury trades of moral misconduct.[125] Again, it must be emphasized that their goals were not at all dissimilar to those of Intieri and Genovesi, for Doria promoted manufacturing as a means of resisting England's "jealousy of trade," and the reason Broggia vilified luxury was that he could conceive of no other way to stop the "wheel of fortune" from churning and yet another wave of rise and decline from overturning Italy.[126]

It is difficult to imagine a field of inquiry further away from Cary's concerns than civil thanatology, but the overpowering memory of repeated decline made it a fundamental subject in the intellectual repertoire of Renaissance and early modern Italian thinkers.[127] In the sixth book of his tremendously influential *Histories,* the second-century BCE Greek historian Polybius had expounded on Platonic and Aristotelian themes to propound his theory of anacyclosis, the cyclical progression of societies. The most influential political reader of Polybius in Renaissance Europe was probably Machiavelli, who, ignoring the original's dream of a perfect, mixed constitution able to withstand the entropy of time, anchored the inevitability of civil death and resurrection in the unruly passions of man, and it was often through his mediation that anacyclosis gained currency in Italy and Europe at large.[128]

Even before the group of philosophers and administrators gathered around the figure of Intieri began their campaign of composing and translating English and French works of political economy in light of Italy's cyclical history, Machiavelli's magnification of the anacyclotic doctrine found its great spokesman in the Neapolitan royal historian Giambattista Vico, an early professor of Genovesi.[129] In an effort to rejuvenate erudition in an age of hard sciences, he published his *New Science,* a Möbius strip of philology and philosophy vindicating the truth of sacred history against the assaults of godless Spinozists, atheists, and Epicureans. Far from an all-out revolt against the teachings of his enemies, however, Vico's work sought to subject the weaponry of their materialist logic to the *nomos* of Christian providence, a rhetorical strategy that has rendered his writings vulnerable to procrustean and often contradictory readings.[130] His moral philosophy is highly contested, his historical vision less so. Only a "poetic" approach to history, Vico argued loudly, could uncover the rules and principles of "providence" guiding all nations, the truth of the Bible, and the cyclical progression of rises and declines, driven by luxury, experienced by all cultures and all societies in the "ideal eternal history." One of the most obsessively repeated phrases in the final, third edition of *New Science,* "the return to barbarism," was thus both a statement of things past and an omen of what was again to come.[131]

This was the intellectual context in which Muratori, though no believer in eternal progress, had dared to speak favorably of parts of the Epicurean thesis of Mandeville and Melon in his *Public Happiness,* adopting their conception of luxury as a positive economic force while entirely rejecting their larger fusion of private vices and public interests.[132] Among those who demonstrated themselves more favorable to Muratori's limited Epicurean-ism than Broggia was the young Galiani. Late in his highly complex 1750 (though it appeared only in 1751) *On Money*, a work set out to map the history and role of money in commercial society, Galiani had presented his *Digression Around Luxury Generally Considered*. Paraphrasing Melon on the "obscure" nature of the term, Galiani defined luxury as the "child of peace, of good government, and of the perfection of the arts useful for society." He did not disagree with those who thought luxury "always" was "an infallible indicator, and the warning that the decline of a state was near," but "it was so no differently than the yellowing of an ear of corn is a sign that it will soon dry." Luxury was the natural autumn of civilization, the last stage before winter set in. In line with other civil thanatologists in early modern Italy, he thought "Kingdoms" and "Empires" were nothing but "noble plants of the august garden of God," and refusing luxury was comparable to letting a hard-fought harvest rot in the fields instead of reaping it.[133] Luxury was an effect, not a cause. Though its most negative consequences to a certain extent could be mitigated, it should not be used as a weapon of policy on the model of Colbert, Melon, and Gournay's circle.

Like his ridicule of original compacts, Vico's theory of historical cyclicality and obsession with Italy's lost greatness were recurring themes in Galiani's work.[134] The relationship Galiani identified between wealth, war, and decline, for example, hardly differed from that of Machiavelli (and Galiani's self-imposed nickname was, incidentally, "il Machiavellino"): poverty brought industriousness and virtue, which facilitated the conquest of a wealthier but less virtuous nation, which created wealth, which engendered luxury and effeminacy, which in turn invited conquest by a poorer and more virtuous nation, and so on ad infinitum. Wars were a necessity, since "the principle of destruction" was a prerequisite for the "principle of new production."[135] Galiani saw nothing but history repeating itself. The scale and terms might have changed, but the only disparity he could find between the "ancient centuries" and "ours" was the "disparity which runs from big to small."[136] This was the essence of cyclical history, and it was not surprising that Italy, after the fall of Rome was triggered by the "decline" of *virtù*, found its provinces "in that state of crudeness and poverty, in which they had been in the times near the flood." Galiani's analytical shortcut to justify the self-destructive nature of greatness relied on the Machiavellian mantra that money was not the "sinews of war." Though many still believed wealth could contribute to war, he thought it "a marvelous and incredible thing, that not reading in two thousand years of history any example at all of a wealthy nation destroying a poor but numerous one, but many in which the poor have preyed on the rich," this idea had not been discarded. This was the very same mantra English economists like Cary actively had begun overturning toward the end of the seventeenth century to formulate a theory of perennial progress through aggressive political economy, a violent vision whose European translation was preceded by the warships of the Royal Navy. The burden of erudition, however, and the memory of Italy's repeated decline, rested too heavily on Galiani's shoulders, who dismissed the idea of perpetual progress and considered commerce no less bellicose than conquest.[137]

The only possible remedy he suggested, the only room he gave for politics to resist the vicissitudes of time, was if a sovereign ensured all luxuries were produced domestically and his "subjects" were not "preyed upon by foreign luxury"; a marked discrepancy, given the work's faith in providence and natural harmonies and equilibriums. Only thus could such goods represent the apex of welfare, the full bloom of civilization on the eve of eschatological fulfillment.[138] Tragically, Melon's attempts to harness luxury to ensure progress were no less doomed at the outset than Broggia's plans for fixing the "wheel of fortune." All that remained, the young Galiani wrote, was to embrace the world's cyclicality and revel in luxury when possible, for it was the deserved fruit of centuries of hard work. The question of enjoying domestic or imported luxuries in the end came down only to whether one should greet the hangman plump or starving. The conclusion of *On Money* is an exercise in almost nihilistic resignation. Italy was doubtlessly seething with the spirit of reform, but Galiani, deploying the venerable analogy of the body politic, found no reason to rejoice over this. Italy was like an old man, and "in old men great ideas and continuous, breathless movement, born from internal anguish and the breakdown of the organs, are always indicators of a near and irreparable death." Utilizing the same verses of Petrarch, the sixth stanza of *My Italy*, with which Machiavelli had concluded *The Prince*, Galiani therefore ascertained it was a mistake to say "That the ancient valor / in Italic hearts is not yet dead." It was stone dead. But his final phrase was even more acquiescent: "but I doubt that finally, given peace, one would not have to begin saying, that *Italy is old, and inclined to barbarism*."[139]

From its opening chapters, *On Money* was haunted by ghosts of ancient Rome. Implicitly calling on Vico's societal inflection of anacyclosis, whereby barbaric youth perpetually would overcome mature civilization, only to in turn grow old and fall victim to yet another more youthful contender, Galiani forecast a cold snap in the "august garden of God," where the flower of Italy already was withering, awaiting distant spring. Reform or not, intervention or trust in providence, it did not matter in *On Money,* which in light of temporal cyclicality forcibly denied politics any more than fleetingly palliative purchase.[140] This was also the harrowing message present in Galiani's correspondence from the period. To an inquiry by Gaspare Cerati about whether Intieri's hopes for the future of Italy were not a tad optimistic, Galiani responded: "[Your opinion] is the same as mine, and you can notice my sentiments well from the conclusion of the work *On Money,* where I judge our age rather declining towards barbarism, which is daughter to tyranny, than rising towards culture. But the good old man [Intieri] has this to console himself in his last age; he always speaks of it, always, and it would be cruel to disillusion him."[141]

Though Genovesi's analysis of luxuries was indebted to this view as well as to that expounded in the *New Science,* his engagement with Cary added important nuances to the picture. Like Vico, Genovesi divided man's existence into distinct stages of increasing welfare, death, being, comfort, and pleasure, recalling also the degrees of liberty a nation could enjoy, and correlated them with parallel categories of goods. As these different stages were reached by an individual, that person's desires shifted from demanding goods of "necessity" to "comfort" and finally to those of "luxury," a stage that was "infinite," given the nature of man's desires. Just as manufactures were imbued economically with the power of infinity, so, conveniently, was man's potential desire for them. This parallel division of the human psyche and the products of humans' labor remains constant throughout the work.[142] Like Melon and Galiani before him, Genovesi thus thought luxury was "as natural as life" and, as an instinct that made people distinguish themselves, indeed the ultimate source of science, art, and culture.[143] Not only did it "stimulate consumption," it also rejuvenated society, for while it "ruins some families," it simultaneously "lifts others."[144] Luxury created wealth through social emulation. The interplay of material oeconomics and shifting social institutions enabled the "vice" of luxury to fuel manufactures by increasing the celerity of production and consumption. It could not, and should not, be extinguished in the manner suggested by Broggia. But how, then, could the "wheel of fortune" be stopped? As it turns out, Genovesi's concern was less with stopping it than with riding it.

That luxury could be a positive force did not entail that it should be nurtured in all its possible manifestations. As in his moral philosophy generally, Genovesi could not entirely abandon the Stagirite's penchant for means, and thus concluded that luxury, like wine, should be enjoyed in moderation.[145] Following Doria in noting that luxury very often only fruitfully connected artists, artisans, and aristocrats, ignoring those employed in subsistence entirely, he likewise maintained that the importation of luxurious goods, as the epitome of importing manufactured goods, was the most "ruinous" activity a merchant could undertake.[146] But even Cary's faith in progress was not enough to banish decline entirely from Genovesi's mind, and although his concept of luxury was more Catholic than Galiani's in emphasizing the concept's redemptive, almost transcendent redistributive capacities, this did not mean they disagreed on its eschatology.[147] Sooner or later, luxury would inevitably progress beyond its appropriate limits to inaugurate the autumn of civilization. Since the benefits of luxury ultimately resulted from the unique power of manufactures, he maintained that if man's desires could only be channeled toward the consumption of domestically produced goods, it would both create wealth and postpone the inevitable. The only way luxuries could be "harmful" was if they made the country politically and economically dependent, in other words if they were imported in exchange for raw materials at a cost "higher" than the wealth they created at home or—reiterating the venerable Machiavellian causation between virtue, empire, luxury, and decline—if they made society "effeminate," "soft," and "decadent," inviting conquest by a more robust and virile people.[148] For all the tortured debates over moral philosophy, the actual economic policies suggested by political economy in the end had preciously little to add to those of the perfidious reason of state, and all Genovesi's erudition in the end hardly amounted to more than a philosophical justification for Serra's and Cary's insights.[149]

History, the *Essay,* and the *New Science*

Yet there were cases where Genovesi decisively parted ways with Cary. For the latter's political economy was not the only thing modulated by Genovesi's historical awareness. "Our author," Genovesi dismissingly wrote in a note accompanying the conjectural economic history with which Cary began his treatise, "has here wished to delve into a subject which does not seem to be of his jurisdiction." Cary had proven himself "a poor philosopher" and "poorly practiced in the history of the human species" in wanting to show that "all the orders of men, that now can be found in civilized nations, are born from Commerce." This idea was nothing less than "out of the way," for though political economy certainly was the means of enlightenment and the vehicle to worldly melioration, this should not tempt people to forget the divine origins—and, importantly, divine *ends*—of society. What Cary had proposed, in his own context, might have seemed somewhat naïve but certainly not subversive. But in a Catholic

Naples besieged, as Genovesi had observed already in his earlier theological works of the 1740s, by Epicureans and Spinozists, Cary's inquiry into the commercial origins of man could not help but recall Bayle's question of whether a society of atheists could possibly exist, a theme with which both Vico and Doria had engaged furiously and at length in writings well known to Genovesi.[150] Indeed, the principal criticism was that Cary had proven himself ignorant of the "light of Divine history." By asserting that the clerical profession emerged to solve a social function like any other in the gradual evolution of commercial society, Cary aligned himself, quite inadvertently (though his readers could not know that), with materialists who thought man was born from the "Earth," in a radical Spinozist manner thinking that "all, not only by nature but also by profession and condition, [were] equal."[151]

This is not to say that Genovesi's criticism derived from simple theological conservatism, for his canonical alternative to Cary was a far cry from the proleptical interpretations of scripture offered by Episcopal authors like Jacques-Bénigne Bossuet.[152] Before charting his own history of civilization, Genovesi explained what men would have been like if they really were born from "the Earth," as argued by those "ignorant of Divine history." Fundamentally, they would all have been "equal," "ignorant," and "barbaric" like those of present-day America. Hunting, fishing, and in constant war, they would have developed some husbandry and little agriculture. But man, as "Sacred History" taught, was created by God, and though men in the wake of the flood were as "rough" and "barbaric" as those made of the "Earth," it was divine providence that got them out of this state. Echoing Vico, he did not doubt that Europeans had been left as primitive as the "huttentotti" of Africa and the natives of the New World when the Noachian floodwaters receded. But, "first of all," even "in this barbarism" there had "always" been those "destined for religious leadership." Because "religion" was "born with mankind and mixed with the souls of men," it could neither be "forgotten nor abolished by the primitiveness and savagery of customs," and so "our Author" was mistaken in arguing that "this class of people was born from Commerce." Rather, religious leaders were the products of a "natural duty and need in the entire human species," and confirmed "by the very oracles of God." By subjecting spiritual concerns to an economic imperative, Cary's account of commercial society was dangerously misleading if not manifestly apostate.[153]

Yet, again, the corrected account Genovesi presented in his annotations was not all that different from the original. "Agriculture" and "Pastoralism" were "peaceful arts" that "sought society, and the dowry of many minor occupations," to the point when they finally brought man out of "savagery" and "banditry." United in one place, and "mostly exercising professions, which usually render more than is needed, a diversity of states with regards to riches" first emerged among men. This created a need for "civil government" alongside that of defense against more primitive and less peaceful neighbors, as shown by Tacitus, and curiously, given the hidden history of Cary's *Essay*, in Locke's *Civil Government* (the Italian title of the French translation of Locke's *Second Treatise*.)[154] This process, Genovesi thought, demonstrated that Cary was wrong yet again, for "militias" were born from the inequality of such stage developments between societies, and not from the development of world commerce itself. As this process churned on and the "multiplication of the human species" continued unabated, nations divided themselves into different cities in need of ruling nobilities. As for Vico and Galiani alike, these were in turn conquered by "nations which still had remained hunters and warriors," and their warlords subsequently established themselves as kings and aristocrats. As time made these institutions hereditary, "the nobility of Europe" grew thanks to "war" and "civil government" rather than the needs of trade. But as wealth increased, so did the realization that commerce was a way of achieving honor through services to the common good just like war and government, inaugurating the age of venality, by which Genovesi demonstrated that commerce had contributed to the development of an already existing class rather than creating it from scratch.

But Cary's mechanisms were never far from view in Genovesi's account, for the next stage, resulting from the infinite increase in ways of making and losing money, gave birth to complex codes of laws and an "infinitely" specialized legal cast to understand them. As sovereigns too needed larger incomes to finance things like wars, alliances, schools, and the "majesty of the kingdom," tributes and tariffs were born along with the specialists to administer them. "Commerce"—Genovesi almost apologized for his reliance on Cary's economic logic—"can be considered the remote cause of these two last classes, but the proximate and immediate one is polishedness, and the new way of living." With "the diversities of classes and conditions," "everyone's natural propensity to distinguish themselves" emerged in full force, "either by distinguishing oneself in a class, or by moving to a superior one," the exact phrase Genovesi used to define luxury. For where people were unable to distinguish themselves "by merit and intrinsic virtue, they tried to do it through external ways of living." This meant that "the arts, which in simple nations did not surpass five or six, reached as far as two hundred, all raising themselves on the ruins of agriculture."[155]

It was beyond doubt for Genovesi that "this new way of life, and the great cities" had greatly "weakened the power and primitive vigor of the human body," creating a demand for "doctors, surgeons, pharmacists, etc.," but it was strange that Cary traced all medicine back to commerce, for people, being mortal, had always needed medical care, "in barbaric and savage nations like as in gentle and cultured ones." As to that cardinal question of whether all of these new classes were "necessary or at least useful to the state," Genovesi positioned himself against those "Angry enemies of the human species who would extirpate them from all civilized nations, and reduce us only to Agriculture, and Militia, in other words to the ancient state of barbarism, as it seems M. Rousseau, bizarre French *spirito* of the Bordeaux Academy, wanted to some years ago."[156] Though he did not agree with Mandeville's *Fable,* which he had read in French translation, on all points, Genovesi wholly agreed that the modern world rested on the laurels of luxury and that this could not be changed without "serious disorders" and a "very great confusion" resulting in "poverty." By ignoring man's natural and divine propensities, plans like those of Broggia and Rousseau could create nothing but havoc.

Genovesi's liberal translation of Mun demonstrates that he was willing to adopt the Francophile culture of translation if need be, so his choice to problematize Cary's history in one of the longest annotations to appear in the Italian rendition of the *Essay* cannot simply be dismissed as prudence in Naples's strictly censored intellectual marketplace.[157] It might, instead, be where Vico's legacy most clearly rears its head. For though the mythical and linguistic interpretation of the past offered by *The New Science* shared little with the *History*'s empiricism, they both agreed on man's intrinsic religiosity—and more specifically the survival of the spiritual vocation through historical epochs characterized by changing epistemes of learning—as a way of counteracting the most heretical traditions of contemporary moral philosophy, and, radically considering Genovesi's reformist zeal, they both held fast to a cyclical conception of time formulated in the Italian context by the so-called civic humanists of Renaissance Italy. "Human history," Genovesi annotated Cary, "teaches us this extremely constant course of nations. I. Roughness, hard work and good manners. II. Wealth, softness, broken morals, decline."[158] Genovesi was making a conscious contribution to his conception of "Enlightenment" and the role of political economy in it. The advocacy of commercial society and a partial adherence to Epicurean influences did not entail putting matter before spirit and could not justify an economic, materialist understanding of civilization and its history. Man was primarily a spiritual being, and though political economy could improve his physical life on this earth, it could never alone provide for his existential needs and never alone counteract the cyclicality of time.[159]

Cary's history of commercial society was unwittingly explosive, for in more learned eyes than his own, it embraced the most radical secularism. Taken out of its Bristol context of Anglicanism and moral reform, Cary's men emerged as aberrations, stunted bundles of greed counterintuitively thriving in each others' company. Harmony and progress resulted from an Epicurean orgy of vices; from commerce and the soulless logic of supply and demand. This was why Genovesi, though accepting the general course of Cary's argument, subjected its economic impetus first to spiritual, then to political, social, and even military concerns. And this was why, though Mandeville wrote his treatise a decade after Cary, his *Fable* seemed the obvious source of Cary's amoral history *and* the authority whose "jurisdiction" Genovesi strikingly did not question but instead delineated as only one element, one incitation, in a much larger history of commercial society built on the providential foundations laid down by Vico. But if the political economy of the *History* had a Vichian beginning, was there really no escape from a Vichian end?

Anacyclosis, Emulation, and Enlightenment

As economic historians have shown, England was *the* overpowering economy with which to struggle, not only for cosmopolitan Neapolitan intellectuals but also for the kingdom's merchants, sailors, peasants, and artisans. English as well as French exports to the Italian states took off generally in the period of Genovesi's economic formation, but it was of a decidedly "colonial" character, particularly in the South; Neapolitan oil, grain, and raw materials were exchanged for foreign manufactures and exotic produce. Equally important, productive investments in Naples were predominantly financed by English loans, whose clauses included sales of English textiles in the Kingdom. The very structures of trade dictated an agricultural Naples contributing to English industrialization. Again, the problem of the structures of international trade and their influence of economic development become paramount. Naples traded abundantly with England, as did other Italian states, but they often found themselves in the wrong, low value added, business. The increasing volume of Anglo-Neapolitan trade in Genovesi's lifetime must be read in light of this asymmetry.[160] (See Figure 4.1.)

Studying history, Genovesi thus found many reasons to emulate England, for history unveiled to him that England's emergence as an economic power coincided closely with Italy's relative decline—that Italy had fallen in England's shadow as England rose out of the "hyperborean mists" that had enveloped it. Juxtaposing the texts of Mun and Cary, Genovesi was consequently able to highlight the way the study of English history became a study of Italian history as well, and the study of England's success likewise the study of Italy's failure. Though different nations, their reciprocal emulation united them at opposing extremes of a common anacyclosis, at opposite ends of Broggia's "wheel of fortune." "Three hundred years ago the manufactures reigned nowhere but in Italy; she was ahead of all other countries," Genovesi noted bitterly. So how "has it been possible that now almost all [other countries] have passed us by?" "How much has changed in a century!" Annotating Mun, he emphasized the irony that the English had looked to Italy as a model in the early seventeenth century. Nowhere in the *History* did the insight emerge with more clarity that the English had succeeded in emulating Italian customs, products, and practices, ultimately beating them at their own game. As Genovesi lectured at the university in the years around his translation of Cary, "the nations to which Italy communicated the arts and manufactures have indeed left us behind."[161]

Now that the secret of economic development had finally been revealed to the world, the countries of Europe all followed England's scheme, to the point where it had become "universal" to differentiate tariffs and discourage prohibitions to promote national manufactures.[162] Europe, in short, was industrializing in accordance with England's, but before that Italy's, example. Had it not been for the differences in climate and natural resources, and the cyclicality of history, one could have hoped for a brighter

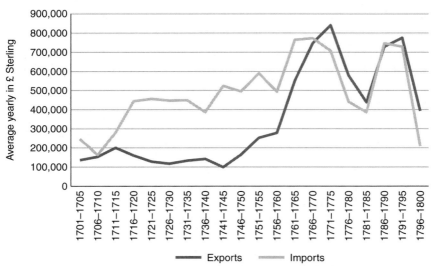

FIGURE 4.1. English and Welsh trade with Italian states, excluding Venice, by quinquennials, 1701–1800 (based on Schumpeter 1960, 17–18)

future in which an "equilibrium of commerce" rendered everyone better off.[163] But were there ways Naples could benefit from the impossibility of perpetual betterment? The realization that the anacyclotic cycles of nations were not synchronized was central to this problem. The great states of the late medieval period had been regions poor in natural resources—like Venice and the Low Countries—that originally arose through effective policies to dominate the trade of the continent. It had only been a matter of time, once these mechanisms were known, before larger states learned to harness their riches.[164] Since Genovesi repeatedly stated that England and France had reached the apex of their power, the question was now how Naples could ride the wheel of fortune toward the top, counterbalanced by the inevitable decline of the great powers. As wages increased in the wealthiest nations in Europe, poor "states" might be able to catch up, the "sweet price" at which their low-wage economies could sell goods giving them "preference in competition."[165] The so-called Rich Country—Poor Country Debate here came to grips with the obsessive eschatology of Italian political theory.[166]

In one of the supportive texts of the *History,* entitled *Philosophical Reasoning on the Strengths and Consequences of Great Riches* and strategically placed between the first two parts of Cary's thesis—demonstrating the economic history of England and the power of its manufactures, respectively—and his translation of Thomas Mun's earlier tract, Genovesi betrayed his profound preoccupation with greatness and decline. Now that he had explained how nations became wealthy, the question of durability remained; a question that brought him dangerously close to the line separating reformism from nihilism. He had already declared, in moralizing terms, that "those, who have read modern history with diligence, assure us, that the cycle of families, and of nations, is this: poverty, and hard work: riches, and luxury, and softness, and decline; and again poverty, and hard work etc." Now, however, his fatalism seemed tempered. "Surplus wealth," he declared, "inevitably brings the decline of the state, if exceptional, and singular prudence is not deployed to maintain it." Were there in fact ways the Polybian specter could be exorcised? It seemed so, and as in Genovesi's discussions of freedom and luxury, this entailed a return to Aristotle and the discovery of a median between excessive poverty and excessive riches. The same prudential vocabulary assisted him in overturning one of the pillars of early modern anacyclotic theory, namely Galiani's Machiavellian insistence that money was not the sinews of war. No less erudite, Genovesi countered with the Periclean dictum that "wars were won with prudence and with money." He in fact theorized the importance of military might in an annotation calling for "government" to step in with arms to protect the commerce of the nation, as the great powers had done so successfully. Harnessing a by now familiar vocabulary, Genovesi observed that countries "have given laws to Europe, when they have been masters of the sea; and have received them, when their navies have been weak."[167]

From the perspective of a weak country, the interconnected cyclicality characterizing the modern order of commercial societies emerged as an uplifting alternative to perpetual enslavement. Emulation, operating as an instrument of anacyclosis, meant that plans for universal economic empires like that proposed by Cary could never work because the "agriculture, manufactures, and navigation are no longer mysteries" but arts "known to all the peoples of Europe."[168] Their emulation would eventually lead poor and dependent countries out of "mediocrity" and out of empire. Even though many said it was "too late," that the great powers had set their zones of influence in stone, Genovesi used his translation of Mun to emphasize that some Englishmen had said the very same thing a century earlier. His translation of Cary was proof of England's success in this process.[169] In fact, in Genovesi's translation of Mun, he notes that Englishmen should "look to the Republics of Venice, Genoa, and Holland," for "nothing is needed apart from doing what they did, with only a little more diligence and *fatiga*." In an annotation, Genovesi remarked: "This is how the Englishmen spoke a century ago. They had a different opinion of themselves, from that Europe generally has of them now."[170]

Similarly, "at that time the best manufactures and the most esteemed in all of Europe were Italian, Spanish, and of the Low Countries. The English and the French were hardly mentioned. How much a single century has been able to change!." The same sentiment is expressed throughout Genovesi's work: "we learn, that little more than a century ago, the English, of whose wealth of traffic we are now envious, were envious of us."[171] Looking back on the history of Europe, he thus had little patience for "disquieted" Englishmen bewailing that other countries were emulating their policies: "[as] the English have either prohibited foreign goods or overburdened them with duties, they cannot reasonably lament that other nations use their same laws with regard to them."[172] Just as England historically had succeeded in emulating and surpassing Italy, Italy and the other laggard nations of the earth could return the favor. This, however, depended on looking beyond their present doctrines to the methods by which they historically had grown wealthy and powerful.

Yet the particular problems that had brought Italy to her knees in the late Renaissance persisted and would have to be addressed if the peninsula were to reclaim her old place in the hierarchy of nations. The "real ruin" of Italy had after all not been softness and luxury but having "her children dismembered in so many small parts." The warring provinces of the peninsula could no longer compete with the consolidated military states of transalpine Europe, and only "concordance and unity," he said, echoing Sarpi, could let summer bloom in Italy once more.[173] If the Italians could only be drawn closer together, the time was right for conquering the world's markets through a gradual development of military and economic power fueled by investments in education and the export of low-cost manufactures. Once a country grew wealthy, there were market mechanisms—the economic manifestations of anacyclosis so to speak—that began eroding its advantages. Wages and food costs would inevitably increase, and with them the price of manufactures, by which the country would no longer "have preference in foreign markets." Exports would decline, and with them wages and the price of foodstuffs, to the point where they would be thrown back into "poverty."[174]

Decline followed greatness like clockwork. The stars were right for a country like Naples to harness its natural resources and encourage its manufactures, which with their "sweet price" could cause the downfall of wealthier nations.[175] Where "everything" was "lacking," as in Naples, the silver lining lay in conquering foreign markets with cheap manufactures.[176] Broggia's "wheel of fortune" would again take an upward turn. Yet the power of civil thanatology meant that Genovesi's thoughts on the matter were far gloomier than those expounded by Hume in his nearly contemporary debate with Josiah Tucker over the fates of rich and poor countries united by international trade. The issue for neo-Polybians like Vico, Galiani, and Genovesi was not simply larger or smaller profit margins, equalization of fortunes versus perpetual disparity amid general development, but the biblical collapse of civilization as they knew it.

Again, this was conceived of as an entirely natural process that should not be overly lamented, for the vicissitudes of anacyclosis would never allow for any extreme state to endure, whether greatness or barbarism. Though Genovesi speculated about whether certain countries might not botch the "age of commerce" entirely, failing to nurture their agriculture and manufactures, becoming dependent, then deserted, demoted as states and cultures alike, he concluded that the destabilizing forces of "Finance" and "War" forever would bar such "theory" from reaching fruition.[177] There is thus an inherent tension in Genovesi's *History* between fate and freedom in economic affairs that is wholly absent from the original *Essay*. On the one hand, time was cyclical, and nature, personified by the most rampant theological Newtonianism, always ensured proper equilibriums.[178] On the other, human agency was the chief prerequisite for worldly melioration, and judicious actions *could* change the structures of the world, whether social, economic, or cultural, for the better.

This dilemma was, of course, by no means a new one, as is evident from Genovesi's engagement with authors like Vico and Machiavelli, and has constituted a topos of the Western tradition in important ways since the time of Homer. To adopt the language of Vico for the occasion, the paradox found its poetic archetype in the Iliadic Achilles, half mortal, half divine, thundering across the fields of Troy, whose wrath unfolded in a tortured mediation between the present and the eternal, between his prophetic knowledge of impending death and his choice to face it heroically. Genovesi's adherence to the values of Enlightenment and worldly melioration was clear cut, but so was his expectation of the eventual return to barbarism, not only for Naples or Italy but eventually for tired old Europe itself:

> The Tartars and the Muscovites are still numerous, and barbaric; we add, they are armed. America is already peopling itself, arming itself, educating itself. Can we persuade ourselves, that the voyage from America to Europe is longer and more exhausting than from Europe to America? Rome would never have believed, that those same barbarians, who she had harnessed in their houses, would have destroyed her.[179]

Commerce, Religion, and Sociability

The result of Genovesi's lengthy engagements with the main intellectual currents of the time was idiosyncratic. He was, as Venturi admitted, "more mysterious than what he seems."[180] Accepting the basic material mechanisms of development expounded by Epicurean authors like Mandeville, but vehemently resisting their presumed atheism, Genovesi, like Vico and Galiani, could simply not let go of the power of providence. He agreed with Cary on the intrinsic interconnectedness of society, politics, and the economy but was unwilling to theorize a cause outside of sacred history.[181] Self-interest and "cupidity," as he thought both sacred history and the English model proved, were important impetuses for general betterment, but could never be assumed to suffice. In fact, he explicitly theorized, on the back of earlier theorists of natural law, that society depended on "centripetal" and "centrifugal" "instincts" in man: on the one hand "sociability," on the other "cupidity." A "legislator" had to grasp that one of them could "not achieve its end without binding itself and remaining united to the other." This was a variation of the eighteenth-century theory of "unsocial sociability" elaborated by Samuel Pufendorf and later lionized by Immanuel Kant, which located the engine of society in the interaction of conflicting instincts; "Sociability" was the force of "gravity" without which a community would dissolve; "cupidity" was what created "industry and the arts." But this synergy was not automatic for Genovesi and depended on "religion" and careful calibration by legislators to "unify men." Similarly, he had no qualms about resorting to Hobbesian fear-based explanations for the emergence of politics within an overarching theological framework.[182] This very same theology of commercial society—ultimately founded on the veracity of scripture—led Genovesi even further along the lines drawn by Butel-Dumont in criticizing the callousness of Cary's project. Genovesi's ideas regarding the economic interests of his homeland in a competitive international arena were nearly identical to those of Cary, but his tolerant approach to cosmopolitanism was nonetheless based on the same faith in providence that had driven men like Fénelon to laissez-faire. Yet, as he resisted ennui in the face of eternal recurrence, so he fused these two seemingly contradictory ideologies of economic policy. One could, he thought, care for one's own citizens without demonizing the rest of humanity.[183]

Government had a duty to educate its entire population, from its own ministers to urban professionals and rural poor, and empower it to better its own condition. Though he certainly employed a vocabulary of "rights" in castigating institutions like slavery, it would remain for his students, like Filangieri, to theorize a political system of natural rights in its entirety.[184] Both agreed on the need for government to ensure these rights and the rightful development of mankind, however, and Genovesi tellingly chose to conclude the enormous enterprise that was his *History* with *Reasoning on Public Faith* [or *Trust*], an exposition on the social and spiritual foundations of his political economy.[185] Strikingly in this context, he began his essay with a eulogy, drawn from Dionysus of Halicarnassus's *Roman Antiquities*, of Numa Pompilius, the axiomatic author of civil theologies.[186] Frolicking with his nymph muse Egeria, Numa had founded the laws of Rome in the wake of Romulus's departure, and his greatest insight, to which Machiavelli would testify, had been the stabilizing function of religion. Yet there was no duplicity in Genovesi's insistence on the religious roots of sociability, for more than a tool for social control his civil theology was the manifestation of transcendent truth.

He repeatedly emphasized that without public "trust" or "faith" there could be no "justice" and no "humanity," the two "foundations" of "civil society."[187] Nothing was therefore more urgent than ensuring the maintenance of "pacts" and "promises" on which not only "civil society" but "public convenience and opulence" depended. As studies of modern savages showed, societies lacking in trust had neither "commerce" nor "culture" nor a "national spirit." Trust could ultimately only be grounded in "religion," and he lauded the example of Peter the Great in spreading the Catechism throughout his realms.[188] Only religion and laws, divine gifts based on "duties," differentiated the "sociability" of "animals" based on "pleasure" from the more complete sociability of "men."[189] And if the Russian autocrat was the model sovereign, there was little doubt that Colbert was the model minister for having "rendered immortal the reign of Louis XIV."[190] But again, if Genovesi employed seemingly Augustinian-Epicurean explanations for economic and social interactions, these mechanisms were everything *but* automatic in his political economy. Crimes reducing the level of trust in society by threatening the social compact, he argued, should be "punished with death," for otherwise "society will either dissolve itself, or it will convert in its entirety into a band of brigands."[191] Few things are further from ideals of spontaneous order through the free interplay of individual agents, an ideology he has been imputed with in recent historiography, than issuing capital punishment for deviant behavior, because "civil society" otherwise would be doomed. As Genovesi succinctly described the importance of higher political authorities in a letter of 1755 bewailing the miserable state of the kingdom,

> It is possible that the cause of all this is not just luxury and the pleasures of our century, which have rendered all minds effeminate and rendered them practical epicureans, but rather the absence of those stimuli, without which human passions never reach enthusiasm, so necessary for accomplishing great enterprises, and especially of premiums, honor, and emulation in schools and nations, all things of which our century is in need.[192]

"Emulation," again, emerged as a cardinal virtue for private as well as national happiness, and it was, from this perspective, natural to conclude that the central architecture of Montesquieu's *Spirit of the Laws*—that tyrannies were based on fear, monarchies on honor, and republics on virtue—was fatally flawed and, in Genovesi's characterization, "very strange." Without the enforcement of virtue and religion from above, and no matter its political constitution, a civil society bound together by laws would fall prey "to fear of one, or the prepotence, and money, of many." All this did not bode well for the future, and "History," Genovesi in fact concluded the third and final volume of his *History*, "is full of examples of those Monarchies, which by lack of virtue, and of Religion have been converted into Despotism, or dissolved in Anarchies."[193]

John Robertson has recently demonstrated the commonality of "Enlightenment" ideas in Scotland and Naples, fruitfully juxtaposing the moral and economic philosophies of Hume and Genovesi. Though their contexts were different, their religious ideas diametrically opposed, and their preoccupations remarkably diverse, they did agree on the fundamentals of economic policy *and* on the way of handling temporal cyclicalities. Genovesi had read Le Blanc's translation of Hume carefully and, though he did not find it worthy of translation, cited it often in his *History*. The concluding passage of Hume's "Idea of a Perfect Commonwealth" seems to address the Neapolitan obsession with anacyclosis directly. "It is needless to enquire," Hume wrote, "whether such a government would be immortal. . . . The world itself probably is not immortal. . . . It is sufficient incitement to human endeavors, that such a government would flourish for many ages; without pretending to bestow, on any work of man, that immortality, which the Almighty seems to have refused to his own productions." Political economy could go on with its business purposefully heedless of eschatology. Its successes might never amount to "progress" in any perennial sense, but worldly melioration in the short term was another matter entirely.[194]

Yet the political constellation the *History* thought most favorable to political economy could not have been further from that preached by the *Essay*, a divergence that sheds significant light on the spectrum of Neapolitan reformism. Considering the contemporary state of affairs, Galiani had argued in private correspondence that "one needs lower houses [of commons], which restrain absolute authority, not books." There were limits to how far reformism could go in the absence of a radical overthrow of existing social and political structures.[195] Genovesi instead thought the only entity capable of implementing necessary reforms was an absolute sovereignty in the image of Peter the Great's, for only "sovereigns" with "omnipotence" could "operate the most powerful levers with which to move men."[196] Genovesi was not the only Neapolitan to react to the pressures of international competition in this way. His sometime colleague Doria too, in reacting to the "jealousy of trade" manifest by the great powers in the 1740s, especially Britain, looked to the executive example of the Ottoman sultan for succor.[197]

At this point, however, Genovesi is no longer translating Cary but overthrowing him. "Civil liberty" did not entail the "license" to import and export goods at will any more than it entailed direct or representative self-government. The world, in short, was ultimately too dangerous for luxuries like those for which Cary fought all his life. England might be in a situation where they were affordable, but Naples was not yet there. Just as Amelot de La Houssaye "hijacked the texts presented in his books"— collating disparate texts to produce new works of his own in what Jacob

Soll has called an exercise of "material rhetoric"—Genovesi combined his own writings with those of Mun, Cary, and Butel-Dumont to produce a unique work of his own.[198]

Building on the economic analysis of foreign and local reason of state authors, Genovesi based his "science" of enlightenment on the power of manufactures to produce disproportionately more wealth with increasing investments. This turned out to have powerful political and philosophical repercussions in the evaluation of personal vices and international economic relations alike. His analytical annotations forcefully supported the conclusions drawn by previous curators of the *Essay* by analyzing and explaining the mechanisms of economic development harnessed by Great Britain after the "Glorious Revolution." The conclusions were clear to all of Genovesi's readers: Following in England's footsteps by encouraging the national production of manufactures and luxuries through asymmetrical trade was the *only* way Naples could become materially and culturally wealthy and retain her hard-won political independence in the face of the pendular movements of history. Even *with* an ostensibly absolute sovereign, however, the process he began of reforming institutions proved frustratingly slow. Neapolitan "civil society," he lamented toward the end of his life, was a "harlequin's dress."[199] And, in one of his last known letters, the elderly abbè synthesized a lifetime of activity:

> I am by now old, and neither hope for nor ask for more from the earth. My end would be to see if I could leave my Italians slightly more enlightened than what I found them when I came, and slightly more subject to virtue, which alone can be the true mother of every good. It is useless to think of art, commerce, government, if one does not think to reform morals.[200]

This was the fundamental program, similar to yet different from that pursued by Cary in Bristol, to which Genovesi dedicated himself until his death in 1769, through his teaching and the publication of his *Lectures of Civil Economics*, his *Diceosina*, and numerous textbooks on economic, philosophical, and moral subjects for students.[201] His final engagement with political economy, which took the form of annotations to an incomplete Italian translation of Montesquieu's *Spirit of the Laws*, clarified whatever doubts the world might have had about his stance on the matter. For did he come around to find succor in laissez-faire and the sweetness of commerce, as has been argued?[202]

> Commerce is the great source of wars. It is jealous, and jealousy arms men. The wars of the Carthaginians, of the Romans, of the Venetians, of the Genoese, of the Pisans, of the Portuguese, of the Dutch, of the French, and of the

English are testimonies of this. If two nations trade out of mutual needs, these needs are what oppose war, not the spirit of commerce.[203]

And again, he noted how England had uniquely mastered the military manifestation of commerce: "England's fort is the sea. It is necessary to arm it with commerce. Commerce forms the navy: the navy is the island's bulwark." Through conquest England had acquired dominion over continental North America; through commerce it had caused the "decline" of Holland and put Portugal in a state of "dependence"; through their union, it now threatened the liberties of Europe.[204]

The *History* across Italy

In a 1765 letter looking back on his career, Genovesi explained how the strands of his enterprise came together. "Every nation," he noted, "which does not have many books of science and the arts in its own language, is barbarian," for "that light, which is not written in one's own language, even though great and very brilliant, nonetheless remains buried in the lanterns of antiquarians, through which they only emit few and tenebrous rays."[205] Emulation required translation. By this standard, his work was a roaring success, for it is difficult to overstate the *History*'s influence. Genovesi's lectures were the focal point of Neapolitan reformism, leaving a lasting mark not only on the city but on Italian economic culture. Italian states began to take ever more care of their domestic manufactures in the second half of the eighteenth century; palliative measures, Venturi argued, against England's intensifying industrial edge, the low cost of its manufactures, and their "penetration" of the peninsula.[206] Genovesi's three-volume translation of Cary was republished in Naples and Venice—another must on the Grand Tour—in 1764; the Venetian edition was sold for 7 lire, roughly the cost of an expensive funeral, by a bookseller in Venice in 1772, and received laudatory reviews in journals across Italy and even in France, where a note in the *Journal Oeconomique* informed its readers of the publication of an Italian translation of the French translation of the *Essay* "with an extensive preface on the subjects of commerce."[207] Genovesi's copious annotations to Cary would form the core of his *Lectures,* which were republished and translated numerous times in the late eighteenth century. Just as Locke had praised Cary's *Essay* on its publication, and Diderot and Grimm had praised Butel-Dumont's French translation of it, the luminaries of the Italian Enlightenment lauded Genovesi's *History,* doubtlessly the most influential work of political economy produced in eighteenth-century Italy.[208] The Venetian *Giornale d'Italia,* one of the first journals on the peninsula to explicitly focus on economic matters, inaugurated its first issue with an extensive review of the 1764 Venetian edition of Genovesi's *History:*

> To some, it will seem strange that we inaugurate a *Giornale d'Italia* pertinent to Commercial things with news of a work written by a Transalpine author; but these must know, that we do this for the same reason that it was brought into our language. We invite our nation to read this book because, if it is convinced to do so, we think it can learn from it how the English lifted every part of their economy to its current greatness, and that from this will come the opportunity to contemplate how, if the right proportion is maintained and the same economy used, every nation can have commerce as great and as rich as the English.[209]

Genovesi's aim in translating Cary could hardly have been better summarized, and he gratefully complimented the journal's editors on their project.[210]

His influence did not stop here, however, as a subsequent review of his *Lectures* rhetorically asked "Who doesn't know the illustrious *Signor Abate Genovesi,* the greatest genius in Italy?" The *Lectures* deserved to be "crowned with gold and citrus."[211] The Milanese statesman and political economist Pietro Verri wrote : "I would like to find the necessary words to inspire my readers to procure for themselves Genovesi's excellent [translation of Cary], which is sufficient to acquire a very extensive understanding of commerce."[212] Even more strikingly, he wrote a letter to Genovesi claiming that "all of Italy" owed him "homage" for his work.[213] Verri's friend and rival Beccaria similarly praised Genovesi in his inaugural lecture at the chair of political economy in Milan as "founder" of economic "science" in Italy, and Paradisi, holder of Italy's third chair at Modena, practically based his entire course on Genovesi's mediation of the English model.[214] Few authors would take the blurred distinction between commerce and conquest championed by the *Essay,* the cyclicality of emulation, or the political economy of decline further than Paradisi, but from Carlo Salerni in Otranto to Andrea Tron in Venice, from Giovanni Attilio Arnolfini in Lucca to Carlo Denina in Turin, Genovesi's inflection of Cary was inescapable among Italian thinkers and statesmen. And so was the transition from secretive reason of state to public political economy that he helped inaugurate.[215]

"These political economic sciences," Genovesi's student Vincenzo Emanuele Sergio lectured from his chair on the subject at the University of Palermo in 1780, "which once were reserved only for the cabinets of princes, must be studied by every citizen." But though Sergio took pride in domesticating foreign economic doctrines such as those promulgated through the Italian translations of Cary and Melon, his purpose was less than cosmopolitan. Only by encouraging "emulation" in Sicily and ensuring that it achieved "superiority" in "competition" with "rivals" through the judicious "protection" of national manufactures could it emerge victorious from the "current war of industry." Quoting Cary frequently, Sergio was instrumental in the establishment of a "public house of industry," explicitly based on Cary's Bristol blueprint, in Palermo in 1800, and he praised technological developments in manufacturing for their ability to "render the toil of man less painful and [for] multiplying annual reproduction." Ultimately, Sergio hoped that the "new lights" offered by ultramontane authors would "restore" Sicily "to that eminent degree of true greatness, splendor, and power which it once enjoyed."[216] The idioms of translation, emulation, protection, industrial warfare, manufacturing multiplication, greatness, and decline that he harnessed should not surprise the reader by this point, though the use to which they were put well might have surprised Cary. For when Pius VI sought ways to rejuvenate the economy of the Papal States on the eve of Napoleon's invasion, his advisor Paolo Vergani too chose the authority of the great "Gioanni Carij" over that of "Adamo Smith."[217] As the papaphobic Cary became papal economist by proxy, the "irony" by which John Dunn has theorized the relation of texts to their original intentions begins to smell ever more of sarcasm. *Traduttore traditore* indeed.[218]

CHAPTER FIVE

Wichmann's Ökonomisch-politischer Commentarius

Conundrum Cameralism

England's American colonies had won independence, France was on the brink of d'Argenson's "total revolution," and Kant had defined "Enlightenment" along the Horatian lines of "dare to know!" when Cary's *Essay* underwent its final translation, into German, in 1788.[1] By this time, it had become a classic in Calvino's sense. On the one hand it depicted the nature of British economic hegemony and codified the policies pursued to achieve it; on the other it conveyed the history of how different European contexts had engaged it.[2] It was an unlikely founding document of political economy, but a founding document all the same. And while the final adaptation of the *Essay* was the least influential of its foreign editions, it was also the most indicative of its standing in Enlightenment Europe, supplying fruitful perspectives on the disciplinary development of political economy as well as the comparative progress of material welfare and political liberty at the time. For like England, France, and the Italian peninsula, so the German lands, as the focal point of an administrative continuum stretching from northern Italy to Scandinavia, were already home to a venerable tradition of economic thought, known as Cameralism, by the time the *Essay* arrived on the scene—a tradition that was both local and cosmopolitan, both idiosyncratic and well versed in the European literature on the subject.

Etymologically, Cameralism derived from the German *Kammer* (a word itself derived from the Latin *camera*), first used to denote the prince's private apartment, then by extension the locus of his administration. The same root survives today in *Kammermusik* as a form of musical expression, lionized by the likes of Haydn and Mozart, proper for performance within a princely chamber and thus distinct in form and origins from sacral and later orchestral compositions.[3] Sweden was not Saxe-Gotha any more than Denmark-Norway was a political community free from conflicting patriotisms, but they all shared, through tradition, emulation, translation, and itinerant university professors, a common discourse of Cameralism, known as such, which, although conversant with other economic traditions, represented a coherent cluster of theories, practices, and preoccupations. For more than a mere economic theory, Cameralism was a technology for governing men and nature; as much a science of forestry and metallurgy as of statecraft. Yet in terms of its aims of harnessing domestic energies, its faith in the information processing faculties of the administrative apparatus, and its trenchant idioms of reason of state, Cameralism had much in common with the sensitivities of Cary, the Gournay circle, and Colbert's legacy of governmental practices in Europe more generally.[4] The Gournayite position had, in fact, been endorsed by a bona fide Cameralist, the Swedish naturalist Carl von Linné, better known as Linnaeus, who in 1752 published his "Principles of Œconomics, founded on the Natural Sciences & on Physics" in the *Journal Économique*. As a manifesto, it clarifies the intellectual ecology that Cary's *Essay* was entering in German translation.[5]

The "science" of Cameralism that informed Linnaeus's entry into the debates derived from rather different premises from those that had given birth to economic discourses in England, France, and Italy. The 1648 Peace of Westphalia concluding the horrors of the Thirty Years' War had recognized more than three hundred German principalities occupying the territories between Poland and France, between the Baltic and the Alps.[6] But much in the same way that Italy, since Petrarch, had mediated its loss of political coherence by nurturing a cultural unity, an *italianità,* so Germans were well aware of their common *Deutschtum*, their shared history, culture, and problems. This political fractionalization had clear economic and demographic consequences also north of the Alps. It created the conditions for what later observers would scorn as *Kleinstaaterei,* the excessive creation of small states, and the population of "the Germanies" therefore grew little in the seventeenth and eighteenth centuries. Historians of urbanization agree that a hierarchical network of urban centers developed in German territories in the absence of a unified state or metropolis, as several cities competed to assume the functions and responsibilities of the emerging economic order.[7] Numerous smaller urban districts emerged there where one single larger city tended to appear in larger unified territorial kingdoms, also partly a consequence of the very tangible rivalry between German sovereigns. Compared to London's 675,000 and Paris's 570,000 inhabitants in 1750, Berlin, the largest Cameralist city, was on a different demographic scale entirely with 113,000, though still far above Copenhagen's 80,000, Stockholm's 70,000, and Christiania's, now Oslo's, 7,000.[8] This, in turn, had serious consequences for industrialization; the intersection of fragmented markets and small cities by default favored imports of foreign manufactures over the development of local industry.[9]

This mosaic of sovereignties competing among themselves and with more unified powers contributed to the emergence of an Aristotelian tradition of administrative theory and practice—conceiving of the prince as a housefather responsible for the material and spiritual well-being of his subject children—very different from the parliamentary focus of Cary's project.[10] Thus born from the needs of smaller states to safeguard and muster their limited resources rather than, as in the case of English "mercantilism"—from vociferous merchants seeking to better the condition of their trades in light of a hegemonic rivalry with France—Cameralism developed, more than immediate counterparts in Europe did, in a dialogue with the emerging science of natural history, for latent resources of the land required discovery, observation, and understanding in order to be harnessed fully, economically as well as scientifically.[11] The eighteenth-century architects of Kew Gardens and the exponents of the "Scottish Enlightenment" were of course well aware of the relationship between natural philosophy and political economy, but this was a much later development in Britain than in continental Europe.[12] Since its origins in the wake of Westphalia, Cameralism consciously incorporated fields of learning as diverse as metallurgy and moral philosophy to codify first an "art" and then a "science" of civil society that was understood as the means of securing the happiness of a people settled in a distinct territory.[13] In terms of Venturi's influential thesis about the conflictual relationship between utopia and reform in the Enlightenment, Cameralists came to accept an inherent interrelationship between the two early on. As the Cameralist and philosopher Christian Wolff put it, "Since nature requires us to strive towards the best as far as we are able, therefore we must also have a conception of the best or most perfect, so we can judge toward what we must strive."[14]

Striving and achieving, of course, were two different things, and the tension between the halcyon ideals and grim realities of Cameralism has doubtlessly contributed to its often derogatory historiography. Far more than the comparable English-speaking scholarship on early English, French, and Italian political economy, that of Cameralism tends explicitly toward ridicule; the Cameralist states, Andre Wakefield recently argued in an incisive reevaluation, were "the Galapagos Islands of state building."[15] It is true that many of the foremost writers of the Cameralist tradition, from Johann Joachim Becher to Johann Gottlob von Justi, can be described as economic adventurers, but in a world populated by truly Münchhausen-like political economists such as Casanova and Major-General Henry Lloyd, this was hardly unique.[16] In effect, part of the problem is that Cameralism, because of its wide field of engagement, too often falls under the historiographical rubric of history of science, a field in which leading scholars have accepted anachronistic stereotypes of neoclassical economics.[17] The assumption that England was some libertarian linchpin of modernity and free trade makes Germanic debates about political economy by necessity aberrant, allowing untenable arguments to go unchallenged.[18] For did Cameralists merely allow "coarse and drunken German princes" to "appropriate the wealth of their subjects"?[19]

One must not succumb to the temptation of equating ideal depictions with actual conditions, but considering Cameralism in the context of the revised English economic persona I expound in this book will help explain many of its traditions and choices. Worldly melioration was a competitive endeavor in early modern Europe, and if the small states of Italy found it difficult to keep up, the often minuscule Cameralist ones seemed doomed to destitution and dependence. The exigencies of jealousy of trade meant that the great powers continued to wreak havoc in German and Scandinavian lands long after the Thirty Years' War. Such was the case when Karl Ludwig, elector of the Palatinate, refounded the city of Mannheim in 1652 hoping that it "would become the Amsterdam of the Rhine." Not surprisingly, as Richard Gawthrop has put it, "the Dutch were not flattered by his attempts at imitation" and dispatched armed forces to end the scheme.[20] So while it is true that Cameralists could evaluate the nature and consequences of "commercial capitalism" in England at a distance, and often drew explicitly on its industrial policies, adopting some while discarding others of its most salient characteristics, said "commercial capitalism" also had ways of affecting them directly.[21] And few phenomena were more conducive to these disruptive mechanisms than the international competition for markets and raw materials raging at the time. "Germany" was one of England's primary trading partners during the long eighteenth century, also because of Hanover's unique position as a "bridgehead for British trade in Germany" following the 1714 coronation of George I.[22] Yet, as in the case of

Italy, this volume of trade must be problematized in light of its structure. As contemporaries noted, English manufactures were flooding Germany, and, echoing the contemporary mainstream of political economy, it was "very impolitic in the Germans" to export raw materials "when they should manufacture their raw materials themselves, and then export them."[23]

While the Cameralist discourse remained one of the liveliest in all of Europe and enthusiastically incorporated foreign works on related subjects, it was seldom translated into other languages except Swedish and Danish. Cameralism was less an isolated archipelago than the end of a funnel of ideas and practices. So when the Leipzig Cameralist professor Daniel Gottfried Schreber composed his *Two Treatises on the History and Necessity of Cameral Sciences in so Far as They are Regarded University Sciences* in 1764, he listed hundreds of authors who had contributed to his discipline, from the thirteenth-century Bolognese jurist Pietro Crescenzi to Botero and Montchrétien to Seckendorff and Linnaeus.[24] Informed with regard to events and traditions elsewhere in Europe, Cameralism developed its own unique practices of engagement with the economic sphere. In a radical rhetorical break with the English and French traditions, for example, Linnaeus's article in the *Journal économique* defined "Oeconomie" as "the Science" that does not study commerce but "teaches us the manner of preparing natural things for our use by means of the elements." Economics, then, was a technology for harnessing nature to the needs of a political community.[25] The "two hinges on which all oeconomie turns" were, in accordance with his Cameralist roots, "knowledge of natural things" and of "the action of elements on bodies, & of the manner of directing this action towards certain ends." Physics, which Linnaeus defined as the science that studied the "elements" of the "globe" and their interaction, found its natural counterpart in "Oeconomics," which, intending to domesticate man's material surroundings, required princes to chart, survey, catalogue, and experiment with all the resources of their land, "plant" new growths and industries, and direct the fortunes of their nations the way a patriarch would those of his family. Though their policy-sensibilities were similar, this was a far cry even from Genovesi's Newtonian mechanics.[26]

By its very nature and localistic focus, the purposes of Cameralist "science" were antagonistic to cosmopolitical arguments for laissez-faire. Economy involved the organization, even disciplining, of man in his material surroundings and as such required purposeful action more than faith in Providence.[27] In terms of the social and cultural history of ideas, it is conceivable that the living memory of the Thirty Years' War and the realities of imperial competition taught Cameralists the dangers of abeyance, of letting be. In fact, while the traditional historiography of Cameralism focuses almost entirely on internal conditions, the lens of international emulation offers fruitful perspectives on its development. For if Cameralism's approach to economic phenomena differed from those of its counterparts elsewhere in Europe, generally focusing on technologies of effective administration rather than on imperialist gambits or sophisticated moral and political theory, its ends were remarkably similar: wealth, independence, and the almighty *Glückseligkeit*—happiness.[28] Not surprisingly, Muratori's 1749 *Public Happiness,* which had so influenced entire generations of Italian reformers, including Genovesi, was nimbly translated into German in 1758 as *On the Happiness of the Commonwealth, as the Principal Purpose of Well Governing Princes.*[29]

And Cameralists, just as other economic "scientists" in Europe, saw a people's happiness and welfare as depending on certain kinds of economic activities. Quite apart from the myriad laws understood to depend on local circumstances, and before worrying about the finer points of financial regulation or the public debt, Cameralist advisors taught the rulers of Germany to appreciate the existential importance of what their peoples produced. The bottom line of increasing princely taxes and popular welfare lay in the development of the nation's industry, its productive capacity, in relation to available natural resources, both in agriculture and, crucially, in manufacturing. As the previous chapters have demonstrated, similar statements of intent were legion across Europe as successful economic policies were codified and institutionalized in the late Renaissance.[30] Seckendorff echoed this tradition in founding the "science of Cameralism" in 1665 when he said Germans "act wrongly in exporting and selling raw materials only to pay a higher price taking them back as manufactures once people have worked them."[31] Industry, both as a personal trait and a synonym for manufacturing, was understood to be the key to human welfare from one end of Europe to the other, but in the Cameralist lands, caught between globalization and exceedingly local constraints, the theory and practice of its encouragement developed in a unique fashion, just as it had in England, France, and Italy.

Ersatz Imperialism

Seckendorff codified Cameralism after observing the flourishing Dutch economy firsthand and produced a set of guidelines for the development of small principalities that focused on the need to encourage emulation, industry, and the production and proliferation of knowledge.[32] His emphasis on these elements found its most central policy implication in import substitution, in the political support for establishing local manufactures to supply local needs as a means of creating domestic "chains" of wealth and escape poverty and dependence on foreigners. This insight echoed throughout the Cameralist tradition and was developed further by men like Linnaeus, who brought the discourse of "planting" to a whole new level of both theory and practice. Not only were foreign industries to be domesticated, but the fruits of foreign soils too should be forcibly transplanted and "acclimatized" to the Cameralist states of Germany and Scandinavia.

In its most extreme manifestation, this autarkism led to extraordinary efforts to simulate the benefits of tropical imperialism in the temperate and arctic territories available to the Cameralist project. In hindsight it is easy to ridicule attempts to domesticate exotic growths in hostile climates, and the vision of mammoth tea plantations spanning the arctic wastes is wondrous at best.[33] Yet the introduction of New World crops like tobacco, potatoes, and the tomato had transformed Old World agriculture and consumption habits, and the immense wealth produced by the cultivation of sugar, coffee, tea, and cotton at the time were understood to result from conscious acts of strategic planting in key colonies employing slave labor, whether of coffee in St. Helena, sugar and coffee in Brazil and Martinique, or cotton in the American South.[34] Central and northern Europeans too had bought into the contemporary crazes for colonial goods, habits that were poignantly debilitating in light of the contemporary theory of the balance of trade. And the impossibility of competing for colonial markets and resources directly channeled many of the energies that drove Englishmen and Frenchmen across the hemispheres in a more local direction, for ideals of self-sufficiency by necessity informed the administrative choices of small states.

Admittedly, the Scandinavian Cameralist states fared better in the colonial race than their largely landlocked German brethren.[35] One of the great powers of the seventeenth century, Sweden controlled a veritable Baltic empire, on the basis of which it established a short-lived presence in Africa, the so-called Swedish Gold Coast, in the seventeenth century, which was soon lost to the Dutch and later to the English. Sweden's imperial misadventures in the Western Hemisphere were only moderately more successful. New Sweden, populated largely by Finns, at the time Swedish subjects, enjoyed a short-lived existence along the Delaware River from 1638 to 1655, when it was captured by the Dutch; nine years later it was captured by the English. In the eighteenth century, Sweden annexed the Caribbean islands of Saint-Barthélemy—whose current capital, Gustavia, named after King Gustav III, still recalls its complex colonial history—and even

Guadeloupe for some time. But the territorial losses Sweden incurred at the end of the devastating Northern War (1709–21) marked its definitive demotion from great power status, inaugurating a period that was known as the "Age of Liberty" for its successful experiment with parliamentary principles and was devoted to intensive internal development rather than international power politics. By the late 1760s, Sweden had, with no funds and only eight serviceable warships, become something of a French protectorate. So throughout the long parliamentary conflicts between the Francophile "Hats" and the Anglophile "Caps," Cameralist reforms (planting industries, emulating policies and technologies, and harnessing latent resources) enjoyed surprisingly wide support; if the "Hats" made Anders Berch Sweden's first professor of Cameralism, at Uppsala in 1741, the country's perhaps greatest economic writer, Anders Nordencrantz, was an inveterate member of the "Caps."[36]

The union of the kingdoms of Denmark and Norway under Danish domination had also brought an empire into existence. This included not only Norway's colonies of Iceland, the Faroe Islands, and Greenland in the icy North Atlantic, which the Lutheran missionary Hans Egede in 1741 optimistically claimed had as strong an economic potential as "anywhere else," but also the Caribbean islands of St. Thomas, St. John, and, after purchasing it from the French in 1733, St. Croix, in addition to Tranquebar in India, seat of the Danish East India Company. Tranquebar, administering a number of smaller trading posts on the Indian subcontinent, would only be bought by the British in the nineteenth century, while Denmark's Levant Company succumbed to poor management and what an envoy referred to, with a vocabulary that by now should be familiar, as the "Envy, Jealousy, and Opposition of certain Nations" who sought to monopolize the "work and industry" of the eastern Mediterranean.[37] Yet none of these overseas efforts could compete with the wealth created by the Norwegian timber trade, which in the seventeenth and eighteenth centuries supplied England with nearly half of its imported wood and generated several times the export value of all trades in the Kingdom of Sweden.[38] Both Denmark-Norway and Sweden also expanded northward, acquiring vast but vague possessions in "Lapland," or present-day Nordkalotten, the "Cap of the North." Even where their empires were formally established, however, Scandinavians simply lacked the administrative capacity and economic power to maintain and expand their influence.

A report prepared for King Frederick IV by the Danish Board of Police and Trade in 1716 tellingly suggests the radical measure of accepting the de facto liberty of Caribbean colonists to trade with other colonial powers. The islands were administered to produce sugar and cotton rather than foodstuffs, and constant warfare rendered it impossible for Danish supply ships to reach St. Thomas more often than once every other year.[39] By comparison, Cary's hometown of Bristol alone sent out an average of eighty-three ships yearly to the West Indies in the period.[40] The Danish colonist's new-found freedom from metropolitan oppression, however, came at a cost. As the governor of St. Thomas wrote to the directors of the Danish West India Company on 25 May 1719, their liberty of trade as a result of Denmark-Norway's failure to administer its empire had made them slaves of another kind: "The English nation is the one that does us the most good, and from which we have most to fear, for truth to say, they hold our very lives in their hands."[41] Failing to provide for the welfare of its overseas citizens and employees, Denmark-Norway allowed them the freedom to trade for their own provisions. This freedom bought them food but also the anxieties of dependence on the goodwill of a competing and often hostile power. Once dependent by ancient rights of conquest, the inhabitants of the Danish West Indies became dependent through modern rights of trade. It was a vice embedded in the contemporary structures of international trade, whereby specialized colonies produced raw materials for the rich and powerful rather than developing holistic economies for themselves. And the Danes, even more so than the Swedes, turned away from delusions of greatness during the eighteenth century, embracing a policy of neutrality in international affairs that would only be ended by British firebombs during the Napoleonic Wars.[42]

The failure of Scandinavia to unify and become a world power in the early modern period, when it controlled the key strategic resources of timber, tar, hemp, and metals, in addition to vast fisheries, remains an enigma of global history, but can only be understood in light of the secular diplomatic and military campaigns of great powers to break Nordic alliances at crucial junctures and hinder the emergence of a centralized monopoly on northern raw materials.[43] In the grand scheme of things, however, if no great Nordic state materialized, Scandinavia fared better in the imperialist game than the smaller states occupying the lands east of the Rhine. Yet these too looked with envy at the riches of empire, seeking ways to emulate the flourishing colonies of western Europe. But this was hardly a Cameralist conceit, and it is easy to forget the legion of political communities that were engaged in early modern imperialism. In 1608–9, even Medici Tuscany planned colonies in Sierra Leone and on the coast of Latin America.[44] And the tiny Cameralist Duchy of Courland, a vassal of the Polish-Lithuanian Commonwealth in present-day Latvia, established colonies on two continents, settling the St. Andres Island near the Gambia River in 1651, and Tobago in 1654, both of which were lost by 1666.[45] German states hardly fared any better. The Brandenburger Gold Coast, settled in 1682, was bought by the Dutch in 1721, the same year in which Brandenburg's colony on Arguin, on the west coast of Mauritania, was taken over by the French. It became ever clearer that the Cameralist empire, barred from the seas, would be realized inward, in the heartlands of Europe, precisely as Seckendorff suggested in his 1665 *Additions* to his *Princely State*. Generations of eighteenth-century Swedes would thus find succor in referring to Lapland as "the Swedish West Indies," an ironic gesture, given that Englishmen had long referred to Sweden itself as part of "the Indyes of the materials of shipping," the economic equivalent of a colony.[46]

It is true that Cameralism—both as an academic discipline and as an administrative and policing practice—also flourished in the Hapsburg monarchy and in Prussia, both great territorial powers on the European stage in the second half of the eighteenth century, but one of its principal tasks remained that of ensuring competitive development in the face of far superior English, French, and for a while, Dutch imperial technologies. Nonetheless, there would be no really durable English or French conquests in continental Europe during the eighteenth century, and the idea of transplanting colonial products back to a relative safety at home was thus a sensible reaction to jealousy of trade in international relations and the ruthless policies pursued by the great powers. Even Frederick the Great, hardly pusillanimous in international relations, preferred "activity" and the "encouragement" of the national economy to "conquest" as a means of "self-aggrandizement." "Manufactures," he wrote, "may be what is most useful and profitable to a state," for not only did they allow for larger and wealthier populations, but they were themselves instruments of international competition; "If France succeeds in ruining the commerce of England, this will increase its power more than the conquest of twenty cities and a thousand villages ever could." In this, and though doubtlessly under the influence of psychological and political imperatives as well, Frederick joined a long line of Cameralists arguing that power was best secured through emulative, if not jealous, development.[47]

The need to "plant" foreign technologies, techniques, and resources represents a pertinent idiosyncrasy through which to contextualize Cary's translation into German. The limits to growth established by geographical, climatic, and imperial conditions in central and northern Europe, by their ecologies, forced statesmen and entrepreneurs to manage resources to a degree never dreamed of by contemporary Englishmen. Cary had pushed for ever greater conquests, for ever-intensifying extraction, manufacturing, and even the provocative burning of valuable raw materials to dominate global trade. The world was his oyster. For Cameralists, whose worlds at times were the size of oysters, such adventurism was unsustainable. Instead, they churned out an extensive literature on the administration and conservation of natural resources, on river fisheries, forestry, and mining. "It is always a bad principle of state," the North-Norwegian author, printer, and later Bengal exile Jacob Christian Bie wrote in 1770, "to look at the present time and advantage alone. A righteous Statesman must have his goals expanded to [include] posterity" in the same way that "a farmer" sells his fruit but not his trees, thus achieving long-term welfare by carefully managing his estate rather than by the myopic spoliation of resources, his own or others'.[48] This was a formulation of a common trope in the Cameralist literature, arrestingly visualized in the frontispiece to a 1752 edition of Wilhelm von Schröder's frequently republished *Princely Tax- and Rent-Chamber*, in which the difference between the true wealth and "happiness" to be had from corralling sheep and shearing them carefully was juxtaposed with the violence and "false profit" one could have from immediately skinning them instead. The image's motto was *"tonderi vult, non deglubi"*—literally "he wants to be shorn, not flayed"—and, through prevalent largely in the early modern context of Cameralism, ultimately derived from ancient accounts of the Roman Emperor Tiberius' good judgment in economic matters after he decided it was better in matters of taxation to shear rather than flay subjects.[49]

This Cameralist preoccupation with planting and cultivation to achieve sustainable wealth-creation was also conditioned by Germany's comparative receptivity to foreign economic works. For just as one sought to "plant" foreign crops and industries in Cameralist lands, while attempts to export bratwurst and cloudberries to the Spice Islands are harder to find, so efforts to "plant" translations could be justified without fear of imbalance, without fear of being overpowered by foreign practices. As the theologian Friedrich Schleiermacher in hindsight argued in his 1813 lecture "On the Different Methods of Translating," delivered to the Royal Academy of Sciences in Berlin:

> Just as our soil itself has no doubt become richer and more fertile and our climate milder and more pleasant only after much transplantation of foreign flora, just so we can sense that our language, because we exercise it less owing to our Nordic sluggishness, can thrive in all its freshness and completely develop its own power only through the most many-sided contacts with what is foreign.[50]

Johan Westerman, the so-called "Swedish Colbert," had encapsulated this process well in his 1768 inaugural lecture to the Swedish Academy of Sciences on how to emulate foreign manufactures.[51] The frontispiece of

Academy publications at the time, framed by palm trees on one side and pine trees on the other, represented a radiant classical building enlightening a bearded man in the act of planting a small palm in temperate Scandinavian soil above the phrase "För Efterkommande," literally meaning for descendents in posterity. Westerman noted the comparative meekness of Swedish industry and proposed ways the Academy could help it catch up with international competitors, among other things by domesticating foreign growths and emulating English "tools and machines." The Academy's official answer to his pamphlet brought the discourse of planting full circle. Traveling around Europe, other members of the institution had also noticed that Swedish not only lacked the word that "Frenchmen call *Industrie*," referring to an economic activity distinct from agriculture, but that Swedes lacked the very "quality" of industry itself, understood as individual industriousness, and praised Westerman's efforts to remedy the situation.[52] Welfare required the translation, the bringing across and planting, not only of growths and industries but of languages, the emulation of economic cultures. In these terms, the final leg of Cary's *Essay* in translation follows the Cameralist logic of acculturation closely. Having already contributed directly to the development of political economy in England, France, and Italy, the *Essay* belonged squarely in this project.

In effect, Seckendorff's foundational acclimatization of foreign thoughts and practices set the pattern for the later development of Cameralism. The influential Johann Friedrich von Pfeiffer, who in a true Cameralist tradition wrote important works on forestry, committed a chapter of his massive 1781 history of economic analysis to Seckendorff's *Princely State,* admitting that "before Seckendorff's time political science in Germany was almost undeveloped and one made do with Italian and French fragments." And in his spirit, Pfeiffer filled his work with chapters dedicated to the greatest foreign thinkers on the subject, from Genovesi to Necker and Adam Smith.[53] The best-selling Johann Heinrich Gottlob von Justi had a similar formation, explicitly drawing on both Seckendorff and non-Germanic authors. He was well versed in English and French debates on political economy, attentively reading the output of Gournay's circle and, strikingly, launching a personal project to encourage industry by translating the "Arts et métiers" volumes published in Diderot and d'Alembert's *Encyclopédie.* And as Genovesi longed for the greatness of Rome and of the Renaissance, so Justi bewailed the loss of Germanic economic preeminence with the decline of the Hanseatic League. The problem now faced by the Cameralist lands was not unlike that faced by Genovesi's Italy. "The English, the Dutch, and the French have such a great head-start," Justi warned, "that a nation that is just beginning will hardly be able to compete with them." Like Cary's translators, Justi suggested turning to the English model of tariffs and prohibitions to forcefully invigorate national industries and relocate manufactures—lucrative both economically and culturally— to German lands. Equally important, he argued and practiced the principle that liberty and material welfare depended on the successful planting not only of exotic growths and foreign industries but of foreign ideas.[54]

As an economic discourse, the Cameralist tradition stretching from Tuscany and Milan, where Cesare Beccaria's university chair was in Cameralism, through the German lands to Scandinavia was not, as some argue, "parochial"; it was eminently receptive to English, French, and Italian ideas yet often going well beyond them in sophistication.[55] Few contemporaries, for example, approached the Dane Carl Christoph Plüer in terms of expounding on the consequences of industrialization in a world that, as he saw it, had overcome "Machiavelli's teachings." In a 1757 pamphlet he laid down the multiplying capacities of manufactures compared to agriculture, explained why gold and silver were mere symptoms of an economy's productive capacity, and why it was that England's prohibitions on the exports of raw materials had been so successful. Explicitly considering not just the home-weaving clusters of division of labor cherished by the historiography of protoindustry but also fire-harnessing factories and furnaces, his work reads as a manifesto for what has been defined as the transition from an "industrious" to an "industrial" revolution. So powerful was industrial production that Plüer envisioned a world, far off in the future, where people traded only in raw materials. The multiplying effects of manufacturing mass production was simply too powerful a weapon in international relations for one state to monopolize. Hence, governments had a duty to encourage the spread of industry and counteract the current climate in which "Capitalists" were "too scared to found factories." And politicians should not heed the fears of merchants that prices would increase. Technological change and improved techniques would always bring costs down over time, Plüer wrote optimistically, eventually making all national industries competitive. It was a peace plan, but opposite in nearly every way to that of Physiocracy.[56] And it was on the heels of this impressive but historiographically ridiculed tradition that Cary's *Essay* neared the end of its remarkable journey.

Northern Lights

The *Essay*'s route through Europe was more circuitous than was statistically probable. Most English works arrived in German directly, some taking a longer route via an intermediary French translation—the capital of commerce reflected through the contemporary capital of culture.[57] But Cary's work steadfastly refused to take the shortest route through the labyrinth of intellectual history, and from one of the southernmost realms in Enlightenment Europe, the *Essay* arrived in Germany via its northernmost territorial power, the Kingdom of Denmark-Norway. Again, the human element in intellectual transmission rears its head. The philosopher Friedrich Heinrich Jacobi lionized Vico's *New Science* in German only after Goethe entrusted him with the copy he had been given by Filangieri during his Grand Tour to Naples; Serra's *Short Treatise* was first republished by Baron Pietro Custodi from a copy that had passed, in Benedetto Croce's apt words, like a "lamp of life" through the hands of Intieri, Galiani, Giuseppe Palmieri, and Francesco Salfi, four of the greatest reformers of eighteenth-century Italy.[58] Similar forces brought Cary to Germany as part of a significant transalpine transmission of Italian economic thought.[59]

Peter Christian Schumacher (1743–1817) was a notable figure in his time, and like many of the major protagonists of this story, he made his way from urban professional—one is tempted to say bourgeois—to nobility by his own merit. Chamberlain to the king of Denmark, formerly longtime Danish consul to Morocco and later St. Petersburg, he was an important architect of the 1780 League of Armed Neutrality and one of Europe's greatest practical Cameralists.[60] His successful career doubtlessly owed much to his being a protégé of the powerful Danish statesman and scholar Ove Høegh-Guldberg (1731–1808), mentor to the young bastard Prince Frederick of Denmark and de facto ruler of the country. Though Høegh-Guldberg is remembered for his ruthlessness, being among those responsible for the fall and ghastly execution of the doctor and Royal usurper Johan Friedrich Struensee, he was also a principal architect of Denmark's successful continuation as a sovereign polity in the late eighteenth century, in precise opposition to Struensee's program of cultural and political Germanification.[61] During the American War of Independence, Count Andreas Peter Bernstorff, minister of foreign affairs during 1773–80, feared that England would emerge too weak from the conflict, thus upsetting the world's balance of power. Instead of following Bernstorff's orders during the negotiations with Russia, however, Schumacher adhered to secret dispatches from Høegh-Guldberg demanding a harder Anglophobic line.[62] Forced to retire from explicit power politics by the new king in 1784, Høegh-Guldberg helped Schumacher go on a Grand Tour to "the Southern Parts of Europe," where he eventually came across Genovesi's translation of Cary.[63]

That he would come across it and find it interesting is not surprising. Ostensibly traveling for reasons of health, escaping the harsh northern winter in favor of Italy, Schumacher was also on a book-buying expedition for the renowned bibliophile Høegh-Guldberg, who had instructed him to buy books for the sum of 100 Rigsdaler, half in incunabula and half in recent publications. At the time, a maid on a large Norwegian estate would have made 6 Rigsdaler per annum, and Høegh-Guldberg's investment would have sufficed to procure several incunabula at contemporary Copenhagen auctions.[64] But while Schumacher had devoted his last Grand Tour fourteen years earlier to learn "languages, politics, and statistics," he now also set out to better understand the principles of the wealth of nations. His "main application" would be to study "agriculture" and the means of improving it, a field in which he hoped to serve his country after his diplomatic career was over. Truth be told, Danes had been emulating foreign technologies and economic practices for a long time, both individually and as a result of conscious policies, and so Høegh-Guldberg was enthusiastic about Schumacher's decision to study "national oeconomy" abroad, hoping he would send him reports and observations on the matter from the continent; "the wise traveler," he instructed him, "sees what he can, and learns what he wants."[65]

The prosperity of their "fatherland" depended on successful espionage and emulation, and the correspondence between these two Cameralists highlights the problems of ersatz imperialism with arresting clarity. Denmark had suffered, Schumacher wrote from Leipzig, from having tried too hard, from having "always wanted to try more, than what we were capable of executing." Danish statesmen cared about "generalia" when the key to worldly happiness lay in the "details," and this was above all true in the realm of political economy. *Generalia* led one to throw "great sums" away to establish "colonies and factories [colonial outposts]"; details assured that expenses in fact were "useful" to the country. "Actually, I believe that Denmark never should think about playing a role abroad; it is not powerful enough for that, and such plans are bound to make it very unhappy. . . . Denmark's situation and the great powers that now have appeared in the North, will certainly not allow us to become conquerors."[66]

Schumacher had taken deep draughts from the bitter cup of realism. By comparison, on the eve of Sweden's disastrous 1741 attack on Russia, one of its noblemen had urged his country to favor a bid for "honourable participation in the general motions of the world" over its current "ignominious quiescence."[67] Its far more ignominious subsequent defeat taught Scandinavians a lesson in humility, and the cruel dynamics of greatness and decline would haunt Schumacher through Germany, Switzerland, and

Italy, directing his travels as he sought remedies for Denmark-Norway's precarious situation in other small states that, like his homeland, had to brave competition with greater powers.

So in addition to marveling at the Venetian Carnival, wondering about the mysteries of magnetism and electricity, and making fun of the Pope, as Protestant travelers were prone to do, Schumacher shaped his Grand Tour around the ideals of political economy. He thus avoided Naples, one of the premier destinations of most Grand Tours and, ironically, a hotbed of political economy, because "it holds so little influence in the European system that it cannot be of particularly dire importance [*magtpaaliggende*] what system they have."[68] Instead, he purposefully went out of his way to visit Tuscany and before that Karlsruhe, on Baden's border with France, for no other reason than to see "whether the Physiocratic system" had "been successful." This was an extremely important question. Baden had actually sought to implement the basic building blocks of Physiocracy, "laying all Taxes solely on the Ground alone," the notorious "single tax" that by 1784 long since had been ridiculed.[69] No early modern economic theory is currently as lionized as Physiocracy, but apart from the abortive and disastrous experiments with it in France, only Tuscany under Leopold II and Baden under Karl Friedrich are ever thought to have implemented it.[70] So how was practical Physiocracy actually received at the time?[71]

On the unification of the two separate branches of the Margravate of Baden in 1771, Karl Friedrich of Baden-Durlach (1728–1811), soon to be Grand Duke, inherited territories along the east bank of the fertile Rhine basin and its mountainous hinterland, including parts of the Black Forest, stretching as far in its southeast corner as Lake Constance. Its rugged terrain held both rich mineral resources and lush agricultural lands. Traveling through the region a few years after Schumacher, Duke Francis Russell of Bedford wrote lyrically of the Rhine's "truly romantic vale," the exquisite wine, the "vast number of manufacturies" in a town he visited, the excellent universities, and the elector's wisdom in requiring a wide university education of all his civil servants. Yet so alien was the Cameralist ideology to him that he had no word for its curriculum, which he noted with surprise included not only "the Sciences" but also "the Laws of Nature and the Country, Eloquence, Farming in all its branches, Politics, Commerce, Knowledge of Trades and Manufactures, &c. &c."[72]

In Baden, Physiocracy emerged from, and gave scientific validity to, an explicitly rural and, in the opinion of its leading historian, "feudal reaction" against urban commercial and manufacturing interests and the complex phenomenon known as the rise of the bourgeoisie.[73] As Marc Bloch ascertained, the economic reality of "feudalism" long outlived its stricter social and political structures, haunting France and other parts of Europe until the revolutionary era.[74] This was the wider sense of the term in which "feudalism," understood as a shorthand for manorial relations between wealthy landowners and hired laborers, could be used, as indeed it was in the eighteenth century, to describe a capitalist system of free wage labor like that proposed by Physiocracy.[75] And even if Karl Friedrich is often mentioned as one of the principal exponents of "enlightened despotism," and though he moved toward ending serfdom in his territories, it is not surprising that he both wrote a treatise on Physiocracy himself and passed a law excluding bourgeois councilors from holding high office in his state.[76] "Nobility," Karl Friedrich wrote, was "a purer race."[77] Yet it had been his last bourgeois minister, Johann Jakob Reinhard, who laid the groundwork for Baden's economic policies in the second half of the eighteenth century, instituting wide-ranging agricultural and industrial reforms already in the 1750s and 1760s. Like a good Cameralist, he aimed to harness the possibilities of the land by putting untapped resources—land, labor, raw materials—to productive use. The Seven Years' War furthermore put an enormous strain on the state's finances, inspiring numerous policies to intensify Baden's productive and thus taxable capacity. Reinhard's solution was to introduce new crops, such as potatoes, tobacco, flax, and mulberry trees to set up a domestic silk industry; breeds of livestock; and import-substituting manufactures. Reinhard's policies would continue to influence Baden's political economy long after Karl Friedrich's turn to Physiocracy, explaining the uninterrupted encouragement of industries there and the continuing survival of tariffs and bounties at a time of ostensibly free trade.[78]

The Margrave decided to adopt Physiocratic reforms around 1768, and initiated a correspondence with Mirabeau over how to successfully implement the doctrine. The epistolary's tendency was clear. Karl Friedrich asked detailed questions about real reforms and the precise means of calculating a "single tax" in an agricultural context of very small-scale cultivation; Mirabeau responded with inspirational slogans about "eternal truths" and the "law of nature."[79] In the absence of concrete guidelines, the Physiocratic experiment began with the simultaneous liberalization of trade and implementation of a single tax in the northern Baden towns of Dietlingen, Theningen, and Bahlingen in 1770. Yet, since the "single tax" was superimposed de facto on already existing structures of taxation, the reforms were hard to swallow for many in the poorer areas. Nor did they work miracles in wealthier regions such as Dietlingen, where the community's debt more than doubled in the first decade of the experiment. Farmers quickly petitioned to return to the old way of doing things, but echoes of the Physiocratic reforms would continue to shape agriculture and rural life there into the nineteenth century.[80]

The experiment was first initiated under Reinhard and then taken over by the Weimar economist Johann August Schlettwein in 1772, a complex thinker who, though embracing many of Quesnay's teachings, was opposed to a wholehearted implementation of Physiocratic doctrines because of the sharp contextual differences between France and Baden. Importantly, he also agreed with Reinhard on the importance of encouraging technological developments to increase agricultural productivity. Where Quesnay seems to have been misunderstood in Baden to have argued that capital investments in technology could slow down growth by derailing resources that otherwise could have been put to use clearing new lands, quite in contrast with his actual writings on economic milling and the nature and benefits of large-scale agriculture, the Cameralist insistence, in light of international rivalries with more powerful states, on improvement rather than expansion inflected the application of Physiocracy in Germany. And Schlettwein's work in Baden was, as Helep Liebel put it, "more cameralist than physiocrat."[81] As such, it was only after his dismissal the following year, when the post of finance minister was taken up by none other than du Pont de Nemours, that a bona fide Physiocrat became involved directly in the reforms.

Not surprisingly, given his self-conscious lack of experience with practical matters, du Pont de Nemours's tenure was a failure, and he returned to Paris only a year later. At this point the Physiocrat and mesmerist Charles de Butré stepped in as his replacement. Though Mirabeau presented him as "the only man in Europe truly admirable and infallible in this genre," he too proved inept and was away from Baden on private business from 1770 to 1786 before finally being banished from the lands. Some positive reforms did, however, occur in this period; the best known was Karl Friedrich's partial abolition of serfdom in 1783, initiated in emulation of his neighbor Joseph II's similar policies. Between this and the planting of new fields, crops, breeds, and technologies in "The Palatinate, Baden and the Swabian circle," agricultural productivity increased "some eight- to tenfold" in the later part of the eighteenth century. Yet, also for geographical reasons, this was not simply the consequence of Physiocracy but of a far wider array of Cameralist reforms, and even Karl Friedrich himself would continue to encourage what Physiocracy would have considered "sterile" domestic industries into the 1780s.[82] As such, Physiocracy was never established in Baden in any meaningful sense, and the verdict of the principal historian of these events is remarkably damning: Karl Friedrich was "an absolute prince who preferred his own pet theories and his own infallibility to the advice of his ablest councillors. It was in this spirit that he tried to introduce the physiocratic system into Baden, also against the counsel of his ministers, and it was because of this mentality that the experiment failed."[83]

The failure of Physiocracy in Baden did not go unnoticed. The English agricultural economist Arthur Young looked at Dietlingen and could only marvel at "what a curse upon the agriculture of a country" Karl Friedrich's Physiocracy was.[84] Somewhat ironically, the debate over Physiocracy in Germany would nonetheless only take off in 1778, after the doctrine already had failed spectacularly in practice in France as well as in Germany and had been criticized even in German journals for its wrongheaded assumptions with regard to the capacity of farmers to carry the state's fiscal burden and the ostensible "sterility" of commerce and manufactures.[85] Galiani's "famous" *Dialogues on the Grain Trade* had been translated into German in 1777—the translator included a history of the text's influence in the French polemic over Physiocracy—and a veritable anti-Physiocratic literature, spearheaded by the likes of Pfeiffer, was well established by the 1780s.[86]

Schumacher knew that travelers before him, particularly the publisher Christoph Friedrich Nicolai, had criticized the practical application of Physiocracy in Baden in harsh terms, but he wanted to see the results with his own eyes and speak to the actual statesmen in charge.[87] "Nicolai," he wrote to Høegh-Guldberg, had "expressed, against Schlettwein, that his [Physiocratic] Plan was unrealizable," and dismissed it on the basis of the "bad outcome" of its implementation, which, he added, had led to a famous and public debate. Unlike most travelers though, Schumacher was a powerful Cameralist whose connections counted, and when he arrived in Baden he had no troubles seeing the Margrave and his remaining ministers personally to hear their side of things. They too, he learned, had "found the Plan unrealizable, and the Marquis himself, who previously has been greatly carried away by the Physiocratic System, [and] even written a piece to explain it, admitted to me, that though he still believed the introduction of this system was [a] happy [occurrence] for his subjects, there still existed too many difficulties in introducing it [so] that he had simply given up on it." So, "soon," Karl Friedrich had confessed to Schumacher, the "Emperor" would enforce new regulations overturning Physiocratic reforms, for his "subjects" were "so heavily burdened by it, that he necessarily must give up on it."[88] Around this time, Mirabeau wrote in private correspondence that he hoped Gustav III of Sweden would visit Baden and learn some "able lessons" from the Physiocratic experiment there. Needless to say, he would not have approved of Schumacher's dispatches, which had their natural effect. Høegh-Guldberg's reply left little doubt as to Physiocracy's relevance for Denmark-Norway: "Everything you write is important to me. The Physiocratic System will never be mine."[89]

Nor would Schumacher's travels onward through the lands of Physiocracy change his initial impression of the doctrine's value for small state reformism. After visiting Baden, he headed southward to the second region outside France where Quesnay's doctrine was thought to have been cultivated: Leopold's Tuscany.[90] While Florence and the Tuscan hills were perennial linchpins of the Grand Tour, Schumacher's reason for visiting defied custom. It was not the Uffizi or Brunelleschi's dome that drew him there but Tuscany's unique history of economic policies. Economic decline had set in centuries before Schumacher visited, and a rich culture of political economy had developed in Tuscany, as it had in the rest of Italy, to come to terms with the vicissitudes of time. When Peter Leopold (1747–92), later Holy Roman Emperor, moved there from Austria to take over the Archduchy in 1765, he officially drew Tuscany into the Cameralist sphere of influence. Not surprisingly, the political economy of his reign shared many preoccupations, not only with the age-old indigenous tradition of reformism and economic legislation but also with Cameralist concerns with the harnessing of natural resources. Relatively protected from the great imperialist gambits of the time by geography and dynastic politics, Leopold could turn his attention to reforming the economy, and under his watch Tuscany became one of the world's most minutely surveyed regions.

And as part of a general preoccupation across Italy with reforms and the emulation of more successful foreign models in the 1750s and 1760s, Tuscan political economists turned to a number of ultramontane authors for inspiration, among whom were Quesnay and Mirabeau.[91] As late as 1781, Mirabeau's Physiocrat envoy to Baden, de Butré, proclaimed for propaganda purposes that Tuscany was realizing Quesnay's ideal, and it has been argued that "Physiocrats were celebrated" there and that Tuscans "naturally had a physiocratic mentality."[92] But were Leopold's reforms strictly Physiocratic, and was Tuscany primarily an "agricultural" economy, as some have insisted?[93] Using official data in 1757, for example, Gianrinaldo Carli calculated that the region exported 372,000 scudi worth of agricultural products versus 1,267,000 worth of manufactures.[94] As it turns out, our impression of the Tuscan economy is not the only thing that has been skewed by historiography.

On 18 September 1767 the first law freeing the internal circulation of grain from most of its barriers was passed, and a number of other laws soon followed, revoking a myriad of regulations. Much has been made of the supposedly Physiocratic inspiration for the restriction of guilds on 1 February 1770, yet the relevant law justifies itself as a means of "increasing the manufactures" of the state, not its agriculture, and in their place Leopold instituted a "Chamber of Commerce, Arts, and Manufactures." Taxes on domestic manufactures were seriously curtailed a few days later to ensure "that honest liberty, which gives birth to the good of commerce," and a decree of 5 February removed all taxes on the export of manufactured linen, hemp, and cotton. Simultaneously, however, the law introduced a uniform tax on their equivalent imports, and measures in those years focused on centralizing and homogenizing the Tuscan economy, not dissolving its territoriality. They sought to "facilitate commerce," but not through laissez-faire. "Arbitrary" street-selling was banned, for example, and strict geographical delineations of commercial spaces were introduced on 23 June 1770. Leopold opened the region for international grain trade but continued to prohibit the export of certain raw materials to ensure the development of domestic manufactures. These laws were far closer to Cary and Genovesi's proposals than Quesnay's.[95] Nor were they isolated atavisms. New tariffs on imported leather goods and textiles followed, and the vocabulary of legislation in the 1770s is replete with calls both for "liberty" and the "protection of industry," just as the tradition from Colbert to Cary, Melon, Gournay, Genovesi, and Necker had argued.[96] Leopold and his advisors were pragmatic, not doctrinaire; when an efficient market for wolf hunting failed to materialize on the abolition of patents (monopolies) on it, they simply renewed privileges.[97]

Leopold opened up the region to a tariff-regulated international grain trade in 1775 and abolished most commercial prohibitions by 1781.[98] He continued, however, to encourage industrial activities during this period; he gave subsidies to exporters of silk manufactures, established successful synergies between governments and individual entrepreneurs, and with time reintroduced a ban on the export of raw materials. And as the reformist minister Francesco Maria Gianni recalled, "subsidies" were given to encourage "emulation" and domesticate foreign manufactures. Furthermore, many of the agricultural reforms embarked on—such as arriving at a Montepulciano wine able to travel as far as England—were not technically Physiocratic in origin. As Eric Cochrane aptly put it, "Florentines were too well read in their own history to believe that manufacturing was really unproductive." Gianni even concluded that the "single tax" was only "so much hot air," and that the Physiocrats, though "beloved names in the subject of political economy," were "the ingredients of charlatanry," authors of a "destructive system." The true source of wealth was "human industries," not the soil per se, and he explicitly favored the protection of domestic manufactures.[99] This was really a typical stance even among the most ardent Tuscan "Physiocrats."[100] Ferdinando Paoletti, for example, a parish priest and agronomist, adapted Physiocracy to Tuscan conditions while citing Cary and insisting on government encouragements for exports of refined goods.[101] That said, agricultural investments were made, also under Physiocratic influence, including, just as in Baden, the widespread planting of new crops, such as tobacco, as a means of supplying domestic demand for colonial goods. Leopold introduced uniform weights and measures, inaugurated one of the most advanced library systems in Europe, and his Penal Code, inspired by Beccaria, enlightened the world entire.[102]

By the early 1780s, the principal Tuscan Physiocrats were dead, and the divergence between ideal and reality became impossible to ignore. Physiocracy had been one influence among many in Tuscany reformism and was, in spite of Mirabeau's assurances, never fully realized there.[103] So did Schumacher draw any positive lessons of political economy on his travels, and did he find any rare books in this unique land of tradition and renovation? As it turns out, he did both, and at the same time. After fruitlessly browsing bookshops and consulting with "antiquarians" around northern and central Italy, he developed an astute sense of contemporary bibliography. First of all, incunabula were nearly impossible to come by at any price. Second, modern works were usually published in Italian, not Latin, reflecting the change from a hierarchical to a horizontal system of European languages at the time.[104] Third, the Tuscan publishing industry had devoted itself to books on "the stewardship of the land and the economy of states":

> I am currently creating for myself a collection of books on politics and state economics, which always will be at Your Highness's command. It is with extreme pleasure that I am reading the famous Geno[v]esi's writings on the economy. I find some new observations in them, of which some must be greatly applicable to Denmark. This book has particularly served as blueprint to the Grand Duke of Tuscany for some good devices that this Duke is introducing in his land, and their consequences will soon have proven the truth of the author's sentences everywhere. Tuscany is truly mounting in wealth, and if this good Duke lives, it will become, from a fallen land, as it was in the time of the Grand Duke's father, one of the happiest States in Europe.[105]

Again comparing his studies of European political economy with the paradigm of Physiocracy, Schumacher concluded that the Grand Duke of Tuscany had "adopted from the Physiocratic System everything that was proven advantageous, and let go everything that rested only on pure political speculations."[106] Was Genovesi's translation of Cary really the blueprint of Tuscan reformism? Probably not, though its influence must have been greater than hitherto acknowledged. All Leopold's measures could, after all, easily be explained within the parameters of political economy as delineated by Cary, Butel-Dumont, and Genovesi, from the importance of abolishing guilds to the need for agricultural reforms and encouragement for manufactures. Comparatively, the core of Physiocracy was deeply anti-thetical to many of Leopold's darling policies. Before leaving Tuscany in 1790, he even justified the continuous support for manufacturing during his reign as part of a substantial description of his lands and reforms aimed at educating his successor. It was a cardinal task of government, he wrote, to "procure those who dedicate themselves to commerce and manufac-tures all ease, assistance, and protection, particularly to ease the export of their products and the import of different dyes for their manufactures, to ease their tariffs and aggravate [those of] foreign goods of the same sort."[107] Leopold had learned his lesson, and so had Schumacher: what a political community produced mattered tremendously.

The key to wealth for small states was neither conquest nor utopian schemes but the full employment of resources, intelligent agriculture, and competitive industry. This depended on support of the "middle class" of urban professionals and independent landowners, on meritocracy and sub-ventions for economic activity and research alike.[108] Tuscany had freed tradesmen from guild regulations, created great projects of public infra-structure, and encouraged industries and the free export of grain, though Schumacher felt they might have wavered too far from the "English ex-ample," not understanding properly the role of the government in instill-ing trust and avoiding food shortages in lean years.[109] In this, he was agreeing with Pfeiffer's assessment, in a passage noticed by contempo-raries, that "the Physiocratic system has not been accepted and put into practice by a single European state."[110]

"The government of Paris alone," Schumacher noted in awe, provided more yearly taxes for its sovereign than did "Denmark, Sweden, and Sar-dinia all three together." All this led him to conclude that a "Country is not happy because it is big, but only because it is administered well," which he realized was easier said than done in a world where the great commercial powers deployed troops for economic advantage. His experiences in Ven-ice, in particular, where he discussed the politics of international trade with the patrician reformer Andrea Tron at length, underlined the fragility of Cameralism in the face of jealousy of trade. Small states needed policies and peace to catch up, but this was difficult when "The Dutch, in a very despotic manner, have sought to *prescribe laws to the* [Venetian] *Repub-lic*" by sabotaging its trade and decimating its navy.[111] The insight that liberty had come to depend on economic superiority in a modern world of warlike competition again reared its head, and great thinkers and statesmen again looked to old books for answers. Symbolically, after weeks of searching, Schumacher finally found incunabula as well. From Siennese "Antiquarii" he bought a 1481 edition of Ephraim's sermons and a 1482 Horace, whose "dare to know!" Kant would symbolically equate with Enlightenment only a few months later.[112]

As Schumacher made his way back to Denmark, he stopped in Leipzig to organize the translation into German of some works he had brought with him from Italy. He and Høegh-Guldberg came to an agreement with Johann Samuel Heinsius to publish books for them, locate texts that might interest them as well as important catalogues, and send them to Denmark, and for their translational needs they turned to one Christian August Wichmann, a political economist in his own right, whose earlier translations of Adam Smith and the Physiocrat Guillaume Le Trosne might have interested the two Danish Cameralists.[113] Not only did Wichmann translate and Heinsius publish a manuscript account by an anonymous Italian nun that Schumacher had discovered in that city, but the two also produced the German edition of Cary's *Essay*, similarly brought from Tuscany by this envoy of the Nordic Enlightenment.[114]

Meet Me at the Fair

So though he was known as a classic of English economic thought in Germany well before that, and though his name had been mentioned often in August Witzman's influential German translation of Genovesi's *Lectures*, Cary himself was first translated into German in 1788. And, selling for 8 Groschen, or a third of a Reichsthaler, he catered to roughly the same market-segment there as he had in Bristol. Comparatively, around 1790 a large book dealer's manager earned 7,200 Groschen a year, his housekeeper 576.[115] It was fitting that the site of Cary's translation would be the city of Leipzig, which with more than thirty thousand inhabitants was the largest city in the Electorate of Saxony.[116] Goethe's impression from his student days there in the late 1760s is telling: "Its monuments proclaim a new, modern epoch redolent of commerce, prosperity and riches."[117] Home to one of the greatest universities in Europe, the city was also renowned for its venerable fair, held twice yearly since 1190. This was one of the supreme commercial events of early modern Europe, dominating the region and drawing merchandise and traders from all corners of the continent. More important for the commerce of culture, Leipzig also hosted a yearly book fair, the largest in Germany after it overtook Frankfurt's in the wake of the Thirty Years' War, and emerged in the eighteenth century as the center of German publishing and a nexus of international influences, famously through the influx of English goods, books, and ideas. Leipzig was, it has been argued, the distinctive home of German "Anglomania."[118] "For one who loves scientific and literary news," Schumacher wrote to Høegh-Guldberg, "Leipzig is extremely pleasant, since this city is the center for the learned of Germany."[119]

Like the majority of figures encountered in this study, Wichmann has largely been ignored by the secondary literature. Neither a lowly miller like Menocchio nor a great theorist like Machiavelli, he is one of many to fall between the interests of cultural and intellectual historiography.[120] The *Essay*'s last translator was born to a licentiate of law in Leisnig, in Mittelsachsen, on 1 November 1735 and passed away, a "Magister der Philosophie," in Leipzig on 14 September 1807. He was instrumental in planting eighteenth-century debates in German soil by translating and publishing some of the greatest works of the Enlightenment.[121] As an anonymous reviewer noted in 1788, Wichmann was known for having "already delivered good translations of various useful books" before turning his attention to Genovesi's rendition of Cary.[122] Canon formation is often a capricious process, but Wichmann's choice of great books for translation differs strikingly from modern counterparts. For alongside works by Hélvetius, Shaftesbury, Adam Smith, Quesnay, and Mirabeau, Wichmann also translated *Antonio Genovesi's Economical-Political Commentary on John Cary's Historical-Political Observations on the Trade and Industry of Great Britain.*[123]

Though Wichmann's choices no doubt were modulated by financial interest to a far greater extent than Gournay's and Genovesi's had been, the logic of translating political economy remained unaltered. The "immensity of the national debt," Wichmann said at the beginning of his introduction, might make "the wealth of the British nation" an "ambiguous" thing, but the "political axiom" that England's "real forces" resulted from its "commerce" "naturally" attracted the "attention of every thinker."[124] The book he "handed over to the German public" was the "composition of at least four originators." The *Essay* had become a written concert, performed by an international quartet of political economists. Wichmann knew that the book's history was curious, marketable precisely on the basis of its unique travels through Europe, and thus recounted his version of it at length. It all began when "the English merchant Johann Cary of Bristol wrote his first small book around 1668 to communicate his thoughts on the possible meliorations of his fatherland's industry and on the ulterior expansion of its commerce." Cary had first spread his ideas by word of mouth, then by circulating manuscripts, until, his fame increasing, he finally published the

Essay so that it could "attract the attention of both the government and the legislative force of the national parliament."[125]

Unknowingly, Wichmann here touched on the very problem of translation and emulation that had distressed Cary in prison. In a world ruled by public discourse rather than by the secret circulation of manuscripts, the very act of influencing a state's political economy paved the way for international emulation through translation. So influential had Cary's *Essay* been that his "opinion" repeatedly was asked for by England's "government," and his book enjoyed the "honor" of repeated republication. The book's success, however, rendered it influential elsewhere too. This, Wichmann noted in the footsteps of Westerman and Pfeiffer, Goudar and Casanova, was because the *Essay* testified to how "questions of industry and commerce proceeded on the basis of different and sound principles" in Great Britain "with respect to other countries." This was why "one or more men of the French government" had turned to Cary for answers "around the middle of this century." The belief that "the concepts of industry and commerce, which, by all appearances, had become extraordinarily dominant among the English through Cary's book, could become passable also in France, pushed the Frenchman Butel-Dumont not only to translate this small work into French, but also to enrich it and enlarge it with very many statistical data."[126]

As elsewhere in Europe, it was understood in Germany that Cary himself had influenced the course of English history, that English political economy and economic policy alike had developed in the image of his *Essay*. The outcome of Butel-Dumont's efforts, however, was "not a simple translation, but rather a historical-statistical composition of its own, to which Cary's work, written more from a political-economic perspective, offered only the outline, to which Dumont has copied and added what he found in a good number of other English writers, and in a small number of French and Nordic ones, the works of which hammered in the present matter [i.e. supported Cary's argument]."[127] Though Wichmann would painstakingly provide detailed bibliographical references to all works mentioned by his predecessors, alongside corresponding German translations, he excused himself to his readers for not having been able to check all of Butel-Dumont's statistical sources. He had done his utmost, but the "public library in Leipzig" simply had "none of the texts being discussed," and no private library in the city was currently up to the task either.[128]

"In Italy," Wichmann continued, it was "probably" only Butel-Dumont's translation that caught Genovesi's attention, because, he wrote with poorly veiled criticism, it seemed that Genovesi had never consulted "Cary's original work." Genovesi had accompanied this translation of Dumont's text with a commentary on the economic-politic outline, with which Cary's text had been enlarged here and there, an outline that he himself considered the correct one, and that he, as a good patriot, driven to favor his own fatherland, considered more useful and necessary the more visibly Naples was in extreme economic decline, and the more severely it, just because of this, was stripped of political power (beyond any proportion with respect to its almost entirely ignored natural forces)—as some still seem to glimpse the fall.[129]

Wichmann had deduced the essence of contemporary political economy; comparative political power in international relations depended on relative economic might.

Genovesi's Italian translation" of Cary had been brought to his attention by his "friend" "Peter Christian von Schumacher, a statesman and businessman" who was "chamberlain" to the king of Denmark. Returning from Italy, Schumacher had recommended that Wichmann make Genovesi's *Lectures* and *History* "available for translation and publication." Why? Because, as Schumacher had written to Høegh-Guldberg, they worked, and because the Grand Duke of Tuscany himself had "constructed his economic system of government, on the basis of which he maintains his own state for the welfare of his own subjects and to the common happiness of all friends of good in Europe, primarily on the principles of this [Genovesi's] doctrine of political economy."[130] In terms of the history of Cary's *Essay*, it was a surprising valediction with which Wichmann could market his book. Leopold had praised what the *Essay* had become and relied on its theoretical message, rendering its proposals into policy. He was not the first, nor would he be the last.

To translate the *Essay* properly, Wichmann emulated Genovesi's erudition, spending years gathering all the necessary books before finally acquiring a working set of Caryana. He candidly affirmed that the "goal of all three authors, the Englishman, the Frenchman, and the Italian" had been "nothing if not that of contributing to the promotion and raising of the economic welfare and political power of their respective motherlands through economic-political maxims that they, on the basis of their persuasion, thought worthy of attention and that every one, in their place, considered salutary." In comparison with the earlier introductions to Cary's *Essay*, Wichmann's nationalist consciousness is indeed striking. And this was precisely what drove him to undertake the translation. For though these authors all had striven for economic betterment, the truth was that most of Europe still lived in abject misery. Thus, Wichmann found that "the proposals of one who wishes to promote the destiny of peoples and the national welfare, as well as he knows and as his best conscience permits, merit—after having been listened to, tested, and, to the extent that they are good and feasible—being accepted and followed." That said, Cary's economic history was "too old and faulty." The original account was "at least 120 years old," and "no few things that once were completely right, have become very wrong in many places." Wichmann was, in essence, rediscovering the problem faced by Butel-Dumont in 1755, but whereas the French statesman took on the task of rewriting his text in light of history's relentless march, the German philosopher chose a very different exit.[131]

History had progressed too quickly for a faithful adaptation. For even if one took the time to update the *Essay* for the year 1788, the result would quickly join its predecessors in antiquarianism because "in some branches of commerce an important change can occur in the space of a few years." In only a few years, Wichmann observed, "change has rendered the thirteen North American provinces completely free from their British dependence, and Irelànd itself has sought to become far more independent of the English monopoly." Instead of undertaking "useless" additions himself, Wichmann encouraged his German readers to consult more recently translated histories and keep up with the current literature on the topic, criticizing Cary's intermediary translators in the meantime. Butel-Dumont, he thought, was a typical example of French arrogance and ignorance, whose text included too many inaccuracies to even begin correcting, and Genovesi was even worse, making mistakes that "even a schoolchild could not make" such as "still counting Holland as a German country." Incessantly, Wichmann underlined that he would have loved to address these mistakes had he found the right books in Leipzig or, he dreamily added, been able to consult magnificent collections such as Dresden's Churfürstliche Bibliothek or the Göttingen University Library.[132]

But it was anyway not the work's historical, statistical, or mercantile aspect that Wichmann thought most important. It was its "political aspect, the reflections of the Englishman Cary and the Commentary of the Italian Genovesi, who infallibly had brought the economical-political observations to the center of attention" and the fact that they were aimed at "studious youths." The *Essay* was, in short, about enlightenment. Wichmann agreed wholeheartedly with this approach to political economy, insisting that "young readers" were a more important audience than "the many who already control the destinies of peoples in the great state offices, and under whom the few, who still believe they can draw a useful lesson from the writings of the political philosophers in the universities, certainly are only an exception to the rule."[133] Yet Wichmann readily admitted that he too had adulterated the text in translation, in terms not only of selecting its content but also of its textual representation, its font and structure. Rather heavy-handedly, he "inserted only the brief observations by Dumont and those of Genovesi that, internally to the text, were similar, and that either appertained to the basic text or that briefly explained things that perhaps are unknown to some young reader, and that, alongside my observation, escape from this duplicitous art in Latin characters." He did, however, include all of "Genovesi's economic-political observations." And though he did not consider them as important as Cary's text, he brought them into the main text principally to speak to his already underlined exception of patriotic statesmen, men who often found footnotes "difficult" to read. Here Wichmann relied on the example of his late friend the Saxonian "minister Gersdorf," probably Karl August von Gersdorf, a Cameralist in his own right, who, reading by nightlight, had been unable to decipher the small footnotes to Wichmann's earlier translation, dedicated to Karl Friedrich of Baden, no less, of the Physiocrat Le Trosne's "erudite concept of the system of government."[134] Again, Cary's *Essay* crystalized the tenuous encounter between two worlds of government—the secretive nocturnal world of reason of state and the enlightened public sphere of published political economy.

Finally, Wichmann concluded his lengthy introduction by saying he was only a translator. He was a communicator of ideas, not an architect of political economies:

> To avoid any misunderstanding, I must furthermore beg the reader not to judge my own principles on the basis of that of which I make myself a simple messenger. Notwithstanding all that which, in my verdict, the book contains that is important, true, and practical, I remain sincere about the fact that, with profound conviction and on different considerable points, I think differently from all three authors, the thoughts of whom the reader finds in the present book.[135]

Though Wichmann was tempted to refute Cary, Butel-Dumont, and Genovesi where he thought it appropriate, he realized that reading "comments on a commentary" (on a commentary, one might add) was "very unpleasant" business, and preferred to eventually write up his thoughts in one volume if his current translation of the *Essay* was met with "some enthusiasm."[136] This was not to happen, and only a single volume of Genovesi's three would be translated into German. History has recorded many reactions to the *Essay,* from Pontoppidan's Bergen to Belgrano's Buenos Aires. His final translator's thoughts about it were not among them.

Translation Anxiety

Wichmann's introduction, as well as his annotations to the translation itself, bring new and contradictory elements into the *Essay*'s story. Cary was born in 1649, making him only nineteen in 1668, when according to

Wichmann he published a work entitled *Observations Concerning Trade and Interest of Money.* He would have had had to write it during his apprenticeship as a linen draper, and a full four years before becoming a merchant and freeman of Bristol, an unlikely preposition even without considering Cary's own account of things. Wichmann, however, relied on textual sources for his narrative, and more specifically on what he referred to as "der Osborneschen Katalogen." These can only be the actual catalogues of the London publisher Thomas Osborne, who published the 1745 edition of Cary's *Essay.* Leipzig was one of the centers of the European book trade, of Anglophilia, and of Enlightenment, and copies of these catalogues made their way to the city's fairs.

Osborne published several catalogues bringing news of the history of English economic thought to Europe. A 1745 leaflet for his publishing house, for example, includes a blurb for Cary's *Discourse of Trade* that lists all the pamphlets that went into it.[137] Osborne's larger catalogues of the 1760s, however, were the ones Wichmann consulted. These were explicitly meant for widespread circulation in European urban centers, and one for 1764 presents an answer to the conundrum. At the bargain price of 1 shilling and 6 pence, Osborne sold copies of "Cary's Observation on Trade and Interest of Money . . . 1668."[138] Osborne's own catalogue had added this work to Cary's bibliography. The only book with a similar title published that year is Joshua Child's *Brief Observations Concerning Trade, and Interest of Money,* a work that very likely influenced Cary's *Essay* and that itself had been translated into French by none other than Butel-Dumont. As it turns out, Child's original 1668 pamphlet was signed J. C., and later editions for which Child was lionized were published with revised titles. To a publisher and bookseller who had several other works by Cary in his catalogue and had demonstrated entrepreneurship enough to produce his own collated edition of them in 1745, it must have seemed either sensible or convenient to market the *Brief Observations* as having been written by one of his best-selling economic authors. But given the current canon of economics, it is almost incomprehensible that a world once existed where Joshua Child could be mistaken for John Cary rather than the other way around.

The bibliographical hurdles Wichmann encountered differentiate his endeavor from those of Cary's other translators. Ann Blair has analyzed the concept of early modern "information overload," and Wichmann suffered from a variation of this pathology.[139] His fear was not that he would be unable to read all the books he could access but that he could not access enough of them, that important works and editions eluded him, weakening his contributions to scholarship. Anxiety haunts sophistication. And in the context of the multiple translations of Cary's work, Wichmann's anxiety speaks clearly to the different cultures of knowledge with which political economy interacted as it first was institutionalized across Europe.

Though his legal reply to Molyneux relied on textual discussions, Cary had unabashedly accepted that he was "not furnish'd with those Books" that his opponent was quoting, and his *Essay* rarely, if ever, relied on bibliographical references more formal than veiled allusions; there was not a single footnote in its 1745 edition, from which all later translations would derive.[140] Cary's "science of trade" was based on the codification of economic norms and practices, not learned theory. Butel-Dumont had treated the "science du commerce" differently. A censor, he was also a foot soldier in Gournay's campaign to create a public debate about political economy. By publishing a critical mass of works on the subject, Gournay's circle created a field from scratch in which books making different but interrelated arguments—Cary's history of English economic policies, Uztáriz's history of Spanish decline, and Coyer's eulogy of commercial nobility—could refer to each other synergetically in the act of weaving together a new economic ideology for France. Individually, these books were mere strands of thought. Together, they formed a thick web of political economy strong enough to support a lively culture of public debate and informed reforms alike. But if Gournay's circle cared deeply about the printed word and the opportunities offered by disseminating economic knowledge, they never worried about missing out on existing publications. When Dangeul didn't find an appropriate English vehicle for his economic ideas, he simply made one up.[141] A university professor, Genovesi approached the "scienza del commercio" differently yet again. He continually referred to a wide variety of texts, but seldom with any rigor in terms of authors, titles, dates, or pages, even mangling the names of his closest colleagues. Whereas Gournay's circle consciously referred to itself and its numerous publications as a means of creating a critical mass of cumulative knowledge, Genovesi actively avoided referring to his Neapolitan contemporaries, preferring to present himself as the local mouthpiece of transalpine wisdom. His *History* thus abounds with vague references to ancient authors, this or that person's "history" or "treatise," at best "Savary's *Dizionario*."[142]

Of all the *Essay*'s de facto authors, Wichmann was the only one to fall into bibliographical despair. Strikingly, practically all the footnotes he added to the translated text were bibliographical references to clarify Genovesi's opaque allusions, and he took the time and effort not only to identify the original editions and those utilized by his predecessor but also to note relevant German translations. So where Genovesi referred only to "Riccardi in the Commerce of Amsterdam," Wichmann inserted a note specifying that the work in question was Jean Pierre Ricard's 1723 work *The Trade of Amsterdam,* published in Rouen in quarto.[143] In other places, Wichmann would even indicate the respective page or chapter probably intended by Genovesi.[144] And when Genovesi, in a relatively rare instance of utilizing notes for bibliographical information, simply footnoted a reference to one "Hum" with "Discours Politiques," Wichmann conscientiously spelled out "David Hume" in the body of the text and footnoted the publication data and paratexts for the English, French, and German editions of the work in question.[145]

In spite of all his caveats, Wichmann painstakingly reconstructed the *Essay*'s shoddy notework, though even he was thwarted in his attempt to come to grips with the different editions and translations of Dangeul's invented alter ego "Chevalier Nikolls."[146] And at times Wichmann's bibliographical anxiety led him to false conclusions, as when he criticized Genovesi's impressionistic reference to "Mister Huet in the History of the Trade of Holland" by stating "I know of no work with this title by Huet . . . probably he just got the author's name wrong."[147] Similarly, where the *Essai* relied on statistical data from Postlethwayte's *Universal Dictionary,* Wichmann insisted this work was first published in 1757, two years after the *Essai* was published, whereas the edition used by Butel-Dumont was that of 1751.[148] And in spite of Wichmann's careful bibliographical research, he concluded that the author of the *History and Commerce of the English Colonies in North America* was one François Dumont, not Cary's translator Butel-Dumont.[149]

So what did Wichmann's edition of the *Essay* consist of apart from anxious footnotes? The final outcome of his efforts was something of a potpourri. Opening with Wichmann's own 1788 introduction, it was followed by Genovesi's 1757 introduction, Butel-Dumont's 1755 introduction, Cary's 1695 dedications to William III and to Parliament, and Cary's 1719 dedication to Spencer Compton, then speaker of Parliament. The first scholarly text included in the volume was Genovesi's 1757 *Treatise on Commerce in General,* which opened up to the main body of the book. This too was disjointed, including only the parts of Butel-Dumont's 1755 translation of Cary's *Essay* that were included in the first of Genovesi's three volumes. Furthermore, since Wichmann only used footnotes to convey bibliographical information and sought to facilitate nighttime reading, he interjected Genovesi's comments on Cary not as annotations but by bringing his footnotes up into the body of the text itself, collating all Genovesi's comments to any given chapter into de facto chapters of their own, by which he alternated the voices of Cary and Genovesi in a dialogue not only of the dead but of the deaf.[150] A reader of Cary's Italian translation could easily follow Genovesi's running commentary on the *Essay*, but this became a much more cumbersome exercise in German. It demanded a constant flipping back and forth between chapters, simultaneously interrupting the flow of the *Essay* and elevating the commentary's relative importance in relation to the original work. Finally, the work concluded with an index to "the first volume," indicating that Wichmann had imagined continuing the translation.[151] Since no further volumes ever appeared, however, Cary arrived seriously truncated in Cameralist lands. The first volume of Butel-Dumont's translation of the *Essay*, the one ostensibly focusing on internal trade, had contained thirteen chapters, the last three—a substantial and central part of the work making up nearly 40 percent of the volume—of which had been devoted to the means of encouraging domestic manufactures, England's historical measures to achieve this, and a summarizing conclusion, respectively. Translating only the first ten chapters of that volume, Wichmann produced not only, as in Vico's celebrated phraseology, "a monster of chronology" but a veritable monster of bibliography.[152]

A Final Insult

In a table concluding his critical 1782 *Inquiry into Physiocracy*, Altdorf Professor Georg Andreas Will contrasted Physiocrats and anti-Physiocrats in Europe. He tellingly could not identify a single Physiocrat in Italy, and though astute enough to list Adam Smith as an anti-Physiocrat, he was tricked by Turgot's deceit to count Gournay as a Physiocrat. In Germany, he identified Karl Friedrich of Baden and, strikingly, Wichmann as representatives of Physiocracy, and it had ultimately been because of Wichmann's translations of Physiocratic works that Will saw the need to write his book. Will did not think it right to judge people by the texts they translated, but Wichmann's "apologetic introductions" made his sympathies explicit. Cary, in short, had been translated by one of Germany's greatest "advocates" of Physiocracy.[153] All said, the final leg of the *Essay*'s travels across Europe was no less ironic than the previous ones. If Cary's Anglicanism and republicanism were smothered in the absolutist ecology of Paris, the emerging ideals of Enlightenment there also curbed the more excessive elements of his racism and the cruelty of his colonial vision. These changes culminated in Italy, where he eventually would become the pope's economist, an instrument for spiritual and secular despotism. Throughout this, his actual economic analysis—that the wealth and independence of a political community had come to depend on governmental encouragement of manufactures—had only been refined. In Germany, this development came to a halt, with the *Essay*'s political economy incompletely translated by an exponent of its antithesis: Physiocracy, and, more generally, the nascent ideology of laissez-faire.

Wichmann had hinted that he disagreed with what he was translating, but since he never elaborated on his objections in print and the translation remained incomplete, his readers were left in the dark. His surviving letters to Schumacher tell a more coherent story. Not only did Wichmann defend "Physiocracy" against "errors" of interpretation, but he criticized Pfeiffer's *Antiphysiocrat* and admitted that though Pfeiffer was "greatly superior" in "style of writing and rendering," he preferred Schlettwein also for his leading an "exemplary life." Schlettwein had furthermore visited him, and the two were "completely convinced" that Schumacher had been misinformed when told that "the Grand Duke [of Tuscany] rules not according to purely Physiocratic principles but according to Genovesian principles. Genovesi has adopted much, very much from Physiocracy," and it was not for lack of "good will" that Genovesi had not accepted Physiocracy fully, but because he had not "grasped the entire system." Finally, his "commentary on Cary" contained ideas that he had "put down" in Genovesi's *Lectures,* a work in which he was "far closer to Physiocracy—and I believe he will be ever closer than before. I am looking for the opportunity to bring him a letter to ascertain this point. Enough—Peter Leopold has given more than one prescription that is not drawn from Genovesi, but ever more, with the passing of time, from Physiocracy; and in this he goes further every day."[154]

Genovesi never gave any indication of knowing Physiocracy existed, and anyway failed to adhere to its most central tenets; he believed in the multiplying effects of manufactures; he preferred small-scale to large-scale landowning; he believed in tariffs to structure international trade. His basic proposals never wavered; and he had been dead for seventeen years. Yet Wichmann drew him, and Leopold's varied policies, into a Physiocratic mold that some historians still see them as occupying.

But what was a reader to make of Wichmann's introduction, and how did it relate to Cary's narrative as rendered by Butel-Dumont and Genovesi's additions to it? Wichmann's fretful annotations proved beyond bibliographical doubts that the work rested on solid foundations. It presented principles and demonstrated how, having been applied in England, then Britain, they had changed world history. Yet the ruthless system they had created seemed to be unraveling. Cary's political economy had led to a greatness greater than Rome's, but Britain, like Rome, had faltered. In light of the American War of Independence, the *Essay*'s principles were no longer those of perpetual progress. Even though Britain with time had perfected the synergy between conquest and commerce, empire still came to an end in the modern world; as the *Chinese Spy* would have put it, Britons had something to live for again, for struggle—emulation—was life itself.[155]

Wichmann's subsequent translation sheds some light on his intentions in composing his introduction to Cary. In 1793, he published a German translation of the French translation of Benjamin Vaughan's 1788 *New and Old Principles of Trade Compared*. Vaughan was a Jamaica-born and Cambridge-educated British commissioner best known for his role as mediator between the warring parties as the American War of Independence came to a close, but he also penned one of the most extreme reactions to Britain's historical interventionism.[156] Wichmann embraced it enthusiastically. There was the corrupt economic system of old, and there was the new system of total liberty ostensibly proclaimed by the likes of Hume and Smith in Scotland, Isaac Iselin and Schlettwein in "Germany," and Genovesi and Filangieri in "Italy." It was a glorious tradition, extending from Locke through Cantillon to Jeremy Bentham, extolling infinite commercial freedom between states as the only means of achieving peace and public happiness, and having already translated Smith, Wichmann relied on Vaughan to carry his message.[157]

But Will was right; Wichmann was not simply in favor of laissez-faire, he was in favor of Physiocracy. An extraordinary footnote, which Wichmann translated conscientiously, Vaughan had identified the "seeds of all principles, yes perhaps even of all doctrines of newer political economy" in "Fénelon's *Telemachus*," and Wichmann himself repeatedly chastised Vaughan for not correctly employing the word "producers" in light of the Physiocratic argument that all activities but agriculture were "sterile." And in case the reader still harbored doubts about the book's new message, he introduced Physiocratic maxims into the footnotes: "Industry, then, is not productive, since its work merely gives shape to a thing first given by the Earth through the productive labor of farmers." Wichmann's emphasis on free international trade was part of an overarching argument for "enlightened" cosmopolitanism, and he wished to fight the political dictum that "Love for one's Fatherland is hatred for the World."[158] Throughout his writings, his lofty goal was to give the lowliest workers of the land their rightful freedom and change people's minds so that, one day, a "war-minister" would be unable to launch an "offensive war" because "the Voice of the People in the Land" would be "universally against it." A clause of this vision was the "naturally free movement" of "trade and exchange." In explicit polemic with Cary's tradition of conceptualizing political economy, which by this time had become the absolute mainstream in Europe, Wichmann thus concluded that "Freedom, unshackled freedom, is unfailingly the most certain rule—a rule that never requires any exception under any circumstance."[159]

This is an important moment in the history of political economy, not because it was particularly influential but because it exemplifies the complex process—and the legerdemain—through which ideological canons can be constructed. For their slippery vocabulary of "liberty," Wichmann rhetorically equated radically interventionist architects of English imperialism such as Locke with authors stretching across time and space, from Swiss Physiocrats to Neapolitan reformers and even Bentham, to create a "liberal" and "modern" economic paradigm. It is a canon with which we still live, but a careful reconstruction of its individual links amply demonstrates the chimerical nature of the chain itself. Then, as now, such misdirection justifies very tangible policies that influence very real lives. A violent backlash against the fundamentalism of Enlightenment libertarianism soon resulted; much as a violent backlash had resulted against the ruthlessness of English imperialism. Political economy remained in thrall to extremism. It is, again, ironic that Smith justified Physiocracy by arguing "If the rod be bent too much one way, says the proverb, in order to make it straight you must bend it as much the other."[160] His much-vaunted "obvious and simple system of natural liberty" was precisely an example of such exaggeration in opposition to the economic program elaborated by Cary and implemented by the English Parliament. The anonymous reviewer of Vaughan's work for the *Monthly Review* was in this regard telling.

It was interesting, the review noted, how "certain notions" of political economy went from being "undeniable axioms" to being "questioned," to the point at which they fell into "disrepute" and eventually were overcome by entirely different core assumptions. Recent events had led to a crisis of the old axioms on which the empire had been built, and the beliefs in "protection" and the "regulating influence" of government had come to be exchanged, by "certain philosophical speculators on legislation," with a stringent doctrine of "free trade" to be adopted "in every case . . . without any encouragement or restriction whatever." One was the "old," the other the "new" principle of trade expounded by Vaughan. This dichotomy puzzled the reviewer, for it did not "appear that, in strict propriety of logical reasoning," the conclusions of the "new" paradigm really resulted from its "premises." Vaughan's conclusions were "assumed," not "proved," by the historical record. "Truth," he argued in an Aristotelian manner, "is generally found to be somewhere about in the middle between two opposite extremes," and without "experimental facts" one should approach political economy with "cautious diffidence." Just as Cary, Butel-Dumont, Genovesi, and Schumacher had argued, the *Monthly Review* believed in drawing "particular conclusions" from specific cases rather than "boldly drawing general conclusions from few facts." The Physiocrats, it strikingly observed, were simply not right in a "general" manner, and "the same thing may be said of the ingenious Dr. Adam Smith, who has frequently fallen into the same error, and by the weight of his great authority has drawn after him a great number of inferior imitators," among them Vaughan. The reviewers did not at all object to new doctrines and new ideas, only the dogmatism by which they were applied: "It does not follow, that because certain powers, when carried to excess, are hurtful, they never can be beneficial when used in moderation. We wish to see the desire of regulating trade very much diminished; but that it ought to be entirely *annihilated,* the state of our knowledge, as yet, does not authorise us to say; and where there is doubt, there is surely room for caution."[161] Economic historians are now painstakingly reconstructing how the British continued to rely on practical reason of state, on high tariffs and military adventurism, as they built their empire in the nineteenth century—the largest the world has ever seen.[162] These actions continued to enjoy widespread and influential intellectual backing long after the publication of Smith's *Wealth of Nations.* Whatever Wichmann's intentions in translating Cary, and there can be no doubt that he would be remembered for decades as one of the "strongest and most cultured teachers and defenders of Physiocracy in Germany," it is worth noting that reviewers again brought lucidity to debates about political economy.[163]

The anonymous reviewer who lauded Wichmann's translation in the *Göttingische Anzeigen von Gelehrnte Sachen* was surprised to note how, in spite of Cary's tremendous "Vaterlandsliebe," the "collaboration of an Englishman, a Frenchman, an Italian, and a German" produced such a "very true" work. Particularly, he praised Genovesi for "powerfully preaching the truth" about the importance of "manufactures and factories," for "dispelling the old myth" that only "Republics could develop a great and enduring commerce," and finally for "correctly defining the concept of free trade, that the *économistes* [Physiocrats] once had twisted so."[164] Though ironic in relation to Wichmann's own ideals of political economy, the cumulative endeavor that the *Essay* had become could not have asked for a more incisive reviewer. Cary dubbed it a "science of trade"; Butel-Dumont a "science du commerce"; Genovesi had alternated between "economia politica" and "economia civile"; Wichmann chose "Staatsoekonomie."[165] All were attempts to codify and promote the ideas and policies responsible for the economic development of states locked in ruthless international competition. As a Cameralist textbook Babelically would put it a year later:

Die Staatswirtschaftslehre—franz. economie politique, Science du commerce et de finance; eng. political oeconomy; ital. economia civile—hat die Gründung, Vermehrung und Verwaltung des *Nationalreichthums*—wealth of nations— zum Gegenstande.[166]

What was this concept all about in its various inflections? Essentially, it was about assuring success in international competition, and, for the historical mainstream, this meant an exercise in industrious and industrial politics. "Industry" had, both as a personal trait and as a distinct sector of the economy, found its champion in early modern England, but this was neither an immemorial characteristic nor a recent mutation: it was the fruit of a carefully cultivated economic culture influenced also by centralized institutions such as tariffs, patents, bounties, and examples. Economics, as it was first codified, was also the "science" of this process. Its history and politics haunted Europe as they haunt us. Anglomania, and its corollary Anglophobia, had carried Cary's message to the continent loud and clear, but it was eventually overshadowed by new waves of British political economy, written after the British Empire itself had matured. As one of Cary's later readers warned his contemporaries, "the needs of a century are not those of that which succeeds it." The needs of the English economy had changed by the nineteenth century, and so had the nature of its political economy. It was thus supremely important that continental legislators kept their eyes fixed on the means by which England historically had grown wealthy and not merely its current doctrines.[167]

Wichmann drew a different conclusion, and the *Essay*'s triumphal march across Europe ended with a proverbial whimper, not a bang. It is telling that when Johann Gottfried von Herder praised the "splendid works" that had come out of Naples in the eighteenth century, he mentioned Genovesi's "Storia," not Wichmann's translation.[168] Where Cary had originally written a robust contribution to one of the most important economic debates in history, and Butel-Dumont and Genovesi had contributed crucial insights in their respective contexts, Wichmann's was an aborted project, a fragmented flurry of anxious annotations and contradictory messages. The legacy of Enlightenment political economy, of the theories and practices responsible for the establishment of the world system as we know it, is not that different.

Epilogue

Translatio Studii, Translatio Imperii

The extraordinary international influence of Cary's *Essay* forces us to rethink the history of political economy, not only in terms of what it originally taught and the policies it helped enact, but also of how it circulated and the extent to which it permeated European culture. Exchange rates in the second half of the eighteenth century were in perpetual flux, and it would be impossible to present accurate price comparisons for the different editions of Cary's *Essay* at the times and places for which data are available. Allowing for the counterfactual conceit of assuming that relevant price information from booksellers were valid for about a decade, that Schumacher exchanged Høegh-Guldberg's 100 Rigsdaler through London in 1775, and that he did not lose out in further exchange rates through intermediary silver currencies such as the German Konventions-thaler, however, one can, on the basis of the ideal silver content of European currencies, roughly estimate how many copies of each edition of the *Essay* he theoretically could have bought. For 100 Rigsdaler Schumacher would have netted £19.9 or ca. 2.2 kilograms of silver. Cary's 1695 *Essay* cost 8.36 grams of silver at the average late eighteenth-century price of 1 shilling 6 pence; at 3 livres 6 sous, Butel-Dumont's 1755 translation cost 16.45 grams in Lausanne in 1772; Genovesi's three volumes sold for 7 Venetian lire, or 16.66 grams, the same year; at 8 Groschen, Wichmann's

1788 translation cost 8.13 grams. Schumacher could, in other words, have bought 265 copies of Cary's *Essay;* 135 copies of Butel-Dumont's *Essai;* 133 copies of Genovesi's *Storia;* or 272 copies of Wichmann's *Commentarius*.[1]

Costs of living differed between these places, and non-monetary components of work-retribution around Europe are often hard to pin down, but comparing contemporary daily wages in silver for building craftsmen in the different cities in which Cary's *Essay* was published can still shed some light on its relative costs. As it turns out, a craftsman in London would have had to work for half a day to buy a copy; in Paris nearly two; a Neapolitan worker buying it in Venice nearly three; and a Leipzig craftsman nearly two days (see Figure E.1).[2] The relatively high cost of the French and Italian editions also depended on their voluminosity, but it is important to emphasize that the work remained accessible to a wide audience throughout its cumulative translations. By comparison, Schumacher would only have been able to afford twelve copies of Adam Smith's *Wealth of Nations,* or five copies of Hume's *History of England* with Smollet's continuation.[3] Political economy emerged in Europe on a more accessible level and influenced wider cultural segments than has often been thought, it taught different lessons, and it did so, to a great extent, through the mediation of international emulation.

This is why Cary's *Essay,* after having been of seminal importance for the institutionalization of political economy in England, France, and Italy,

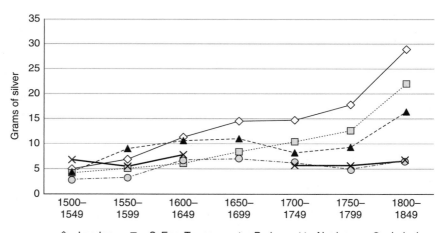

FIGURE E.1. Nominal daily wages for building craftsmen, by fifty-year periods, 1500–1849 (based on Allen 2001, 416)

and contributed to the venerable tradition of German and Scandinavian Cameralism, eventually reached even farther shores. Cary inspired books and translations, and these in turn ventured out on Grand Tours of their own. Butel-Dumont's works entered new contexts in Spanish and German, and his translation of Cary was read by the Spanish reforming minister Pedro Rodriguez de Campomanes and by the editor of a Dano-Norwegian economic journal, on the very frontier of European civil society.[4] Genovesi's *Lectures,* elaborating on his annotations to the *Storia,* were similarly translated both into German—in which language it was brought to Catherine II's St. Petersburg—and into Spanish. Perhaps because of the extensive cultural transfer before and after Charles III left Naples to take up the crown of Spain in 1759, the Spanish translation was adopted as a textbook of political economy at the Seminary of Nobles in Madrid and at universities in Salamanca, Majorca, and Zaragoza, where, as a Genoese spy reported, not only Genovesi's teachings but the very institution through which he taught them was emulated. With time, the *Lectures* even made their way to Cuba, and curricula at the University of Quito, in the faraway Viceroyalty of New Granada.[5]

By way of this Atlantic translation, and the explicit teaching of his political economy in the New World, some of Genovesi's worst fears were realized. Overcome by anacyclotic anxieties, he had argued in his *Lectures* that the Old World's colonies would eventually want to share its wealth, liberty, and happiness by developing their "arts and sciences" on the "European model," embarking on a process that would lead them beyond mere "independence from the Metropoles." With time, "those colonies could be our Metropoles."[6] It was a melancholy idea to which he returned at the end of his life, annotating his translation of Montesquieu's *Spirit of the Laws.* Had Hannibal won the Second Punic War against Rome, Genovesi mused, Carthage itself would have been consumed by its enterprise, the colonizing power biting off more than any polity could digest: "Once Italy had been conquered, so Sicily would have been. And once Sicily had been conquered, Carthage would have become a Province of the Italian Carthaginians; just as if Canada remains an English possession, England might one day become a Province of the English Americans."[7]

It is thus striking that when Manuel Belgrano, father of Argentine independence, wrote his economic articles for the Buenos Aires *Correo de Comercio,* in 1809–11 he reiterated the maxims of "useful foreign trade" that Genovesi had taken from Cary.[8] He had studied Genovesi's textbook at the University of Salamanca and turned to political economy expressly to arm himself in the fight against the "perverse intentions of the metropolitans."[9] Tools of empire became instruments of independence. By "multiplying" manufactures on the European model Argentina could "become more powerful than the other [countries]," and it should follow "all States" in carefully encouraging them through judicious "taxes" and even "prohibitions," through both tariffs and the occasional trade ban. This "right" could "not be disputed in any independent society." Argentina's colonial past and economic structures meant that its agricultural sector could be a source of immense wealth, and he translated Quesnay and Karl Friedrich of Baden into Spanish precisely for that reason, but agriculture and raw materials could never be enough to safeguard a state's welfare and liberty in the modern world.[10] As Belgrano noted in his translation of the latter, Physiocracy was to be approached through the lens of Galiani's *Dialogues,* which taught the need to adapt policies to "circumstances" because "the most minimal variation produces incredible mutations, and above all *nihil repente.*"[11] So much for Belgrano the Physiocrat.

That said, it would be an untranslated emulation of England's political economy that enabled the most direct *translatio* of empire. For after decades of nervous debates over the future of independence and the possibility that virtuous free trade agrarianism could save the former colonies from Old World corruption, the United States of America embarked on Hamilton's program of development—a program based on the aggressive conquest of lands and markets, state-supported industrialization, and wide arrays of tariffs—to create an empire of their own, and in so doing they made extensive use not only of British imperial theories but of British imperial and manufacturing technologies.[12] A review of the French translation of Child undertaken by Gournay and Butel-Dumont had warned in 1755 that the "Navigation Acts" were what "bound" the colonies to England and "subjected" them, and that "without this dependence the colonies would raise themselves on the ruins of their metropolis."[13] In hindsight, these fears for the future were vindicated. With time, the former colonial subjects harnessed the very political economy by which imperial powers had usurped their wealth and liberty to forcibly turn the tables. Around 1720, the Swedish polymath and engineer Christopher Polhem explained how Holland had succeeded in usurping Sweden's riches for so long only because of Sweden's ignorance. Through the rapacious system of trade they had established in Europe, the Dutch had "bought [the power of] Disposition over them," in effect giving Sweden laws. "Time," however, had finally "put glasses on the Swedes' noses," and the kingdom was learning to industrialize and benefit from its own resources.[14] With time, the American colonies oppressed by Cary's system were also cured of their myopia.

America's rise to economic hegemony, however, was neither absentminded nor providential, though its reliance on the vocabulary of liberty no doubt facilitated its conflation with the rhetoric of laissez-faire. Well into the twentieth century, the wealth, power, and freedom of the United States and other relative latecomers in continental Europe were the result of precisely the sort of purposeful political economy England had mastered before them, and the "American System" owed far more to Cary than to Quesnay. This brings us back to the role played by economic policy in the rise of the West.[15]

It has recently been argued that the Industrial Revolution first took place in Britain because its remarkably high costs of labor and abundance of cheap capital and nonorganic energy compared to conditions in continental Europe created a situation in which industrial investments paid off and the Industrial Revolution could take hold. As Craig Muldrew further has argued, such a situation resulted from extraordinary increases in agricultural productivity from the late seventeenth century onward, which freed up labor for industrial pursuits, and from the emergence of a purposeful "doctrine of industriousness' " and general "improvement" in the country.[16] These economic mechanisms, and their concomitant progressive ideology, cannot be divorced from the spirit of Cary's enterprise to encourage high wages and the diehard history of English economic policies to ensure the development of domestic manufactures and with them widespread technical knowledge, the democratization of useful learning, and the aggressive intercontinental quest for raw materials and coerced markets. Adam Smith was right that "the division of labour" depended on the "extent on the market," but said market could be extended through a variety of means, some less peaceful than others.[17]

Margaret C. Jacob has argued that "central government" played a "key role" in bringing about the "Industrial Revolution" and in nurturing a "culture" favoring entrepreneurship and industrialization in late eighteenth-century Britain, but this was not simply about building canals and improving infrastructure for free-trading agents.[18] It was about the most self-conscious industrialization policy in history to that date, theorized and justified by an emerging discipline of political economy, which was emulated internationally alongside the techniques and inventions by which it was inspired and which it in turn inspired. The high domestic wages that ended up channeling investments and entrepreneurship into mechanized industry cannot be explained without recourse to England's success in the centuries preceding its industrial takeoff, a success secured through political and military investments in achieving a global superiority in manufacturing. This is not to argue that interventions were the *only* cause of England and later Britain's rise to greatness, far from it, only that the conscious role of government in encouraging industrialization too often has been sidelined in historiography, and that a more rigorous understanding of the history of political economy can illuminate the history of economic development.

In hindsight it is ironic that the same theory by which the *Essay* suppressed and oppressed colonial subjects and independent states with time became the vehicle of their liberty. Nietzsche might have remarked in *The Gay Science* that "translation was a form of conquest" in Roman times, when poets such as Horace and Propertius absorbed Greek texts for the Roman present as part of a protocol of cultural annexation, but "economic" translations could serve precisely the opposite purpose. Resisting a conquering economy implied countervailing its measures and emulating the instruments of its empire, and translation was a primary medium of this process.[19] With time, the world's great powers industrialized along the nationalist lines previously embraced by England. This suggests that a profound reconceptualization of early political economy is in order: "Enlightenment economics" cannot be equated with laissez-faire.[20] Nor, however, was the turn of the eighteenth century any kind of watershed, and Friedrich List, for one, explicitly accused later British economists of continuing counter-emulation, of wishing "to conceal the true policy of England," and all its violent interventionism, "in order to induce foreign nations not to imitate that policy."[21] As England maintained higher tariff levels than even France into the 1870s, though never giving up its gunboat political economy of free trade abroad, the founding influence on the British economy of men like Cary was felt until its imperial apotheosis, when it literally gave laws to a quarter of the earth.[22]

The *Essay/Essai/Storia/Geschichte* remains a unique litmus test of the centripetal and centrifugal forces at play in the eighteenth-century world and, simultaneously representing universal problematics and the sequential expression of local concerns, a clear contribution to the growing debate over the plurality or singularity of "Enlightenments." As Venturi intuited years ago, the eighteenth-century "Enlightenment" can only be understood through the attentive study of different contexts: the local, regional, and global.[23] And translations were a vinculum binding them together. One of the purposes of this study has been to demonstrate the historical complexity of England's role in such an Enlightenment, through which the entire construct must be reassessed. For the *Essay* was only one manifestation of a larger cultural reaction to the expansionism of the English and later British empire. Albion's forceful ascendancy had profound consequences for not only the economic and political but also the social and symbolic life of its rivals, instilling anxieties and inflecting rituals from the quotidian to the

identity-defining, from the breaking of bread in Paris and the cultural coherence of Newfoundland settlers to the terror of British bombardments in
coastal Europe. The globally coercive capacity of the English "model" was
the subject of fear and emulation but never indifference, which is why
Anglomania and Anglophobia were so hard to separate: the power with
which England infatuated the minds of Europe was the power not only to
give them laws, but to destroy them.

The Dangers of Emulation

On 22 January 1799, Naples became a republic. Its architects were students of Genovesi, who for decades had nurtured the English and more
recent French examples, not only of political economy but of how to overcome despotism and arbitrary rule. But, as Locke had preached liberty at
home and struck it down abroad, so his legacy remained dangerously ambivalent. On 21 June 1799, besieged by Royalists and their far more powerful British allies, the republic capitulated after its enemies granted the
republicans and their families safe passage to France in a treaty also signed
by the English. As soon as the revolutionaries put down their arms, however, Admiral Horatio Nelson annulled the agreement and imprisoned
them. The Neapolitan republican admiral Prince Francesco Caracciolo,
who had served the British well during the American War of Independence,
was charged with high treason aboard the HMS *Foudroyant* in the Bay of
Naples on 29 June 1799, and after the British denied his plea to summon
witnesses in his defense as well as his request to be shot like a gentleman
rather than hanged like a buccaneer, he was summarily lynched, at Nelson's express order: hanged from the yardarm of the HMS *Minerva* that
same afternoon, his body dropped into the sea at sundown. Several thousand were tried, almost five hundred were exiled, and 216—among them
the republic's leading intellectuals—were executed in Naples alone.[24]

In 1791, the Neapolitan abbé Sotira had warned Frenchmen against taking English claims about the causes of their own greatness at face value,
arguing that they instead were undertaking a campaign of conscious
counter-emulation to distract Europeans from the real issues of relative
military power and manufacturing industry. One could not straightforwardly adopt England's political institutions without regard for underlying economic structures and think that all else would immediately follow.
As he put it, the "English themselves, out of interest and out of vanity,
have accredited such errors, which *serve greatly to render their emulation*

by other Peoples more difficult."[25] A variation of this caveat became a common criticism of the 1799 revolutionaries in the early years of the nineteenth century. Incensed with emulating foreign ideas and practices, influential thinkers like Vincenzo Cuoco argued, the republicans had failed to respect the real conditions, traditions, and national character of more backward regions such as Naples.[26] Again, emulation, in this case of political and economic ideas, was a hazardous gambit.

Truth be told, Europeans knew the lesson well. The fabular literature was replete with caveats against the dangers of emulation. Æsop put it succinctly in a tale about a raven and an eagle elaborated by the French poet Jean de La Fontaine twenty-three centuries later, and both versions were among the most widely translated and best-selling fiction of the early modern period. The story told the sad tale of a raven who, witnessing an eagle swoop down to snatch a lamb from its flock, was "moved with emulation" to attempt the same. Inevitably, the raven's smaller claws got stuck in the animal's thick fleece, his wings not powerful enough to lift off with his intended prey. As an eighteenth-century edition of Æsop explained the tale: "he that dareth to attempt any thing beyond his strength, doth only bring this about, *that he falls too often into adversity."* La Fontaine's moral differed little: "One must measure oneself," for "example is a dangerous lure." Another of his fables, "The Frog that endeavours to swell her self to the Size of an Ox," explicates the same point at gory lengths as a diminutive frog, wishing to match his cloven neighbor, huffs and puffs until she literally explodes through emulation.[27] Naples, in the logic of these fables, had the will, but no ability to fly; it was small, but it wished to be big. And as a consequence the dangerous lure of emulation proved fatal.

But as Nelson's reprobate actions bore witness to, small states had more to fear than the counter-emulation of the great powers or their own hubristic mimesis. They had to fear the British Empire itself. For while the fables' powerful beasts cared little for the meeker creatures of their allegorical world, their equivalents in the early modern states-system ravaged the weak with abandon. In 1806, the Royal Navy firebombed civilian targets in Copenhagen for three days straight, killing approximately 5 percent of its population before Denmark-Norway abandoned its hopes of neutrality and surrendered its entire navy to the British.[28] And as something eerily similar to the world-system sketched out by Cary finally materialized in the wake of Waterloo, with Napoleon perambulating around St. Helena and no earthly power being able to resist Albion giving the world both laws and manufactures, the conflation of conquest and commerce in international relations became impossible to ignore. This was no sudden occurrence but a culmination of a project of political economy that had long been in the making.

Montesquieu's ideas of *doux commerce* were ancient history when foreign support for the Bourbon Restoration of Naples in 1816 was rewarded with "colonial" commercial privileges. Over the next decades, Neapolitan foreign trade gradually came to be carried on British vessels, through which the kingdom supplied the "workshop of the world" with raw materials.[29] To break out of a cul-de-sac of poverty and dependence, the Neapolitan finance minister Luigi de' Medici launched a massive program of economic policies in 1823, inspired by Genovesi, to industrialize the kingdom and achieve autonomy. Tariffs were introduced on foreign manufactures to encourage English-style import-substituting industrialization, focusing particularly on "textiles, shipbuilding, and engineering." Their success was immediate: Neapolitan shipyards soon launched the first Italian steamships; its engineers constructed the peninsula's first railway. By the early 1830s, Naples was by some accounts the most industrialized state in Italy. Yet it was not to last. Britain retaliated against Neapolitan exports and, when this did not dissuade the kingdom from seeking economic and political independence, dispatched gunboats—with orders to seize Neapolitan shipping—to the Bay of Naples for the fourth time in about a century. Under the threat of bombardments the Neapolitans caved in, paying "heavy indemnities" and dismantling their tariff system.[30]

By this time, "free trade" simply meant England's freedom to export manufactured goods in exchange for foreign raw materials, a practice oxymoronically known as "free trade imperialism."[31] Decades ago, Enrico de Mas noted the "substantial equivalence of economic and political protectionism" for Genovesi.[32] Through active economic policies, Genovesi had hoped Naples would find the means of defending and developing its polity. The political liberty of Naples depended on its liberty to selectively curtail foreign trade. Freedom in the latter turned out to be a death knell to the former. What Doria had identified as "gelosia di commercio," d'Argenson as "jalousie de commerce," and Hume as "jealousy of trade" was not only an eighteenth-century phenomenon. It was painfully present as today's world took form, casting into relief the means by which the great power rose to prominence and the practical limits of emulation in international relations. Where Genovesi failed, Hamilton succeeded, but conceptually their problems were remarkably similar.

Strikingly, even the changes incurred by Cary's *Essay* in translation testify to the growing hostility of the world economy and the increasing care with which it was understood one had to calibrate the economy to safeguard liberty, development, and the common good. Cary had warned about the importance of keeping commerce political, "it being possible for the Public to grow Poor, whilst private Persons encrease their Fortunes." In France, Butel-Dumont rendered the same passage more urgently: *"Car il est très-possible quìun état s'appauvrisse, tandis qu'un petit nombre de Particuliers augmentent leur fortune."* In Italy, Genovesi wrote: *"Perciocchè egli è cosa la più facile del Mondo, che uno Stato impoverisca, mentre un piccol [sic] numero di particolari ingrandisce il suo patrimonio."* Wichmann's German translation followed suit: *"es ist nichts in der Welt leichter, als daß ein Staat zu eben der Zeit verarmt, da indessen eine Anzahl von Privatleuten in eben diesem Staat ihr Vermögen immer mehr vergrößert."* A situation in which the private wealth of a few increased while the nation as a whole suffered in international trade went from being "possible" in 1695 Bristol through "very possible" in 1755 Paris to "the easiest thing in the world" in 1757 Naples before the 1788 Leipzig edition similarly concluded there was "nothing easier in the world." As more came to depend on international trade, its implicit dangers became more acute.[33]

Like the Acadian genocide, Nelson's extermination of the Neapolitan republic in 1799, and the gunboat episode in 1823, the echoes of Cary's political economy have largely been ignored by historiography. A recent work on the history of English national character fails to mention the historically omnipresent "jealousy," and if award-winning popular historians now praise the Anglo-American continuum as the "most decent, honest, generous, fair-minded and self-sacrificing *imperium*" in history, that says less about the moral integrity of English-speakers over the past five centuries than it does about the corrupting quintessence of empire. That said, it might also, comparatively, be true.[34] The history and longevity of Enlightenment political economy demonstrate the shaky foundations on which some of our most cherished assumptions about commerce, liberty, and modernity rest.

Contemporaries across Europe were all too aware of what was at stake in international competition: nothing less than political existence itself. Between the Peace of Westphalia and World War II, literally hundreds of once viable political entities were absorbed by a diminishing number of growing territorial states that had mastered the political organization of material life. Even the most autarkic writers conceived of independence in relation to their competitors' military and commercial aggressions.[35] Wealth and liberty were competitively interdependent phenomena, and the Seven Years' War was an axiomatic event in this process.[36] International emulation could of course be cumulative, and with time the emulatee might in turn emulate the emulator, but it would be unethical, not to mention wrong, to claim that nobody suffered in the process; historically, there have been cases and forms of economic competition as devastating for political communities as they daily are for businesses.

Enlightened Economics

Of course, political economy had many origins, took many forms, and relied on a variety of justifications across very different contexts during the long eighteenth century. This study has only explored one tradition (rather literally), as well as some it intersected, and demonstrated its immense influence throughout the continent as thinkers and statesmen sought to come to grips with the politics of emulation and industrialization. And this tradition was widely implemented; the general trend of the eighteenth century was clear: European states powerful enough to decide on their own economic policies selectively curtailed their international trade to ensure the development of domestic productive capacity.[37] This specific tradition developed out of a realist insight into the power of manufacturing industry and the seminal importance of disseminating useful knowledge.[38] Only by furthering education and industrial pursuits, both carefully fostered and safeguarded against rivals by political will, could a polity flourish and be free in a world of cutthroat competition.

Quite contrary to the Physiocrats, who preached the universality of their maxims, this tradition was eminently aware of the importance of contexts for economic policies.[39] "As the state of a Nation alters," Cary surmised, "so must our measures in *Trade*"; and Gournay warned that "it amounts to insulting the great Colbert to think that, because he set a few limits to our trade, he intended them to last forever."[40] As one Grand Tourist followed suit, observing the European economy in 1786: "the nations" that could "give laws in matters of commerce" all pursued dynamic economic policies. The "chimerical system" of Physiocracy, on the other hand, spelled "certain ruin." Quesnay had ultimately composed an "elegant and ingenious poem" rather than "useful theories to experiment with"; economic "betterment" required "corrections, but without violence." Policies had to be tailored to the changing needs of a political community. "Limitations," he thus argued, "are as damaging to a country after industries have been established, as they are useful to introduce them."[41]

Something akin to an economic language has emerged from the foregoing pages, replete, to borrow Anthony Pagden's definition, with "precise vocabularies, metaphors and topoi, even recognised authorities, all readily identifiable and easily transmitted from one author to another." But this language did not derive primarily from the discourses of "civic humanism and natural jurisprudence."[42] Across Europe, its vocabulary consisted of concepts like "emulation," "industry," and "multiplication"; its idioms were "jealousy of trade" and "giving laws"; its authorities were figures like Colbert, Cary, and Melon, a heterogenous triumvirate united by a faith in the revolutionary consequences of manufacturing and the ability of political communities to actively shape their material destinies; and it echoed well beyond the writings of political economists. The Genoese scientist and ambassador Pietro Paolo Celesia, for example, reported at length about England's role in the world in the wake of the American War of Independence, a world he found to be under the influence of *"avarice of commerce"* and in which one could *"give the law"* through international trade. And no country embodied this better than England, which harbored "arcane Designs" and sought to use the "superiority of its industry" to render other countries "tributaries" with the "immense variety of its extremely exquisite manufactures."[43]

A striking aspect of this "language" is how nimbly its basic preoccupation with the role of industry in international relations catered to disparate moral, political, and intellectual needs. The *Essay* was at times parliamentary and Protestant; at times absolutist and Catholic; at times mercantile; at times learned. It is hard to argue that the doctrines that usually interest intellectual historians were ever more than window dressing in the *Essay*'s larger history. This is not to say that Cary and Genovesi did not take their political and religious convictions seriously, only that some of the building blocks of their shared political economy indeed existed, to summon a much-maligned argument, in a distinct sphere of knowledge.[44] As a vehicle of emulation and worldly melioration, political economy was a unifying discourse of "the Enlightenment," but there is a danger in making this "science" too dependent on specific confessional and philosophical preferences. Though Anglicanism, Epicureanism, and Spinozism informed some of its now most celebrated manifestations, the mainstream discourse of political economy was a far more practical creature, generally inspired by the exigencies of economic and military competition rather than by their moral-philosophical justifications.[45] Part and parcel of "Enlightenment" aims of reform and worldly melioration, the European discourse of political economy informed and was informed by the entire spectrum of Enlightenment spirituality, from the radical materialist through the moderate to the religious.[46] Economic concerns transcended confessional concerns on the continent, all the while that specific theories about them reflected and shaped spiritual preferences in individual contexts.

But, whatever one's prejudices, it is worth emphasizing again: "Enlightenment" economics cannot be equated with laissez-faire, and there is little heuristic value in continuing to equate, for good and bad, "economic liberalism" with "the Enlightenment Project," whatever any of those phrases may mean. As argued by luminaries such as Galiani, political economy was essentially about mediating between relatively simple general theories and inordinately complex local realities. The Physiocrats had mistakenly emphasized the "economic" dimensions of their science at the expense of the "political."[47] Dangeul observed the pragmatic rather than idealist nature of political economy when, criticizing the Dutch for not allowing the French to fish off their own shores, he noted that "two great and learned treatises on the Dominion of the Sea were written by Selden, and Grotius; the question has remained undecided, and the Dutch have continued in possession."[48] To a greater extent than historiography so far has insisted, early modern political economy engaged actively with the exigencies of knowledge, productivity, and the political technologies of power in international relations. And texts such as Botero's *Reason of State,* Cary's *Essay,* and Diderot's *Encyclopédie,* at times woven together explicitly, contributed more to the language of political economy in Europe than "civic humanism" did.[49] In short, they contributed to what Joseph Schumpeter referred to as "economic analysis."[50]

Scholars and laypeople alike continue to be obsessed by Adam Smith, but by the most lenient standards of historical evidence, we must accept that he was a treacherous guide to his age. For he was either eerily duplicitous or remarkably ignorant in claiming that "every town and country . . . in proportion as they have opened their ports to all nations, instead of being ruined by this free trade, as the principles of the commercial system would lead us to expect, have been enriched by it."[51] Too many cities and states had been impoverished through trade by 1776 to allow for alternative explanations.[52] In effect, the extent to which Smith was off the mark cannot but invoke doubts about the Scotsman's intentions. In the text known as the *Early Draft of the Wealth of Nations* he warned that "a nation is not always in a condition to imitate and copy the inventions and improvements of its more wealthy neighbours; the application of these frequently requiring a stock with which it is not furnished."[53] That he decided to cut this truism in favor of conjectures about the universal benefits of international trade is telling with regard to the nature of his enterprise. During the ardent debates leading up to the new Tuscan tariff of 1781, the reformist minister Luigi Tramontani feared that "emulating nations" circulated abstract treatises on laissez-faire to "obscure enlightenment" abroad, peddling theories that were not "followed by the[ir own] national legislation." Laissez-faire, Tramontani was not the last to claim, was a good that powerful nations wished to export to latecomers as a means of keeping them from catching up, of keeping them from emulating the ways and means by which they themselves had gotten ahead.[54]

And history, many argued, was the principal laboratory available to political economy: "There is no better way of understanding the uses of a machine," Paradisi lectured on this topic, "than to observe the process of its construction."[55] Because of Italy's unique history of rise and decline, this sentiment reached its greatest level of theoretical sophistication there, but it was widespread and influential throughout the European world, from St. Petersburg to Philadelphia.[56] Such a historical approach to political economy was also humbling. De Jorio warned that "all sciences have their chimera" and compared the quest for universal happiness in political economy with the mathematician's quest to "square the circle."[57] In this context, it is noteworthy that Quesnay himself, from whom modern economists derive their pedigree, hubristically claimed to have done precisely this toward the end of his life.[58] And as for the importance of the past, "let us not seek into the history of nations or the mistakes of men," Quesnay proclaimed, "for that only presents an abyss of confusion . . . [These] do not serve to throw a light which can illuminate the darkness."[59] Economics has long followed in Quesnay's footsteps, but it is a mistake to believe the path he charted was representative of political economy as the West and the rest diverged in the long eighteenth century.

In effect, the types of "political economy" expounded in the foregoing pages have little to do with "economics" as it developed in the wake of David Ricardo. Though their chosen activities differed, the heirs of Cary and Quesnay both feared that specializing in the wrong kind of trade would lead a country astray. Ricardo solved the issue in 1817 by de facto claiming that manufactures and agriculture were qualitatively alike. "Under a system of perfectly free commerce," as he famously adumbrated the theory now known as "comparative advantage,"

> each country naturally devotes its capital and labour to such employments as are most beneficial to each . . . It is this principle which determines that wine shall be made in France and Portugal, that corn shall be grown in America and Poland, and that hardware and other goods shall be manufactured in England.[60]

Conceptually, this is the negation of emulation.[61] Nobody should seek to catch up with industrial England because it did not matter what a country produced; there were no differential returns in economics and market mechanisms would automatically ensure a fair and optimal distribution of

wealth and power. So it was not inherently better to specialize in one economic activity rather than another. And it is conspicuous that Ricardo
used the examples of Portugal and England to prove this theory. For at the
time, the former's comparative advantage lay precisely in being poorer and
dependent on the latter. Schumpeter wrote of Ricardo's efforts that "it is
an excellent theory that can never be refuted and lacks nothing save
sense."[62] But for anyone wishing to devote the time and energy to consult
the historical record, it is eminently refutable.

Cary Redivivus

Nearly a century after Cary's writings, Gaetano Filangieri neatly encapsulated how Europe felt about England after it embraced the *Essay*'s message
and sought to convince the world to exchange raw materials for its manufactured goods:

> I am sympathetic to this spirit of *vendetta,* to this nearly universal hatred of a
> nation that has acquired it with its injustices; of a republic that has always
> been more inclined to grieve over the wealth of others than to enjoy its own;
> of a people, finally, that has not been content with becoming wealthy, but has
> sought to be the only one wealthy. Its exclusive patriotism, similar to that of
> the Romans, has provoked the hatred of all commercial nations.[63]

Such wishes for "vendetta" against England's political economy would
haunt Europe for centuries, justifying central claims of twentieth-century
totalitarianism, sometimes even with specific reference to Cary.[64] Modern
economic growth and exceptionalism in Britain—counterfactual questions
of whether its development was optimal or not aside—were based on commerce as well as conquest: on systematic state intervention, walls of tariffs
and subsidies to encourage manufactures, and arbitrary violence on a
global scale.[65] And it was the harrowing success of these policies that rendered them worthy of hatred, but also of guarded emulation abroad. Yet
the beneficial economic consequences of imperialism for England go far
further, still inflecting the basic way our world engages with itself: its languages. The rise of English from being a minor, peripheral language in the
late Renaissance to being the principal language of global communication
today cannot be divorced from Britain's historical success in conquest and
commerce.[66] Schleiermacher once argued that "a person deserves to be
heard beyond his immediate environment only to the extent to which he
influences language."[67] Though no poet, Cary contributed to influencing
languages on a scale equaling any Dryden of his era. Giuseppe Mazzini's

criterion for intellectual greatness might, however, in the end be more fitting: "an idea becomes great only insofar as it reaches beyond one's own
national boundaries."[68] That, Cary's ideas did.

The eventual overthrow of Cary's imperial vision by its offspring was
only one element in a larger story of *translatio imperii*. For just as his intellectual progeny turned against him, so his real bloodline played a role in
the collapse of Britain's old colonial system and the erection of a new empire across the Atlantic. Cary's children populated the early colonies from
Jamaica to Massachusetts, giving birth to new generations of merchants
and statesmen whose outlooks and loyalties came to differ greatly as settlers became colonials and Britons gradually turned American. As the interactions of consumption, industry, and welfare became ever clearer
during the eighteenth century and colonial inhabitants realized the injustice by which Britain's metropolis monopolized manufactures at their expense, the foot soldiers of empire renegaded. Carys, subsequently, were
legion in the American War of Independence.[69]

An anonymous Englishman writing in 1737 had feared that in "*bullying*
Mankind" England not only risked losing "her natural Influence, but likewise her Commerce" through "*Don Quixot* Atchievements [*sic*]."[70] Cer-
vantes' ghost again stalks the world economy, for states struggle, as then,
to remain viable in a context shaken by the dangers and opportunities of
economic globalization. The pursuit of power in international relations
through economic means was once known as "jealousy of trade." Though
now nearly forgotten, Cary's brutal vision of economic empire was one of
that jealousy's primary vehicles, carrying it from England to France to Italy
to Germany and into the New World. That journey, however, profoundly
changed his *Essay*. With time, the book would, incredibly, also provide a
possible remedy for this economic pathology: the exercise of active policy
to ensure worldwide industrialization, and the subsequently fruitful interaction of equi-powerful economies and cultures; neither empire nor cosmopolitanism but respectfully competitive coexistence: *emulation,* in the
term's ideal meaning.

To return to Hamilton again: "it is one thing for a country to be in a
posture not to receive the law from others, and a very different thing for
her to be in a situation which obliges others to receive the law from her."[71]
But given the mechanisms that we now know as increasing and diminishing returns to scale, liberty and development had to happen through industry, not agriculture alone. From Galiani to Smith, the greatest economic
minds of the eighteenth century explicitly theorized the role of industrialization in abolishing not only poverty and famine but also superstition and
extremism.[72] Civilized life was inconceivable without the manufacturing

process, which Cary and the British Empire sought to safeguard for England alone. And even the Physiocrat du Pont de Nemours became an enthusiast of manufacturing on his arrival in the United States.[73] This is a lesson worth remembering, for the legacy of the Cold War has led the historiography of economic analysis exasperatingly astray; scholarship has almost entirely lost touch with the texts and policies that historically were consequential and the complex causes of economic and political development. The procrustean dichotomy between planning and laissez-faire that crystallized in the wake of World War II has long outlived its usefulness, and so has the historiography which supports it.[74]

Of course, the eighteenth century is not the twenty-first. Heraclitus was right, you cannot step into the same river twice.[75] The mechanisms of early modern industrial emulation are today voided by laws of international copyright, and many of the basic building-blocks of early political economy have been greatly transformed, from the meaning of "free trade" to the qualitative differentiation between diverse economic activities. Even the idiom of "giving laws" was radically transmuted during the nineteenth century. From being an expression of imperialism, it became its justification as Britons employed the very same phraseology to explain their civilizing mission abroad. The British Parliament, a speaker in the House of Lords mused in 1813, had "now once more to give laws to India," but it should do so for the sake of India's own "welfare" and "moral improvement."[76] This was the ironic origin of a still extant tradition of globalization known as "liberal imperialism."[77] But if political economy fundamentally is about change, it is, as the Norwegian-American economist Thorstein Veblen intuited, essentially "evolutionary" and path-dependent.[78] History therefore can, and must, be the lodestar of our political economies.

The journey that took the *Essay* from Bristol to Leipzig and made Cary's name familiar from Copenhagen to Quito has not yet come to an end. The words of Edmund Bohun, one of his first critics, can serve to remind us of that fact. All nations, he argued, would be able one day to "enlarge their trades *prope ad infinitum,* without any damage to each other if the monopolizing humour, envy, and an insatiable avarice supported by fraude and violence, did not mislead them."[79] That day has not yet come. Empire remains ever present and ever evanescent, and the one vied for by Cary and his successors has been translated numerous times over the last three hundred years, transversing, as feared, both the Atlantic and, now, the Pacific.[80] From Athens to Washington, D.C., the translation of economic power took place within a cultural continuum originating in Ancient Greece. It will be up to future historians to analyze the consequences of economic power leaving this political and philosophical legacy behind. In the meantime, *translatio imperii* will not falter. To again invoke William Marlow's extraordinary painting of St. Paul's on a Venetian canal, future *Capriccios* might depict the Statue of Liberty in the Forbidden City, the Troll A oil-rig looming over Wall Street, or, who knows, moais along the majestic Zambezi. Whatever happens, how we go about our quests for freedom and worldly melioration cannot but remain a moral question of ancient and urgent pertinence.

Abbreviations

AMAE	Archives du Ministère des Affaires Étrangères, Paris, France
ANF	Archives Nationales de France, Paris, France
ASG	Archivio di Stato di Genova, Genoa, Italy
ASL	Archivio di Stato di Lucca, Lucca, Italy
ASN	Archivio di Stato di Napoli, Naples, Italy
AST	Archivio di Stato di Torino, Turin, Italy
BA	Biblioteca Ambrosiana, Milan, Italy
BI	Bibliothèque de l'Institut, Paris, France
BL	British Library, London, United Kingdom
BLO	Bodleian Library, Oxford, United Kingdom
BNCF	Biblioteca Nazionale Centrale di Firenze, Florence, Italy
BNF	Bibliothèque Nationale de France, Paris, France
BNN	Biblioteca Nazionale di Napoli, Naples, Italy
BNT	Biblioteca Nazionale di Torino, Turin, Italy
BP	Biblioteca Panizzi, Reggio Emilia, Italy
BRO	Bristol Record Office, Bristol, United Kingdom
BTE	Bernardo Tanucci, *Epistolario*. Edited by R. P. Coppini et al. Rome, 1980–2007, 18 vols.
Chicago	University of Chicago Press
Cornell	Cornell University Press
CSP—Colonial	*Calendar of State Papers, Colonial Series*. 42 vols. Edited by W. Noël Sainsbury et al. London, 1860–1953.
CSP—Domestic	*Calendar of State Papers, Domestic Series* [William and Mary—William III]. 11 vols. Edited by William John Hardy and Edward Bateson. London, 1895–1937.

CSP—Venetian *Calendar of State Papers and Manuscripts, Relating to English Affairs, Existing in the Archives and Collections of Venice, and in Other Libraries of Northern Italy.* 38 vols. Edited by Rawndon Brown et al. London, 1864–1947.
CUL Cambridge University Library, Cambridge, United Kingdom
CUP Cambridge University Press
FM Fondazione Mattioli, Milan, Italy
GFS *Ove Høegh Guldbergs og Arveprins Frederiks brevveksling med Peter Christian Schumacher 1778–1807.* Edited by J. O. Bro-Jørgensen. Copenhagen: Nyt Nordisk Forlag Arnold Busck, 1972.
Harvard Harvard University Press
Hopkins Johns Hopkins University Press
IC *Il Caffè: 1764–1766.* Edited by Gianni Francioni and Sergio Romagnoli. Turin: Bollati Boringhieri, 1998.
IISF Istituto italiano per gli studi filosofici, Naples, Italy
OUP Oxford University Press
Princeton Princeton University Press
PRO Public Record Office, Kew, United Kingdom
RC Rigsarkivet, Copenhagen, Denmark
SHL Senate House Library, London, United Kingdom
SNSP Società Napoletana di Storia e Patria, Naples, Italy
UFEG Universitäts- und Forschungsbibliothek Erfurt/Gotha, Schloss Friedenstein, Gotha, Germany
Yale Yale University Press

Notes

Introduction

1. Bacon 1597; similarly Hobbes 1656, 5.
2. Smith 1976, I, 35; Hobbes 1651, 35, 41. The first mention of the phrase "political economy" seems to have been Mayerne 1611, 558, on which see King 1948.
3. On "useful" knowledge and development see Mokyr 2002.
4. E.g. Mokyr 2006, to mention only one example of a tradition explored in Reinert 2010.
5. I am of course not the first to argue for the need to think more historically about the canon of economics and the history of industrial policies. Reinert 1980 and 1999 sketched out the basic premises of this reevaluation, and it was developed by Chang 2002 also as a result of conferences organized by The Other Canon Foundation, the most mature expression of which can be found in Reinert 2007.
6. I agree with Poni 2009, 61–2 that there are no grounds for refusing the moniker "industrial" to the sorts of manufacturing complexes that bloomed in the most advanced areas of Europe before the so-called "Industrial Revolution," on which see Horn, Rosenbad, and Smith 2010. On the "industrious" revolution see de Vries 2008 and Muldrew 2011. On European proto-industry see Ogilvie and Cerman 1996.
7. For a similar perspective, see Kocka 2003, 44. On these traditions see also Werner and Zimmermann 2006.
8. Meusel 1806–7, I, 599.

9. Gould 1989. See similarly Montgomery 2000, 14. On the interpretation of strata see Zalasiewicz 2008, 19.
10. For analytical frameworks see Hont 2005; Vietor 2007.
11. On which see Pocock 1999–2011, III, 98–100.
12. Murray 2008; McMurran 2010, 7.
13. On emulation see Hont 2005, 115–122; Resende-Santos 2007, 1–92. On its historical importance for development see Henderson 1972; Greenfeld 2001, 37–58; Lancas 2003, 124; Foucault 2007, 294; de Vries 2008, 46–50.
14. Montchrétien 1615, 44, 134–137, 141–143, on which see Keohane 1980, 163–168. On Montchrétien and imitation see Panichi 1989, 295–353; on "political economy" as the unifying discourse of "The Enlightenment" see Venturi 2001; Robertson 2005.
15. Botero 1589; ANF K/909, no. 27, "Établissement à Paris d'un Manufacture de tapisserie façon de Flandre, 1607–1630." On Seckendorff see Reinert 2005. On Hamilton see McCoy 1980; McNamara 1998. On the geography of "the Enlightenment" see Venturi 2001; Withers 2007.
16. On the importance of translations see Kelley 1979; Steiner 1998. For translations and Enlightenment see Withers 2007, 50–57. For approaches to studying the fortunes of texts see St. Clair 2004, 3.
17. Calvino 2002, 7–8.
18. On canons in economics see Schumpeter 1954, 10.
19. Nye 2007, 112.
20. Krugman 1998, 69–84; Rice 2004; Blair 2004. Cf. Barbieri 2002.
21. See for discussions Hirschman 1977 and 1992; Pagden 1995, 115–125, 178–200; Pocock 1999–2011; Dickey 2001–2; Pocock 2003, 570; Hont 2005; Robertson 2005. For analyses of this paradigm in modern political philosophy, see Mansfield and Pollins 2003.
22. In the wake of Hont 2005, we can see this idiom was omnipresent. E.g. Doria 1979–82, I, 173–174; Anonymous 1732, 11; Kelly 1732–37, III, 91; Anonymous 1741, 7; Skelton 1741, 53; Anonymous 1747, I, 26; Smith 1747, I, 215; Nugent 1750, II, 49; Guglielmo de Ludolf to Bernardo Tanucci, 11 February or March 1758, in BTE, V, 829n; Hume 1758, 187–189; Tucker 1763, 40; Baggs 1774, xv; Raynal 1780, 598; Malaspina 1786, 100–101; Filangieri 2004, II, 150–163.
23. Madison, Hamilton, and Jay 1987, 104–108.
24. See, among others, Braudel 1977, 66, 88–89; Findlay and O'Rourke 2007; Tabak 2008.
25. Fitzmaurice 2003, 4.
26. Martines 1963, 25.
27. Carpenter 1975 and 1977.
28. Skinner 2002, I, 73; Rothschild 2001, 40–41.
29. Robertson 2005, 9.
30. Makato 1899, 9, 36.
31. Freeborn 1985.
32. Rothschild 2006, 219.
33. Burke 1996a, 3; Burke and Hsia 2007.

34. See similarly Koehn 1994, xi.
35. Ballaster 2005, 202–203.
36. Dunn 1996, 24.
37. Chartier 1994, 1.
38. "Las versiones Homéricas," in Borges 1996, I, 239. See similarly Beebee 1990, 178.
39. On *translatio imperii* see Pocock 1999–2011, III, 98–100.
40. Hont 2005, 155–156.
41. "Dei difetti della letteratura e di alcune loro cagioni," in IC, 543.

1. Emulation and Translation

1. On this war see Anderson 2001 and Szabo 2007.
2. Anonymous 1765, IV, 1. Emphasis added. On Casanova's involvement with the work, see Casanova 1997, IX, 287. On the two, see Hauc 2004.
3. Vico 2000, 120; Kennett with Percivale 1703, 53; Anonymous 1715, I, 17; Nugent 1748, 138; Anonymous 1787, 468.
4. Anonymous 1765, IV, 186, 215.
5. Smith 1976, II, 486.
6. Anonymous 1765, IV, 59. On England's penchant for imitation, see Defoe 1737, 300–301, and Voltaire 1733, 222. On the economic history of this phenomenon, see Harris 1998, 559–560; MacLeod 2004 and 2008.
7. Anonymous 1765, IV, 6–7, V, 203–204. Emphasis added.
8. Pietro Mocenigo, "Account of England," read to the Senate 9 June 1671, CSP—Venetian, 37, 1671–72, 64, 54–73.
9. Anonymous 1787, 468. Emphasis added. See similarly the Abbé Coyer in Greenfeld 2001, 136.
10. Beccaria 1984, 24; echoed by Paolini 1785–86, I, 39.
11. Accarias de Sérionne 1766, I, 3–4, on which see Hasquin 1974. See also the review in *Giornale d'Italia,* 27 December 1766, 203–206.
12. FM Archivio Verri, 380.4. Sebastiano Franci, "La guerra senza sangue," ed. Pietro Verri.
13. "Proposizione per la riforma delle Tariffe, ossia dato della mercanzia" [1764], in Verri 2006–7, II, 735–749, 745. For context see Capra 2002.
14. On autonomy see Tuck 1999, 226.
15. Hobbes 1651, 63. E.g. Caton 1988, 464; Gerace 2004.
16. Hirschman 1997, 117–118, 130, 135; Locke 1692, 15; Constant 1988, 5; Neff 1990.
17. Rousseau 1761, 15–16. Emphasis added.
18. A tradition more resonant with Hirschman 1945.
19. Mun 1621, 1.
20. Colbert to A. Rochefort, 11 January 1666 and "Dissertation sur la question: quelle des deux alliances de France ou de Hollande peut-être plus avantageuse à l'Angleterre," in Colbert 1861–82, III:1, 37 and VI:269 respectively.
21. Leti 1676, I, pt. VI, 15.
22. On such goods see Verdoorn 1949 and 1980.

23. Griffin 1969.
24. Raynal 1780, 598.
25. ANF K/907, no. 14: "Mèmoire sur les moyens d'augmenter la navigation et le commerce, les revenus du Roi, et les droits de l'amiraté," 12–[13].
26. *Giornale d'Italia,* 12 April 1766, 327.
27. In Cerutti 2009, 205. On this long-lived dream, see Scuccimarra 2006, 376–388.
28. In Hont 2008, 299.
29. CSP—Domestic, 1 March–31 October 1673, 304. On Florentine reactions to earlier English protectionism, see Malanima 1988.
30. Giovanni Giacomo Corniani to the Doge and Senate, 22 July 1673, CSP—Venetian, 38, 1673–75, 114, 77–78.
31. Piero Duodo, Venetian Ambassador in Prague, to the Doge and Senate, 22 May 1600, in CSP—Venetian, 9, 1592–1603, 883, 409–410.
32. Marin Cavalli, Venetian Ambassador in France, to the Doge and Senate, 21 October 1602, CSP—Venetian, 9, 1592–1603, 1097, 598–509; Giovanni Carlo Scaramelli, Venetian Secretary in England, to the Doge and Senate, 20 March 1603, CSP—Venetian, 9, 1592–1603, 1160, 555–557.
33. It was a trope that united such disparate observers as Bernardo Tanucci to Michelangelo Giacomelli, 16 April 1746, in BTE, II, 28; Herder 2002, 381, 386, 407; Saint-Simon 1976, 84–6, 93; all the way to Scarfoglio 1937 and Corpaci 1941.
34. Hont 2005, 5–6.
35. Baggs 1774, xv.
36. On Melon see the essays introducing Melon 1983 and Megnet 1955; Hont 2005, 30–36; Robertson 2005, 340–346.
37. Melon 1736, 1–11. Emphasis added.
38. Melon 1736, 79–91; Reinert 2010.
39. In Bonno 1948, 51.
40. Dryden 1694, unpaginated prologue. For context see Winn 1987, 445.
41. Montesquieu does not mention "England" as the subject of this passage but hints of it in 1989, 156–166, 325. For the marginalia see Voltaire 1979–94, V, 748, and similarly 757. On Montesquieu's debt to Melon, see Shackleton 1961, 39, 238–239; Bouzinac 1970, 23; Hont 2006, 410; Sonenscher 2007a, 111. On England in Montesquieu's thought see Landi 1981.
42. Montesquieu 1989, 328–329. Emphasis added. On Anglomania and Anglophobia see Acomb 1950; Grieder 1985; Perrot 1992, 305–331; Buruma 1999. On the Italian case see Graf 1911; on the German see Maurer 1987, 432.
43. On fears of Britain becoming a union of Rome and Carthage in the French context, see Dziembowski 1998.
44. In Fusaro 2008, 71. See similarly Findlay and O'Rourke 2007, 244.
45. On the concomitant changes in England's linguistic and imperial status see Burke 2004, 13, 80–81.
46. Pecchio 1829, 135.

47. ANF T 1545, Papiers Sotira, "Discorsi politici sopra la forma del governo d'Inghilterra e sopra le cagioni della Grandezza, e decadenza di Quel Regno dell'' Abate Gaetano Sotira," 2r.
48. See the astute discussion in Bernardo Tanucci to Montealegre, 10 October 1758, in Migliorini 1984, 144.
49. Meyssonnier 1989; Harris 1998, 563; Alimento 2009.
50. Gournay 2008, 242. Emphasis added. See also Crouzet 2008, 8.
51. *Journal de Trévoux,* January 1755, 39.
52. Reinert 2010.
53. Belloni and Zanobetti 1751, 70n. On Belloni see Belloni 1965; on Zanobetti see Alimento 2008.
54. Algarotti 1823, I, 452. Emphasis added.
55. See particularly Machiavelli's letters to Francesco Vettori of 10 and 26 August 1513, in Machiavelli 1971, 1147–1150, 1154–1157; Najemy 1993, 159, has convincingly shown that "Machiavelli invented the Prince" in these two letters.
56. This dichotomy, promulgated above all by Pocock 1975, is nearly ubiquitous in the secondary literature. See also Pocock 1985, 48, and Pocock 1999–2011. For discussion see Jurdjevic 2001.
57. De Jorio 1979, I, 105, 127.
58. Galiani 1770, 65, and 1974, 78. For context see Kaplan 1976.
59. BP MSS. REGG: E 139, Agostino Paradisi, "Lezioni di economia civile," II, 129.
60. AST, Materie di Commercio, 3 Categoria, Mazzo d'addizione 1 [Mazzo 1 da ordinare], no. 20, no date, "Pensieri d'un' anonimo sul Commercio in generale, 'Del Commercio del Piemonte,'" 3v.
61. In Devine 2004, 44.
62. Armitage 1995.
63. Anonymous 1754a, 338–339.
64. On the long history of this economic relationship, see Abulafia 1977.
65. Genovesi 1757–58, I, lxxxv–lxxxvi, 35n–36n, 220n–221n, 367. Emphasis added. On this work see Reinert 2007b. On Genovesi see Pii 1984; on his chair see Di Battista 1992 and Iovine 2001.
66. De Jorio 1778–83, I, 24. See similarly De Jorio 1979, I, 82.
67. De Jorio 1778–83, I, 2–4, 18–19. Also De Jorio 1979, I, 198, 212. See practically the same passage in Accarias de Sérionne 1766, I, 1–2, and Franci, "Alcuni pensieri politici," in IC, 143–150.
68. Cf. among others Pocock 1999–2005, I, 109, and II, 169.
69. De Jorio 1778–83, I, 21, 24. Emphasis added. On how popular awareness of these mechanisms informed the American Revolution, see Breen 2004, 329–331.
70. De Jorio 1778–83, IV, 299; 1979, I, 91–93.
71. Skinner 2008, 63–72, 173–177.
72. Livy, *History of Rome* 34.57; Virgil, *Aeneid* 12.112; Parry 1787, I, 183. See also, for biblical occurrences, Exodus 24:12; Deuteronomy 5:31, 7:11, 12:1,

17:11; John 17:1. For different usages of this idiom see Harrington 1659, 7–9; Chacón 1727, 113; Bernardo Tanucci to the Count of Cantillana, 27 May 1757, in BTE, V, 24. For other explicitly economic uses see Serra 1613, 95; Barbon 1690, 92; Alessandro Verri, "Di alcuni sistemi del pubblico diritto," in IC, 725–739; Arriquibar 1779, I, 165.

73. Bodin 1576, 173; Botero 1589, 144, 303.
74. Locke 1988, 367–368; Greenfeld 2001, 1–58.
75. Connelly 1797–98, pt. 2, I, 554.
76. *Digest* 1.6.4, in Skinner 2008, x–xii.
77. Machiavelli 1971, 282; Thucydides in Knox 1989, 92–109, 107–108.
78. Diderot 1992, 186. See similarly S. X. 1755, 33; Hamilton in Walling 1999, 23.
79. De Jorio 1979, I, 302.
80. Skinner 2008, 49–50.
81. Melon 1736, 9; Anonymous 1747, II, 91–93, 347–348, 353; Montesquieu 1989, 328–329; Butel-Dumont 1755c, I, 75; Genovesi 1757–58, I, lxxxv–lxxxvi, 35n–36n, 220n–221n, 367, and II, 31n–32n.
82. Davenant 1771, II, 254.
83. Ward 1779, 256.
84. Worsley 1651, 9–12; Anonymous 1747, II, 347–348.
85. Gifford 1795, 293; Høegh-Guldberg to Schumacher, 23 January 1803, in GFS, 534.
86. Filangieri 2004, II, 138–139 and n, but see also I, 138–139. See similarly delle Mallere (1776?), 24–25. On Filangieri and his impact see Ferrone 2003 and Trampus 2005. On delle Mallere see Monestarolo 2006.
87. Machiavelli 1971, 148. For founding statements of this tradition see Botero 1589; Serra 1613. For some later expressions, see Justamond 1798, IV, 470, V, 281, VI, 66; Burnaby 1775, 159.
88. For Blenheim's importance for political thought, see Rahe 2005; Claydon 2007, 125–132. For war as a "heuristic shortcut," see Resende-Santos 2007, 81. This fear was evident in Italy already in the early 1740s; see S. Reinert 2009. On French propaganda to weave this image on the eve of the Seven Years' War, see Shovlin 2010.
89. Møller 1983, 124.
90. Uztáriz 1724, 123.
91. Anonymous 1712, 19. Emphasis added.
92. As explicitly theorized by De Jorio 1979, I, 91–93, building on Genovesi 1757–58, I, 28, 247–248.
93. See, however, on the theorists of closed commercial states, Nakhimovsky 2011.
94. Davenant 1771, II, 75, discussed differently in Pocock 2003, 443. See similarly De Jorio 1979, I, 152, 169.
95. Hume 1994, 51–57, 52.
96. Anonymous 1765, I, 82–83.
97. Burke 1998, 66; Barkan 1999.
98. Hobbes 1681, 66–69.

99. Coles 1677, unpaginated entry for "Emulation"; Bayley 1727, unpaginated entry for "To Emulate." See also Bayley 1800, unpaginated entry for "Emulation."

100. Chambers 1738, 1, unpaginated entry for "emulation." Notice the difference in a later edition, 1778–88, 2, unpaginated entry for "Emulation." Nonetheless, the *Encyclopædia Britannica* for the same years (1778–83, IV, 2723) reprinted Chambers's definition verbatim.

101. Thomas 1758, unpaginated entries.

102. Cited in Iverson 2003, 218; for a juxtaposition of emulation and jealousy, see Delany 1747, 374–375.

103. Coke 1670, 55.

104. Altieri 1726–27, 1, unpaginated entries for "Emulazione" and "Gara"; 2, unpaginated entry for "Emulation." Ash 1775 registered his unpaginated entry for "emulation" as an alternative to "Contend" and "Contention."

105. Reynolds 1853, 103–104; Crow 2006, 314.

106. N.H. 1694, 274. For another cupidic use of emulation, see Anonymous 1753, unpaginated entry for "Fashion"; Anonymous 1747–66, I, viii, and V, 3053–3054; Anonymous 1777a, title pages. On conjugal emulation see Mandeville 1988, I, 134–147.

107. Barrow 1759–60, 2, unpaginated entry for "Oswestry"; see similarly Mandeville 1988, I, 134–147.

108. E.g. Cary 1717a, 112; Anonymous 1738, 17; Beawes 1754, 608; C.K. 1756, A2r; Galiani 1974, 79. See also Schytte 1773–76, IV, 130, and Anonymous 1776–77, I, 159, entry for 18 May 1776.

109. See for example Justamond 1798, III, 186; Casanova quoted in Moe 2002, 47; d'Argenson 2004, 82.

110. Harrison 1999; Maza 2003, 198.

111. Anonymous 1765, I, 1.

112. Anonymous 1776–77, I, 32.

113. Phillips 1658, unpaginated dedication and entry for "Emulation." Anonymous 1756d, iv–v. See also Rhudde 1757. On the survival and consequences of such institutions see among others Greenfeld 2001, 144; Maza 2003; and similarly Reddy 1984, 147. On goods and emulation, see Berg 2005, 110.

114. In Bell 2003, 2. See similarly Forbonnais 1753c, iv; Rhudde 1757, 20.

115. *Weekly Account*, 29 February 1644; Anonymous 1765, I, 210; Justamond 1798, II, 435.

116. Postlethwayte 1757a, 233–235, 276. See also Genovesi 1777, II, 214n.

117. Francesco Giannetti in Becagli 1983, 120.

118. Justamond 1798, VI, 230.

119. Hume 1758, 22, 67, 97–98, 155, 186, 188.

120. Ferguson 1995, 29, see also 52–53, 95, 202.

121. Ferguson 1769, 101, but see also 99, 102; Hume 1758, 22, 67, 97–98, 155, 186, 188. For this analysis see Hont 2005, 85, 122. For Hobbes's conflation of jealousy and emulation, see 1995, 66–67.

122. Smith 1776, II: 100–101, and II: 363.

123. Boudard 1766, I, 182, and II, 141.

124. Hont 2005, 118.
125. Burke 1993, 63–77.
126. See similarly Girard 1978, vii–xiii; Saint-Amand 1996, 1–14.
127. Ever since, at least, Gonzáles de Cellorigo 1600, 38.
128. Anonymous 1770, 35–36.
129. Borst 1957–63.
130. On early modern gardens, see Drayton 2000. On early commentaries on Babel see Fyler 2007, 1–59.
131. Rossi 1960 and Eco 2004.
132. See similarly Sher 2006, 597; Yeo 2001, 57–58.
133. *Giornale d'Italia,* 17 October 1767, 127.
134. Chambers 1728, I, xxi.
135. See, for the darker fears of early modern language theory, Dawson 2007.
136. Steiner 1998, 253.
137. BNCF NA 050, Giuseppe Pelli Bencivenni, *Efemeridi,* I series, III, c. 35, 18 July 1760, and c. 39
138. BNCF NA 050, Giuseppe Pelli Bencivenni, *Efemeridi,* I series, XVIIII, c. 39, 9 February 1767. For a modern theory of such translations, see Reiss and Vermeer 1984.
139. Pocock 1999–2011, III, 206.
140. Pluche 1751, on which see Eco 2004, 364–365.
141. Kippax 1751, I, vii.
142. In Beaurepaire 2007, 100–101.
143. BNCF NA 050, Giuseppe Pelli Bencivenni, *Efemeridi,* II series, IV, c. 593, 13 March 1776.
144. Burke 1966, 138–139.
145. Becagli 2003, 69.
146. Anonymous 1775, unpaginated introduction entitled "El traductor."
147. Stierle 1996, 65; Cinquemani 2006, 79.
148. Barbapiccola 2005, 55–56.
149. Anonymous 1765, I, 171.
150. Helgerson 2007, 13.
151. Anonymous 1714b, 2.
152. See the example of Beecher 2006, 103–121.
153. Franci, "Alcuni pensieri politici," in IC, 143–150; BP TURRI: C 56, Agostino Paradisi, "Miscellanea di scritti," II, [1].
154. On the Roman canon see Pagden 1995, 11–28, and MacCormack 2007. On this see also Reinert 2010.
155. Campbell 1750, 486; Forbonnais 1753c, iv–v.
156. Reinert 2010.
157. Johns 2009, 41–56.
158. White 1792, II, l.
159. Child 1690, 131, 42.
160. Child 1740, 85–86. Emphasis added. For other discussions of emulation, see Cary 1745, 113; Decker 1744, 13; Defoe 1745, I, 315; T.W. 1746, 27;

Hutcheson 1747, 30; Tucker 1749, 27, 35; Postlethwayte and Royston 1750, 41, 44, 60.

161. Pagden 2007. For "capitalism" understood as a system of "ceaseless and merciless competition" see McCraw 1995, 6.

162. *Journal de Trévoux,* January 1755, 6–7, 10, 39–40. Emphasis added.

163. Anonymous 1756c, ii.

164. On the Savarys see Cipolla 1994, 63–91.

165. Postlethwayte 1749, 23, 30–31, 51–52.

166. Pombal 1986, 158. I owe this reference to Gabriel Paquette.

167. Defoe 1737, 300–301.

168. Justamond 1798, III, 366. Emphasis added. See similarly Goudar 1756; De Jorio 1979, I, 186; Torres 1781, I, 109, on how Britain "gave the law" to Portugal; Pombal 1986, 76. On this see also Shaw 1998.

169. Raynal 1780, III, 447–448; Justamond 1798, IV, 462–463.

170. Alessandro Verri, "Dei difetti della letteratura e di alcune loro cagioni," in IC, 543.

171. E.g. Anonymous 1705, translator's preface. See, for a complementary perspective, McMurran 2010, 19.

172. Noboa y Lisasueta 1753, 13.

173. Child 1668, 42; Anonymous 1747, II, 92; Butel-Dumont 1755b, II, 128–129; Anonymous 1765, I, 18; De Jorio 1979, I, 179.

174. Genovesi 1757–58, I, 22–23. On this problem see Abramowitz 1986; Anderson 1991, 155–156; Horn 2006, 5.

175. Antonio Serristorio in Becagli 1983, 32.

176. Butel-Dumont 1755b, I, 188–189, 327. This precise argument was picked up by the work's reviewer in the *Journal de Trévoux,* August 1755, 2077–2096; Genovesi 1757–58, II, 80n–81n.

177. ANF, T 1545, Papiers Sotira, *Discorsi politici . . .* , 45r.

178. List 1844, 501. Emphasis added. See on this Tribe 1995; Chang 2002; James 2006, 53; and earlier Galiani 1975, 735–741; Genovesi 1757–58, I, 249, 289; Hamilton, "The Federalist VI," in Madison, Hamilton, and Jay 1987, 104–108.

179. E.g. AST, *Materie di Commercio,* 3 Categoria, Mazzo d'addizione 1 [Mazzo 1 da ordinare], no. 2: "1757 Parere del Consiglio del Commercio per la soppressione di corporazioni. Con uno scritto intitolato *Extrait du Mémoire de Mr. de Gournay Intendant du Commerce/1756/*"; Butel-Dumont 1755b, II, 128–129; Schröderstierna 1756. For sovereigns emulating see among others Catherine II of Russia 1977 and Ferdinand IV of Naples to John Acton, 25 May 1785, in Nuzzo 1990, 74.

180. E.g. de Graef 1996, 130–132; Anonymous 1747, II, 209; Montesquieu 1989, xliii, 18–19, 310, 345, 602; Anonymous 1756c, ii; Anonymous 1756a, 1–10; many of the articles in *Danmarks og Norges Oeconomiske Magazin* (1757–64); Arnolfini 2001, 95–216, 192; Marcoleta 1771, [vii–viii]; Hamilton, "The Federalist VI," in Madison, Hamilton, and Jay 1987, 104–108. For Russia see Venturi 1972, 178.

181. Genovesi 1757–58, I, ix–x, echoing Muratori 1749, 84. See also Genovesi to Camillo Tori, 20 March 1759, and Genovesi to Cristofero Migliarini, 21 December 1762, in Genovesi 1962, 123–124 and 140–141, respectively. On history as a "propedeutic" of other sciences for Genovesi see Marcialis 1999a, 103–134, and similarly Di Liso 1997, 269–312.

182. [Nordencrantz] 1730, 213–270, particularly 215–216 and 227; similarly Cortanze's 1726 ambassadorial report from London (1911) as well as the similar AST *Materie di Commercio,* 3 categoria, mazzo 2, no. 28: "Memoria circa i motivi della decadenza del Commercio, e de' mezzi per contenere i Fallimenti," pamphlet no. 2, 2v. See similarly Bernardo Tanucci to the Count of Cantillana, 21 May 1757, in BTE, V, 4, and De Jorio 1979, I, 301, 313. On this see also Reinert 2006a. On how the "models" of England and Spain served opposite purposes, see Cheney 2010, 38, 45, 122–128.

183. Galiani 1975, 735.

184. Milo 1984.

185. On which see Chartier 1994.

186. One example would be the anonymous and undated eighteenth-century manuscript translation of Locke's economic works into French, "Considérations sur l'effet que pourrait avoir une loi qui reduirait le taux de l'usure" and "Considérations sur l'augmentation de la valeur nominale des monnaies," in my private collection.

187. Mazzini 2009, 201.

188. Anonymous 1654, translator's introduction; Harris 1998, 544.

189. Zanden 2009, 185.

190. The decree is reprinted in Berge 1998, 9–10.

191. Bruhns 2004, 31, 162–163.

192. Berge 1998, 10; Bruhns 2004, 163; Amdisen 2002, 103–105, 156–157; Glebe-Møller 2007, 99, 103.

193. In Benjamin 1999, 60.

194. Calculations are based on Maddison 2006, 244–247, 263–265. Numbers are in 1990 U.S. dollars and are historical projections of the performance of current regions.

195. Allen 2009, 17.

196. Allen 2001.

197. Burke 2004, 13, 80–81; Fabian 1992, 110.

198. Quoted in Phillipson 1992, 31, and Helgerson 2007, 5. On the deep historical relation between economic, military, and linguistic power, see Anthony 2007, 464.

199. Frederick of Prussia 1981, 75. On this theme see Hont 2005 and the essays in Dunn 1990.

200. On economic theory codifying historically successful practice, see already Laspeyres 1863.

201. In Shovlin 1998, 1.

202. Burke 1996a, 61; Sherman 2004.

203. Compare United Nations 1999, 6, and Jefferies 2005, 3.

204. Braudel 1982. On this emulative arms race see Conway 2006 and Harris 2002.
205. Schmoller 1897; Cipolla 1969.
206. Compare, say, Anonymous 1743, ix–xi, to Kippax 1751, I, iv. I here follow Carpenter 1977, 22–23.
207. Kippax 1751, I, viii. Spanish prohibitions on manufactures from some nations would soon justify such caution; see Bernardo Tanucci to the Marquis of Caraccioli, 21 May 1757, in BTE, V, 8.
208. Genovesi 1757–58, I, ii.
209. de Graef 1996, 130–132.
210. Marcoleta 1771, 6–7, 9–10.
211. Anonymous 1972; Llombart 2004; Paquette 2007.
212. Court 1662, on which see Carpenter 1975, 7.
213. *Danmarks og Norges Oeconomiske Magazin* 1757, I: X3v, XXr; see for a similar sentiment C.K. 1756, A2r, and, for an academy, Westerman 1768.
214. *Journal Oeconomique*, January 1756, 16.
215. This from comparing the data on translations with the total numbers estimated in Théré 1998, on which see Shovlin 2006, 2.
216. Guasti 1995–96 and similarly Cheney 2010, 38, 45, 122–128.
217. *Journal de Trévoux*, January 1755, 5.
218. In Carpenter 1977, 8–9.
219. Anonymous 1754b, frontispiece and introduction. For the Danish, see Anonymous 1756a, 1–10.
220. Almodóvar 1784–90, III, appendix, 68, on which see Paquette 2007.
221. Grieder 1985.
222. In Pocock 1999–2011, I, 241.
223. Oz-Salzberger 1995, 59.
224. On German translation culture, see Huber 1968.
225. Humpert 1937. On the origins of political economy in Germany see Backhaus 1994. For its later development see Tribe 1988 and 1995 as well as Lluch's 1997 corrective.
226. Moser 1771, 20.
227. In Fabian 1992, 77.
228. Beaurepaire 2007, 183.
229. Anonymous 1717, 5, on which see Cheney 2010, 28–30. On Huet, see DeLater 2002.
230. St. Luke, Acts 2:1–15.
231. Vico 2002, 60–61; d'Alambert 1752, x, on which see Goodman 1994, 26; Hume 1994, 107.
232. In Genovesi 1757–58, II, 413n; III, 15n. On Huet and translations, see Rapetti 1999; Knecht 1999. On the longevity of his paradigm, see Grafton 1999.
233. Hieronymus Stridonensis, Epistula LVII, ad Pammachium: "De optimo genere interpretandi" (c. AD 375), in Migne 1844–55, XXII, 570. See also Horace in Lefevere 1992, 15. On this tradition of translation, see Weissbort and Eysteinsson 2006, 20–33.

234. Steiner 1998. Examples are endless, but see the colorful Anonymous 1705, iv, and Noboa y Lisasueta 1753, 12.
235. In Weissbort and Eysteinsson 2006, 25.
236. In Lefevere 1992, 87; Montgomery 2000, 34; Weissbort and Eystensson 2006, 26–27.
237. BNF ms. N.A.F. 1359, Antoine Le Maistre, *Regles de la Traduction,* 1r; Anonymous 1705, A2v; Dryden in Lefevere 1992, 24, and Goethe in Lefevere 1992, 24–25; Baggs 1774, i–iv; Stockdale 1776, I, X. On translation as commerce, see Zinsser 2002.
238. Giovio 1781, 61.
239. Gibbon in Pocock 1999–2011, I, 242; Goethe and Schlegel in Lefevere 1992, 75, 78. See, for French justifications, Charles 2008, 186; Lefevere 1992, 28–29, 39–40, 111.
240. Zinsser 2002, 616.
241. Diderot 1755, 637–637v.
242. In Viano 2005a, 108.
243. Chambers, 1778–88, I, unpaginated entry for "agriculture." Emphasis added.
244. Mah 2003, 45–46.
245. Rousseau 1953, 325.
246. Secondo 1747–54, I, "Prefazione del traduttore."
247. In Farinella 1996, 124–125.
248. Though not always; see McMurran 2010.
249. Anonymous 1777c, v–vi. On Beccaria's influence in England see Draper 2000.
250. In Davenant 1771, I, 307.
251. Anonymous 1798, v; Anonymous 1736, iv.
252. Forster 1772, vi–vii.
253. There are, of course, exceptions such as Stockdale 1776, I, xi–xii.
254. Alessandro Verri to Pietro Verri, 22 February 1771, in Verri and Verri 1910–1942, IV, 147–148. On this see Scalvini 1998.
255. Lai 2000; Howland 2002; Zhiri 2006. See, however, Beebee 1990, ix, for an inter-European translation problem.
256. Gladwin 1783–86, I, viii.
257. Legrand 2005.
258. Soll 2005.
259. Findlen, in Messbarger and Findlen 2005, 37.
260. Beecher 2006, 105, 113.
261. Toland 1695, 25, on which see Locke 1991, I, 34–35n. On Davanzati see Cochrane 1973, 119–122.
262. See, for a similar argument focused on technological emulation, the editors' introduction to Horn, Rosenband, and Smith 2010, 6.
263. Smith 1976, I, 449. E.g. Josiah Tucker to Lord Kames, 6 July 1758, in Hume 1955, 202–205; BP MSS. REGG: E 139, Agostino Paradisi, *Lezioni di economia civile,* II, 134–135; De Jorio 1979, I, 5. On this problem see Porta and Scazzieri 1997.

264. Compare the historical understanding behind Smith 1976, I, 522–523, to Justamond 1798, III, 366, Goudar 1756, and Anonymous 1765, VI, 116. See also Genovesi 1777, II, 204, and Torres 1781, I, 109, on how Britain "gave the law" to Portugal, in addition to Pombal 1986, 76. See also Shaw 1998.

265. Hamilton 1795, 36. Emphasis added. See also Hamilton in Harper 2004, 135, and his "Federalist VI" and "Federalist VII," in Madison, Hamilton, and Jay 1987, 104–113.

266. Coxe 1787, 29–30. On Coxe see Cooke 1975. Similar examples are legion, but see for a contemporary historiographical discussion, De Jorio 1979, I, 1–44. On the difference between emulating real and "conjectural" history see McNamara 1998, 102. On the "realism" and "pragmatism" of political economy in the early republic, see still Johnson 1973.

267. De Jorio 1979, I, 40, 91–92, 103, 152, 166–171, 236–237, 245–246, 272–273.

268. See, for different perspectives on this, de Vries 1976; Lane 1979; Tilly 1990; Levy and Ali 1998; Vries 2002; Gerace 2004; Foucault 2007; Findlay and O'Rourke 2007; Cheney 2010.

269. Hont 2005, 267–322, and 2008, as well as Reinert 2010; see similarly Mably in Sonenscher 2008, 389, and Genovesi 1757–58, II, 22–23n, 189–190n, 248–249n.

270. See Gould 2003, 51, and Brown 2001, 96.

271. Anonymous 1765, IV, 110. See also de Vries 2008, 20–25.

272. Gibbon 1994, I, 83.

273. Hale 1781, 33. Emphasis added. Cf. Thucydides 5.85–113.

274. Reinert 2010.

275. In Wyatt 2005, 1–2.

276. See similarly Pomian 2005.

277. Soll 2009.

278. Bruni 1978, 146.

279. Bacon 1985, 78.

280. Girolamo Alberti to the Doge and Senate, 16 September 1672, CSP—Venetian, 37, 294, 282–283.

281. In Schui 2005, 68.

282. Verri 1939, 202.

283. Alessandro Verri, "Dei difetti della letteratura e di alcune loro cagioni," in IC, 543.

284. Koepp 1986; Yeo 2001, xiv–xv, 146–147, 243.

285. On which see Grafton 2009.

286. For a powerful statement see Melon 1736, 390–393; on which see Voltaire in Anonymous 1764 (but written 1738), 183; Diderot in Bouzinac 1970, 17. See also Ives 2003.

287. Kaplan 1976; on actual economic best sellers, see Carpenter 1975.

288. See similarly St. Clair 2004.

289. Pocock 1987, 20, 37.

290. Goethe and Carlyle 1887, 26, on which see Steiner 1998, 262.

2. Cary's *Essay on the State of England*

1. Pocock 1975; Eglin 1999; Liversidge 2000. The painting is Marlow's *Capriccio: St. Paul's and a Venetian Canal* (c. 1795), N06213, Tate Gallery, London. For a typical, if later Anglo-Venetian comparison, see Lockman 1750a, 7. An example of an anxious Venetian is UFEG ms. Ch. A, no. 217: *Relatione del Clarissimo M. Gio Micheli, ritornato Ambasciatore alla Regina d'Inghilterra.* On how England "copied" Italy see Braudel 1977, 66 among many others.

2. The best biographical sketches of Cary are Lane 1932, Sacks 1991, Morgan 2002, and Barry 2005. Cary does not appear in most of the famous histories of economic thought, among which are Bell 1953; Blanqui 1880; Ekelund and Hébert 1997; Ferguson 1950; Ingram 1919; Negishi 1989; Redman 1997; Robbins 1998; Roll 1953; Roncaglia 2001; Rothbard 1995; Routh 1989; Rubin 1979; Screpanti and Zamagni 1993; Staley 1989; Taylor 1960; Vaggi and Groenewegen 2003.

3. Letwin 1963, 235; Magnusson 1994, 116; Armitage 2000a, 163; Buck 1942, 59, 93–94; Johnson 1937, 267.

4. Viner 1937, 10, 21, 75; Appleby 1992, 43.

5. Schumpeter 1954, 197; Horsefield 1960, 44.

6. Schumpeter 1954, 197; Gunn 1969, 261. On Cary's free trade see Hont 2005, 228; Groenewegen 1994, 122; Haslam 2002, 139–140. On Cary's mercantilism see Thomas 1926, 69.

7. See the many entries in BRO K.R. Port Books for Bristol, e.g. for 1671; BRO College of Heralds, Funeral Certificates I. 24, 87v; BRO J/BRS/32, The Great White Book of Bristol, *Folio* 82 [1573]. On Cary's family see briefly Harrison 1919; Lane 1932. For a genealogical tree see Hall 1949, insert between 110 and 111.

8. Sacks 1991; Morgan 1993; Fissel 1991, 4. This was recognized in a petition signed by Cary, BRO Hall Book II, 487 (17 November 1691) and by those responsible for his French translation, see Gournay 2003, 382. Glass 1950 places Bristol's 20,000 inhabitants at roughly one-thirtieth of London.

9. Cruickshanks, Handley, and Hayton 2002, II, 209–210; Barry 1993, 193; Fissel 1991, 6.

10. See on these phenomena Hutchison 1988, 56; Ashcraft 1969, 744; Hoppit 2006.

11. McGrath 1955, x.

12. Cary's papers are kept in the untitled and haphazardly ordered folder BL Add. MS. 5540. For the specific references mentioned here see 19r–21v, 34r–35v; BRO Exchequer Queen's Remembrancer E 190/1140 no. 3; BRO Hall Book II, 461, 490–491, Hall Book III, 122; Calendar of Treasury Books, XIV, 6 June 1699, 379; XV, 26 April 1700, 333; BL Add. MS. 5540 19r–21v, 34r–35v. On the world of Atlantic merchants, see Rediker 1987 and Gauci 2004.

13. BRO Hall Book II, 114, 219–222; Apprent. List. 1/6/1672; "Burgess Book, 1662–89, 162. On Cary's apprentices, see Lane 1932, 24; BL Add. MS. 5540. On the "Glorious Revolution," see Pincus 2009.

14. E.g. Cary 1718, 40.
15. Cary 1695, 163–165; Cary 1719, 109, 117; Cary 1745, 110 and 118.
16. On English national identity at the time expressed in such terms, see Claydon and McBride 1998; Blanning 2001, 301.
17. BL Add. MS. 5540, 21v. On his argument for *"Liberty of Conscience"* see Cary 1695, 42–43.
18. BL Add. MS. 5540, 45; Cary 1695, A3; Cary 1718, 79.
19. John Cary's first letter to John Locke, 11 January 1696, in Locke 1976–89, V, 515. This was noticed by Locke, who thought it "a very civill letter," Locke to Edward Clarke, 12 April 1696, in Locke 1976–89, V, 603.
20. Cary 1718, 1. On "English liberties" and Protestantism in the period, see Pincus 1998b.
21. On such movements for social reform, see Bahlmann 1957; Hundert 1972; Curtis and Speck 1976, 45–61; Hayton 1990; Hunt 1999, 42; Gregg 2001.
22. Cary to Locke, 5 January 1697, in Locke 1976–89, V, 746. This is a recurring idiom in Cary's political vocabulary: Cary 1695, 49–50, 88, 91, 151; Cary 1696b, 8–9, 33; Cary to Locke, 11 January 1696, in Locke 1976–89, V, 516; Cary to Benjamin Coole, 24 November 1695, BL Add. MS 5540, 75. It was, however, well represented in his wider tradition, see among others Reynell 1674, 12; Petyt 1680, 8; N.C. 1697, 8; Locke to William Molyneux, 22 February 1697–98, in Locke 1976–89, VI, 7; Locke 1997, 342.
23. Calendar of Treasury Books, X, pt. II, 1694, 847. Echoes of this incident can be heard in Cary 1695, 28. On Cary's legal troubles in relation to international trade during times of war, see BL Add. MS. 5540, 27v–28r.
24. Hakluyt 1584, 36–44.
25. Cary 1696a; 1696b; 1696c; 1698a; 1698b; 1700a; 1700b; 1700c; 1704; 1717b.
26. BRO Hall Book III, 59–60, 62–64, three entries dated 17 and 21 January 1695.
27. Lane 1932.
28. On this council and its initial composition, see Lee 1939 and Sainty 1974, 28–37.
29. Cary to Locke, 9 May 1696, in Locke 1976–89, V, 634. See also Kelly 1980, 28, and Morgan 2002. Cary received less than 8 percent of the votes at the parliamentary election of 1698. The winning politicians—Robert Yate and Thomas Day—received roughly 31.5 and 27 percent of the votes, respectively. Calculations made from statistics in Cruickshanks, Handley, and Hayton 2002, II, 209; for short biographies of Day and Yate see III, 863–865, and V, 949–953.
30. Hall 1951.
31. Cary 1695, 85. For his alchemical treatise see his "Sundry Collections touching Gold & Silver, & ye Manner of Making Essays [Alloys]," BL Add. MS 5540, 10v–17r; for the astronomical observations see 112; for the curing of a horse's sore eye see 21. He also copied a cure for diabetes, 7v–8v.
32. This is a historiographical trope. See Paolo Sarotti to the Doge and the Senate of Venice, 8 November 1675, CSP—Venetian, 1675, 577, 474–476 and Dave-

nant 1771, IV, 389, among others. On English national identity in this context see Brewer 1988, 140.

33. On the war's economic origins see Clark 1954, 173. Pincus 1998b emphasizes its "multiconfessional" character, but Cary is an exception. On Williamite England and the "Protestant international" see Claydon 2007.
34. N.C. 1697, 2.
35. See, for the French case, Sonenscher 2007a.
36. Davenant 1695, 26–27. On Davenant see Casper 1930 and Waddell 1958. See, for similar statements about wealth and war, Trevers 1675, 52; Carter 1681, II, 2; Barbon 1690, A3r–v; Carew 1675, 1; Defoe 1730, 52, 54. See on this Pincus 1998a, 713–717.
37. Cary 1695, dedication.
38. Davenant 1695, 15; Davenant 1701. See similarly Fletcher 1997, 83–117. On "universal monarchy," see Pincus 1995 and Robertson 1995. On its shifting focus, see Claydon 2007, 136–140, 152–160.
39. For Cary's papophobia see 1695, 98; 1696a, 6; 1700b, 8.
40. Cary 1695, 31; see similarly Davenant 1695, 29.
41. Cary 1695, dedication. Cary drew on a wide variety of Locke's writings, such as his conceptualization of the body politic in 1988, 332. On this tradition see Kantorowicz 1957 and Skinner 1997.
42. Cary to Locke, 11 January 1696, in Locke 1976–89, V, 516. For a similar argument about eighteenth-century France, see Shovlin 2006, 11.
43. Cary 1719, 3.
44. Unlike, for example, Barbon 1690, A3r–v and later Hume 1994, 52.
45. Cary 1695, 151–152. For an allusion to Æsop see 85–86.
46. See the very similar (in many ways) Anonymous 1689c, 1–3, but also [Wellingborough 1650]; Willan 1670, 88; Taylor 1675, 78; Manton 1681, 1018; Pierce 1686, 603; Locke 1988, 291–292. See also Genesis 3:19 and St. Paul's letter to the Thessalonians 2, 3:10, used to justify the idea of "deserving poor" at the time, on which see Hindle 2004, 38. For other biblical references see Cary 1695, 90, 100.
47. Cary to Locke, 11 January 1695, and Locke to Cary, 2 May 1696, in Locke 1976–89, V, 515–516, 625–627. Tellingly, Locke argued that Latin was "necessary for a gentleman but useless to a merchant," in Grassby 1995, 181.
48. Cary 1695, 23–42, 48, 55–56, 61, 71, 91, 106.
49. Cary 1695, 1.
50. E.g. Anne Bradshaw in Shields 1990, 15; AST *Materie di Commercio,* 3 Categoria, Mazzo 3, no. 5, 1756, "Scritto datato dalla Segreteria di Guerra contenute diversi suggerimenti relativi al Commercio ne' Stati di S.M. . . . ," 12. On the classical roots of this way of justifying international trade, see Pagden 2003, 186.
51. Pincus 2009. See similarly Brewster 1695, iv, and earlier Anonymous 1641.
52. E.g. Cary 1695, 2; also 50–51.
53. E.g. Carter 1669, 2; Brewster 1695, i–iv. Cf. Serra 1613.
54. Pincus 2009, 373.

55. North 1691, preface. For hagiographies of North see McCulloch 1856, xii–xiv; Letwin 1963, 213; Wilson 1965, 184; Appleby 1978. On this revolt against earlier scholarship see Grafton 1991.

56. E.g. the self-propagandizing Barbon 1690, A4v–A5r; Barbon 1684; Barbon 1685, republished 1689.

57. Cary to Locke, 9 May 1696, in Locke 1976–89, V, 633–635; Bohun 1853, 131; see also the letter from an undecipherable sender to Cary and that from Cary to Thomas Long, 19 August 1696, in BL Add. MS. 5540, 74v and 76v, respectively; Locke to Cary, 2 May 1696, in Locke 1976–89, V, 625–627. On Cary as a "Great Projector" see Anonymous 1711, 12; Barry 2005.

58. Locke 1988, 276–277.

59. On Garcilaso's work, context, and historiographical tradition see Valcarcel 1995; MacCormack 2007.

60. de la Vega 1609, 7r–9v.

61. Baudoin 1633, 34–42.

62. Rycaut 1688, 5.

63. Locke 1988 277n; item 3058 in Harrison and Laslett 1965, 257. On translations of Garcilaso generally, see Garcés 2006.

64. Cary 1695, 4–7. On how money and exchange entered Cary's conjectural history see Monroe 1966, 81–83. Locke 1692, 34, had presented a similar synergy, but to another effect. Both seem inspired by the likes of Reynell 1674, 21, 48, echoed closely again in Locke 1692, 59–60, and drawn on in Locke 1997, 221–222.

65. Cary 1695, 75.

66. Locke 1988, 269; Rousseau 1997a.

67. On balance of trade theories, see Perrotta 1991; Finkelstein 2000.

68. Cary 1695, 164. See similarly Anonymous 1697b, 11. On chrysohedonism see Perrotta 2004.

69. Pincus 2009, 366–399, particularly 383.

70. Locke 1988, 296–297. Cary was thus particularly fond of *"Clockwork"* because they were "nothing but Art and Labour," see 1695, 2, 12, 22. Similarly, see Locke 1692, 42, and 1997, 323. Both probably drew on Petty 1683, 36–37. On the influence of this analysis see Hont 2005, 253n.

71. Cary 1695, 143–148.

72. Cary 1695, 145–147. See similarly Cary 1704, 10, perhaps drawing on Reynell 1674, 49, 86–87, on inventions, and Fortrey 1663, 27, on manufactures and ingenuity.

73. Cary 1695, 147; BRO 10531. On the Atlantic sugar industry at the time see Drayton 2002.

74. Cary 1695, 149–150.

75. Cary 1695, 150.

76. Cary 1695, preface. See similarly Anonymous 1689c, 9–10. Pagden 1995, 66–73, shows this became a classic criticism of Spanish imperialism.

77. John Cary, "An Abstract delivered Mr. Thru[p?] Attorney to Mr. Abraham E Hon and other the Merc.ts of Bristoll in the Suit w.th the King ab.t the Wollen Bay Irish Yarn, Showing how the Trade of England would receive prejudice

in the Woollen Manufactures by its paying [word crossed out] Duty as Worssed Yarn," BL Add. MS. 5540, 6v–7v.

78. Lane 1932 traces Cary's family's involvement in woolens to the fourteenth century. Locke 1991, II, 488–489, agreed on their importance, but they both relied on a venerable phraseology employed by May 1613, 1; Mun 1621, 48–49; Malynes 1622; Fortrey 1663; Carter 1669, 2; Reynell 1674; Petyt 1680; Barbon 1690; Charles Davenant to Lowndes, 4 April 1712, in Clark 1938, 57–59; Anonymous 1737, 43. For the same mythological reference see Anonymous 1647; W.S. 1656, 1; Carter 1669, 8; Trevers 1675, unpaginated introductory poems, 22; Carter 1681, II, 1, and, quoting Virgil, 20. See similarly foreign observers in Wyatt 2005, 22.

79. "Henry Martyn's Report to the Board of Trade," in Clark 1938, 62–69.

80. Morgan 1996, 33.

81. McCloskey 1994, 256 and 2009, 208. See similarly Mokyr 1985 and 2009, 163, 438.

82. Buchanan 1979, 236, on which see Reinert 2007, 109.

83. Perez 2002; Reinert 2007.

84. Rapp 1976, 139n; Sella 1968, 109–110.

85. Smith 1995b, 577.

86. Daudin, O'Rourke, and Prados de la Escosura 2008, 19.

87. Morgan 1996, 26–27.

88. Inikori 2002, 362; Ashworth 2007, 352.

89. Mokyr 2006, 269.

90. Cary 1695, 154–155. On England's fashion economy see Berg 2005. On social anxieties see Cowan 2005. Cary did, however, embrace tobacco, 1696b, 38. For arguments regarding the economic dynamics of fashion see Child 1693, 55; Barbon 1690, 15, 65–67; North 1691, 15. A critical view of such emulation was voiced by Locke 1692, 93, and Locke 1997, 271–272.

91. Cary's insistence on moral rectitude, close to Locke 1997, 296–297, marks a sharp distinction from authors like Mandeville. On this spectrum, see Baroncelli 1981.

92. Cary 1695, 156.

93. Cary 1695, 158.

94. Cary 1695, 158, 161–162.

95. Cary 1695, 163–165.

96. Dyer 1757, 98.

97. Cary 1695, 7; for terminological caveats see Skinner 2002, II, 368–413.

98. Parker 1648, 36, echoed by Hobbes 1651, 120; Bland 1659, 45–46; Coke 1675, 115; Anonymous 1678, 50. Later, see Anonymous 1737, 66–67. On Parker see Mendle 2003. On England's transition from decentralized to centralized imperialism, see Games 2008.

99. Worsley 1651, 9–12, emphasis added; see also Worsley 1652, 7. On Worsley and the Navigation Acts see Brenner 2003, 625–631, and Leng 2005. For the act see Parliament 1651.

100. Cary 1695, 49.

101. Cary 1696b, 30; Cary 1745, 87. This passage resonated in the literature on the subject, being quoted from Cary 1745 in Postlethwayte 1774, un-paginated entry for "Chamber of Commerce"; Mortimer 1774, 193; Levi 1849, 22.

102. Child had presented such lists, but insisted that a low interest rate was "the *Causa Causans* of all the other causes" of the wealth of nations, 1690, 9. For Cary, this was auxiliary. For similar lists see 1663; Reynell 1674; and Locke 1692.

103. Cary 1695, 23–42. See similarly Fortrey 1663, 28–29.

104. Cary 1745, 57.

105. See similarly his "Queries offered to the House of Commons against the East India Comp.a. by John Cary Merch.t. wch were spoken so in the House Anno 7° & 8° Guilelmi 3," BL Add. MS. 5540, 115v–116v. On the historical meanings of "free trade" see Seligman 1920, ix.

106. E.g. Cary's undated (but pre-1696) "An Abstract delivered Mr. Thru[p?] . . . ," BL Add. MS. 5540, 6v–7v.

107. For an unapologetically partisan account of these debates, see Thomas 1926.

108. BRO Hall Book II, 482 (10 November 1691), 487 (17 November 1691). See also his "Queries offered to the House of Commons . . . " BL Add. MS. 5540, 115v–116v. Cary also copied the "Bill for restraining the wearing of all Wrought Silks, Bengalls, & dyed, printed, & stained Calicoes, imported into the Kingdom of England" for his personal papers, BL Add. MS. 5540, 113v.

109. Anonymous 1692a, 75–76.

110. Cary 1695, 74–78; Cary 1712

111. Cary 1712; BRO Hall Book II, 461. On slavery in Bristol in the period, see Richardson 1986.

112. Cary to Thomas Day and Major Yate, 14. December 1695, BL Add. MS. 5540, 83.

113. Wm. Swimmer, Micha. Pope, John Cary, Wm. Andrews, Geo Mason &c to Sir Thomas Day and Major Yate, undated, BL Add. MS. 5540, 84. A similar fear is repeated in a letter to the same dated 21 December 1695, BL Add. MS. 5540, 87. Cary voiced an analogous fear in 1696b, 32.

114. Thomas Day and Robert Yate to Alderman Swymer, 23 December 1695, BL Add. MS. 5540, 88.

115. Cary to Benjamin Cole, 24 November 1695, BL Add. MS. 5540, 75. This dichotomy played a prominent part of the early modern cultural lexicon. See Cary 1695, 66, 152, 164; Cary to Benjamin Coole, 24 November 1695, BL Add. MS 5540, 75, and similarly Anonymous 1689c, 33, and, for the idea that *working* people were a nation's weath, Temple 1673, 2; Trevers 1675, 4–5; Firmin 1681; Davenant 1695, 111; Anonymous 1737, 42. On bees and commercial society see de Vries 2008, 62.

116. Cary 1719, 1; Cary 1745, introduction.

117. Cary 1695, dedication. This is the focal point of Cary 1745, 93, described more poetically in Cary to Long, 19 August 1698, BL Add. MS. 5540, 76.

118. See again his undated (but pre-1696) "An Abstract delivered Mr. Thru[p?] . . . ,"
     BL Add. MS. 5540, 6v–7v. This was a general problem in contemporary co-
     lonial debates; see Crowley 1993, 1–12.
119. Cary 1695, 11, 89, 113, 117, 128.
120. Cary 1695, 136; Cary 1745, 79–80.
121. On Edward III's protectionism and the origins of English "Woollen-
     manufacture" see Anonymous 1641, 9; Anonymous 1677, first page; Carter
     1669, 2–3; Carew 1675, 2; Trevers 1675, 3; Defoe 1730, 126–127.
122. Cary 1695, 119–120. See similarly Davenant 1771, IV, 40. On the theoretical
     history of "preemptive strikes" see Tuck 1999, 18–31.
123. Cary 1695, 132–136; Cary 1719, 79–84; Cary 1745, 79–84.
124. Cary 1695, preface.
125. Cary might have drawn on Sheridan 1677, 203–204, and Haines 1679a, 4.
     For an astute contrary statement, see the anonymous "Essay towards finding
     the balance of our whole trade annually from Christmas 1698 to Christmas
     1719," in Clark 1938, 69–150, particularly 75–76.
126. Fisher and Jûrica, 1977, 288; Tawney and Power 1924, II, 6.
127. Maffio Michiel to the Doge and Senate, 22 February 1603, in CSP—Venetian,
     9, 1592–1603, 1140, 536–537.
128. Giovanni Carlo Scaramelli to the Doge and Senate, 6 March 1603, CSP—
     Venetian, 9, 1592–1603, 1152, 548–549.
129. E.g. Carter 1669, 3. Cf. Grassby 1995, 211–212.
130. E.g. Berenberg (Jr.) to LM & PJ, 5 April 1672, and C. Bene to JD, 23 April
     1678, in Roseveare 1987, 345, 504.
131. Lawrence 1682, pt. 1, 9. On this see Armitage 2000b, 227. See, for a later
     and almost literal adaptation of this principle, ANF K/907, no. 14: "Mèmoire
     sur les moyens d'augmenter la navigation et le commerce, les revenus du Roi,
     et les droits de l'amiraté" [1744], 12–[13]. For Davenant's statement see BL
     Harleian MS. 1223, 184r–188v, which are paginated internally 1–10; quota-
     tion from 186r, 5.
132. Davenant 1695, 24; Nye 2007, 23; a stance satirized in Fletcher 1997, 201.
133. Cary 1695, 132. See similarly Carter 1669, 2.
134. Barbon 1690, 77–79.
135. Cary 1695, 33.
136. Anonymous 1761, pt. 1, 30. On the mechanisms of this public debt see Car-
     ruthers 1999, 71–91.
137. Anonymous 1761, pt. 1, 59–73.
138. Clapham 1944, I, 19.
139. Brewer 1988, 34, 114.
140. Brewer 1988; O'Brien 2002; Ashworth 2003; Findlay and O'Rourke 2007,
     256–257.
141. Cary 1695, 140. On this Whig mantra, see Pincus 2009, 388–389.
142. On this topos see Macdonald 2003.
143. Echoes of the old order are nonetheless present in his insistence that "Ser-
     vants" and "People of mean Qualities" were not to bear arms, Cary 1695,
     162. See similarly Locke et al. 1670, 24, reprinted in Locke 1997, 181.

144. Kleer 2004, 534.
145. Kleer 2004, 535, citing Kelly's introduction to Locke 1991, 116. For context see Wennerlind 2004.
146. Cary 1696a, 6. Emphasis added.
147. On Locke and the recoinage, see Laslett 1957, particularly 378; Finkelstein 2000, 150–155. On the recoinage see Horsefield 1960; Kwarteng 2000.
148. Cary to Locke, 11 January 1696, in Locke 1976–89, V, 515.
149. Locke to Cary, 2 May 1696, in Locke 1976–89, V, 626. Emphasis added. This said, Locke failed to mention Cary in his 1703 reading list for gentlemen, 1997, 348–355.
150. Locke 1692, 87.
151. Cary to Locke, 24 October 1696, and Cary to Locke, 5 January 1697, in Locke 1976–89, V, 710 and 746, respectively. De Beer overlooked that Cary sent Locke two *different* pamphlets on the public debt. They are items 611 and 612 in Locke's library, Harrison and Laslett 1965, 102.
152. Cary 1696c, 4.
153. On alchemy and "infinity" in contemporary monetary theory see Finkelstein 2000; Wennerlind 2003, 234–236. Cary was familiar with the alchemical tradition, but seems to have ignored this element of it. See his "Sundry Collections . . . ," which concludes with a list of foreign coins, their supposed values, and their real values according to gold/silver content, BL Add. MS. 5540, 10v–17r.
154. Cary 1696b, dedication, followed with a quote from Juvenal: "Dulcis odor lucri ex re qualibet." For this, something like the merchant handbook Davies 1656, 152, is a more plausible source than a Latin original.
155. Cary 1696b, 8–11.
156. Locke 1692, 4.
157. Locke 1692, 32. On his anachronisms see Finkelstein 2000, 153.
158. On the political aims of his economic policy see Viano 1960, 189. For Locke's manuscripts on natural law see Locke 1997, 79–133. On their economics see Hutchison 1988, 60–73.
159. Hall 1949, insert between 110 and 111; Hall 1951.
160. Cary 1696c, 2.
161. Cary 1696b, 1; perhaps echoing Toland 1695, 19–22.
162. Cary 1696b, 26–27; 1696c, 2.
163. Cary 1696b, 8, 28–29, 36, 40.
164. Cary 1696c, 7. Emphasis added.
165. Cary 1696c, 7–8; 1717b, 15; and also the editor's introduction to 1745, xi.
166. Locke may well have avoided the issue in memory of Shaftesbury's freezing of repayments during the Anglo-Dutch war in 1672; see Viano 1960.
167. Hont 2005, 325–353.
168. Cary 1717b, 6, 9–10.
169. Cary 1717b, 11–12.
170. Cary 1700a, 4, 9. On this issue see Grassby 1995, 283–286.
171. On Cary and the Society for Reformation of Manners, see Slack 1998, 106–109.

172. If not representative of Weber's 1930 "Protestant work ethic," Cary's efforts fit the "petty-bourgeois ethic" discussed in Burke 1996b, 213. On contemporary work ethics see Grassby 1995, 271–301.

173. Butcher 1932, 1; Butcher 1972, 3. On Fletcher and slavery see Cambiano 2000, 321–322. See similarly Raeff 1983, 32; Burke 1996b, 243.

174. On the idea of "Foreign Paid Incomes" see Johnson 1932; Perrotta 1988; Perrotta 1991; Magnusson 1994, 134–138. The efforts of the Bristol MPs to ensure the implementation of Cary's proposals reconciled the Merchant Venturers of Bristol and their parliamentary representatives, see Cruickshanks, Handley, and Hayton 2002, II, 212.

175. Anonymous 1697b, 13.

176. Child 1690; 1693; 1698; e.g. Haines 1679b; on Firmin, see Anonymous 1698e; Sherwin 1950. Firmin suggested woolworking for the idle to Locke, [8 or 9 April 1697?], in Locke 1976–89, V, 84. On the legacy on which Firmin built, see Willen 1988, 564–565. On these themes see Davis 1980; Davison et al. 1992; Slack 1998.

177. Mason 1991, 270–271. Locke 1997, 182–198, 326–328; see similarly Davenant 1695, 142. Cary sent Locke the workhouse's act of incorporation, see Locke 1976–89, V, 635n. Cf. Tully 1993, 237.

178. Cary 1700a, 4, 9. Cary generalized from these findings in 1700b. His account was republished, among other places, in Eden 1797, I, 275n–282n. For context see Burke 1996b, 207–286.

179. Cary 1700a, 10. Cary's poor worked relatively short hours. Firmin wrote of "16 howers" to Locke, [8 or 9 April 1697?], in Locke 1976–89, V, 84. See also the general scenario in Mendelson and Crawford 1998, 262. On reformers and the rise of literacy, see Burke 1996b, 252. On the relations between reformers and reformees in Bristol, see Fissel 1991, 81.

180. Cary 1700a, 15.

181. Cary 1695, 29.

182. Cary 1695, 150–170; 1700a, 15; 1700b; 1700c.

183. Cary 1700b. His targets were the likes of Anonymous 1677.

184. On early European *settlements* in the area see Forbes 2007, 159–167.

185. Faragher 2005, 99–101.

186. Pritchard 2004, 353.

187. "Petition of the Merchants of Bideford to the King," CSP—Colonial, XV, 12 November 1696, 211. See also 211 and 305–306.

188. "Memorial of Sir Robert Robinson to the King," CSP—Colonial, XV, 23 November 1696, 222.

189. "Council of Trade and Plantations to the King," CSP—Colonial, XV, 3 December 1696, 235, and J. Ellis to William Popple, 21 January 1697, 314; Richard Usticke to William Popple, CSP—Colonial, XV, 396, 12 March 1697; Council of Trade and Plantations to Secretary Trumbull, CSP—Colonial, XV, 452–453, 17 April 1697.

190. "Memorial of the Merchants of Bristol, trading to Newfoundland, to Council of Trade and Plantations," CSP—Colonial, XV, 11 February 1697, 359.

191. For Gibsone's correspondence with the War Office, both before and after his stay in Newfoundland, see BL Add. Ms. 33278, 19, 58, 60, 66–82. See also BL Stowe 463, Journals of M. Richards 1696–1700, XVII, "Journal from London to Newfoundland"; Morgan 1932; Murray 1951; Pritchard 2004.

192. J. Burchett to William Popple, 19 April 1697, CSP—Colonial, XV, 453. See similarly Council of Trade and Plantations to Secretary Trumbull, 28 January 1697, CSP—Colonial, XV, 337; William Popple to William Hammond and John Cary, 20 April 1697, CSP—Colonial, XV, 454.

193. "List of Ships of the Royal Navy" presented to the House of Commons by the Lords Commissioners of the Admiralty, Journals of the House of Commons, XII, 21 December 1698, 361–364.

194. Journal of General Assembly of Massachusetts, 26 May 1697, CSP—Colonial, XV, 493–494; Colonel Gibsone to Council of Trade and Plantations, 28 June 1697, CSP—Colonial, XV, 522–524. See similarly Lieutenant Governor Stoughton to Council of Trade and Plantations, 30 September 1697, CSP—Colonial, XV, 624–626.

195. Pritchard 2004, 351.

196. Calculations based on Pope 2004, 38; Brewer 1988, 34; Woodward 2002, 177.

197. James Vernon to Council of Trade and Plantations, 19 October 1697, CSP—Colonial, XV, 641. The full account is given by Gibsone's narrative of the expedition, CSP—Colonial, XVI, 39–42.

198. Pritchard 2004, 326–333; De la Matta Rodriguez 1979; Morgan 1932; Anonymous 1740, 829; BL Stowe 463, Journals of M. Richards 1696–1700, XVII, "Journal from London to Newfoundland," 15–16.

199. Colonel Gibsone to Council of Trade and Plantations, 28 June 1697, CSP—Colonial, XV, 523.

200. Lieutenant Governor Stoughton to Council of Trade and Plantations, 30 September 1697, CSP—Colonial, XV, 625.

201. For the correspondence relating to Cary's schemes for Newfoundland, see CSP—Colonial, XV, 15 May 1696–31 October 1697, 596–597, 705, 729.

202. John Cary and Edwd Hacket to Sir Thomas Day and Major Yate, BL Add. MS. 5540, 78. See similarly Wm. Swimmer, Micha. Pope, John Cary, Wm. Andrews, Geo Mason &c to Sir Thomas Day and Major Yate, undated, 84.

203. Wm. Swimer, Wm. Daines, Geo. Mason, Jno. Cary, Jno. Swimer, Wm. Andrews to Sir Thomas Day and Major Yate, 21. December 1695, BL Add. MS. 5540, 87.

204. Thomas Day and Robert Yate to Alderman Swymer, 23 December 1695, BL Add. MS. 5540, 88.

205. Kearney 1959, 484, argued that "for practical purposes, the attack on the woolen industry of Ireland may be said to have been launched by the Bristol economist, John Cary." For antecedents, see Armitage 2000b.

206. Cary 1698a, 3–4.

207. Fitzmaurice 2003, 35–39; Canny 1973. On Ireland as a "laboratory" of empire, see Ohlmeyer 2004.

208. Ohlmeyer 2000.
209. Carter 1669, 18; Temple 1673, 10; Yarranton 1677, 101–103; Trevers 1675, 21–22. On these debates see also Hely-Hutchinson 1779, 30–31, and Woodfall 1785, 55. For their development see Kearney 1959; Kelly 1980; Hont 2008. Bills prohibiting the export of Irish wool to the continent were venerable institutions, though not always enforced, see Anonymous 1674, 1.
210. Armitage 2000a, 151, and 2000b, 229. On Petty's Irish policies see McCormick 2009.
211. Against it being "bloodless," see Anonymous 1689a and Hayton 1991, 186, quoting William III on 187.
212. Sydney 1692, 2. As Anonymous 1688, 4, put it, William III "is come with a Resolution to have the Government settled on its true Basis." On Irish optimism following the revolution see Israel 1991, 24.
213. E.g. Cocks 1996, 34.
214. Kelly 2000.
215. Anonymous 1697a, 4, 8.
216. E.g. Anonymous 1697a, 19; reprinted as Anonymous 1698b, 10; Anonymous 1698c, 21.
217. Kelly 1980, 34; Kelly 2000, 86–87.
218. Simms 1982.
219. William Molyneux to John Locke, 19 April 1698, in Locke 1976–89, VI, 376. See also Clement 1698, 5.
220. Clement 1698, unpaginated *Epistle;* Cary 1698b, 101; Davenant 1771, II, 240–250.
221. Cobbett 1812–20, V, 1181–1182; CSP—Domestic, IX, 25 October 1698, 409; *Journal of the House of Commons,* XII, 21 May 1698, 281, 22 June 1698, 324–327, 23 June 1698, 328, 24 June 1698, 329, 27 June 1698, 331.
222. Kelly 2000, 104; CSP—Domestic, IX, 21 and 24 May, 1698, 261–263.
223. Molyneux 1698, 153.
224. Molyneux 1698, 115. On this dynamic see Pocock 1957, 188–238; Kelly 2000, 91, and 2005; Hont 2005, 227. On Molyneux's work from the perspective of a union that failed to happen, see Hill 1995.
225. Pocock 1957, 235; Laslett's introduction to Locke 1988, 67–79.
226. Kelly 2005, 338.
227. Molyneux 1698, 24, 46, 58.
228. Molyneux 1698, 33–36; on this see Locke 1988, 384–397. I owe this reading to Kelly 2005.
229. William Molyneux to John Locke, 26 September 1696, in Locke 1976–89, V, 704; Temple 1673, 7, had argued similarly.
230. Molyneux 1698, 17–18.
231. Nicholson 1724, 138. The immediate replies were Atwood 1698; Cary 1698b; Leslie 1698; Clement 1698.
232. *Post Boy,* London, 5 July 1698, iss. 495, r. The same news was repeated in iss. 496.
233. Cary 1695, 89, 101, discussed in Heckscher 1994, II, 314.
234. Cary 1695 90, 100.

235. Cary 1695, 93. This would also make Ireland more "secure," 96. On Irish wool see similarly Cary 1696a, 35.

236. Cary 1695, 109–110. This division of textiles between England and Ireland was a common trope. See Temple 1673, 12–13; Locke to William Molyneux, 10 January 1698, in Locke 1976–89, VI, 296; Anonymous 1698d, 12; Anonymous 1698f, 7, 15.

237. Cary 1698b, 21; Molyneux 1698, e.g. "proof," 20, 28, 58, 89, 150; "testimonium," 11, 163; "testifying," 12; "evident," 150.

238. Cary 1698b, 10, 127. His papers in the British Library include "A Breviate of the proper method for electing officers in the City of Bristoll," which demonstrates his familiarity with the city's legal history, BL Add. MS. 5540, 37v–42v.

239. Nicholson 1724, 139.

240. Cary 1695, 133.

241. Cary 1698b, 4.

242. Hamilton 1783, 251.

243. Molyneux 1698, 39; William Molyneux to John Locke, 15 March 1698, in Locke 1976–89, VI, 349; Locke to Edward Clarke, 30 May; 1698, in Locke 1976–89, VI, 410.

244. Laslett's introduction to Locke 1988, 15.

245. For perspectives on his paradoxical stance see Keynes 1936, 343; Laslett 1957, 371; Finkelstein 2000, 147.

246. Locke 1997, 170; 1670, 11; 1988, 408, on which see Goldie's introduction to Locke 1997, xxiv. On Locke and America see Arneil 1996; Armitage 2004. Hallmark 1998 considers Locke's Carolina a full civil society but ignores its economic elements. Contemporaries like Amy 1682, 35, emphasized Carolina's continuing lack of manufacturing.

247. On Locke's work on Virginia, see his *Some of the Chief Grievances of the Present Constitution of Virginia*, BLO Locke MSS e.9, 7, on which see Ashcraft 1969. The manuscript was edited by Hartwell, Blair, and Chinton 1727, on which see Bain 1971. See particularly 3–4, 11–12, and 17–19 of the printed edition for Locke's economic proposals, and compare to Locke 1988, 290.

248. Locke 1997, 252–259. See similarly his note on 270–271.

249. On Locke's work on the Board of Trade in the case of Ireland see Laslett 1957.

250. Clement 1698, 14, 30–32.

251. Leslie 1698, 3.

252. Atwood 1698, 210–211. On his problems with the "fellow anti-Filmerian John Locke" see Ludington 2000, 250.

253. Cary 1698b, 94.

254. Cary 1698b, 103.

255. Cary 1695, 68, 105–106, 113, 128.

256. Cary 1695, 70. For the erudite tradition of interpreting this trope, see Stacey 2007, 46–52.

257. Cary to Edmund Bohun, 31 January 1695–96, in Bohun 1853, 135.

258. On the debates over power or plenty, see Magnusson 1994. On their relation to imperialism, see Semmel 1993, 2.

259. Cary to Long, 19 August 1698, BL Add. MS. 5540, 76.

260. Cary to Bohun, 31 January 1695–96, in Bohun 1853, 135.

261. Cary 1695, 71, 98. See also Cary to Long, 19 August 1696, BL Add. MS. 5540, 76. Very similar arguments, also related to the Hobbesian mantra of submission for protection, appear in Anonymous 1698d, 23; Anonymous 1698f, 7, 15; Cox 1698, 17; and Atwood's 1698 reply to Molyneux, 196, 208, 214. On Whig uses of this Hobbesian argument see Goldie 1977, 570; Skinner 2002, II, 209–237, 238–263.

262. Cary 1718, 1; Cary 1698b, 96.

263. Cary 1698b, 94. Cf. Leslie 1698, 3.

264. Cox 1749, 9–10.

265. Anonymous 1698a, 50.

266. Cox 1698, 9, 16.

267. Edmund Bohun to John Cary, 2 January 1695–96, in Bohun 1853, 131. On Bohun see Goldie 1977. Bohun's papers contain numerous pamphlets on the Irish and Scottish parliaments, see CUL Sel. 3. 230238.

268. On which see Pocock 1999–2005, II, and O'Brien 1997.

269. Edmund Bohun to John Cary, 18 January 1695–96, in Bohun 1853, 132–135. Bohun and Cary may both have relied on Anonymous 1689c, preface 2Av. A similar argument to Bohun's was voiced by North 1691, viii. On such laissez-faire arguments see Letwin 1963 and Appleby 1976, 507. But even "libertarian" economic arguments could be deeply bellicose; see Anonymous 1737, 55–56.

270. See, for a similar historiographical point, Cheney 2010, 11–13.

271. Edmund Bohun to John Cary, 18 January 1695–96, in Bohun 1853, 132–135. See for a similar argument about manufacturing and civility, Anonymous 1698d, 12.

272. Cary to Bohun, 31 January 1695–96, in Bohun 1853, 136.

273. Davenant 1771, I, 99; Machiavelli 1971, 295. On Davenant's Machiavellianism see Pocock 1975; Multamäki 1999; and Hont 2005, 185–266.

274. Davenant 1771, II, 236, 247–248, 254 (emphasis added), 257. The anonymous marginalia appear in II, 236, in the copy in my private collection.

275. Davenant 1771, II, 259. Either Waddell's 1958, 288, verdict regarding Davenant's mercenary tendencies was right, or the Irish case led him to reconsider his entire policy worldview.

276. The anonymous marginalia appear in Davenant 1771, IV, 388, in the copy in my private collection. Cf. Machiavelli 1971, 262.

277. Anonymous c. 1696b. It has gone unnoticed that their argument sketched out Martyn 1701, on which see Hont 2005, 246–258.

278. Anonymous c. 1696b, 2.

279. Anonymous c. 1696b, 3; Anonymous c. 1696a, 1.

280. Anonymous c. 1696a, 1.

281. As summarized in Cary 1696d, 1.

282. North 1691, 14. See a similar argument empowered by a Cary-like technological insight in Martyn 1701.

283. Cary 1695, 135, had already attacked such arguments. See also Reinert 2007, 8.

284. Cary 1696d, 1–2.

285. Girolamo Alberti to the Doge and Senate, 16 September 1672, in CSP—Venetian, XXXVII, 282–283.

286. E.g. Anonymous 1689c, 9–10; Locke 1692, 116.

287. Cary 1695, 51. Even monopolies *could* be fruitful, 86–87.

288. Cary 1696d, 3. On the difference between commercial republics and nation-states at the time, see Hont 2005, 185–266. Cary's argument was echoed in Etienne de Silhouette's 1747 manuscript "Observations sur les finances, le commerce, et la navigation d'Angleterre," in Cheney 2010, 34. He might have encountered Cary's work in London.

289. Cary 1696d, 4.

290. Kearney 1959; Kelly 1980; Sundell 2002.

291. ASG Archivio Segreto, busta 2275, Inghilterra anni 1664–99, mazzo 3, Lettere del M.tro Giustiniano, e dell'Agente Viceti Alferini, al Governo di Genova, [22?] October 1698.

292. Berg 2005, 78–79. On the organization of England's customs system in the period, see Hoon 1968; Ashworth 2003.

293. Simms 1956, 118–119.

294. Cary 1704, 6. See similarly CSP—Domestic, III, 104, and Locke to Molyneux, 10 January 1698, in Locke 1976–89, VI, 296, on which see Kearney 1959, 489.

295. Cary 1704, 7, revisited in 1717b, 14.

296. Harris 1998, 539; Cullen 1968, 45.

297. Cary 1704, 10–14.

298. Bartlett 1998, 256.

299. E.g. Cary 1718, 47.

300. Cary 1698b; Cary 1718, iii. He uses variations of "Proof" on 8, 58, 114, 119, 120, and 121. For variations of "Argument" see 15, 32, 35, 38, 46, 75, 103, 111, 115, 117, 119–124, 127. For "Testimony" see 32 and 82. Note also words like "Evidence" on 32, "witness" on 81, and "truth" on 104. For "evidence" see Cary 1718, 20, 21. For "proof" see Cary 1718, 19, 43. On the evolution of this terminology see Serjeantson 1999. On contemporary legal thought and the "culture of fact" see Shapiro 2000.

301. Cary 1718, 2. See similarly Cary 1698b, 68.

302. Cary 1718, 43; see similarly Tucker in Armitage 2004, 620; Hume 1994, 7, 9.

303. For "evidence" see Cary 1717a, 81; 1719, 81; 1745, 81. For "proof" see Cary 1717a, 94; Cary 1719, 94; Cary 1745, dedication, 93.

304. Cary 1718, 28.

305. Cary 1717a, 2. This was noted by Magnusson 1999, 142.

306. Locke 1690, 14, and passim; Child 1694, 108; Hoock, Jeannin, and Kaiser 1991–2001.

307. Reinert 2007, 88; Johns 2009, 20–21, 59–82.

308. Sprat 1667, 67, discussed in Klein 1997, 25–53.

309. Petty 1687; Gregory King, "Natural and Politicall Observations and Conclusions on the State and Condition of England, 1696," BL Harleian Mss. 1898; Davenant 1771. On "political arithmetick" see McCormick 2009.

310. Shapin 1996.

311. E.g. Dobbs 1991; Osler 2000; Findlen 2000.

312. See Cary's "Sundry Collections . . . ," BL Add. MS. 5540, 10v–17r.

313. For the perspective of the *Wunderkammern,* see Smith and Findlen 2001.

314. Anonymous 1706, 305.

315. Cary 1717a, 20, 47, 90; 1719, 16, 47, 90; 1745, 20, 47, 91. Cary had already used the word "Experiment" in 1696b, 12.

316. On these issues see Dear 1995, 124–150; Shapin and Schaffer 1985, 22–27; Burke 2000, 15.

317. Dear 2009, 164.

318. See Newball 1750, 33–34; Hay 1751, 12–13.

319. Cary 1717a, iv–ix; Cary 1745, unpaginated advertisement. On Osborne see Raven 2007, 217–219.

320. Cary to Locke, 28 November 1696, in Locke 1976–89, V, 726; Hall 1951. For Cary's change of title see 1719. On the size of the gentry, see Laslett 2005, 27.

321. Shapin 1994, 42–64.

322. Heckscher 1994, II, 24–25; Buck 1942, 28–30. Cf. Wiles 1974; Andrew 2002. See also Cary to Bohun, 31 January 1695–96, in Bohun 1853, 132–136.

323. For a typical "*popish* conspiracy" see Anonymous 1689b.

324. Cary 1695, 140. On this "French Model" in England, see Berg 2005, 94. For England emulating France, see Defoe 1737, 300–301; Voltaire 1733, 222. Colbert's policies had been brought to England already by Wase's 1671 translation of Priolo, 434. For encouragements to emulate Colbert see Sheridan 1677, 211; Anonymous 1684, 96. See also Phillips 1690, 51, 56. Cf. Packard 1923.

325. Tuck 1999; Pocock 1999–2005, III; Armitage 2002.

326. Gérando 1839, I, xix, and Kelly 1980, 28, mention usages of Cary, but see also N.C. 1697, 19; Bohun to Cary, 2 January 1695–96, in Bohun 1853, 131; Locke to Cary, 2 May 1696, in Locke 1976–89, V, 625. Cary himself contributed to the spreading of his works, see Bohun to Cary, 31 July 1696, in Bohun 1853, 138. For his readership in the colonies see Cary to Long, 19 August 1696, BL Add. MS. 5540, 76. See also important engagements in Postlethwayte 1757b, 142; Postlethwayte 1774, entries for "Assurance" and "Chamber of Commerce." See also Weskett 1781, unpaginated list of "authorities" relied on. For probable echoes see Seton 1705, 57; Janssen 1713; Gee 1738; Defoe 1737, 251.

327. Cock 1725, 163, 1s (shilling); Molini 1765, 51, 1717 edition 1s; White 1766a, 106, 1s; Carter 1768, 63, 2s; White 1770, 107, 1s; White 1772, 121, 1s; Davis 1785, 200, 1s and 1s 6d (pence); Payne and Son 1788, 139, 1s; Robson and Clarke 1789, 172, 1s 6d; Thomas 1793, 90, 6d; Arrowsmith

1800?, 72, 1s. It was bound with other pamphlets including one by Hobbes for 2s 6d in Davis 1771, 66, who also sold the *Essay*'s chapter on the East India Trade, 44, 1s.

328. Anonymous 1717?, 106; Sare 1740, 33, 1s 6d; Wilson 1788?, 55, 1s 6d; Egerton 1793, 204, 2s.

329. Osborne 1735, 150; Osborne 1761, 236, 1s 6d and 1s; Osborne 1745b, 328, on which see Raven 2007, 194; Osborne and Shipton 1754, 207, but see also their 1756 catalogue; Hildyard 1751, 379, 2s; Whiston 1754, 106, 2s 6d; White 1766a, 106 , 2s; White 1766b, 107, 2s; White 1771, 124, 2s; White 1774, 135, 2s; White 1775, 155, 2s; White 1780, 173, 2s; Whiston and White 1762?, 129, 2s; Robson 1782, 110, 1s 6d; Payne and Son 1788, 139, 2s; Tupman 1790, 19, 1s; Todd 1792, unpaginated, 1s 6d; Cooke 1793?, 59, 1s 6d; Binns 1795?, 72, 9d; Binns 1797?, 76, 1s; Fletcher and Hanwell Booksellers 1798?, 77, 1s, 6d.

330. Olsen 1999, 198–201.

331. Whiston 1754, 34, 106, 115.

332. Cooke 1793?, 54, 55, 59, 65, 101.

333. Raven 2007, 240.

334. See on these patterns Hoon 1968; Wright 1986, 156–157; O'Brien 1998; Ashworth 2003; Berg 2005, 95, 189; Findlay and O'Rourke 2007; Nye 2007; Pincus 2009, 384–385.

335. Lévi-Strauss 1995, 14.

336. Thomson 1740, 43. On Thornhills's ceilings, see Armitage 2000, 167–168.

337. In Oz-Salzberger 1995, 48.

338. On this tension see Robertson 2005, 358; Soll 2009.

339. Habermas 1989, 51.

340. Jon Cary and Edwd Hacket to Sir Thomas Day and Major Yate, 2 December 1695, BL Add. MS 5540, 78.

341. See similarly Barry 2005, 206.

342. Cary 1719, ix.

3. Butel-Dumont's *Essai sur l'État du Commerce d'Angleterre*

1. Voltaire 1733, 109. See also Casanova 1997, IX, 161.

2. Anonymous 1747, I, 105–106, II, 344–345, as well as Le Blanc 1754, vii. For an earlier statement regarding the comparative advantages of being an island, see ASG Archivio Segreto, busta 2276, Inghilterra anni 1700–1703, mazzo 4, Inghilterra 1700 orpoi e 1702, lettere orig.li del S.r Viceti Agente Al Ser.mo Governo di Genova, 13 December 1700.

3. In Sonenscher 2007a, 115. On "fashion's empire," see Sonenscher 2008, 77–101.

4. See, from different perspectives, Schui 2005, 7; Cheney 2010.

5. On Anglomania see Grieder 1985 and Buruma 1999; on Anglophobia see Acomb 1950.

6. d'Argenson 1902, II, 11 February 1750, 95. See also the earlier Anonymous 1700b, 35.

7. Anonymous 1747, I, 296. Shovlin 2006, 6–7, makes a similar point.

8. Anonymous 1689c, 29–30.

9. For a revolutionary reevaluation of the subsistence history of the Industrial Revolution, see Muldrew 2011.

10. Barbon 1690, 42, and similarly Tucker 1749, 9; Montesquieu's son's translation of Gee, Jean-Baptiste Secondat Montesquieu 1749, 202. For an exception see Carter 1669, 2.

11. d'Argenson 1902, I, 243; Kaplan 1976, 6.

12. Linguet 1777–92, V, 429–450, on which see Levy 1980, 84–127; Voltaire 1733, 89. This obsession united the extremes of the political spectrum, from Anonymous 1700b, 39, to La Bruyère in Rothkrug 1965, 239–240.

13. d'Argenson 1902, II, 144, 151, 162, 172, 190, 198–199, 212–214, 228.

14. d'Argenson 1902, II, 145, and I, 242. On the cultural and symbolic "empire" of bread in France and its policing, see Kaplan 1976; 1984; 1996, particularly 1–60.

15. LaCapra 2001.

16. Kaplan 1982. On the dearth of 1751–52 see 47–51. This was an anomalous year; see Kaplan 1996, 550.

17. d'Argenson 1902, II, 151, 159. On apocalyptic political prophecies at the time, see Sonenscher 2007a, 28–32.

18. See on this climate Anonymous 1790, I, 223–238.

19. For context see Collins 2009, 222–225.

20. Murphy 1997, 331. See also Pritchard 2004, 25–26; Sonenscher 2007a, 108–120; Sonenscher 2008, 261.

21. For a typical statement see Anonymous 1737, 15.

22. North 1691, 15; Cary 1695, 154–155, 162.

23. Mandeville 1988, on which see Hundert 1994 and 1995; Robertson 2005, 260–280.

24. Smith 2002, 63, 73–76.

25. Anonymous 1790, I, 228–229.

26. See generally de Vries 2008, 44–45.

27. See on this debate Barry 1994; Hont 2006.

28. Théré 1998.

29. Shovlin 2006, 2.

30. Perrot 1984, 95.

31. Laffemas 1597, 17, and 1602, 123. On this topos in Montchrétien and Colbert, see Rothkrug 1965, 7–85.

32. On the complexity of Colbert's stance see Kaplan 1996, 158. On Enlightenment Colbertism see Minard 1998 and 2000. Similarly, Cary was not received as antiagriculture merely because he was promanufacture; e.g. Societé d'Agriculture, de Commerce et des Arts de Bretagne 1760, I, 9–10, 36, 114, 138, 244.

33. Kanter 1966, 323–324; on his influence see Hont 2006 and Sonenscher 2008.

34. Fénelon 1994, 297; Hont 2005, 24–29, and 2006, 383–387; Shovlin 2006, 21, 28. There exists a literature on Fénelon and Physiocracy that insists that

they were right in their criticisms of Colbert on this point. As Rothkrug 1965, 243–244 and Kaplan 1976 have demonstrated, it is entirely misleading.

35. Fénelon 1994, 259.
36. Anonymous 1700b, 7, 17, 45.
37. Hundert 1995.
38. Rothkrug 1965; Reinert 2006a.
39. Contemporaries too noted the differences between the oceanic and agricultural paths to subsistence safety. See Lockman 1750a, 4. On such Braudelian "geographic possibilism," see Marino 2002, 17, and similarly Cheney 2010, 73.
40. Rousseau 1997a, 84, against which see Voltaire in Anonymous 1764 (written 1738), 185. On Rousseau's "virtue," see Rosenblatt 1997, 43.
41. d'Argenson 1902, I, 299; II, 100, 151, 285, 335, 337.
42. d'Argenson 1902, I, 6, 186; II, 9, 196, 212, 244. For a similar statement see Cerati to Galiani, 17 December 1755, in Galiani and Cerati 2008, 99–101. On the Anti-Gallicans see A True Anti-Gallican 1758; Anonymous 1756d; Anonymous 1757. On outrage at English economic policies in France, see Acomb 1950, 8–9.
43. "Arguments en faveur de la liberté du commerce des grains," *Journal économique*, May 1754, 64–79, reprinted in Klotz 1995, 45–54, 54.
44. On the importance of this battle for political philosophy see Rahe 2005; Claydon 2007, 125–132.
45. Resende-Santos 2007, 81.
46. Anonymous 1747, I, 15, and again II, 60. On early French emulation of English economic thought and practice see Bonno 1948, 50–52, 149–155.
47. In Rahe 2005, 51–52.
48. Yeo 2001, 155–156.
49. Voltaire 1733, 51–53, 59. On the Fénelonianism of this phrase see Sonenscher 2007a, 102.
50. Voltaire 1733, 69, 71.
51. Mantoux 1907.
52. Voltaire 1733, 54–55, 67, 72, 88, 222.
53. Condorcet 1791, I, 47.
54. Montesquieu 1989, xliii, 18–19, 310, 602.
55. Montesquieu 1989, 338, 389–390.
56. Cf. e.g. Spector 2001, 8–12, and 2004, 195.
57. Sonenscher 2007a, 135.
58. Montesquieu 1989, 343–347.
59. Montesquieu does not mention "England" as the subject of this passage but hints of it in 1989, 156–166, 325. For the marginalia see Voltaire 1979–94, V, 748, and similarly 757. On England in Montesquieu's thought see Landi 1981.
60. Montesquieu 1989, 327.
61. Montesquieu 1989, 328–329, 362; see also Montesquieu 2003, 441–442. Cf. Spector 2004, 195.
62. Montesquieu 1989, 391.

63. Montesquieu 1989, 352.
64. E.g. Morilhat 1996, 85; Spector 2006, 462 among many others.
65. In Genovesi 1777, II, 217–219n.
66. Montesquieu 2000, 74–75.
67. Montesquieu 1989, 353. In a manuscript, he suggested this was what Spain should do, 1943, 115.
68. Montesquieu 1989, 349–345, on which see Sonenscher 2007a, 107–108.
69. Montesquieu 1989, 18–19. "Tyranny," after all, followed "democracy" like clockwork already in Plato 2000, 255, 545a.
70. Montesquieu 1989, 63.
71. Montesquieu 1989, 19. See also Pii 1998, 180.
72. Courtney 1993, 53; Spector 2004, 197. This was another issue uniting Montesquieu and Gournay's circle, despite other differences. See also Anonymous 1747, I, 12–15 and passim.
73. Montesquieu 1943, 100–101. This passage would be reformulated in 2000, 105.
74. Anonymous 1747, I, 2.
75. Anonymous 1747, I, 35, 208, 401. See also Le Blanc's very favorable mention of Montesquieu in the introduction to his 1754 translation of Hume, xi–ii, as well as his mention of Melon, xv.
76. Anonymous 1747, II, 91–93, 353. On the possibility of an economic science based on experience see II, 354–355.
77. Harris 1998, 555–556.
78. For contemporary accounts of England's iron industry, see Birch 1955.
79. See, for the historical importance of England's early lead in iron and important caveats, MacLeod 2008, 136–137.
80. Harris 1998, 535.
81. Anonymous 1747, I, 101, II, 118–119, 347–348. Emphasis added.
82. Montesquieu 1999, 302. Gee was quoted favorably by Le Blanc, one of very few economic authors (alongside Melon) mentioned in Anonymous 1747, II, 94.
83. Montesquieu 1749.
84. On Gee see Schumpeter 1954, 372 and the manuscripts in SHL GB 0096 MS 99. For his will see PRO 11/640. He was the second owner of Fenton House, a Quaker, personal friend of William Penn (for which see Penn 1720) and coinvestor of George Washington's father in the Principio pig iron company of Maryland, see the National Trust website at www.nationaltrust.org.uk/main/w-vh/w-visits/w-findaplace/w-fentonhouse/w-fentonhouse-history.htm. Last accessed 15/05/2011. Incidentally, Gee suggested all manufactures but "pig iron" be prohibited in the colonies, 1738, 102. On Principio see May 1945. Benjamin Franklin was impressed enough to publish an extract of Gee in the *Pennsylvania Gazette,* 5 January 1731.
85. Anglo-French emulation was a recurring theme in Gee. I use his 1738 edition, which was the one translated, xxx, 59, 105, 201, 206.
86. Gee 1738, xxiii, and similarly 121.

87. Gee 1738, xxx.
88. On the "universal panic" Gee's predictions caused, see Hume's dismissal, 1994, 137.
89. Gee 1738 quotes, among others, Hale and Child, 60, 88, 130, Pufendorf, 93, and Huet, 203–205. He followed Cary closely, down to Bristol workhouses, xxxiii–xxxiv 2, 17, 56–58, 113–114, 200.
90. Gee 1738, xxxviii, 117–118.
91. Gee 1738, 120–126, 215. Not surprisingly, Montesquieu 1749, 210–215, concluded with an appendix titled "Articles principaux de l'Acte de la Navigation Anglaise."
92. Gee 1738, xvi–xvii.
93. On the anxiety over these measures in England, and Lord Townshend's attempt to establish a prize for works on trade at the University of Cambridge, see Raven 1985.
94. Anonymous 1747, I, 105, echoed Cary on this already before England's victory in the war and before Gournay's circle was formed.
95. Schumpeter 1954, 244.
96. du Pont de Nemours 1768–69, III, 11; Twiss 1847, 152; Blanqui 1880, 353; Oncken 1886; Schelle 1897; Ingram 1919, 58; Roberts 1935, 339; Liggio 1985, 298; Vaggi 1987, 22; Ekelund and Hébert 1997, 75–78; Hamilton 2008, 8–11; McCabe 2008, 270–271.
97. Ashley 1898; Secrestat-Escande 1911; Meek 1962, 33; Gournay 1983 and 1993; Larrère 1992; Pitavy-Simoni 1997; Miller 2000; Shovlin 2006; Sonenscher 2007a; Cheney 2010.
98. Acomb 1950, 12–13; Meyssonnier 1989, particularly 168–236, 1990, 1995, and her introduction to Gournay 2008.
99. On the political culture of Gournay's circle see Ives 2003; Shovlin 2003 and 2006.
100. Hutchison 1988, 224.
101. Turgot 1997, 125; Morellet 1821, I, 36. The best definition of this science offered by Gournay's group was Forbonnais 1754, I, 87.
102. [Gournay] to Maurepas, 5 March 1747, in Gournay 1993, 93–102; for his network see the 124 letters in Gournay 1993, 112–216; on such networks and how they changed with the rise of Gournay, see Smith 1995, 571–572; on Gournay's economic espionage see Minard 1998, 212–218; on the Bureau of Commerce, see Harris 1998, 562.
103. Gournay to Trudaine, [1758], in Gournay 1993, 105. See similarly 134.
104. Expressed already in Gournay 2003, 373, 375–376, 381–382, 384, 387. Bonno 1948, 149–155, traces French emulation of English political economy back to the late seventeenth century. Shovlin 2003 opts for a more recent origin.
105. Anonymous 1747, II, 36–37, 351, 357.
106. E.g. Butel-Dumont 1755b, I, introduction and 109, 141, 188; II, 210.
107. Sonenscher 2007a, 180–181.
108. Yeo 2001, 54.
109. Anonymous 1747, II, 145.

110. Coyer 1756. See similarly Montesquieu 1749, 8, and Butel-Dumont 1755b, I, 457. Their circle could also draw on the authority of Savary (e.g. 1675, 14), Voltaire, and the French translations of the *Spectator,* the *Freeholder,* and the *Tatler* on this matter. See Bonno 1948, 50–52. On Coyer see Adams 1974; the debate has been studied thoroughly, see Smith 2005; Shovlin 2006; Cheney 2010.
111. On patronage see Boissevain 1966, 19.
112. For this term see St. Clair 2004, 4. For the circle's roster see Meyssonnier 1989, 179–188.
113. Venturi 1969–90, I, 683.
114. Charles 2008, 197. Butel-Dumont himself prodded Malesherbes for quick publications of his works; see his letters in BNF M. Fr. 22147, 42, and BNF M. Fr. 22135, 38. As late as 1761, Forbonnais similarly had Malesherbes approve a translation of Hume's *History,* full of suspect musings on religious and political issues; see their epistolary in Shaw 1952, 1188–1190.
115. Charles n.d., 6; Morellet 1821 I, 38. On this see also Weulersse 1910, I, 28; Diaz 1962, 29; Murphy 1986a, 299–321. For a discursive catalogue of contemporary economic translations see Le Blanc 1755, II, 250–274. For an insightful contemporary reaction, see *Journal de Trévoux,* January 1755, 5–40. See, for what the circle read, Alimento 2006.
116. Gournay 1983, 370.
117. Forbonnais 1753c, x.
118. Roche 2006, 189; Koepp 1986, 240.
119. On Diderot's striking reliance on Bacon, see Cru 1913 and Luxembourg 1967.
120. Diderot 1992, 5.
121. Diderot 1992, 5–6; Smith 1976, I, 8.
122. Diderot 1751b, 717.
123. In Carter 2001, 36.
124. Muthu 2003, 153–154.
125. Groenewegen 2002, 255.
126. Murphy 1986b, 309. Cary had been mentioned already by Forbonnais 1753b, II, 122.
127. CL, 15 March 1755, I, 320.
128. Pott 1772, 27; Braudel 1992, I, 132; Darnton 1986, 274–275.
129. Haney 1920, 180. On Butel-Dumont see Borghero 1974, 107; Hanley 2005, 376–381; Cheney 2002, 103–115, and 2010, 103–110. Child 1668 was translated as Gournay and Butel-Dumont 1754, Jefferys 1754 as Butel-Dumont 1755a, Cary 1745 as Butel-Dumont 1755b. Initially received very critically in the CL, December 1754, I, 449. The CL recanted its criticism in January 1755, I, 466.
130. Butel-Dumont to Hennin, 23 August 1756, BI MS 1266, 446–447, in Charles n.d., 7. Given Gournay's 1747 letter to Maurepas, in Gournay 1993, 93, it is not surprising that he would ask a young acolyte to write the *Histoire.* On his circle's fear of England in the New World, see Gournay 2003, 381; Forbonnais 1754; Gournay 1983.

131. Butel-Dumont himself realized his works were interconnected, and in 1755a, 28n, referred to his own 1755c.
132. See his censorial report in BNF, Ms fr. 22137, 83r–83v, discussed in Henley 2005, 380.
133. Marlborough and Townshend to Boyle, 21 May 1709, BL Add. Ms. 36795, 4v–53.
134. Anonymous 1714a, 273–275, X.
135. On the ensuing "war of maps" see Pedley 1998. Confusion regarding the contours of Acadia predated Utrecht; see the documents in BL Add. Ms. 31147, 130v–141r, dating from 1711–12. See also BL Add. 35913–35915, Hardwicke Papers, DLXV–DLXVII, 1712–64, I. Diderot 1751a defined Acadia as occupying "Long.311–316. lat.43–46."
136. Dull 2005, 13–14. On Newfoundland as a "nursery" see for example the many petitions by English merchants for the government to conquer it definitely, among which BL Add. Ms. 38350, 124; Add. Ms. 61620, 53r–54v; Add. Ms. 61620, 55r–56v; Add. Ms. 61620, 57r–58v; Add. Ms. 6162, 61v–65r; Add. Ms. 36795, 131r; Lockman 1750b.
137. Gournay to Maurepas, 5 March 1747, in Gournay 1993, 98.
138. Shovlin 2010.
139. Beaurepaire 2007, 192.
140. Harley 1966, 38.
141. Jefferys 1754, 1–4, 70, 72. For earlier claims see Pagden 1995, 80–82.
142. d'Argenson 1902, II, 26 May 1755, 317.
143. Dull 2005, 18–19; Beaurepaire 2007, 191.
144. Faragher 2005, 328–329, 350–357, 366, 409–410. On England's brutality, see Dull 2005, 34; Mayers 2007, 104. For later accounts rehabilitating British actions, see for example BL Add. Ms. 19071, 255v–258r, and BL Add. Ms. 19071, 259v–263r. Both emphasized that the Acadians had lived "in A mere State of Nature." On the earlier history of forced migrations in the English empire, see Games 2008, 256–257. Compare to Numbers 22:50–56; Deuteronomy 7.
145. Justamond 1798, V, 353.
146. For Butel-Dumont's authorship see the CL, September 1755, 89. For context see also Beaurepaire 2007, 190–211.
147. Positively reviewed in the CL, August 1758, II, 25. On these colonies see also Gournay 2003, 380–381.
148. Butel-Dumont 1755b, vi. He repeated his criticism of Savary in 1755c, I 391.
149. Butel-Dumont 1755b, viii–xi.
150. *Journal des sçavans,* January 1755, 54.
151. Butel-Dumont 1755c, xi; Mangio 2006, 165.
152. Butel-Dumont 1755c, xiii–xiv, 1–3. On this tradition see Hirschman 1997, 12–14. See similarly Rousseau 1953, 377.
153. Butel-Dumont 1755c, 9, 35–37.
154. Butel-Dumont 1755c, 38, 113, 117, 226, 279, 284–285, 334.
155. Butel-Dumont 1755c, 164, 209–210, 240, 252, 257–261, 267–268.

156. Butel-Dumont 1755c, 55. The importance of the Acadian question in Butel-Dumont's work was noted also in the *Journal des sçavans,* January 1755, 55.
157. Butel-Dumont 1755a, iii–iv, vii, 5n, 6n–24n, 263n. For an example of how contemporaries understood the historical evolution of universal monarchy see Davenant 1771, IV, 3–41.
158. For a late use of Cary in France, see Clark 2007, 27.
159. *Journal Oeconomique,* January 1756, 19–20. See also des Pommiers 1763, xv; *Journal des sçavans,* June 1755, 352; *Journal de Trévoux,* August 1755, 2077–2096. Butel-Dumont 1755b, 19, emphasized Cary's celebrity, echoed in Coster 1762, 337; Morellet 1769, 30; Lacretelle 1786, 24.
160. Butel-Dumont 1755b, I, 4–8. Châtelet's translation of Mandeville had been driven by the same search for universality, see Zinsser 2002, 606.
161. Butel-Dumont 1755b, I, 9–10. Genovesi made the same methodological caveat in a letter to an anonymous recipient, 30 March 1765, ASN *Casa Reale Antica, Diversi,* MS fasc. 868.
162. This was also pointed out by the *Journal de Trévoux,* August 1755, 2077–2096.
163. Butel-Dumont 1755b, I, 21–22. An example of this awareness of differences appears in I, 372–373. Butel-Dumont furthermore claims to have used an unidentified second edition of 1715 on 21.
164. Anonymous 1747, II, 389–390; Butel-Dumont 1755b, I, 17. See similarly his fake translation in 1772, 6–9, 17–20.
165. Butel-Dumont 1755b, I, 16–17.
166. Reviewed separately in the *Journal des sçavans,* June 1755, 352–357, and *Journal des sçavans,* June 1755, 436–441, and together but in separate sections in the *Journal de Trévoux,* August 1755, 2077–2096.
167. Butel-Dumont 1755b, I, 22–23. Coster 1762, 337–338, indirectly observed that Cary's nationalism remained.
168. Davenant 1771, II, 239; Butel-Dumont 1755b, xxii–xxiii, 75.
169. Butel-Dumont 1755b, 50. England's tyranny over Ireland was mentioned often in the French literature; see among others Montesquieu above; Bellepierre de Neuve-Église 1761–63, VIII, 118–119; Linguet 1777–92, V, 490; and the review of Forbonnais's *Le Négociant Anglois* in the *Journal de Trévoux,* July 1754, 1870–96, particularly 1878–79, as well as that of Child in the *Journal de Trévoux,* January 1755, 5–40. On Ireland, the Gournay circle, and peripheral development, see Shovlin forthcoming.
170. Anonymous 1747, II, 209. Ironically, Le Blanc went on to castigate the English for having ignored historical studies for too long. On such economic histories in Enlightenment France, see Cheney 2010.
171. ANF, Minutier Céntral, etude XXVI, Jean-Antoine Dosfant, 971, 11 March 1789, "Inventaire aprèce le Décès de Georges Marie Butel Dumont." The striking lack of economic titles among those mentioned in Butel-Dumont's estate might reflect that those responsible for the list prioritized the financial value of his library.

172. On such "Enlightenment narratives" see again Pocock 1999–2005, II, 20–21.
173. Butel-Dumont 1755b, I, 1–7. See again Anonymous 1747, II, 354–355.
174. Butel-Dumont 1755b, I, 7–11.
175. Butel-Dumont 1755b, I, 22, 31–34, 137–161. See also Forbonnais 1758, II, 122–123, on Cary and textile regulations.
176. Butel-Dumont 1755b, I, 405.
177. Butel-Dumont 1755b, I, 141–144, 185–189, 209, 292–302, 320–325. See on Cary and English emulation also the *Journal des sçavans,* June 1755, 353.
178. Butel-Dumont 1755b, I, 49–52, 75, 300, 388, II, 259, 274–277, 369–370.
179. Melon 1734, 138; Hume 1994, 105; Le Blanc 1754, I, 26. Cf. Fénelon 1994, 297.
180. See, for example, Cary 1695, dedication, and 1, 6, 50, 119, 122, 131, 154, 162, 165, and Cary 1745, 2, 5, 70, 79, 110. On "luxe" see Butel-Dumont 1755b, I, viii, 2, and II, 133. On such strategies see Shovlin 2006, 14–15.
181. Butel-Dumont 1755b, I, 141, 218, 220, 297, 312, versus Cary 1695, 53, 59.
182. CL, 15 March 1755, I, 318–328.
183. Butel-Dumont 1755b, I, 52–67. See also Tucker 1749, 9; Dangeul 1754a, 57; Montesquieu 1749, 202.
184. Butel-Dumont 1755b, I, 86–113, particularly 99, 107, II, 5–6.
185. For a similar contemporary strategy, see Fox-Genovese 1976, 229–230.
186. Voltaire to Marie Louise Denis, 24 July 1750, in Schui 2005, 41. See similarly A.R. [1760?], 12.
187. In Rothkrug 1965, 239–240. The same alarmist prose appeared again in the anonymous 1688 *Mémoire sur les Finances* submitted to the king, BNF, Fds. Fr. MS 11149, in Rothkrug 1965, 249–258.
188. Kaplan 1996, 24.
189. Fogel 2004, 9; Muldrew 2011.
190. A similar tactic is evident in Anonymous 1747, I, 296–297.
191. Particularly Linguet 1774, on which see Kaplan 1996, 26–30, and Levy 1980, 84–136.
192. Orwell 1972, 91.
193. Butel-Dumont 1755b, I, 109, 315.
194. Butel-Dumont 1755b, I, 111–113, 198–199, 208–209, 416–419.
195. Butel-Dumont 1755b, I, 457.
196. Butel-Dumont 1755c, 117.
197. Smith 2005, 104–142; Shovlin 2006, 58–65.
198. Coyer 1756, 131–132, 150, in Smith 2005, 117; Gournay 1983, 212.
199. Butel-Dumont 1755b, I, 116, 125–130, 174–178.
200. Harris 1998, 557.
201. Butel-Dumont 1755b, I, 246–259, 289–290. See again II, 208–225. This should be read in the context of Forbonnais's (1753a) analysis of "competition."
202. Butel-Dumont 1755b, I, 192–194, 268, 288–294, II, 292. On England's technological and manufacturing success and the difficulty of emulating it, see also Anonymous 1747, I, 48–49.

203. Butel-Dumont 1755b, I, 259–260, and again I, 272–273. The *Journal des sçavans,* June 1755, 357, concluded its review by highlighting this precise passage. See similarly Anonymous 1747, I, 176–179.

204. Butel-Dumont 1755b, I, 398–400. For the concept of an economist at the time, see Steiner 1997.

205. Butel-Dumont 1755b, I, 273–274. He made the same argument for exporting manufactured goods and importing raw materials under prohibitions and tariffs defended by Melon 1736, 131, and by Cantillon 1755, 301–323.

206. Butel-Dumont 1755b, I, 238–242, 243, 265–266. On this see also Anonymous 1747, II, 37.

207. Butel-Dumont 1755b, I, 197, 188–189, 327. This argument was picked up by the *Journal de Trévoux,* August 1755, 2077–2096.

208. Butel-Dumont 1755b, I, 293.

209. Butel-Dumont 1755b, I, 293, 331, II, 102–112.

210. Foucault 2007, 333.

211. Butel-Dumont 1755b, I, 373–378 and passim. On the Welsh prince see Williams 1987.

212. Butel-Dumont 1755b, II, 310–331, echoed in *Journal des sçavans,* June 1755, 438–440.

213. Crouzet 2008, 295–311.

214. Butel-Dumont 1755b, II, 328–329.

215. Butel-Dumont 1755b, II, 90. Yet the Gournay circle never neared the universalism of Raynal 1781, V, 2, discussed in Pagden 1993, 160; Muthu 2003, 74; Pocock 1999–2005, IV, 279.

216. Butel-Dumont 1755b, II, 128–129, 222. See similarly Anonymous 1747, II, 92.

217. Gournay and Butel-Dumont 1754 in 1983, 425; Butel-Dumont 1755b, II, 111. On the importance of the Navigation Acts and the need to emulate them carefully, see also *Journal de Trévoux,* January 1755, 2077–2096; Butel-Dumont 1758, 130–284, particularly 138; Butel-Dumont 1760, i–ii, xxxv–xxxvi.

218. Butel-Dumont 1755b, II, 409–420.

219. Butel-Dumont 1755b, I, 129–130.

220. *Journal des sçavans,* June 1755, 356.

221. There exists a vast and favorable literature on Physiocracy. For recent overviews see Sonenscher 2007a and 2008; Théré and Charles 2008.

222. On the evolution of Physiocracy see Fox-Genovese 1976; Kaplan 1976, II, 603–606, and 1979, 21, 29.

223. Bourde 1953, 20; Fox-Genovese 1976, 93; Shovlin 2006, 52–53. On the techniques of the agricultural revolution see Riches 1967.

224. Shovlin 2006, 54.

225. Duhamel du Monceau 1750–61; Réamur, Duhamel, and Perronet 1761.

226. Shovlin 2005, 126–129.

227. Sonenscher 2007b; Vardi 2010.

228. Guiraudet 1790, 101–110; Vergani 1794, 77; Luigi Tramontani in Becagli 1983, 125n. On the Physiocrats' critiques of "feudalism" see Mackrell 1973.

229. Quesnay 1736; Larrère 1992, 17–19; Riskin 2002, 112; Charles 2003 and 2004 building on Reiter 1990.
230. Quesnay's first article in the *Encyclopédie* drew authority from a supposed Sullyan pedigree. Even Quesnay's "maxims" of economic governance were initially presented as "Sully's maxims." See Quesnay 2005, 128–159; du Pont de Nemours 1984, 239; Buisseret 1962; Shovlin 2006, 56. For a later version of this argument see Smith 1976, I, 9, 115–120, II, 197. See on this Reddy 1984, 40–43; Biernacki 1995, 251–253.
231. Quesnay 2005, 198–206; Quesnay 1973, 14, emphasis in original; Groenewegen 2002, 222–262.
232. du Pont de Nemours 1984, 238, 244. On this vocabulary of constitutions, see Cheney 2010.
233. Kaplan 1976 and 1982, 52–57.
234. Turgot to Hume, 25 March 1767, in Hume 1955, 210–213. Cf. his 1759 statement about productive industry while eulogizing Gournay in Turgot 1997, 133–134.
235. Turgot to Hume, 23 July 1766, in Hume 1955, 205–206.
236. Quesnay to Mirabeau, September 1760, ANF M/784 no.72–14(27), also in Quesnay 2005, 1190. On the two networks see Théré and Charles 2008.
237. The letter might be the "Lettre sur la Théorie de l'impôt," ANF K/910, no. 28, discussed in Quesnay 2005, 1322.
238. Letter from Quesnay to Mirabeau, no date but end of 1760, in Quesnay 2005, 1208.
239. *Depenses du revenue*, ANF M/784 no. 72–14(14), in Quesnay 2005, 699.
240. In Borghero 1974, 107.
241. Longhitano 2009, 19. On Physiocracy as Enlightenment, see, among others, Backhouse 2002; Bell 1953; Ekelund and Hébert 1997; Ferguson 1950; Galbraith 1991; Landreth and Colander 1994; Negishi 1989; Redman 1997; Robbins 1998; Roll 1953. For antidotes, see Larrère 1992, 5; Shovlin 2006, 3, 113; Cheney 2010, 10.
242. An argument made most forcefully by Galiani 1770.
243. du Pont de Nemours 1984, 226, 231–232.
244. Hume 1777, 13.
245. Hume to Morellet, 10 July 1769, in Hume 1955, 214–216.
246. Rousseau to Mirabeau, 26 July 1767, in Rousseau 1997b, 268–271; Mercier in Kaplan 1976, 591, 603. On *The Year 2240*, see Darnton 1996, 300–336.
247. Kaplan 1976.
248. Graslin 1767; Galiani 1770; Schumpeter 1954, 175.
249. Guiraudet 1790, 101–110.
250. Vergani 1794, 77.
251. ANF B4/68, 1754–56, no. 23.
252. In Beaurepaire 2007, 193, 199. See generally 194–211 and for context Dziembowski 1998 and Shovlin 2010.
253. Galiani 1975, 718–719.
254. Butel-Dumont 1760.
255. Williams 1979.

256. Newbigging 1998, 165.
257. Butel-Dumont 1761, 33.
258. Anonymous 1765, I, 21–22; II, 73–74; V, 61. Emphasis added.
259. Harris 1998, 558–559; Inikori 2002.
260. AMAE, correspondance politique, Russie, LIII, 131v–136r, in Henley 2005, 377.
261. Butel-Dumont to Benjamin Franklin, 8 February 1778, in Wolf and Hayes 2006, 168. Franklin had, it seems, asked for his books on America, and Butel-Dumont sent them both in addition to his treaty on luxury.
262. Butel-Dumont 1771, 44, 133.
263. Butel-Dumont 1772 and 1776.
264. Nerval 1852, 216–217; Coward 1991, 112; Hanley 2005, 378. On Réstif see also Manuel and Manuel 1979, 548–555.
265. Réstif de la Bretonne 1889, xxxviii, 19–24, 163n; Poster 1971, 11; Hanley 2005, 378.
266. Butel-Dumont 1779, 480–481.
267. Métra 1787–90, VII, 377–378.

4. Genovesi's *Storia del commercio della Gran Brettagna*

1. Venturi 2001, 31; Ruffolo 2004; Reinert 2010. For eighteenth-century observations see Verri 1939, 11; Franci, "Alcuni pensieri politici," in IC, 143–150.
2. Brucker 2005, 42–61.
3. Thompson 1744, I, 67; Anonymous 1765, V, 61.
4. Braudel 1992, II, 569 and passim; Wallerstein 1974–89; Krantz and Hohenberg 1974; Tabak 2008. For Italy see Cipolla 1969; Thomson 1998, 97–134.
5. Cipolla 1969, 133; Mori 1951, 7.
6. Machiavelli in Skinner 2001, 7–9; Goldsmith 1770, II, 205; on these changes, see Arnaldi 2005; Shaw 2006.
7. Anonymous 1765, II, 4; V, 216.
8. Paolo Sarpi to Dudley Carleton, [summer 1614?], in Sarpi 1979, 210.
9. In Silvestri 1968, 144.
10. Berkeley 1979, 135; Montesquieu 1995; Smith 1980, 243; Linguet, 1777–92, I, 7.
11. White 1964, 57–58, and Graf 1911. On the war see the epistolary between Celesia and Galiani, particularly the letters of 15 February 1755, 19 April 1755, and 23 June 1759, in Rotta 1974, I, 161–167, 174–177, 202–205, and Venetian spy reports such as G. B. Manuzzo, 26 June 1757, in Comisso 1984, 83. On the Seven Years' War and Italy, see Migliorini 1984 and Mangio 2006.
12. Quazza 1971; Venturi 1973, 999; Waquet 1989; Moe 2002, 1–81; Alimento (ed.) 2009.
13. AST *Materie di Commercio,* 3 categoria, mazzo 3, no. 4, 1751, "Pensèes diverses sur les moïens de rendre le Commerce florissant en Piemont . . . ," with

a translation of Cox 1749. Quotations are from another copy, unnumbered but bound as no. 12 with a slightly different title (the first spells "after" correctly, suggesting the second copier did not realize the archaic *f* in the original was not an *s*), 9–12, 112, 118, 195. Legislative emulation made the Savoy procure a manuscript of parts of Gournay's memoirs in 1757. AST *Materie di Commercio*, 3 categoria, mazzo d'addizione 1 [mazzo 1 da ordinare], no. 2, "1757 Parere del Consiglio del Commercio per la soppressione di corporazioni. Con uno scritto intitolato *Extrait du Mémoire de Mr. de Gournay Intendant du Commerce /1756/.*" These memoirs circulated more widely than hitherto assumed; see for example Schröderstierna 1756.

14. Astarita 2002, 12.

15. Serra 1613; similarly Montesquieu 1989, 341; Hume 1994, 161; Spinelli 1750, 25; Genovesi 1753, 251, and 1757–58, I, 228n.

16. Ferdinando Galiani to Antonio Cocchi, 20 February 1753, in Venturi 1959, 452–454. On Spanish economic mismanagement of Naples see Calabria 1991. For the consequences of this for political thought there, see Pagden 1990, 65–89. For the connection between backwardness and its image, see Moe 2002, 52.

17. Burckhardt 1944, 2–3, on which see Abulafia 1988 and the introduction to Calabria and Marino 1990.

18. De Rosa 1971, 185.

19. Marino 1988, 261–265; Astarita 2002. On Neapolitan intellectual life, see, for different periods, Bentley 1987; Ferrone 1984; Robertson 2005.

20. AST *Materie di Commercio*, 3 categoria, mazzo 2, no. 23: "Progetto di Giò. Nicola Morena di stabilire un Commercio tra il Regno di Napoli, ed il Piemonte . . . colla risposta al d. Progetto fatta dal Conte di Monestarolo . . . ," 1r. See also Botero 1603, 36; Genovesi 2005, 36; Astarita 2005, 242, 250.

21. For different perspectives on early modern feudalism in southern Italy, see Rao 1984; Petrusewicz 1990; Astarita 2002, 202–232; Robertson 2008.

22. Anonymous 1765, III, 251–252.

23. Croce 1927, I, 68–86, discussed in Calaresu 1999, 138, and Moe 2002, 38, 46–52.

24. Pii 1984, 30; Venturi 1969–90, I, 523–644; Gittermann 2008. For a peninsular survey of the period, see Rao 2002. Genovesi, too, would echo these nationalist sentiments, see Genovesi to Giuseppe de Sanctis, 3 June 1754, in Genovesi 1977, 248.

25. Maiorini 2000, 10.

26. Brosses 1973, vi, 253–256; Calaresu 1999, 144–145.

27. Intieri 1716 and 1754, the prototype (on which see Rotta 1974, I, 152–155) of which inspired Duhamel du Monceau 1753. On this see Galiani to Gaspare Cerati, 5 March 1754, 2 September 1754, and 17 December 1755, in Galiani and Cerati 2008, 56–57, 69–70, and 99–100, respectively. See also Galiani to Lorenzo Mehus, 7 May 1754, in Galiani and Mehus 2002, 66.

28. See fragments of Intieri's letters in Venturi 1959, 417–419. On Intieri see Galanti 1772, 92–101; Genovesi 1962, 29–35; Venturi 1959.

29. Venturi 1959, 421–422; Ferrone 1984; see also Ajello 1976, 422–426; Pii 1984, 11; Bellamy 1987, 278; Stone 1997; Robertson 2005.
30. Galanti 1772, 29.
31. Genovesi 1962, 29; Genovesi to Romualdo Sterlich, 23 February 1754, in Genovesi 1962, 78. On Genovesi's travails, see Villari 1959, 15–19; Zambelli 1972; Venturi 1969–90, I, 536.
32. Genovesi 1762, unpaginated epistle to the reader; Garin 1985, 11.
33. Villari 1959, 19–20; Mastellone 1969; Ferrone 2003.
34. Genovesi to Romualdo Sterlich, 27 October 1753, in Genovesi 1977, 241–243.
35. Genovesi to Romualdo Sterlich, [c. 1754], and Genovesi to Giuseppe de Sanctis, 21 April 1759, in Genovesi 1977, 245, and 253–254 respectively; Genovesi to Pasquale Saffiotti, 30 July 1763, in Genovesi 1962, 149–150.
36. Genovesi's critiques of Rousseau became increasingly polemical (e.g. Genovesi 1764, 405). On this see Pii 1984, 28–29; Bellamy 1987, 292; Imbruglia 2000, 74.
37. Genovesi 1753, 245. For contrasting interpretations of this essay, see Marcialis 1999b and Garin 1985.
38. Genovesi 1753, 231.
39. Genovesi 1757–58, II, 39.
40. Genovesi 1753, 273–274; see also Genovesi 1757–58, I, 225n; II, 217. On his diverse reception, see Villari 1959, 36–37.
41. Genovesi to Ludovico Antonio Muratori, 29 June 1747, in Genovesi 1962, 59–60; Genovesi 1757–58, III, 475–507. Genovesi's veneration of English publishing practices resurfaced again in his work on Cary, 1757–58, II, 348n. For his wide readings at the time see Zambelli 1972, 74; Pii 1984, 12–21; di Battista 2007. On foreigners noting Genovesi's familiarity with the European literature see Venturi 1969–90, I, 536–537.
42. E.g. Genovesi 1745; Genovesi 1757–58, II, 276, III, 501; Genovesi 1962, 33. Literacy was particularly important to him; see Genovesi 1753, 241.
43. Genovesi to Giuseppe de Sanctis, 20 June 1758, in Genovesi 1977, 252.
44. Genovesi 1768, I, 21; Genovesi to N.N., no date, in Genovesi 1962, 47–54; Genovesi to Romualdo Sterlich, 11 September 1756, in Genovesi 1962, 101–107.
45. On Genovesi's interest in education, see Genovesi to N.N., 8 May 1750, Genovesi to Romualdo Sterlich, 23 June 1753, Genovesi to Cristofero Migliarini, 21 December 1762, Genovesi to Francesco Loffredi, 22 September 1764, in Genovesi 1962, 63–64, 72–73, 140–141, and 174–175 respectively. Genovesi employed the term "enlighten" to describe his pedagogical project already in his letter to Antonio Conti, 15 January 1746, in Genovesi 1962, 54–56. On Genovesi and education see De Luca 1970, 27–37; Cerrone 2000.
46. On the group's emphasis on political economy, see Genovesi 1962, 32. For praise of specific authors, see Bartolomeo Intieri to Celestino Galiani, 29 November 1738, SNSP XXXI.A.7, 17r; Genovesi 1757–58, I, 5–10; Genovesi 1757, II, xiii. On Melon see also Genovesi to De Gemmis Maddalena, 30 March 1754, Genovesi to N.N., 13 June 1761, in Genovesi 1962, 80–81, and

135–136 respectively. On Montesquieu see Genovesi to Alessandro Serti, 13 March 1749, in Genovesi 1977, 238–241, and Genovesi to Alessandro Serti, 26 March 1754, in Genovesi 1977, 257. Genovesi met Dangeul late in life, discussed in a letter to Gioseppe de Sanctis, 20 June 1758, in Genovesi 1962, 252.

47. Genovesi 1777. On Genovesi and Montesquieu, see de Mas 1971.

48. Reinert 2011.

49. Ferdinando Galiani to Gaspare Cerati, 23 December 1755, in Galiani and Cerati 2008, 106.

50. On his chair see Di Battista 1992; Iovine 2001. It was not, however, the first of its kind, as usually argued. Simon Peter Gasser was given the chair of political economy in Halle already in 1727; see Schrebers 1764, 58–59.

51. Galiani to Mehus, 28 May 1754, in Galiani and Mehus 2002, 74–75.

52. Discussed in Bellamy 1987, 277n, but the principal division separates Venturi 1969–90 from Villari 1959, Zambelli 1972, and Garin 1985.

53. Genovesi to Alessandro Serti, 25 November 1754, in Genovesi 1977, 250.

54. Genovesi to Gioseppe de Sanctis, 3 June 1754, in Genovesi 1977, 248–249.

55. Genovesi to Gioseppe de Sanctis, 23 November 1754, in Genovesi 1977, 249–250.

56. Robertson 2005, 254, argues that Melon's *Essai* was "used to propagate political economy in Naples." Melon's work was discussed like those of Serra, Child, Dangeul, Forbonnais, Ulloa, and Ustariz, but only Cary was translated, annotated, and made into a university textbook.

57. There are, however, numerous mentions of his work on Cary in his private correspondence: Genovesi to Ignazio Roderique, 2 Novembre 1756, in Genovesi 1844, 138; Genovesi to Ferrate de Gemmis, 1757, in Genovesi 1844, 140; Genovesi to Luigino Fiorini, 4 July 1757, in Genovesi 1844, 143; Genovesi to Ferrante de Gemmis, 10 April 1758, in Genovesi 1844, 148.

58. E.g. Bartolomeo Intieri to Celestino Galiani, 4 October 1738, SNSP XXXI.A.7, 3v.

59. See Intieri's letter of 16 May 1750, in Venturi 1959, 425; Galiani 1962, 34, and, on his aborted translation of Locke, Galiani 1780, note II; de Felice 1755, xxv–xxvii. On de Felice and Genovesi, see Venturi 1969–90, I, 549–551. Cf. Duranti 1998, 478.

60. Genovesi to Gian Vincenzo Petrini, 24 December 1757, in Genovesi 1977, 241n. On Genovesi and English political economy see still Sampaoli 1949.

61. Genovesi to De Gemmis Maddalena, 30 March 1754, in Genovesi 1962, 80–81. He had an almost Lutheran appreciation of theological translations, see Genovesi to F. Basiolio N., 12 April 1755, in Genovesi 1962, 94–95. He was generally more perplexed by emotional than by technical aspects of translation; see Genovesi to Luigi Martini, 3 August 1764, Genovesi to Antonio Jerocades, 28 November 1767, in Genovesi 1962, 170–171, 209–210. On his censorship see Venturi 1969–90, I, 550; Farinella 1996, 109–110.

62. Genovesi 1753, 256; Genovesi to Gioseppe de Sanctis, 23 November 1754, in Genovesi 1977, 249–250. On the importance of Genovesi's example for the vernacularization of Italian academia, see Villari 1959, 36; De Luca 1970, 31. He would reiterate the relationship between national language and devel-

opment at the end of his life, Genovesi to anonymous, 4 October 1765, in Genovesi 1977, 269.

63. Genovesi 1745 in Garin 1985, 15. See also Genovesi to Romualdo Sterlich, 23 February 1754, in Genovesi 1977, 245–247. Nor would these sentiments change with time, see Genovesi to Francesco Griselini, 25 June 1764, in Genovesi 1977, 257. Consonantly, Genovesi's work has been assessed in Habermasian terms, Imbruglia 2000, 78; Robertson 2005, 371. On the Neapolitan public sphere see Calaresu 2005.

64. In Bronner 2004, 5. See also Genovesi 1768, I, chap. viii.

65. Galiani to Bernardo Tanucci, 12 November 1764, in Galiani 1975, 914.

66. Diderot 1755. See also Genovesi 1757–58, I, 44n.

67. Genovesi 1757–58, I, viii.

68. Muratori 1749, 161.

69. Muratori 1749, 84, similarly 147.

70. Genovesi to Camillo Tori, 20 March 1759, in Genovesi 1962, 123–124. Garin 1985, 19, discusses this in the context of Genovesi's Vichian influences.

71. Genovesi 1757–58, I, ix–x. See later also Genovesi to Cristofero Migliarini, 21 December 1762, in Genovesi 1962, 140–141. On history as a "propedeutic" of other sciences for Genovesi see Di Liso 1997; Marcialis 1999a, 123–126.

72. Genovesi to Alessandro Serti, 13 March 1749, in Genovesi 1977, 241.

73. Botero 1589, 204; BNF Ital. 875, "Di fra Tomaso Campanella Discorsi della Monarchia di Spagna . . . ," 161r–v, on the complex philology of which see Headley 1997. On Campanella drawing on Botero see Russi 1992. See similarly Shirley 1613, 32. For later occurrences known to Genovesi see Anonymous 1722, 13; Uztáriz 1751, 9; Forbonnais 1753c, 8.

74. Serra 1613, 24. Emphasis added.

75. Reinert 2011.

76. Genovesi to Giuseppe Calzerani, 15 April 1761, in Genovesi 1844, 178; Genovesi 1757–58, II, xiv. Genovesi did not know Butel-Dumont had translated Cary, but was aware of his work on America, Genovesi 1757–58, III, 60n.

77. O'Brien 1997, 21–55.

78. Le Blanc 1755, 252. For an example of Genovesi's consciously "liberal" translation, see Genovesi 1757–58, II, 426.

79. Genovesi 1757–58, III, 136–146.

80. Genovesi 1757–58, II, 145–146.

81. Genovesi 1757–58, I, v.

82. Genovesi 1757–58, II, iv.

83. Galanti 1772, 102.

84. Perna 1984, 1293.

85. Genovesi 1757–58, II, 271. Genovesi's Mun indeed spoke of the "sciences" of "commerce," 273. This passage was praised in the *Novelle letterarie* 2, 11 January 1760, 25–26.

86. Carpenter 1975.

87. Genovesi 1757–58, I, i–iii.

88. Genovesi 1757–58, I, lxxxiii. And again I, 358.
89. Forbonnais 1753c; Dangeul 1754b; Galiani to Cerati, 23 December 1755, in Galiani and Cerati 2008, 106. Their echoes are evident in Genovesi's discussion of "dependence" and "manufactures," 1757–58, I, 159n, 310.
90. Genovesi 1757–58, I, ii.
91. "Elementi di Commercio," BNN Ms. XIII.B.92; Perna 1984, 1289.
92. Genovesi 1753, 251, and again 1757–58, I, ci, 1.
93. Genovesi 1757–58, I, iix, 160n.
94. *Giornale d'Italia*, 21 July 1764, 17.
95. Cary 1745, I, 1; Butel-Dumont 1755a, I, 1; Genovesi 1757–58, I, 1.
96. Genovesi was certain of England's imminent decline, Genovesi 1757–58, III, 390n.
97. Anderson 1991, 155–156; see similarly Horn 2006, 5.
98. Genovesi 1757–58, I, 22–23, and passim.
99. Genovesi to Angelo Pavesi, 12 February 1765, in Genovesi 1962, 264–265. For similar statements with which Genovesi was familiar, see Serra 1613; Hume 1994, 64–65.
100. Genovesi to A.A., 19 May 1761, in Genovesi 1962, 133–134. Cf. Pii 1984, 51.
101. Marcialis 1999a; Di Liso 1997.
102. See similarly Gaspare Cerati to Galiani, 17 December 1755, in Galiani and Cerati 2008, 100.
103. Genovesi 1757–58, I, xviv, xxvi, xx–xxiii, xxxvii, xliv–xlvii, lvi, lx–lxi, 38n; II, 3n–17n. Genovesi quotes Cantillon on circulation; Tull and Duhamel de Manceau on agricultural academies. On the problem of feudalism see also I, 108n; on vagrancy II, 3n–17n; on emulation I, 316.
104. Genovesi 1757–58, I, lxix, 2–7.
105. Genovesi 1757–58, I, lxxxv–lxxxvi, 35n–36n, 189n–190n, 212n–214n, 220n–221n, 367.
106. Genovesi 1757–58, I, LXXXVIII, 2, 8n, 52n, 220n, 310n, 359–360n, 362n; II, 2–3, 35, 188n. On England and Spain choosing "opposite" paths, see I, lxxxvii, xcv–xcvi, 34n–35n.
107. Galiani 1780, note XXIX.
108. Galiani 1770, 150–151. On Galiani and the Physiocrats see Kaplan 1976; Galiani 1979; Goodman 1994. On his relation to Serra see Reinert 2011. For his attempts to republish Serra, see a manuscript by Galiani in SNSP xxxi.c.8. fasc. 18, 129–36v, on which see Stapelbroek 2008, 200.
109. Genovesi 1757–58, I, xxxi, lv–lvi, lxvii, 52n, 159, 180n–181n, 195n; II, 2–3; see also his Serra-like argument that Roman law could not explain political economy in Genovesi 2005, 5.
110. Genovesi 1757–58, I, xlix. He also quotes Hume, Dutot, and Galiani as authorities on this, II, 50n.
111. Genovesi 1757–58, I, 244n.
112. Genovesi 1757–58, II, 252.
113. Genovesi 1757–58, I, 244–249; see also 18n.

114. Genovesi 1757–58, I, 247–248, see also I, 28. Genovesi cites Huet 1718 on this. Compare also to Hume 1994, 54.
115. Genovesi 1757–58, I, 292–293n.
116. Genovesi 1757–58, II, 289.
117. Genovesi 1757–58, I, 249. See also his lectures of those years, Genovesi 2005, 15–20.
118. Genovesi 1757–58, II, 21n–29n; Genovesi 1765, I, 227, and 311. Cf. the bizarre Wahnbaeck 2004, 61, and critiques of Genovesi's "mercantilism": De Luca 1956, 115; Ferguson 1950, 37; Villari 1959, 49–50; Ingram 1919, 64. Strikingly, Genovesi, Melon, Montesquieu, and Forbonnais were seen to represent a coherent line of argument regarding the real meaning of "free trade" well into the nineteenth century, see for example Martinengo 1833, 95.
119. Genovesi 1757–58, I, 371n–373n.
120. Genovesi 1757–58, I, 295n.
121. Genovesi 1757–58, II, 80n–81n.
122. Genovesi 1757–58, II, 30. See also his lectures of those years, Genovesi 2005, 15.
123. Genovesi 1757–58, I, 285n.
124. Bertrand 1740.
125. Broggia 1743, 228, 242–249, passim. On this see Wahnbaek 2004, 63; S. Reinert 2009. On this debate see Berry 1994, 126–176, and Hont 2006.
126 S. Reinert 2009; Broggia, "Memoria ad oggetto di varie politiche ed economiche ragioni," in Ajello 1978, 1044–1045.
127. Reinert 2010.
128. Polybius, *Histories* 6.4.7–10. On these issues see Sasso 1958; Podes 1991.
129. See, for a historiographical introduction to his discussion of cyclicality, Breisach 1994, 210–214. On Vico and his context see Stone 1997 and Robertson 2005.
130. Compare Israel 2001 and Robertson 2005.
131. Vico 2001, 171, 173, 174, 177, 178, 461, among others. See similarly, in a different context, Hume 1994, 75. On the two, see again Robertson 2005.
132. Muratori 1749.
133. Galiani 1750, 287–289.
134. E.g. Galiani to Cerati, 23 December 1755, in Galiani and Cerati 2008, 103–108. On Galiani's Vichianism see Tagliacozzo 1969.
135. Nietzsche was an avid reader of Galiani, and might have drawn on this for his theory of creative destruction. On creative destruction in economics, see Reinert and Reinert 2006.
136. Galiani 1750, 9, 299.
137. Galiani 1750, 15, 150, 17, but also Galiani 1770, 65, and Galiani 1974, 78.
138. Galiani 1750, 291.
139. Galiani 1750, 370; Petrarca 2006, canzone CXXVIII, 162–165, lines 95–96; Machiavelli 1971, 298; Venturi 1969–90, I, 502.
140. Strikingly, Galiani had not yet read Hume 1994, 19, but would draw on him in 1770; discussed in Faccarello 1994.
141. Galiani to Cerati, 2 September 1754, in Galiani and Cerati 2008, 69.

142. Genovesi 1757–58, I, xlviii–xlix. This was lauded by Moreno at the Intierian chair as late as 1845–48, 179. The three-partite vision had been voiced by Vico 2002, 82, but was widely shared. Smith 1976, I, 34 picked it up from Cantillon 1755, 1–2, an author also known to Genovesi, who employed it in his lectures; Genovesi 2005, 9–10.
143. Galiani 1751, 287–292.
144. Genovesi 1757–58, I, 269n–283n, particularly 269n–271n and 282n. See similarly Galiani 1751, 290.
145. Genovesi 1757–58, II, 252–253.
146. Genovesi 1757–58, I, xcvi–xcvii, 322; S. Reinert 2009.
147. Wahnbaeck 2004, 65.
148. Genovesi 1757–58, I, 269n–282n, particularly 280n, II, 233–237.
149. Cf. Robertson 2005, 154.
150. On the religious context of Neapolitan reformism, see Chiosi 1992 and Robertson 2005.
151. Genovesi 1757–58, I, 19–20n.
152. Bossuet 1990.
153. Genovesi 1757–58, I, 19–20n.
154. Genovesi read Locke in the 1691 French translation, on which see Savonius 2004.
155. Genovesi 1757–58, I, 19n. The reference is, ironically given their differences, to Boisguilbert 1695.
156. Genovesi 1757–58, I, 26n.
157. On which see Galiani to Cerati, 2 September 1754, in Galiani and Cerati 2008, 70.
158. Genovesi 1757–58, I, 12n. See similarly Vico 2002, 82–83, 288.
159. See similarly Rossi 2003, 131.
160. Romano 1951, 23; Villari 1959, 127; Chorley 1965, 20; Salvemini 2000, 48–49.
161. Genovesi 1757–58, I, 190n, II, 291 and n, 294n, 408n. See similarly his manuscript BNN Ms. XIII.B.92, 42v, now published in Genovesi 2005, 44–46, but also 35–36. See on this Venturi 1969–90, I, 574–575.
162. Genovesi 1757–58, II, 21n.
163. Genovesi 1757–58, II, 21n–22n.
164. Genovesi 1757–58, II, 23n.
165. Genovesi 1757–58, I, 222n.
166. On which see Hont 2005 and 2008. For a particularly acute later statement see Malaspina 1786, 111.
167. Genovesi 1757–58, II, 31n–32n, drawing on Boterian theorems, and 207–268, particularly 219–220, 242, 247, 262–263. For a nearly contemporary English account of the cyclicality of emulation, see Postlethwayte 1749, 23, 30–31.
168. Genovesi 1757–58, I, lxxv–lxxvi.
169. Genovesi 1757–58, I, 116n, 188–189n.
170. Genovesi 1757–58, II, 291 and n. Genovesi's translation is here close to literal. Cf. Mun 1664, 23–24.

171. Genovesi 1757–58, II, 294n; II, 303 and 325n, see also 414–415n.
172. Genovesi 1757–58, II, 81n, annotates Butel-Dumont's description of anxious Englishmen, 1755, vol I, 188, based on Cary 1695, 41–42. See also Genovesi 1757–58, III, 146. For other "anxious" Englishmen in the tradition of Cary, see Fortrey 1663, 28–29, Reynell 1674, 9, N.C. 1697, 4, and Anonymous 1692b. For a similar argument see Bernardo Tanucci to the Count of Cantillana, 21 May 1757, in BTE, V, 4.
173. Genovesi 1757–58, II, 36n. See also Genovesi 2005, 36. On Italian unity in Genovesi, see De Luca 1970, 24.
174. The same penchant for equilibriums, perhaps a remnant of Genovesi's Vichian and Newtonian heritages, is observable in his critique of Petty's writings on the forced relocation of populations; Genovesi 1757–58, II, 195n.
175. Genovesi 1757–58, II, 189n, 248n–249n.
176. Genovesi 1757–58, II, 190n, see also 22n–23n.
177. Genovesi 1757–58, II, 24n.
178. Genovesi 1757–58, II, 195.
179. Genovesi 1757–58, II, 251. This was the civic humanist cyclical temporality manifest in Hume 1994, 145. See on this Reinert 2010.
180. Franco Venturi to Leo Valiani, 16 February 1960, in Valiani and Venturi 1999, 305.
181. Genovesi 1757–58, I, lxvii.
182. Genovesi 1757–58, II, 212–214; similarly III, 503; Genovesi 2008b, 378–381; Genovesi to Angelo Pavesi, 21 of an unknown month 1765, in Genovesi 1962, 263–264. On "unsocial sociability" see Hont 2005, 175.
183. E.g. his praise of the *Code Noir*, Genovesi 1757–58, II, 15n.
184. Filangieri 2004; Ferrone 2003.
185. On Genovesi and trust see Pagden 1990, 65–89.
186. Dionysius of Halicarnassus, *Roman Antiquities* 2.75, on which see Viano 2005b.
187. Genovesi 1757–58, III, 475. Genovesi's term is "fede," translated as "trust" and "faith." On the problems of translating it, see Pagden 1990, 65–89.
188. Genovesi 1757–58, III, 480–483.
189. Genovesi 1757–58, III, 485–488.
190. Genovesi 1757–58, III, 493.
191. Genovesi 1757–58, III, 498.
192. Genovesi to Ferrante De Gemmis Maddalena, 21 June 1755, in Genovesi 1962, 95–96. See also Genovesi 1757–58, I, 316–317.
193. Genovesi 1757–58, III, 506–507.
194. Hume 1994, 233. On Hume in Naples see Baldi 1983 and Robertson 2005. This section builds on Reinert 2010.
195. Galiani to Cerati, 25 February 1755, in Galiani and Cerati 2008, 89.
196. Genovesi 1753, 244; Genovesi 1757–58, I, lxiii, III, 483; Genovesi to Emilio Pacifico, 20 July 1765, in Genovesi 1962, 185; Genovesi 2005, 39.
197. S. Reinert 2009.
198. Soll 2005, 13.
199. As he told Giovanni Attilio Arnolfini, in Arnolfini 2001, 47.

200. Genovesi to Angelo Pavesi, 12 February 1765, in Genovesi 1962, 264.
201. Chorley 1965; Marcialis 1987; Guasti 2006.
202. Wahnbaeck 2004, 61.
203. Genovesi 1777, II, 195n.
204. Genovesi 1777, II, 202n, 255n.
205. Genovesi to N.N., 4 October 1765, in Genovesi 1977, 269.
206. Venturi 1973, 1074–1075.
207. Remondini 1772, 128; Vaussard 1959, 227; *Novelle della repubblica letteraria* 34, 26 August 1758, 369–371; *Novelle letterarie* 2, 11 January 1760, 25–26; *Journal Oeconomique* 1761, 6.
208. Cary was used as an authority by Romualdo de Sterlich, in Cepparrone 2008, 73; Bernardo Tanucci, see BTE, IX, 433n; Fortunato 1760, xv, 98; Betti 1765, 245; Pagnini 1765–66, II, 102–103; Zanon 1766, VI, 257–258; Grimaldi 1770, 9; Todeschi 1770, 73; Roberti 1772, II, 44; Gemelli 1776?, I, xiv; de Jorio 1773–83, I, 31; Cantalupo 1785, 144; Targioni 1786, 58; Azuni 1788, III, 49, 157, 289; Pini 1791, 29, 42, 46, 76, 154, 157; Mengotti 1792, lxxv, xl; Mengotti 1797, 199, 230; Baldessaroni 1801–4, II, 57; Isola 1811, 74; Fanucci 1822, IV, 272; Bianchini 1828, 37–38, 57, 94–95; [Rotondo] 1834?, 6; *Ape delle Cognizioni Utili* 1838, 346–347; he is one of the main sources of Miselli 1802; Martinengo 1833; Bianchini 1845; Moreno 1845–48, 179, among many others. Graf 1911, 402–403, traced economic Anglomania in Italy to Genovesi's translation of Cary.
209. *Giornale d'Italia*, 7 July 1764, 7–8, continuing 21 July 1764, 17–20.
210. See his letter to the editor, *Giornale d'Italia*, 28 July 1764, 31–32.
211. *Giornale d'Italia*, 3 December 1768, 177–183, continued on 10 December 1768, 188–191; 17 December 1768, 193–195; 24 December 1768, 204–207; and 31 December 1768, 209–212.
212. "Sulla spensieratezza nella privata economia," in IC, 327. On Verri see Capra 2002; Porta and Scazzieri 2002. On Genovesi's influence on his group see Ruđer Josip Bošković to Giovanni Attilio Arnolfini, 26 November 1768, in Arrighi 1965, 35–36.
213. FM Ms. Corrispondenza di Pietro Verri a vari destinatori 1763–95 (ex CAR 083.01–11), fasc. 7, Antonio Genovesi—Milano (CAR 083.07).
214. Anonymous 1769, 42; Reinert 2010.
215. Salerni 1782; Tron 1784, on which see Tabacco 1980; Arnolfini 2001 and ASL *Carteggio Arnolfini*, R., on which see Croccolo 1932; Denina 1829 and BNT *Libreria scelta di autori e traduttori italiani*, Q2–12, 97, on which see Reinert 2006b.
216. Sergio 1993, 18, 43, 48, 56n, 97, 166, 171, 179.
217. Vergani 1794, 78–81, 283.
218. Dunn 1996, 24.

5. Wichmann's *Ökonomisch-Politischer Commentarius*

1. On the slogan see Venturi 1972 and Ginzburg 1989.
2. Calvino 2002, 7–8.

3. Tribe 1988, 6; Lluch 1997. On Cameralism see still Small 1909 and Zielenziger 1914.
4. For perspectives, Raeff 1983; Foucault 2007; Soll 2009.
5. Linnaeus 1752. On this article see Steiner 1998, 13–17.
6. Wilson 2009.
7. de Vries 1984, 116, 153.
8. Bairoch, Batou, and Chèvre 1988, 4, 14, 28, 33, 52, 66.
9. Bruford 1935, 155.
10. Backhaus 1994; Bauer 1997.
11. On this see Raeff 1983, 100; Cooper 2007, 96–98; Backhaus and Wagner 2005, 317–318; Reinert 2005.
12. See on some of these issues Drayton 2000.
13. Hull 1996, 161.
14. In Hull 1996, 156. See similarly Raeff 1983, 29; Venturi 2001.
15. Wakefield 2009, 24.
16. Smith 1997 and Wakefield 2009. Cf. Reinert 2007a.
17. E.g. Koerner 1999.
18. Raeff 1983, 255; Wakefield 2009, 140.
19. Koerner 1999, 3, 97.
20. Gawthrop 1992, 251.
21. Raeff 1983, 70; Hull 1996, 155.
22. Bertram 2007, 125; Harding 2000.
23. Wendeborn 1791, I, 104–105. See, for analysis, Arup 1907, 284–285; Inikori 2002, 57–58.
24. Schrebers 1764, 16, 39–53.
25. For an unsympathetic account of Linnaeus's "economics" in these terms, see Koerner 1999.
26. Linnaeus 1752, 41.
27. Raeff 1983.
28. Cortekar 2007.
29. Anonymous 1758c.
30. Ortiz 1558; Hales 1581, 59; Laffemas 1597 and 1602; Montchrétien 1615; Botero 1589; Serra 1613.
31. Seckendorff 1665, 188.
32. Reinert 2005.
33. Koerner 1999.
34. See, among others, Mintz 1986; Drayton 2000, 72–73 and passim; Schiebinger 2004, 1–12.
35. But see Maseng 2005, I, 16.
36. Roberts 1986, 25, 140–141; Liedman 1986, 27; Söderpalm 1993.
37. Egede 1926, 140. On Danish colonial history see Larsen 1907–8; Feldbæk 1969; Ustvedt 2001; Bregnsbo and Jensen 2004. On its botched efforts in the Levant see Wandel 1927. For Sigurd Wilhelm de Gähler's account of 15 June 1754, see 21–24.
38. Tveite 1961; Kent 1973, 39–58; Rian 2008, 41.

39. Reproduced in Westergaard 1916, 306–314.
40. Morgan 1993, 14.
41. Governor Erik Bredal to Directors of the West India Company, 25 May 1719, in Westergaard 1916, 315–317.
42. Feldbæk 1971 and 1980; Mentz 2009.
43. Maseng 2005, I, 32–33, passim.
44. Spini 1999, 86.
45. Lavasse 1820, 344–345; Kirby 1990.
46. Johannisson 1988, 98; Sörlin 1990, 109–122; Maseng 2005, I, 34.
47. Frederick of Prussia 1981, 133–135; Wichmann 1793, 36n.
48. Bie 1998, 107.
49. Schröder 1752, frontispiece. For its ancient usage, see Dio 57.10, on which see Sharp 1999; on its Cameralist echoes see Simon 2004, 470.
50. In Weissbort and Eysteinsson 2006, 209.
51. Bain 1894, I, 163.
52. Westerman 1768, 30, 33.
53. Pfeiffer 1781–84, I, 387. See for Seckendorff's explicit influence on the first chair of Cameralism, Gasser 1729.
54. Justi 1758–1761, I, 27–28; Adam 2006, 43, 51, 56, 192–193; Wakefield 2009, 110.
55. Cf. Schabas 2005, 32.
56. Plüer 1757, 17–20, 23, 55–56, 67, 84–85. Interestingly, one of his sources was the "famous Englishman Josias Child," 73. German translation Anonymous 1758a. On "industrious" and "industrial" revolutions, see de Vries 1994; Muldrew 2011.
57. Roche 2001.
58. Becchi 1986, 20–36; Reinert 2011; see similarly Gotha 1985, 42.
59. Venturi 1973, 1076–1086.
60. Friis 1899, 200–206.
61. Friis 1899; Amdisen 2002, 146.
62. Bain 1905, 408–410; Vedel 1901; Madariaga 1962, 233; Feldbæk 1971.
63. Schumacher to Høegh-Guldberg, 28 June 1784, in GFS, 281.
64. Høegh-Guldberg to Schumacher, 19 November 1784, in GFS, 304; Coldevin 1950, I, 403; Ilsøe 2007, 188, 232.
65. Schumacher to Høegh-Guldberg, 12 August 1784, and Høegh-Guldberg to Schumacher, 31 August 1784, in GFS, 288 and 291, respectively. On Danish technological emulation, see Strømstad 1991.
66. Schumacher to Høegh-Guldberg, 1 September 1784, in GFS, 293. See similarly Høegh-Guldberg's caveat in Rian 2008, 36–37.
67. In Roberts 1986, 35.
68. Schumacher to Høegh-Guldberg, 2 April 1784, in GFS, 329.
69. Voltaire 1768; Galiani 1770. See also Kotta 1966, 38–83.
70. Schumacher to Høegh-Guldberg, no date but around New Year's Eve 1784, in GFS, 306.
71. See generally Tribe 1988, 126.

72. Bedford 1786, 9, 39, 44–46.
73. Liebel 1965, 14; Gray 2008, 119.
74. Bloch 1989, II, 169.
75. E.g. Vergani 1794, 77.
76. Baden 1782; Black 1999, 136.
77. Liebel 1965, 22.
78. Liebel 1965, 36–47; Karl Friedrich to Mirabeau, 22 September 1769, in Baden 1892, I, 3–5.
79. See Karl Friedrich to Mirabeau, 22 September 1769, 13 October 1769, and no date [1770], in Baden 1892, I, 3–5, 10, and 18–20 respectively; Mirabeau to Karl Friedrich, 4 October 1769, no date [probably 1769], 31 March 1770, in Baden 1892, I, 5–9, 10–17, 20–38. But see, for Mirabeau's more practical side and the differences between his "public" and "private" opinions of the Margrave, Becagli 1977, 163.
80. Emminghaus 1872, 36.
81. Liebel 1965, 48–49, 74–77.
82. Mirabeau to Carl Fredrik Scheffer, 16 October 1784, in Becagli 1977, 194–195; Liebel 1965, 53–54, 96, 98, 100; Beales 1987–2009, II.
83. Liebel 1965, 13.
84. Young 1774, 252–253.
85. Gray 2008, 109–113. See, for example, Anonymous 1772 and later Dohm 1778, on which see Bernardini 1989. See also Verri 2006–7, II, 404, translated into German as Anonymous 1774, 35, and Galiani 1770, 150, translated as Barkhausen 1777, 201. The Baden-Durlach experiment would remain fundamental to the Physiocratic debate in Germany, see Anonymous 1780, [iv]; Will 1782, 30–34.
86. Barkhausen 1777, 1–10.
87. Nicolai 1783–96, I, 265–266. On Nicolai see Selwyn 2000.
88. Schumacher to Høegh-Guldberg, no date but around New Year's Eve 1784, in GFS, 306; Nicolai 1783–96, III, 86–87.
89. Mirabeau to Carl Fredrik Scheffer, 16 October 1784, in Becagli 1977, 194–195; Høegh-Guldberg to Schumacher, 17 March 1785, in GFS, 324.
90. Tuscan ministers were well aware of the Baden experiment, see Becagli 1977, 140n13. On Physiocracy in Tuscany, see also Alimento 1995; Becagli 2003; Mirri 2009.
91. Cochrane 1973, 429, 435–437, 447.
92. Butré 1781, 144–157, discussed in Becagli 1977, 170. On the celebration of Physiocrats, see Charles and Théré 2011, 38. On Physiocratic mentalities, see Jonard 1969, discussed in Wahnbaeck 2004, 131
93. E.g. Holmes 1997, 137; Wahnbaeck 2004, 84.
94. Carli 1784–94, I, 337–338.
95. E.g. Gianni 1790, 20–21.
96. Genovesi 1757–58, II, 30; Minard 1998, 294; Pitavy-Simoni 1997.
97. Cantini 1800–1808, XXIX, 46–55, 325, 335–337, 339–340; XXX, 34–38, 69, 83, 92–93, 107–108, 151–153, 244–245, 255; XXXI, 109–115.
98. On the debates surrounding these reforms, see Becagli 1983.

99. Cantini 1800–1808, XXXI, 73; Gianni 1790, 28; Gianni 1848–49, I, 12, 28–29; Miselli 1802, 35; Mori 1951, 84–85; Cochrane 1973, 435–437, 445–452, quotation from 450.

100. Mori 1951, 28, 142–143; Schumpeter 1954, 374n; Cochrane 1961, 232–248.

101. Paoletti 1772, 35, on which see Mirri 2009, 406–421.

102. On the reforms, from different perspectives, see Cochrane 1961, 243–244; Diaz 1966, 90; Litchfield 1986, 297–298; Sordi 1991; Chapron 2009.

103. Becagli 1977, 155, 168.

104. Stierle 1996, 65; Cinquemani 2006, 79.

105. Schumacher to Høegh-Guldberg, 2 April 1785, in GFS, 327–328. In translating "landhusholdning" I follow Lerche 1999, 21. Cochrane 1973, 446, noted the influence of Cary and other foreign authors in Tuscany in the 1750s and 1760s, also through the mediation of Genovesi's mediation, whose inward-looking conception of economic greatness Mori 1951, 67, shows was mirrored by the Tuscan mainstream.

106. Schumacher to Høegh-Guldberg, 2 April 1785, in GFS, 327–328. See similarly the methodological caveat about the dangers of abstraction in Høegh-Guldberg to Schumacher, 7 May 1787, in GFS, 394. Cochrane 1973, 446, echoes Schumacher's verdict on Tuscan emulation.

107. Leopold II 1769–74, I, 294.

108. On Cameralism and meritocracy see Bleek 1972.

109. Schumacher to Høegh-Guldberg, 14 May 1785, in GFS, 340, 343.

110. Pfeiffer 1779, II, 62 (see also 1780); Will 1782, 35.

111. Schumacher to Høegh-Guldberg, 23 April 1785, in GFS, 334.

112. Schumacher to Høegh-Guldberg, 23 April 1785, in GFS, 338; Kant 1996.

113. Wichmann 1780.

114. Wichmann 1786. Høegh-Guldberg to Schumacher, 10 October, 21 November 1786, and 22 December 1786, in GFS, 375, 379, and 382, respectively.

115. For earlier mentions of Cary in Germany see Rohr 1755, 625; Anonymous 1758b, 309; Hirsch 1760?, 23, 156; Achenwall 1768, 314. Genovesi's *Lezioni* were translated by Witzman in 1772–74, republished in 1776. On these translations of Genovesi see Pfeiffer 1781–84, II, 355–470. Damianoff 1908, 65–68, discusses Pfeiffer's debt to Genovesi. On the German *Essay*'s price, compare Bouginé 1789–1802, V, 74, to Selwyn 2000, 166.

116. Bairoch, Batou, and Chèvre 1988, 7.

117. In Beachy 2005, 99.

118. Febvre and Martin 1997, 233. See also the essays in Martens 1990; Meise 1997, 16–18.

119. Schumacher to Høegh-Guldberg, no date but around New Year's Eve 1784, in GFS, 305.

120. A divide separating Ginzburg 1999 from Skinner 2001. See on this also Rothschild 2006, 222.

121. Weiz 1780, 275–276; Goedeke 1893, 253.

122. *Göttingische Anzeigen von gelehrten Sachen*, 1788, 1077. For a critical assessment, see Johann Heinrich Merck to Christoph Martin Wieland, 1 March 1773, in Merck 2007, 362–365.

123. Wichmann 1768; 1774; 1776–78; 1788; 1797–98; 1798.
124. Wichmann 1788, iii.
125. Wichmann 1788, iv–v.
126. Wichmann 1788, iv–v.
127. Wichmann 1788, v–vi.
128. Wichmann 1788, vi.
129. Wichmann 1788, vii.
130. Wichmann 1788, viii.
131. Wichmann 1788, viii–xi.
132. Wichmann 1788, ix–xiii.
133. Wichmann 1788, xiv. Cf. 234n.
134. Wichmann 1788, xv–xvi; Wichmann 1780, iii, referred to also in 1793, 68n. On Gersdorf see Zinzendorf 2009, IV, 224. Wichmann 1758 was dedicated to Gersdorf.
135. Wichmann 1788, xvi.
136. Wichmann 1788, xvi–xvii.
137. Osborne 1745?a, 6.
138. Osborne 1764?, 141; Wichmann 1788, xxxv.
139. Blair 2010.
140. Cary 1698b, 10, 127.
141. Dangeul 1754a.
142. Pii 1984, 16. E.g. Genovesi 1757–58, I, x.
143. Genovesi 1757–58, I, x; Wichmann 1788, 7n. See similarly 52n, 53n, 72n, 73n.
144. E.g. Wichmann 1788, 349.
145. Genovesi 1757–58, I, l; Wichmann 1788, 41n.
146. Wichmann 1788, 110n–113n.
147. Genovesi 1757–58, I, x; Wichmann 1788, 6n. See similarly 168–169.
148. Butel-Dumont 1755b, I, 62; Wichmann 1788, 237n; Postlethwayte 1751; Postlethwayte 1757b.
149. Wichmann 1788, 320–321.
150. Throughout, he generally differentiated between footnotes that were Genovesi's, the rare ones by Butel-Dumont, and those of his own making. For a rare note by Butel-Dumont that survived all translations, see Butel-Dumont 1755b, I, 186n; Genovesi 1757–58, I, 290n; Wichmann 1788, 403n.
151. The sections of Wichmann 1788 are paginated i–xvi, xviii–xxii, xxiii–xxxv, xxxvi–xl, xli–xlii [misprinted xii], xliii–liv, 1–94, 95–584, 585.
152. Vico 2001, 36. Wichmann did not translate Butel-Dumont 1755b, I, 291–466, corresponding to Genovesi 1757–58, II, 1–206.
153. Will 1782, [1], 28–30, 71–72. Yet he included the caveat that his verdict on Gournay relied on secondary sources; 6–7.
154. See Wichmann to Schumacher, 25 April 1786, 3v and "undated fragment," 2r, in RC 06312 *Schumacher, Peter Chr., 1762–1817 Breve, kopibøger, optegnelser m.m.*, 7: *Breve fra private V-Æ, A. I. 3: Breve fra Christian August Wichmann, Leipzig.*
155. Cf. Anonymous 1765, IV, 110.

156. Vaughan 1788; Rayneval 1789; Wichmann 1793. On Vaughan see Hamilton 2008.
157. Wichmann 1793, iv.
158. On this argument in the longer tradition of nationalism, see among others Viroli 1995.
159. Wichmann 1793, xixn–xxn, 46n, 75n, 147–149n, 175n, 220n. For the original see Vaughan 1788, vii. On Wichmann's democratic approach see Gagliardo 1969, 106–107, 153–154.
160. Smith 1776, II, 182–183.
161. *The Monthly Review* 59 (January–June 1789), 417–419.
162. See, again, O'Brien 2002 and Nye 2007, among others.
163. Steinlein 1831, 77.
164. *Göttingische Anzeigen von gelehrten Sachen,* 1788, 1077–1079. On the meanings of *Vaterlandsliebe,* see Oz-Salzberger 1995, 197.
165. See also *Allgemeine Literatur-Zeitung* 264, Wednesday, 26 August 1789, 562–564.
166. In Tribe 1988, 133.
167. Misellli 1802, 1.
168. Herder 2002, 393.

Epilogue

1. Compare earlier mentions of prices for Cary's work to McCusker 1992, 17, 81–86; Malanima 2002, 409; Edvinsson 2010, 251–254.
2. Allen 2001, 416.
3. See again Chapter 2.
4. Anonymous 1755; 1756b; 1768. For notable readings, see Llombart 1992, 329–335; Anonymous 1756d, 2, 0, 1–52; Uhlich 1755; *Oeconomiske Tanker til Høiere Efter-Tanke* 1759, VI, 87.
5. On the impact of Genovesi in Russia see Venturi 1973, 1089; in the Spanish-speaking world see Chiaramonte 1964; Keeding 1983, 208, 301, 307, 314; Cervera Ferri 1998; Astigarraga 2001 and 2004; Astigarraga and Usoz 2007. On Charles III bringing Neapolitan thinkers to Spain see Gittermann 2008; Cheney 2010, 123. For the spy's report see that of Pietro Paolo Celesia, 50 October 1784, in ASG *Archivio Segreto* 2482y.
6. Genovesi 1768, I, 436. See also Genovesi 1777, II, 207, and Raynal in Sonenscher 2007a, 31.
7. Genovesi 1777, I, 293n.
8. Belgrano 1954, 113–336. See, for Belgrano's reliance on Genovesi, Lluch 1984, 76; López 2007, 227–228.
9. Belgrano 1954, 47–62, particularly 48.
10. "De las manufacturas," *Correo de Comercio,* 27 October 1810, 265–272.
11. Belgrano 1927, 203–204. On this slogan see Faccarello 1994.
12. McCoy 1980; McNamara 1991; Hietala 2003; Ben-Atar 2004; Austin 2009.
13. *Journal de Trévoux,* January 1755, 21.

14. Polhem 1947–54, II, 131, 146. See similarly Bernardo Tanucci to the Duke of Montallegre, 26 April 1757, in BTE, IV, 513.
15. For this longer story of industrial emulation, see among others Landes 2003; Amsden 2001.
16. On these dynamics see Allen 2009; Wrigley 2010; Muldrew 2011, 2–3, 320–323.
17. Smith 1976, I, 21.
18. Jacob 1997, 204.
19. Nietzsche 1974, 173.
20. E.g. Backhouse 2002; Bell 1953; Dickey 2001–2, 272; Ekelund and Hébert 1997; Ferguson 1950; Galbraith 1991; Landreth and Colander 1994; Mokyr 2006, 283–286, 290; Negishi 1989; Redman 1997; Robbins 1998; Roll 1953. Even critics such as Bronner 2004, 155, and Gray 2007, 135, also equate Enlightenment with laissez-faire.
21. List in James 2006, 45.
22. Nye 2007.
23. Reinert 2006b.
24. Robertson 2000; Davis 2006, 92–93.
25. ANF T 1545, Papiers Sotira, *Discorsi politici* . . . , 45r. Emphasis added.
26. Cuoco 1929. For similar critiques of emulation from the perspective of the emerging discourse of nationalism, see Viroli 1995, 139.
27. Anonymous 1723, 174; La Fontaine 1708, 64; 1734, 25.
28. Compare Feldbæk 2004, 64 to Bairoch, Batou, and Chèvre 1988, 14.
29. Davis 2006, 289.
30. Davis 2006, 325–326.
31. Semmel 1970; see also Drayton 2000, 272.
32. De Mas 1971, 160.
33. Cary 1745, 1–2; Butel-Dumont 1755b, 2; Genovesi 1757–58, I, 2–3; Wichmann 1788, 98.
34. Langford 2000; Roberts 2008, 648.
35. Reinert 2005; S. Reinert 2009.
36. E.g. Anonymous 1765, II, 109.
37. Davis 1969, 102.
38. On this, see again Mokyr 2002 and 2006.
39. du Pont de Nemours 1984, 238, 244.
40. Cary 1695, 51; Gournay 2003, 387.
41. Malaspina 1786, 31, 124–125.
42. Pagden 1987, 1, 11–12.
43. Pietro Paolo Celesia to the Genoese Senate, 7 March 1786, 17 October 1786, 14 November 1786, 17 February 1787, 9 October 1787, 26 February 1788, 15 July 1788, in Celesia 1995, 46, 63, 66, 69–70, 88, 98, and 111–112, respectively. Emphasis added. On this correspondence, see Bernardini 1994.
44. But by no means "autonomous," see Schabas 2005.
45. Pomian 2005.
46. On this spectrum, see Sorkin 2008.

47. Galiani 1975, 735.
48. Anonymous 1754a, 97.
49. E.g. Todeschi 1770 and 1774.
50. Schumpeter 1954.
51. Smith 1976, I, 522–523.
52. See similarly Miselli 1802, 95.
53. Smith 1982, 579.
54. In Becagli 1983, 128; see also List 1844, 501, and untold others.
55. BP MSS. REGG: E 139, Agostino Paradisi, *Lezioni di economia civile*, II, 102–103.
56. Reinert 2010.
57. De Jorio 1979, I, 171.
58. Fox-Genovese 1976, 269.
59. In Olson 1993, 132.
60. Ricardo 1817, 156–157.
61. E. Reinert 2009.
62. Schumpeter 1954, 473.
63. Filangieri 2004, II, 156–157. See also his echoes in Herder 2002, 381, 386, 407. For a similar, earlier indictment see Bernardo Tanucci to Michelangelo Giacomelli, 16 April 1746, in BTE, II, 25–29.
64. E.g. Corpaci 1941, 52, 55, 57–58, 105–106; Scarfoglio 1937, 6, 21, 34, 95, 231. See also Schacht 1900. Curiously, as Cary and what he represented were claimed by the extreme right, so was he claimed by Keynesianism, see Lane 1932.
65. For different takes on the economic policies by which England conquered the world see Williams 1972; de Vries 1976; Braudel 1977; Wallerstein 1974–89; Perrotta 1988; Reinert 1995; O'Brien 1998; Pomeranz 2000, 194–207; Jones 2001; Vries 2002; Ashworth 2003; Ormrod 2003, 337; O'Brien 2002; Allen 2004; Hobson 2004, 243–280; MacLeod 2004; Wrigley 2004; O'Brien 2005; Horn 2006; Maddison 2006, 264; Ashworth 2007; Findlay and O'Rourke 2007, 238–262; Nye 2007; Reinert 2007b. See on the synergy between power and plenty, Lane 1979; Tilly 1990; Findlay and O'Rourke 2007, 261.
66. In Phillipson 1992, 7.
67. In Weissbort and Eysteinsson 2006, 206.
68. Mazzini 2009, 240.
69. Cary 1907; Harrison 1919, 55–56; Brock 1937.
70. Anonymous 1737, 8, 33.
71. Hamilton 1795, 36; see similarly Hamilton in Harper 2004, 135.
72. See, among others, Hume 1763, III, 312; Galiani 1770, 121; Smith 1776, II, 394; Anonymous 1799, 26, 52–55.
73. Peskin 2003, 203.
74. See similarly Harcourt 2011.
75. Plato, *Cratylus,* 402a4–b4.
76. Hansard 1812–20, XXV, 714–715.

77. On this tradition, see Pitts 2005 and Mantena 2010.
78. Veblen 1898, which helps explain his analysis of industrial emulation in Veblen 1915.
79. Edmund Bohun to John Cary, 18 January 1695–96, in Bohun 1853, 132–135.
80. On America as the end point of a "final *translatio*," see Pagden 2002, 268.

Bibliography

Given the changes early modern books often underwent in translation, contemporary translations of primary sources are listed under the names of their translators. Full manuscript sources are referenced only in the notes for reasons of space.

Archival Abbreviations

AMAE	Archives du Ministère des Affaires Étrangères, Paris, France
ANF	Archives Nationales de France, Paris, France
ASG	Archivio di Stato di Genova, Genoa, Italy
ASL	Archivio di Stato di Lucca, Lucca, Italy
ASN	Archivio di Stato di Napoli, Naples, Italy
AST	Archivio di Stato di Torino, Turin, Italy
BA	Biblioteca Ambrosiana, Milan, Italy
BI	Bibliothèque de l'Institut, Paris, France
BL	British Library, London, United Kingdom
BLO	Bodleian Library, Oxford, United Kingdom
BNCF	Biblioteca Nazionale Centrale di Firenze, Florence, Italy
BNF	Bibliothèque Nationale de France, Paris, France
BNN	Biblioteca Nazionale di Napoli, Naples, Italy
BNT	Biblioteca Nazionale di Torino, Turin, Italy
BP	Biblioteca Panizzi, Reggio Emilia, Italy
BRO	Bristol Record Office, Bristol, United Kingdom
CUL	Cambridge University Library, Cambridge, United Kingdom
FM	Fondazione Mattioli, Milan, Italy
PRO	Public Record Office, Kew, United Kingdom
RC	Rigsarkivet, Copenhagen, Denmark

SHL   Senate House Library, London, United Kingdom
SNSP Società Napoletana di Storia e Patria, Naples, Italy
UFEG Universitäts- und Forschungsbibliothek Erfurt/Gotha, Schloss Friedenstein, Gotha, Germany

Primary Sources

Journals

Allgemeine Literatur-Zeitung (Jena, 1785–1841).
L'Ape delle cognizioni utili (Capolago then Milan, 1833–47).
Il Caffé (Milan, 1764–6).
Correo de Comercio (Buenos Aires, 1810–11).
Correspondance Littéraire (Paris, 1747–93).
Danmarks og Norges Oeconomiske Magazin (Copenhagen, 1757–63).
Giornale d'Italia spettante alla scienza naturale, e principalmente all'agricoltura, alle arti, ed al commercio (Venice, 1764–76).
Göttingische Anzeigen von gelehrten Sachen (Göttingen, 1739–1801).
Journal Oeconomique, ou Memoires, Notes et Avis sur les Arts, l'Agriculture, le Commerce . . . (Paris, 1751–72).
Journal of the House of Commons (London, 1802–).
Mémoires pour servir à l'histoire des sciences et des arts [Journal de Trévoux] (Trévoux, 1701–67).
The Monthly Review (London, 1749–1845).
Novelle della repubblica letteraria (Venice, 1729–62).
Novelle letterarie (Florence, 1740–92).
Oeconomiske Tanker til Høiere Efter-Tanke (Copenhagen, 1756–61).
The Pennsylvania Gazette (Philadelphia, 1728–1815).
Post Boy (London, 1695–1728).

Printed Books

Accarias de Sérionne, Jacques (1766). *Les intérêts des nations de l'Europe, dévélopés relativement au commerce.* 2 vols. Leiden: Luzac.
Achenwall, Gottfried (1768). *Staatsverfassung der heutigen vornehmsten europäischen Reiche und Völker im Grundriss* . . . 5th ed. Göttingen: Vandenhoeck.
Adair, Robert (1795). *A Whig's Apology for his Consistency* . . . London: Debrett.
Ajello, Raffaele, et al. (eds.) (1978). *Politici ed economisti del primo Settecento.* Milan: Ricciardi.
Algarotti, Francesco (1823). *Opere scelte.* 3 vols. Milan: Società tipografica de' classici italiani.
Almodóvar, Eduardo Malo de Luque, Duke of (1784–90). *Historia Política de los Establecimientos Ultramarinos de las Naciones Europeas.* 5 vols. Madrid: de Sancha.
Altieri, Ferdinando (1726–27). *Dizionario Italiano ed Inglese* . . . 2 vols. London: William and Innys.

Amy, Thomas (1682). *Carolina* . . . London: W.C.

Anonymous (1641). *An Humble Petition and Remonstrance . . . Concerning the Insupportable Grievance of the Transportation of Leather.* N.p.

—— (1647). *The Golden Fleece Defended.* N.p.

—— (1654). *A Discourse Touching the Spanish Monarchy . . .* London: Stephens.

—— (1674). *Account of the Late Design of Buying up the Wooll of Ireland . . .* London.

—— (1677). *Reasons for a Limited Exportation of Wooll.* N.p.

—— (1678). *The Ancient Trades Decayed, Repaired Again.* London: T.N.

—— (1684). *Monsieur Colbert's Ghost . . .* Cologne: Marteau.

—— (1688). *A Review of the Reflections on the Prince of Orange's Declaration.* London: Churchil.

—— (1689a). *An Account of the Present, Miserable, State of Affairs in Ireland . . .* London: Wilkens.

—— (1689b). *An Account of the Reasons which Induced Charles II, King of England to declare War against the States-General of the United Provinces in 1672 . . .* London: Chiswell.

—— (1689c). *A Discourse of the Necessity of Encouraging Mechanick Industry . . .* London: Chiswell.

—— (1692a). *Fables of AEsop and other Eminent Mythologists . . .* London: Sare.

—— (1692b). *To the Honourable Members, Assembled in Parliament.* N.p.

—— (1697a). *A Letter from a Gentleman in the Country . . . Together with An Ansvver . . .* Dublin: Campbell.

—— (1697b). *A Letter to a Member of the Honourable House of Commons . . .* London: Whitlock.

—— (1698a). *A Discourse Concerning Ireland . . .* London: Nott.

—— (1698d). *The Interest of England, As it stands with Relation to the Trade of Ireland . . .* London: Atwood.

—— (1698e). *The Life of Mr. Thomas Firmin . . .* London: Baldwin.

—— (1698f). *The Substance of the Arguments For and Against the Bill, for Prohibiting the Exportation of Woollen Manufacture from Ireland . . .* London: Atwood.

—— (1698b). *An Answer to a Letter from a Gentleman in the Country . . .* Dublin: Crook.

—— (1698c). *An Answer to a Letter from a Gentleman in the Country . . .* London: Huddleston.

—— (1700a). *Arrest portant establissement d'un Conseil de Commerce . . .* Paris.

—— (1700b). *Critical Remarks upon the Adventures of Telemachus son of Ulysses.* London: Rhodes and Bell.

—— (1705). *The Letters of Monsieur l'Abbe dè Bellegarde* [sic] . . . London: Trahan.

—— (1706). *Æsop's Fables.* London: Phillips, Rhodes, and Taylor.

—— (1711). *Some Considerations offered to the Citizens of Bristol relating to the Corporation of the Poor in the said City.* N.p.

—— (1712). *A Long Ramble, or Several Years Travels, in the Much Talk'd of, but Never Before Discover'd, Wandering Island of O'Brazil* ... London.

—— (1714a). *A Collection of Treaties of Peace and Commerce* ... London: Baker.

—— (1714b). *Fishery, A Poem* ... London: J.M.

—— (1715). *Of the Rights of War and Peace.* 3 vols. London: Brown, Ward, and Meares.

—— (1717). *A Memoir of the Dutch Trade in all the States, Kingdoms, and Empires of the* World. London: Sackfield.

—— (1717?). *A Catalogue of the Libraries of Mr. John Warre* ... London.

—— (1722). *A View of the Dutch Trade* ... *translated from the French of Monsieur Huet.* 2nd ed. London: King et al.

—— (1723). *Æsopi fabulæ* ... London: Read.

—— (1732). *An Address to the Proprietors of the South-Sea Capital* ... London: Austen.

—— (1736). *Cardinal Alberoni's Scheme for Reducing the Turkish Empire to the Obedience of Christian Princes* ... London and Dublin: Faulkner.

—— (1737). *Seasonable Observations on the Present Fatal Declension of the General Commerce of England.* London: Hugginson.

—— (1738). *An Enquiry into the Causes of the Encrease and Miseries of the Poor of England.* London: Bettesworth and Hitch.

—— (1740). *A Genuine and Particular Account of the Taking of Carthagena by the French and Buccaniers* ... *By the Sieur Pointis* ... London: Payne.

—— (1741). *An Essay on the Improvement of the Woollen Manufacture* ... London: Cooper.

—— (1743). *An Essay on Maritime Power and Commerce* ... *By M. Deslandes.* London: Vaillant.

—— (1747). *Letters on the English and French Nations; By Mons. l'Abbé Le Blanc* ... 2 vols. London: Brindley et al.

—— (1747–66). *Biographia Britannica* ... 7 vols. London: Innys et al.

—— (1753). *Dictionary of Love.* London: Griffiths.

—— (1754a). "Memorial concerning the trade of the republic of GENOA." In *Select Essays on Commerce, Agriculture, Mines, Fisheries, and Other Useful Subjects.* London: Wilson and Durham, 336–371.

—— (1754b). *Remarks on the Advantages and Disadvantages of France and of Great-Britain* ... London: Osborne.

—— (1755). *Der Engländischen Pflanzstädte in Nord-America: Geschichte und Handlung.* Stuttgart: Metzlers.

—— (1756a). *Anmærkninger over Frankriges og Engellands Fordeele og Mangeler* ... Copenhagen: Lillie.

—— (1756b). *Geschichte und Handlung der Französischen Pflanzstädte in Nordamerika* ... Stuttgart: Weiler.

—— (1756c). *Le peuple instruit.* N.p.

——— (1756d). *Useful Remarks on Privateering. Addressed to the Laudable Association of Anti-Gallicans.* London: Hooper.

——— (1757). *The Anti-Gallican . . .* London: Lownds.

——— (1758a). *Gedanken und Nachrichten von den Manufacturen und der Handlung in Ansehung Dänemarks . . .* Copenhagen and Leipzig: Mummens.

——— (1758b). *Gedanken vom Gelde und von der Handlung nebst einem Vorschlage dem Geldmangel in Schottland abzuhelften . . .* Vienna, Prague, and Trieste: Trattnern.

——— (1758c). *Von der Glückseeligkeit des gemeinen Wesens, als dem Hauptzweck gut regierender Fürsten . . .* Munich: Osten.

——— (1761). *The History of our Customs, Aids, Subsidies, National Debts, and Cares . . .* London: Kearsley.

——— (1764). *Dialogues and Essays Literary and Philosophical . . .* Glasgow: Urie.

——— (1765). *The Chinese Spy . . .* 6 vols. London: Bladon.

——— (1768). *Historia del establecimiento y comercio de las colonias inglesas en la America septentrional . . .* Madrid: Ibarra.

——— (1769). *A Discourse on Public Economy and Commerce.* London: Dodsley and Murray.

——— (1770). *Lettere sopra lo studio del commercio.* Venice: Baglioni.

——— (1772). *Anmerkungen über die französische Schrift: Moyens d'arrêter la misère publique.* Frankfurt.

——— (1774). *Betrachtungen über die Staatswirtschaft.* Dresden: Waltherischen Hofbuchhandlung.

——— (1775). *Dialogos sobre el comercio de trigo, atribuidos al abate Galiani . . .* Madrid: Ibarra.

——— (1776–77). *Diario económico di agricultura, manifatture, e commercio.* 2 vols. Rome: Casaletti.

——— (1777a). *The Beauties of Biography . . .* 2 vols. London: Kearsley.

——— (1777b). *On Crimes and Punishments . . .* London: Almon.

——— (1778–83). *Encyclopædia Britannica . . .* 10 vols. Edinburgh: Black.

——— (1780). *Die Kontribuzion oder Übersicht des Kontribuzionstandes in Beziehung auf das phisiokratische Sistem.* Vienna.

——— (1787). *The Law of Nations.* Dublin: White.

——— (1790). *Fragments of Original Letters, of Madame Charlotte Elizabeth of Bavaria, Duchess of Orleans; written from the year 1715 to 1720 . . .* 2 vols. London: Hookham.

——— (1798). *Memoirs, Illustrating the Antichristian Conspiracy . . .* Dublin: Watson and Son.

——— (1799). *Three Letters to A Noble Lord on the Projected Legislative Union of Great Britain and Ireland.* London: Sidney.

——— (c. 1696a). *An Answer to Mr. Cary's Reply, &c.* N.p.

——— (c. 1696b). *The Linnen Drapers Answer to that Part of Mr. Cary his Essay on Trade, that Concerns the East India Trade.* N.p.

A. R. (1760?). *The Curiosities of Paris . . .* London: Owen.

Arnolfini, Giovanni Attilio (2001). *Giovanni Attilio Arnolfini ed il Trattato del ristabilimento dell'Arte della Seta.* Edited by Renzo Sabbatini. Lucca: Fazzi.

Arrighi, Gino (1965). *Carteggi di Giovanni Attilio Arnolfini.* Lucca: Azienda Grafica Lucchese.

Arriquibar, Nicolás de (1779). *Recreación Política: Reflexiones sobre el Amigo de los Hombres . . .* 2 vols. Vitoria: de Robles y Navarro.

Arrowsmith, Thomas (1800?). *A Catalogue . . .* London: Arrowsmith.

Ash, John (1775). *The New and Complete Dictionary of the English Tongue.* London: Dilly and Baldwin.

A True Anti-Gallican (1758). *Albion Restored . . .* London: Seymour.

Atwood, William (1698). *The History, and Reason, of the Dependency of Ireland upon the Imperial Crown of the Kingdom of England . . .* London: Brown and Smith.

Azuni, Domenico Alberto (1788). *Dizionario universale ragionato della giurisprudenza mercantile.* 4 vols. Nice: Societá Tipografica.

Bacon, Francis (1597). *Meditationes Sacrae.* London: Hooper.

——— (1985). *The Essays.* Edited by John Pitcher. London: Penguin.

Baden, Karl Friedrich von (1782). "Kurzer Abriss von den Grundsätzen der politischen Oekonomie." *Archiv für den Menschen und Bürger* 4, 234–63.

——— (1892). *Brieflicher Verkehr mit Mirabeau und Du Pont.* Edited by Carl Knies. 2 vols. Heidelberg: Carl Winter's Universitätsbuchhandlung.

Baggs, S. (1774). *An Essay on Circulation and Credit . . . From the French of Monsieur De Pinto.* London: Ridley.

Baldessaroni, Ascanio (1801–4). *Delle assicurazioni maritime, trattato.* 2nd ed. 5 vols. Florence: Bonducciana.

Barbapiccola, Giuseppa Eleonora (2005). "The Translator to the Reader: Preface to René Descartes's Principles of Philosophy." In Rebecca Messbarger and Paula Findlen, eds., *The Contest for Knowledge: Debates over Womens' Learning in Eighteenth-Century Italy.* Chicago: Chicago, 47–66.

Barbon, Nicholas (1684). *An Advertisement . . .* London: Darker and Newman.

——— (1685). *An Apology for the Builder.* London: Pullen.

——— (1690). *A Discourse of Trade.* London: Milbourn.

Barkhausen, Heinrich L. W. (1777). *Des Abts Galiani Dialogen über die Regierungskunst.* Lemgo: Meyerschen Buchhandlung.

Barrow, John (1759–60). *A New Geographical Dictionary . . .* 2 vols. London: Coote.

Baudoin, J. (1633). *Le commentaire royal, ou L'histoire des Yncas, rois du Péru.* Paris: Courbé.

Bayley, Nathan (1727). *An Orthographic Dictionary . . .* 2 vols. London: Cox.

——— (1800). *An Universal Etymological English Dictionary . . .* London: Neill.

Beawes, Wyndham (1754). *Lex mercatoria rediviva . . .* Dublin: Wilson.

Beccaria, Cesare Bonesaria, Marquis of (1984). *Dei delitti e delle pene.* Edited by Gianni Francioni. Milan: Mediobanca.

Bedford, Francis Russell, Duke of (1786). *A Descriptive Journey Through the Interior Parts of Germany and France.* London: Kearsley.

Belgrano, Manuel (1794). *Maximas generales del gobierno economico de un reyno agricultor* . . . Madrid: Ruiz.

———— (1927). "Nota de Belgrano a la traducción del resumen del Margrave de Baden." In Luis Roque Gondra, ed., *Las Ideas Económicas de Manuel Belgrano*. Buenos Aires: Imprenta de la Universidad, 203–204.

———— (1954). *Escritos económicos*. Edited by Gregorio Weinberg. Buenos Aires: Raigal.

Bellepierre de Neuve-Église, Louis-Joseph (1761–63). *L'agronomie et l'industrie* . . . 10 vols. Paris: Despilly.

Belloni, Girolamo, and Giovanni Battista Zanobetti (1751). *Del Commercio* . . . Leghorn: Fanteschi, e Compagni.

Belloni, Girolamo (1965). *Scritture inedite e dissetazione "Del commercio."* Edited by Alberto Caracciolo. Rome: Istituto per la storia del risorgimento italiano.

Berkeley, George (1979). *Viaggio in Italia*. Edited by Thomas E. Jessop and Mariapaola Fimiani. Naples: Bibliopolis.

Bertrand, Jean (1740). *La fable des abeilles* . . . London.

Betti, Zaccaria (1765). *Il baco da seta*. 2nd ed. Verona: Moroni.

Bianchini, Lodovico (1828). *Dell'influenza della pubblica amministrazione sulle industrie nazionali* . . . Naples: Trani.

———— (1845). *Della scienza del ben vivere sociale e della economia degli stati*. Palermo: Lao.

Bie, Jacob Christian (1998). "Philopatreias trende Anmærkninger. 1. Om de dyre Tider og Handelens Svaghed. 2. Om Rettergang. 3. Om Geislighedens Indkomster." In Kjell Lars Berge (ed.), *Å beskrive og forandre verden: En antologi tekster fra 1700-tallets dansk-norske tekstkultur*. Oslo: Norges Forskningsråd, 103–122.

Binns, John (1795?). *A Catalogue of Books, for 1795* . . . [Leeds?].

———— (1797?). *A Catalogue of Books, for 1797* . . . [Leeds?].

Bland, John (1659). *Trade Revived*. London: Holmswood.

Bodin, Jean (1576). *Les six livres de la repvbliqve* . . . Paris: du Puys.

Bohun, Edmund (1853). *The Diary and Autobiography of Edmund Bohun, Esq.* Edited by S. W. Rix. Beccles: Privately Printed.

Boisguilbert, Pierre Le Pesant, sieur de (1695). *Le detail de la France* . . . N.p.

Bolingbroke, Henry St. John (1997). *Political Writings*. Edited by David Armitage. Cambridge: CUP.

Borghero, Carlo (ed.) (1974). *La polemica sul lusso nel Settecento francese*. Turin: Einaudi.

Bossuet, Jacques-Benigne (1990). *Politics Drawn from the Very Words of Holy Scripture*. Edited by Patrick Riley. Cambridge: CUP.

Botero, Giovanni (1589/1956). *The Reason of State*. Translated by P. J. and D. P. Waley. New Haven: Yale.

———— (1603). *An Historicall Description of the Most Famous Kingdomes and Common-weales in the Worlde*. London: Iaggard.

Boudard, J. B. (1766). *Iconologie*. 4 vols. Vienna: Trattnern.

Bouginé, Karl Joseph (1789–1802). *Handbuch der allgemeinen Litterargeschichte* . . . 7 vols. Zurich: Orell, Geßner und Füßli.

Brewster, Francis (1695). *Essay on Trade and Navigation in Five Parts.* London: Cockerill.

Broggia, Carlo Antonio (1743). *Trattato de' tributi, delle monete, e del governo politico della sanità.* Naples: Palombo.

Brosses, Charles de (1973). *Viaggio in Italia: Lettere familiari.* Edited by Carlo Levi. Bari: Laterza.

Bruni, Leonardo (1978). "Panegyric to the City of Florence." In Benjamin G. Kohl and Ronald G. Witt (eds.), *The Earthly Republic: Italian Humanists on Government and Society.* Philadelphia: University of Pennsylvania Press, 135–175.

Burke, Edmund (1993). *Pre-revolutionary Writings.* Edited by Ian Harris. Cambridge: CUP.

Burnaby, Andrew (1775). *Travels Through the Middle Settlements in North-America.* 2nd ed. London: Great Seals.

Butcher, E. E. (1932). *Bristol Corporation of the Poor: Selected Records 1696–1834.* Bristol: Bristol Record Society.

—— (1972). *Bristol Corporation of the Poor 1696–1898.* Bristol: Bristol Branch of the Historical Association, The University, Bristol.

Butel-Dumont, Georges-Marie (1755a). *Conduite des François, par rapport a la Nouvelle Ecosse . . .* London: Vaillant.

—— (1755b). *Essai sur l'etat du commerce d'Angleterre.* 2 vols. Paris: Guillyn.

—— (1755c). *Histoire et commerce des colonies angloises, dans l'Amerique septentrionale.* London: Le Breton et al.

—— (1758). *Histoire et commerce des Antilles anglaises.* N.p.

—— (1760). *Acte du Parlement d'Angleterre, connu sous le nom d'Acte de Navigation, passé en 1660 . . .* Amsterdam and Paris: Jombert.

—— (1761). *Point de vue sur les suites que doit avoir la rupture, par les Anglois, de la négociation de la France et de l'Angleterre, depuis le 26 mars jusqu'au 20 septembre 1761, ou lettre à M*** banquier à Bordeaux.* Amsterdam.

—— (1771). *Théorie du luxe.* N.p.

—— (1772). *Journées mogoles, opuscule decent d'un docteur chinois.* 2 vols. Dély [Paris]: Costard.

—— (1776). *Essai sur les causes principales qui ont contribué à détruire les deux premières races des rois de France . . .* Paris: Duchesne.

—— (1779). *Recherches historiques et critiques sur l'administration publique et privée des terres chez les Romains . . .* Paris: Duchesne.

Butré, Charles de (1781). *Loix naturelles de l'agriculture et de l'ordre social.* Neufchatel: Imprimérie de la société typograhique.

C.K. (1756). *Davenants Afhandling, Angående Sætt och Utvægar, Hvarigenom et Folk kan Winna uti Handels-Wägen.* Stockholm: Grefing.

Campbell, John (1750). *The Present State of Europe . . .* London: Longman.

Cantalupo, Domenico di Gennaro (1785). *Annona o sia piano economico di pubblica sussistenza.* 2nd ed. Nice: Societá tipografica.

Cantillon, Richard (1755). *Essai sur la nature du commerce in general.* London [but Paris]: Gyles.

Cantini, Lorenzo (1800–1808). *Legislazione Toscana*. 32 vols. Florence: Fantosini.

Carew, George (1675). *Several Considerations offered to the Parliament concerning the Improvement of Trade* . . . N.p.

Carli, Gianrinaldo (1784–94). *Delle opere* . . . 19 vols. Milan: Nell'Imperial Monistero di S. Ambrogio Maggiore.

Carter, William (1669). *England's Interest Asserted* . . . London: Smith.

——— (1681). *A Summary of Certain Papers about the Woollen-Manufacture* . . . London: Streater.

Carter, William (1768). *A Catalogue* . . . London: Carter.

Cary, John (1695). *An Essay on the State of England in Relation to its Trade, its Poor, and its Taxes, for Carrying out the Present War against France*. Bristol: Bonny.

——— (1696a). *A Discourse Concerning the Trade of Ireland and Scotland as they stand in Competition with the Trade of England, Being taken out of an Essay on Trade*. N.p.

——— (1696b). *An Essay on the Coyn and Credit of England as They Stand in Respect to its Trade*. Bristol: Bonny.

——— (1696c). *An Essay Towards the Settlement of a National Credit in the Kingdom of England*. London: Collins.

——— (1696d). *A Reply to a Paper delivered to the Right Honourable the Lords Spiritual and Temporal, Entituled, The Linnen-Drapers Answer to that part of Mr. Cary's Essay on Trade that concerns the East-India Trade*. N.p.

——— (1698a). *To the Freeholders and Burgesses of the City of Bristol*. N.p.

——— (1698b). *A Vindication of the Parliament of England, in Answer to a Book, Written by William Molyneux of Dublin, Esq; Intituled, The Case of Ireland's being Bound by Acts of Parliament in England, Stated*. London: Collins.

——— (1700a). *An Account of the Proceedings of the Corporation of Bristol, in Execution of the Act of Parliament for the Better Employing and Maintaining of the Poor of that City*. London: F. Collins.

——— (1700b). *A Proposal Offered to the Committee of the Honourable House of Commons, Appointed to Consider of Ways for the Better Providing for the Poor* . . . N.p.

——— (1700c). *Reasons for Passing the Bill for Relieving and Employing the Poor of this Kingdom Humbly Offered*. N.p.

——— (1704). *Some Considerations Relating to the Carrying on the Linnen Manufacture in the Kingdom of Ireland by a Joint Stock*. N.p.

——— (1712). *A Discourse of the Advantage of the African Trade to this Nation, Extracted out of an Essay on Trade*. N.p.

——— (1717a). *An Essay Towards Regulating the Trade and Employing the Poor of this Kingdom*. London: Collins and Mabbat.

——— (1717b). *A Proposal for Paying off the Public Debts by Erecting a National Credit*. London: Collins and Mabbat.

——— (1718). *The Rights of the Commons in Parliament Assembled Asserted; And the Liberties of the People Vindicated*. London: Collins and Mabbat.

———— (1719). *An Essay Towards Regulating the Trade and Employing the Poor of this Kingdom*. 2nd ed. London: Collins and Mabbat.

———— (1745). *A Discourse on Trade and Other Matters Relative to it*. 3rd ed. London: Osborne.

Cary, Henry Grosvenor (1907). *The Cary Family in America*. Boston: Murray and Emery.

Casanova, Giacomo (1997). *History of My Life*. Translated by Willard R. Trask. 12 vols. Baltimore: Hopkins.

Catherine II of Russia (1977). *Catherine the Great's Instruction (Nakaz) to the Legislative Commission, 1767*. Edited by Paul Dukes. Newtonville, Mass.: Oriental Research Partners.

Celesia, Pietro Paolo (1995). *Le corrispondenze diplomatiche di Pietro Paolo Celesia dalla Corte di Spagna: Una scelta (1784–1788)*. Edited by Paolo Bernardini. Genoa: Civico Istituto Colombiano.

Chacón, José Alonso (1727). *Tradiciones, y Memorias Historiales, de la Vida, y Muerte del Ilustrissimo Señor D. Gonzalo de Stuñiga . . .* Madrid: Imprenta Real.

Chambers, Ephraim (1728). *Cyclopædia . . .* 2 vols. London: Knapton et al.

———— (1738). *Cyclopædia . . .* 2 vols. London: Midwinter et al.

———— (1778–88). *Cyclopædia . . .* 5 vols. London: Strahan et al.

Chiaramonte, José Carlos (1992). *Pensamiento de la Ilustracion: Economía y sociedad iberoamericanas en el siglo XVIII*. 2nd ed. Caracas: Biblioteca Ayacucho.

Child, Josiah (1668). *Brief Observations Concerning Trade and the Interest of Money*. London: Calvert.

———— (1690). *A Discourse about Trade*. London: Sowle.

———— (1693). *A Discourse Concerning the East-India Trade*. London: Baldwin.

———— (1694). *A New Discourse of Trade*. London: Crouch et al.

———— (1698). *A New Discourse of Trade*. London: Sowle.

———— (1740). *A New Discourse of Trade*. London: Hodges.

Clement, Simon (1698). *An Answer to Mr. Molyneux his Case of Ireland's being Bound by Acts of Parliament in England . . .* London: Parker.

Cobbett, William (1812–20). *The Parliamentary History of England*. 36 vols. London: Hansard.

Cock, Christopher (1725). *Bibliothecæ Bridgesianæ . . .* London: Cock.

Cocks, Richard (1996). *The Parliamentary Diary of Sir Richard Cocks 1698–1702*. Edited by D. W. Hayton. Oxford: Clarendon Press.

Coke, Roger (1670). *A Discourse of Trade . . .* London: Brome.

———— (1675). *England's Improvements*. London: Brome.

Colbert, Jean-Baptiste (1861–82). *Lettres, instructions et memoires de Colbert*. Edited by Pierre Clément. 10 vols. Paris: Imprimerie Nationale.

Coles, Elisha (1677). *An English Dictionary Explaining the Difficult Terms that are Used*. London: Parker.

Comisso, Giovanni (ed.) (1984). *Agenti Segreti di Venezia 1705–1797*. Vicenza: Neri Pozza.

Condorcet, Jean-Antoine-Nicolas de Caritat, Marquis de (1791). *Vie de Voltaire*. 2 vols. London [but Paris].

Connelly, William (1797–98). *Diccionario Nuevo y Completo de las Lenguas Española é Inglesa* . . . 4 vols. Madrid: Imprenta Real.

Constant, Benjamin (1988). *Political Writings*. Edited by Biancamaria Fontana. Cambridge: CUP.

Cooke, Joshua (1793?). *A Catalogue of Useful and Valuable Books* . . . Oxford.

Cortanze, Hercules Tomaso Rovero, Marquese di (1911). "Relazione del commercio della Grande Bretagna e specialmente dell'Inghilterra . . . " In Giuseppe Prato (ed.), *L'espansione commerciale inglese nel primo Settecento in una relazione di un inviato Sabaudo*. Turin: OPES, 4–24.

Coster, Joseph-François (1762). *Lettres d'un citoyen a un magistrate, sur les raisons qui dolvent affranchir le commerce des duchés de Lorraine & de Bar, du tariff general* . . . N.p.

Court, Pieter de la (1662). *Interest van Holland*. Amsterdam: Gracht.

[Cox, Richard] (1698). *Some Thoughts on the Bill* . . . *For Prohibiting the Exportation of the Woolen Manufactures of Ireland* . . . Dublin and London.

——— (1749). *A Letter* . . . *Shewing, from Experience, a Sure Method to Establish the Linen-Manufacture* . . . Dublin and London.

Coxe, Tench (1787). *An Address to an Assembly of the Friends of American Manufactures* . . . Philadelphia: Aitken.

Coyer, Gabriel François (1756). *La noblesse commerçante*. London: Duchesne.

Cuoco, Vincenzo (1929). *Saggio storico sulla rivoluzione napoletana del 1799* . . . Edited by Fausto Nicolini. Bari: Laterza.

d'Alembert, Jean-Baptiste Le Rond (1752). "Discourse preliminare." In d'Alembert and Denis Diderot (eds.), *Encyclopédie*. Vol. 1. Paris and Neufchatel, i–xlv.

Dangeul, Plumard de (1754a). *Remarques sur les Avantages et les Désavantages de la France et de la Grande Bretagne*. Leiden.

——— (1754b). *Rétablissement des manufactures et du commerce d'Espagne* . . . 2 vols. Amsterdam: Estienne.

d'Argenson, René-Louis de Voyer (2004/1764). *Considerazioni sul governo passato e presente della Francia*. Edited by Claudio Tommasi. Turin: La Rosa.

——— (1902). *Journal and Memoirs* . . . Translated by K. P. Wormeley. 2 vols. London: Heinemann.

Davenant, Charles (1695). *An Essay on the Ways and Means of Supplying the War*. London: Tonson.

——— (1701). *Essays* . . . London: Knapton.

——— (1771). *The Political and Commercial Works of that Celebrated Writer Charles D'Avenanti*. 5 vols. London: Horsefield.

Davies, John (1656). *The Question Concerning Impositions, Tonnage, Poundage, Prizage, Custom, &c* . . . London: S.G. for Twyford.

Davis, Lockyer (1785). *A Catalogue* . . . London: Davis.

Davis, Thomas (1771). *A Catalogue* . . . London: Davis.

Decker, Matthew (1744). *An Essay on the Causes of the Decline of the Foreign Trade* . . . London: Brotherton.

de Felice, Fortune Barthelemy (1755). *Scelta de' migliori opuscoli . . . Tradotti in italiana favella . . .* Naples: Raimondi.

Defoe, Daniel (1730). *A Plan of the English Commerce.* London: Rivington.

——— (1737/1969). *A Plan of the English Commerce.* New York: Kelley.

——— (1745). *The Complete English Tradesman.* 5th ed. 2 vols. London: Rivington.

de Graef, Juan Enrique (1996). *Discursos mercuriales económico-políticos (1752–1756).* Edited by Francisco Sáncez-Blanco. Seville: Fundación El Monte.

de Jorio, Michele (1778–83). *Storia del commercio e della navigazione . . .* 4 vols. Naples: Stamperia Simoniana.

——— (1979). *Il codice marittimo del 1781 di Michele de Jorio per il Regno di Napoli.* Edited by Cesare Maria Moschetti. 2 vols. Naples: Giannini.

Delany, Patrick (1747). *Twenty Sermons on Social Duties, and their Opposite Vices.* London: Rivington.

de la Vega, Garcilaso (1609). *Comentarios Reales de los Incas.* Lisbon: Crasbeeck.

delle Mallere, Ignazio Donaudi (1776?). *Saggio di economia civile.* Turin: Avondo.

Denina, Carlo (1829). *Rivoluzioni d'Italia.* 9 vols. Turin: Pomba.

De Rosa, Loise (1971). *Napoli aragonese nei ricordi di Loise De Rosa.* Edited by Antonio Altamura. Naples: Libreria scientifica editrice.

des Pommiers, Matthieu Auroux (1763). *L'art de s'enrichir promptement par l'agriculture, prouvé par des experiences.* New éd. Paris: Guillyn.

Diderot, Denis (1751a). "Acadie." In Jean-Baptiste Le Rond d'Alembert and Diderot (eds.), *Encyclopédie.* Vol. 1. Paris and Neufchatel, 57.

——— (1751b). "Art." In Jean-Baptiste Le Rond d'Alembert and Diderot (eds.), *Encyclopédie.* Vol. 1. Paris and Neufchatel, 713–717.

——— (1755). "Encyclopédie." In Jean-Baptiste Le Rond d'Alembert and Diderot (eds.), *Encyclopédie.* Vol. 5. Paris and Neufchatel, 635–648.

——— (1992). *Political Writings.* Edited by John Hope Mason and Robert Wokler. Cambridge: CUP.

Dohm, Wilhelm (1778). "Ueber das physiokratische System." *Deutsches Museum* 10, 289–324.

Doria, Paolo Mattia (1979–82). *Manoscritti napoletani di Paolo Mattia Doria.* Edited by Giulia Belgioioso et al. 5 vols. Galatina: Congedo.

Dryden, John (1694). *Amphitryon, or The Two Sosias.* London: Tonson.

Duhamel du Monceau, Henri-Louis (1753). *Traité de la conservation des grains . . .* Paris: Guerin & Delatour.

——— (1750–61). *Traité de la culture des terres . . .* 6 vols. Paris: Guerin.

Du Pont de Nemours, Pierre Samuel (1768). *De l'origine et des progrès d'une science nouvelle.* Paris: Desaint.

——— (1768–9). *Physiocratie . . .* 6 vols. Yverdon.

——— (1984). *Autobiography.* Edited by Elizabeth Fox-Genovese. Wilmington, Del.: Scholarly Resources.

Dyer, John (1757). *The Fleece . . .* London: Dodsley.

Eden, Frederick Morton (1797). *The State of the Poor . . .* 3 vols. London: Davis.

Egede, Hans (1926). *Grønlands Beskrivelse*. Oslo: Brøggers Boktrykkeris Forlag.

Egerton, John (1793). *A Catalogue* . . . London: Egerton.

Fanucci, Giovanni Battista (1822). *Storia dei tre celebri popoli marittimi dell'Italia* . . . 4 vols. Pisa: Pieraccini.

Fénelon, François de Salignac de La Mothe (1994). *Telemachus, Son of Ulysses*. Edited by Patrick Riley. Cambridge: CUP.

Ferguson, Adam (1769). *Institutes of Moral Philosophy*. Edinburgh: Kinkaid & Bell.

———— (1995). *An Essay on the History of Civil Society*. Edited by Fania Oz-Salzberger. Cambridge: CUP.

Filangieri, Gaetano (2004). *La scienza della legislazione*. Edited by Vincenzo Ferrone et al. 7 vols. Venice: Centro di Studi sull'Illuminismo Europeo "G. Stiffoni."

Firmin, Thomas (1681). *Some Proposals for the Imploying the Poor* . . . London: Grover.

Fisher, H. E. S., and A. R. S. Jûrica (1977). *Documents in English Economic History: England from 1000 to 1760*. London: Bell.

Fletcher and Hanwell Booksellers (1798?). *A Catalogue of Useful and Valuable Books* . . . Oxford: Fletcher and Hanwell.

Fletcher, Andrew (1997). *Political Writings*. Edited by John Robertson. Cambridge: CUP.

Forbonnais, F. Véron Duverger de (1753a). "Commerce." In Jean-Baptiste Le Rond d'Alembert and Denis Diderot (eds.), *Encyclopédie*. Vol. 4. Paris and Neufchatel, 690–699.

———— (1753b). *Le Négotiant anglois* . . . 2 vols. Dresden: Estienne.

———— (1753c). *Theorie et pratique du commerce et de la marine* . . . Paris: Estienne.

———— (1754). *Éléments du commerce*. Leiden and Paris.

———— (1758). *Recherches et considérations sur le finances de France* . . . 6 vols. Leiden [but Paris].

Forster, John Reinhold (1772). *A Voyage Round the World* . . . *By Lewis de Bougainville* . . . London: Nourst and Davies.

Fortrey, Samuel (1663). *Englands Interest and Improvement*. Cambridge: Field.

Fortunato, Nicola (1760). *Riflessioni* . . . *Intorno al commercio antico, e moderno del regno di Napoli*. Naples: Stamperia Simoniana.

Frederick of Prussia (1981). *The Refutation of Machiavelli's Prince or Anti-Machiavel*. Edited by Paul Sonnino. Athens: Ohio University Press.

Galanti, Giuseppe Maria (1772). *Elogio storico del signor abate Antonio Genovesi*. Naples.

Galiani, Ferdinando (1750 [but 1751]). *Della moneta*. Naples: Raimondi.

———— (1770). *Dialogues sur le commerce des bleds*. London [but Paris].

———— (1780). *Della moneta*. 2nd ed. Naples: Stamperia Simoniana.

———— (1962). *Sullo stato della moneta ai tempi della Guerra Trojana*. Edited by Fausto Nicolini. Naples: Banco di Napoli.

———— (1974). *Nuovi saggi inediti di economia*. Edited by Achille Agnati with an introduction by Giovanni Demaria. Padua: Cedam.

———— (1975). *Opere*. Edited by Furio Diaz and Luciano Guerci. Milan and Naples: Ricciardi.

———— (1979). *La Bagarre: Galiani's "Lost" Dialogue*. Edited by Steven Laurence Kaplan. The Hague: Nijhoff.

Galiani, Ferdinando, and Lorenzo Mehus (2002). *Carteggio (1753–1786)*. Edited by Giuseppe Nicoletti. Naples: Bibliopolis.

Galiani, Ferdinando, and Gaspare Cerati (2008). *Carteggio (1749–1758)*. Edited by Giuseppe Noceletti. Naples: Bibliopolis.

Gasser, Simon Peter (1729). *Einleitung zu den Oeconomischen, Politischen und Cameralwissenschaften*. Halle: Verlegung des Wäysenhauses.

Gee, Joshua (1738). *The Trade and Navigation of Great-Britain Considered* . . . London: Bettesworth and Hitch.

Gemelli, Francesco (1776?). *Rifiorimento della Sardegna proposto nel miglioramento di sua agricoltura*. 2 vols. Turin: Briolo.

Genovesi, Antonio (1745). *Elementorum artis logico-criticae* . . . Naples: Palumbo.

———— (1753/1962). "Discorso sopra il vero fine delle lettere e delle scienze." In Genovesi, *Autobiografia e lettere*. Edited by Gennaro Savarese. Milan: Feltrinelli, 227–276.

———— (1757–58). *Storia del commercio della Gran Brettagna scritta da John Cary* . . . 3 vols. Naples: Casari.

———— (1762). *Elementa metaphysicae mathematicum in morem adornata* . . . Naples: Simoniana.

———— (1764). *Storia del commercio della Gran Brettagna scritta da John Cary* . . . 3 vols. Venice: Bassanese.

———— (1765). *Lezioni di commercio o sia d'economia civile*. Venice: Remondini.

———— (1765–67). *Lezioni di commercio o sia d'economia civile*. 2 vols. Naples: Simone.

———— (1768). *Lezioni di commercio o sia d'economia civile*. 2 vols. Milan: Agnelli.

———— (1777). *Spirito delle leggi del signore di Montesquieu*. 2 vols. Naples: Terres.

———— (1844). *Lettere familiari*. 2 vols. Venice.

———— (1962). *Autobiografia e lettere*. Edited by Gennaro Savarese. Milan: Feltrinelli.

———— (1977). *Scritti*. Edited by Franco Venturi. Turin: Einaudi.

———— (2005). *Delle lezioni di commercio o sia di economia civile con Elementi di commercio*. Edited by Maria Luisa Pesante. Naples: IISF.

———— (2008a). *Della Diceosina*. Edited by Niccolò Guasti. Venice: Centro di Studi sull'Illuminismo Europeo "G. Stiffoni."

———— (2008b). *Dialoghi e altri scritti*. Edited by Eluggero Pii. Naples: IISF.

Gérando, Joseph-Marie, Baron de (1839). *De la bienfaisance publique*. 4 vols. Paris: Renouard.

Gianni, Francesco Maria (1790). *Governo della Toscana sotto il regno di Sua Maestà il Rè Leopoldo II*. Florence: Cambiagi.

———— (1848–49). *Scritti di pubblica economia*. 2 vols. Florence: Niccolai.

Gibbon, Edward (1994). *The Decline and Fall of the Roman Empire*. Edited by David Womersley. 3 vols. London: Penguin.

Gifford, John (1795). *The Reign of Louis the Sixteenth*. London: Lowndes.

Giovio, Giambattista (1781). *Pensieri varii . . .* Como: Scotti.

Gladwin, Francis (1783–6). *Ayeen Akbery: or, The Institutes of the Emperor Akber, Translated from the Original Persian*. 3 vols. Calcutta.

Goethe, Johann Wolfgang von, and Thomas Carlyle (1887). *Correspondence between Goethe and Carlyle*. Edited by Charles Eliot Norton. London: Macmillan.

Goldsmith, Oliver (1770). *The History of England*. 2 vols. London: Carnan and Newbery.

Gonzáles de Cellorigo, Martín (1600). *Memorial de la politica necessaria, y útil restauración à la República de España . . .* Valladolid: de Bostillo.

Gotha, August von (1985). *Das italienische Reisetagebuch des Prinzen August von Sachen-Gotha-Altenburg, des Freundes von Herder, Wieland und Goethe*. Edited by Götz Eckardt. Stendal.

Goudar, Ange (1756). *Discours politique sur les avantages que les Portugais pourroient retirer de leur malheur: et dans lequel on developpe les moyens que l'Angleterre avoit mis en usage pour ruiner le Portugal*. Lisbon [but Paris].

Goudar, Ange, [and Giacomo Casanova] (1764). *L'espion chinois*. 6 vols. Cologne.

Gournay, Jacques-Claude-Marie-Vincent de (1983). *Traites sur le commerce de Josiah Child avec les remarques de Gournay*. Edited by Takumi Tsuda. Tokyo: Kinokuniya.

——— (1993). *Mémoires et lettres de Vincent de Gournay*. Edited by Takumi Tsuda. Tokyo: Kinokuniya.

——— (2003). "Mémoire." In Henry C. Clark (ed.), *Commerce, Culture, and Liberty: Readings on Capitalism before Adam Smith*. Indianapolis: Liberty Fund.

——— (2008). *Traites sur le commerce de Josiah Child suivis des Remarques de Jacques Vincent de Gournay*. Edited by Simone Meysonnier. Paris: L'Harmattan.

Gournay, Jacques-Claude-Marie-Vincent de, and Georges-Marie Butel-Dumont (1754). *Traités sur le commerce et les avantages de la reduction de l'intérêt de l'argent*. Amsterdam and Berlin: Neaulme, Guérin & Delatour.

Graslin, Jean-Joseph-Louis (1767). *Essai analytique sur la Richesse et sur l'impôt*. N.p.

Grimaldi, Domenico (1770). *Saggio di economia campestre per la Calabria ultra*. Naples: Orsini.

Guiraudet, Charles Philippe Toussaint (1790). *Erreurs des économistes sur l'impot . . .* Paris: Lejay.

Haines, Richard (1679a). *A Breviat of some Proposals*. London: Langley Curtis.

——— (1679b). *A Method of Government for such Publick Working Alms-Houses*. London: Curtis.

Hakluyt, Richard (1584/1877). *A Discourse concerning Western Planting.* Edited by Charles Deane. Cambridge, Mass.: Wilson and Son for the Maine Historical Society.

Hale, John (1781). *A Letter to the People of England* ... London: Faulder.

Hales, John (1581). *Compendious or Briefe Examination of Certayne ordinary Complaints divers of our Countrymen in these our Dayes.* London: Marshe.

Hamilton, Alexander (1795). *A Defence of the Treaty of Amity, Commerce, and Navigation, Entered into Between the United States of America & Great Britain* ... New York: Childs and Co.

Hamilton, William (1783). *A History of Ireland from the Earliest Period, to the Present Time* ... Strabane: Bellew.

Hansard, Thomas Carson (ed.) (1812–20). *The Parliamentary Debates from the Year 1803 to the Present Time.* 41 vols. London: Longman et al.

Harrington, James (1659). *Aphorisms Political.* London: J.C. for Fletcher.

Harrison, J., and Peter Laslett (1965). *The Library of John Locke.* Oxford: OUP.

Hartwell, Blair, and Chilton (1727). *The Present State of Virginia, and the College.* London: Wyat.

Hay, William (1751). *Remarks on the Laws Relating to the Poor* ... N.p.

Hely-Hutchinson, John (1779). *The Commercial Restraints of Ireland considered* ... Dublin: Longman.

Herder, Johann Gottfried von (2002). *Philosophical Writings.* Edited by Michael N. Forster. Cambridge: CUP.

Hildyard, John (1751). *A Catalogue of Several Libraries and Parcels of Books* ... York.

Hirsch, Johann Christoph (1760?). *Bibliotheca numismatica.* Nuremberg: Felseckeri.

Hobbes, Thomas (1651). *Leviathan.* London: Crooke.

——— (1656). *Elements of Philosophy* ... London: Crooke.

——— (1681). *The Art of Rhetoric* ... London: Crooke.

——— (1995). *Three Discourses: A Critical Modern Edition of Newly Identified Works of the Young Hobbes.* Edited by Noel B. Reynolds and Arlene W. Saxonhouse. Chicago: Chicago.

Hornigk, Philip Wilhelm von (1684). *Österreich über alles wann es nur will.* N.p.

Huet, Pierre-Daniel (1718). *Mémoires sur le commerce des Hollandois dans tous les états et empires du monde.* Amsterdam: Du Villard and Changuion.

Hume, David (1758). *Essays and Treatises on Several Subjects. A New Edition.* London and Edinburgh: Millar, Kincaid and Donaldson.

——— (1763). *The History of England* ... 8 vols. London: Millar.

——— (1777). *The Life of David Hume* ... Dublin: Williams.

——— (1955). *Writings on Economics.* Edited by Eugene Rotwein. Edinburgh: Nelson.

——— (1994). *Political Essays.* Edited by Knud Haakonssen. Cambridge: CUP.

Hutcheson, Francis (1747). *A Short Introduction to Moral Philosophy.* Glasgow: Foulis.

Intieri, Bartolomeo (1716). *Nuova invenzione di fabbricar mulini a vento* ... Naples: Mosca.

———— (1754). *Della perfetta conservazione del grano*. Naples: Raimondi.

Isola, Francesco (1811). *Instituzioni di commercio e di economia civile*. Rome: de Romanis.

[Janssen, Theodore] (1713). *General Maxims of Trade . . .* London: Buckley.

Jefferys, T. (1754). *The Conduct of the French, With Regard to Nova Scotia . . .* London: Jefferys.

Justamond, J. O. (1798). *Philosophical and Political History of the . . . East and West Indies*. 6 vols. London: Cadell.

Justi, Johann Heinrich Gottlob von (1758–61). *Vollstaendige Abhandlung von den Manufakturen und Fabriken*. 2 vols. Copenhagen: Rothen.

Kant, Immanuel (1996). "An Answer to the Question: What Is Enlightenment? (1784)." In James Schmidt (ed.), *What Is Enlightenment? Eighteenth-Century Answers and Twentieth-Century Questions*. Berkeley: University of California Press, 58–64.

Kelly, John (1732–37). *The History of England. Written originally in French by M. Rapin de Thoyras*. 3 vols. London.

Kennett, Basil, with William Percivale (1703). *Of the Law of Nature and Nations*. Oxford: Lichfield.

King, Charles (ed.) (1721). *The British Merchant . . .* 3 vols. London: Darby.

Kippax, John (1751). *The Theory and Practice of Commerce and Maritime Affairs . . .* 2 vols. London: Rivington.

Klotz, Gérard (1995). *Politique et économie au temps des Lumières*. Saint-Étienne: Publications de l'Université de Saint-Étienne.

Lacretelle, Pierre-Louis de (1786). *Mémoire á consulter, et consultation pour les négoicians faisant le commerce des merchandises des Indes . . .* N.p.

Laffemas, Barthélemy de (1597). *Reiglement [sic] general pour dresser les manufactures en ce rayaume . . .* Paris: de Monstr'oil and Richter.

———— (1602). *Lettres et examples de feu de la Royne mere*. Paris: Pautonnier.

La Fontaine, Jean de (1708). *Fables choices*. London: Vaillant.

———— (1734). *Fables and tales from La Fontaine . . .* London: Bettsworth, Hitch, and Davis.

Lavasse, Jean-J. Dauxion (1820). *A Statistical, Commercial, and Political Description of Venezuela, Trinidad, Margarita, and Tobago . . .* London: Whittaker.

Lawrence, Richard (1682). *The Interest of Ireland in its Trade and Wealth Stated*. Dublin: Ray.

Le Blanc, Jean Lambert (1754). "Notice de quelques-uns des principaux ouvrages Anglois sur le commerce." In *Discours politiques . . .* Dresden: Groell, 250–259.

Lefevere, André (ed.) (1992). *Translation/History/Culture: A Sourcebook*. Shanghai: Shanghai Foreign Language Education Press.

Leopold II (1969-74). *Relazioni sul governo della Toscana*. Edited by Arnaldo Salvestrini. 3 vols. Florence: Olschki.

[Leslie, Charles] (1698). *Considerations of Importance to Ireland*. N.p.

Leti, Gregorio (1676). *Li segreti di stato . . .* 3 vols. Cologne: Turchetto.

Levi, Leone (1849). *Chambers and Tribunals of Commerce and Proposed General Chamber of Commerce in Liverpool*. London: Simpkin, Marshall.

Linguet, Simon-Nicolas-Henri (1774). *Du pain et du bled.* London [but Paris].

—— (1777–92). *Annales politiques, civiles et littéraires.* 19 vols. London [but Paris]

Linnaeus, Carl von (1752). "Principes de l'Oeconomie, fongés sur la Science naturelle & sur la Physique." *Journal Oeconomique,* May, 40–65.

List, Friedrich (1844). *Das nationale System des politischen Oekonomie.* Stuttgart and Tübingen: Cotta.

Locke, John (1690). *An Essay Concerning Humane Understanding* . . . London: Basset.

—— (1692). *Some Considerations of the Consequences of the Lowering of Interest, and Raising the Value of Money* . . . London: Awnsham and Churchill.

—— (1976–89). *The Correspondence of John Locke.* Edited by E. S. de Beer. 8 vols. Oxford: OUP.

—— (1988). *Two Treatises of Government.* Edited by Peter Laslett. Cambridge: CUP.

—— (1991). *Locke on Money.* Edited by Patrick H. Kelly. 2 vols. Oxford: OUP.

—— (1997). *Political Essays.* Edited by Mark Goldie. Cambridge: CUP.

Locke, John, et al. (1670). *The Fundamental Constitution of Carolina.* N.p.

Lockman, John (1750a). *Britannia's Gold-Mine; or, the Herring-Fishery for Ever* . . . London: Owen.

—— (1750b). *The Vast Importance of the Herring Fishery* . . . London: Owen.

Machiavelli, Niccolò (1971). *Tutte le Opere.* Edited by Mario Martelli. Florence: Sansoni.

Madison, James, Alexander Hamilton, and John Jay (1987). *The Federalist Papers.* Edited by Isaac Kramnick. London: Penguin.

Malaspina, Luigi (1786). *Relazione di una scorsa per varie provincie d'Europa* . . . Pavia: Nella Stamperia del R. Im Monastero di S. Salvatore.

Malynes, Gerard (1622). *The Maintenance of Free Trade* . . . London: Legatt.

Mandeville, Bernard de (1988). *The Fable of the Bees.* 2 vols. Edited by F. B. Kaye. Indianapolis: Liberty Fund.

Manton, Thomas (1681). *One Hundred and Ninety Sermons on the Hundred and Nineteenth Psalm.* London: Parkhurst.

Marcoleta, D. Domingo de (1771). *Observaciones sobre las ventajas, y desventajas de la Francia, y la Gran Bretaña* . . . Madrid: Blas Roman.

Martinengo, Michel Antonio (1833). *Del sistema proibitivo* . . . Turin: Stamperia Reale.

Martyn, Henry (1701). *Considerations upon the East-India Trade.* London: Churchill.

May, John (1613). *A Declaration of the Estate of Clothing now Used within this Realme of England.* London: Islip.

Mayerne, Louis Turquet de (1611). *La monarchie aristodémocratique* . . . Paris: Berjon and Bouc.

Mazzini, Giuseppe (2009). *A Cosmopolitanism of Nations: Giuseppe Mazzini's Writings on Democracy, Nation Building, and International Relations.* Edited by Stefano Recchia and Nadia Urbinati. Princeton: Princeton.

McCulloch, John Ramsay (1856). *Early English Tracts on Commerce*. London: Political Economy Club.

Melon, Jean François (1734). *Essai politique sur le commerce*. N.p.

——— (1736). *Essai politique sur le commerce*. 2nd ed. N.p.

——— (1983). *Opere*. Edited by Onofrio Nicastro and Severina Perona. 2 vols. Pisa: Libreria Testi Universitari.

Mengotti, Francesco (1792). *Ragionamento . . . presentato alla Real società economica fiorentina pel concorso al problema del 1791 . . .* Florence: Pagani e compagni.

——— (1797). *Del commercio de' Romani ed il Colbertismo*. Verona: Giuliani.

Merck, Johann Heinrich (2007). *Briefwechsel*. Edited by Ulrike Leuschner. Göttingen: Wallstein Verlag.

Messbarger, Rebecca, and Paula Findlen (eds.) (2005). *The Contest for Knowledge: Debates over Women's Learning in Eighteenth-Century Italy*. Chicago: Chicago.

[Métra, François (ed.)] (1787–90). Correspondance secrète, politique et littéraire . . . 18 vols. London: Adamson

Meusel, Johann Georg (1806–7). *Litteratur der Statistik*. 2 vols. Leipzig: Fritsch.

Migne, J. P. (1844–55). *Patrologia Latina*. Paris: Garnier.

Miselli, Vincenzo Colizzi (1802). *Memoria sulle lane greggie, e manifatturate dello Stato Pontificio*. Rome: Salvioni.

Molini, Peter (1765). *A Catalogue . . .* London: Molini.

Molyneux, William (1698). *The Case of Ireland's being Bound by Acts of Parliament in England, Stated*. Dublin: Ray.

Montchrétien, Antoine de (1615/1889). *Traicté de l'oeonomie politique*. Edited by Th. Funck-Brentano. Paris: Plon.

Montesquieu, Charles Secondat de (1943). *Riflessioni e pensieri inediti (1716–1755)*. Turin: Einaudi.

——— (1989). *The Spirit of the Laws*. Edited by Anne M. Cohler, Basia C. Miller, and Harold S. Stone. Cambridge: CUP.

——— (1995). *Viaggio in Italia*. Edited by Giovanni Macchia and Massimo Colesanti. Bari: Laterza.

——— (1999). *Catalogue de la Bibliothèque de Montesquieu à la Brède*. Edited by Louis Desgraves and Catherine Volpilhac-Auger with Françoise Weil. Naples: Liguori Editore; Paris: Universitas; Oxford: Voltaire Foundation.

——— (2000). *Réflexions sur la monarchie universelle en Europe*. Edited by Michel Porret. Geneva: Droz.

——— (2003). *Voyages*. Paris: Arléa.

Montesquieu, Jean-Baptiste Secondat (1749). *Considérations sur le commerce et la navigation de la Grande-Bretagne*. London: Bettesworth & Hitch.

Morellet, André (1769). *Examen de la réponse de M.N. au Mémoire de M. l'Abbé Morellet, sur la Compagnie des Indes*. Paris: Desaint.

——— (1821). *Mémoires inédites . . .* 2 vols. 2nd ed. Paris: Baudouin.

Moreno, Vincenzio (1845–48). *Lezioni di publica economia*. Naples: Virgilio.

Mortimer, Thomas (1774). *The Elements of Commerce, Politics and Finances*. London: Hooper.

Moser, Johann Jacob (1771). *Anti-Mirabeau*. Frankfurt and Leipzig: Meizer.

Mun, Thomas (1621). *A Discourse of Trade* . . . London: Okes for Pyper.

———— (1664). *England's Treasure by Forraign Trade*. London: Clark.

Muratori, Antonio (1749) *Della pubblica felicità, oggetto de' buoni principi*. Lucca.

Møller, Anders Monrad (1983). *Frederik den Fjerdes Kommercekollegium og Kongelige Danske Rigers Inderlig Styrke og Magt*. Copenhagen: Akademisk Forlag.

N.C. (1697). *The Great Necessity and Advantage of Preserving our own Manufacturies* . . . London: Newborough.

N.H. (1694). *The Ladies Dictionary* . . . London: Dunton.

Nerval, Gérard de (1852). *Les illumines: Récits et portraits*. Paris: Lecou.

Newball, John (1750). *Proposals to Preserve the Publick Roads* . . . London: Cooper.

Nicholson, William (1724). *The Irish Historical Library*. Dublin: Rhames.

Nicolai, Friedrich (1783–96). *Beschreibung einer Reise durch Deutschland und die Schweiz, im Jahre 1781*. 12 vols. Berlin and Stettin: Nicolai.

Nietzsche, Friedrich (1974). *The Gay Science*. New York: Vintage.

Noboa y Lisasueta, Benito de (1753). *Consideraciones sobre el comercio, y la navegacion de la Gran-Bretaña* . . . Madrid: San Martin.

[Nordencrantz], Anders Bachmansson (1730). *Arcana oeconomiæ et commercii* . . . Stockholm: Horn.

North, Dudley (1691). *Discourses upon Trade*. London: Basset.

Nugent, Thomas (1748). *The Principles of Natural Law*. London: Nourse.

———— (1750). *The Spirit of the Laws*. 2 vols. London: Nourse and Vaillant.

Ortiz, Luis (1558/1957). "Memorial a Felipe II [1558]." Edited by Manuel Fernandez Álvarez. *Anales de Economia* 17, no. 63, 117–200.

Osborne, Thomas (1735). *Bibliotheca splendidissima* . . . London: Osborne.

———— (1745?a). *Books Just Published by Thomas Osborne* . . . London: Osborne.

———— (1745b). *Catalogus bibliothecæ Harleianæ, V*. London: Osborne.

———— (1761). *A Catalogue* . . . London: Osborne.

———— (1764?). *A Catalogue for the Year 1764*. London: Osborne.

Osborne, Thomas, and J. Shipton (1754). *A Catalogue* . . . London: Osborne and Shipton.

———— (1756). *A Catalogue* . . . London: Osborne and Shipton.

Pagnini, Gianfrancesco (1766–67). *Della decima e delle altre gravezze* . . . 4 vols. Lisbon and Lucca [but Florence].

Paoletti, Ferdinando (1772). *I veri mezzi di render felici le società*. Florence: Stecchi and Pagani.

Paolini, Aldobrando Giovanni Battista (1785–86). *Della legittima libertà del commercio*. 2 vols. Florence: Pagani.

Parker, Henry (1648). *Of a Free Trade*. London: Neile.

Parliament (1651). *An Act for Increase of Shipping, and Encouragement of the Navigation of this Nation*. London: Field for The Parliament.

Parry, R. (1787). *The Life of Scipio Africanus, and of Epaminondas* . . . 2 vols. London: Richardson.

Payne, Thomas, and Son (1788). *A Catalogue* . . . London: Payne and Son.

Pecchio, Giuseppe (1829). *Storia dell'economia pubblica in Italia.* Lugano: Ruggia.

Penn, William [1720]. *The case of William Penn* . . . N.p.

Petrarca, Francesco (2006). *Canzoniere.* Milan: Feltrinelli.

Petty, William (1683). *Another Essay in Political Arithmetick* . . . London: H.H. for Pardoe.

———— (1687). *Five Essays in Political Arithmetick.* London: Mortlock.

[Petyt, William] (1680). *Britannia Languens.* London: Dring and Crouch.

Pfeiffer, Johann Friedrich von (1779). *Natuerliche, aus dem Endzweck der Gesellschaft entstehende allgemeine Polizeiwissenschaft.* 2 vols. Frankfurt am Main: Esslingerische Buchhandlung.

———— (1780). *Der Antiphysiocrat* . . . Frankfurt am Main: Esslingerische Buchhandlung.

———— (1781–84). *Berichtigungen berühmte Staats-, Finanz-, Policei-, Cameral-, Commerz- und ökonomischer Schriften dieses Jahrhunderts.* 6 vols. Frankfurt am Main: Esslingerische Buchhandlungen.

Phillips, Edward (1658). *The New World of English Words* . . . London: Olms.

Phillips, John (1690). *The Secret History of the Reigns of K. Charles II and K. James II.* N.p.

Pierce, Thomas (1686). *The Law and Equity of the Gospel* . . . London: Roycroft for Clavell.

Pini, Giovambattista (1791). *Memoria . . . coronata dalla Societá patria delle arti e manifatture.* Genoa: Eredi di Scionico.

Plato (2000). *The Republic.* Edited by G. R. F. Ferrari. Translated by Tom Griffith. Cambridge: CUP.

Pluche, Noël-Antoine (1751). *La mécanique des langues et l'art de les enseigner.* Paris: Estienne.

Plüer, Carl Christoph (1757). *Patriotiske Tanker over Manufactur- og Fabrik-Væsenet.* Copenhagen: Lillie.

Polhem, Christopher (1947–54). *Christopher Polhems efterlämnade skrifter.* Edited by Henri Sandblad et al. 4 vols. Uppsala: Alqvist & Wiksells Boktryckeri.

Pombal, Sebastião José de Carvalho e Melo, Marquis of (1986). *Escritos Económicos de Londres (1741–1742).* Lisbon: Biblioteca Nacional.

Postlethwayte, Malachy (1749). *A Dissertation on the Plan, Use, and Importance, of the Universal Dictionary of Trade and Commerce* . . . London: Knapton.

———— (1751). *The Universal Dictionary of Trade and Commerce* . . . 2 vols. London: Knapton.

———— (1757a). *Great Britain's True System.* London: A. Millar et al.

———— (1757b). *The Universal Dictionary of Trade and Commerce* . . . 2nd ed. 2 vols. London: Knapton.

———— (1774). *The Universal Dictionary of Trade and Commerce* . . . 4th ed. 2 vols. London: Stratham.

Postlethwayte, Malachy, and James Royston (1750). *British Mercantile Academy* . . . London: Knapton.

Pott, Jules Henri (1772). *Catalogue de livres françois.* Lausanne: Pott.

Quesnay, François (1736). *Essai phisique sur l'oeconomie animale.* Paris: Cavelier.

———— (1973). *Quesnay's Tableau économique.* Edited by Marguerite Kuczynski and Ronald L. Meek. London: Macmillan.

———— (2005). *Œuvres Économiques Completes et Autres Textes.* Edited by Christine Théré, Loïc Charles, and Jean-Claude Perrot. Paris: INED.

Raynal, Guillaume-Thomas (1780). *Histoire philosophique et politique des établissemens et du commerce des européens dans les Deux Indes.* Geneva: Pellet.

Rayneval, J. M. Gérard de (1789). *Principes de commerce entre les nations.* London.

Réamur, René-Antoine Ferchaut de, Henri-Louis Duhamel du Monceau, and Jean-Rodolphe Perronet (1761). *Art de l'épinglier.* Paris: Saillant and Nyon.

Remondini, Giuseppe (1772). *Catalogus novissimus . . .* Bassano del Grappa: Remondini.

Réstif de la Bretonne, Nicolas-Edme (1889). *Mes inscriptions.* Paris: Plon, Nourrit et Cie.

Reynell, Carew (1674). *The True English Interest . . .* London: Gile's Widowess.

Reynolds, Joshua (1853). *The Life and Discourses of Sir Joshua Reynolds.* Hudson: Sawyer, Ingersoll and Company.

Rhudde, Durand (1757). *The Love of our Country Recommended and Inforced . . .* London: Johnson.

Ricardo, David (1817). *On the Principles of Political Economy and Taxation.* London: John Murray.

Roberti, Giovanni Battista (1772). *Del lusso: Dialogo cristiano.* 2 vols. Bassano del Grappa: Remondini.

Robson, James (1782). *A Catalogue . . .* London: Robson.

Robson, James, and W. Clarke (1789). *A Catalogue . . .* London: Robson and Clarke.

Rohr, Julius Bernhard von (1755). *Haushaltungs Bibliothek.* 3rd ed. Leipzig: Wendlern.

Roseveare, Henry (ed.) (1987). *Markets and Merchants of the Late Seventeenth Century: The Marescoe-David Letters 1668–1680.* London: British Academy.

[Rotondo, Mario Luigi] (1834?). *Osservazioni sul progetto presentato al Real Governor dal signor Commendatore D. Carlo Afan de Rivera relative alle basi di una banca rurale . . .* N.p.

Rotta, Salvatore (ed.) (1974). *L'illuminismo a Genova: Lettere di P. P. Celesia a F. Galiani.* 2 vols. Florence: La Nuova Italia.

Rousseau, Jean-Jacques (1761). *Extrait du Projet de Paix Perpétuelle de Monsieur l'Abbé de Saint-Pierre.* Amsterdam: Rey.

———— (1953). *The Confessions.* London: Penguin.

———— (1997a). *The Discourses and Other Early Political Writings.* Edited and translated by Victor Gourevitch. Cambridge: CUP.

———— (1997b). *The Social Contract and Other Later Political Writings.* Edited and translated by Victor Gourevitch. Cambridge: CUP.

Rycaut, Paul (1688). *The Royal Commentaries of Peru . . .* London: Flesher.

Saint-Simon, Claude-Henri de (1976). *The Political Thought of Saint-Simon*. Edited by Ghita Ionescu. Oxford: OUP.

Salerni, Carlo (1782/1996). *Riflessioni sull'economia della provincia d'Otranto*. Lecce: Centro di studi salentini.

Sare, William (1740). *A Catalogue* . . . London: Sare.

Sarpi, Paolo (1979). *Dai consulti; Il carteggio con l'ambasciatore inglese Sir Dudley Carleton*. Edited by Gaetano and Luisa Cozzi. Turin: Einaudi.

Savary, Jacques (1723). *Dictionnaire universel de commerce*. 2 vols. Paris: Estienne.

Schrebers, Daniel Gottfried (1764). *Zwo Schriften von der Geschichte und Nothwendigkeit der Cameralwissenschaften in so ferne sie als Universitätswissenschaften anzusehen sind*. Leipzig: Onckischen Buchandlung.

Schröder, Wilhelm von (1752). *Fürstliche Schatz- und Rent-Kammer*. Königsberg and Leipzig: Hartung.

Schröderstierna, Samuel (1756). *Tvänne Memorialer angående Frihet i Handel och Slögde-Näringar*. Stockholm: Grefing.

Schytte, Andreas (1773–76). *Staternes indvortes regiering*. 5 vols. Copenhagen: Gyldendals forlag.

Seckendorff, Veit Ludwig von (1665). *Additiones oder Zugaben und Erleuterungen zu dem Tractat des Teutscher Fürsten-Staats*. Frankfurt: Göken.

Secondo, Giuseppe Maria (1747–54). *Ciclopedia* . . . 8 vols. Naples: De Bonis.

Sergio, Vincenzo Emanuele (1993). *Lezioni di economia civile e di commercio*. Edited by Laura Pulejo. Messina: Sicania.

Serra, Antonio (1613). *Breve trattato delle cause che possono far abbondare li regni d'oro & argento dove non sono miniere*. Naples: Scorriggio.

[Seton, William] (1705). *Some Thoughts, on Ways and Means For making This Nation a Gainer in Foreign Commerce* . . . Edinburgh: Watson.

Shaw, Edward (1952). "Unpublished Correspondence Relating to M. de Malesherbes." *Proceedings of the Modern Language Association*, 67, no. 7, 1184–1190.

Sheridan, Thomas (1677). *A Discourse on the Rise & Power of Parliaments* . . . N.p.

Shirley, Anthony (1613/1961). *Peso politico de todo el mundo del conde D. Antonio Xerley*. Edited by Carmelo Viñas y Mey. Madrid: Instituto "Balmes" de Sociologia.

Skelton, Philip (1741). *The Necessity of Tillage and Granaries*. Dublin.

Smith, Adam (1776). *An Inquiry into the Nature and Causes of the Wealth of Nations*. 2 vols. London: Strahan and Cadell.

——— (1976). *An Inquiry into the Nature and Causes of the Wealth of Nations*. Edited by Edwin Cannan with a preface by George J. Stigler. 2 vols. Chicago: Chicago.

——— (1980). *Adam Smith: Essays on Philosophical Subjects*. Edited by W. P. D. Wightman and J. C. Bryce. Oxford: OUP.

——— (1982). *Lectures on Jurisprudence*. Edited by R. L. Meek, D. D. Raphael, and P. G. Stein. Indianapolis: Liberty Fund.

——— (2002). *The Theory of Moral Sentiments*. Edited by Knud Haakonssen. Cambridge: CUP.

Smith, John (1747). *Chronicon rusticum-commerciale* . . . 2 vols. London: Osborne.

Societé d'Agriculture, de Commerce et des Arts de Bretagne (1760). *Corps d'Observation de la Societe d'Agriculture de Commerce & des Arts, 1757–8.* 2 vols. Rennes: Vatar.

Spinelli, Trojano [1750]. *Riflessioni politiche sopra alcuni punti della scienza della moneta.* N.p.

Sprat, Thomas (1667). *History of the Royal Society.* London: Martyn and Allestry.

Steinlein, Karl (1831). *Handbuch der Volks-Wirthschafts-Lehre: Mit drei synoptischen Tafeln.* Munich: Literarisch-Artistischen Anstalt.

Stockdale, Percival (1776). *The Institutions, Manners, and Customs of the Ancient Nations* . . . 2 vols. London: Becket.

Sydney, Henry (1692). *Speech* . . . *to Both Houses of Parliament Assembled at Dublin. October 5. 1692.* N.p.

S.X. (1755). *A letter concerning prerogative. Addressed to C-r N-n, Esq.* Dublin: Cooper.

Targioni, Luigi (1786). *Saggi fisici politici ed economici* . . . Naples: Campo.

Tawney, R. H., and Eileen Power (1924). *Tudor Economic Documents.* 3 vols. New York: Longmans Green.

Taylor, Jeremy (1675). *Antiquitates christianae* . . . London: Norton for Royston.

T.W. (1746). *The Present Condition of Great Britain.* London: J. Robinson et al.

Temple, William (1673). *Essay upon the Advancement of Trade in Ireland.* Dublin.

Thomas, Lucas (1793). *A Catalogue* . . . Birmingham: Thomas.

Thomas, Mr. (1758). *An Abridgement of Ainsworth's Dictionary of the Latin Tongue.* 2 vols. London: Mount et al.

Thompson, Charles (1744). *The Travels of the Late Charles Thompson.* 3 vols. Reading: Newbery and Micklewright.

Thomson, James (1740). *Alfred: A Masque.* London: Millar.

Thott, Otto (1983). "Allerunderdanigste uforgribelige Tanker om Commerciens Tilstand og Opkomst." In Kristof Glamann and Erik Oxenbøll, *Studier i dansk merkantilisme: Omkring tekster af Otto Thott.* Copenhagen: Akademisk Forlag, 169–220.

Todd, John (1792). *J. Todd's Catalogue for 1792* . . . London: Todd.

Todeschi, Claudio (1770). *Saggi di agricoltura, manifatture, e commercio* . . . Rome: Casaletti.

———— (1774). *Pensieri sulla pubblica felicità.* Rome: Casaletti.

Toland, John (1695). *A Discourse upon Coins by Signor Bernardo Davanzati* . . . London: Awnsham and Churchill.

Torres, Antonio de (1781). *Saggio di riflessioni sulle arti, e il commercio europeo dei nostri tempi, e degli antichi* . . . 2 vols. Pesaro: Gavelli.

Trevers, Joseph (1675). *An Essay to the Restoring of our Decayed Trade.* London: Gile's Widdowess.

Tron, Andrea (1784/1994). "Serenissimo Principe." In Paolo Gaspari (ed.), *Il testamento morale dell'aristocrazia veneziana.* Udine: Istituto editoriale Veneto friulano, 90–125.

Tucker, Josiah (1749). *A Brief Essay on the Advantages and Disadvantages, which Respectively Attend France and Great Britain, with Regard to Trade.* London: Trye.

—— (1763). *The Case of Going to War, for the Sake of Procuring, Enlarging, or Securing of Trade, Considered in a New Light.* London: Dodsley et al.

Tupman, Samuel (1790). *A Catalogue* . . . Nottingham: Tupman.

Turgot, Anne Robert Jacques (1997). *Formation et distribution des richesses.* Paris: Flammarion.

Uhlich, Adam Gottfried (1755). *Geschichte und Handlung der Englischen Colonien in dem nördlichen America.* Frankfurt am Main: Andreä.

Uztáriz, Géronimo de (1724). *Theorica y practica de comercio, y de marina* . . . Madrid.

Vaughan, Benjamin (1788). *New and Old Principles of Trade Compared* . . . London: Johnson and Debrett.

Vergani, Paolo (1794). *Della importanza e dei pregi del nuovo sistema di finanza dello Stato Pontifico.* N.p.

Verri, Pietro, and Alessandro Verri (1910–42). *Carteggio di Pietro e di Alessandro Verri.* 12 vols. Milan: Cogliati et al.

Verri, Pietro (1939). *Considerazioni sul commercio dello stato di Milan.* Edited by C. A. Vianello. Milan: Università L. Bocconi.

—— (2006–7). *Scritti di economia finanza e amministrazione.* Edited by Giuseppe Bognetti et al. 2 vols. Rome: Edizioni di storia e letteratura.

Vico, Giambattista (2000). *Universal Right.* Edited by Giorgio Pinton and Margaret Diehl. Amsterdam: Rodopi.

—— (2001). *The New Science.* Translated by David Marsh. Edited by Anthony Grafton. London: Penguin.

—— (2002). *The First New Science.* Edited by Leon Pompa. Cambridge: CUP.

Voltaire [Francois Marie Arouet] (1733). *Letters Concerning the English Nation.* London: C. Davis.

—— (1768). *L'Homme aux Quarante Ecus.* Paris.

—— (1979–94). *Corpus des notes marginales de Voltaire.* 5 vols. Berlin: Akademie Verlag.

—— (1994). *Political Writings.* Edited by David Williams. Cambridge: CUP.

W.S. (1656). *The Golden Fleece* . . . London: Grismond.

Ward, Bernardo (1779). *Proyecto Economico* . . . Madrid: Ibarra.

Wase, Christopher (1671). *The History of France under the Ministry of Cardinal Mazarine* . . . London: Starkey.

Weissbort, Daniel, and Astradur Eysteinsson (2006). *Translation—Theory and Practice: A Historical Reader.* Oxford: OUP.

Weiz, Friedrich August (1780). *Das gelehrte Sachsen* . . . Leipzig: Schneidern.

[Wellingborough] (1650). *A Declaration of the Grounds and Reasons why the Poor Inhabitants of the Town of VVellinborrow* . . . *have Begun and Give Consent to Dig Up, Manure and Sow Corn Upon the Common* . . . London: Calvert.

Wendeborn, Gebhard Friedrich August (1791). *A View of England.* 2 vols. London: Sleater.

Weskett, John (1781). *A Complete Digest of the Theory, Laws, and Practice of Insurance* . . . London: Frys, Couchman, & Collier.

Westerman, Johan (1768). *Inträdes-Tal, om Svenska Näringarnes Undervigt emot de Utländske, förmedelst en trögare Arbets-drift.* Stockholm: Salvius.

Whiston, John (1754). *A Catalogue* . . . London: Whiston.

Whiston, John, and Benjamin White (1762?). *A Catalogue* . . . London: Whiston and White.

White, Benjamin (1766a). *A Catalogue of a Valuable Collection of Books* . . . London: White.

———— (1766b). *A Catalogue of the Entire Libraries* . . . London: White.

———— (1770). *A Catalogue* . . . London: White.

———— (1771). *A Catalogue* . . . London: White.

———— (1772). *A Catalogue* . . . London: White.

———— (1774). *A Catalogue* . . . London: White.

———— (1775). *A Catalogue* . . . London: White.

———— (1778). *A Catalogue* . . . London: White.

———— (1780). *A Catalogue* . . . London: White.

White, James (1792). *Speeches by M. de Mirabeau the Elder* . . . 2 vols. London: Debrett.

Wichmann, Christian August (1758). *Herrn Carl Christian Krausens . . . Abhandlung von den Muttermälern* . . . Leipzig: Gollner.

———— (1768) . . . *Characteristics* . . . Leipzig: Heinsiussischen Buchhandlung.

———— (1774) . . . *Helvetius hinterlassenes Werk vom Menschen* . . . 2 vols. Breslau: Meyer.

———— [with Friedrich Schiller] (1776–78). *Untersuchung der Natur und Ursachen von Nationalreichtümern* . . . 2 vols. Leipzig: Weidemanns Erben und Reich.

———— (1780). *Lehrbegriff der Staatsordnung.* Leipzig: Jacobäer und Sohne.

———— (1786). *Die entlarvte Heilige oder die neue Katharina von Siena in der Geschichte einer Nonne* . . . Leipzig: Heinsius.

———— (1788). *Anton Genovesi, ökonomisch-politischer Commentarius zu Johann Carys historisch-politischen Bemerkungen über Grossbritanniens Handel und Gewerbe.* Leipzig: Heinsius.

———— (1789). *Geschichte des französischen Reichstages vom Jahr 1789* . . . Leipzig: Göschen.

———— (1793). *Ueber Freyheit und Einschränkung der Handelsgeschäffte* . . . Leipzig: Jacobäer.

———— (1797–98). . . . *Landwirtschaftsphilosophie oder Politische Ökonomie der gesammten Land-und Staats-Wirtschaft.* Liegnitz: Siegert.

———— (1798). *Flor und Verfall der Länder* . . . Züllichau: Darnmann.

Will, Georg Andreas (1782). *Versuch über die Physiokratie* . . . Nuremberg: Raspe.

Willan, Leonard (1670). *The Exact Politician, or, Compleat Statesman* . . . London: Newman.

Wilson, Thomas (1788?). *Catalogue* . . . York: Wilson.

Witzman, August (1772–74). *Grundsätze der bürgerlichen Oekonomie* . . . Leipzig: Saalbach.

——— (1776). ... *Grundsätze der bürgerlichen Oekonomie* ... Leipzig: Kummer.

Wolf, Edwin, and Kevin J. Hayes (2006). *The Library of Benjamin Franklin.* Philadephia: American Philosophical Society.

Woodfall, William (1785). *An Impartial Sketch of the Debate in the House of Commons of Ireland.* Dublin: White.

Worsley, Benjamin (1651). *The Advocate.* London: Du-Gard for the Council of State.

——— (1652). *Free Ports, the Nature and Necessitie of them Stated.* London: Du-Gard for the Council of State.

Xenophon (1984). *Poroi.* Edited by E. C. Merchant. Cambridge, Mass.: Harvard.

Yarranton, Andrew (1677). *England's Improvement by Sea and Land to Out-do the Dutch without Fighting* ... London: Everingham.

Young, Arthur (1774). *Political Arithmetic* ... London: Nicoll.

Zanon, Antonio (1766). *Dell'agricoltura, dell'arti, e del commercio* ... 6 vols. Venice: Fenzo.

Zinzendorf, Karl von (2009). *Europäische Aufklärung zwischen Wien und Triest: Die Tagebücher des Gouverneurs Karl Graf Zinzendorf 1776–1782.* Edited by Grete Klingenstein, Eva Faber, and Antonio Trampus. 4 vols. Vienna: Böhlau.

Secondary Sources

Abramowitz, Moses (1986). "Catching Up, Forging Ahead, and Falling Behind." *Journal of Economic History* 46, no. 2, 385–406.

Abulafia, David (1977). *The Two Italies: Economic Relations between the Norman Kingdom of Sicily and the Northern Communes.* Cambridge: CUP.

——— (1988). *Frederick II: A Medieval Emperor.* London: Allen Lane.

Acomb, Frances (1950). *Anglophobia in France, 1763–1789: An Essay in the History of Constitutionalism and Nationalism.* Durham, N.C.: Duke University Press.

Adam, Ulrich (2006). *The Political Economy of J. H. G. Justi.* Oxford: Peter Lang.

Adams, Leonard (1974). *Coyer and the Enlightenment.* Banbury: Voltaire Foundation.

Ajello, Raffaele (1976). *Arcana Juris: Diritto e politica nel Settecento italiano.* Naples: Jovene.

Alimento, Antonella (1995). "La réception des idées physiocratiques à travers les traductions: le cas toscan et vénetien." In Bernard Delmas, Thierry Demals, and Philippe Steiner (eds.), *La Diffusion Internationale de la Physiocratie (XVIIIe–XIXe).* Grenoble: Presses Universitaires de Grenoble, 297–313.

——— (2006). "Passione e disincanto nella vita di un economista 'scomodo': La biblioteca di Véron de Forbonnais." In Carlo Mangio and Marcello Verga (eds.), *Il Settecento di Furio Diaz.* Pisa: Edizioni Plus, Pisa University Press, 47–60.

——— (2008). "Tra Bristol ed Amsterdam: Discussioni livornesi su commercio, marina ed impero negli anni Cinquanta del Settecento." In Donatella Balani et al. (eds.), *Dall'origine dei lumi alla rivoluzione: Scritti in onore di Luciano Guerci e Giuseppe Ricuperati*. Rome: Edizioni di storia e letteratura, 25–45.

—— (2009). "Entre animosité nationale et rivalité d'émulation: La position de Véron de Forbonnais face à la compétition anglaise." In Manuela Alberatone (ed.), *Governare il mondo: L'economia come linguaggio della politica nell'Europa del Settecento*. Milan: Fondazione Giangiacomo Feltrinelli, 125–148.

—— (ed.) (2009). *Modelli d'oltre confine: Prospettive economiche e sociali negli antichi stati italiani*. Rome: Edizioni di storia e letteratura.

Allen, Robert C. (2001). "The Great Divergence in European Wages and Prices from the Middle Ages to the First World War." *Explorations in Economic History* 38, 411–447.

—— (2004). "Britain's Economic Ascendancy in a European Context." In Leandro Prados de Escosura (ed.), *Exceptionalism and Industrialisation: Britain and Its European Rivals, 1688–1815*. Cambridge: CUP, 15–34.

—— (2009). *The British Industrial Revolution in Global Perspective*. Cambridge: CUP.

Amdisen, Asser (2002). *Til Nytte og Fornøjelse: Johann Friedrich Struensee, 1737–1772*. Copenhagen: Akademisk Forlag.

Amsden, Alice H. (2001). *The Rise of "The Rest": Challenges to the West from Late-Industrializing Economies*. Oxford: OUP.

Anderson, Benedict (1991). *Imagined Communities: Reflections on the Origin and Spread of Nationalism*. New York: Verso.

Anderson, Fred (2001). *The Crucible of War: The Seven Years' War and the Fate of Empire in British North America, 1754–1766*. New York: Faber & Faber.

Andrew, Bradley B. (2002). "Unfair Trade, Mercantilism and Economic Development: Great Britain: 1660–1800." Ph.D. diss., University of Connecticut.

Anonymous (ed.) (1972). *Las Reales Sociedades Economicas de Amigos del Pais y su Obra*. San Sebastian: Izarra.

Anthony, David W. (2007). *The Horse, the Wheel, and Language: How Bronze-Age Riders from the Eurasian Steppes Shaped the Modern World*. Princeton: Princeton.

Appleby, J. O. (1976). "Ideology and Theory: The Tension between Political and Economic Liberalism in Seventeenth-Century England." *American Historical Review* 81, no. 3, 499–515.

—— (1978). *Economic Thought and Ideology in Seventeenth-Century England*. Princeton: Princeton.

—— (1992). *Liberalism and Republicanism in the Historical Imagination*. Cambridge, Mass.: Harvard.

Armitage, David (1995). "The Scottish Vision of Empire: Intellectual Origins of the Darien Venture." In John Robertson (ed.), *A Union for Empire: Political Thought and the Union of 1707*. Cambridge: CUP, 97–120.

—— (2000a). *The Ideological Origins of the British Empire*. Cambridge: CUP.

—— (2000b). "The Political Economy of Britain and Ireland after the Glorious Revolution." In J. H. Ohlmeyer (ed.), *Political Thought in Seventeenth-Century Ireland: Kingdom or Colony?* Cambridge: CUP, 221–243.

———— (2002). "Empire and Liberty: A Republican Dilemma." In Martin van Gelderen and Quentin Skinner (eds.), *Republicanism: A Shared European Heritage*, vol. 2, *The Values of Republicanism in Early Modern Europe*. Cambridge: CUP, 29–46.

———— (2004). "John Locke, Carolina, and the *Two Treatises of Government*." *Political Theory* 32, no. 5, 602–627.

Arnaldi, Girolamo (2005). *Italy and Its Invaders*. Translated by Antony Shugaar. Cambridge, Mass.: Harvard.

Arneil, Barbara (1996). *John Locke and America: The Defence of English Colonialism*. Oxford: Clarendon Press.

Arup, Erik (1907). *Studier i Engelsk og Tysk Handels Historie*. Copenhagen: Gyldendalske Boghandel—Nordisk Forlag.

Ashcraft, Richard (1969). "Political Theory and Political Reform: John Locke's Essay on Virginia." *Western Political Quarterly* 22, no. 4, 742–758.

Ashley, William (1898). "Review of *Vincent de Gournay* by G. Schelle." *Political Science Quarterly* 13, no. 2, 342–344.

Ashworth, William J. (2003). *Customs and Excise: Trade, Production, and Consumption in England, 1640–1845*. Oxford: OUP.

———— (2007). "The Intersection of Industry and the State in Eighteenth-Century Britain." In Lissa Roberts, Simon Schaffer, and Peter Dear (eds.), *The Mindful Hand: Inquiry and Invention from the Late Renaissance to Early Industrialisation*. Amsterdam: Koninklijke Nederlandse Akademie van Wetenschappen, 349–377.

Astarita, Tommaso (2002). *The Continuity of Feudal Power: The Caracciolo di Brienza in Spanish Naples*. Cambridge: CUP.

———— (2005). *Between Salt Water and Holy Water: A History of Southern Italy*. New York: Norton.

Astigarraga, Jesús (2001). "The Light and Shade of Italian Economic Thought in Spain (1750–1850)." In P. F. Asso (ed.), *From Economists to Economists: The International Spread of Italian Economic Thought, 1750–1950*. Florence: Polistampa, 227–253.

———— (2004). "Diálogo económico en la "otra" Europa: Las traducciones españolas de los economistas de la Ilustración napolitana (A. Genovesi, F. Galiani y G. Filangieri)." *Cromohs* 9, 1–21. www.cromohs.unifi.it/92004/astigarraga .html.

Astigarraga, Jesús, and Javier Usoz (2007). "From the Neapolitan A. Genovesi of Carlo di Borbone to the Spanish A. Genovesi of Carlos III: V. De Villava's Spanish Translation of 'Lezioni di Commercio.'" In Bruno Jossa, Rosario Patalano, and Eugenio Zagari (eds.), *Genovesi economista*. Naples: IISF, 193–220.

Austin, Ian Patrick (2009). *Common Foundations of American and East Asian Modernisation: From Alexander Hamilton to Junichero Koizumi*. Singapore: Select.

Backhaus, Jürgen (1994). "The German Economic Tradition: From Cameralism to the Verein Für Socialpolitik." In Maria Albertone and Alberto Masoero (eds.), *Political Economy and National Realities*. Turin: Fondazione Einaudi, 329–357.

Backhaus, Jürgen, and Richard E. Wagner (2005). "From Continental Public Finance to Public Choice: Mapping Continuity." In Steven G. Medema and Peter Boettke (eds.), *The Role of Government in the History of Economic Thought*. Durham, N.C.: Duke University Press, 314–332.

Backhouse, Roger E. (2002). *The Penguin History of Economics*. London: Penguin.

Bahlman, Dudley W. R. (1957). *The Moral Revolution of 1688*. New Haven: Yale.

Bain, Robert Nisbet (1894). *Gustavus III and His Contemporaries, 1746–1792*. 2 vols. London: Kegan Paul, Trench, Trübner.

——— (1905). *Scandinavia: A Political History of Denmark, Norway and Sweden from 1513 to 1900*. Cambridge: CUP.

Bain, Robert (1971). "The Composition and Publication of *The Present State of Virginia and the College*." *Early American Literature* 6, no. 1, 31–54.

Bairoch, Paul, Jean Batou, and Pierre Chévre (1988). *La population des villes européennes de 800 à 1850—The Population of European Cities from 800 to 1850*. Geneva: Droz.

Baldi, Marialuisa (1983). *David Hume nel Settecento italiano: Filosofia ed economia*. Florence: La Nuova Italia.

Ballaster, Rosalind (2005). *Fabulous Orients: Fictions of the East in England, 1662–1785*. Oxford: OUP.

Barbieri, Katherine (2002). *The Liberal Illusion: Does Trade Promote Peace?* Ann Arbor: University of Michigan Press.

Barkan, Leonard (1999). *Unearthing the Past: Archaeology and Aesthetics in the Making of Renaissance Culture*. New Haven: Yale.

Baroncelli, Flavio (1981). "Tra Locke e Smith: Alcune immagini del rapporto col 'povero.'" *Studi Settecenteschi* 2, 135–151.

Barry, Christopher (1994). *The Idea of Luxury: A Conceptual and Historical Investigation*. Cambridge: CUP.

Barry, Jonathan (1993). "Cultural Patronage and the Anglican Crisis: Bristol c. 1689–1775." In John Walsh, Colin Haydon, and Stephen Taylor (eds.), *The Church of England c. 1689–1833*. Cambridge: CUP, 191–208.

——— (2005). "The 'Great Projector': John Cary and the Legacy of Puritan Reform in Bristol, 1647–1720." In Margaret Pelling and Scott Mandelbrote (eds.), *The Practice of Reform in Health, Medicine, and Science, 1500–2000*. Aldershot: Ashgate, 185–206.

Bartlett, Thomas (1998). "'This Famous Island set in a Virginian Sea': Ireland in the British Empire, 1690–1801." In P. J. Marshall (ed.), *The Oxford History of the British Empire*, vol. 2, *The Eighteenth Century*. Oxford: OUP, 253–275.

Bauer, Volker (1997). *Hofökonomie: Der Diskurs über den Fürstenhof in Zeremonialwissenschaft, Hausväterliteratur und Kameralismus*. Vienna: Böhlau Verlag.

Beachy, Robert (2005). *The Soul of Commerce: Credit, Property, and Politics in Leipzig, 1750–1840*. Leiden: Brill.

Beales, Derek (1987–2009). *Joseph II*. 2 vols. Cambridge: CUP.

Beaurepaire, Pierre-Yves (2007). *Le mythe de l'Europe française au XVIIIe siècle: Diplomatie, culture et sociabilités au temps des Lumières.* Paris: Éditions Autrement.

Becagli, Vieri (1977). "Il 'Salomon du Midi' e l'"Ami des Hommes.' Le riforme Leopoldine in alcune lettere del marhese di Mirabeau al Conte di Scheffer." *Ricerche storiche* 7, no. 1, 137–195.

———— (1983). *Un unico territorio gabellabile: La riforma doganale leopoldina: Il dibattito politico 1767–1781.* Florence: Università degli studi di Firenze.

———— (2003). "La diffusione della fisiocrazia nell'Italia del Settecento: Note per una ricerca." In Piero Barucci (ed.), *Le frontiere dell'economia politica: Gli economisti stranieri in Italia: dai mercantilisti a Keynes.* Florence: Polistampa, 63–82.

Becchi, Paolo (1986). *Vico e Filangieri in Germania.* Naples: Jovene.

Beebee, Thomas O. (1990). *Clarissa on the Continent: Translation and Seduction.* University Park: Pennsylvania State University Press.

Beecher, Donald (2006). "John Frampton, Translator, Traveler." In Carmine G. Di Biase (ed.), *Travel and Translation in the Early Modern Period.* Amsterdam: Rodopi, 103–121.

Bell, David A. (2003). *The Cult of the Nation in France: Inventing Nationalism, 1680–1800.* Cambridge, Mass.: Harvard.

Bell, John Fred (1953). *A History of Economic Thought.* New York: Ronald Press.

Bellamy, Richard (1987). "'Da metafisico a mercatante': Antonio Genovesi and the Development of a New Language of Commerce in Eighteenth-Century Naples." In Anthony Pagden (ed.), *The Languages of Political Theory in Early-Modern Europe.* Cambridge: CUP, 277–299.

Ben-Atar, Doron S. (2004). *Trade Secrets: Intellectual Piracy and the Origins of American Industrial Power.* New Haven: Yale.

Benjamin, Walter (1999). *Illuminations.* London: Pimlico.

Bentley, Jerry H. (1987). *Politics and Culture in Renaissance Naples.* Princeton: Princeton.

Berg, Maxine (2005). *Luxury and Pleasure in Eighteenth-Century Britain.* Oxford: OUP.

Berge, Kjell Lars (1998). "Å beskrive og forandre verden: om tekstkulturen i dansk-norsk 1700-tall og studiet av den." In Berge (ed.), *Å beskrive og forandre verden: En antologi tekster fra 1700-tallets dansk-norske tekstkultur.* Oslo: Norges Forskningsråd, 7–40.

Bernardini, Paolo (1989). "Aufklärung e Beamtentum: I. Metodo storiografico e teoria dell'economia in C. W. Dohm (1773–1779)." *Annali della Fondazione Luigi Einaudi* 23, 371–470.

———— (1994). *Magnifici e re: Le corrispondenze diplomatiche di Pietro Paolo Celesia dalla Corte di Spagna. Gli ultimi anni di regno di Carlo III, 1784–1788.* Genoa: Civico Istituto Colombiano.

Berry, Christopher J. (1994). *The Idea of Luxury: A Conceptual and Historical Investigation.* Cambridge: CUP.

Bertram, Mijndert (2007). "The End of the Dynastic Union, 1815–1837." In Brendan Simms and Torsten Riotte (eds.), *The Hanoverian Dimension in British History, 1714–1837*. Cambridge: CUP, 111–127.

Biernacki, Richard (1995). *The Fabrication of Labour: Germany and Britain, 1640–1914*. Berkeley: University of California Press.

Birch, Alan (1955). "Foreign Observers of the British Iron Industry during the Eighteenth Century." *Journal of Economic History* 15, no. 1, 23–33.

Bisgaard, H. L. (1902). *Den Danske Nationaløkonomi i det 18. Århundre*. Copenhagen: Hagerup.

Black, Jeremy (1999). *Eighteenth-Century Europe*. Basingstoke: Palgrave Macmillan.

Blair, Ann (2010). *Too Much to Know: Managing Scholarly Information before the Modern Age*. New Haven: Yale.

Blair, Tony (2004). "Doctrine of International Community." In Irwin Stelzer (ed.), *The Neocon Reader*. New York: Grove Press, 107–116.

Blanning, T. C. W. (2001). *The Culture of Power and the Power of Culture: Old Regime Europe, 1660–1789*. Oxford: OUP.

Blanqui, Jérôme-Adolphe (1880). *History of Political Economy in Europe*. New York: G. P. Putnam's Sons.

Bleek, Wilhelm (1972). *Von der Kameralausbildung zum Juristenprivileg*. Berlin: Colloquium.

Bloch, Marc (1989). *Feudal Society*. Translated by L. A. Manyon. 2 vols. London: Routledge.

Boissevain, Jeremy (1966). "Patronage in Sicily." *Man* 1, no. 1, 18–33.

Bonno, Gabriel (1948). "La Culture et la civilisation britanniques devant l'opinion française de la paix d'Utrecht aux Lettres philosophiques (1713–1734)." *Transactions of the American Philosophical Society* 38, pt. 1.

Borges, Jorge Luis (1996). *Obras Completas*. 4 vols. Buenos Aires: Emecé.

Borst, Arno (1957–63). *Der Turmbau von Babel: Geschichte der Meinungen über den Ursprung und Vielfalt der Sprachen und Völker*. 6 vols. Stuttgart: Hiersemann.

Bourde, André J. (1953). *The Influence of England on the French Agronomes, 1750–1789*. Cambridge: CUP.

Bouzinac, J. (1970). *Les doctrines économiques au dix-huitième siècle: Jean-Francois Melon: Économiste*. New York: Burt Franklin.

Braudel, Fernand (1977). *Afterthoughts on Material Civilization and Capitalism*. Translated by Patricia M. Ranum. Baltimore: Hopkins.

——— (1982). *On History*. Translated by Sarah Matthews. Chicago: Chicago.

——— (1992). *Civilization and Capitalism*. 3 vols. Berkeley: University of California Press.

Breen, T. H. (2004). *The Marketplace of Revolution: How Consumer Politics Shaped American Independence*. New York: OUP.

Bregnsbo, Michael, and Kurt Villads Jensen (2004). *Det Danske Imperium: Storhed og Fald*. Copenhagen: Aschehoug.

Breisach, Ernst (1994). *Historiography: Ancient, Medieval, and Modern*. 2nd ed. Chicago: Chicago.

Brenner, Robert Paul (2003). *Merchants and Revolution: Commercial Change, Political Conflict, and London's Overseas Traders, 1550–1653*. London: Verso.

Brewer, John (1988). *The Sinews of Power: War, Money and the English State, 1688–1783*. Cambridge, Mass.: Harvard.

Brock, Robert K. (1937). *Archibald Cary of Ampthill: Wheelhorse of the Revolution*. Richmond, Va.: Garrett and Massie.

Bronner, Stephen Eric (2004). *Reclaiming the Enlightenment: Toward a Politics of Radical Engagement*. New York: Columbia University Press.

Brown, Laura (2001). *Fables of Modernity: Literature and Culture in the English Eighteenth Century*. Ithaca, N.Y.: Cornell.

Brucker, Gene (2005). *Living on the Edge in Leonardo's Florence*. Berkeley: University of California Press.

Bruford, Walter Horace (1935). *Germany in the Eighteenth Century: The Social Background of the Literary Revival*. Cambridge: CUP.

Bruhns, Svend (2004). *Bibliografiens historie i Danmark, 1700- og 1800-tallet*. Aalborg: Aalborg Universitetsforlag.

Buchanan, James (1979). *What Should Economists Do?* Indianapolis: Liberty Fund.

Buck, Philip W. (1942). *The Politics of Mercantilism*. New York: Holt.

Buisseret, D. J. (1962). "The Legend of Sully." *Historical Journal* 5, no. 2, 181–188.

Burckhardt, Jacob (1944). *The Civilization of the Renaissance*. London: Phaidon Press.

Burke, Peter (1966). "A Survey of the Popularity of Ancient Historians, 1450–1700." *History and Theory* 5, no. 2, 135–152.

——— (1996a). *The Fortunes of the Courtier*. Philadelphia: University of Pennsylvania Press.

——— (1996b). *Popular Culture in Early Modern Europe*. Aldershot: Ashgate.

——— (1998). *The European Renaissance: Centres and Peripheries*. London: Blackwell.

——— (2000). *A Social History of Knowledge*. Cambridge: Polity.

——— (2004). *Languages and Communities in Early Modern Europe*. Cambridge: CUP.

Burke, Peter, and R. Po-chia Hsia (eds.) (2007). *Cultural Translation in Early Modern Europe*. Cambridge: CUP and the European Science Foundation.

Buruma, Ian (1999). *Voltaire's Coconuts: Or, Anglomania in Europe*. London: Weidenfeld and Nicolson.

Calabria, Antonio (1991). *The Cost of Empire: The Finances of the Kingdom of Naples in the Time of Spanish Rule*. Cambridge: CUP.

Calabria, Antonio, and John A. Marino (eds.) (1990). *Good Government in Spanish Naples*. New York: Peter Lang.

Calaresu, Melissa T. (1999). "The End of the Grand Tour and the Cosmopolitan Ideal: Neapolitan Critiques of French Travel Accounts (1750–1800)." In J. Elsner and J. P. Rubiés (eds.), *Voyages and Visions: Towards a Cultural History of Travel*. London: Reaktion Books, 138–161.

──── (2001). "Constructing an Intellectual Identity: Autobiography and Identity in Eighteenth-Century Naples." *Journal of Modern Italian Studies* 6, no. 2, 157–177.

──── (2005). "Coffee, Culture and Consumption: Reconstructing the Public Sphere in Late Eighteenth-Century Naples." In Andrea Gatti and Paola Zanardi (eds.), *Filosofia, scienza, storia: Il dialogo fra Italia e Gran Bretagna*. Padua: Il Poligrafo, 135–174.

Calvino, Italo (2002). *Perché leggere i classici*. Milan: Oscar Mondadori.

Cambiano, Giuseppe (2000). *Polis: Un modello per la cultura europea*. Bari: Laterza.

Canny, N. (1973). "The Ideology of English Colonisation: From Ireland to America." *William and Mary Quarterly* 30, 575–598.

Capra, Carlo (2002). *I progressi della ragione: Vita di Pietro Verri*. Bologna: Il Mulino.

Carpenter, Kenneth (1975). "The Economic Bestsellers before 1850." *Bulletin of the Kress Library of Business and Economics* 11. Boston: Harvard Business School.

──── (1977). *Dialogue in Political Economy: Translations from and into German in the Eighteenth Century*. Kress Library Publication no. 23. Boston: Baker Library, Harvard Business School.

Carruthers, Bruce G. (1999). *City of Capital: Politics and Markets in the English Financial Revolution*. Princeton: Princeton.

Carter, April (2001). *The Political Theory of Global Citizenship*. London: Routledge.

Casper, Willy (1930). *Charles Davenant: Ein Beitrag zur Kenntnis des englischen Merkantilismus*. Jena: Gustav Fischer.

Caton, Hiram (1988). *The Politics of Progress: The Origins and Development of the Commercial Republic, 1600–1835*. Gainsville: University of Florida Press.

Cepparrone, Luigi (2008). *L'Illuminismo europeo nell'epistolario di Romualdo De Sterlich*. Bergamo: Bergamo University Press.

Cerrone, Andrea (2000). *Antonio Genovesi: Sacerdote ed educatore*. Salerno: Elea Press.

Cerutti, Simona (2009). "Società di 'eguali' e 'comune umanità': La critica al processo tra il Piemonte e la Francia del Settecento." In Antonella Alimento (ed.), *Modelli d'oltre confine: Prospettive economiche e sociali negli antichi stati italiani*. Rome: Edizioni di storia e letteratura, 191–208.

Cervera Ferri, Pablo (1998). "Las Lecciones de Economía Civil ó de el Comercio de B. J. Danvila y Villarasa." *Cuadernos Aragoneses de Economía* 8, no. 1, 143–162.

Chang, Ha-Joon (2002). *Kicking Away the Ladder: Development Strategy in Historical Perspective*. London: Anthem.

Chapron, Emmanuelle (2009). *"Ad utilità pubblica": Politique des bibliothèques et pratique du livre à Florence au XVIIIe siècle*. Geneva: Droz.

Charles, Loïc (2003). "The Visual History of the *Tableau Économique*." *European Journal of the History of Economic Thought* 10, no. 4, 527–550.

———— (2004). "The *Tableau Économique* as Rational Recreation." *History of Political Economy* 36, no. 3, 445–474.

———— (2008). "French 'New Politics' and the Dissemination of David Hume's *Political Discourses* on the Continent." In Carl Wennerlind and Margaret Schabas (eds.), *David Hume's Political Economy*. London: Routledge, 181–202.

———— "French Political Economy and the Making of Public Opinion as a Political Concept (1750–1765)." Manuscript.

Charles, Loïc, and Christine Théré (2007). "François Quesnay: A 'Rural Socrates' in Versailles?" *History of Political Economy* 39 (supp.), 195–214.

———— (2011). "From Versailles to Paris: The Creative Communities of the Physiocratic Moment." *History of Political Economy* 43: 1, 25–58.

Chartier, Roger (1994). *The Order of Books*. Stanford: Stanford University Press.

Cheney, Paul (2010). *Revolutionary Commerce: Globalization and the French Monarchy*. Cambridge, Mass.: Harvard.

Cheney, Paul Burton (2002). "The History and Science of Commerce in the Century of Enlightenment: France, 1713–1789." Ph.D. diss., Columbia University.

Chiaramonte, José Carlos (1964). "Gli illuministi napoletani nel Río de la Plata." *Rivista storica italiana* 76, no. 1, 114–132.

Chiosi, Elvira (1992). *Lo spirito del secolo: Politica e religione a Napoli nell'età dell'illuminismo*. Naples: Giannini.

Chorley, Patrick (1965). *Oil, Silk and Enlightenment: Economic Problems in XVIIIth Century Naples*. Naples: IISF.

Cinquemani, Anthony M. (2006). "Milton Translating Petrarch: *Paradise Lost* VIII and the *Secretum*." In Carmine G. Di Biase (ed.), *Travel and Translation in the Early Modern Period*. Amsterdam: Rodopi, 65–88.

Cipolla, Carlo M. (1969). "The Economic Decline of Italy." In Brian Pullan (ed.), *Crisis and Change in the Venetian Economy in the Sixteenth and Seventeenth Centuries*. London: Methuen, 127–145.

———— (1994). *Tre storie extra vaganti*. Bologna: Il Mulino.

Clapham, John Harold (1944). *The Bank of England: A History*. 2 vols. Cambridge: CUP.

Clark, G. N. (1938). *Guide to English Commercial Statistics, 1696–1782*. London: Royal Historical Society.

Clark, George (1954). "The Character of the Nine Years War, 1688–97." *Cambridge Historical Journal* 11, no. 2, 168–182.

Clark, Henry C. (2007). *Compass of Society: Commerce and Absolutism in Old-Regime France*. Lanham, Md.: Lexington Books.

Claydon, Tony (2007). *Europe and the Making of England, 1660–1760*. Cambridge: CUP.

Claydon, Tony, and Ian McBride (eds.) (1998). *Protestantism and National Identity: Britain and Ireland, c. 1650–1850*. Cambridge: CUP.

Cochrane, Eric (1961). *Tradition and Enlightenment in the Tuscan Academies, 1690–1800*. Chicago: Chicago.

———— (1973). *Florence in the Forgotten Centuries, 1527–1800*. Chicago: Chicago.

Coldevin, Axel (1950). *Norske storgårder.* 2 vols. Oslo: Aschehoug.

Collins, James B. (2009). *The State in Early Modern France.* Cambridge: CUP.

Conway, Stephen (2006). *War, State, and Society in Mid-Eighteenth-Century Britain and Ireland.* Oxford: OUP.

Cooke, Jacob E. (1975). "Tench Coxe, Alexander Hamilton, and the Encouragement of American Manufactures." *William and Mary Quarterly* 32, no. 3, 369–392.

Cooper, Alix (2007). *Inventing the Indigenous: Local Knowledge and Natural History in Early Modern Europe.* Cambridge: CUP.

Corpaci, Francesco (1941). *Nazione e stato in Antonio Genovesi.* Rome: Soc. Editrice del libro italiano.

Cortekar, Jörg (2007). *Glückskonzepte des Kameralismus und Utilitarismus.* Marburg: Metropolis Verlag.

Courtney, C. P. (1993). "Montesquieu and Revolution." In Edgar Mass et al. (eds.), *Lectures de Montesquieu.* Naples, Paris, and Oxford: Liguori Editore, Universitas, and Voltaire Foundation, 41–61.

Cowan, Brian (2005). *The Social Life of Coffee: The Emergence of the British Coffeehouse.* New Haven: Yale.

Coward, David (1991). *The Philosophy of Restif de la Bretonne.* Oxford: Voltaire Foundation.

Croccolo, Giulia (1932). *Un economista lucchese del Settecento: Giovanni Attilio Arnolfini.* Lucca: Tip. Editrice G. Giusti.

Croce, Benedetto (1927). *Uomini e cose della vecchia Italia.* 2 vols. Bari: Laterza.

Crouzet, François (2008). *La guerre économique franco-anglaise au XVIIIe siècle.* Paris: Fayard.

Crow, Thomas E. (2006). *Emulation: David, Drouais, and Girodet in the Art of Revolutionary France.* Rev. ed. New Haven: Yale.

Crowley, John E. (1993). *The Privileges of Independence: Neomercantilism and the American Revolution.* Baltimore: Hopkins.

Cru, R. Loyalty (1913). *Diderot as a Disciple of English Thought.* New York: Columbia University Press.

Cruikshanks, Eveline, Stuart Handley, and D. W. Hayton (2002). *The House of Commons, 1690–1715.* 5 vols. Cambridge: CUP for the History of Parliament Trust.

Cullen, L. M. (1968). *Anglo-Irish Trade, 1660–1800.* New York: Augustus M. Kelley.

Curtis, T. C., and W. A. Speck (1976). "The Societies for the Reformation of Manners: A Case Study in the Theory and Practice of Moral Reform." *Literature and History* 3, 45–61.

Damianoff, Michael D. (1908). *Die volkswirtschaftlichen Anschauungen Johannes Friedrich von Pfeiffers.* Borna-Leipzig: Buchdruckerei Robert Noske.

Darnton, Robert (1986). *The Business of Enlightenment: A Publishing History of the Encyclopédie, 1775–1800.* Cambridge, Mass.: Harvard.

——— (1996). *The Forbidden Best-Sellers of Pre-revolutionary France.* New York: Norton.

Daudin, Guillaume, Kevin H. O'Rourke, and Leandro Prados de la Escosura (2008). "Trade and Empire, 1700–1870." OFCE Document de travail No. 200824. www.ofce.sciences-po.fr/pdf/dtravail/WP2008-24.pdf.

Davis, J. C. (1980). *Utopia and the Ideal Society: A Study of English Utopian Writing, 1516–1700*. Cambridge: CUP.

Davis, John A. (2006). *Naples and Napoleon: Southern Italy and the European Revolutions, 1780–1860*. Oxford: OUP.

Davis, Ralph (1969). "English Foreign Trade, 1700–1774." In W. E. Minchinton (ed.), *The Growth of English Overseas Trade in the Seventeenth and Eighteenth Centuries*. London: Taylor and Francis, 99–120.

Davison, Lee, et al. (1992). *Stilling the Grumbling Hive: The Response to Social and Economic Problems in England, 1689–1750*. London: Palgrave Macmillan.

Dawson, Hannah (2007). *Locke, Language and Early-Modern Philosophy*. Cambridge: CUP.

Dear, Peter (1995). *Discipline and Experience: The Mathematical Way in the Scientific Revolution*. Chicago: Chicago.

——— (2009). *Revolutionizing the Sciences: European Knowledge and Its Ambitions, 1700–1800*. 2nd ed. Princeton: Princeton.

De La Matta Rodriguez, Enrique (1979). *El asalto de Pointis a Cartagena de Indias*. Seville: Escuela de estudios hispano-americanos de Sevilla.

DeLater, James Albert (2002). *Translation Theory in the Age of Louis XIV: The 1683 De optimo genere interpretandi (On the Best Kind of Translating) of Pierre-Daniel Huet (1630–1721)*. Manchester: St. Jerome.

De Luca, Mario (1956). "Attualità dei pensieri di Antonio Genovesi sul problema dello sviluppo delle economie arretrate." In Domenico Demarco (ed.), *Studi in onore di Antonio Genovesi nel bicentenario della istituzione della cattedra di economia*. Naples: L'Arte Tipografica, 115–125.

——— (1970). *Scienza economica e politica sociale nel pensiero di Antonio Genovesi*. Naples: Unione regionale delle camere di commercio, industria, e agricoltura della Campania.

De Mas, Enrico (1971). *Montesquieu, Genovesi e le edizioni Italiane dello Spirito delle leggi*. Florence: F. Le Monnier.

Devine, T. M. (2004). *Scotland's Empire and the Shaping of the Americas, 1600–1815*. Washington, D.C.: Smithsonian Books.

de Vries, Jan (1976). *The Economy of Europe in an Age of Crisis, 1600–1750*. Cambridge: CUP.

——— (1984). *European Urbanization, 1500–1800*. Cambridge, Mass.: Harvard.

——— (1994). "The Industrial Revolution and the Industrious Revolution." *Journal of Economic History* 54, no. 2, 249–270.

——— (2008). *The Industrious Revolution: Consumer Behavior and the Household Economy, 1650 to the Present*. Cambridge: CUP.

Diaz, Furio (1966). *Francesco Maria Gianni: Dalla burocrazia alla politica sotto Pietro Leopoldo di Toscana*. Milan: Ricciardi.

——— (1962/1973). *Filosofia e politica nel Settecento francese*. Turin: Einaudi.

Di Battista, Francesco (1992). "Per la storia della prima cattedra universitaria d'economia. Napoli 1754–1866." In Massimo M. Augello et al. (eds.), *Le cattedre di economia politica in Italia: La diffusione di una disciplina "sospetta."* Milan: Franco Angeli, 31–92.

Di Biase, Carmine G. (ed.) (2006). *Travel and Translation in the Early Modern Period.* Amsterdam: Rodopi.

Dickey, Laurence (2001–2). "Doux-Commerce and Humanitarian Values." *Grotiana* 22–23, 271–318.

Di Liso, S. (1997). "Ragione e autorità negli scritti filosofici di Antonio Genovesi." *Annali della Facoltà di Filosofia dell'Università di Bari* 40, 269–312.

Dobbs, B. J. T. (1991). *The Janus Faces of Genius: The Role of Alchemy in Newton's Thought.* Cambridge: CUP.

Draper, Anthony J. (2000). Cesare Beccaria's Influence on English Discussions of Punishment, 1764–1789." *History of European Ideas* 26, 177–199.

Drayton, Richard (2000). *Nature's Government: Science, Imperial Britain, and the "Improvement" of the World.* New Haven: Yale.

——— (2002). "The Collaboration of Labour: Slaves, Empires and Globalizations in the Atlantic World, c. 1600–1850." In A. G. Hopkins (ed.), *Globalization in World History.* London: Pimlico, 98–114.

Dull, Jonathan R. (2005). *The French Navy and the Seven Years' War.* Lincoln: University of Nebraska Press.

Dunn, John (ed.) (1990). *The Economic Limits to Modern Politics.* Cambridge: CUP.

——— (1996). *The History of Political Theory and Other Essays.* Cambridge: CUP.

Duranti, Riccardo (1998). "Italian Tradition." In Monica Baker (ed.), *Routledge Encyclopedia of Translation Studies.* London: Routledge, 474–484.

Dziembowski, Edmond (1998). *Un nouveau patriotisme français, 1750–1770: La France face à la puissance anglaise à l'époque de la guerre de Sept Ans.* Oxford: Voltaire Foundation.

Eco, Umberto (2004). *La ricerca della lingua perfetta nella cultura europea.* 4th ed. Bari: Laterza.

Edvinsson, Rodney (2010). "Foreign Exchange Rates in Sweden 1658–1803." In Rodney Edvinsson et al. (eds.), *Historical Monetary and Financial Statistics for Sweden: Exchange Rates, Prices and Wages, 1277–2008.* Stockholm: Sveriges Riksbank, 238–290.

Eglin, John (1999). "Venice on the Thames: Venetian *Vedutisti* and the London View in the Eighteenth Century." In Shearer West (ed.), *Italian Culture in Northern Europe in the Eighteenth Century.* Cambridge: CUP, 101–115.

Ekelund, Robert, and Robert Hébert (1997). *A History of Economic Theory and Method.* 4th ed. New York: McGraw-Hill.

Emminghaus, A. (1872). "Carl Friedrichs von Baden physiokratische Verbindungen, Bestrebungen und Versuche, ein Beitrag zur Geschichte des Physiokratismus." *Jahrbücher für Nationalökonomie und Statistik* 19, 1–63.

Fabian, Bernhard (1992). *The English Book in Eighteenth-Century Germany.* London: British Library.

Faccarello, Gilbert (1994). " 'Nil Repente!': Galiani and Necker on Economic Reforms." *European Journal of the History of Economic Thought* 1, no. 3, 519–550.

Faragher, John Mack (2005). *A Great and Noble Scheme: The Tragic Story of the Expulsion of the French Acadians from Their American Homeland.* New York: Norton.

Farinella, Calogero (1996). "Le traduzioni italiane della *Cyclopedia* di Ephraim Chambers." *Studi Settecenteschi* 16, 97–160.

Febvre, Lucien Paul Victor, and Henri-Jean Martin (1997). *The Coming of the Book: The Impact of Printing 1450–1800.* Translated by David Gerard. London: Verso.

Feldbæk, Ole (1969). *India Trade under the Danish Flag, 1772–1808.* Lund: Studentlitteratur.

——— (1971). *Dansk Neutralitetspolitik under Krigen, 1778–1783.* Copenhagen: Akademisk Forlag.

——— (1980). *Denmark and the Armed Neutrality, 1800–1801.* Copenhagen: Akademisk Forlag.

——— (2004). "Denmark-Norway 1720–1807: Neutral Principles and Practice." In Rolf Hobson and Tom Kristiansen (eds.), *Navies in Northern Waters, 1721–2000.* London: Frank Cass, 59–65.

Ferguson, John M. (1950). *Landmarks of Economic Thought.* 2nd ed. New York: Longmans, Green.

Ferrone, Vincenzo (1984). *Scienza, natura, religione: Mondo newtoniano e cultura italiana nel primo Settecento.* Naples: Jovene.

——— (2003). *La società giusta ed equa: Repubblicanesimo e diritti dell'uomo in Gaetano Filangieri.* Rome-Bari: Laterza.

Findlay, Ronald, and Kevin O'Rourke (2007). *Power and Plenty: Trade, War, and the World Economy in the Second Millennium.* Princeton: Princeton.

Findlen, Paula (2000). "The Janus Faces of Science in the Seventeenth Century: Athanasius Kircher and Isaac Newton." In Margaret J. Osler (ed.), *Rethinking the Scientific Revolution.* Cambridge: CUP, 221–246.

Finkelstein, Andrea (2000). *Harmony and the Balance: An Intellectual History of Seventeenth-Century English Economic Thought.* Ann Arbor: University of Michigan Press.

Fissel, Mary E. (1991). *Patients, Power, and the Poor in Eighteenth-Century Bristol.* Cambridge: CUP.

Fitzmaurice, Andrew (2003). *Humanism and America: An Intellectual History of English Colonization, 1500–1625.* Cambridge: CUP.

Fogel, Robert William (2004). *The Escape from Hunger and Premature Death, 1700–2100: Europe, America, and the Third World.* Cambridge: CUP.

Forbes, Jack D. (2007). *The American Discovery of Europe.* Urbana: University of Illinois Press.

Foucault, Michel (2007). *Security, Territory, Population: Lectures at the Collège de France, 1977–1978.* London: Palgrave Macmillan.

Fox-Genovese, Elizabeth (1976). *The Origins of Physiocracy: Economic Revolution and Social Order in Eighteenth-Century France.* Ithaca, N.Y.: Cornell.

Freeborn, Richard (1985). *The Russian Revolutionary Novel: Turgenev to Paster-nak*. Cambridge: CUP.

Friis, Aage (1899). *Andreas Peter Bernstorff og Ove Høegh Guldberg: Bidrag til den Guldbergske Tids Historie (1772–1780)*. Copenhagen: Det Nordiske For-lag.

Fusaro, Maria (2008). *Reti commerciali e traffici globali in età moderna*. Bari: Laterza.

Fyler, John M. (2007). *Language and the Declining World in Chaucer, Dante, and Jean de Meun*. Cambridge: CUP.

Gagliardo, John G. (1969). *From Pariah to Patriot: The Changing Image of the German Peasant, 1770–1840*. Lexington: University Press of Kentucky.

Galbraith, John Kenneth (1991). *A History of Economics: The Past as Present*. London: Penguin.

Games, Alison (2008). *The Web of Empire: English Cosmopolitans in an Age of Expansion, 1560–1660*. Oxford: OUP.

Garcés, Marìa Antonia (2006). "The Translator Translated: Inca Garcilaso and English Imperial Expansion." In Carmine G. Di Biase (ed.), *Travel and Trans-lation in the Early Modern Period*. Amsterdam: Rodopi, 203–225.

Garin, Eugenio (1985/1999). "Antonio Genovesi metafisico e storico." Introduc-tion to Antonio Genovesi, *Dello stato e delle naturali forze del Regno di Na-poli per rispetto all'arti e al commercio*. Naples: Città del Sole, 3–32.

Gauci, Perry (2004). *The Politics of Trade: The Overseas Merchant in State and Society, 1620–1720*. Oxford: OUP.

Gawthrop, Richard L. (1992). "The Social Role of Seventeenth-Century German Territorial States." *Sixteenth Century Essays and Studies* 18, 243–258.

Gerace, Michael (2004). *Military Power, Conflict and Trade*. London: Frank Cass.

Geuss, Raymond (2008). *Philosophy and Real Politics*. Princeton: Princeton.

Ginzburg, Carlo (1989). "The High and the Low: The Theme of Forbidden Knowl-edge in the Sixteenth and Seventeenth Centuries." In Ginzburg, *Clues, Myths, and the Historical Method*. Baltimore: Hopkins, 60–76.

——— (1999). *Il formaggio e i vermi: Il cosmo di un mugnaio del '500*. Turin: Einaudi.

Girard, René (1978). *"To Double Business Bound": Essays on Literature, Mime-sis, and Anthropology*. Baltimore: Hopkins.

Gittermann, Alexandra (2008). *Die Ökonomisierung des politischen Denkens: Neapel und Spanien in Zeichen der Reformbewegungen des 18. Jahrhunderts unter der Herrschaft Karls III*. Stuttgart: Franz Steiner.

Glamann, Kristof, and Erik Oxenbøll (1983). *Studier i dansk merkantilisme: Om-kring tekster af Otto Thott*. Copenhagen: Akademisk Forlag.

Glass, D. V. (1950). "Gregory King's Estimate of the Population of England and Wales, 1695." *Population Studies* 3, no. 4, 338–374.

Glebe-Møller, Jens (2007). *Struensees vej til Skafottet: Fornuft og Åpenbaring i Oplysningstiden*. Copenhagen: Museum Tusculanums Forlag.

Goedeke, Karl (1893). *Grundriss zur Geschichte der Deutschen Dichtung aus den Quellen*. 2nd ed. Vol. 5. Dresden: L. Ehlermann.

Goldie, Mark (1977). "Edmund Bohun and Jus Gentium in the Revolution Debate, 1689–1693." *Historical Journal* 20, no. 3, 569–586.

Goodman, Dena (1994). *The Republic of Letters: A Cultural History of the Enlightenment.* Ithaca, N.Y.: Cornell.

Gould, Philip (2003). *Barbaric Traffic: Commerce and Antislavery in the Eighteenth Century Atlantic World.* Cambridge, Mass.: Harvard.

Gould, Stephen Jay (1989). *Wonderful Life: The Burgess Shale and the Nature of History.* New York: Norton.

Graf, Arturo (1911). *L'Anglomania e l'influsso inglese in Italia nel secolo XVIII.* Turin: Casa Editrice Ermanno Loescher.

Grafton, Anthony (1991). *Defenders of the Text: The Traditions of Scholarship in an Age of Science, 1450–1800.* Cambridge, Mass.: Harvard.

——— (1999). "The Humanist as Reader." In Giuglielmo Cavallo and Roger Chartier (eds.), *A History of Reading in the West.* Cambridge: Polity, 179–212.

——— (2009). *Worlds Made by Words: Scholarship and Community in the Modern West.* Cambridge, Mass.: Harvard.

Grassby, Richard (1995). *The Business Community of Seventeenth-Century England.* Cambridge: CUP.

Gray, John (2007). *Enlightenment's Wake.* London: Routledge.

Gray, Richard T. (2008). *Money Matters: Economics and the German Cultural Imagination, 1750–1850.* Seattle: University of Washington Press.

Greenfeld, Leah (2001). *The Spirit of Capitalism: Nationalism and Economic Growth.* Cambridge, Mass.: Harvard.

Gregg, Stephen H. (2001). " 'A Truly Christian Hero': Religion, Effeminacy, and Nation in the Writings of the Societies for Reformation of Manners." *Eighteenth-Century Life* 25, 17–28.

Grenier, Jean-Yves (1996). *L'économie d'Ancien Régime: Un monde de l'échange et de l'incertitude.* Paris: Albin Michel.

Grieder, Josephine (1985). *Anglomania in France, 1740–1789: Fact, Fiction, and Political Discourse.* Geneva-Paris: Librairie Droz.

Griffin, Keith (1969). *Under-development in Spanish America.* London: Routledge.

Groenewegen, Peter (1994). "Pietro Verri's Mature Political Economy of the *Meditazioni:* A Case Study of the Highly Developed International Transmission Mechanism of Ideas in Pre-revolutionary Europe." In Manuela Albertone and Alberto Masoero (eds.), *Political Economy and National Realities.* Turin: Fondazione Luigi Einaudi, 107–125.

——— (2002). *Eighteenth-Century Economics: Turgot, Beccaria and Smith and Their Contemporaries.* London: Routledge.

Guasti, Niccolò (2006). "Antonio Genovesi's *Diceosina:* Source of the Neapolitan Enlightenment." *History of European Ideas* 32, no. 4, 385–405.

——— (1995–96). "Uztáriz, Forbonnais e la 'Theorica y practica de comercio y de marina': Prime ricerche." Tesi di laurea, University of Florence.

Gunn, J. A. W. (1969). *Politics and the Public Interest in the Seventeenth Century.* London: Routledge and Kegan Paul.

Habermas, Jürgen (1989). *The Structural Transformation of the Public Sphere.* Cambridge: Polity Press.

Hall, I. V. (1949). "John Knight, Junior, Sugar Refiner at the Great House on St. Augustine's Back (1654–1679): Bristol's Second Sugar House." *Transactions of the Bristol and Gloucestershire Archaeological Society* 68, 110–164.

—— (1951). "The Grant of Arms to the Cary Family." *Transactions of the Bristol and Gloucestershire Archaeological Society* 70, 155–156.

Hallmark, Terrell L. (1998). "John Locke and the *Fundamental Constitution of Carolina.*" Ph.D. diss., Claremont Graduate University.

Hamilton, Andrew (2008). *Trade and Empire in the Eighteenth-Century Atlantic World.* Newcastle upon Tyne: Cambridge Scholars.

Haney, Lewis H. (1920). *History of Economic Thought.* New York: Macmillan.

Hanley, William (2005). *A Biographical Dictionary of French Censors, 1741–1789.* Vol. 1. *A–B.* Ferney-Voltaire: Centre International d'étude du XVIIIe siècle.

Harcourt, Bernard E. (2011). *The Illusion of Free Markets: Punishment and the Myth of Natural Order.* Cambridge, Mass.: Harvard.

Harding, Nicholas B. (2000). "North African Piracy, the Hanoverian Carrying Trade, and the British State, 1728–1828." *Historical Journal* 43, no. 1, 25–47.

Harley, J. B. (1966). "The Bankruptcy of Thomas Jefferys: An Episode in the Economic History of Eighteenth Century Map-Making." *Imago Mundi* 20, 27–48.

Harper, John Lamberton (2004). *American Machiavelli: Alexander Hamilton and the Origins of U.S. Foreign Policy.* Cambridge: CUP.

Harris, Bob (2002). *Politics and the Nation: Britain in the Mid-Eighteenth Century.* Oxford: OUP.

Harris, J. R. (1998). *Industrial Espionage and Technology Transfer: Britain and France in the Eighteenth Century.* Aldershot: Ashgate.

Harrison, Carol (1999). *The Bourgeois Citizen in Nineteenth-Century France: Gender, Sociability, and the Uses of Emulation.* Oxford: OUP.

Harrison, Fairfax (1919). *The Virginia Carys: An Essay in Genealogy.* New York: Privately printed.

Haslam, Jonathan (2002). *No Virtue like Necessity: Realist Thought in International Relations since Machiavelli.* New Haven: Yale.

Hasquin, Hervé (1974). "Jacques Accarias de Serionne économiste et publiciste français au service des Pays-Bas autrichiens." *Etudes sur le XVIIIe siècle* 1, 159–170.

Hauc, Jean-Claude (2004). *Ange Goudar: Un aventurier des Lumières.* Paris: Honoré Champion.

Hayton, David W. (1990). "Moral Reform and Country Politics in the Late Seventeenth-Century House of Commons." *Past and Present* 128, 48–91.

—— (1991). "The Williamite Revolution in Ireland, 1688–91." In Jonathan I. Israel (ed.), *The Anglo-Dutch Moment: Essays on the Glorious Revolution and Its World Impact.* Cambridge: CUP, 185–213.

Headley, John M. (1997). *Tommaso Campanella and the Transformation of the World.* Princeton: Princeton.

Heckscher, Eli F. (1994/1931). *Mercantilism*. Edited by Lars Magnusson. 2 vols. London: Routledge.

Helgerson, Richard (2007). *A Sonnet from Carthage: Garcilaso de la Vega and the New Poetry of Sixteenth-Century Europe*. Philadelphia: University of Pennsylvania Press.

Henderson, W. O. (1972). *Britain and Industrial Europe, 1750–1870: Studies in British Influence on the Industrial Revolution in Western Europe*. Leicester: Leicester University Press.

Hietala, Thomas R. (2003). *Manifest Design: American Exceptionalism and Empire*. Rev. ed. Ithaca, N.Y.: Cornell.

Hill, Jacqueline (1995). "Ireland without Union: Molyneux and His Legacy." In John Robertson (ed.), *Union for Empire: Political Thought and the British Union of 1707*. Cambridge: CUP, 271–296.

Hindle, Steve (2004). "Civility, Honesty and the Identification of the Deserving Poor in Seventeenth-Century England." In Henry French and Jonathan Berry (eds.), *Identity and Agency in English Society, 1500–1800*. Houndmills: Palgrave Macmillan.

Hirschman, Albert O. (1945). *National Power and the Structure of Foreign Trade*. Berkeley: University of California Press.

—— (1997/1977). *The Passions and the Interest: Political Arguments for Capitalism before Its Triumph*. Princeton: Princeton.

—— (1992). *Rival Views of Market Society*. Cambridge, Mass.: Harvard.

Hobson, John M. (2004). *The Eastern Origins of Western Civilisation*. Cambridge: CUP.

Holmes, George (1997). *The Oxford Illustrated History of Italy*. Oxford: OUP.

Hont, Istvan (2005). *The Jealousy of Trade: International Competition and the Nation-State in Historical Perspective*. Cambridge, Mass.: Harvard.

—— (2006). "The Early Enlightenment Debate on Commerce and Luxury." In Mark Goldie and Robert Wokler (eds.), *The Cambridge History of Eighteenth-Century Political Thought*. Cambridge: CUP, 379–418.

—— (2008). "The 'Rich Country–Poor Country' Debate Revisited: The Irish Origins and French Reception of the Hume Paradox." In Carl Wennerlind and Margaret Schabas (eds.), *David Hume's Political Economy*. London: Routledge, 243–323.

Hoock, Jochen, Pierre Jeannin, and Wolfgang Kaiser (1991–2001). *Ars mercatoria: Handbücher und Traktate für den Gebrauch des Kaufmanns, 1470–1820*, 3 vols. Paderborn: Schöning.

Hoon, Elizabeth Evelynola (1968). *The Organization of the English Customs System, 1696–1786*. Newton Abbot: David & Charles.

Hoppit, Julian (2006). "The Contexts and Contours of British Economic Literature, 1660–1760." *Historical Journal* 49, no. 1, 79–110.

Horn, Jeff (2006). *The Path Not Taken: French Industrialization in the Age of Revolution, 1750–1830*. Cambridge, Mass.: MIT Press.

Horn, Jeff, Leonard N. Rosenband, and Merrit Roe Smith (eds.) (2010). *Reconceptualizing the Industrial Revolution*. Cambridge, Mass.: MIT Press.

Horsefield, J. Kenneth (1960). *British Monetary Experiments, 1650–1710*. Cambridge, Mass.: Harvard.

Howland, Douglas R. (2002). *Translating the West: Language and Political Reason in Nineteenth-Century Japan*. Honolulu: University of Hawai'i Press.

Huber, Thomas (1968). *Studien zur Theorie des Übersetzens im Zeitalter der Deutschen Aufklärung, 1730–1770*. Meisenheim am Glan: Verlag Anton Hain.

Hull, Isabel V. (1996). *Sexuality, State, and Civil Society in Germany, 1700–1815*. Ithaca, N.Y.: Cornell.

Humpert, Magdalene (1937). *Bibliographie der Kameralwissenschaften*. Cologne: Balduin Pick.

Hundert, E. J. (1972). "The Making of Homo Faber: John Locke between Ideology and History." *Journal of History of Ideas* 33, no. 1, 3–22.

——— (1994). *The Enlightenment's Fable: Bernard Mandeville and the Discovery of Society*. Cambridge: CUP.

——— (1995). "Bernard Mandeville and the Enlightenment Maxims of Modernity." *Journal of the History of Ideas* 56, no. 4, 577–593.

Hunt, Alan (1999). *Governing Morals: A Social History of Moral Regulation*. Cambridge: CUP.

Hutchison, T. W. (1988). *Before Adam Smith: The Emergence of a Political Economy*. Oxford: Blackwell.

Ilsøe, Harald (2007). *Biblioteker til salg: Om danske bogauktioner og kataloger, 1661–1811*. Copenhagen: Museum Tusculanums Forlag.

Imbruglia, Girolamo (2000). "Enlightenment in Eighteenth-Century Naples." In Girolamo Imbruglia (ed.), *Naples in the Eighteenth Century: The Birth and Death of a Nation-State*, Cambridge: CUP, 70–94.

Ingram, John Kells (1919). *A History of Political Economy*. New and enl. ed. London: A. & C. Black.

Inikori, Joseph E. (2002). *Africans and the Industrial Revolution in England: A Study in International Trade and Economic Development*. Cambridge: CUP.

Iovine, Raffaele (2001). "Una cattedra per Genovesi: Nella crisi della cultura moderna a Napoli (1744–1754)." *Frontiera d'Europa*, 7 359–532.

Israel, Jonathan I. (1991). General introduction to Israel (ed.), *The Anglo-Dutch Moment: Essays on the Glorious Revolution and Its World Impact*. Cambridge: CUP, 1–43.

——— (2001). *Radical Enlightenment: Philosophy and the Making of Modernity, 1650–1750*. Oxford: OUP.

Iverson, John (2003). "Forum: Emulation in France, 1750–1800." *Eighteenth-Century Studies* 36, no. 2, 217–223.

Ives, Robin J. (2003). "Political Publicity and Political Economy in Eighteenth-Century France." *French History* 17, no. 1, 1–18.

Jacob, Margaret C. (1997). *Scientific Culture and the Making of the Industrial West*. Oxford: OUP.

James, Harold (2006). *The Roman Predicament: How the Rules of International Order Create the Politics of Empire*. Princeton: Princeton.

Jefferies, Julie (2005). "The UK Population: Past, Present, and Future." In Office for National Statistics (ed.), *Focus on People and Migration*. Houndmills: Macmillan, 1–18.

Johannisson, Karin (1988). *Det Mätbara Samhället: Statistik och Samhällsdröm i 1700-Talets Europa*. Stockholm: Norstedts Förlag.

Johns, Adrian (2009). *Piracy: The Intellectual Property Wars from Gutenberg to Gates*. Chicago: Chicago.

Johnson, E. A. J. (1932). "British Mercantilist Doctrines Concerning the 'Exportation of Work' and 'Foreign-Paid Incomes.' " *Journal of Political Economy* 40, no. 6, 750–770.

——— (1937). *Predecessors of Adam Smith: The Growth of British Economic Thought*. New York: Prentice Hall.

——— (1973). *The Foundations of American Economic Freedom: Government and Enterprise in the Age of Washington*. Minneapolis: University of Minnesota Press.

Jonard, Norbert (1969). "Le Problème du luxe en Italie au XVIIIe siècle." *Revue des études italiennes* 15, 295–321.

Jones, D. W. (2001). "Sequel to Revolution: The Economics of England's Emergence as a Great Power, 1688–1712." In Jonathan I. Israel (ed.), *The Anglo-Dutch Moment: Essays on the Glorious Revolution and Its World Impact*. Cambridge: CUP, 389–406.

Jurdjevic, Mark (2001). "Virtue, Commerce, and the Enduring Florentine Republican Moment: Reintegrating Italy into the Atlantic Republican Debate." *Journal of the History of Ideas* 62, no. 4, 721–743.

Kanter, Sanford B. (1966). "Archbishop Fenelon's Political Activity: The Focal Point of Power in Dynasticism." *French Historical Studies* 4, no. 3, 320–334.

Kantorowicz, E. H. (1957). *The King's Two Bodies: A Study in Mediaeval Political Theology*. Princeton: Princeton.

Kaplan, Steven Laurence (1976). *Bread, Politics, and Political Economy in the Reign of Louis XV*. The Hague: Nijhoff.

——— (1979). *La Bagarre: Galiani's "Lost" Parody*. The Hague: Nijhoff.

——— (1982). *The Famine Plot Persuasion in Eighteenth-Century France*. Philadelphia: American Philosophical Society.

——— (1984). *Provisioning Paris: Merchants and Millers in the Grain and Flour Trade during the Eighteenth Century*. Ithaca, N.Y.: Cornell.

——— (1996). *The Bakers of Paris and the Bread Question, 1700–1775*. Durham, N.C.: Duke University Press.

Kearney, H. F. (1959). "The Political Background to English Mercantilism, 1695–1700." *Economic History Review* 11, no. 3, 484–496.

Keeding, Ekkehart (1983). *Das Zeitalter der Aufklärung in der Provinz Quito*. Cologne: Böhlau.

Kelley, L. G. (1979). *The True Interpreter: A History of Translation-Theory in the West*. Oxford: Blackwell.

Kelly, Patrick (1980). "The Irish Woollen Export Prohibition Act of 1699: Kearney Re-Visited." *Irish Economic and Social History* 7, 484–496.

———— (2000). "Recasting a Tradition: William Molyneux and the Sources of *The Case of Ireland . . . Stated* (1698)." In Jane H. Ohlmeyer (ed.), *Political Thought in Seventeenth-Century Ireland: Kingdom or Colony?* Cambridge: CUP, 83–106.

———— (2005). "Conquest versus Consent as the Basis of the English Title to Ireland in William Molyneux's *Case of Ireland . . . Stated (1698)*." In Ciaran Brady and Jane Ohlmeyer (eds.), *British Interventions in Early Modern Ireland*. Cambridge: CUP, 334–356.

Kent, H. S. K. (1973). *War and Trade in Northern Seas: Anglo-Scandinavian Economic Relations in the Mid-Eighteenth Century*. Cambridge: CUP.

Keohane, Nannerl O. (1980). *Philosophy and the State in France: The Renaissance to the Enlightenment*. Princeton: Princeton.

Keynes, John Maynard (1936). *The General Theory of Employment, Interest, and Money*. London: Harcourt, Brace.

King, James E. (1948). "The Origin of the Term 'Political Economy.'" *Journal of Modern History* 20, 230–231.

Kirby, David (1990). *Northern Europe in the Early Modern Period: The Baltic World, 1492–1772*. London: Longman.

Kleer, Richard A. (2004). "'The Ruine of Their Diana': Lowndes, Locke, and the Bankers." *History of Political Economy* 36, no. 3, 533–556.

Klein, Judy L. (1997). *Statistical Visions in Time: A History of Time Series Analysis, 1662–1938*. Cambridge: CUP.

Knecht, Daniel (1999). "De optimo genere interpretandi van Pierre Daniel Huet." *Filter: Tijdschrift voor vertalen en vertaalwetenschap* 6, no. 4, 50–59.

Knox, Bernard (1989). *Essays Ancient and Modern*. Baltimore: Hopkins.

Kocka, Jürgen (2003). "Comparison and Beyond." *History and Theory* 42, no. 1, 39–44.

Koehn, Nancy F. (1994). *The Power of Commerce: Economy and Governance in the First British Empire*. Ithaca, N.Y.: Cornell.

Koepp, Cynthia J. (1986). "The Alphabetical Order: Work in Diderot's *Encyclopédie*." In Cynthia J. Koepp and Steven L. Kaplan (eds.), *Work in France: Representations, Meaning, Organization, and Practice*. Ithaca, N.Y.: Cornell, 229–257.

Koerner, Lisbet (1999). *Linnaeus: Nature and Nation*. Cambridge, Mass.: Harvard.

Kotta, Nuçi (1966). *L'Homme aux Quarante Écus: A Study of Voltairian Themes*. With a foreword by George R. Havens. The Hague: Mouton.

Krantz, Frederick, and Paul Hohenberg (eds.) (1974). *Failed Transitions to Modern Industrial Society: Renaissance Italy and Seventeenth Century Holland*. Montreal: Interuniversity Centre for European Studies.

Krugman, Paul (1998). *Pop Internationalism*. Cambridge, Mass.: MIT Press.

Kwarteng, Kwasi (2000). "The Political Thought of the Recoinage Crisis of 1695–7." Ph.D. diss., University of Cambridge.

LaCapra, Dominick (2001). *Writing History, Writing Trauma*. Baltimore: Hopkins.

Lai, Cheng-chung (2000). "Adam Smith and Yen Fu: Western Economics in Chinese Perspective." In Lai (ed.), *Adam Smith across Nations: Translations and Receptions of The Wealth of Nations*. Oxford: OUP, 16–26.

Landes, David (2003). *The Unbound Prometheus: Technological Change and Industrial Development in Western Europe from 1750 to the Present.* 2nd ed. Cambridge: CUP.

Landi, Lando (1981). *L'Inghilterra e il pensiero politico di Montesquieu.* Padua: Cedam.

Landreth, Harry, and David C. Colander (1994). *History of Economic Thought.* 3rd ed. Boston: Houghton-Mifflin.

Lane, Frederic C. (1979). *Profits from Power: Readings in Protection Rent and Violence-Controlling Enterprises.* Albany: State University of New York Press.

Lane, H. J. (1932). "The Life and Writings of John Cary." M.A. diss., University of Bristol.

Langford, Paul (2000). *Englishness Identified: Manners and Character, 1650–1850.* Oxford: OUP.

Larsen, Kay (1907–8). *De Dansk-Ostindiske Koloniers Historie.* 2 vols. Copenhagen: Centralforlaget.

Larrère, Catherine (1992). *L'invention de l'économie au XVIIIe siècle.* Paris: Presses Universitaires de France.

Laslett, Peter (1957). "John Locke, the Great Recoinage, and the Board of Trade: 1695–1698." *William and Mary Quarterly* 14, no. 3, 370–402.

―――― (2005). *The World We Have Lost: Further Explored.* London: Routledge.

Laspeyres, Etienne (1863). *Geschichte der Volkswirtschäftlichen Anschauungen der Niederländer und ihrer Literatur zur Zeit der Republik.* Leipzig.

Lee, R. M. (1939). "Parliament and the Proposal for a Council of Trade, 1695–6." *English Historical Review* 54, no. 213, 38–66.

Legrand, Pierre (2005). "Issues in the Translatability of Law." In Sandra Bermann and Michael Wood (eds.), *Nation, Language, and the Ethics of Translation.* Princeton: Princeton, 30–50.

Leng, Thomas (2005). "Commercial Conflict and Regulation in the Discourse of Trade in Seventeenth-Century England." *Historical Journal* 48, no. 4, 933–954.

Lerche, Grith (1999). *The Royal Veterinary and Agricultural University: Its Contribution to Rural Education and Research in Denmark.* Frederiksberg: KVL.

Letwin, William (1963). *The Origins of Scientific Economics, English Economic Thought, 1660–1776.* London: Methuen.

Lévi-Strauss, Claude (1995). *Myth and Meaning: Cracking the Code of Culture.* New York: Schocken Books.

Levy, Darline Gay (1980). *The Ideas and Careers of Simon-Nicolas-Henri Linguet: A Study in Eigtheenth-Century French Politics.* Urbana: University of Illinois Press.

Levy, Jack S., and Salvatore Ali (1998). "From Commercial Competition to Strategic Rivalry to War: The Evolution of the Anglo-Dutch Rivalry, 1609–52." In Paul F. Diehl (ed.), *The Dynamics of Enduring Rivalries.* Urbana: University of Illinois Press, 29–63.

Liebel, Helep (1965). "Enlightened Bureaucracy versus Enlightened Despotism in Baden, 1750–1792." *Transactions of the American Philosophical Society,* new ser., 55, no. 5, 1–132.

Liedman, Sven-Eric (1986). *Den Synliga Handen: Anders Berch och Ekonomiämnena vid 1700-Talets Svenska Universitet.* Stockholm: Arbetarkultur.

Liggio, Leonard (1985). "Richard Cantillon and the French Economists: Distinctive French Contributions to J. B. Say." *Journal of Libertarian Studies* 7, no. 2, 294–304.

Litchfield, R. Burr (1986). *Emergence of a Bureaucracy: The Florentine Patricians, 1530–1790.* Princeton: Princeton.

Liversidge, Michael (2000). " '. . . A Few Foreign Graces and Airs . . . ': William Marlow's Grand Tour Landscapes." In Clare Hornsby (ed.), *The Impact of Italy: The Grand Tour and Beyond.* London: British School at Rome, 83–99.

Llombart, Vincent (1992). *Campomanes: Economista y politico de Carlos III.* Madrid: Alianza Editorial.

———— (2004). "Traducciones españolas de economía política (1700–1812): Catálogo bibliográfico y una nueva perspectiva." *Cromohs* 9, no. 1–14. www.cromohs.unifi.it/92004/llombart.html.

Lluch, Ernst (1984). *Acaecimientos de Manuel Belgrano, Fisiócrata, y su Traducción de las "Máximas Generales del Gobierno Económico de un Reyno Agricultor" de François Quesnay.* Madrid: Ediciones Cultura Hispánica, Instituto de Cooperación Iberoamericana.

———— (1997). "Cameralism beyond the Germanic World: A Note on Tribe." *History of Economic Ideas* 5, no. 2, 85–99.

Longhitano, Gino (2009). "François Quesnay: Una scienza per la politica." In Manuela Albertone (ed.), *Governare il mondo: L'economia come linguaggio della politica nell'Europa del Settecento.* Milan: Fondazione Giangiacomo Feltrinelli, 3–19.

López, Manuel Fernández (2007). "Genovesi's Influence on Argentine Political and Economic Independence." In Bruno Jossa, Rosario Patalano, and Eugenio Zagari (eds.), *Genovesi economista.* Naples: IISF, 221–229.

Ludington, C. C. (2000). "From Ancient Constitution to British Empire: William Atwood and the Imperial Crown of England." In Jane H. Ohlmeyer (ed.), *Political Thought in Seventeenth-Century Ireland: Kingdom or Colony?* Cambridge: CUP, 244–270.

Luxembourg, Lilo K. (1967). *Francis Bacon and Denis Diderot: Philosophers of Science.* New York: Humanities Press.

MacCormack, Sabine (2007). *On the Wings of Time: Rome, the Incas, Spain, and Peru.* Princeton: Princeton.

Macdonald, James (2003). *A Free Nation Deep in Debt: The Financial Roots of Democracy.* Princeton: Princeton.

MacLeod, Christine (2004). "European Origins of British Technological Predominance." In Leandro Prados de Escosura (ed.), *Exceptionalism and Industrialisation: Britain and Its European Rivals, 1688–1815.* Cambridge: CUP, 111–126.

———— (2008). *Heroes of Invention: Technology, Liberalism and British Identity, 1750–1914.* Cambridge: CUP.

Macrell, J. Q. C. (1973). *The Attack on "Feudalism" in Eighteenth-Century France.* London: Routledge.

Madariaga, Isabel de (1962). *Britain, Russia, and the Armed Neutrality of 1780: Sir James Harris's Mission to St. Petersburg during the American Revolution.* New Haven: Yale.

Maddison, Angus (2006). *The World Economy.* Paris: OECD.

Magnusson, Lars (1994). *Mercantilism: The Shaping of an Economic Language.* London: Routledge.

—— (1999). *Merkantilism: Ett ekonomiskt tänkande formuleras.* Stockholm: SNS Förlag.

Mah, Harold (2003). *Enlightenment Phantasies: Cultural Identity in France and Germany, 1750–1914.* Ithaca, N.Y.: Cornell.

Maiorini, Maria Grazia (2000). "The Capital and the Provinces." In Girolamo Imbruglia (ed.), *Naples in the Eighteenth Century: The Birth and Death of a Nation-State.* Cambridge: CUP, 4–21.

Makato, Tentearo (1899). *Japanese Notions of European Political Economy.* Philadelphia: printed under the supervision of Kuya Shihoshio.

Malanima, Paolo (1988). "An Example of Industrial Reconversion: Tuscany in the Sixteenth and Seventeenth Centuries." In Herman Van der Wee (ed.), *The Rise and Decline of Urban Industries in Italy and the Low Countries.* Leuven: Leuven University Press, 63–74.

—— (2002). *L'economia italiana: Dalla crescita medievale alla crescita contemporanea.* Bologna: Il Mulino.

Mangio, Carlo (2006). "In margine a una memoria presentata nel gennaio 1759 al Sacro Romano Imperatore: Alcuni osservatori italiani di fronte alla crisi marittima e coloniale della Francia." In Carlo Mangio and Marcello Verga (eds.), *Il Settecento di Furio Diaz.* Pisa: Edizioni Plus—Pisa University Press, 151–168.

Mansfield, Edward D., and Brian M. Pollins (2003). *Economic Interdependence and International Conflict: New Perspectives on an Enduring Debate.* Ann Arbor: University of Michigan Press.

Mantena, Karuna (2010). *Alibis of Empire: Henry Maine and the Ends of Liberal Imperialism.* Princeton: Princeton.

Mantoux, Paul (1907). "French Reports of British Parliamentary Debates in the Eighteenth Century." *American Historical Review* 12, no. 2, 244–269.

Manuel, Frank E., and Fritzie Manuel (1979). *Utopian Thought in the Western World.* Cambridge, Mass.: Harvard.

Marcialis, Maria Teresa (1987). "Natura e sensibilità nell'opera manualistica di Antonio Genovesi." In G. Solinas (ed.), *Ricerche sul pensiero del secolo XVIII.* Cagliari: Istituto di filosofia della facoltà di lettere dell'università di Cagliari, 83–124.

—— (1999a). "Antonio Genovesi e la costruzione scientifica dell'economia civile." In Marcialis (ed.), *Ragione, natura, storia: Quattro quadri sul Settecento.* Milan: Franco Angeli, 103–134.

—— (1999b). "Genovesi e Wolff." In Giuseppe Cacciatore et al. (eds.), *La filosofia pratica tra metafisica e antropologia nell'età di Wolff e Vico.* Naples: Alfredo Guida Editore, 47–69.

Marino, John A. (1988). *Pastoral Economics in the Kingdom of Naples.* Baltimore: Hopkins.

———— (2002). "On the Shores of Bohemia: Recovering Geography." In Marino (ed.), *Early Modern History and the Social Sciences: Testing the Limits of Braudel's Mediterranean*. Kirksville, Mo.: Truman State University Press, 3–32.

Martens, Wolfgang (ed.) (1990). *Leipzig: Aufklärung und Bürgerlichkeit*. Heidelberg: Verlag Lambert Schneider.

Martines, Lauro (1963). *The Social World of the Florentine Humanists, 1390–1460*. London: Routledge & Kegan Paul.

Maseng, Einar (2005). *Utsikt over de Nord-Europeiske Staters Utenrikspolitikk*. Edited by Lars Mjøset. 3 vols. Oslo: Universitetsforlaget.

Mason, M. G. (1991). "John Locke's Proposals on Work-House Schools." In Preston King (ed.), *John Locke: Critical Assessments*. London: Routledge, 269–280.

Mastellone, Salvo (1969). *Francesco D'Andrea politico e giurista (1648–1698): L'ascesa del ceto civile*. Florence: Olschki.

Maurer, Michael (1987). *Aufklärung und Anglophilie in Deutschland*. Göttingen: Vandenhoeck und Ruprecht.

May, Early Chapin (1945). *Principio to Wheeling, 1716–1945: A Pageant of Iron and Steel*. New York: Harper.

Mayers, David (2007). *Dissenting Voices in America's Rise to Power*. Cambridge: CUP.

Maza, Sarah (2003). *The Myth of the French Bourgeoisie: An Essay on the Social Imaginary, 1750–1850*. Cambridge, Mass.: Harvard.

McCabe, Ina Baghdiantz (2008). *Orientalism in Early Modern France: Eurasian Trade, Exoticism, and the Ancient Régime*. Oxford: Berg.

McCloskey, Deirdre (2006). *Bourgeois Virtues: Ethics for an Age of Commerce*. Chicago: Chicago.

———— (2010). *Bourgeois Dignity: Why Economics Can't Explain the Modern World*. Chicago: Chicago.

McCloskey, Donald (1994). "1780–1860: A Survey." In Roderick Floud and Donald McCloskey (eds.), *The Economic History of Britain since 1700*. 2nd ed. 3 vols. Cambridge: CUP, 1:242–270.

McCormick, Ted (2009). *William Petty: The Ambitions of Political Arithmetick*. Oxford: OUP.

McCoy, Drew R. (1980). *The Elusive Republic: Political Economy in Jeffersonian America*. Chapel Hill: University of North Carolina Press.

McCraw, Thomas K. (ed.) (1995). Editor's introduction to *Creating Modern Capitalism: How Entrepreneurs, Companies, and Countries Triumphed in Three Industrial Revolutions*. Cambridge, Mass.: Harvard, 1–18.

McCusker, John J. (1992). *Money and Exchange in Europe and America, 1600–1775*. Chapel Hill: University of North Carolina Press.

McGrath, Patrick (1955). *Merchants and Merchandise in Seventeenth-Century Bristol*. Bristol: Bristol Record Society.

McMurran, Mary Helen (2010). *The Spread of Novels: Translation and Prose Fiction in the Eighteenth Century*. Princeton: Princeton.

McNamara, Peter (1998). *Political Economy and Statesmanship: Smith, Hamilton, and the Foundation of the Commercial Republic.* DeKalb: Northern Illinois University Press.

Meek, Ronald L. (1962). *The Economics of Physiocracy.* Cambridge, Mass.: Harvard.

Megnet, Franz (1955). *Jean-François Melon (1675 bis 1738): Ein origineller Vertreter der vorphysiokratischen Oekonomen Frankreichs.* Winterthur: Verlag P. G. Keller.

Meise, Jutta (1997). *Lessings Anglophilie.* Frankfurt am Main: Peter Lang.

Mendelson, Sara, and Patricia Crawford (1998). *Women in Early Modern England: 1550–1720.* Oxford: OUP.

Mendle, Michael (2003). *Henry Parker and the English Civil War.* Cambridge: CUP.

Mentz, Søren (2009). "Neutralitetens Sammenbrudd: Skæbneåret 1807." In Bård Frydenlund and Rasmus Glenthøj (eds.), *1807 og Danmark-Norge: På Vei mot Atskillelsen.* Oslo: Unipub, 11–23.

Meyssonnier, Simone (1989). *La balance et l'horloge: La genèse de la pensée libérale en France au XVIIIe siècle.* Montreuil: Les Editions de la Passion.

——— (1990). "Vincent de Gournay (1712–1759) et la 'Balance des hommes.'" *Population* 45, no. 1, 87–112.

——— (1995). "Deux négociants économistes: Vincent de Gournay et Véron de Forbonnais." In Daniel Roche (ed.), *Cultures et formations négociantes dans l'Europe moderne.* Paris: Éditions de l'EHESS, 513–553.

Migliorini, Anna Vittoria (1984). *Diplomazia e cultura nel Settecento: Echi italiani della Guerra dei sette anni.* Pisa: ETS.

Miller, Judith A. (2000). "Economic Ideologies, 1750–1800: The Creation of the Modern Political Economy?" *French Historical Studies* 23, no. 3, 497–511.

Milo, Daniel (1984). "La bourse mondiale de la traduction: Un baromètre culturel?" *Annales: Économies, sociétés, civilizations* 39, 93–115.

Minard, Philippe (1998). *La fortune du colbertisme: État et industrie dans la France des Lumières.* Paris: Fayard.

——— (2000). "Colbertism Continued? The Inspectorate of Manufactures and Strategies of Exchange in Eighteenth-Century France." *French Historical Studies* 23, no. 3, 477–496.

Mintz, Sidney W. (1986). *The Place of Sugar in Modern History.* London: Penguin.

Mirri, Mario (2009). "Fisiocrazia e riforme: Il caso della Toscana e il ruolo di Ferdinando Paoletti." In Manuela Albertone (ed.), *Governare il mondo: l'economia come linguaggio della politica nell'Europa del Settecento.* Milan: Fondazione Giangiacomo Feltrinelli, 323–441.

Moe, Nelson (2002). *The View from Vesuvius: Italian Culture and the Southern Question.* Berkeley: University of California Press.

Mokyr, Joel (1985). *The Economics of the Industrial Revolution.* Lanham, Md.: Rowman and Littlefield.

———— (2002). *The Gifts of Athena: Historical Origins of the Knowledge Economy*. Princeton: Princeton.

———— (2006) "Mercantilism, the Enlightenment, and the Industrial Revolution." In Ronald Findlay et al. (eds.), *Eli Heckscher, International Trade, and Economic History*. Cambridge, Mass.: MIT, 269-303.

———— (2009). *The Enlightened Economy: An Economic History of Britain, 1700–1850*. New Haven: Yale.

Monestarolo, Giorgio (2006). *Negozianti e imprenditori nel Piemonte d'Antico Regime: La cultura economica d'Ignazio Donaudi delle Mallere (1744–1795)*. Florence: Olschki.

Monroe, A. E. (1966). *Monetary Theory before Adam Smith*. New York: Augustus M. Kelley.

Montgomery, Scott L. (2000). *Science in Translation*. Chicago: Chicago.

Morgan, Kenneth (1993). *Bristol and the Atlantic Trade in the Eighteenth Century*. Cambridge: CUP.

———— (1996). "Atlantic Trade and British Economic Growth in the Eighteenth Century." In Peter Mathias and John A. Davis (eds.), *International Trade and British Economic Growth: From the Eighteenth Century to the Present Day*. Oxford: Blackwell, 14–33.

———— (2002). "Cary, John." In *The Oxford Dictionary of National Biography*. Oxford: OUP, 10:434-436. www.oxforddnb.com/view/article/4840.

Morgan, William Thomas (1932). "The Expedition of Baron de Pointis against Cartagena." *American Historical Review* 37, no. 2, 237–254.

Mori, Renato (1951). *Le riforme leopoldine nel pensiero degli economisti toscani del '700*. Florence: G. C. Sansoni.

Morilhat, Claude (1996). *Montesquieu: Politique et richesse*. Paris: Presses Universitaires de France.

Muldrew, Craig (2011). *Food, Energy and the Creation of Industriousness: Work and Material Culture in Agrarian England, 1550–1780*. Cambridge: CUP.

Multamäki, Kustaa (1999). *Towards Great Britain: Commerce and Conquest in the Thought of Algernon Sidney and Charles Davenant*. Helsinki: Academia Scientiarum Fennica.

Murphy, Antoin E. (1986a). "Le developpement des idées économiques en France (1750–1756)." *Revue d'histoire moderne et contemporaine* 33, 521–541.

———— (1986b). *Richard Cantillon: Entrepreneur and Economist*. Oxford: Clarendon Press.

———— (1992). "Le Groupe de Vincent de Gournay." In Alain Béraud and Gilbert Faccarello (eds.), *Nouvelle Histoire de la Pensée Economique I*. Paris: Editions La Découverte, 199–203.

———— (1997). *John Law: Economic Theorist and Policy-Maker*. Oxford: Clarendon Press.

Murray, John J. (1951). "Anglo-French Naval Skirmishing off Newfoundland, 1697." In J. J. Murray (ed.), *Essays in Modern History Written in Memory of William Thomas Morgan*. Bloomington: Indiana University Press, 71–85.

Murray, K. Sarah-Jane (2008). *From Plato to Lancelot: A Preface to Chrétien de Troyes*. Syracuse, N.Y.: Syracuse University Press.

Muthu, Sankar (2003). *Enlightenment against Empire*. Princeton: Princeton.

Najemy, John M. (1993). *Between Friends: Discourses of Power and Desire in the Machiavelli-Vettori Letters of 1513–1515*. Princeton: Princeton.

Nakhimovsky, Isaac (2011). *The Closed Commercial State: Perpetual Peace and Commercial Society from Rousseau to Fichte*. Princeton: Princeton.

Neff, Stephen (1990). *Friends but No Allies: Economic Liberalism and the Law of Nations*. New York: Columbia University Press.

Negishi, Takashi (1989). *History of Economic Theory*. Amsterdam: North-Holland.

Newbigging, William James (1998). "The Cession of Canada and French Public Opinion." In David Buisseret (ed.), *France in the New World*. East Lansing: Michigan State University Press, 163–176.

Nuzzo, Giuseppe (1990). *A Napoli nel tardo Settecento: La parabola della neutralità*. Naples: Morano.

Nye, John V. C. (2007). *War, Wine, and Taxes: The Political Economy of Anglo-French Trade, 1689–1900*. Princeton: Princeton.

O'Brien, Karen (1997). *Narratives of Enlightenment: Cosmopolitan History from Voltaire to Gibbon*. Cambridge: CUP.

O'Brien, Patrick K. (1998). "Inseparable Connexions: Trade, Economy, Fiscal State, and the Expansion of Empire, 1688–1815." In P. J. Marshall (ed.), *The Oxford History of the British Empire*, vol. 2, *The Eighteenth Century*. Oxford: OUP, 53–77.

—— (2002). "Fiscal Exceptionalism: Great Britain and Its European Rivals from Civil War to Triumph at Trafalgar and Waterloo." In Donald Winch and Patrick O'Brien (eds.), *The Political Economy of British Historical Experience, 1688–1914*. Oxford: OUP, 245–265.

—— (2005). "Fiscal and Financial Preconditions for the Rise of British Naval Hegemony 1485–1815." *LSE Economic History Working Papers 91/05*. London: London School of Economics and Political Science.

Ogilvie, Sheilagh C., and Markus Cerman (eds.) (1996). *European Proto-Industrialization*. Cambridge: CUP.

Ohlmeyer, Jane H. (ed.) (2000). *Political Thought in Seventeenth-Century Ireland*. Cambridge: CUP.

—— (2004). "A Laboratory for Empire? Early Modern Ireland and English Imperialism." In Kevin Kenny (ed.), *Ireland and the British Empire*. Oxford: OUP, 26–60.

Olsen, Kirstin (1999). *Daily Life in Eighteenth-Century London*. Santa Barbara: Greenwood.

Olson, Richard (1993). *The Emergence of the Social Sciences, 1642–1792*. New York: Wiley.

Oncken, August (1886). *Die Maxime laissez faire et laissez passer, ihr Ursprung, ihr Werden*. Bern: Wyss.

Ormrod, David (2003). *The Rise of Commercial Empires: England and the Netherlands in the Age of Mercantilism, 1650–1770*. Cambridge: CUP.

Orwell, George (1972). *The Road to Wigan Pier.* New York: Harvest Books.

Osler, Margaret J. (ed.) (2000). *Rethinking the Scientific Revolution.* Cambridge: CUP.

Oz-Salzberger, Fania (1995). *Translating the Enlightenment: Scottish Civic Discourse in Eighteenth Century Germany.* Oxford: OUP.

Packard, Laurence Bradford (1923). "International Rivalry and Free Trade Origins, 1660–78." *Quarterly Journal of Economics* 37, no. 3, 412–435.

Pagden, Anthony (1987). Editor's introduction to *The Languages of Political Theory in Early-Modern Europe.* Cambridge: CUP, 1–17.

———— (1990). *Spanish Imperialism and the Political Imagination: Studies in European and Spanish-American Social and Political Theory 1513–1830.* New Haven: Yale.

———— (1993). *European Encounters with the New World.* New Haven: Yale.

———— (1995). *Lords of All the World: Ideologies of Empire in Spain, Britain and France, c. 1500–c. 1800.* New Haven: Yale.

———— (2002). "Plus Ultra: America and the Changing European Notions of Time and Space." In John A. Marino (ed.), *Early Modern History and the Social Sciences: Testing the Limits of Braudel's Mediterranean.* Kirksville, Mo.: Truman State University Press, 255–273.

———— (2003). "Human Rights, Natural Rights, and Europe's Imperial Legacy." *Political Theory* 31, no. 2, 171–199.

———— (2007). "The Immobility of China: Orientalism and Occidentalism in the Enlightenment." In Larry Wolff and Marco Cipolloni (eds.), *The Anthropology of the Enlightenment.* Stanford: Stanford University Press, 50–64.

Panichi, Nicola (1989). *Antoine de Montchrétien: Il circolo dello stato.* Milan: Guerini e Associati.

Paquette, Gabriel (2007). "Enlightened Narratives and Imperial Rivalry in Bourbon Spain: The Case of Almodóvar's Historia Política de los Establecimientos Ultramarinos des las Naciones Europeas (1784–1790)." *Eighteenth Century: Theory and Interpretation* 48, no. 1, 61–80.

Pedley, Mary (1998). "Map Wars: The Role of Maps in the Nova Scotia/Acadia Boundary Disputes of 1750." *Imago Mundi* 50, 96–104.

Perez, Carlota (2002). *Technological Revolutions and Financial Capital: The Dynamics of Bubbles and Golden Ages.* Cheltenham: Edward Elgar.

Perna, Maria Luisa (1984). "Nota critica." In Perna (ed.), *Antonio Genovesi: Scritti economici.* Naples: IISF, 2:1269–1312.

Perrot, Jean-Claude (1984). "Nouveautés: L'économie politique et ses livres." In Henri-Jean Martin and Roger Chartier (eds.), *Histoire de l'édition francçaise.* 4 vols. Paris: Fayard, 2:240–257.

———— (1992). *Une histoire intellectuelle de l'èconomie politique (XVIIe–XVIIIe siècle).* Paris: Éditions de l'École des Hautes Études en Sciences Sociales.

Perrotta, Cosimo (1988). *Produzione e lavoro produttivo nel mercantilismo e nell'illuminismo.* Galatina: Congedo.

———— (1991). "Is the Mercantilist Theory of the Favorable Balance of Trade Really Erroneous?" *History of Political Economy* 23, no. 2, 301–336.

———— (2004). *Consumption as an Investment: I. The Fear of Goods from Hesiod to Adam Smith*. London: Routledge.

Peskin, Lawrence A. (2003). *Manufacturing Revolution: The Intellectual Origins of Early American Industry*. Baltimore: Hopkins.

Petrusewicz, Marta (1990). *Latifondo: Economia morale e vita materiale in una periferia dell'Ottocento*. 2nd ed. Venice: Marsilio.

Phillipson, Robert (1992). *Linguistic Imperialism*. Oxford: OUP.

Pii, Eluggiero (1977). "Montesquieu e Véron de Forbonnais: Appunti sul dibattito settecentesco in tema di commercio." *Pensiero politico* 10, 362–389.

———— (1984). *Antonio Genovesi dalla politica economica alla "politica civile."* Florence: Olschki.

———— (1998). "Montesquieu e l'esprit de commerce." In Domenico de Felice (ed.), *Leggere l'Esprit de Loix: Stato, società e storia nel pensiero di Montesquieu*. Naples: Liguori, 165–201.

———— (2002). "Republicanism and Commercial Society in Eighteenth-Century Italy." In Martin van Gelderen and Quentin Skinner (eds.), *Republicanism: A Shared European Heritage*. 2 vols. Cambridge: CUP, 2:249–274.

Pincus, Steven (1995). "The English Debate over Universal Monarchy." In John Robertson (ed.), *A Union for Empire: Political Thought and the Union of 1707*. Cambridge: CUP, 37–62.

———— (1998a). "Neither Machiavellian Moment nor Possessive Individualism: Commercial Society and the Defenders of the English Commonwealth." *American Historical Review* 103, 703–736.

———— (1998b). "To Protect English Liberties: The English Nationalist Revolution of 1688–89." In Ian McBride and Tony Claydon (eds.), *Protestantism and National Identity: Britain and Ireland, c. 1650–c. 1850*. Cambridge: CUP, 75–104.

———— (2009). *1688: The First Modern Revolution*. New Haven: Yale.

Pitavy-Simoni, Pascale (1997). "Vincent de Gournay, or 'Laissez-Faire without Laissez-Passer.'" In James P. Henderson (ed.), *The State of the History of Economics*. London: Routledge, 173–193.

Pitts, Jennifer (2005). *A Turn to Empire: The Rise of Imperial Liberalism in Britain and France*. Princeton: Princeton.

Pocock, J. G. A. (1957). *The Ancient Constitution and the Feudal Law: A Study of English Historical Thought in the Seventeenth Century*. Cambridge: CUP.

———— (1975). *The Machiavellian Moment: Florentine Political Thought and the Atlantic Republican Tradition*. Princeton: Princeton.

———— (1985). *Virtue, Commerce, and History*. Cambridge: CUP.

———— (1987). "The Concept of Language and the Métier d'historien: Some Considerations on Practice." In Anthony Pagden (ed.), *The Languages of Political Theory in Early-Modern Europe*. Cambridge: CUP, 19–38.

———— (1999–2011). *Barbarism and Religion*. 5 vols. Cambridge: CUP.

———— (2003). *The Machiavellian Moment: Florentine Political Thought and the Atlantic Republican Tradition*. With a new afterword by the author. Princeton: Princeton.

Podes, Stephan (1991). "Polybius and His Theory of *Anacyclosis:* Problems of Not Just Ancient Political Theory." *History of Political Thought* 12, no. 4, 577–587.

Pomeranz, Kenneth (2000). *The Great Divergence: China, Europe, and the Making of the Modern World Economy.* Princeton: Princeton.

Pomian, Krzysztof (2005). "Illuminismo e illuminismi." *Rivista di filosofia* 1, 13–32.

Poni, Carlo (2009). *La seta in Italia: Una grande industria prima della rivoluzione industriale.* Bologna: Il Mulino.

Pope, Peter Edward (2004). *Fish into Wine: The Newfoundland Plantation in the Seventeenth Century.* Chapel Hill: University of North Carolina Press.

Porta, Pier Luigi, and Roberto Scazzieri (1997). "Towards an Economic Theory of International Civil Society: Trust, Trade, and Open Government." *Structural Change and Economic Dynamics* 8, 5–28.

——— (2002). "Pietro Verri's Political Economy: Commercial Society, Civil Society, and the Science of the Legislator." *History of Political Economy* 34, no. 1, 83–110.

Poster, Mark (1971). *The Utopian Thought of Restif de la Bretonne.* New York: New York University Press.

Pritchard, James (2004). *In Search of Empire: The French in the Americas, 1670–1730.* Cambridge: CUP.

Quazza, Guido (1971). *La decadenza italiana nella storia europea: Saggi sul Sei-Settecento.* Turin: Einaudi.

Raeff, Marc (1983). *The Well-Ordered Police State: Social and Institutional Change through Law in the Germanies and Russia, 1600–1800.* New Haven: Yale.

Rahe, Paul A. (2005). "The Book That Never Was: Montesquieu's *Considerations on the Romans* in Historical Context." *History of Political Thought* 26, no. 1, 43–89.

Rao, Anna Maria (1984). *L'amaro della feudalità: La devoluzione di Arnone e la questione feudale a Napoli alla fine del '700.* Naples: Guida.

——— (2002). "Enlightenment and Reform." In John A. Marino (ed.), *Early Modern Italy.* Oxford: OUP, 229–252.

Rapetti, Elena (1999). *Pierre-Daniel Huet: Erudizione, filosofia, apologetica.* Milan: Vita e Pensiero.

Rapp, Richard Tilden (1976). *Industry and Economic Decline in Seventeenth-Century Venice.* Cambridge, Mass.: Harvard.

Raven, J. R. (1985). "Viscount Townshend and the Cambridge Prize for Trade Theory, 1754–1756." *Historical Journal* 28, no. 3, 535–555.

Raven, James (2007). *The Business of Books: Booksellers and the English Book Trade.* New Haven: Yale.

Reddy, William M. (1984). *The Rise of Market Culture: The Textile Trade and French Society, 1750–1900.* Cambridge: CUP.

Rediker, Marcus (1987). *Between the Devil and the Deep Blue Sea: Merchant Seamen, Pirates, and the Anglo-American Maritime World, 1700–1750.* Cambridge: CUP.

Redman, Deborah A. (1997). *The Rise of Political Economy as a Science.* Cambridge, Mass.: MIT Press.

Reinert, Erik S. (1980). "International Trade and the Economic Mechanisms of Underdevelopment." Ph.D. diss., Cornell University.

―――― (1995). "Competitiveness and Its Predecessors—a 500-Year Cross-national Perspective." *Structural Change and Economic Dynamics* 6, 23–42.

―――― (1999). "The Role of the State in Economic Growth." *Journal of Economic Studies* 26, no. 4/5, 268–326.

―――― (2007). *How Rich Countries Got Rich . . . and Why Poor Countries Stay Poor.* London: Constable and Robinson.

―――― (2009). "Emulation vs. Comparative Advantage: Competing Principles in the History of Economic Policy." In Mario Cimoli et al. (eds.), *Industrial Policy and Development: The Political Economy of Capabilities Accumulation.* Oxford: OUP, 79–106.

Reinert, Erik S., and Hugo Reinert (2006). "Creative Destruction in Economics: Nietzsche, Sombart, Schumpeter." In Jürgen Backhaus and Wolfgang Drechsler (eds.), *Friedrich Nietzsche 1844–2000: Economy and Society.* New York: Springer, 55–85.

Reinert, Sophus A. (2005). "Cameralism and Commercial Rivalry: Nationbuilding through Economic Autarky in Seckendorff's 1665 *Additiones.*" *European Journal of Law and Economics* 19, no. 3, 271–286.

―――― (2006a). "Blaming the Medici: Footnotes, Falsification, and the Fate of the "English Model" in Eighteenth-Century Italy." *History of European Ideas* 32, no. 4, 430–455.

―――― (2006b). "In margine a un bilancio sui lumi europei." *Rivista storica italiana* 118, no. 3, 975–986.

―――― (2007a). " 'One Will Make of Political Economy . . . What the Scholastics Have Done with Philosophy': Henry Lloyd and the Mathematization of Economics." *History of Political Economy* 39, no. 4, 643–677.

―――― (2007b). "Traduzione ed emulazione: La genealogia occulta della *Storia del Commercio.*" In Bruno Jossa, Rosario Patalano, and Eugenio Zagari (eds.), *Genovesi economista.* Naples: IISF, 155–192.

―――― (2009). "The Sultan's Republic: Jealousy of Trade and Oriental Despotism in Paolo Mattia Doria." In Gabriel Paquette (ed.), *Enlightened Reform in Southern Europe and Its Atlantic Colonies, c. 1750–1830.* Farnham: Ashgate, 253–269.

―――― (2010). "Lessons on the Rise and Fall of Great Powers: Commerce, Conquest, and Decline in Enlightenment Italy." *American Historical Review* 115, no. 5, 1395–1425.

―――― (2011). Introduction to Antonio Serra, *Short Treatise on the Wealth and Poverty of Nations (1613),* translated by Jonathan Hunt and edited by Sophus A. Reinert. London: Anthem.

Reiss, Katharina, and Hans J. Vermeer (1984). *Grundlegung einer allgemeinen Translationstheorie.* Tübingen: Niemeyer.

Reiter, Hans (1990). "Quesnays Tableau Économique als Uhren-Analogie." In Harald Scherf (ed.), *Studien zur Entwicklung der ökonomischen Theorie IX.* Berlin: Duncker & Humblot, 57–94.

Resende-Santos, João (2007). *Neorealism, States, and the Modern Mass Army.* Cambridge: CUP.

Rian, Øystein (2008). "Christiania-Elitens Politiske Betydning i det Dansk-Norske Eneveldet—Med Hovedvekt på Forholdet til Imperiehovedstaden København." In John Peter Collett and Bård Frydenlund (eds.), *Christianias Handelspatrisiat: En Elite i 1700-Tallets Norge.* Oslo: Andresen & Butenschøn, 29–46.

Rice, Condoleezza (2004). "The President's National Security Strategy." In Irwin Stelzer (ed.), *The Neocon Reader.* New York: Grove Press, 81–87.

Richardson, David (1986). *Bristol, Africa and the Eighteenth-Century Slave Trade to America.* Vol. 1. *The Years of Expansion, 1698–1729.* Bristol: Bristol Record Society.

Riches, Naomi (1967). *The Agricultural Revolution in Norfolk.* London: Frank Cass.

Riskin, Jessica (2002). *Science in the Age of Sensibility: The Sentimental Empiricists of the French Enlightenment.* Chicago: Chicago.

Robbins, Lionel (1998). *A History of Economic Thought: The LSE Lectures.* Princeton: Princeton.

Roberts, Andrew (2008). *A History of the English-Speaking Peoples since 1900.* New York: Harper Perennial.

Roberts, Hazel van Dyke (1935). *Boisguilbert: Economist of the Reign of Louis XIV.* New York: Columbia.

Roberts, Michael (1986). *The Age of Liberty: Sweden 1719–1772.* Cambridge: CUP.

Robertson, John (1995). "Empire and Union: Two Concepts of the Early Modern European Political Order." In Robertson (ed.), *A Union for Empire: Political Thought and the Union of 1707.* Cambridge: CUP, 3–36.

—— (1997). "The Enlightenment above National Context: Political Economy in Eighteenth-Century Scotland and Naples." *Historical Journal* 40, no. 3, 667–697.

—— (2000). "Enlightenment and Revolution: Naples 1799." *Transactions of the Royal Historical Society,* 6th ser., 10, 17–44.

—— (2005). *The Case for the Enlightenment: Scotland and Naples, 1680–1760.* Cambridge: CUP.

—— (2008). "Political Economy and the 'Feudal System' in Enlightenment Naples: Outline of a Problem." *Studies on Voltaire and the Eighteenth Century* 1, 65–86.

Roche, Daniel (1993). *France in the Enlightenment.* Cambridge, Mass.: Harvard.

—— (2006). "Encyclopedias and the Diffusion of Knowledge." In Mark Goldie and Robert Wokler (eds.), *The Cambridge History of Eighteenth-Century Political Thought.* Cambridge: CUP, 172–194.

Roche, Geneviève (2001). *Les traductions-relais en Allemagne au XVIIIe siècle: Des letters aux sciences.* Paris: CNRS Editions.

Roll, Eric (1953). *A History of Economic Thought.* London: Faber and Faber.

Romano, Ruggiero (1951). *Le Commerce du Royaume de Naples avec la France et les pays de l'Adriatique au XVIIIe siècle.* Paris: S.E.V.P.E.N.

Roncaglia, Alessandro (2001). *La ricchezza delle idée*. Bari: Laterza.

Rossi, Paolo (1960). *Clavis universalis: Arti mnemoniche e logica combinatoria da Lullo a Leibniz*. Milan: Riccardo Ricciardi.

—— (2003). *I segni del tempo: Storia della Terra e storia delle nazioni da Hooke a Vico*. Milan: Feltrinelli.

Rothbard, M. N. (1995). *Economic Thought before Adam Smith: An Austrian Perspective on the History of Economic Thought*. Aldershot: Ashgate.

Rothkrug, Lionel (1965). *Opposition to Louis XIV: The Political and Social Origins of the French Enlightenment*. Princeton: Princeton.

Rothschild, Emma (2001). *Economic Sentiments: Adam Smith, Condorcet, and the Enlightenment*. Cambridge, Mass.: Harvard.

—— (2006). "Arcs of Ideas: International History and Intellectual History." In Gunilla Budde, Sebastian Conrad, and Oliver Janz (eds.), *Transnationale Geschichte: Themen, Tendenzen und Theorien*. Göttingen: Vandenhoeck und Ruprecht, 217–226.

Routh, Guy (1989). *The Origin of Economic Ideas*. London: Macmillian.

Rubin, Isaac I. (1979/1929). *A History of Economic Thought*. London: Ink Links.

Ruffolo, Giorgio (2004). *Quando l'Italia era una superpotenza: Il ferro di Roma e l'oro dei mercanti*. Turin: Einaudi.

Russi, Luciano (1992). "Il Botero di Rodolfo de Mattei." In A. Enzo Baldini (ed.), *Botero e la "Ragion di Stato."* Florence: Olschki, 449–462.

Sacks, David Harris (1991). *Widening Gate: Bristol and the Atlantic Economy, 1450–1700*. Berkeley: University of California Press.

Saint-Amand, Pierre (1996). *The Laws of Hostility: Politics, Violence, and the Enlightenment*. Translated by Jennifer Curtiss Gage. Foreword by Chantal Mouffe. Minneapolis: University of Minnesota Press.

Sainty, J. C. (1974). *Office-Holders in Modern Britain*. Vol. 3. *Officials of the Boards of Trade, 1660–1870*. London: Institute of Historical Research.

Salvemini, Biagio (2000). "The Arrogance of the Market: The Economy of the Kingdom between the Mediterranean and Europe." In Girolamo Imbruglia (ed.), *Naples in the Eighteenth Century: The Birth and Death of a Nation State*. Cambridge: CUP, 44–69.

Sampaoli, Antonio (1949). "Economia e politica inglese nel pensiero di Antonio Genovesi." *Rivista di politica economica* 39, no. 5, 655–670.

Sasso, Gennaro (1958). "Machiavelli e la teoria dell'anacyclosis." *Rivista storica italiana* 70, 333–375.

Savonius, S.-J. (2004). "Locke in French: The *Du gouvernement civil* of 1691 and Its Readers." *Historical journal* 47, no. 1, 47–79.

Scalvini, Barbara (1998). "*L'Iliade* tra compendio e dramma: Alessandro Verri traduttore d'Omero." *Studi Settecenteschi* 18, 159–178.

Scarfoglio, Carlo (1937/1999). *Dio stramaledica gli inglesi! L'Inghilterra e il continente*. Milan: Società Editrice Barbarossa.

Schabas, Margaret (2005). *The Natural Origins of Economics*. Chicago: Chicago.

Schacht, Hjalmar Horace Greeley (1900). *Der theoretische Gehalt des englischen Merkantilismus*. Berlin: Mann.

Schelle, Gustave (1897). *Vincent de Gournay*. Paris: Guillaumin.

Schiebinger, Londa (2004). *Plants and Empire: Colonial Bioprospecting in the Atlantic World.* Cambridge, Mass.: Harvard.

Schmoller, Gustav von (1897). *The Mercantile System and Its Historical Significance.* New York: Macmillan.

Schui, Florian (2005). *Early Debates about Industry: Voltaire and His Contemporaries.* London: Palgrave Macmillan.

Schumpeter, Elizabeth Boody (1960). *English Overseas Trade Statistics, 1697–1808.* Oxford: Clarendon Press.

Schumpeter, Joseph Alois (1954). *A History of Economic Analysis.* Oxford: OUP.

Screpanti, E., and Stefano Zamagni (1993). *An Outline of the History of Economic Thought.* Oxford: OUP.

Scuccimarra, Luca (2006). *I confini del mondo: Storia del cosmopolitismo dall'Antichità al Settecento.* Bologna: Il Mulino.

Secrestat-Eslande, G. (1911). *Les idees economiques de Vincent de Gournay.* Bordeaux: Cadoret.

Seligman, E. R. A. (1920). *Curiosities of Early Economic Literature.* San Francisco: privately printed by John Henry Nash.

Sella, Domenico (1968). "The Rise and Fall of the Venetian Woollen Industry." In Brian Pullan (ed.), *Crisis and Change in the Venetian Economy in the Sixteenth and Seventeenth Centuries.* London: Methuen, 106–126.

Selwyn, Pamela Eve (2000). *Everyday Life in the German Book Trade: Friedrich Nicolai as Bookseller and Publisher in the Age of Enlightenment, 1750–1810.* University Park: Pennsylvania State University Press.

Semmel, Bernard (1970). *The Rise of Free Trade Imperialism: Classical Political Economy, the Empire of Free Trade and Imperialism, 1750–1850.* Cambridge: CUP.

——— (1993). *The Liberal Ideal and the Demons of Empire: Theories of Imperialism from Adam Smith to Lenin.* Baltimore: Hopkins.

Serjeantson, Richard W. (1999). "Testimony and Proof in Early-Modern England." *Studies in the History and Philosophy of Science* 30, no. 2, 195–236.

Shackleton, Robert (1961). *Montesquieu: A Critical Biography.* Oxford: OUP.

Shapin, Steven, and Simon Schaffer (1985). *Leviathan and the Air-Pump.* Princeton: Princeton.

Shapin, Steven (1994). *A Social History of Truth.* Chicago: Chicago.

——— (1996). *The Scientific Revolution.* Chicago: Chicago.

Shapiro, Barbara J. (2000). *A Culture of Fact: England, 1550–1720.* Ithaca, N.Y.: Cornell.

Shaw, Christine (ed.) (2006). *Italy and the European Powers: The Impact of War, 1500–1530.* Leiden: Brill.

Shaw, L. M. E. (1998). *The Anglo-Portuguese Alliance and the English Merchants in Portugal, 1654–1810.* Aldershot: Ashgate.

Sharp, Michael (1999). "Shearing Sheep: Rome and the Collection of Taxes in Egypt, 30 BC – AD 200." In Werner Eck (ed.), *Lokale Autonomie und römische Ordnungsmacht in den kaiserzeitlichen Provinzen vom 1. bis 3. Jahrhundert.* Munich: Oldenbourg, 213–242.

Sherman, William H. (2004). "Bringing the World to England: The Politics of Translation in the Age of Hakluyt." *Transactions of the Royal Historical Society* 14, 199–207.

Sher, Richard B. (2006). *The Enlightenment and the Book: Scottish Authors and Their Publishers in Eighteenth-Century Britain, Ireland and America.* Chicago: Chicago.

Sherwin, Oscar (1950). "Thomas Firmin: Puritan Precursor of WPA." *Journal of Modern History* 22, no. 2, 38–41.

Shields, David S. (1990). *Oracles of Empire: Poetry, Politics, and Commerce in British America, 1690–1750.* Chicago: Chicago.

Shovlin, John (1998). "Luxury, Political Economy, and the Rise of Commercial Society in Eighteenth-Century France." Ph.D. diss., University of Chicago.

—— (2003). "Emulation in Eighteenth-Century French Economic Thought." *Eighteenth-Century Studies* 36, no. 2, 224–230.

—— (2005). "Political Economy and the French Nobility, 1750–1789." In Jay M. Smith (ed.), *The French Nobility in the Eighteenth Century: Reassessments and New Approaches.* University Park: Pennsylvania State University Press, 111–38.

—— (2006). *The Political Economy of Virtue: Luxury, Patriotism, and the Origins of the French Revolution.* Ithaca, N.Y.: Cornell.

—— (2010). "Selling American Empire on the Eve of the Seven Years War: The French Propaganda Campaign of 1755–1756." *Past and Present* 206, 121–149.

—— (forthcoming). "The Society of Brittany and the Irish Economic Model: International Competition and the Politics of Provincial Development." In Koen Stapelbroek and Jani Marjanen (eds.), *Patriots and Reformers: The Rise of Economic Societies in the Eighteenth Century.* Basingstoke: Palgrave.

Silvestri, Giuseppe (1968). *Scipione Maffei: Europeo del Settecento.* Verona: Neri Pozza Editore.

Simon, Thomas (2004). *"Gute Policey": Ordnungsleitbilder und Zielvorstellungen politischen Handelns in der Frühen Neuzeit.* Frankfurt am Main: Vittorio Klostermann.

Simms, J. G. (1956). *The Williamite Confiscation in Ireland, 1690–1703.* London: Faber & Faber.

—— (1982). *William Molyneux of Dublin, 1656–1698.* Dublin: Irish Academic Press.

Skinner, Quentin (1997). *Liberty before Liberalism.* Cambridge: CUP.

—— (2001). *Machiavelli: A Very Short Introduction.* Oxford: OUP.

—— (2002). *Visions of Politics.* 3 vols. Cambridge: CUP.

—— (2008). *Hobbes and Republican Liberty.* Cambridge: CUP.

Slack, Paul (1998). *From Reformation to Improvement: Public Welfare in Early Modern England.* Oxford: Clarendon.

Small, Albion W. (1909). *The Cameralists: The Pioneers of German Social Polity.* Chicago: Chicago.

Smith, David Kammerling (1995). " 'Au bien du commerce': Economic Discourse and Visions of Society in France." Ph.D. diss., University of Pennsylvania.

Smith, Jay M. (2005). *Nobility Reimagined: The Patriotic Nation in Eighteenth-Century France.* Ithaca, N.Y.: Cornell.

Smith, Pamela H. (1997). *The Business of Alchemy: Science and Culture in the Holy Roman Empire.* Princeton: Princeton.

Smith, Pamela H., and Paula Findlen (eds.) (2001). *Merchants and Marvels: Commerce, Science, and Art in Early Modern Europe*. London: Routledge.

Smith, S. D. (1995a). "British Exports to Colonial North America and the Mercantilist Fallacy." *Business History* 37, no. 1, 45–63.

——— (1995b). "Prices and the Value of English Exports in the Eighteenth Century: Evidence from the North American Colonial Trade." *Economic History Review* 48, no. 3, 575–590.

Soll, Jacob (2005). *Publishing the Prince: History, Reading, and the Birth of Political Criticism*. Ann Arbor: University of Michigan Press.

——— (2009. *The Information Master: Jean-Baptiste Colbert's Secret State Intelligence System*. Ann Arbor: University of Michigan Press.

Sonenscher, Michael (2007a). *Before the Deluge: Public Debt, Inequality, and the Intellectual Origins of the French Revolution*. Princeton: Princeton.

——— (2007b). "French Economists and Bernese Agrarians: The Marquis de Mirabeau and the Economic Society of Berne." *History of European Ideas* 33, 411–426.

——— (2008). *Sans-Culottes: An Eighteenth-Century Emblem in the French Revolution*. Princeton: Princeton.

Sordi, Bernardo (1991). *L'amministrazione illuminata: Riforma delle comunità e progetti di costituzione nella Toscana leopoldina*. Milan: Giuffrè.

Sorkin, David (2008). *The Religious Enlightenment: Protestants, Jews, and Catholics from London to Vienna*. Princeton: Princeton.

Söderpalm, Kristina (1993). "Handel och sjöfart: Svenska Ostindiska Kompaniet." In Pontus Grate (ed.), *Solen och Nordstjärnan: Frankrike och Sverige på 1700-talet*. Stockholm: Nationalmuseum, 172–175.

Sörlin, Sverker (1990). "Guldet från Norden: Norrlandsvisioner från Olaus Magnus till Johan Galtung." In Sune Åkermann and Kjell Lundholm (eds.), *Älvdal i norr*. Umeå: Universitetet i Umeå, 83–147.

Spector, Céline (2001). *Le vocabulaire de Montesquieu*. Paris: Ellipses.

——— (2004). *Montesquieu: Pouvoirs, richesses et societies*. Paris: Presses Universitaires de France.

——— (2006). *Montesquieu et l'émergence de l'économie politique*. Paris: Honoré Champion.

Spini, Giorgio (1999). *Michelangelo politico e altri studi sul Rinascimento fiorentino*. Milan: Edizioni Unicopli.

Stacey, Peter (2007). *Roman Monarchy and the Renaissance Prince*. Cambridge: CUP.

Staley, C. E. (1989). *A History of Economic Thought from Aristotle to Arrow*. Oxford: OUP.

Stapelbroek, Koen (2008). *Love, Self-Deceit, and Money: Commerce and Morality in the Early Neapolitan Enlightenment*. Toronto: University of Toronto Press.

St. Clair, William (2004). *The Reading Nation in the Romantic Period*. Cambridge: CUP.

Steiner, George (1998). *After Babel: Aspects of Language and Translation*. 3rd ed. Oxford: OUP.

Steiner, Philippe (1997). "Storm over Economic Thought: Debates in French Economic Journals, 1750–70." In James P. Henderson (ed.), *The State of the History of Economics*. London: Routledge, 194–213.

——— (1998). *La "science nouvelle" de l'économie politique*. Paris: Presses Universitaires de France.

Stierle, Karlheinz (1996). "Translatio Studii and Renaissance: From Vertical to Horizontal Translation." In Sanford Budick and Wolfgang Iser (eds.), *The Translatability of Cultures: Figurations of the Space Between*. Stanford: Stanford University Press, 55–67.

Stone, Harold (1997). *Vico's Cultural History: The Production and Transmission of Ideas in Naples, 1685–1750*. Leiden: Brill.

Strømstad, Poul (1991). "Artisan Travel and Technology Transfer to Denmark, 1750–1900." In Kristine Bruland (ed.), *Technology Transfer and Scandinavian Industrialisation*. New York and Oxford: Berg.

Sundell, Kirsten Ewart (2002). "The 'Dangerous Authors': Dublin's Economic Pamphleteers, 1727–1732." Ph.D. diss., University of Notre Dame.

Szabo, Franz A. J. (2007). *The Seven Years' War in Europe*. London: Longman.

Tabacco, Giovanni (1980). *Andrea Tron e la crisi dell'aristocrazia senatoria a Venezia*. 2nd ed. Udine: Del Bianco.

Tabak, Faruk (2008). *The Waning of the Mediterranean, 1550–1870: A Geohistorical Approach*. Baltimore: Hopkins.

Tagliacozzo, Giorgio (1969). "Economic Vichianism: Vico, Galiani, Croce—Economics, Economic Liberalism." In Tagliacozzo et al. (eds.), *Giambattista Vico: An International Symposium*. Baltimore: Hopkins, 349–368.

Taylor, Overton H. (1960). *A History of Economic Thought*. New York: McGraw-Hill.

Théré, Christine (1998). "Economic Publishing and Authors." In Gilbert Faccarello (ed.), *Studies in the History of French Political Economy: From Bodin to Walras*. London: Routledge, 1–56.

Théré, Christine, and Loïc Charles (2008). "The Writing Workshop of François Quesnay and the Making of Physiocracy." *History of Political Economy* 40, no. 1, 1–42.

Thomas, P. J. (1926). *Mercantilism and the East India Trade*. London: Frank Cass.

Thomson, J. K. J. (1998). *Decline in History: The European Experience*. Cambridge: Polity Press.

Tilly, Charles (1990). *Coercion, Capital, and European States*. Cambridge, Mass.: Blackwell.

Tompkins, M. M. (1962). "The Two Workinghouses of Bristol, 1692–1735." M.A. diss., University of Nottingham.

Trampus, Antonio (ed.) (2005). *Diritti e costituzione: L'opera di Gaetano Filangieri e la sua fortuna europea*. Bologna: Il Mulino.

Trevelyan, George Macaulay (1945). *History and the Reader*. London: CUP for the National Book League.

Tribe, Keith (1988). *Governing Economy: The Reformation of German Economic Discourse, 1750–1840*. Cambridge: CUP.

───── (1995). *Strategies of Economic Order German Economics, 1750–1950.* Cambridge: CUP.

Tuck, Richard (1999). *The Rights of War and Peace: Political Thought and the International Order from Grotius to Kant.* Oxford: OUP.

Tully, James (1993). *An Approach to Political Philosophy: Locke in Contexts.* Cambridge: CUP.

Tveite, Stein (1961). *Engelsk-Norsk Trelasthandel, 1640–1710.* Bergen: Universitetsforlaget.

Twiss, Travers (1847). *View of the Progress of Political Economy in Europe since the Sixteenth Century.* London: Longman, Brown, Green, and Longmans.

United Nations (1999). *The World at Six Billion.* New York: United Nations Population Division.

Ustvedt, Yngvar (2001). *Trankebar: Nordmenn i de Gamle Tropekolonier.* Oslo: Cappelen.

Vaggi, Gianni (1987). *The Economics of François Quesnay.* Durham, N.C.: Duke University Press.

Vaggi, Gianni, and Peter Groenewegen (2003). *A Concise History of Economic Thought from Mercantilism to Monetarism.* New York: Palgrave Macmillan.

Valcarcel, Carlos Daniel (1995). *Garcilaso: El Inca Humanista.* Lima: Universidad Nacional Mayor de San Marcos.

Valiani, Leo, and Franco Venturi (1999). *Lettere 1943–1979.* Edited by Edoardo Tortarolo. Florence: La Nuova Italia.

Vardi, Liana (2010). "Physiocratic Visions." In Dan Edelstein (ed.), *The Super-Enlightenment: Daring to Know Too Much.* Oxford: Voltaire Foundation, 97–122.

Vaussard, Maurice (1959). *La vie quotidienne en Italie au XVIIIe siècle.* Paris: Hachette.

Veblen, Thorstein Bunde (1898). "Why Is Economics Not an Evolutionary Science?" *Quarterly Journal of Economics* 12, no. 4, 373–397.

───── (1915). *Imperial Germany and the Industrial Revolution.* New York: Macmillan.

Vedel (1901). "Schumacher, Peter Christian." In C. F. Bricka (ed.), *Dansk Biografisk Lexikon*, vol. 15, *Scalabrini-Skanke.* Copenhagen: Gyldendalske Boghandels Forlag.

Venturi, Franco (1959). "Le *Lezioni di commercio* di Antonio Genovesi: Manoscritti, edizioni e traduzioni." *Rivista storica italiana* 3, 511–530.

───── (1969–90). *Settecento riformatore.* 7 vols. Turin: Einaudi.

───── (1972). *Italy and the Enlightenment: Studies in a Cosmopolitan Century.* Translated by Susan Corsi. With an introduction by S. J. Woolf. London: Longman.

───── (1973). "L'Italia fuori d'Italia." In Ruggiero Romano and Corrado Vivanti (eds.), *Storia d'Italia*, vol. 3, *Dal primo Settecento all'unità.* Turin: Einaudi, 985–1481.

───── (2001). *Utopia e riforma nell'illuminismo.* Turin: Einaudi.

Verdoorn, Petrus Johannes (1949). "Fattori che regolano lo sviluppo della produttivitá del lavoro." *L'industria* 1, 3–10.

——— (1980). "Verdoorn's Law in Retrospect: A Comment." *Economic Journal* 90, no. 358, 382–385.

Viano, Carlo Augusto (1960). *John Locke: Dal razionalismo all'illuminismo.* Turin: Einaudi.

——— (2005a). "L'Illuminismo tra risurrezioni e miraggi." *Rivista di filosofia* 1, 91–120.

——— (2005b). *Le imposture degli antichi e i miracoli dei moderni.* Turin: Einaudi.

Vietor, Richard. H. (2007). *How Countries Compete: Strategy, Structure, and Government in the Global Economy.* Cambridge, Mass.: Harvard.

Villari, Lucio (1959). *Il pensiero economico di Antonio Genovesi.* Florence: Felice le Monnier.

Viner, Jacob (1937). *Studies in the Theory of International Trade.* London: Allen & Unwin.

Viroli, Maurizio (1997). *For Love of Country: An Essay on Patriotism and Nationalism.* Oxford: OUP.

Vries, P. H. H. (2002). "Governing Growth: A Comparative Analysis of the Role of the State in the Rise of the West." *Journal of World History* 13, no. 1, 67–138.

Waddell, David (1958). "Charles Davenant (1656–1714)—A Biographical Sketch." *Economic History Review* 11, no. 2, 278–288.

Wahnbaeck, Till (2004). *Luxury and Public Happiness: Political Economy in the Italian Enlightenment.* Oxford: OUP.

Wakefield, Andre (2009). *The Disordered Police State: German Cameralism as Science and Practice.* Chicago: Chicago.

Wallerstein, Immanuel (1974–89). *The Modern World System.* 3 vols. San Diego: Academic Press.

Walling, Karl-Friedrich (1999). *Republican Empire: Alexander Hamilton on War and Free Government.* Lawrence: University Press of Kansas.

Wandel, C. F. (1927). *Danske Handelsforsøg paa Levanten i det Attende Aarhundrede.* Copenhagen: C. A. Reitzels Forlag.

Waquet, Françoise (1989). *Le modèle française et l'Italie savante: Conscience de soi et perception de l'autre dans la république des lettres, 1660–1750.* Rome: École Française de Rome.

Weber, Max (1930/2001). *The Protestant Ethic and the Spirit of Capitalism.* London: Routledge.

Wennerlind, Carl (2003). "Credit-Money as the Philosopher's Stone: Alchemy and the Coinage Problem in Seventeenth-Century England." *History of Political Economy* 35, annual supp., 234–261.

——— (2004). "The Death Penalty as Monetary Policy: The Practice and Punishment of Monetary Crime, 1690–1830." *History of Political Economy* 36, no. 1, 131–161.

Werner, Michael, and Bénédicte Zimmermann (2006). "Beyond Comparison: *Histoire Croisée* and the Challenge of Reflexivity." *History and Theory* 45, no. 1, 30–50.

Westergaard, Waldemar (1917). *The Danish West Indies under Company Rule (1671–1754) with a Supplementary Chapter, 1755–1917.* New York: Macmillan.

Weulersse, Georges (1910). *Le mouvement physiocratique en France.* 2 vols. Paris: Alcan.

White, D. Maxwell (1964). *Zaccaria Seriman 1709–1784 and the Viaggio di Enrico Wanton: A Contribution to the Study of the Enlightenment in Italy.* Manchester: Manchester University Press.

Wiles, R. C. (1974). "Mercantilism and the Idea of Progress." *Eighteenth-Century Studies* 8, no. 1, 56–74.

Willen, Diane (1988). "Women in the Public Sphere in Early Modern England: The Case of the Urban Working Poor." *Sixteenth Century Journal* 19, no. 4, 559–575.

Williams, David (1979). "Voltaire's War with England: The Appeal to Europe 1760–1764." In *Studies on Voltaire and the Eighteenth Century* 179, *Voltaire and the English.* Oxford: Voltaire Foundation, 79–100.

Williams, Gwyn A. (1987). *Madoc: The Legend of the Welsh Discovery of America.* Oxford: OUP.

Williams, Judith Blow (1972). *British Commercial Policy and Trade Expansion, 1750–1850.* Oxford: Clarendon Press.

Wilson, Charles (1965). *England's Apprenticeship, 1603–1763.* New York: Longmans, Green.

Wilson, Peter H. (2009). *Europe's Tragedy: A History of the Thirty Years War.* London: Allen Lane.

Winn, James Anderson (1987). *John Dryden and His World.* New Haven: Yale.

Withers, Charles W. (2007). *Placing the Enlightenment: Thinking Geographically about the Age of Reason.* Chicago: Chicago.

Woodward, Donald (2002). *Men at Work: Labourers and Building Craftsmen in the Towns of Northern England, 1450–1750.* Cambridge: CUP.

Wright, Esmond (1986). *Franklin of Philadelphia.* Cambridge, Mass.: Harvard.

Wrigley, E. A. (2004). *Poverty, Progress, and Population.* Cambridge: CUP.

—— (2010). *Energy and the English Industrial Revolution.* Cambridge: CUP.

Wyatt, Michael (2005). *The Italian Encounter with Tudor England: A Cultural Politics of Translation.* Cambridge: CUP.

Yeo, Richard (2001). *Encyclopaedic Visions: Scientific Dictionaries and Enlightenment Culture.* Cambridge: CUP.

Zalasiewicz (2008). *The Earth after Us: What Legacy will Humans leave in the Rocks?* Oxford: OUP.

Zambelli, Paola (1972). *La formazione filosofica di Antonio Genovesi.* Naples: Morano.

Zanden, Jan Luiten van (2009). *The Long Road to the Industrial Revolution: The European Economy in a Global Perspective, 1000–1800.* Leiden: Brill.

Zhiri, Oumelbanine (2006). "Leo Africanus and the Limits of Translation." In Carmine G. Di Biase (ed.), *Travel and Translation in the Early Modern Period.* Amsterdam: Rodopi, 175–186.

Zielenziger, Kurt (1914). *Die alten deutschen Kameralisten.* Jena: Fischer.

Zinsser, Judith (2002). "Entrepreneur of the 'Republic of Letters': Emilie de Breteuil, Marquise du Châtelet, and Bernard Mandeville's *Fable of the Bees.*" *French Historical Studies* 25, no. 4, 595–624.

Acknowledgments

On the occasion of his invitation to deliver the Third Annual Lecture of the National Book League on 30 May 1945, the great Cambridge historian George Macaulay Trevelyan voiced his supreme fear for the future. It was neither Bolshevism nor bombs. Rather, it was the "disappearance of the private library." These had been "among the best things in the Victorian civilization," he soliloquized, but "in the brave new world of the near future, our one-class society will be housed in small houses where there is little room for bookshelves. And when the motor car and its petrol are paid for there will be little money left over for books." Appropriately never getting a car, I have yet had the immense privilege of growing up in a library of the Victorian variety. This book originated there, through familial discussions amidst the Proustian smell of old folios. Some of its basic ideas were adumbrated at Cornell University, it took form at the University of Cambridge, and was completed while I was a Research Fellow there at Gonville & Caius College. I will remain forever grateful to its Master Sir Christopher Hum and its Fellows for the great honor with which they entrusted me. Finally, this book went to press after I was elected to a position in the Business, Government, and the International Economy Unit of the Harvard Business School, a symbolic event given the many ways, both personal and professional, in which this project grew out of the Kress Collection at HBS's Baker Library.

My research for this book was undertaken with the support of The

Other Canon Foundation, the Norwegian State Educational Loan Fund, the South-South Exchange Programme for Research on the History of Development of the Dutch Ministry of Foreign Affairs, the Centro di Studi sull'Illuminismo Europeo "G. Stiffoni" at the University of Ca'Foscari in Venice, a Carl Schurz Fellowship at the University of Erfurt, a fellowship at the Fondazione Luigi Einaudi in Turin, and an inaugural grant from the Institute for New Economic Thinking. My work has depended on all of these institutions and on the staffs of libraries and archives across Europe and the Americas.

For fruitful discussions about, and comments on, various aspects of this book, I am grateful to David Abulafia, Doohwan Ahn, Antonella Alimento, David Armitage, Jesus Astigarraga, Niall Atkinson, Jürgen G. Backhaus, Francesco di Battista, Vieri Becagli, Duncan Bell, Paul Binski, Chris Brooke, Peter Burke, Melissa Calaresu, John Casey, Loïc Charles, Paul Cheney, Samuel J. Coldicutt, Richard Drayton, Wolfgang Drechsler, Vincenzo Ferrone, Gianni Francioni, Anthony Grafton, Felicity Green, Norbert Häring, Torbjørn Holt, Alizah Holstein, Isabel V. Hull, Joel Isaac, Samuel James, Gareth Stedman Jones, Rainer Kattel, Jim Kloppenberg, Isaac Kramnick, Peter Mandler, John Marino, Philippe Minard, Mario Mirri, Sarah Mortimer, Craig Muldrew, Isaac Nakhimovsky, Michael O'Brien, Patrick O'Brien, William O'Reilly, Gabe Paquette, Ionuṭ Epurescu-Pascovici, K. J. Patel, Maria Luisa Perna, Cosimo Perrotta, Steve Pincus, Pier Luigi Porta, Will Provine, Anna Maria Rao, Giuseppe Ricuperati, Pernille Røge, Alessandro Roncaglia, Emma Rothschild, Joan-Pau Rubiés, Sami-Juhani Savonius, Roberto Scazzieri, Richard and Deirdre Serjeantson, John Shovlin, Quentin Skinner, Sophie Smith, Koen Stapelbroek, William St. Clair, Andrew Taylor, Anoush Terjanian, André Tiran, Antonio Trampus, Keith Tribe, Liana Vardi, and Cara Warner. And I would particularly like to thank John Robertson and Michael Sonenscher for invaluable advice in the preparation of this book. My heartfelt thanks to Michael O'Brien are long overdue, and Jan Kregel, Jomo K. S., and Carlota Perez remain to me models of moral integrity and intellectual excellence. Additionally, audiences in Belgirate, Boston, Cambridge, Heilbronn, London, Naples, Oslo, Pisa, Rio de Janeiro, Turin, and Venice greatly furthered my understanding of the project. Though the end result differed considerably, I first adumbrated what this book might become in the article "Traduzione ed emulazione: La genealogia occulta della *Storia del Commercio*," which Rosario Patalano kindly invited me to present in Naples years ago and which later appeared in his co-edited 2007 volume *Genovesi economista*. At Harvard University Press, Mike Aronson believed in my book from before the word go, and I am immensely grateful for the cheerful assistance of Kathleen Drummy. I would, in this context, also like to thank Isabelle Lewis for her wonderful maps and Tonnya Norwood for her expert project management. I am of course solely responsible for whatever mistakes may still remain.

That said, I also have more personal debts to acknowledge. For invaluable bibliographical assistance over the years, I owe generational debts to Wilhelm Hohmann of Antiquariat Hohmann and the inimitable Ian Smith of Bernard Quaritch. Jacob Soll has taught me much about life, work, and wines with characteristic flair, and his support has been relentless. Were it not for Ken Carpenter's pioneering work and wonderful character, this book could not exist; he put his vast learning and years of research at my disposal, and carefully read the entire manuscript. I hope it is up to his standards. At Cornell, my *maître* Steven L. Kaplan taught me the true meaning of "food for thought," and he has continued to encourage me with scorching wit and epic acuity for more than a decade. Though impossible to emulate, he has provided and continues to provide endless inspiration. Also in Ithaca, John M. Najemy left an important mark on my work with formative friendship and erudition, and I will forever be grateful to him for introducing me to the wonders of archival research and the marvels of the Italian Renaissance. But this has principally been a Cambridge project, and, since my first chance encounter with him at the Trinity Street CUP bookstore, Istvan Hont has galvanized me personally and intellectually; only time will tell if the final product has warranted his formidable critiques and granitic support.

My best man Robert Fredona has been an extraordinary companion in arms, and I am greatly indebted to his friendship and frightening rigor. Carlo Augusto and Giorgina Viano have offered me shelter from many a storm and took me in as a son. My brother Hugo was awarded a PhD from the University of Cambridge on the same day as I was, and taught me the meaning of emulation of hard way. And I want to thank our parents, Erik and Fernanda Reinert, for investing in us with such boundless generosity and for ensuring that dinners were never boring. They have given me all that books are written about and because of, and I can only hope that they find room for one more.

Finally, Francesca Lidia Viano has been my muse and my rock throughout the writing of this book. She has debated my every idea with grace and genius, and taught me that sometimes what is most important is not lost in translation; it is found. As fate would have it, our son Erik August's first smiles coincided with the closing of this book. I can think of no better ending.

Index

Science of Legislation (Filangieri), 28
Scientific Revolution, 122–123
Scottoni, Giovanni Francesco, 34
Seckendorff, Veit Ludwig von, 5, 237–238, 242, 244; founding Cameralism, 5, 60, 223, 238, 244; on industry, 238
Secondat, Jean-Baptiste, 149–150
Second Treatise (Locke), 82–83, 218
Self-interest, 76, 134–135; Cary on, 76; Genovesi on, 225; Montesquieu on, 139–142
Sergio, Vincenzo Emanuele, 231–232
Sérionne, Jacques Accarias de, 15–16
Serra, Antonio, 194, 199–200, 203–205, 207–208, 210, 216, 246; on agriculture 199–200, 205; on economic development, 200; Galiani on, 199–200, 207, 246; and Genovesi, 199–200; on industry, 199–200; and reason of state, 207
Serrano, Pedro, 82–83
Seven Years' War, 11, 13, 21, 53, 59, 68, 146, 182–183, 188; Acadia and, 153–154; Anglomania/Anglophobia and, 181; Baden and, 249
Shaftesbury. See Ashley-Cooper, Anthony, 1st Early of Shaftesbury; Ashley-Cooper, Anthony, 3rd Earl of Shaftesbury
Short Treatise on the Causes that make Kingdoms Abound in Gold and Silver even in the Absence of Mines, with Particular Reference to the Kingdom of Naples (Serra), 194, 199–200, 246
Skinner, Quentin, 27
Slavery, 91–92, 157–158, 173–174, 239
Smith, Adam, 1, 70, 151, 232, 244, 269; in canon, 70, 269, 283, 286; costs of, 126, 272; on division of labor, 275; on emulation, 32–33, 134; on emulation of the rich, 134; on imperialism, 14; on industry and society, 151–152; influence of, 283–284; on Italy, 188; List on, 43; on Physiocracy, 180, 265, 268; on political economy as science, 1; on power, 1; translations of, 65, 256–257, 269
Sociability, 129, 225–230; emulation and, 31; Genovesi on, 225–230; Mandeville on, 144; Pufendorf and, 225
Social contract, 82–83
Social mobility, 89, 133–135; Butel-Dumont on, 168–169; Gournay and, 148–149; Physiocracy and, 176–181
Society: anacyclosis of, 212–216, 220–225; Butel-Dumont on, 163, 168–169, 170, 184; Cary on development of, 81–84; Gee on, 144–146; Genovesie on, 192–200, 225–230; Gournay on, 147–149; luxury and, 222; modernity and, 133–136; Montesquieu on,

139–142; religion and, 216–220; in small states, 255–256; sociability and, 225–230; trust and, 226–227
Society of Merchant Venturers of Bristol, 74–75, 77, 101, 106
Society for the Reformation of Manners of Bristol, 76, 101
Soll, Jacob, 65, 228–229
Sotira, Gaetano, 43, 277
South Sea Bubble, 128, 133
Sovereignty, 26; Genovesi on, 206–207, 228; Irish, 106–107; protecting, 280–281. See also Autonomy
Spain: colonies and wealth of, 202–203; decline of, 53–56; economic translations in, 55–56; manufacturing in, 143; universal monarchy of, 28
Specialization, 20, 145, 284–285
Spenser, Edmund, 38
Spirit of the Laws (Montesquieu): in economic discourse, 139–142; on economic empires, 21; Genovesi translation of, 194, 196, 273; on tyranny, 227
Storia del commercio della Gran Brettagna (Genovesi), 191–232; annotations in, 200; on civil decline, 211–216; fate vs. freedom in, 224–225; influence of, 230–232; on luxury, 207, 208, 211–216; on merchandizing vs. commerce, 205–207; objectives of, 202–203; scientific perspective in, 193–194; on society's origins and functions, 215–220; source documentation in, 201–202; supplementary texts in, 200, 201–202; Wichmann translation of, 257, 258–259. See also Genovesi, Antonio
Struensee, Johan Friedrich, 47, 246
Subsistence, 130–133, 166–168, 178, 209. See also Agriculture
Sweden, 25, 47, 57, 234, 239–240, 247, 251, 255, 274

Tacitus, 1, 69, 79, 154, 218
Tanucci, Bernardo, 197
Tariffs, 67, 91, 170, 221; in Baden, 241; Belgrano on, 274; Butel-Dumont on, 163–164, 166–167, 170, 174; Cary on, 91, 93, 95, 123, 135, 168, 170, 218, 221, 245; Davenant on, 116; English, 164, 166, 182, 269–270, 276, 285; and Enlightenment economics, 71; French, 276; Genovesi on, 209–210, 218, 266; Hamilton on, 274; in historiography, 7; Leopold II on, 255; Neapolitan, 279; and patents, 122; in Tuscany, 253, 255, 283. See also Government intervention
Technological development, 18, in Baden, 250; Butel-Dumont on, 170; Cameralism